THE DYNAMICS OF ANCIENT EMPIRES

OXFORD STUDIES IN EARLY EMPIRES

Series Editors
Nicola Di Cosmo, Mark Edward Lewis, and Walter Scheidel

The Dynamics of Ancient Empires: State Power from Assyria to Byzantium
Edited by Ian Morris and Walter Scheidel

Rome and China: Comparative Perspectives on Ancient World Empires
Edited by Walter Scheidel

The Dynamics of Ancient Empires

State Power from Assyria to Byzantium

Edited by
Ian Morris and Walter Scheidel

OXFORD
UNIVERSITY PRESS

OXFORD

UNIVERSITY PRESS

Oxford University Press, Inc., publishes works that further
Oxford University's objective of excellence
in research, scholarship, and education.

Oxford   New York
Auckland   Cape Town   Dar es Salaam   Hong Kong   Karachi
Kuala Lumpur   Madrid   Melbourne   Mexico City   Nairobi
New Delhi   Shanghai   Taipei   Toronto

With offices in
Argentina   Austria   Brazil   Chile   Czech Republic   France   Greece
Guatemala   Hungary   Italy   Japan   Poland   Portugal   Singapore
South Korea   Switzerland   Thailand   Turkey   Ukraine   Vietnam

First published by Oxford University Press, Inc., 2009
198 Madison Avenue, New York, New York 10016

www.oup.com

First issued as an Oxford University Press paperback, 2010

Oxford is a registered trademark of Oxford University Press

Library of Congress Cataloging-in-Publication Data
The dynamics of ancient empires : state power from Assyria to Byzantium /
edited by Ian Morris and Walter Scheidel.
p. cm.
Includes bibliographical references.
ISBN 978-0-19-975834-0
1. State, The—History.   2. Imperialism—History.   3. Mediterranean Region—
History—To 476.   I. Morris, Ian, 1960–   II. Scheidel, Walter, 1966–
JC51.D96 2009
320.93—dc22   2008004179

Maps in the front matter were previously published in the following books, published
by Oxford University Press: W.R.F. Browning, *A Dictionary of the Bible*;
Sarah B. Pomeroy, Stanley M. Burstein, Walter Donlan, and Jennifer Tolbert Roberts,
Ancient Greece; Mary T. Boatwright, Daniel J. Gargola, and Richard J. A. Talbert,
The Romans; and Cyril Mango, *Oxford History of Byzantium*.

Printed in the United States of America
on acid-free paper

Preface

The world's first known empires took shape in Mesopotamia between the eastern shores of the Mediterranean Sea and the Persian Gulf, beginning around 2350 B.C.E. The next 2,500 years witnessed sustained imperial growth, bringing a growing share of humanity under the control of ever-fewer states. Two thousand years ago, just four major powers—the Roman, Parthian, Kushan, and Han empires—ruled perhaps two-thirds all the people on Earth. Yet, despite empires' prominence in the early history of civilization, there have been surprisingly few attempts to study the dynamics of ancient empires in the western Old World comparatively. Such grand comparisons were popular in the eighteenth century, but scholars then only had Greek and Latin literature and the Hebrew Bible as evidence and necessarily framed the problem in different, more limited, terms. Near Eastern texts, and knowledge of their languages, appeared in large amounts only in the late nineteenth century. Neither Karl Marx nor Max Weber could make much use of this material, and not until the 1920s were there enough archaeological data to make syntheses of early European and west Asian history possible. But one consequence of the increase in empirical knowledge was that twentieth-century scholars generally defined the disciplinary and geographical boundaries of their specialties more narrowly than their Enlightenment predecessors had done, shying away from large questions and cross-cultural comparisons. As a result, Greek and Roman empires have been studied largely in isolation from those of the Near East. Our book is designed to address these deficits and to encourage dialogue across disciplinary boundaries by examining the fundamental features of the successive and partly overlapping imperial states that dominated much of the Near East and the Mediterranean in the first millennia B.C.E. and C.E.: the Neo-Assyrian, Achaemenid Persian, Athenian, Roman, and Byzantine empires.

This volume has grown out of a series of conferences sponsored by Stanford University's Social Science History Institute (SSHI). Founded as an interdepartmental program involving faculty and graduate students from the Departments of Anthropological Sciences, Classics, Economics, History, Political Science, and

Sociology, SSHI aimed to combine the analytical tools and techniques of the social sciences with the appreciation for institutions and evidence associated with the discipline of history. From the start, ancient history occupied a prominent position in SSHI's research agenda. Following a conference on the ancient economy in 1998 that resulted in a collection of essays edited by Joe Manning and Ian Morris,[1] SSHI sponsored a conference titled "Empires and Exploitation in the Ancient Mediterranean" at Stanford in May 2000, organized by the editors of this book. Follow-up meetings at Stanford in May 2001 and a final gathering at the University of Western Australia at Perth in August 2002 allowed the contributors to present and discuss revised papers and strengthen the thematic and methodological coherence of their studies.

At these meetings, internationally recognized experts in the history of the principal empires of ancient western Eurasia addressed a set of key issues such as the nature of the evidence, geographical context, the main historical developments, the role of material resources and modes of exploitation and redistribution, economic development, institutional frameworks, administrative and political practices, ideology, center-periphery relations, and the demise of imperial states. We did not impose a rigid template but left it to each contributor to emphasize some of these features in accordance with the potential of the source material and the preoccupations of pertinent scholarship. As a result, the individual chapters differ in terms of focus and scope, yet they also address the same crucial problems: how empires were run, how they extracted resources, and what their long-term consequences were.

A substantial introductory discussion of recent thought on the mechanisms of imperial state formation prefaces the five case studies of the Neo-Assyrian, Achaemenid Persian, Athenian, Roman, and Byzantine empires. Coauthored by a sociologist with strong historical interests (Jack Goldstone) and a historian with strong sociological interests (John Haldon), this introductory chapter situates the study of ancient empires within the broader context of related work in historical sociology and political science. The final chapter, on the sexual dimension of empire, adopts an explicitly comparative and multidisciplinary perspective, drawing on the findings of evolutionary psychology to improve our understanding of ultimate causation in imperial predation and exploitation in a wide range of historical systems from all over the globe.

We hope that, taken together, these seven contributions will encourage more systematic and comparative thinking about the nature and development of imperial states in early history, and serve as building blocks for cross-cultural studies. This project has inspired all the participants to engage in more explicitly comparative and multidisciplinary work on early empires, and we will measure this book's success by its capacity to motivate our present and future colleagues to do the same.[2]

We particularly want to thank our longtime colleague Steve Haber, SSHI's founder and director, for his invaluable intellectual and financial support. This volume would never have been conceived without his generosity and example. We are also grateful to the University of Western Australia at Perth for hosting the group's third meeting. We especially thank our host on that occasion, Brian Bosworth, who also delivered a paper at the first conference at Stanford, as did William Harris. Lance Davis, Erich Gruen, Steve Haber, David Laitin, and Gavin Wright kindly offered valuable comments on the papers presented at our first event.

The meetings that led to this volume were greatly enriched by the formidable presence of Keith Hopkins, who did more than anyone else to hold ancient historians to the standards of social scientific research.[3] He died in March 2004, before he was able to complete the final revision of his contribution. With the kind permission of his literary executor, Christopher Kelly, it is published here for the first time with editorial additions by Walter Scheidel. This book is dedicated to his memory.

NOTES

1. Manning and Morris, eds. 2005.
2. The cross-cultural study of ancient empires need not be confined to historically related entities: for comparative perspectives on the ancient Mediterranean and ancient China, see Scheidel, ed., forthcoming, complemented by an investigation organized by Morris and Scheidel of divergent processes of state formation in Europe and China after the Roman period. Cf. also Scheidel, in preparation, on models of causality in the study of ancient empires and now especially the international research project "Tributary Empires Compared," directed by Peter Bang and focusing on the Roman, Mughal, and Ottoman empires.
3. Osborne 2004; Harris 2005.

Contents

Contributors

PETER R. BEDFORD is John and Jane Wold Professor of Religious Studies in the Departments of Classics and History at Union College (N.Y.). The author of *Temple Restoration in Early Achaemenid Judah* (2001), he focuses his research on ancient Jewish history and the social and economic history of the Near East in the first millennium B.C.E. He is currently preparing a study on Judean nationalism in the context of the Neo-Assyrian Empire and editing a volume to be titled *The Idea of History in the Ancient Near East*.

JACK A. GOLDSTONE is Hazel Professor and director of the Center for Global Policy at George Mason University and a Scholar at the Mercatus Center. He is the author of *Revolution and Rebellion in the Early Modern World* (1981) and editor of *The Encyclopedia of Political Revolutions* (1998). He has received the Distinguished Contribution to Scholarship award of the American Sociological Association, the Arnoldo Momigliano Prize of the Historical Society, and fellowships from the ACLS and the MacArthur Foundation. He is currently working on two books: *Why Europe?: The Rise of the West in World History* and *A Peculiar Path: The Rise of the West in Global Context 1500–1850*.

JOHN F. HALDON is professor of Byzantine history at Princeton University. His research focuses on the history of the early and middle Byzantine Empire, especially from the sixth to twelfth centuries C.E., on state systems and structures across the European and Islamic worlds, and on the production, distribution and consumption of resources in the late Roman and medieval world. He is director of the international project "Medieval Logistics: Movement, Demography and Warfare." He has published many books and articles, including *The State and the Tributary Mode of Production* (1993), *Byzantium in the Seventh Century* (1997), *Warfare, State and Society in the Byzantine World* (1999), *Byzantium: A History* (2006), and *The Palgrave Atlas of Byzantine History* (2005).

Keith Hopkins was professor of ancient history in the University of Cambridge, a Fellow and vice-provost of King's College, Cambridge, and a Fellow of the British Academy. He is best known for his research on Roman social and economic history and on the history of early Christianity. He is the author of *Conquerors and Slaves* (1978), *Death and Renewal* (1983), *A World Full of Gods* (1999), and *The Colosseum* (2005, with Mary Beard) and the editor of *Hong Kong: The Industrial Colony* (1971). A collection of his articles will be edited by Christopher Kelly. He died in 2004.

Ian Morris is Jean and Rebecca Willard Professor of Classics and professor of history at Stanford University. He works on ancient Greek and Mediterranean history and archaeology and directs an excavation at Monte Polizzo in Sicily. He has authored or (co-)edited ten other books, including *Burial and Ancient Society* (1987), *Death-Ritual and Social Structure in Classical Antiquity* (1992), *Archaeology as Cultural History* (2000), *The Greeks: History, Culture, and Society* (2005, with Barry Powell), *The Ancient Cconomy: Evidence and Models* (2005, co-edited with Joe Manning), and *The Cambridge Economic History of the Greco-Roman World* (2007, co-edited with Walter Scheidel and Richard Saller). He is currently working on two studies of world history.

Walter Scheidel is professor of classics and, by courtesy, history at Stanford University. His research focuses on ancient social and economic history, historical demography, and comparative and transdisciplinary world history. He has authored or (co-)edited eight other books, including *Measuring Sex, Age and Death in the Roman Empire* (1996), *Death on the Nile: Disease and the Demography of Roman Egypt* (2001), *Debating Roman Demography* (2001), and *The Cambridge Economic History of the Greco-Roman World* (2007, with Ian Morris and Richard Saller). He is currently editing *Rome and China: Comparative Perspectives on Ancient World Empires* and *The Cambridge Companion to the Roman Economy*, co-editing *The Oxford Handbook of Roman Studies* and *The Oxford Handbook of the Ancient State*, and working on monographs on ancient empires and ancient demography.

Josef Wiesehöfer is professor of ancient history at the University of Kiel (Germany) and director of its Institute for Classical Studies. He is a member of the Center for Asian and African Studies at Kiel University, editor of the series *Oriens et Occidens*, and co-editor of the series *Asien und Afrika*, *Achaemenid History*, and *Oikumene*. His main interests are the history of the ancient Near East and its relations with the Mediterranean world, social history, the history of early modern travelogues, and the history of scholarship. He has written and edited numerous books, including *Der Aufstand Gaumatas und die Anfänge Dareios' I.* (1978), *Die 'dunklen Jahrhunderte' der Persis* (1994), *The Arsacid Empire: Sources and Documentation* (1998), *Ancient Persia: From 550 B.C. to 650 A.D.* (2001), and *Das frühe Persien* (2006).

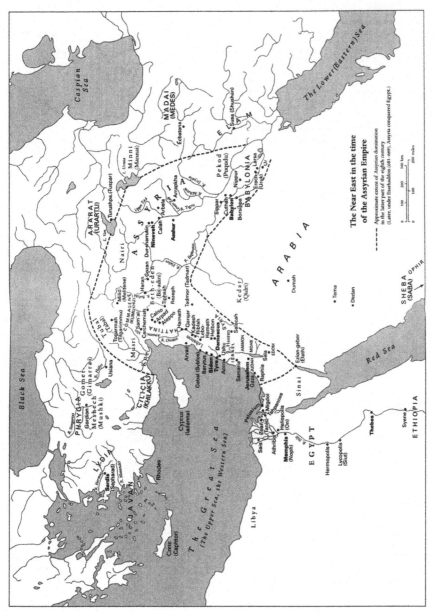

The Neo-Assyrian Empire

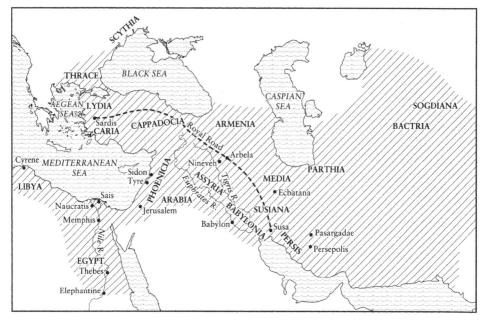

The Achaemenid Empire

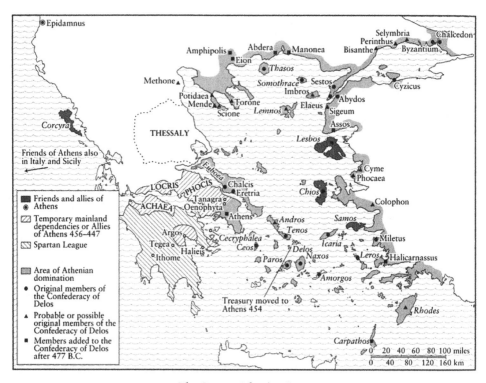

The Greater Athenian State

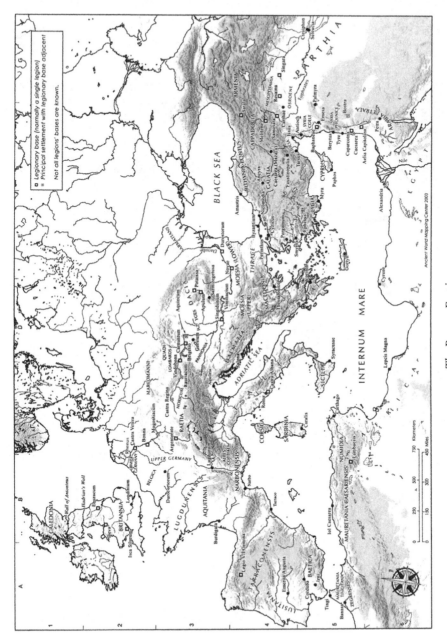

The Roman Empire

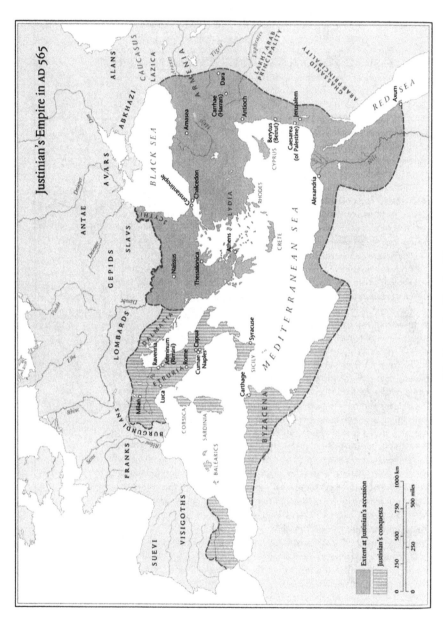

Justinian's Empire in AD 565

ALANS

ABKHAZI

CAUCASUS

LAZICA

A R M E N I A

LAKHMID ARAB
PRINCIPALITY

GHASSANID
PRINCIPALITY

ARAB PRINCIPALITY

Euphrates

Tigris

Amasea

Carrhae
(Harran)

Antioch

Dara

RED SEA

Axum

Berytus
(Beirut)

Jerusalem

BLACK SEA

Constantinople

Chalcedon

CYPRUS

Caesarea
(of Palestine)

LYDIA

RHODES

Alexandria

Nile

AVARS

ANTAE

Dnieper

Dniester

SLAVS

SCYTHIA

Naissus

Athens

Thessalonica

CRETE

M E D I T E R R A N E A N   S E A

GEPIDS

Danube

LOMBARDS

DALMATIA

Ravenna

Ariminum
(Rimini)

Capua

Syracuse

Cumae

Rome

Naples

ETRURIA

Carthage

SICILY

BYZACENA

Vistula

Elbe

BURGUNDIANS

Milano

Luca

CORSICA

SARDINIA

BALEARICS

FRANKS

Rhine

Seine

SUEVI

VISIGOTHS

The Byzantine Empire (1)

Extent at Justinian's accession

Justinian's conquests

0   250   500   750   1000 km

0   250   500 miles

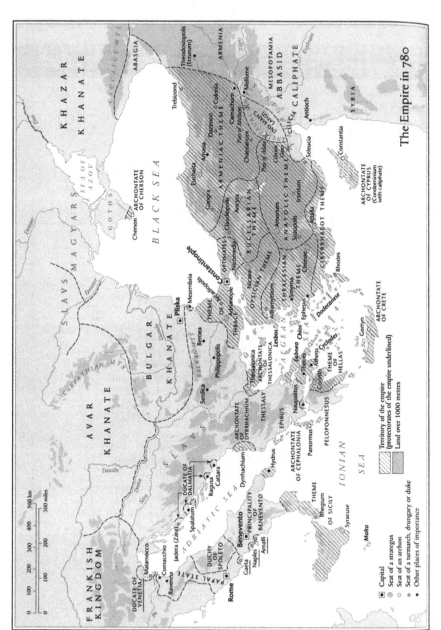

The Byzantine Empire (2)

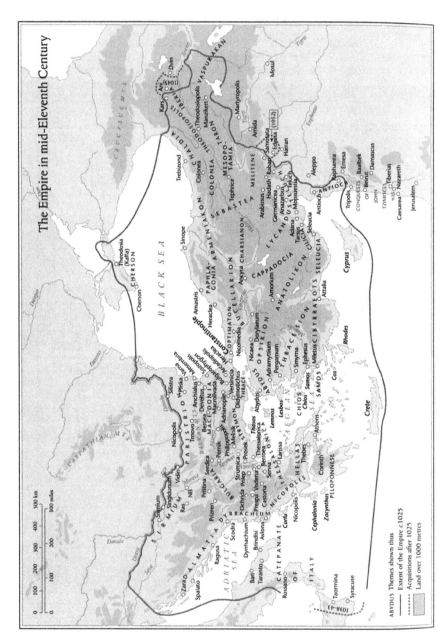

The Empire in mid-Eleventh Century

The Byzantine Empire (3)

ABYDUS Themes shown thus

- - - - - Extent of the Empire c.1025

········· Acquisitions after 1025

Land over 1000 metres

CAUCASUS MTS

Ani [1045]
Dvin
Kars
IBERIA
Theodosiopolis
VASPURAKAN
Manzikert
Martyropolis
TARON
MESOPO-
TAMIA
Amida
[1052]
Melitene
Samosata
Edessa
Harran
Mosul
CHALDIA
COLONEA
Colonea
Trebizond
Tephrice
SEBASTEA
Rabat
Hadath
Germanica
Arabissus
Aleppo
Apamea
Emesa
Baalbek
Damascus

PAPHLA-GONIA
ARMENIAKON
CHARSIANON
Anazarbus
Adana
Mopsuestia
LYCANDUS
Tarsus
Seleucia
Antiocheia
ANTIOCH
Tripolis
CONQUESTS
Beirut
JOHN
935
Tiberias
TZIMISCES
Caesarea
Nazareth
Jerusalem

Amastris
Heraclea
CAPPADOCIA
Amorium
ANATOLIKON
SELEUCIA
CILICIA
Attalia
Cyprus

BLACK SEA

Sinope

Theodosia (Kaffa)
CHERSON
Cherson

Danube

Constantinople
OPTIMATON
Nicomedia
OU CELLARION
Heraclea
Nicaea
OPSIKION
Doryleum
Pergamum
THRACESION
Adramyttium
Smyrna
Ephesus
Miletus
CIBYRRAEOTS
Rhodes

Amastris

Mesembria
Develtus
Anchialus
Varna
Pliska
Silistra
PARISTRION
Nicopolis
Preslav

Adrianople
Arcadiopolis
Versinicia
Didymoticho
THRACE
Abydus

Lesbos
Chios
CHIOS
SAMOS
Samos
Cos
AEGEAN
SEA

Berroea
Timovo
Serdica
Pernik
MACEDONIA
Philippopolis
BULGARIA
Nis
STRYMON
Melnik
Strumica
Prilep
Prosek
Vodena
Berroea
THESSALONICA
Thessalonica
Thasos
Lemnos

Singidunum
Sirmium
Ras
Prizren
SIRMIUM
Vidin
Skopje
Ochrida
Servia
Castoria
Larissa
THESSALY
Thebes
Athens

Danube

CARPATHIAN MTS

Drava

Zara
Spalato
DALMATIA
Ragusa
Scodra
Dyrrhachium
DYRRACHIUM
Avlona
ADRIATIC SEA
Brindisi
Bari
Taranto
CATEPANATE OF
ROSSANO
Rossano

Nicopolis
NICOPOLIS
Corfu
Cephalonia
Zacynthus
HELLAS
Corinth
PELOPONNESE
Crete

ITALY
Taormina
Syracuse
EP. RI 1031

0   100   200   300   400   500 km
0   100   200   300 miles

THE DYNAMICS OF ANCIENT EMPIRES

Ancient States, Empires, and Exploitation

Problems and Perspectives

Jack A. Goldstone and John F. Haldon

Τ HE RISE AND FALL OF ANCIENT EMPIRES AND STATES HAS BEEN A POPULAR theme in comparative social and political history for many years, yet we still find the whole process fascinating—perhaps because, in the modern world, notions of the "end of history" and "imperial overstretch" have raised questions about whether decline and fall affect the modern Western world as well as the past. Yet beyond such simple slogans lies a deeper truth: the dynamics of historical social change remain problematic because there are no simple answers to the question "Why did such-and-such an empire rise when it did, and why did it collapse or succumb to external pressures when it did?" The resurgence of interest in the fates of empires, as well as in meta-theoretical discussion about the structures of historical change on the grand scale, is evidenced in a number of current projects and recent publications.[1]

In the past thirty years or so, questions regarding the dynamics of empires have also been related to wider issues of cultural transformation, in which the appearance of particular religious-ideological and intellectual tendencies has been seen to play a more important and causal role. The impact of religious and intellectual change has especially been highlighted in the evolution of the political systems and state structures of a range of "axial civilizations," in relation to both their impact on the formation and developmental trajectory of social and political elites and the psychological-ideological systems that underpin forms of political and social power. The phrase "axial age" was coined in 1949 by Karl Jaspers to characterize the period of formation of the world's major religions as distinct belief systems based on canonical texts, roughly from 600 B.C.E. to 600 A.D., and which, it was argued, were one result of the evolution of cultural elites that were able to theorize a transcendental vision of their world and "the order of things," exemplified in the cultural-intellectual traditions of Judaism, Hinduism, and Buddhism, of the ancient Greek cities and early Christianity, of Zoroastrianism and, by extension, of Islam. Several comparative sociological-historical analyses have tried to build on this.[2] But the premise on which concepts of "axial civilizations" was constructed has been

3

challenged, partly because it failed to grapple adequately with the multiplicity of cultural and political forms and the divergences between different cultural systems that supposedly shared a common "axial" significance.[3] A more fruitful approach, although it, too, has been subjected to some criticism, was outlined by Mann, in which the role of the major transcendental religions holds the key to the dynamic of the cultures in which they came to dominate, in respect of control over ideological as well as material resources, the articulation of power-structures, and elite identities.[4] What is clear is that understanding the dynamics of empires requires us to grapple with the tensions among the political/military, economic, and ideological/religious structures and elites that together constitute imperial power systems. To return to the notions with which we opened this essay, it may be that the United States and other Western powers face a reduction in their relative military and political power at the very same time that Western ideology regarding human rights and democracy becomes dominant, precisely because the ideals of spreading global democracy and economic development that have been used to justify Western domination are inconsistent with indefinite continuation of that domination.

The contributions to this volume discuss these issues in respect of a number of premodern states or empires and attempt to put them into a comparative context based on a presentation of their economic, social, and political-cultural systems and a comparison of the systemic similarities and dissimilarities they displayed. The neo-Assyrian Empire, Achaemenid Persia, Athens, Rome, Byzantium, and the early Islamic caliphates (Umayyad and Abbasid dynasties) provide the main case histories, although other comparative material is also drawn upon. The contributors in each case do not present their discussions from within any single standpoint but try to draw on a range of sociological and comparative perspectives that may suggest a range of possible approaches.

Yet we may attempt to derive certain general conclusions from the sum of these discussions. The first issue is to define the terms of the discussion. What is an empire? Indeed, how should we define a state? What differentiates "empire" from "state," if there is a difference? Should our definitions be descriptive (i.e., empires are just big states) or analytical (i.e., empires operate on different structural bases from simple states)?[5]

1. States

To begin with the notion of the state:[6] no agreement has ever been reached on a universally acceptable general definition that has any real analytic value, partly because historians and anthropologists tend to define "the state" in terms of the different questions they wish to ask. Indeed, for much of human history the state is not a relevant concept to the forms and functions of social and political organization. It is difficult to point to institutions that formally constitute "the state" until the evolution from the third millennium B.C.E. of sacred monarchical authority concentrated in the hands of an individual supported by an intellectual-religious elite.

Yet thereafter, too rigid a definition merely acts as a conceptual straitjacket that ignores the fundamentally dynamic and dialectical nature of human social organization, and so, as with any definition, the notion of "the state" must remain flexible if it is to generate explanations; it should function as a heuristic tool.

A great deal of ink has flowed in attempts to generate all-embracing concepts of the state, ranging from Marx's various definitions of the state as the embedded forms of property relations and social power in social formations, in which religious-ideological power was the form through which political structures were expressed (his "Asiatic" mode, for example), and also as the instrument of domination by a ruling class, to Max Weber's concept of the state as a system of institutions and impersonalized relationships evolving out of late medieval society or as a territorial entity with a central power monopolizing coercive power. At the same time, emphasis has been placed by some, following the approach elaborated by Norbert Elias, on tracing the points or periods at which differential rates of socioeconomic and institutional change attain a certain qualitative evolutionary departure, during which modes of resource extraction and the political forms through which these were achieved undergo transformative changes, and studying how these impact upon yet are also affected by the processes of sociocultural class formation, awareness, and conflict.[7] Modern discussion has tended to focus around efforts to reconcile these alternative and in many respects conflicting approaches centered on "structure" or "process"—Mann's approach, for example, which sees the state as both an instrument of coercive and ideological power and an organ through which elites may reproduce their domination and which places emphasis on process as much as on structure.[8]

Adopting a provisional working definition of the "state" that encompasses yet allows us to identify what is unique about "empires" would therefore seem appropriate at this stage (although we shall see in what follows that the contributors vary in both their emphases and their perspectives). At one extreme of social-political organization, the term "state" can refer to a relatively short-lived grouping of tribal or clan communities united under a warlord or chieftain who is endowed with both symbolic and military authority—in anthropological terms, a "Big-man" confederacy. Such "states" rarely survive for long, however, and are sometimes referred to as "proto-states," since they have not yet attained a degree of institutional permanence and authority is generally exercised over a mobile people rather than a sovereign territory. Examples include the majority of the "nomad empires" that arose on the Eurasian steppe zone from the beginning of the first millennium B.C.E. and periodically re-appeared until the seventeenth century C.E., with the possible exception—although the point is certainly debateable—of the postconquest Mongol "hordes" in the early thirteenth and fourteenth centuries, and certainly of Nurhaci's formation of the Manchu Empire.[9] At the other extreme we find more or less territorially unified political entities, with an organizational "center" (which may be peripatetic) from which a ruler or ruling group exercises political authority and that maintains its existence successfully over several generations; a key element in the formation and degree of permanence of such formations is that the authority of the ruler or ruling group is recognized as both legitimate and exclusive. In this respect, the ideological aspect is absolutely fundamental to state-building, a point to which we will return later.

This more permanent type of state formation might be defined in the first instance as a territorially demarcated region* controlled by centralized governing or ruling establishments, which may or may not have a monopoly over the use of coercion but which usually have the coercive power to assert their authority over the territories they claim, at least on an occasional "punitive" basis when needed. If the central state had a monopoly on coercive power, this would fit Weber's "ideal type" definition of the state.

How exactly such central authorities achieve these ends varies enormously from state to state and society to society. In all premodern states there have been gaps in the extent of state authority—border or mountainous regions, for example, difficult of access and untouched by state supervision, or "tribal" groups nominally owing allegiance and occupying territory claimed by the state but not always easily brought under the state's authority or control. Where geography has favored a tribal pastoral and/or nomadic economy, the nomads have frequently formed important elements in the armies of conquest states, certainly in the initial stages of their evolution. However, this has also meant that, because of the mobility of such pastoralists, because of their internal social cohesion and self-sufficiency, and because their wealth is generally easily moved out of the reach of state officials, they are both able and sometimes inclined to resist any central authority that does not directly favor their own interests.

By the same token, the relative patchiness of central control may represent a point on the line from local state to supra-local state to empire (and back again), as with Assyrian control over neighboring territories in the early period of expansion (ninth century B.C.E.). Ideological power can overcome this at certain times, but by itself generally remains a short-term means of cementing such power relationships.[10] The very different configuration of power relationships within three late ancient or early medieval states, for example—late Rome and early Byzantium, Sasanian Iran, and the early Umayyad caliphate, partly discussed in chapter 6—provides striking examples of the ways in which the features of official military versus nomad militias, and central control versus central authority with varying local control, were combined.

A key element in state formation is the generation of fairly complex ideological and legitimating systems, on the one hand, and at the same time more

---

* Although lands may well have been geographically dispersed and frontiers ill defined or fluctuating, reflecting the process of formation through amalgamation, conquest, inheritance, and so forth.

impersonalized and institutionalized modes of surplus extraction than proto-states or clan or tribal groupings are capable of developing. In Weber's concept, a focus around sacred monarchical and priestly authority is seen as one important initial stimulus to the formation of administrative-bureaucratic institutions evolved to secure the surpluses required for the temple and related religious-social functions. Administration based on kinship and lineage relationships, and the exploitation of kin-based modes of subordination, tend then gradually to be replaced by non-kinship-based bureaucratic or administrative systems (although kin and lineage are rarely entirely absent—again, the Assyrian example, on the one hand, with provincial governors appointed from among the ruling families, and that of the later Byzantine Empire, with its close familial networks, provide useful but very different illustrations). In most examples, a bureaucratic-administrative structure of some sort confers a clear advantage and appears to be a necessity if the political system is to retain its nontribal existence and cohesion. This point was made already by the Muslim philosopher and political analyst Ibn Khaldun, who saw this process as generally following the initial formation of a supra-tribal political entity from tribal elements under a chieftain of some sort, in which a crucial role was played by religion as a unifying element providing a new, supra-kinship set of relationships, identities, and loyalties. While Ibn Khaldun was clearly working on the basis of his knowledge of the evolution of Islamic states, his main point remains valid for any state formative process.[11]

A relatively open-ended account, allowing for both variety and evolution in state forms, is thus to be preferred to a closed and descriptive formulation, which would otherwise exclude features found in some state formations but perhaps not in others. An obvious reason for this preference is the fact that the formation of a state, and the civilizational system it may represent, is never a single event but rather a longer-term evolutionary process in which social habits and institutions and state organizations respond to changing conditions through what Runciman refers to as "competitive selection" of practices—where they fail to respond adequately, the state fails to develop further and fails. There are many different shades of "state-ness," both in respect of the degree of actual physical control and in the degree of ideological integration of the varying and often antagonistic elements occupying the territory claimed by a given central authority. Some historical states have been represented by claims to legitimacy based on consensus, having little or no power of coercion, and have survived generally for only a relatively short time. Those state elites that have military coercion at their disposal, at least in the early stages of their development, may remain relatively isolated from the social structures they live off, surviving only as long as they are able effectively to coerce or persuade support and resources. Others may move toward the establishment of a permanent and self-regenerating body of administrators, which draws its recruits from either specific groups within the state (tribal groups, for example), from particular family dynasties, or from those of a particular social or cultural background (which includes the establishment of slave bureaucracies and armies, deracinated from their original social and cultural context and dependent entirely on the system to which they owe their position). They thus tend to evolve institutional structures—fiscal systems, military organizations, and so forth—that establish their own sets of roles and discourses, divorced from the daily practices of "ordinary" society. The state becomes a specialized and dominant set of institutions, which may even undertake the creation *ab initio* of its own administrative personnel and that can survive only by maintaining control over the appropriation and distribution of surplus wealth that this specialized personnel administers.[12] This certainly became the case in Rome and Byzantium, in the Umayyad and Abbasid caliphates, and in the Ottoman and Mughal empires, for example. And it seems also that this distancing of administrative apparatus from social base as well as from the kinship ties of the royal household represents a developmental shift, a process of maturation, as we follow the evolution of state formation through time. Where the Assyrian and Achaemenid empires recruited their administrative infrastructure from the elite families of the center and provinces, bound through kinship ties or vested interests shared with the ruling dynasty and its kin, more developed bureaucratic systems recruited their personnel from a wider social range and depended upon more broadly available literary and educational possibilities. Of course, the picture is in all cases uneven and patchy, a mix of both "types," and this simplification does a certain amount of injustice to the historical cases we examine. But where we find these phenomena, we have also found "states" in the more modern sense of the term.

A key issue is clearly the potential for state formations to reproduce themselves, in contrast to the potential of a particular dynasty with its retinues based upon personal loyalties and notions of honor, obligation, and reciprocity, to maintain itself in power over a number of generations. A crucial factor in state reproduction is the evolution of a bureaucratic elite that has a sense of its own function within the state or society, even if this elite remains closely tied to a particular social stratum (such as the slave administrators of the imperial household in first-century imperial Rome or the royal household in Assyria and Persia). At higher levels of state development, this elite identifies with a particular set of ideological and symbolic narratives and can recruit and train its personnel into the institutional roles and behavioral patterns relevant to the maintenance and even expansion of these structures. The relative success of the first Islamic caliphates, the Roman and Byzantine, or the Chinese and Ottoman states, in their different forms over time in this regard, to name just a few examples, provides good illustrations of the ways in which some political formations evolved stable yet flexible structures sufficient to permit their survival over a long period, despite often major shifts in dynastic arrangements and the nature of the central authority itself. The relative failures of the early Frankish kingdoms illustrate the fate of political formations that failed to generate such structures.

The case of the Athenian Empire may be used as an illustration. In spite of its success in mobilizing a vast resource catchment area, in the form of allies and dependent cities and territories, Athens remained remarkably jealous of its rights of citizenship, although this by no means reflected a wholly impermeable system (see Morris, in this volume). But the failure to expand citizenship and to create identities between center and periphery (with notable exceptions—Samos, for example, toward the end of the Peloponnesian War) reflected the failure to evolve an integrated imperial elite based on a broad tax base within the core territories. Athens was thus always parasitical in respect to its allied and subordinate territories, and this deprived it of the sort of structural flexibility that would have permitted it to survive the crisis of 405–404 B.C.E. and the defeat at Aegospotamoi. The failure to generate common identities within Athenian tributary territories vitiated Athenian strength at precisely the point at which it was most severely challenged.

Failure to bridge both regional and lineage identities (however spurious or artificial the latter may usually in fact have been) thus dramatically vitiated attempts by a central authority, even when supported by elements of a permanent civil or military bureaucracy, to maintain itself as an effective power with real coercive potential over more than a few generations. A similar situation was evident when the Spanish conquistadors entered Mesoamerica. The Aztec Empire they faced was not a centralized and ideologically unified organization but rather a loose tribute federation in which different Native American nations with distinct identities had been forced to pay tribute to, and recognize the suzerainty of, the Aztec leadership in Tenochtitlan. Instead of the various domains of the Aztec Empire uniting against the foreign invaders, the Tlaxcalans and other former tributary tribes took advantage of the opportunity to join with the Spanish invaders to destroy the Aztecs' power.

In general, the maintenance of ideological legitimacy and hegemony must accompany the maintenance of appropriate coercive potential in situations during which external pressures build up, and the combination is central to the long-term survival of state systems. The relatively short lifespan of the Athenian Empire and the rapid collapse of the Aztecs after the arrival of the Europeans must owe something to these systemic weaknesses. In contrast, the neo-Assyrian state of the tenth through the eighth centuries B.C.E. does appear to have been able to maintain an administrative apparatus that, although dependent upon a social and ethnic identity within the palace, was supported by the spread of a unifying religious belief in the cult of Assur. The taxation and tribute raising (and associated bureaucratic skills) that provided a stable basis for supporting this apparatus was integrated into a system of vassalage and dependency upon both the royal dynasty and the cult of Assur, which was quite deliberately introduced into the pantheon of conquered peoples.[13]

The late ancient and early medieval Persian kingdom of the Sasanids provides a good example of a remarkably successful dynasty in which ideological legitimacy and a bureaucratic administrative structure were successfully combined to hold in check powerful centrifugal tendencies, including competition among several equally powerful clans, for some four centuries. The power of the Sasanid royal house depended very largely on two interlinked factors: an ideological commitment by a powerful group of regional clan or dynastic chiefs (the Sasanian "aristocracy," from whom the royal house was itself drawn) to the legitimacy of the dominant dynasty (which claimed politico-religious authority sanctioned both by a claim to ancient lineage and military leadership) and the willingness of that dynasty to rule without challenging the key ideological, political, or economic interests of the aristocracy upon which it was in part dependent.[14]

The failure to maintain these two interlinked factors in the course of dynastic rivalries, as well as questions of honor, shame and competition, inevitably undermined central authority. The Abbasid caliphate (750–1258) can be understood from this perspective, for already by the later ninth century the central power was heavily compromised by the growing autonomy of provincial governors and by generals commanding armies in the central lands. It could be argued that it was only the need to attain ideological legitimacy within Islam that held the wider polity together, and successful religious-ideological opposition in Africa, Egypt, and the Arabian peninsula led to its disintegration into multiple caliphates.

2. State Success and Ideological Integration

The preceding discussion emphasized the importance of an integrated bureaucratic elite with its own resource base, as well as an ideologically rooted identity and legitimacy, to sustain state formation. Yet it is clear from a cursory comparison of a number of ancient and medieval state formations that a central authority can survive for substantial periods simply through the manipulation of key ideological and symbolic elements in the cultural system of the social formation as a whole. South Indian temple culture and the attendant state structures, particularly as exemplified in the Chola and Vijayanagar empires, provide classic examples. They also illustrate the central importance of legitimation within symbolic terms of reference—that is, within the symbolic universe of a given cultural formation—and of the social and cultural groups that are generally responsible for their maintenance, whether priestly groups or official churches or cult organizations or aristocratic elites endowed with particular symbolic authority.[15]

Thus, states may have ideological lives that are not necessarily tied to their actual political and institutional efficacy or power. Political ideologies and belief systems, once in existence, are sometimes well able to adapt and to survive in conditions that have evolved significantly from those within which they were originally engendered, provided the contradictions between the two are not too extreme or insurmountable in terms of social praxis and psychology. Those that respond to long-term functional needs in human society provide the best examples and include religious systems in particular, such as Hinduism, Islam, and Christianity. These systems did, to a greater or lesser degree, free themselves in certain respects from both the political and the social and economic conditions that produced them (although they may at the same time constrain the direction of social-economic evolution within those societies).

Political ideologies too can be extremely flexible. They may provide a rationale for conflict where no visible or obvious reason in terms of competition for material resources exists, for example. And they can also be extremely powerful. Many states were, in effect, little more than territories under the nominal authority of a ruler but in which actual power was exercised by a tribal-, clan- or family-based socioeconomic elite. The position of such an elite might originally have depended upon the central ruler and/or the conditions in which the state came into being (by conquest, for example), but, because of their actual control over resources or because of other historical conditions, that elite became in practice independent of the center. Yet, in such cases, we find that the very idea of a centralized kingdom or state, together with the residual power of concepts such as honor or loyalty to a particular dynastic succession or to a set of constitutional arrangements, was enough to maintain at least a fictional unity of identity. The later history of the Byzantine state from the thirteenth century to its final extinction in 1453 exemplifies this particular type of development. The Assyrian Empire in the late ninth century and the first half of the eighth century B.C.E. survived partly at least, it appears, because of the strength of these symbolic and ideological relationships, in spite of political strife at the center and the loss of certain more distant western territories. The Holy Roman Empire provided an expanded base for Hapsburg rule in central Europe up to the seventeenth century primarily through the ideological power of the Roman imperial ideal, rather than through the dynasty's coercive or organizational strength. The Japanese shogunate continued to derive legitimacy from the concept of the semidivine emperor's dominion over all Japanese, long after the role of the imperial court in national politics had become insignificant. Finally, the repeated unification of China after its initial integration under the Qin and early Han appears to be at least partly rooted in the persistent ideal of a single Chinese imperium, an ideal that survived multiple defeats and disintegrations of particular dynasties.

These points suggest that a crucial element in the longer-term success of a state formation is a degree of acceptance of that state as normatively desirable, especially by elites, but even by the broader populace from which it draws its resources. We do not mean to revive the "consensus" theory of state formation but rather to stress the significance in the structuring of political relations of power and resource distribution of rules, "law," and forms of normative behavioral patterns. These differed enormously in different historical cases. Some states survived only by virtue of their ability to coerce submission and the extraction of revenues and resources on a more or less continuous basis, such as the Aztec Empire of Mesoamerica or the empires of the Mongol "hordes." But, over the longer term, this has not been a particularly effective way of evolving or maintaining state power. A good example of more lasting imperial power is provided by the case of Rome, in which a conquest state was able to evolve an ideological hegemony that in turn generated a consensual identity among the conquered territories.[16] Although most states first evolved in the context of an imbalance between military coercion and cooperative participation, those that have been most successful have usually generated increasingly complex relationships of reciprocity, consensus, and interdependence with leading elements of conquered groups or previous political formations, such as tribal and clan leaders, merchant elites, or aristocracies.

Many states, established after a relatively brief period of military expansion and conquest, came to rest very heavily on such ideological structures for gaining the support of varied elites, and the Indian examples mentioned already provide a good illustration of such systems. Equally, the Merovingian kingdom during the sixth and seventh centuries depended very heavily on the support and goodwill of the preexisting Gallo-Roman elite and the episcopal establishment (the two were anyway very closely integrated), especially in its southern regions,[17] while the Ottoman rulers during the fifteenth century in particular relied on their Christian vassals as a counterweight to the power of the Turkish tribal and clan elites both in the Balkans and in Asia Minor.

In the Western tradition, this ideological integration has generally been seen, until recently, at least, as a secondary aspect of state formation, a reflection, perhaps, of the dominance of military institutions and coercion in the political history of the western Eurasian world. In fact, comparison with different types of state suggests that this prioritization may be misplaced. In the southern Indian state of Vijayanagar, political power rested on the exploitation of a core region, the source of immediate royal income, while the areas furthest away from the center of military and political coercion were attached primarily through occasional military expeditions and by connections of a ritual nature. Royal rituals were centered on key religious centers and temples, through whose religious-ideological authority the rulers reinforced their legitimacy and claims to overlordship, in return for which they undertook to support such institutions through a variety of endowments, regular gifts in cash and in kind, grants of labor services, and so on. It was through their involvement in such rituals that members of dominant social groups could be incorporated within what was in practice a network of royal and spiritual patronage. At the same time, the rituals legitimated more localized authority and power, so the system as a whole provided a rationale for the prevailing political institutions and social-economic relations.

To some extent, this set of structured relationships can also be approached from Durkheim's perspective of religion as the primary and totalizing set of practices through which societies become both self-aware and can realize their identity through various political-institutional arrangements: stable and coherent social organization requires not just a degree of unifying coercion and/or lineage-based vested interests but also a normative level of mutually accepted perceptions, which exist outside such "secular" relationships yet at the same time serve to explain or situate the position of the individual or group within them. This is the function and effect of ritual observance and "religion," in the broadest sense, so that the state can also be understood—following Durkheim's logic—as the interface or instance at which religion and the institutionalized practice of a political elite meet and integrate.[18]

The political relationships of the Vijayanagar state, and to a degree the Egyptian, Assyrian, Babylonian, and other empires in which religious or priestly elites and temple economies played a central role, have been described by the concept "ritual polity"[19] or as the "intense ritual penetration of everyday life." But there is, of course, a danger in this notion of turning these specifically structured systems of governance into an idealist notion of theocratic, "Asiatic" stability, in which the rise and fall of states and power elites is determined by "religion" and in which economic relationships are created by the demands of religious observance and beliefs or perceptions.

In fact, it is clear that rulers were generally quite aware of the process of religious-political manipulation necessary to the maintenance of their power and especially of the need to maintain control over resources in order to invest in this ritual system on a grand scale in order to continually legitimate their position. More significant, it is clear that, when we examine a number of ancient state formations more closely, this ritual incorporative facet and the ways in which cultic systems function at both the political and the economic levels to bind a wider territory together was widespread and represented in practice one of the commonest means of empire building—whether we are concerned with the Babylonian, Assyrian, or any of the other early Near Eastern empires. The point is clear in the contributions to this volume that deal with the Assyrian and Achaemenid Persian empires, where the rulers of both empires became actively involved in the dominant cults of conquered territories, which were then assimilated into a broader network of divine relationships, participation in which guaranteed both continuing divine support and therefore political and institutional stability. Indeed, the "ritual penetration" of a society as represented by specific sets of social practices that express the legitimacy and belief system underpinning elite and central authority and that generally express and reinforce the structure of social relations of production is common to all premodern (precapitalist) social formations, but in different degrees.

The differing combinations of a specific political universe, ecological context, kinship structure, and religious configuration promoted the varying role and position of such ritual, transactional networks. In southern India, the centering of social life around a temple-oriented system of redistribution of surplus wealth and political legitimacy, combined with the particular, highly fragmented character of the political geography of the region, meant that the process of state formation was always inscribed within such relationships and the structures they generated, producing a highly inflected set of political-religious relationships in which legitimacy depended to a very great extent on consensual acceptance. The situation was not so different in ancient Assyria and Babylon.

But, in the case of Indian states, there is an additional factor to be taken into account. The ideological structures of Hinduism, and its contingent social practices, which marked every aspect of Hindu social and political life across the whole subcontinent, tended under certain conditions to render the functions normally assumed and required of any state structure, especially those of maintaining order and internal cohesion, dangerously redundant. If we assume that states provide both centralized authority and, more important, normative rules for legal, social and economic relationships, then it becomes clear that in the Hindu context these characteristics of state organization are already present in the internal order of religious and social life—the lineage structures and caste attributions alone provide for much of this.[20] Given the permeative strength of Shari'a as a guide to day-to-day patterns of behavior down to the humblest levels of household existence, a similar case could, in fact, be made for certain varieties of Islam, although the two cases have rarely been compared, while in a few cases within Christianity—especially in certain post-Reformation movements—one could draw similar conclusions about the interface between state structures (and their functions), law, and normative social behavior. It would be interesting to examine some of the ancient state formations about which we have evidence in an attempt to see whether similar relationships did, or could, prevail, or whether, as argued by Mann, it is only the most recent salvationist systems that can achieve these results.[21]

The persistence of ideological integration can allow states to survive even with considerable administrative decentralization. State centers that are unable to maintain control and participation in the process of primary surplus distribution (through direct taxation, for example, or the ability always to coerce militarily) must attempt to survive by promoting their interests through alternative, *secondary* means of surplus *re*-distribution. Such means include the "devolution" of military and other authority, for example, to the level of the fief or an equivalent institution, as in western Europe during the period from the sixth to the sixteenth century. They include also networks of redistribution reinforced and operated through primarily religious structures.

Of course, both Islamic and Christian rulers in East and West legitimated the extraction and distribution of surplus—which is to say, in effect, the continued existence of their respective states—through political theologies, ideological narratives that highlighted the necessary duty of the state and its rulers to defend the faith and to promote the variety of associated activities which this entailed. At the same time, they had to be seen to reinforce and reaffirm their particular symbolic universe through ritualized expressions of faith and the redistribution of considerable amounts of surplus wealth to religious foundations of various types or through certain ideologically legitimating ritual actions. In the Byzantine world, the complex ceremonial of the imperial palace, the close relationship between the emperor (with the state) and the Church, and the supervision by the Church of popular beliefs and kinship structures created an impressive ideological and symbolic system of legitimation. Yet, in this particular formation, in contrast with the South Indian examples, it did not itself express also, or serve as, a key institution of surplus *distribution* necessary to the economic survival of the state institution. Similar ritual networks can be seen in the Islamic world, in western Christendom, and in the Chinese Empire. And, in the case of both Christianity and Islam, ritual incorporation (that is to say, conversion) served as a fundamental tool of political integration and domination. The "segmentary" states (discussed later) of South and Central America provide closer parallels to the South Indian case, for here temple-centered redistribution of surplus and tribute was a crucial means through which surplus appropriation and political authority were maintained.[22]

An additional point should be made: such ideologically integrative systems coexist at varying levels and interact differentially with local or group-based "social memories," that is, the narratives peculiar to particular socially and/or culturally distinct groups within a social formation.[23] Various elites—religious, political, warrior, mercantile—may each have their own ideological basis for defining their identity and their relationship and integrating ties with the central authorities. Similarly, different popular groups likely have their own group narratives that establish both their identity and the accepted basis of their relationships to local elites and to central state powers. To varying degrees, these legitimating narratives for various groups need to overlap and interpenetrate in a way that creates a network of ties that supports the authority of the state. However they may have evolved, such narratives serve not only to differentiate particular sets of individuals or subgroups—families, clans, kinship units, functionally distinct entities (craftsmen and artisans, slaves, servants, soldiers, clerics, aristocrats and so forth)— from one another (dependent on cultural, political, and geographical context) but at the same time to offer a source of common ideas and shared identities when the group as a whole is confronted with something external or imposed from outside. The historical context will determine how this takes place, but it is clear that both commemorative practices and public or private ritual observance derive from such narrative structures and can offer both oppositional and integrative possibilities to both subjects and rulers of empires.[24]

3. States and Elites

Since S. N. Eisenstadt's classic study of the dynamics of empires, the pursuit of resources by elites has been seen as central to understanding imperial states. Particularly important is the nature of the power-relations that dominated elite relationships—both within state apparatuses and between elites and the broader social formation.[25] How independent of society were state functionaries, individually or as a group? How limited was state power by the social and economic relationships that dominated a given society? Was the state, as a set of institutions, dependent upon a social and economic elite or "ruling class," or upon an alliance of tribal lineages and identities (which may or may not have had any historical substance), or upon some combination of these?[26] To what extent did emergent states incorporate existing elites? The relationships between these considerations and the origins of a given state system, on the one hand, and the appropriation, allocation, and distribution or redistribution of resources, on the other, constitute a series of focal issues.

These considerations are important because the state, through its need to establish and then maintain a regular and predictable structure for extracting revenues and resources, also enables or facilitates the evolution of new practices and relationships. This is clear in the evolution of the Roman state and empire, outlined in chapter 5, as well as in the way in which the East Roman/Byzantine state transferred the focus of its attention in fiscal matters away from urban centers to village communities during the course of the seventh and eighth centuries, thereby radically altering the ways in which social relationships between landlords and tenants, on the one hand, and between peasant producers, the state, and towns, on the other, functioned.[27] Similar examples exist in the cases of the Ottoman and Mughal states. In the Ottoman case, the growth during the seventeenth century of a local "nobility," together with the garrisoning of imperial salaried troops and Janissaries in the provinces on a permanent basis, radically altered the relationship between central government and regions (generally seen as to the disadvantage of the former); yet, such changes were made possible precisely because of the state's perceived fiscal and military requirements.[28]

Thus, the state also created spaces in which new developments could take place—the role of tax farmers in the Byzantine, Ottoman, and Mughal contexts, for example, both as extractors of revenue and as potential stimulants to changed patterns of investment or consumption of wealth, to changed structures of money use on the part of both producers and state administrations, and so on. In some cases, the existence of a central fiscal administration may have given hitherto unimportant local leaders—village headmen, small-scale local landlords—a more significant role in the process of fiscal extraction and accumulation, leading to shifts in the political order of power at the local level and ultimately reacting back on the state itself. In sixteenth- and seventeenth-century Indian states, the role of pre-imperial village elites and rank attributions had a significant influence on the ways the Mughal state, for example, and its regional predecessors and successors could organize, just as the existence of centralized state apparatuses and their demands for revenue in turn affected the ways in which these local relationships worked, shaping the social space within which they could evolve.[29]

As we shall see again and again in the chapters that follow, the evolution of states, as well as considerations bearing on their stability and collapse, turned on how rulers sought new ways to maintain control over state (and often nonstate) elites, while elites sought to maintain their authority, whether at the expense of the state or of rivals for local power. And this leads in turn to a consideration of how such state-elite relationships form part of a social totality, especially in the context of both local and international pools of influence—the concentric, overlapping, and reciprocally (but unevenly) influencing relationships that cross the boundaries of social formations.[30]

4. STATES, EMPIRES, AND COMPLEXITY

One important aspect of any discussion of states and their histories must be the differential processes of evolution reflected in their age or maturity. "Mature" states must confront very different problems from "young" states. The degree to which their various institutional and ideological systems become well established and embedded into the basic fabric of the social formations that support them must play an important role.

In newly formed conquest states, the conquerors are rarely integrated into the wider structure of social and economic relationships; they remain, in effect, parasitic consumers of wealth extracted by force, or the threat of force, alone. The "empire" of the late Roman Republic can be examined from this perspective. In others, while this may once have been the case, centuries of "state embedding" have occurred, so that the state elite, its apparatuses, and its ideology are inextricably interwoven into the social fabric of society at large.

Mature states also have a sense of identity and tradition, one based on generations of continuity of ideological and power structures, that is very different from that of newly founded states. These factors also influence both the contemporary and the modern views of certain states. The Byzantine "empire" was, in many respects, just a small, territorially unified state; its "imperial" aspect was both short lived and occasional, yet it retains the image of an empire because of its "imperial" origins, as part of the Roman imperial system.

This brings us at last to the question at the heart of this volume: the nature, constitution, and dynamics of empires. In a recent discussion, empires have been described very straightforwardly as the effects of the imposition of political sovereignty by one polity over others, however achieved, and the key marker of an "imperial" state was thus the degree of "foreign-ness" perceived to exist between rulers and ruled, conquerors and conquered.[31] In the simplest terms, then, the study of empires becomes the study of the subordination of one "state" or social formation by another and the extent to which the conquerors are successful in converting these peripheral zones into a part of their original state, both ideologically and in terms of fiscal, military, and administrative structures.

In some respects, this definition overlaps with the notion of the "segmentary" state, intended to suggest a multicentered, confederated political structure in which ideological elements and consensus play as great a role as centrally exercised coercive power.[32] Although many early states functioned on the basis of a series of concentric zones of power distribution, focused around a political core, we might reasonably describe "empires" on the same lines, in which case the issue of their success and longevity will revolve around the same key questions: to what extent are empires of conquest able to impose upon the conquered lands and cultures their own ideological and cultural values and patterns of administration and elite formation and thereby create out of a range of different sociocultural formations a more or less homogeneous set of political values and ideological identities? Of all the "empires" discussed in this volume, the Roman—and its successor in the east Mediterranean basin, the Byzantine—states were perhaps the most successful in this respect. Of those not discussed here, the various Chinese states, especially from the T'ang onwards, and perhaps with the exception of the Mongol Yuan and Manchu Qing dynasties, achieved similar rates of successful integration, although the vastness of the Chinese lands and the regionalization of Chinese elites meant that this process was always contested and achieved at some cost.

Historians have generally referred to the expansive political entities of the East and pre-Renaissance Europe as "empires"—whether that of China, of Charlemagne, of Rome, Russia, Persia, Byzantium, or many others. The "national state" is then something that emerges with the renaissance monarchies of Europe. Yet in fact most so-called national states emerged through conquest or inheritance of previously distinct political or cultural domains, even in Western Europe. This was true of the integration of Ireland into the British monarchy (or monarchies, as Scotland remained institutionally distinct as well until the eighteenth century); it was true of the French incorporation of regions such as Flanders, Alsace-Lorraine, and the Burgundian inheritance; it was true of various Italian peninsular states; and it was a fortiori true for such expansive multinational entities as the properly named Prussian, Russian, and Austro-Hungarian empires. In the nineteenth century, much of Africa and south Asia was then forcibly incorporated into empires ruled from European metropoles. "Empire" was thus arguably the normal or modal form of large political entity throughout Eurasia until quite recently.

The true national state claimed by citizens as their own through their identification with a ruling elite to which *all* (or very nearly all) members of society could legitimately aspire is a quite recent phenomenon, perhaps visible only from the end of the eighteenth century in the United States and France and from the nineteenth century in South America and most of Europe. In terms of political, cultural, and social integration and ideological unity, the late Byzantine, Ming Chinese, and Tokugawa Japanese states were more "national" territorial states than was the late-eighteenth-century British monarchy, which ruled over Ireland, Scotland, and England and parts of North America, India, and the Caribbean, as well as other overseas possessions.

While some empires evolved through strategic alliances based on kinship or inheritance through gift or marriage, the majority of those political formations that we conventionally label empires were the direct result of military conquest. However, the key element that defines "empires" here is not simply their origins but rather the mode through which states and elites exercised power and defined their relationships to each other and the broader society. In our terms, an "empire" is a territory (contiguous or not) ruled from a distinct organizational center (which may be mobile) with clear ideological and political sway over varied elites who in turn exercise power over a population in which a majority have neither access to nor influence over positions of imperial power. Such empires may over time acquire a great deal of cultural unification and identification between rulers and ruled (as in Ming China or late Imperial Rome), or there may be a clear gulf between rulers and ruled (as in the Ottoman rulers of Christian territories in Europe and most of the Mongol empires); or there may be partial integration of local elites and even limited pathways for certain ordinary individuals into broader imperial structures (as in the Janissary recruitment system of the late Ottoman Empire or the multinational elite of the Austro-Hungarians). While the particular patterns of state/elite relations and how they were institutionalized in systems of revenue extraction and distribution varied over space over time, "empire" in this sense was the typical formation by which large territorial states were ruled for most of human history, from several thousand years B.C.E. until the past century or two. While this volume concentrates on those empires that spanned the Middle East and eastern Mediterranean regions—largely because the states of Europe and China have been so often the basis for comparative analyses—the theoretical issues raised here thus are the same basic ones encountered throughout political history.

The following chapters describe and analyse such formations in respect of four key questions: how did they come into being? How did they survive? What was the structure of military/political and ideological power relations that facilitated this (or not)? And what was their economic basis in respect of the production, distribution, and consumption of wealth and also of the expansion of the base upon which wealth could be generated—whether quantitative (territorial expansion, for example), or qualitative (changing technologies of production, expanding trade, or shifts in the structures of capital investment)?

To answer any of these questions, we need first of all to determine at what level of explanatory power we wish to situate our discussion. It seems to us that there are at least three temporal frameworks across which the generation of states may be understood, which we may call for the sake of argument macro-, meso-, and micro-levels. While these are not equivalents for Braudel's long, medium, and short *durées*, they are similar in concept. The macro-level is perhaps best illustrated in the recent work by Diamond, which posits very long-term evolutionary pathways determined primarily by ecological conditions. Once a particular set of conditions has stimulated a particular set of responses in terms of demography, reproductive patterns, nutritional systems and technologies, then micro-level shifts and causal relationships are determined in their effects entirely within that set of constraints. In this framework, once the appropriation of surpluses from nature reach a certain level, and this circumstance is combined with a certain density of settlement and ability to transmit coercive force, then states and empires become possible. Ecological and evolutionary pathways then lead to further increases in density, surplus, extraction, and concentration of coercive force, or not. On these grounds, the geography, flora, and fauna of the fertile crescent at the end of the last ice age (ca. 11,000 B.C.E.) conferred specific advantages that gave the human societies that evolved there a permanent advantage over those in other areas that were unable to offer those conditions.[33] At this level of generality, of course, the value of specific data in terms of historical political systems is merely that it should not contradict the evolutionary pathways thus sketched out, and it is of little help in determining the causal relationships behind the rise and fall of specific imperial formations within ecological regions.

At the meso-level of explanation, however, we can begin to grasp issues pertaining to specific empires and peoples and the way they affected a particular trajectory of development. Here, we are confronted with particular but broadly located cultural systems set within specific geopolitical contexts (for example, the fertile crescent, the Indus valley, the Eurasian steppe, the central and western European zone, the mountain and plateau regions of central and south America) associated with particular types of political structure. Such differences tend to reflect fairly straightforwardly geographical catchment areas—contrast China, with its extensive cereal and rice culture, extensive power relationships, vast manpower resources, and consequent assumptions about use and availability of labor and so on, and the microcosmic systems of the southern Balkans, Asia Minor and the Mediterranean basin, or again the Indian subcontinent, with its contiguous zones of relatively open plain, semi-arid coastal and plateau regions, mountains, and forest.

At the micro-level, finally, we need to differentiate within these broader contexts and interrogate local variations (in both time and space) in social, cultural, and political life, including fortuitous shifts in social relations instigated by issues of resource availability, competition, and access to centers of production and distribution, density and rate of reproduction of population groups, and the relations of social *re*-production. That is to say, within the broad parameters of a given imperial system, we need to recognize the contingent patterns of kinship, control of resources, and allocation of power and authority, which can vary over time and space in response to highly specific conditions.

The contributions in this volume range from the macro- to the micro-level, although the emphasis is, for most contributors, on the meso- and micro-levels. One of the most important issues that emerges is that of avoiding an overly reductionist model—although lack of firm empirical data often makes this problematic—in grasping the actual workings of a given state formation in its social, economic, and political context. For several of the empires covered in this volume, the preponderance of archaeological and documentary evidence concerns the state, its projects and operations. Thus, an imbalance naturally emerges, with attention to the state's internal structure and its relations to elites playing a far greater role in analysis than the equally important–from a theoretical point of view—relationship between elites and local populations or the social relations governing daily life within the empire.

The limitations of definitions of state organization confined for the most part to governmental and administrative structures must be obvious, yet the discussion has generally been confined—with some exceptions—to this level. Thus, the role and function of the different elements that constitute the "ordinary" populations of states and their day-to-day activities have been generally ignored. Sadly, concepts of state power and authority have too often built upon this imbalance as if it were natural, so that the study of the state has for the most part been confined by the limits imposed by nineteenth- and twentieth-century concepts of centralized states and societies. This has meant, in particular, that historians have been constrained by notions of societal evolution that begin with "the primitive" and end up with the modern nation state, a teleology that has generally placed Western European societies at the forefront of "progress" and "development" and makes the rest of the world, in consequence, either a victim or a benefactor of Western "advances." While this strongly ideological perspective has been challenged sufficiently strongly in recent decades to merit only a mention here, we should be aware that it continues to exercise a certain attraction, especially when "ancient" empires are discussed as precursors to a later "rise of the West."

Equally suspect has been "state centrism," an approach that conceives of imperial states as sets of centralized operational processes and that denies local infrastructural autonomy to regions away from the central territories. This approach tends also to encourage a cyclical approach to historical change, in which the rise and decline of central state power is seen as a wholly internal process that occurs abstracted from any change in the broader society and its economic and social relations. In contrast to Europe, for example, some regions, such as South Asia, the Islamic realm, and China, are seen as lacking in cumulative and consequential processes. Each polity is taken as an object of research in itself and, usually, in isolation, so that it is characterized as having a period of growth, expansion, and consolidation, followed by a period of decline, to be replaced eventually by a new and, at the same time, derivative political structure, each of which is founded on the same unchanging social base. Again, this has been challenged and a more sophisticated approach proposed in more recent debate.[34]

One way of challenging these assumptions—where the empirical data are available, of course—is to attempt a detailed analysis of the evidence for what have been referred to as the "unofficial infrastructures" within which and upon which the more obvious "official" or public forms of government and state administration in most states are built. This may take a variety of forms, but its premise is that only rarely do novel forms of political structure arise from a vacuum (i.e., the complete annihilation of all that went before). Rather, elements of processual and structural continuity as well as change are universally present in the growth of any "new" system. The analysis may be focused on a range of themes, including, for example, the role of household administrations, of accounting systems, of clerical and exchange media, of networks of inherited rights and jurisdictional claims, and of popular socioeconomic solidarities and local ideologies and identities.

Wider structures of governmental administration arise out of a multiplicity of infrastructural relationships, many of which may remain entirely invisible to the historian because of the nature of the available evidence but which should always be borne in mind when describing the results of research based upon what data is at hand. There is a personal, career-oriented, family- and individual-centric core to all historically attested organizational infrastructures, for example, in which the power to control wealth and its distribution may also coincide in both delegated and inherited forms. State systems are usually the result of a long-term evolution of a wide range of highly inflected localized modes of micro-structural social organization, each operating in its own immediate context according to local traditions and practices, which coalesce at a higher level to produce interlocal and interregional networks of resource management, distribution, and exchange. Such networks always preexist the actual state formative moment itself (although such a moment can usually be precisely identified only in very recent cases). For some societies we have enough material actually to identify these relational systems, at least to a limited extent—the later Roman Republic and Empire, the Byzantine state, especially in its last four centuries or so, the Ottoman Empire and some of the more recent state formations in the Indian subcontinent, and the more recent Chinese and Japanese state systems, for example. For the temporally more distant empires, it is not always possible, although a surprising amount of detail for such aspects of middle- and late-kingdom Egypt and the empires of the Near East (including Assyria) can in fact be elicited.

The reason for emphasizing this collective, many-headed, and sometimes random development is that it provides the essential ground in which systems of rule and administration began to develop, and these are fundamental elements in the medium- and long-term success of state-like political entities. Networks of elite household administrations, the "bundles" of rights and privileges they gained over productive resources, through both long-term processes of kin-based inheritance and rights granted from higher political authorities, and their intra-elite relationships, all contributed to situations in which "states" were in effect many-centered, functioning through progressively decentralized pools of administrative effectiveness, and dependent upon mutually beneficial relations of support, tribute, and upward redistribution of revenues and resources.

These are only rarely visible in the case of the majority of the ancient states for which we have evidence, but they can be highlighted and brought out in the analysis of more recent state formations, as in Frank Perlin's discussion of the ways in which the heritable rights and "property brotherhood" described by the concept *vatan* functioned in the Maratha "state" in the seventeenth and eighteenth centuries. There a web of jurisdictional and property privileges coexisted and meshed with a state-centered hierarchic set of rights, an understanding of which must inform any attempt to come to grips with the origins of Maratha power in the region.[35] While they may not be attainable through the limited ancient source material for many ancient empires, they should perhaps be assumed more widely when we examine the inner dynamic of any such political formation.

One aspect that arises indirectly from most of the discussions in this volume but that directly addresses the micro-level of state development is the importance of the extensive keeping of records and accounts. These appear to be a key element in the structural underpinning of state systems, not only stimulating the growth of a specialist, literary/clerical elite but also functioning as determinants of the directions in which power and administration might evolve. Each imperial system appears to develop, to a greater or lesser degree, a "library" of categories, techniques, and measurement systems, along with their organizational prerequisites; and these demand in turn a certain input of wealth and resources, a certain mode of social-economic organization. They were an important feature of the Achaemenid administration and of the interprovincial economy that flourished under Achaemenid rule. With obvious regional and local exceptions, they became an important element in the economies of the Roman imperial state and remained so throughout the history of the Byzantine Empire. They were equally significant at the ideological level, symbolizing the power of the ruling house or the state administrative apparatus.

Systems of accounts, records, and measurement are thus essential features of the broader historical developments in which we are interested and exemplify two fundamental points: first, that state and governmental/administrative "systems" cannot be the product of individual "reforms" or planning (even if individuals introduce changes or innovations into preexisting structures) and, second, that infrastructural networks of administration, exchange, reciprocity, and appropriation represent a constant element of any wider set of political power relations. Such networks both support the latter and at the same time continue to lead an existence that, while not autonomous, nevertheless is also relatively independent of the higher-order authority at progressively more localized levels of activity; that is, the greater the social distance between them and the paramount political-economic power, the greater the degree of their autonomy.

Moreover, there need not necessarily be a thoroughgoing uniformity across an empire's territory, either geographically or in respect of social use. Indeed, a multiplicity of systems could often coexist, and the more geographically, socially, and politically diverse an empire or state, the more varied the subsystems of exchange and measurement might be beneath the surface created by the "official" systems. Even in the most uniform of monetary systems, such as Byzantium, for example, there existed local and regional variations determined by social as well as geographical locus.[36] In this respect, we need to keep in mind the specificity of infrastructural social organization and at the same time its integration into wider networks of relationships, a focus emphasized also by Mann, who has also stressed the open and nonbounded nature of social structures at certain levels by approaching the problem from the point of view of the distribution of networks of social power.[37]

The issues raised by these questions are especially pertinent to the problem of how empires arise and evolve, since we are confronted in most cases by a process in which a wide range of neighboring systems and subsystems of power over resources and ideas are subsumed or incorporated by an aggressive external power but in which the aggressors themselves are always affected in some form by the process of conquest and by the nature of the systems conquered. In all the historical examples dealt with by the contributors to this volume, this was the case, although the modalities through which these relations were expressed varied enormously from case to case. What we see, inevitably, is the complexity of state and empire building, both in terms of origins and genesis of empire and in terms of structure and function.

5. HISTORY AND THE EVOLUTION OF IMPERIAL FORMS

It is a striking pattern in the history of empires that the succession of empires also presents us with a succession of imperial forms. That is, as we view the Assyrian, Persian, Macedonian, Roman, and Byzantine empires, to name just a few, we also see imperial formations that differ in degree of power over their territories, the integrations of their elites, and the patterns of ideological integration and institutionalized resource extraction and redistribution. To a surprising degree, it is as if a given imperial formation emerges as a response or solution to a particular problem of power extension or integration and then persists as long as that solution holds. Yet, when changes in broader social relations, resource balances, or external relationships with other territorial powers threaten given imperial institutions, that empire often fails. A new empire, more successful in solving that problem (or able to solve new ones that have arisen) then arises, and its imperial structures remain more or less stable for long periods.

Thus, for example, if we view the relationships between the imperial center and recently subordinated regions, we find that the Assyrian Empire imposed a simple binary choice on such regions: recognize Assyrian suzerainty and pay tribute or be destroyed. There was no question of ideological integration of distant territories into the Assyrian national character or of absorption of local rulers or elites into the Assyrian elite. The Persian Empire, by contrast, approached the problem of relations with subordinated regions more peaceably, seeking to co-opt local rulers and elites into an alliance (often cemented by marriage) with Persian notables sent to govern these territories. Persian satraps thus created a successful "straddle," maintaining power relationships both within local regional societies and within the Persian imperial elite. Local societies, however, were largely unaffected. The Roman Empire went still further and sought to remodel conquered territories by creating a full ideological and institutional integration with Roman practices. Local elites could (and did) adopt Roman names and religion and obtain positions in the imperial bureaucracy—but local institutions, cultural and religious practices, and power networks were deprived of any political significance. States became Roman provinces, local deities were absorbed into the Roman pantheon, and even local kings were subordinated to Roman governors.

Some empires—such as those of Rome and Byzantium—of course evolved through several stages, experiencing institutional collapse (as at the end of the Roman Republic or the decline of the Western empire) and then re-emerging in new forms. But, for the most part, imperial structures have been both fairly rigid and persistent. In some ways, this has been a source of imperial strength; when a particular set of institutions of imperial authority and imperial center/elite relations has been well fitted to mesh with existing patterns of elite relationships and social patterns of ordinary life and local authority, that has endowed imperial structures with long life. In this way, the "fit" or equilibrium between the often invisible infrastructures of local and everyday power and the overarching institutions of imperial power are as important to the origins and maintenance of particular imperial formations as the initial facts of conquest (or sometimes inheritance) that incorporated certain territories. Yet, it can also be a critical weakness, for, as underlying conditions change, the "fit" or equilibrium among economic, social, and political relationships that span local, imperial, and "international" levels and the specific institutions of imperial rule can become impaired, leading to conflicts among rulers, elites, and even popular groups over the terms and extent of each group's claims on the others.

Historians—and many sociologists—have typically adopted static metaphors for imperial institutions, speaking of the "architects" of "structures" of authority. Yet, recognizing the ongoing equilibrium between the infrastructures of everyday social and economic life and the reproduction of overarching imperial authority, it may well be wise to adopt a more dynamic metaphor. In this view, the "stability" of an imperial system would not be the result of a fixed institutional structure of authority; rather it would be the dynamic result of an ongoing equilibrium, the maintenance of a balance between the demands of the state upon elites and the underlying economy, between the authority of rulers over elites and the authority of elites within their local or particular sphere, and of the ideological integration of diverse cultural, regional, and economic groups into imperial systems of meanings, values, and responsibilities.[38]

Instability or change then becomes a matter not simply of internal decay, of conflicts or problems within the central regime, but of the breakdown of the dynamic equilibrium that maintains apparent stability. Of course, internal decay (as in fiscal affairs or military discipline), internal factional conflicts, and problems of central versus regional control may well be a part of the story of imperial decline. But such factors often appear in the course of ongoing dynasties without toppling the overarching framework of imperial rule. When an imperial system falls, we generally need to look at failures of the existing institutions to maintain their dynamic "fit," or ability to reproduce themselves, given changes in underlying economic, political, social, or international conditions. Major demographic shifts that create, reduce, or redistribute revenues and resources; new modes of economic activity that create free resources outside the accustomed local and imperial channels of resource flows; changes in patterns of social mobility that unsettle local, regional, and intra-elite relationships and thus undermine elite relationships with the central authorities; waves of conquest that offer new opportunities to elites and popular groups or destroy earlier patterns of local or imperial authority; and the emergence of new belief systems (or the increased salience of old heterodoxies) that weaken the hegemony and integration of imperial ideology—some or all of these are likely to lurk behind the sudden dramatic collapse of imperial regimes.[39]

When we speak of the "evolution of imperial forms," it should be clear that we are *not* using a unilinear metaphor of progressive improvement or a "stage theory" of social history, à la Spencer. Rather, the terminology of evolution here is meant to invoke the more precise usage of evolutionary biology, in which evolution represents the diversity of life as resulting from a series of unpredictable, highly diverse, many-branched pathways of change and development, including dead ends, regressions, and certain innovations that allow species a greater range or special adaptations. Somewhat analogously, we suggest that the variety of imperial formations reflects a series of unpredictable, highly diverse, many-branched pathways of political, social, and economic development, in which imperial forms arise and succeed as they develop a dynamic equilibrium with their "niche" of local economic, political, and social relationships in the societies they rule (and border). Some such forms prosper for greater or less periods, then may fail and be replaced by other forms as conditions change.

To point to a familiar example, the alternation of imperial control in Asia between nomadic hordes that create conquest empires and settled communities with long-standing ideological, political, and social regimes has been a long-recognized rhythm that is quite similar to the cycles of predator-prey populations in simple ecological models. In both cases, the precise timing and magnitude of the shifts from domination by nomads (or predators) to their retreat is chaotic and unpredictable. However, the general pattern of ebb and flow, of stability and instability of the equilibrium of a particular institutional setting, is inherent in the nature of the underlying relationships—namely that at any given time apparent stability is merely the result of a dynamic equilibrium among many forces, so that equilibrium can be lost (or regained) as conditions shift, and new equilibria arise.

For the purposes of this volume, we thus suggest (and it must remain no more than a suggestion at this point, whose value is to be tested in the specific studies that follow) that the series of empires that has arisen and fallen in overlapping succession in the Middle East and eastern Mediterranean region represents a series of equilibria, stable formations in which imperial structures have managed to find a balance with the resource production and distribution, the local elite authority, the settlements and networks of social interaction, and the belief systems that characterized varying swathes of this region. Of course, rulers and imperial systems act to restructure resource production and distribution, local authority, population settlements and networks, and belief systems, sometimes quite radically, as with Babylonian deportations of conquered people or with Roman assimilation of conquered peoples as citizens and their states as provinces. Yet, imperial states rarely have total control over their infrastructure and their physical and political environment. They are thus subject to both sharp shocks and to gradual changes in those environments. In this way, the "meso-" and even "micro-" levels of social and political relationships influence the longer-term Braudelian "deep structures" to which imperial structures are generally fitted during their periods of inception, growth, and success. Reproduction—in both the literal biological form (as in chapter 7) and the more metaphorical form applied to institutions, beliefs, and practices—thus is central to understanding the full cycle of the rise, stability, decay, and displacement of empires.

The essays in this volume examine, in various ways, the institutions and "reproductive processes" of ancient, classical, and early medieval empires. Each makes its own choice of focus on micro- or meso-processes, although with some attention to the very macro-level of general ecological, economic, and international conditions in the eastern Mediterranean and Middle East region. While we do not propose to develop anything like an integrated history of the region as a whole, we do hope that by bringing together these cases, we can produce greater insights into the varied bases for imperial "success" at different times and places and into the pattern of imperial declines and successions that have characterized world history for most of the past five millennia.

NOTES

1. The discussion is complex, and a range of different perspectives have been expressed in the recent literature. For a representative sample, see Di Cosmo 1999; Lieberman 1999; Tilly 1992; Goldstone 1991; McNeil 1989; Mann 1986a (reviewed by Wickham 1988); Carneiro 1987; Tainter 1988; Runciman 1989 (reviewed by Wickham 1991: 188–203); Skocpol 1979; Rueschemeyer, Evans and Skocpol 1985; Eisenstadt 1986; Jessop 1990; Block 1988; Sanderson 1999; Steinmetz 1999; Alcock et al. 2001; Bang and Bayly 2003; Trigger 2003.

2. See Jaspers 1949; Schwartz 1975; and in particular Eisenstadt 1986a and 1886b; Arnason, Eisenstadt, and Wittrock 2005.

3. See, for example, Assmann 1992, 290–1.

4. Mann 1986a.

5. Similar questions posed, e.g., in Morrison 2001a.

6. For a recent survey see Goldstone 2000; for some older literature, see Cipolla 1970; Cohen and Service 1978; Claessen and Skalník 1978, 1981; Eisenstadt 1967, 1978; Kautsky 1982, Poggi 1990.

7. Elias 1967, esp. vol. 2.

8. Weber 1921; 1972: vol. 3, 619–30, 650–78; Mann 1986a: 20–32. See the useful summaries of concepts and theories in Giddens 1993: 50–2, 308–11, and the discussions in Sanderson 1999; Trigger 2003. The general discussion in Bang and Bayly 2003 and Bang 2003 reflects the current diversity of approach. Bang's paper, which deals with "tributary empires," in recognition of the difficulties of establishing a functionally agreed general definition, takes the term "tributary" for granted without further elaboration, which itself leads to some difficulties, of course.

9. See Runciman 1989: 152–53, for example.

10. This is not only a premodern phenomenon: see, e.g., Fabietti 1982.

11. See Ibn Khaldun 1958: I 247 ff.

12. There has been a great deal of discussion in recent years on the nature and form of state power in premodern state formations. See in particular Mann 1986a and Runciman 1989, both of which discuss, from very different perspectives, the ways in which structures of social power are generated within the institutional framework of state apparatuses, on the one hand, and social praxis, on the other. For Mann's useful summary of the key elements in state formation as argued here, see Mann 1986a: 112.

13. See chapter 2.

14. For Sasanid Persia (3rd–7th c. c.e.), see Rubin 1995; Howard-Johnston 1995. The points made here can be read without difficulty from the political history of the Sasanian kingdom and the pattern of power relations over the fourth to the seventh centuries, which it exemplifies. See also Rubin 2004.

15. See, e.g., Appadurai and Breckenridge 1976.

16. See chapter 5.

17. See especially the valuable discussion of Wood 1977/79; Heinzelmann 1975; and Lewis 1976. Bishops represented a very important focus of spiritual power and authority, backed by sometimes quite extensive ecclesiastical revenues, quite independent of the royal and lay establishment. By the middle of the seventh century, the blending of Frankish and Gallo-Roman elites meant that the episcopate was more closely connected, through kinship, to the secular elites of the Merovingian kingdom.

18. See Stein 1989: 18 ff. on the evolution of the Vijayanagar state, and 102 ff. on the nature and function of ritual incorporation; and see for further discussion Tambiah 1976: 114 ff.; Stein 1980: esp. 264 ff. For a useful account of the ways in which dissent and opposition to central authority, or particular forms of central authority, were expressed, see Morrison 2001b. For Durkheim's approach, see Durkheim 1976.

19. See Heitzman 1991; Preston 1980; Spencer 1969: 42–56.

20. See in particular Stein 1985: esp. 74 ff.; and in general Saraswati 1977. For a detailed discussion of these points, with further literature, see Haldon 1993: 242 ff.

21. Mann 1986a: 301–40, and esp. 341–72.

22. For "ritual penetration," see Mann 1986a: 361; but against his argument that it was *only* the major world—salvationist—religious systems that offered such possibilities, see Wickham 1988: esp. 68–72. For the function of "ritual enclosure" in pre-Columbian South American cultures, see Marcus 1976, and esp. 1984.

23. For studies of "social memory," see Fentress and Wickham 1992; Connerton 1989; Appadurai 1981, for example.

24. See Woolf 2001, 1998; Assmann 1992. On theories of narrative and the construction of political identities, see Haldon 1986.

25. Eisenstadt 1967. The concept "society" needs also to be employed circumspectly: in how inclusive or exclusive a sense is it to be taken? To what extent does it embrace smaller or less extensive sets of social relations and cultural identities? This is a point taken up by, among others, Mann 1986a: 1 ff., who rejects the term entirely, along with the notion that societies form unitary wholes that are in some way "bounded," preferring to speak of multiple overlapping and intersecting power networks. We are not sure that this is necessarily a *better* way to theorize "society," but it does at least ask the right questions. For historically grounded discussion for the late Roman and early Islamic period, see Haldon and Conrad 2004.

26. See for discussion Haldon 1993: 140 ff.

27. See Haldon 1997: esp. 132 ff.

28. See, for example, Goffman 1990: 26 ff; Barkey 1997.

29. See on these issues the excellent discussion of Perlin 1993: esp. 36 ff., 51–74.

30. For the "overlapping" character of socioeconomic and cultural structures, and the ways in which such reciprocal influences are hierarchized according to the relative strengths of the state, social, or cultural forms, see Rowlands 1987 and Hedeager 1987.

31. Doyle 1986, 45.

32. For the "segmentary" state, see Southall 1956, 1965; also Stein 1977. For criticisms of the way this concept has been used, however, see Champakalakshmi 1981; Kulke 1982.

33. Diamond 1997.

34. Rueschemeyer et al. 1985.

35. Perlin 1993: esp. 60–74.

36. For Indian examples, see ibid. 178–228.

37. See Mann 1986a and 1986b.

38. See Morrison 2001b: 277, for example.

39. Eisenstadt 1978; Goldstone 1991.

2

The Neo-Assyrian Empire

Peter R. Bedford

1. Introduction

The Neo-Assyrian (hereafter NA) Empire is the name given to a polity centered on the upper Tigris River that at its height in the seventh century B.C.E. controlled territory extending from the Zagros Mountains in the east to the Levant (Syria-Palestine) and much of Egypt in the west and from the Persian Gulf in the south to the headwaters of the Tigris and Euphrates in southeastern Anatolia in the north. It was the largest polity seen in western Asia up until that time. The NA period is technically a linguistic designation, denoting the third and last period of the Assyrian dialect of Akkadian (Old Assyrian period c.2000–c.1800 B.C.E.; Middle Assyrian period c.1400–c.1050 B.C.E.), although this period is coincident with the empire in which the texts were generated. While dates for the beginning of the empire can be disputed, it is generally accepted that the empire existed from the late tenth century until the late seventh century (c.934–c.605 B.C.E.), more than three hundred years. It was therefore also the most durable empire seen until then in western Asia. There had been a smaller Assyrian Empire for part of the Middle Assyrian (hereafter MA) period that extended across northeastern Mesopotamia (now northern Iraq, northeastern Syria, and southeastern Turkey) and after which the NA Empire was initially fashioned. Previous to this, the empires based in Mesopotamia were centered in the south (Babylonia) and, while extending along the Euphrates Eiver valley into northern Syria, were much more modest in their territorial reach. The best known of the southern-based empires are those founded by Sargon of Akkad (c.2340–c.2159 B.C.E.)[1] and Hammurabi of Babylon (he of the famous "law code"; 1863–1712 B.C.E. [middle chronology]). Arguably these third- and early-second millennium "empires" were rather different in their forms of maintenance and political integration from what one sees in the NA Empire.

With this empire lasting some three hundred years, it is possible to identify changes in its character, not simply its geographic extent, but also its organization and modes of political domination and economic exploitation. This chapter offers a description of aspects of these changes by means of an historical overview of the period. In so doing, it attempts to elucidate, with varying degrees of success, a number of questions that should prove useful for the comparative study of empires: how did the empire begin? How was it maintained and expanded? How did it end? How was it ruled? Given the constraints of space and the nature of the available sources, it is possible to offer here an extended consideration of two areas closely related to the second and fourth questions, namely principles or beliefs that provided legitimacy and identity to both rulers and the ruled and mechanisms of imperial control, including the classification of regions of the empire into different categories. The NA Empire is significant not only for the new and distinctive ways in which it justified and attempted to integrate the empire. It also bequeathed modes of imperial organization and legitimation to the ensuing Neo-Babylonian and Achaemenid Persian empires. Before turning to the historical outline of the NA Empire, however, the chapter briefly sets out by way of orientation the sources available for the study of the empire and the types of questions they can address, and it briefly introduces certain aspects of NA culture and society.

2. Orientation and Background

Various categories of evidence are available for the study of the NA Empire. Written sources include chronological texts, such as king lists, chronicles, and eponym lists (year-names taken from the names of officials),[2] and royal inscriptions, such as annals, display inscriptions, votive inscriptions, and "letters to the god" (reports on military campaigns).[3] As these texts are primarily royal commemorative texts, they have proved to be useful sources for the study of royal ideology and the ideological justifications for Assyrian imperialism. They also include important information concerning the political geography of the empire, types and amount of tribute and booty obtained, chronology of reigns, and political history. These types of texts cover the whole period, but not in uniform depth. More inscriptions, for example, were produced in periods of Assyrian ascendancy (in periods 1a, 1b, 2a, and 2b, in the historical overview provided later in this chapter). Officials' inscriptions include texts written by NA governors in their provinces[4] and others written by indigenous ruling houses that were retained in power by the Assyrians, as evidenced in Neo-Hittite and Aramean and Phoenician texts from Syria-Palestine.[5] As the Tell Fekherye inscription (midnorthern Mesopotamia) shows,[6] these two types were not mutually exclusive categories, since local rulers could represent themselves as governors as well as indigenous monarchs (in this bilingual stele the local ruler is termed "governor" in the Akkadian text and "king" in the Aramaic text). Royal inscriptions were composed by independent Babylonian kings.[7]

Loyalty oaths and treaties are the oaths sworn by client kings and also by Assyrian officials.[8] Probably to be included here are the Aramaic treaties from Sifre, which are thought by some to be between an Assyrian provincial governor and a client king.[9] Administrative texts deal with the palace and temple, with provincial and military administration. Administration often includes economic matters.[10] Legal texts deal with decisions before a judge over matters such as murder, theft, and debt[11] or concern conveyances (of persons or property, including land), contracts (loans and promissory notes), and receipts (as proof that a debt had been discharged).[12] There are also legal and economic texts from Babylonia.[13] Also to be included here are royal grants and decrees giving land and tax concessions to senior administrators.[14]

About 2,500 letters and fragments survive mainly from historical period 2 (discussed later), although a preponderance of all datable letters come from two brief periods in period 2b)—"ten years at the end of Sargon's reign and nine years at the beginning and end of Esarhaddon's and Assurbanipal's reigns, respectively."[15] The letters are written to and from the royal court, dealing with administrative matters (only in part to do with the provinces), and about half of them deal with matters of medicine, extispicy, astrology, and omen interpretation.[16] Oracular material was largely generated for the royal court by cultic experts in response to enquiries to deities, particularly Shamash, the god of justice.[17] Whereas in the "letters to the king" it is commonly unsolicited omens being reported, the extispicy reports are solicited by the king to obtain divine advice. A related category of texts consists of "prophecies" delivered to the king from the goddess Ishtar (the god of war [and love], so often the message is an encouragement for the battle).[18] The date of these texts is quite late (historical period 2b), but they offer insight into the types of political decisions that had to be made by kings, the ways in which they were reached, and other concerns of the kings (illness, loyalty of officials and clients). Together with the annals, they also help to track military campaigns, since the kings always sought divine support and the divine timetable in undertaking military activities. Finally, there are also literary texts, some of which give insight into royal ideology.[19]

Nontextual information comes from surface surveys, undertaken for sections of the upper Habur Valley and northern Jezirah (both north-central Mesopotamia),[20] and above all from excavations, mainly of cities, notably the Assyrian royal (capital) cities in the homeland (such as Kalhu [Nimrud]; Dur-Sharrukin [Khorsabad]; Nineveh; Aššur) as well as some provincial capitals (for example, Til Barsip/Kar Shalmaneser [Tell Ahmar] on the Euphrates bend; Dur-katlimmu on the Habur).[21] The emphasis has been on palatial buildings, which has led to the discovery of texts but leaves us with little understanding of urban sites as a whole. Assyrian palace reliefs have been analyzed in detail, particularly with an eye to their ideological import. There is also interest in influence on Assyrian art from western (that is, Aramean and Neo-Hittite) artistic traditions.[22]

The preponderance of written sources date from the later period (historical period 2b). We rarely obtain anything from the subjugated peoples themselves, so our view of them is from the perspective of the dominant Assyrian power. The biblical texts from Israel and Judah ascribed to this period are about our only source for the views of subjugated peoples. Texts such as First Isaiah (Isaiah 1–39), Amos, and Deuteronomy document knowledge of Assyrian literary traditions.[23] Much of the Assyrian source material, both written and archaeological, is skewed toward the royal court and the king in particular. The types of sources, their provenances, and their dates circumscribe to a great degree the analysis of the empire that is possible.

Both Assyriology and the historical study of ancient western Asia based on the cuneiform sources (as distinct from classical or biblical sources) are still relatively young academic fields, only about 150 years old. Much of that time has been spent deciphering the texts, establishing a reliable chronology, and outlining the political history. For the NA period, deciphering the texts has proven to be particularly demanding, with a number of false steps along the way. Take the letters mentioned earlier. They were rather poorly copied in the 1890s through the 1910s and similarly poorly edited in the 1930s; they thus proved to be of limited historical use. It was not until the 1970s that reliable translations of them began to appear, thanks largely to the work of Simo Parpola. Similarly, hand copies of the economic and administrative texts had been published,[24] but they were not always accurate and often proved hard to understand, not the least because it proved difficult to establish a context for them and they are filled with specialist terminology. Nicholas Postgate's work since the late 1960s has helped immensely to clarify the meaning of these texts. Having said that, I must admit that there is much that we cannot deduce simply because we have no clear knowledge of the context of the texts. Parpola's team that produced the State Archives of Assyria (that is, the complete corpus of NA texts produced by the empire)[25] has rendered an invaluable service to those who do not want to be burdened with deciphering the texts. That does not mean, of course, that a firsthand familiarity with the texts and an intimate knowledge of the language are unimportant for historians of the NA Empire.

The upshot of all this is that a number of questions pertinent to those interested in the comparative study of empires cannot be readily answered with any assurance. Take demography, for example. Ancient Near Eastern historians have been reticent to offer even guesses at the population of western Asia for any pre-Hellenistic period. It might be possible to estimate the population by extrapolating from the number of deportees given in NA annals, if we knew what percentage of the conquered population they represented and if we could trust the numbers given. Estimates of the overall number of people deported in the NA period range from 1.5 to 4.5 million.[26] But even the lower of these figures is commonly considered to be impossibly high, not least because of the logistical problems facing the Assyrian administration in moving, in the largest contingent, some 208,000 persons (from Babylonia to Assyria). Even if this latter figure is interpreted as the number of persons deported in a series of movements, logistical problems remain. While we cannot trust the figures sufficiently to extrapolate an accurate population count, the general settlement pattern clearly underwent a change, with more villages appearing across northern Mesopotamia and signs of increased settlement in Babylonia.[27] Urbanism, not the least in the Assyrian heartland, is also a feature, with royal cities either being newly built or being refurbished and expanded (Aššur 75 ha; Nimrud 360 ha; Khosabad 300 ha; Nineveh 700 ha). Provincial capitals were also constructed or refurbished, with their populations increased by new settlers (for example, Kar Shalmaneser 60 ha; Dur-katlimmu 55 ha). The populations of these royal cities were mostly settled by the crown, and arguably the same obtains for most, if not all, the new agricultural settlements across northern Mesopotamia. Rather than reflecting population increase, changing settlement patterns were an outcome of a government policy that included the resettlement of people after deportation and the sedentarizing of semi-nomadic Arameans and Chaldeans. It points to a restructuring of the agricultural economy; exploiting labor in new ways and opening up new lands.[28]

We are only a little better served in respect of technology.[29] Assyria lagged behind both the Hittites and Syria-Palestine in the use of iron. As Brinkman notes: "The Hittites had mastered the methods of producing significant amounts of iron by at least the thirteenth century, and Syria-Palestine was making wide use of the technology by the tenth century. Assyria at the beginning of the ninth century was still largely dependent on bronze for weapons and for agricultural and household implements."[30] Iron was seemingly appropriated by Assyrians for military use from caches captured in Syria-Palestine, but by the third quarter of the eighth century it was undoubtedly a producer. This slow introduction of the technology for iron production did not hamper Assyrian military success. Much of what we know of technological improvements pertains to the military—the development of more advanced chariotry, particularly the development of a platform that could support three (and sometimes four) men (the driver, the bowman, and the shield bearer), and of highly specialized siege warfare, including the development of the battering ram, the construction of earthen ramps, and the use of sappers. Something more substantial can be said on the topics of Assyrian political and religious institutions and class structure, although it must be stressed that the vast bulk of our information pertains to the upper echelons of society. We really know very little about the ordinary members of society.[31]

Assyria seems to have formed in the early fourteenth century when a territory at the eastern edge of the northern Mesopotamian Hurrian kingdom of Mitanni extricated itself. In wresting its independence, Assyria was born. This polity needs to be distinguished from the ancient city-state of Aššur (Ashur), although there is clear continuity with it, not the least in Ashur initially being the capital, and that city's tutelary deity (also named Ashur) becoming the paramount deity of the new polity. MA and NA king lists and lists of officals present Assyria as being an unbroken continuation of the city-state, and cultural continuity is evident in language and religion. The territory of Assyria was much larger than that controlled by the city-state, however. It encompassed a triangular area from Ashur in the south, to Dur-Sharrukin (Khorsabad) in the north, across to Arbela in the east (see map 2.1). This was the Assyrian homeland. To this was attached a number of provinces in northern and northeastern Mesopotamia taken from the declining Mitanni.

NA notions of kingship and the political and religious institutions and beliefs that obtained are all indebted to the MA period. More will be said on royal ideology in a later section, but here it should be noted that the king was viewed as having an intimate relationship with the god Ashur, and he implemented the divine will.[32] He enjoyed absolute power over the state and had responsibility for good governance, which included the care and feeding of gods and the maintenance of their shrines. He was the supreme and sole legislator and chief justice. No formal law codes are known to us. Most legal matters were regulated by custom, and the judicial system operated without the king's personal intervention.[33] While the king was the supreme human being in Assyrian thought, he was a mortal all the same, and Assyrians resisted the deification of their ruler, which had been known in Sumer and early Babylonia. Assyria was a militaristic state, and the king was the chief military leader, although he did not always lead the army in person. In marching to war, the army was a sort of religious procession, led along by priests and statues of the gods. All wars were religious wars, justified by the will of Ashur.[34]

Our knowledge of religion is limited to the state cults. Little is known of personal piety or the religious beliefs and practices of ordinary Assyrians. Assyrian religion was polytheistic, with the gods organized as in a hierarchy under the chief deity, Ashur.[35] They each had assigned roles (for example, Ishtar: battle and love; Shamash: justice), and each had a primary residence in one of the main cities (Ishtar: Arbela; Ninurta: Kalhu; Ashur: Ashur), although they all had shrines in various cities. Babylonian deities such as Enlil, Marduk, and Nabu were also worshipped in Assyria, and Babylonian ceremonies such as the *akitu* ritual were borrowed.[36] The center of the cult was the temple and the divine statue. The temple was a monumental structure housing the cult statue in a central shrine and provided space for other deities in ancillary chapels. It also had rooms for storage and the activities of various personnel who worked there: artisans, scribes, kitchen staff, and domestic servants, as well as cultic functionaries. A temple was a self-contained community with its own hierarchy of personnel and its own economic resources, which were mainly in the form of land holdings, although increasingly they were dependent on royal benefits, including donations of tribute and booty, specific taxes levied on certain provinces, and ex voto offerings. The head of the temple was the "chief administrator," who was responsible to the king. Given that the king had ultimate responsibility for the cults, temples and their senior personnel can be viewed as part of the state bureaucracy. Divination (specifically astrology and extispicy) also fall within the bounds of religion, since the Assyrian worldview understood that deities communicated with the terrestrial world, in particular with the king, through such means. There were numerous specialists in both astrology and extispicy attached to the royal court and within the state bureaucracy generally (as temple personnel or attached to the palace of a provincial governor).[37]

In the administration of the empire[38] there was a clear distinction between, on the one hand, Assyria (the home provinces) and the northern Mesopotamian provinces that paid taxes of various kinds and, on the other hand, the subjugated client states from which tribute was exacted. There were some similarities in organization, since the king placed each province under the control of a governor[39] or in client states, particularly earlier in the empire and in territories more distant from the Assyrian heartland, under a member of an indigenous ruling house as a loyal servant of Assyria. Beneath the governor and his bureaucracy were local town and village mayors. Some agricultural lands were placed at the disposal of governors, leading bureaucrats of the central administration, and members of the leading Assyrian families, often including the labor to work the land (for example, appendix, text no. 4).

The Assyrian state, including the administration, was essentially militaristic in organization, and there was usually little distinction between military service and civil service. The chain of command was not always from one level to that immediately adjacent; the crown gave direct orders to some officials far down the pyramid, and the king had the right to intervene at any level in any matter. While the authority of the king was technically unlimited, it was checked by religion, legal precedent, and the temper of his nobles and officials; this last group effectively ran the empire on the king's (and the deity's) behalf.[40] At the royal court there were six senior officials (the following English titles are attempts to make some sense of their position): the major domo, the vice-chancellor, the field marshal, the palace herald, the chief butler, and the (chief) steward. The first two were royal advisers (the former alone having direct access to the king), the third headed the army, the fourth was the chief administrative officer of the realm, the fifth acted as the king's plenipotentiary, and the sixth undertook special royal commissions. We do not know much about their actual duties. Some of these officials had provinces ceded to them, which were administered by others in view of the owner's absence at court.[41] Land grants were also given to certain administrators at the next level down: viziers, the chief eunuch, and the chief justice. At this level also were the provincial governors, basically organized in a hierarchy (most prestigious in the homeland or near it). Their responsibilities were military and civil. Technically, they were members of the court, but they served in the provinces. Also outside the court, but of high standing in the administration, were the chief administrators of the main temples and the mayors of the major cities in the Assyrian heartland. There were numbers of lower-level administrators ("courtiers") attached to the palace who were organized under the chief baker (note that often the titles of senior bureaucrats reflect their origins in domestic service). There were also tax collectors for royal lands and for the provinces. Some of these were assigned specialized tasks such as the collection of horses for the army. Army officers should also be mentioned among important, but lower-level, officials. Captains commanded a company of fifty men. Charioteers were viewed as the elite fighting forces within an army that also included cavalry, engineers, and infantry, the last forming the majority of the troops. What we know of the class structure arises out of this bureaucracy, since it reflected the social order.[42] At the top was the king; next came those attached to the royal court or the court of the crown prince, then administrators at various levels, officers in the army, ordinary Assyrian "citizens" (there is no Assyrian term), and semifree laborers (made up of deportees who worked on state land). At the bottom were slaves (never a very large number; some were Assyrians reduced to debt bondage, others prisoners of war).

Assyrians belonged to family groups or clans that were in turn part of larger groupings usually called tribes. One's social status, and thus access to administrative posts and the emoluments that came with them, depended on the family or clan to which one belonged. It was possible, although not common, for families to move up in social status given one or more generations of sterling service to the state by an individual. In this way, one successful family member could enhance the social and economic standing of the whole family. Some foreigners were integrated into the Assyrian social system, since by the late eighth century Aramean names appear at very high levels in the class structure. There were a number of other "free" foreigners who also attained high rank in the bureaucracy. Generally foreigners did forced labor on building and agricultural projects or were otherwise employed in menial capacities in temples and palaces.

The vast majority of the population were farmers who worked family-owned land. Families and clans lived together in villages near their agricultural holdings. We do not know how these villages were organized beyond each having a mayor who represented them before state bureaucrats and who also acted as the local judge (a traditional role rather than one given by the state; many bureaucrats [palace officials, temple officials] acted in a judicial capacity, with their role more like that of a counselor to the parties involved than a judge who passed judgment). Babylonian villages, towns, and cities were characterized by councils of "citizens" who made determinations in certain legal cases. Whether or not something similar obtained in Assyria is not known. We might assume so, but such a body is not mentioned in any text. There is no popular assembly of any kind or any quasi-representative body that could make known the concerns of the people to their rulers. Perhaps the mayors played this role. There were never any popular uprisings by Assyrians against the crown or its administrative appointees. The only rebellions by Assyrians were those of the provincial governors, which reflect tensions within the elite class.

The state dominated ownership of the means of production, but there was also a vibrant private economic sector with property rights ensured by the state. All large-scale investment, such as the construction of monumental buildings, construction of infrastructure such as roads, expansion of agriculture into new areas, and mineral exploration and exploitation, was undertaken by the crown. Most of the trade was also in government hands, although some may have been contracted to private operators. Private contractors could be used for major construction work, as is clear in the construction of the new royal city Dur-Sharrukin.[43] But in this project a levy of labor, tools, animals, and raw materials was laid on provincial governors, so it was mainly construction undertaken by the state. Private investment and the wealth it generated were dwarfed by the state. It was the largest employer of labor, including semifree labor (deportees), controlled a large portion of the land (and thus agricultural production), controlled much of the manufacturing, and held a monopoly in the exploitation of minerals.

The economy was structured in such a way that surpluses flowed to the center or were used for the maintenance of the state in the provinces (including provincial courts). It was the Assyrian elite that was most advantaged by this. Postgate sees three sectors of the NA economy: palace sector, government sector, and private sector.[44] This tripartite division has not convinced everyone. The government sector seems to overlap both the other two rather than being completely discrete. For example, when a high government official is involved in trading activities for personal gain, one must assume that this is part of the private sector, not part of the government sector, even though it may be his government position that affords him opportunity to trade.[45] However, when an official trader is sent out by the crown to undertake trading activities, this must be seen as part of the palace sector.[46]

The palace sector comprised all things owned by the royal family. Included in this sector as consumers were the royal palaces, royal family, domestic staff, administrators and military, and court officials. Income was in the form of booty, tribute, "gifts," produce and rents from lands owned, credit activities, slave sales, appropriations, and confiscations. Expenditures covered the subsistence of palace residents and staff, equipment of military staff, luxuries, gifts, regular temple offerings, and building operations. The government sector (including the army) drew on the private sector to provide resources for civil and military operations via taxation and conscription. The backbone of the government sector was the provincial system. The government subordinates were responsible for the collection of payments of all kinds from their province and for conscription and supply of soldiers and civil laborers. Village inspectors were responsible to the provincial administration for the assessment of taxation. There is no evidence of a conscious effort by the crown to control or monopolize trade, although both the crown and government officials were involved in it via agents. The private sector is hard to document because of scarcity of sources, although there is evidence for trading in private hands.[47]

Liverani, in contrast, has used a two-sector model of "palace" and "family" to examine trends in land tenure and inheritance from the mid-third through the mid-first millennium.[48] He sees two processes at work in the first millennium that I believe are apt particularly for the NA period (at least in the Assyrian homeland and northern Mesopotamia).[49] First, the palace sector directed to members of the palace organization (high officials at court and in the provinces) land, labor, and surpluses as it decentralized control of its lands.[50] Some (most?) of these lands may well have been prebendary holdings accompanying the office, rather than actually "owned" by the officials.[51] Much of the labor on these estates would have been deportees from elsewhere in the empire, some of whom were put to work in (new) royal cities. We should expect this to have increased agricultural output and thus the overall wealth of the empire, but it is impossible to obtain figures to show its actual scale. Much (or all, in the case of state land) of this wealth would have gone to the state or enriched the elite families to whom the king had granted the land and labor.

The second process noted by Liverani is the erosion of the connection between land lot and a family or kinship group that had characterized earlier periods. Eventually, land became freely alienable. The upshot of this is that some families were completely deprived of landed property (and enslaved for debts), while other families accumulated large extensions of land that in the "free" sector came to be the exact counterpart of the large landed properties that belonged to the high officials in the Palace sector.[52]

Both processes led to ownership of landed property being concentrated in the hands of only some individuals or families, whereas in the second millennium landed properties were equally distributed among different family units in the family sector and centralized by the great organization in the Palace sector.[53] Both these models recognize that wealth came to be concentrated in the hands of the leadings families that held the top administrative positions in the empire. Liverani's model points to the impoverishment of an increasing number of Assyrians who lost their family lands, but the size of this change is impossible to judge.

3. Historical Overview

The following schematic outline of the history of the NA Empire helps to contextualize our main concerns. This history has been divided a number of ways, depending on whether a reign has been interpreted as marking the beginning of a new epoch or as belonging with the reigns that preceded it. Some of these divisions are fairly arbitrary, so I offer here one way of organizing the period:[54]

1. From territorial state to imperial power—934–745 B.C.E
   a. Recovery of areas dominated in the MA period—934–884 B.C.E. (Ashur-dan II, Adad-nirari II, Tukulti-ninurta II)
   b. Extension of control to areas further west, south, and east—883–824 B.C.E. (Ashurnasirpal II and Shalmaneser III)
   c. Internal problems in Assyria—823–745 B.C.E. (Shamshi-Adad V — Ashur-nirari V; five kings)
2. Imperial expansion and consolidation—744–c.630 B.C.E.
   a. Second expansion and further provincial organization—744–722 B.C.E. (Tiglath-pileser III and Shalmaneser V)
   b. Imperial apogee—721–c.630 B.C.E. (Sargon II, Sennacherib, Esarhaddon, Ashurbanipal)
3. The fall of Assyria—c.630–609 B.C.E. (Ashur-etel-ilani, Sin-shar-ishkin, Ashur-uballit II)

3.1. Period 1a

What seemed to be driving expansion westward, northward, and eastward from the Assyrian heartland was a desire to reclaim territories that had been gained in the MA period after the demise of the Hurrian state of Mitanni/Hanigalbat in the mid-fourteenth century.[55] Assyria had lost control of these territories in the mid-eleventh century after the death of Tiglath-pileser I. Around this time, Assyria, with the rest of western Asia and the eastern Mediterranean, was plunged into something of a "dark age" usually connected to climatic change[56] and events surrounding the movements of the Sea Peoples in Anatolia and along the Levantine coast. When written sources reappear in the early first millennium, a quite different political landscape obtains in western Asia. Whereas before 1200 a group of major powers (Egypt, Hatti, Assyria [replacing Mitanni], Babylonia) was involved in international diplomacy and rivalry,[57] no such polities now existed. The Hittite empire was defunct, Egypt had retreated within its traditional borders, and Babylonia was stable but lacked rulers with imperial aspirations. In the place of city-states in Syria-Palestine, over which Egypt and Hatti had struggled for dominance in the mid- to late second millennium, there was a series of independent kingdoms (such as Israel, Aram, Moab, Edom). A similar political geography was evidenced across northern Mesopotamia (Aramean kingdoms) and into northern Syria (Neo-Hittite and Aramean kingdoms).[58] As at the end of the MA period, Aramean pastoral nomads were found across northern Mesopotamia, and there were Aramean and Chaldean semi-nomadic and sedentary tribes in Babylonia. There were no major powers contesting control of northern Mesopotamia, which was obviously a prerequisite for Assyrian expansion. Assyria had a clear military advantage over the smaller polities in northern Mesopotamia, as it was able to muster more resources to overpower these smaller states if they were not immediately intimidated into submission. In this period, Assyrian expansion stayed well within the limits of the area controlled during the MA period.[59] If one considers the military activities in this period as the (re)taking of territory deemed to be historically Assyrian, it is interesting that there was no attempt to integrate all of this territory into Assyria immediately. The "control" was not marked by the immediate institution of provincial administration. Rather, it took the form of a series of raids, collecting tribute and confirming local rulers as Assyrian administrators and governors. A number of these local rulers were in fact the descendants of Assyrian governors who had served in the MA provincial system. The royal annals record these (usually) annual "tours" of Assyrian-controlled areas, and the itineraries in the annals give us a clear idea of the geographic extent of Assyrian power. Even though these lands were viewed as properly Assyrian territory, the Assyrian kings took advantage of the internal organization of these territories that had developed in the interim between the MA and the NA periods. The formation of kingdoms in this region, as with the rest of northern Syria and Palestine in the aftermath of the demise of the great second-millennium powers, was seen not as something that needed to be completely overturned but rather as something that could be exploited. The problem was that these territories were not submissive to Assyria, not that they had the wrong form of political organization.

It is likely, then, that this first period should be viewed as an attempt to return to the political conditions of the MA period. From the Assyrian perspective, this might be considered not a new act of imperialism but rather the re-establishment of control over territories in rebellion against their long-standing overlord. They had tried to withdraw from the natural condition of belonging to Assyria. The significance of this is that it is possible to construe the Assyrian Empire as beginning in the fourteenth century (MA period), then experiencing a hiatus in the eleventh century, followed by recovery in the tenth century.[60] Thus, the mechanisms of imperialism may in fact derive from a period earlier than the first millennium. That the NA kings saw themselves as standing in a tradition that reached back into the MA period is evidenced not only by the occasional reference by name to military exploits of MA kings but also by reference to the fact that "Assyrians" lived in these territories and had been displaced by Arameans and others. The Assyrian king was seeking to return to political normalcy by reasserting Assyrian rule and returning Assyrians to towns and lands from which they had been displaced. So one motivation for the territorial expansion in this period, as well as in the next, was the correction of perceived political anomalies. Another motivation would seem to be economic, since the annals register the tribute exacted from these traditionally subjugated areas as well as the booty taken in one-off raids into territory (notably in Babylonia) that Assyrian kings recognized could not be retained. Also, in reconstituting "Assyria," polities abutting the territories under Assyrian control began to send gifts acknowledging Assyria's status.

3.2. Period 1b

This period has two identifiable sections.[61] The first half of this period (reign of Ashurnasirpal II, 883–859) saw the continued expansion westward, northward, and southward within the limits of Assyrian control marked out in the MA period, as well as the development of the imperial administrative system.[62] In this period, the construction of garrisons on borders or at strategic points in Assyrian-controlled territory was undertaken. Unsurprisingly, borders became contested places, not least because, prior to NA annexation, many of these subjugated polities had developed political and economic arrangements with their neighbors with which Assyrian hegemony interfered. Territories outside Assyria proper (say, west of the Habur River in central north Mesopotamia) were often initially dealt with in terms of treaty agreements (and at least sometimes under threat of Assyrian invasion), which afforded Assyria income in the form of tribute and the opportunity to intervene in their client's affairs if the partner did not meet treaty obligations. In that event, a client state (commonly termed "vassal" in the scholarly literature) might have its ruler replaced with a more compliant member of the indigenous ruling house or might be turned into a province (one result of resistance to the Assyrian army can be seen in appendix, text no. 2). In the second half of this period (reign of Shalmaneser III, 858–824), a number of north Syrian states beyond the Euphrates bend, which had marked the limit of Assyrian control, were made clients.[63] A coalition of these states successfully challenged Assyrian influence, but only for a time. Only by forming coalitions could the smaller states, for example the northern Syrian kingdoms in period 1b and by Syro-Palestinian kingdoms in periods 1b and 2a, have any hope of successfully resisting Assyria. Quite often these coalitions were initially successful, but they proved difficult to maintain in the longer term. Once they broke up due to internal wrangling or Assyrian meddling in an effort to win favor with some of the allies, the Assyrians subjugated their territories. These polities were not provincialized but remained clients. A few others became clients in period 2a by calling on Assyrian aid against former coalition partners. Period 1b also saw the beginning of direct Assyrian involvement in Babylonian political affairs, with Shalmaneser intervening militarily to secure the Babylonian throne for the incumbent royal house against a usurper. The Babylonian king returned the favor in the next period. The character of Assyrian control in this period continues to be debated. It is indisputable that, over time, members of the ruling Assyrian families were installed as provincial governors. Provincialization across northern Mesopotamia was, however, sporadic, with client states and provinces intermixed. For Liverani, the control of newly acquired territories was a web or a network with a series of control points or nodes ("islands," "outposts") connected by roads but with much of the territory not directly under Assyrian administrative control. From these centers the Assyrians could strike out against Aramean tribes or others who were causing problems. Thus, "the empire is not a spread of land but a network of communications over which material goods are carried."[64] This can be contrasted with the more common view of Assyrian expansion and administrative control as an "oil stain" that slowly spread across northern Mesopotamia and that covered everything in its path.[65] It is a question of how tightly controlled these holdings were in administrative practice. This issue continues to be relevant throughout the history of the NA Empire, particularly on the northern frontier.[66]

It is in this period that the lines of the NA administrative system, characterized by client states and provinces, clearly appear. The development of provincialization marked a higher level of integration. Here the Assyrians ruled directly through their own Assyrian appointees, commonly from the elite families. Why move from using the local political structures to having an Assyrian ruler? One argument is that this was a more efficient means of domination and economic exploitation. When Assyria relied on local rulers and structures, it incurred the costs of the annual "visits" needed to collect or demand the tribute. Provincialization, as a system in which the tribute moved naturally, without the costs of direct coercion but certainly because of the threat of coercion if there was a rebellion, arguably lowered the costs of running the empire. In theory, however, the system of clientship should have delivered this "natural," regular sending of tribute.

Perhaps one aspect of provincialization in this period was the reinforcement of ties to the crown afforded by the appointment of members of the leading Assyrian families to governorships or other administrative positions. Also, this practice arguably extended the territory of "Assyria," since these lands were now ruled by Assyrians, not by locals. Here we may observe in the royal inscriptions the beginnings of a changing notion of what constituted "Assyria" and "Assyrians."

3.3. Period 1c

This period is particularly interesting as we reflect on the structure and cohesion of the empire. In the late MA period, central weakness led the provinces in northern Mesopotamia to establish independent polities of their own. Assyria in period 1c also exhibited central weakness, marked by wrangling over the kingship and the cessation of annual military campaigns. While the western client states took advantage of this and ceased sending tribute, the status of the provinces closer to the Assyrian homeland is unclear. There is no indisputable evidence for a loss of provinces similar to the end of the MA period. When the annals start again, in period 2a, Assyria did not have to reassert authority over these territories, so it may have been possible for the weak center to hold onto these territorial gains. Perhaps the administrative structure (provincialization) was able to continue to function regardless of events in the center so long as the governors' commitment to the center was maintained. That is, a weak center did not mean that the Assyrian governors declared independence, nor were the local populations in a position militarily to overthrow the governors. Perhaps, then, the idea of the "weak center" is incorrect if the center could still command the allegiance of the provinces despite turmoil among the Assyrian elite concerning who should be king.

Another interpretation of the relationship between provincial governors and the central administration in this period emphasizes the role of the former, as members of elite families, in confirming an incoming king. The beginning of period 1c saw a major rebellion of cities (capitals of provinces?) within the empire, which Postgate suggests reflects factionalism among the provincial governors over the coming to power of Shamsi-Adad V, Shalmaneser's successor.[67] So divided was the Assyrian elite that he needed Babylonian support to secure the throne.[68] The independence of some governors in this period is thought to be seen in the Aramaic treaties from Sifire between the western ruler Mati'ilu of Arpad and Bar Gay'ah of KTK.[69] Bar Gay'ah was the dominant partner, and he has been identified by some commentators with Shamash-ili,[70] Assyrian governor of Bit Adini (Bit Adini is then identified with the otherwise unknown KTK). Shamash-ili would then have been acting independently of the Assyrian crown in making a client treaty with Mati'ilu. Others counter that the texts should be interpreted as presenting Shamash-ili as acting in the interests of the central administration by binding to Assyria a client who would otherwise have become delinquent.[71] This would mean that the governor had not rebelled against the incumbent king. A third alternative is that Bar Gay'ah was an independent king (location of KTK unknown) who was able to poach a former Assyrian client due to the weak center. The matter continues to be debated.

3.4. Period 2

This period is commonly identified as the NA Empire proper. The frontier of Assyria continued to press westward, northward, and southward beyond the limits set in period 1b, confronting other sovereign territories that had not traditionally been under Assyrian control (see map). Claims to them could not therefore be made on the basis of tradition, although it could be affirmed that at some previous time Assyrian kings had received occasional tribute or gifts of recognition from such territories (including in period 1b). Perhaps, on the western frontier at least, the borders were unstable, and so, in order to secure them, the area beyond the periphery had to be brought under Assyrian control.[72] Thus, the frontier kept moving. Did Assyria somehow "blunder" into confrontation with those territories neighboring to the west (Syria-Palestine), east (Zagros Mountains), north (Urartu), and southeast (Elam) in period 2a due to border conflicts and a concern to retain the allegiance of clients, or was there some overarching policy goal that Assyria was trying to attain but that it was in fact not successful in fully realizing until period 2b?[73] It is widely thought that there was a specific purpose in pushing westward beyond the Euphrates in period 2, although not in fulfilment of some long-held "policy" from period 1, and that its primary motivation was economic. Assyria sought a stranglehold on all the trade routes in western Asia. It wanted to divert to the center the luxury goods and as much as possible of the surplus produced in the subjugated territories, which were then largely devoted to the building of palaces and new royal cities (the first of which was constructed as early as period 1b). Driving westward to the Mediterranean, it gained access to the Phoenician seaports, with their exotic wares, and to Lebanese cedar, while by pushing north into eastern Anatolia and east into the Zagros it obtained control over mineral deposits. In the west, at least, trade had to pass through Syria-Palestine, coming from the Aegean or further west in the Mediterranean or coming from the southwest (Arabia). That trade was probably both state controlled and in private hands (maybe no difference, since the "private" operators may in fact have been government officials), and the Assyrians were thus dependent on these other states for the goods. Demands for tribute may have been a way of enforcing terms of trade (in one direction) that were economically advantageous for Assyria.[74] Assyria obtained the goods and materials it wanted "free" (minus the costs to enforce compliance, which could be high; notice that the Assyrians had to keep going back to the West to militarily enforce these demands). This is not primarily about the control of territory, but of goods and surpluses. I contend that at this stage the Assyrians were not thinking that they needed more land or that they wanted to appropriate and redeploy the labor available there.

The last point is significant because it is commonly supposed that Assyria had a voracious appetite for territories and populations, not just for extracting their surpluses through ruthless military aggression. Here we need to make a distinction between those territories east of the Euphrates bend and those to the west. Territories to the east were seemingly incorporated into Assyria. Territories to the west were not initially, and the Assyrians did not want to run these territories. That is to say, the westward push was not some sort of land grab, nor a grab for labor. Assyria would have preferred that these territories remain under their indigenous ruling houses and send tribute and goods to the center of the empire. This was the purpose of the system of clientship.

In this system, the Assyrian king intimidated the kings of the smaller western polities into submitting to his overlordship, legally binding themselves to the service of the Assyrian king through the swearing of oaths of obedience by both local and imperial gods. Part of the act of obedience was the annual sending of tribute to the Assyrian king. Thus, the Assyrians were to be guaranteed regular tribute income and access to trade goods without the costs of regular military "trips" to extort it, unless the client broke the agreement and refused to pay. In return for submission, the local polity would retain a level of self-determination and territorial integrity. The system did not work, however. The Assyrians may have felt that the coercive power of oaths sworn by the gods, coupled with the threat of military intervention if the oaths were broken, would effectively bind the client; but it did not. This is why, throughout period 2, the Assyrians moved to provincialize most of the western polities. It was not out of the desire (or a specific policy) to control these lands directly (otherwise they could have been provincialized from the outset); rather, it was in response to the failure of the client system. If a kingdom repeatedly dishonored its oaths by refusing to pay the tribute, then the polity had to be dissolved and turned into a province ruled by an Assyrian governor. In that way, the flow of income to the center could be assured. The ideological underpinning of these actions will be explored in the following section. The failure in the client system was in no small way a result of the meddling of Assyria's powerful neighbors—Urartu, Elam, and Egypt. As early as period 1b, Urartu had sought to obtain the allegiance of Assyrian clients across northern Mesopotamia and north Syria. This continued into period 2b. Elam in period 2 persistently provided support for Chaldean rebellion in Babylonia, and Egypt similarly in period 2b encouraged and aided rebellion among south Syrian and Palestinian clients. So provincialization, and the military action on which it depended, can be seen as responses to the influence and interference of powerful polities bordering on Assyrian-controlled territories. These polities wanted to put a break on Assyrian expansion, if only to preserve their own economic interests in their respective areas. Political destabilization would also check the integration of the empire. These polities may properly have feared that stable Assyrian clients would offer a staging ground for a move against their territory. Assyria attacked them in any case, but its purpose appears to have been to stop their political meddling with Assyrian clients rather than to subjugate them and incorporate them into Assyria. Although kings in period 2b made successful military incursions into Egypt, with Ashurbanipal reaching as far south as Thebes, Egypt was never subjugated in any real sense. Assyrian authority there was limited to making clients of Delta kings.[75] A long border war with Urartu was fought from period 1c throughout period 2a and into period 2b, until Sargon II made a successful raid into Urartian territory and as a result managed to stabilize the border.[76] In the case of Elam, Ashurbanipal (period 2b) successfully attacked its capital, Susa, and claimed to have sacked it, but he immediately withdrew and made no attempt to retain control of the territory. Hallo is seemingly right in noting of period 2b that "Assyrian power was in fact approaching the natural limits of which it was capable, and the thrusts that were now made into more distant regions such as Persia [Elam], central Anatolia [Urartu], or Egypt were either repulsed or only temporarily successful."[77]

What did clients get from siding with a powerful neighbor against Assyria? Although there is no direct evidence, these large polities must have been offering terms that were deemed more beneficial to the ruling elites. In both southern Syria-Palestine and Babylonia, the offer seems to have been independence, although Egypt and Elam, respectively, might have expected more in return for their military investment than just a check on Assyrian expansion. In northern Syria, there is evidence that, at least in some instances, Urartu demanded by military threat that Assyrian clients transfer their allegiance to them. Clients were in an invidious position. They not only had to weigh up the putative benefits of accepting aid, breaking with Assyria, and realigning themselves with the powerful neighbor but also had to judge the military strength and resolve of the neighbor to resist the Assyrian retaliation that was sure to come. Elam turned out to be a reliable ally to Chaldean Babylonia, whereas Egypt proved to be fundamentally useless to the south Syrian and Palestinian states. It was thus a highly dangerous political game to play off Assyria against other powerful polities. The potential gains were improved terms of clientship (since all the states in Syria-Palestine would need to be in a relationship with one major power or another), which could also include something approaching "independence." The risk was political extermination through provincialization. All the clients opted for the former status, but most of these polities by the end of period 2b had obtained the latter.

In period 2b, Assyria had basically won out over its potential rivals and stabilized the internal organization of the empire, with the exception of Babylonia, which proved to be an intractable problem (on which see the next section). It is for this reason that Hallo terms period 2b *pax assyriaca*.[78] Culturally, economically, and territorially, this was the empire's zenith. Agriculture was greatly expanded, and vast amounts of wealth were invested in monumental building projects in the Assyrian homeland and in artistic displays in palaces as the provincial system successfully delivered taxes and labor to meet Assyrian economic objectives.

The relationship among elite families, provincial governors, clients, and the king is evidenced in an interesting set of texts known as the Vassal Treaties of Esarhaddon.[79] These are not client treaties in the regular sense but binding agreements for the groups named earlier to support the succession to the throne of Ashurbanipal, Esarhaddon's son and heir (period 2b). Sargon II, Esarhaddon's grandfather, had usurped the throne, although he was a member of the royal family, and there is some suggestion the Esarhaddon was not his father's first choice for king. His father, Sennacherib, had been murdered in a palace conspiracy.[80] Since the succession to the throne was potentially fraught with problems, at the height of the empire's power no less, Esarhaddon wanted to secure Ashurbanipal's position before his death. He used this legal instrument to obtain the commitment of the ruling elites across the empire to ensure it.

3.5. Period 3

The rapid demise of Assyria from its zenith under Ashurbanipal (668–631) to its defeat at the hands of the Medes and the Babylonians (612–605) has long confounded historians.[81] The sources are scant and problematical. In the late 620s, Babylonia again wrested its independence from Assyria. It has been thought that some military or organizational weakness must have been exploited by Assyria's enemies, but what seems likely is that Assyria could not withstand a loosely coordinated two-pronged attack by two strong armies, particularly from directions in which it was less well defended (the south and east). The fact that Babylonia could become so economically and politically buoyant as to challenge militarily the Assyrian home-land highlights a serious inadequacy in the Assyrian administration of Babylonia and the failure of the Assyrians to integrate Babylonia fully into the empire. In this regard, Assyria may have fallen victim to the privileged view it held of Babylonia and its culture, manifested not least in the privileges it granted the ancient Babylonian cities. It is noteworthy that the provincial administrative system stayed in place, inherited by the Babylonians who continued to use it successfully, as did the Achaemenid Persians later. The overall strength of this system can be seen in the ease with which political power was transferred with little fragmentation of territorial holdings. The empire did not end, therefore. Rather, its center shifted from the upper Tigris south to Babylon, arguably continuing under the Persians with its center shifted again further east.

4. Constructing "Assyria": Imperial Ideology, Administrative Organization, and Techniques of Imperial Control

One topic that has been of considerable interest to students of the NA Empire is the ideology of Assyrian imperialism. The annals and other royal inscriptions, together with artistic representations on the walls of Assyrian palaces depicting victorious battles and the king's reception of subjugated peoples with their tribute, lend themselves to this analysis. A number of themes have been identified: royal ideology; the legitimacy of the king to subjugate foreign lands and to appropriate surpluses; the rule of the god Ashur (= Assyria) bringing "order" to nations that are disordered (that is, outside Assyrian control); defining "Assyria"; and the view of foreigners.[82] These themes are interlinked and are closely aligned with modes of imperial organization and the construction of imperial identity.

Economic gain has been commonly accepted as the primary motivation for Assyrian territorial expansion. The ruling elite sought to organize territory and people for its own economic benefit, to maximize agricultural output through a more efficient use of labor on newly opened cultivatable lands, to enhance the flow of luxury goods and raw materials to the center, and to keep the costs of running the empire as low as possible by lessening the threat of internal revolt. How was the empire administratively organized to attain these goals? Basically, it was through a mixed system of direct and indirect rule. Direct rule took the form of incorporating territory into the Assyrian provincial system with an Assyrian administrator appointed as governor. Indirect rule drew on a long-standing form of international relations between politically superior and inferior rulers. This is the vassal or client system.

While it is no doubt true that an economic motive was driving imperial aspirations, it is notable that Assyrian texts, particularly the annals and court literature focusing on royal ideology, are at pains to legitimate both direct and indirect forms of Assyrian domination. As mentioned in the historical overview, a case can be made to justify the initial territorial expansion (periods 1a and 1b) on the basis of historical precedent: these lands had been under Assyrian control in the MA period. Further, Assyrian texts expound a imperial ideology claiming that Ashur was the preeminent deity who ruled over all the gods, and, as a corollary, the political reality on Earth should be that all peoples acknowledged the sovereignty of Ashur's representative, the Assyrian king. To that end, the king was charged at his coronation to "extend the borders" of Assyria.[83] Territories beyond Assyrian control were held to be disordered, chaotic realms that did not conform to proper conduct. Charged with bringing more peoples under the shadow of Ashur, the Assyrian king was a divine agent for order in the world.[84]

The superior military power on which Assyrian hegemony was founded was thus a reflection of the will of Ashur and the divine mandate to bring territories under his control (appendix, texts nos. 1, 3, 6). Assyrian expansion was construed in theological and moral terms: it was right and proper that neighboring peoples submit to Assyrian sovereignty, a circumstance sanctioned by the gods. The Assyrian Empire was bringing into earthly political reality the order that obtained in the heavenly realm where the gods of all the peoples and polities of western Asia acknowledged Ashur as their lord. Resistance to Assyrian sovereignty of course meant resistance to the divine will, which marked one as a reprobate deserving of the most stringent punishments (see appendix, texts no. 2, 8).

This ideology served as an important impetus for and a legitimation of Assyrian imperialism.[85] At its heart, beside the god Ashur, stood the Assyrian king.

Traditionally, the Assyrian king was a religious functionary; at least his title in the Old Assyrian period (early second millennium), "vicar of Ashur," marked him off as such. Another common title was "administrator of Ashur" (formerly translated "priest of Ashur"), which probably has cultic overtones given that the king held ultimate administrative responsibility for the cult of Ashur and other leading state deities. His role as cultic administrator may in fact be symbolic of his rule over the polity as a whole, if one accepts that Assyria was understood to be the domain of the god Ashur. Technically, it was the deity who ruled over the land, with the divine will implemented by his executive, the "administrator." It is not until the MA period, probably in response to the need to represent himself as an equal of the other "Great Kings" among whom western Asia was then divided, that one sees the consistent use of the term "king" for the Assyrian ruler. This club of "Great Kings" in western Asia during the mid-second millennium recognized its members as political equals, as well as trading partners and potential competitors, and they called each other "brother."[86] The basic criterion for membership was sovereignty over territories outside one's homeland, which led to recognition of one's status by the existing members of the group. As in the case of Egypt and Hatti, this sovereignty could be expressed in the submission of neighboring polities, the recognition by lesser kings of the authority of the Great King. Submission was ratified through vassal treaties and the swearing of oaths. The MA Assyrian kings joined the club of Great Kings not through treaties with vassals but by occupying and provincializing territory west and southwest of their homeland from which they had displaced Mitannian rule.[87] These relationships of "brotherhood" among political equals and vassalage of smaller polities were the mechanisms by which international relations were played out in this period.

Assuming that recollection of the control of territories bordering the homeland by the MA Great King underpinned initial NA expansion, it is notable that by period 1b this area included examples of both direct (provincialization) and indirect (clientship) rule. In fact, a number of independent polities that had developed west of the Assyrian homeland during the so-called dark age were seemingly remnants of the MA provinical system whose governors had established independent dynasties as a result of the weak center. For Assyria, the outcome of indirect rule was much the same as that of direct rule, except that the client state retained vestiges of independence. On the economic level, Assyrian interests were met through the payment of tribute and privileged trading arrangements. In some ways, being a client king was similar to being a provincial governor. Governors also swore oaths of allegiance to the king, and in return the king granted them not only political power over a territory but also economic rewards and privileges.[88] If we consider client kings to be on a similar administrative level and to have similar administrative responsibilities vis-à-vis the Assyrian king, we could conclude that the empire was run by an administrative elite, some Assyrian, some native, who all ascribed to the Assyrian imperial ideology and who were linked to the king through a relationship of oaths, mutual obligations, and responsibilities. As the Assyrian king was Ashur's vice-regent, so client kings and provincial governors served and represented the Assyrian king and maintained imperial interests. Imperial ideology acted as a mechanism for giving the empire some cohesion at the elite level. As will be seen, it also justified the eradication of polities ruled by recalcitrant clients and their incorporation into the provincial system.

While it is possible to identify similarities in the roles of clients and governors within the provincial administrative system, there are important differences that help to focus our attention on the problem of the type of polity Assyrian imperialism was forming. Provinces had their local political institutions replaced by Assyrian governors, who were commonly members of leading Assyrian families. Their appointment was an act of political largesse that served the king's political interests, since the support of these families secured his position. Client states retained local rulers and political institutions. The client relationship was also a form of benefaction, but it should be construed after the model of international relations in the mid-second millennium in which the "Great King" accepted homage (marked by tribute, gifts, and subservience) from lesser kings, as was his due. The innovation in NA royal ideology lies in the fact that the Assyrian king was no longer *a* Great King among a group of "brothers" but *the* Great King. It was to the Assyrian king alone that Ashur, supreme among the gods, had given authority to rule. In the divinely instituted order of things (imperial ideology) it was appropriate for small kings to acknowledge the Great King; indeed, the Assyrian king was impelled to make them submit. The character of the relationship between the client and the Great King arose directly out of Assyrian royal ideology, which reinforced the relative status of the two parties. In response to submission, the Assyrian king, as Ashur's representative, confirmed and legitimated the rule of the junior partner, committing himself to supporting that royal line against usurpers and defending the kingdom's territorial integrity against foreign encroachment. The Assyrian king acted as the protector of good order in the kingdom that had submitted itself to the (indirect) rule of Ashur. The client king recognized that his legitimacy flowed from the Assyrian king and was dependent on the maintenance of good relations with him as a faithful servant. The two kings formed a pact or political relationship with mutual obligations. It was, of course, an unequal relationship both politically and economically. Nevertheless, it can properly be described as a reciprocal relationship: the client gave the Assyrian king tribute, allegiance, and adherence to imperial goals, and the Assyrian king gave legitimacy, tenure of rule, and promises of protection.

In assuming his obligations to the client, the Assyrian king exercised royal responsibilities, just as he did in the Assyrian homeland. This alerts us to the fact that the client kingdom could be considered a part of "Assyria." If Assyria was the domain of the god Ashur, then client kingdoms fell within this domain, but they were of a category or status different from that of the homeland or the provinces. This difference is evident not only in the form of administrative leadership—local client kings versus Assyrian provincial governors—but is reinforced in the language used to describe their economic relationship with the center. Provinces (including the homeland) paid taxes into the Assyrian treasury that are described in a vocabulary quite distinct from that used to describe the tribute and gifts paid to the Assyrian king by client kings. Gifts and tribute reflected an acknowledgment of Assyrian sovereignty, rather than a tax that was placed on a province as part of Assyria. So "Assyria" can be understood in a number of ways. It can refer to the homeland and to the homeland plus provinces. But its meaning can also seemingly encompass the client states, as well. When historians write of "the Assyrian Empire," these client states are always in view. It is important to consider, however, how the status of these clients within the Assyrian "Empire" makes the character of this emerging polity somewhat complex.

In order to meet his obligation to "extend the borders" of Ashur's rule, the Assyrian king drew on the model of mid-second-millennium international relations in which independent polities entered, voluntarily or not, into to a submissive political relationship with Assyria. Other territories were immediately incorporated into the Assyrian provincial system. Thus, the "empire" was constituted as a homeland surrounded by a network of provinces and client kingdoms of various sizes. In respect to the client states, this may not have been an "empire," since they were still semi-independent and had indigenous political institutions. They did, however, have a living memory of being an autonomous polity. I suppose it turns on how we view the NA-type of overlord-client relationship. To the extent that territories were provincialized, they qualify as imperial possessions, although much of the territory east of the Euphrates had formerly been under Assyrian rule (MA period) and from the Assyrian perspective should never have been independent.

This mixed system of direct and indirect rule is consonant with many studies of modern imperialism, which include both direct and indirect rule within their definition of empire.[89] But why were some territories immediately provincialized while others were made clients? The answer is unfortunately not as simple as identifying the reaction of these polities to the claim of Assyrian hegemony: those that submitted were permitted to become clients, while those that resisted were made into provinces. The evidence from the annals and province lists shows that some polities that were initially unwilling to acknowledge Assyria had a compliant local ruler set on the throne who was made a client, whereas some submissive territories became provinces. Further, should we perhaps view the provincialization throughout period 1 of an increasing number of the territories formerly under Assyrian control in the MA period as an attempt to create a "Greater Assyria"? That is, should this be construed an act of state formation rather than as empire? And if it should be, what are the boundaries of the state? Should a distinction be made between the territories west of the Habur River (central north Mesopotamia) and those east of it—the former being beyond the limits of the state proper, while the latter were annexed to an expanded Assyrian homeland? This consideration is made all the more challenging given the thorough provincialization of the territories between the Habur and the Euphrates (that is, the territories west of the Habur) into what appears to be a "Greater Assyria" by the end of period 1b. To be sure, this "Greater Assyria" might not have held together during the period of central weakness in period 1c, but it is the political reality that was immediately reinstated in period 2a. In period 2a, the client system was extended to encompass all of Syria-Palestine. Throughout period 2a and 2b, almost all these clients were provincialized in response to persistent rebellion. What, then, should be made of the change of status of many of the Syro-Palestinian kingdoms from client to province in period 2? If incorporation of provinces east of the Habur (or also east of the Euphrates?) could be considered the formation of a Greater Assyria and perhaps reflect the process of state formation, can the incorporation of the Syria-Palestine clients as provinces be viewed similarly? In discussing how administrative organization reflected and reinforced the developing understanding of imperial identity, we must consider that period 2 offers clear evidence from Syria-Palestine of how subjugated polities moved from the status of client to that of province, how the appropriation of lands and peoples was justified, how the territories and peoples were viewed, and how they were integrated into the empire. To highlight the complexity of Assyrian views on subjugated territories, the discussion juxtaposes the treatment of Syro-Palestinian polities with that of Babylonian polities. It is to a consideration of the role of client states in period 2 that our attention now turns.

Syria-Palestine was unambiguously outside Assyria. Occasionally, MA period kings had marched westward to the Mediterranean, collected gifts from local rulers, and erected a stele noting the accomplishment, the latter perhaps marking the nominal limits of Ashur's rule. Assyrian kings in period 1b did likewise. Assyrian territorial ambitions in period 1b (specifically, during the rule of Shalmaneser III) may have run to the control of northern Syria, but temporary coalitions of Syro-Palestinian states successfully resisted Assyrian military encroachments. In period 2 a, by which time the territory east of the Euphrates had been provincialized, a concerted effort was made by Assyrian kings to bring Syria-Palestine under Assyrian control. Why was this? Economic gain and royal ideology again feature as the two main reasons. The economic motive is obvious enough. As a Mediterranean coastal region, Syria-Palestine had a different climate and therefore produced different agricultural products from the rest of Assyrian-controlled territory. Most significant, however, was the role of the Phoenician cities as trade centers, which was promoted by the Assyrians' demand for exotic goods. Via these centers, the empire could control Mediterranean commerce.[90] Royal ideology arguably features in the need for successive kings to "extend the borders" of Assyria. To do so would make one a "good" king who obeyed the will of Ashur, and it is possible that the Assyrian elite expected this of its rulers. Kings would therefore need to undertake successful campaigns in order to keep the support of elites, who were also undoubtedly economically advantaged through such activities.

In period 2, Syro-Palestinian states subjugated by Assyria, a few voluntarily, the sizable majority involuntarily, were all made clients. To be a client was to come within the economic and ideological orbit of Assyria. It was to recognize that Assyria was your overlord to whom homage was due in the form of annual tribute; it was also to recognize the legitimacy of Assyrian sovereignty in terms articulated by the Assyrians themselves: that Ashur, the great lord, the lord of all gods (including the gods of the client territory), had commissioned the Assyrian king to superintend this land, which the deities of this land themselves affirmed. Clients were bound to the Assyrian king by oaths sworn by both the local and the Assyrian gods. This made the relationship one that was divinely sanctioned, although in effect it meant that the client was no longer a sovereign state. The legitimacy of the local king to rule now depended on his loyalty to the Great King, which itself was construed as an act of obedience to the local gods. As the local gods served Ashur, the imperial deity, so the local king served the vice-regent of Ashur, the king of Assyria. The earthly political reality was to mirror the cosmic political reality. If the oath was broken by nonpayment of tribute (= rebellion), the Assyrians were justified in undertaking drastic action against the perpetrators who had committed an offense against the gods.

The ideological reason for not immediately incorporating these territories into the provincial system may have been respect for the deities of these lands. These deities had not wronged Ashur and had arguably served him appropriately in the heavenly realm, where all things are done in good order. Thus, on the ground, as it were, these polities were afforded the opportunity of serving Ashur's vice-regent, the Assyrian king (a service marked by the prompt payment of annual tribute). If they did so, well and good. But if they did not, then they had offended divine order and their own gods. This in part explains the confiscation of cult statues from recalcitrant clients. If a people did not know how to honor their deity by keeping the oaths sworn by that deity, then clearly that deity needed to be taken into Assyrian care. Indeed, the Assyrian king claimed that the local deity had called on him to punish the deity's own people because they had broken their oath (see also appendix, text no. 7). The removal of the deity from its shrine was not a mark of disrespect; rather, it was interpreted as the result of that deity's will—he or she wished to go to Assyria to pay homage to Ashur. The local deity is said to have abandoned its people because of the effrontery of oath violation and to have permitted the Assyrian army to capture the kingdom, replace its monarchy, and take the local god back to Assyria, where it would be properly cared for. (And as the deity was being removed to Assyria or elsewhere in the empire, so too that deity's people could follow it into exile.) The spoliation of the divine images of rebellious vassals and the destruction of shrines was thus viewed as just punishment for unwillingness to submit to Ashur and his king.

There has been a long-running debate over whether the Assyrians imposed on client states the obligation to worship Assyrian gods as a gesture of submission and as a means of "Assyrianizing" them. The balance of opinion is against such an imposition.[91] Client states, as distinct from provincial territories in northern Meso-potamia, were spared direct Assyrian interference in religious affairs, even though tribute payments and loyalty oaths were required to demonstrate allegiance to the Assyrian overlord. Assyrians permitted local cults to continue even after the spolia-tion of divine images.[92] That this was the case even in provincial territories may be shown by II Kings 17:24–34, where the worship of Yahweh was officially sanctioned in the former kingdom of Israel. Peoples deported to this territory were also permit-ted to worship their traditional gods that they had brought with them. The threat of destruction of shrines or the removal of deities from the shrines in their home-lands was an important means by which the NA Empire managed relationships with its client states. NA monarchs did not sanction the wanton destruction of the shrines and cult objects of subject peoples.[93] The images of minor deities could be destroyed, while the images of the main deities of the subjugated territory, together with accompanying religious objects, were removed to Assyria. There they were commonly treated with respect and placed in a shrine in Assyria or in an outlying district. One reason for the spoliation of divine images was to secure loyalty oaths from vassals, after which the cult images could be returned.[94] Shrines were destroyed and divine images destroyed and/or removed in territories unwilling to submit to the Assyrian king or in rebellious vassal states, especially when there was resistance on the arrival of the army of the empire. There does not seem to have been a con-sistent policy, however, since not all territories appear to have suffered the loss of divine images or shrines. From Tiglath-pileser III (period 2a) on, states in Syria-Palestine suffered this fate if they proved to be consistently recalcitrant vassals.[95]

Ostensibly, while subjugated peoples were responsible for their own local and national cults, the king of Assyria had final responsibility for them. The royal inscrip-tions of Esarhaddon and Ashurbanipal (period 2b) not only speak of the normal-ization and regulation of Assyro-Babylonian cults and cult centers but also include references to the repatriation of captured foreign deities (that is, deities outside the Assyro-Babylonian cultural sphere) and the re-establishment of regular offerings and income for these foreign cults.[96] There is also a reference to the restoration of shrines of foreign deities. Esarhaddon claims to have proclaimed a general amnesty for all gods who had been taken to Assyria:

> [I am he] who returned the pillaged gods of the countries from Assyria and Elam to their shrines, who let them stay in comfortable quarters until he completed temples [for them], and could set the gods upon daises as a lasting abode. In all cult centers, [it was] I, who established the necessary accessories.[97]

The result of military action to restore divine order to the territories of rebellious clients normally was incorporation into the Assyrian provincial system, the sec-ond category of administration, with an attendant loss of autonomy. Peoples who rebelled were seen as criminals against the divine order and thus had to be severely punished (appendix, text no. 8). Their indigenous leaders had forfeited the right to rule the territory, and, for the sake of good order and the well-being of gods and people, the territory had to be ruled directly by an Assyrian governor and incorporated into the provincial system. Much of the local population would be deported and peoples from elsewhere in the empire relocated to the region. Religion was thus clearly used by the Assyrians as a tool of subjugation, and Assyrian gods were used to that end. The use of the client states' own deities as an ideological tool of control, as part of the imposition of Assyrian imperial ideology to recast national self-understanding, might also be seen as a form of "Assyrianization." The claim that the Assyrian king was the final protector of religion in both the provinces and client states undermined traditional national understandings of the relationship between deities and their polities and peoples and brought them all within the Assyrian worldview.

As noted in the historical overview (period 2a), the Assyrians arguably preferred that the territories west of the Euphrates remain in a client status. This form of subjugation as an administrative tactic expressed an Assyrian imperial ideology that ascribed an identity and location to these polities within the Assyrian worldview. The changing of status between client and province demanded a change in the view of territory and also in the view of the subjugated population. What had been a client state with a level of autonomy and territorial integrity was now incorporated under direct Assyrian control, as were its people. This was not only another level of administrative integration into the empire; the territory and people occupied a different place in the Assyrian worldview. It marked a different relationship between the empire and the territory and people and moved the territory into a different category. "Client" as an ascribed identity with certain characteristics was replaced by "province" as a different ascribed identity with different characteristics. Clients were accorded the right to retain their national ideology and territorial integrity, and thus their "national" identity, albeit within the context of the Assyrian "symbolic universe." But once a territory was incorporated into the provincial system, the Assyrian claim was that the territory and people now belonged to the Assyrian Empire. This then became the ideological justification for deportation, since the subjugated peoples were informed that they were now, after a fashion at least, "Assyrians" and that they now lived in "Assyria," so they could legitimately be moved anywhere within that realm without ever leaving "their" territory and even take their gods with them. There was an economic spin-off from this. As new agricultural lands, including some in quite marginal areas in northern Mesopotamia (successful crops two in five years), were opened up, much of the labor on these estates was performed by deportees from elsewhere in the empire (see appendix, text no. 4). The populations of provinces became viewed as labor that could be best utilized on projects (usually agricultural projects, although there is evidence for building projects such as new royal cities) that served imperial needs. This concern with the efficient use of labor was sometimes couched in terms of political expediency: people had to be moved from their homeland in order to quell rebellion. However, these people were usually those deemed to be less economically productive and so were put to use in fertile agricultural areas (for example, urbanites who had been using up the local surplus; Arameans, Chaldeans, and other pastoral nomads who were not sedentary agriculturalists and who were settled to become such). Their status was not the same as that of "ethnic" Assyrians, however. The legal status of these deportees was not "slave" but "dependent labor," since they were tied to a particular estate. Postgate views them as "helots," borrowing a category applied to western Asia by Diakonoff.[98]

As client kingdoms were turned into provinces, peoples and deities were no longer tied to a particular place but now belonged to the empire. In breaking the traditional nexus of people, place, and gods (divine rule), the Assyrian elite dissolved the basis for existing national and ethnic identities and ascribed to subjugated peoples a new identity. Deportation was a mechanism for breaking old and constructing new identities, since peoples from various locations were mixed in new settlements. Thus, deportation achieved two complementary goals for the central administration: it dissolved national and ethnic identies that were risked fragmenting the empire (even though client status sought to bring all such polities within a single "symbolic universe"), and it legitimated the movement of labor within Assyria to locations where it could be more economically exploited. So far as I can tell, this attitude toward and use of provincialization and deportation was an innovation, certainly on this scale. It also might be termed "Assyrianization," if by that one means turning populations from whatever they were (e.g., "Israelites," "Bit Adinians") into "Assyrians" (see appendix, texts nos. 3, 4, 5).

Provincialization was qualitatively different from clientship both administratively and ideologically. In considering the evidence from NA royal inscriptions pertaining to the incorporation of territories and peoples into the empire, Machinist reviews a number of key phrases such as "accounted to/with the people of Assyria/my land," "added to the border of Assyria/my land/a particular district or province of Assyria," "I (= the king) imposed upon them my yoke/the yoke of my rule/the yoke of Ashur, my lord," and the claim to have imposed taxes on subjugated peoples "like Assyrians," among others. He concludes that "the terms 'Assyria' and 'Assyrian,' in the royal inscriptions, are not really, or at least essentially, ethnic terms but rather political ones, defining a region and people that manifest the required obedience [to Ashur/the Assyrian king]."[99] This, of course, need not suggest that "Assyria" did not also refer specifically to the Assyrian homeland in contradistinction to the subjugated territories or that "Assyrian" referred specifically to the indigenous inhabitants of the homeland. In the latter case, "Assyrian" was arguably an ethnic designation.[100] It is perhaps notable, although unremarked by Machinist since he was concerned solely with royal inscriptions, that in NA administrative texts, subjugated peoples, including those who had been deported to the Assyrian homeland, were never termed "Assyrians." They were always denoted by their ethnic designation or by reference to their place of origin. Despite the evidence of the administrative texts, the royal inscriptions make clear that the Assyrian elite viewed subjugated peoples and lands, particularly when they had been incorporated into the provincial system, as "Assyrians" and "Assyria," respectively. This was a direct challenge to the identity affirmed by the subjugated peoples themselves. The Syro-Palestinian kingdoms, for example, had articulated "national" and ethnic identities that clearly referred to a political and social identity tied to a particular place (the kingdom ruled over by the divinely appointed indigenous king) and (a) particular national god(s).[101] Assyrian hegemony contravened that, initially by imposing client status and, more violently, by turning the state into a province. The Assyrians were not consistent in their treatment of Syro-Palestinian polities. The positive outcomes to the empire from provincialization needed to be evaluated against possible negatives. The clear example of this is the Phoenician cities Tyre, Sidon, and Byblos. Their economic significance to Assyria was such that they were never brought into the provincial system but were instead permitted to retain a level of self-determination as client states even after episodes of rebellion. Babylonia offers a starker contrast with the experience of Syro-Palestinian states. Babylonia was seen to have close cultural connections to Assyria, with major temples of deities revered by the Assyrians long established in Babylonian cities. Assyrians recognized their culture as younger than Babylonia's and as in some sense derivative of it. Assyrians and Babylonians spoke dialects of the same language, and Assyrians had borrowed the Babylonian cuneiform writing system. Babylonia was effectively turned into a province in period 2a, regained its independence in period 2b with Elamite support (reign of Sargon II), only to be subjugated soon after (reign of Sennacherib). Assyrian kings were so concerned to legitimate their rule there that more than one Assyrian king in period 2 assumed the throne of Babylon and ruled (perhaps in name only) the two states concurrently. Assyria never did resolve how to govern Babylonia. When Shamash-shuma-ukin, the brother of Ashurbanipal (late period 2b), was installed as king of Babylon, a bloody civil war between them followed.

Babylonia was the only subjugated territory in which the Assyrian king assumed the indigenous kingship. Other recalcitrant territories were quashed and indigenous kingship eradicated, and while it is true that the city of Babylon was razed by Sennacherib out of frustration at the population's recalcitrance, it was almost immediately rebuilt by Esarhaddon and Ashurbanipal, who claimed to have been called by Marduk, the god of Babylon, to restore cultic normality to Babylonia. They undertook rebuilding projects in this conquered territory and sought to have themselves portrayed as legitimate kings of Babylon rather than as foreign usurpers.[102] To this end, they not only had royal inscriptions written proclaiming such but also adopted the titulary of the king of Babylon, as evidenced in economic and legal texts written during their reigns. There were also deportations (mainly of Arameans and Chaldeans), but the royal inscriptions make it clear that Babylonia was a special place culturally and so had to be treated in a special way. This marks a different conception of Babylonia as a territory within the orbit of Assyrian control. Nominally, one might expect the king of Assyria to be king over all the subjugated territories. While this was so, the important thing to note is that in all locations other than Babylonia either the Assyrian king either recognized the local king as a client and thus retained him or eradicated the indigenous monarchy and replaced it with the Assyrian king, who ruled via an appointed Assyrian governor. The Assyrian king did not have himself crowned king according to the rites of the subjugated territory. This consideration was afforded Babylonia alone. The local traditions of legitimate kingship were not set aside as they were when other territories were made into provinces. They were retained in Babylonia, and the Assyrian king was seemingly at pains to legitimate himself by keeping them (although not necessarily all of them; see, for example, his absence from the annual *akitu* ritual at which the Babylonian king's presence was normally required).[103] Following the tradition of Babylonian kings, the *kiddinutu* status of the ancient Babylonian cities with their long-standing legal rights and tax concessions for their citizens, including curtailment of the king's authority to exact taxes, fines, labor service, and army service, were recognized by the Assyrians.[104]

Babylonian cities were centers of culture and the economy, so it is hardly surprising, given the Assyrians' attitude toward Babylonia, that they displayed a generally positive disposition to them. It was also politically expedient to do so. Tribal Chaldeans and Arameans whose power base lay in regional Babylonia needed the support of urban elites and institutions (specifically, temples) to mount rebellions against Assyrian rule. Throughout period 2, they had some success in unifying urban, elite, and regional interests to resist Assyrian hegemony. The Assyrians themselves countered by acting like indigenous Babylonian monarchs. This positioning was deliberately targeted at the urban elites and institutions and sought to undermine Chaldean coalition building. In the struggle for the hearts and minds of the Babylonian urban elites, the Chaldeans were ultimately successful.

By the end of period 2, the empire consisted largely of provinces across northern and southeastern Mesopotamia, Syria, and northern Palestine. Southern Palestinian kingdoms such as Judah were some of the few remaining clients. Babylonia vacillated among being a province, being a kingdom ruled by the Assyrian king, and being independent. The administrative status of subjugated territories reflected their particular relationship to the Assyrian king and their position within the Assyrian "symbolic universe." The ideology of empire was impressed on both Assyria and the subjugated polities, since to the Assyrian ruling elite they were part of a single system, even though they belonged in distinct categories. Structurally, the empire looked much like it had at the end of period 1b. It was a nexus of homeland, provinces, and clients, but now Babylonia was included as a seemingly different type of territory. The question of what type of polity the Assyrian Empire was remains. In fact, the extension of the provincial system into Syria exacerbates the problem of defining "Assyria," especially since deportation to various parts of the empire and ethnic mixing might be construed as a form of state formation. It is a problematic notion, though, given that provincialized populations and deportees did not have the same legal standing as Assyrian "nationals." To make matters more complex, it is unclear exactly how an Assyrian "national" should be defined, since if it is done on the basis of birth in the homeland (or of descent from one born there), the boundaries of the homeland are debatable. My suspicion is that by period 2b it would be the territory east of the Habur.

In this section I have emphasized (1) aspects of the ideology underpinning Assyrian imperialism; (2) some mechanisms for controlling, organizing, and integrating the empire; and (3) problems in elucidating the character of the polity being formed by Assyrian imperialism; I have attempted to show how they are interconnected. It seems to me that the problem of integration plagued the empire. It is that problem, no doubt exacerbated by the empire's vast (for the time) territorial reach, that constantly demanded the attention of Assyrian rulers, strained their system of administrative organization, and exercised their powers of coercion. The process of integrating an empire may prove to be one of the areas that could be fruitfully further pursued in comparative research.

5. Conclusion: What's "New" About the Neo-Assyrian Empire?

In his study of ancient Near Eastern imperialism, Michael Mann devotes most of his attention to the late-third-millennium empire of Sargon of Akkad.[105] This is understandable, not only because it is the earliest of the "empires" but also because it affords Mann the opportunity to lay out his interpretative strategy for this and later empires. I am somewhat surprised, though, that he devotes comparatively little space (only some seven pages) to the much better attested NA Empire. In any case, since he has treated both empires, it affords an opportunity to relate my discussion in this chapter to his work and to reflect on the relationship between the NA and earlier western Asian empires.

In his study of the empire of Sargon of Akkad, Mann elucidates the four principal strategies in the development of genuine imperial domination: rule through clients; direct army rule; "compulsory cooperation" (indicating "that economic development and repression could go together," with economic benefits depending "on the provision of certain uniform and repressive services by the state": 153); and the development of a common ruling-class culture (where the place of religion as "ideological power" is recognized, noting its role in the development of "ruling-class community"). Mann holds that, generally, the first two strategies dominated in the earliest empires, with the balance shifting to the latter two strategies by the time of the Roman empire. It would seem that Sargon of Akkad's empire emphasized rule through clients and direct army rule, although elements of compulsory cooperation and common ruling-class culture can be detected. By comparison, the

NA Empire was marked by a strategy that "combined ruling through the army and a degree of compulsory cooperation with a diffused upper-class 'nationalism' of their own core" (231). Mann notes regarding this empire that "the 'army option' [was] pursued to its most ferocious known limits in our historical traditions," marked by large conquests, the control of subjugated populations "by threat and occasional use of ruthless militarism," and deportations (234). The compulsory cooperation resulted in a number of claimed economic benefits through expenditure on the building of palaces, royal cities, and other administrative centers, through investment in the provision of plows and the acquisition of draught horses, and through the storing of grain reserves. While these two strategies have much in common with those of earlier empires, for Mann the NA Empire introduces a new element: "a form of 'nationalism'" (235). This is not "a cohesive ideology that spreads vertically through all classes of the 'nation,'" since Assyria was too hierarchical a society, unlike the Greeks, whose nationalism "was dependent on rough equality and a measure of political democracy." It was only the Assyrian upper classes— nobility, landowners, merchants, officials—that, together with the army, conceived of themselves as belonging to the same nation. "*They* seem to have participated in a common ideology, a normative community that diffused universally among the upper classes" (235, author's emphasis). "Their community seems to have ended abruptly at the boundaries of what was called the Assyrian nation, consigning the outer provinces to a clearly subordinate status. This was probably the most novel technique of rule, adding to the cohesion of the empire's core. Ideological power as immanent *ruling-class morale* seems to make its clearest historical entry so far in this narrative" (235, author's emphasis; cf. 160–1). Thus, with the emergence of "nationalism," "more diffuse, universal sources of social identity grew at the expense of particularistic, local ones" (236).

I agree with Mann that we see the emergence of a sense of Assyrian national identity in the NA period, although I think that it may well go somewhat deeper in Assyrian society than he allows. Be that as it may, what Mann's analysis misses, and what I have tried to emphasize in this essay, is the use of imperial ideology to integrate subjugated peoples into the Assyrian "symbolic universe." Mann is correct to note that the Assyrian ruling elite looked on subjugated peoples and territories differently from the way they looked on Assyria and "ethnic" Assyrians, but it is significant that this ruling-class ideology also articulated the ways in which various types of subjugated peoples related to and were placed within the empire. This ideology was diffused throughout the empire, at least at the level of elites.

One could therefore view clientship not simply as an example of ruling through a conquered elite (as in earlier empires), but as a means, articulated through imperial ideology, of integrating this elite within an empire-wide ruling-class culture. The conquered elite now belonged to the Assyrian ruling elite, albeit on the second tier. They were legally recognized as ruling their territory under the patronage of the Assyrian king, and they became representatives of Assyrian rule and imperial values and ideology. Subjugated peoples and their rulers who were submissive and continued to be obedient were applauded for their moral virtues and for acting "like Assyrians." The ideology underpinning clientship articulated a relationship between Assyria and the subjugated polity that placed the latter in a position inferior to Assyria even as it drew the ruling elite into an association with the Assyrian king and the imperial ruling structures.

Provincialization can also be viewed similarly. It did indeed reinforce the status of the territory as something considerably less than Assyria proper, as Mann avers (at least in the sense that it was a territory in need of correct ordering by an Assyrian governor), but it also integrated the territory and population closely with Assyria, spreading the notion of Assyria beyond the boundaries of the home provinces. This is seen most clearly for provinces east of the Euphrates bend, but it is arguable also for provinces in Syria-Palestine. Provincialization in particular led the peoples and territories to become "Assyrian," even if that "Assyria" can de distinguished in some sense from the homeland.

This highlights the issue of the type of polity the Assyrians were forming. Earlier empires espoused religio-political ideologies to legitimate the subjugation of neighboring territories. But I do not think that prior to the Assyrians there was an attempt to articulate an imperial ideology that sought to integrate the subjugated polities into the ruling-class worldview and then, if necessary, to change where they "fitted" into that worldview (moving from client to province). Assyrian imperial ideology was diffused across the empire and should be seen as an innovative means of integrating the empire, expressing power, and maintaining control. We might want to draw a distinction between an Assyrian national and ethnic identity and an Assyrian imperial identity, although the two are obviously related. All subjugated territories and peoples found a place in the latter, whether in the administrative category of client or province. These peoples may not have had a place in ethnic or national Assyria, but the issue needs further research.

APPENDIX: ASSYRIAN TEXTS

1. Tiglath–pileser, strong king, unrivalled king of the universe, king of the four quarters, king of all princes, lord of lords, chief herdsman, king of kings, attentive purification priest, to whom by the command of the god Shamash the holy scepter was given and who had complete authority over the people.... The god Ashur [and] the great gods who magnify my sovereignty, and who granted as my lot power and strength, commanded me to extend the border of their land. They placed in my hands their mighty weapons, deluge in battle. I gained control over lands, mountains, towns, and princes who were hostile to Ashur and I subdued their districts. I vied with 60 crowned heads kings and achieved victory over them in battle. I have neither rival in strife nor equal in conflict. I added territory to Assyria [and] people to its population. I extended the border of my land and ruled over all their lands. (Tiglath-pileser I, MA period) (Grayson 1991b: 13)

2. In strife and conflict I besieged [and] conquered the city. I felled 3,000 of their fighting men with the sword. I carried off prisoners, possessions, oxen, [and] cattle from them. I burnt many captives from them. I captured many troops alive: I cut off some of their arms [and] hands; I cut off of others their noses, ears [and] *extremities*. I gouged out the eyes of many troops. I made one pile of the living (and) one of heads. I hung their heads on trees around the city. I burnt their adolescent boys [and] girls. I razed, destroyed, burnt, [and] consumed the city. (Ashurnasirpal II, 883–859 B.C.E.; period 1b) (Grayson 1991b: 201)

3. When Ashur, the great lord, chose me in his steadfast heart [and] with his holy eyes and named me for the shepherdship of Assyria, he put in my grasp a strong weapon which fells the insubordinate, he crowned me with a lofty crown, [and] he sternly commanded me to exercise dominion over and to subdue all the lands insubmissive to Ashur....I uprooted 17,500 of his troops. I took for myself Ahunu together with his troops, gods, chariots, [and] horses, brought [them] to my city Ashur, [and] regarded them as people of my land. (Shalmaneser III, 858–824 B.C.E.; period 1b) (Grayson 1996: 8, 29–30)

4. [Of] those [Ara]means [whom] I despoiled, X thousand to the province of the *turtanu*, 10,000 [to] the province of the Palace-Herald, [...] thousand [to] the province of the Chief Cupbearer, [...thousand [to] the province] of Barha[l]zi, 5,000 [to] the province of Mazamua [I divid]ed and settled [therein]. I made them of one mouth. [I considered them as] inhabitants of [Assyria]. [I placed upon them] the yoke of Ashur my lord, as upon the Assyrians. The abandoned settlements in the periphery of my [land], which had go[ne] to ruin [during the reign of my royal ancestors, the kings of Assyria], I restored. (Tiglath-pileser III, 744–727 B.C.E.; period 2b) (Tadmor 1994: 44–45)

5. The population of the four [quarters], of foreign tongue and divergent speech, inhabitants of mountain and plain, all of whom the Light of the gods, the lord of all, shepherded, whom I had carried off with my powerful scepter by the command of Ashur, my lord—I made them of one mouth and put them in its [= the new city; Dut-katlimmu] midst. Assyrians [lit., sons of Assyria], versed in all the proper culture, I ordered as overseers and supervisors to give them instruction in fearing god and king. (Sargon II, 721–705 B.C.E.; period 2b) (Machinist 1993: 95)

6. May Shamash, king of heaven and earth, elevate you to shepherdship over the four regions! May Ashur, who gave you the scepter, lengthen your days and years! Spread your land wide at your feet!...Ashur is king—indeed Ashur is king! Ashurbanipal is the representative of Ashur, the creation of his hands. May the great gods make firm his reign, may they protect the life of Ashurbanipal, king of Assyria! May they give him a straight scepter to extend the land and his peoples! May his reign be renewed, and may they consolidate his royal throne for ever! (Ashurbanipal, 668–631 B.C.E; period 2b) (Livingstone 1989: 26–27)

7. The goddess X, beloved of Tel.unu, priestess of the land of [Arabia], who, angered at Haza'el, king of Arabia,...handed him over to Sennacherib, my own grandfather, and caused his defeat. She [i.e., the goddess] determined not to remain with the people of Arabia and set out for Assyria....Hazail, king of the Arabs, came before him [i.e., Esarhaddon] with [his rich] gifts, kissed his feet, and appealed to him concerning the return of his goddess. He had mercy on him and agreed....Esharhaddon had a star of red gold made, which was studded with precious stones,...and presented it for a healthy life and long days, the prosperity of his descendants, the constancy of his rule, and the overthrow of his enemies. He showed kindness toward captured gods of all lands, whose sanctuaries had been trampled, so that the gods might grant him the blessing of long life and permit his offspring to rule over humanity. (Ashurbanipal, 668–631 B.C.E.) (Cogan 1974: 16–17)

8. Uate' together with his army, who had not kept the sworn oaths (and) who had fled before the weapons of Ashur my lord, Erra the strong overcame them. Disaster broke out among them so that they ate the flesh of their children to keep from starving. [The Assyrian gods] quickly inflicted all the curses which are written in the sworn oaths (including that) a camel-foal, a donkey-foal, a calf, a lamb might suck at seven milk-giving animals yet could still not satisfy their bellies with milk. The people in Arabia asked each other: "Why has such a disaster fallen on Arabia?"— "Because we did not abide by the great oaths of Ashur, and sinned against the kindness of Ashurbanipal, the king who pleases the heart of Enlil!" (Ashurbanipal, 668–631 B.C.E.; period 2b) (Streck 1916: 2:76–79)

Notes

1. Liverani 1993.
2. Grayson 1975; Millard 1994.
3. For example, Streck 1916; Luckenbill 1926–27; Borger 1956; Grayson 1991b, 1996; Tadmor 1994. For an overview see Grayson 1980.
4. Frame 1995: 11.
5. Gibson 1975, 1982.
6. Abou-Assaf, Bordreuil, and Millard 1982.
7. Frame 1995.
8. Watanabe 1987; Parpola and Watanabe 1988; Brinkman 1990.
9. Fitzmyer 1995.
10. Menzel 1981; Fales and Postgate 1992, 1995.
11. Jas 1996; see Radner 2003 for a review of types of legal texts.
12. Postgate 1976; Kwasman 1988; Kwasman and Parpola 1991; Mattila 2002.
13. Brinkman and Kennedy 1983.
14. Postgate 1969; Kataja and Whiting 1995.
15. Parpola 1981: 120.
16. Parpola 1970–83; Lanfranchi and Parpola 1990; Hunger 1992; Parpola 1993; Cole and Machinist 1998; Fuchs and Parpola 2001; Luukko and Van Buylaere; Dietrich 2003; Reynolds 2003.
17. Starr 1990.
18. Parpola 1997; Nissinen 1998.
19. Livingstone 1989.
20. Kühne 1991; Kühne 1995; Wilkinson 1995; Wilkinson and Tucker 1995; Wilkinson 2000: 232; Wilkinson, Wilkinson, Ur, Altaweel 2005: 37–44.
21. Nimrud: Oates and Oates 2001; Khorsabad: Loud 1936, Loud and Altman 1938; Nineveh: Layard 1849, Stronarch and Lumsden 1992; Aššur: Andrae 1977; Til Barsip: Bunnens 1993–94; Dur-katlimmu: Kühne 1991.
22. Reade 1979; Winter 1997; Russell 1991; Lamprichs 1995: 269–326; Cifarelli 1995, 1998.
23. Weinfeld 1972; Machinist 1983; Paul 1991; Steymanns 1995; Otto 2002: 94–219.
24. Johns 1898–1923.
25. Parpola 1987.
26. Oded 1979: 19–22.
27. For northern Mesopotamia see the studies cited in n. 20; for Babylonia see Brinkman 1984: 3–10.
28. Bedford 2007: 307–8, 315–17.

29. Moorey 1999, esp. 278–292 on iron technology.
30. Brinkman 1999: 7. See also Waldbaum 1978; Wertime and Muhly 1980.
31. For an overview of Assyrian society and political and religious institutions, see Grayson 1991a; on senior officials see Mattila 2000.
32. Oppenheim 1977: 98–100, 102–3; Maul 1999.
33. Radner 2003: 883, 886–87.
34. Oded 1992.
35. Porter 2000.
36. Pongratz-Leisten 1994.
37. Pongratz-Leisten 1999; Fales 2001: 244–83.
38. Pecírková 1977, 1987; Allen 2005.
39. Postgate 1980.
40. Grayson 1999; Holloway 2002: 223–24.
41. Grayson 1991a: 200–1, cf. Mattila 2000; Postgate 1995 on provinces.
42. Fales 2001: 53–71.
43. Parpola 1995.
44. Postgate 1979.
45. Cole 1996: 56–68; cf. Oppenheim 1967.
46. Elat 1987; Radner 1999: 101–9.
47. Radner 1999: 109–19.
48. Liverani 1984.
49. See also Fales 1984a, 1984b, but cf. Postgate 1989.
50. Liverani 1984: 39–40.
51. Postgate 1989: 147.
52. Liverani 1984: 42.
53. Liverani 1984: 40.
54. Partially indebted to Kuhrt 1995, cf. Liverani 1988a, both of whom offer extended historical overviews.
55. Kühne 1995: 69–79.
56. Neumann and Parpola 1987.
57. See Liverani 1990.
58. Hawkins 1995.
59. Liverani 1992: 103–10.
60. Postgate 1992.
61. Liverani 2004a.
62. Liverani 1992: 111–15.
63. Yamada 2000.
64. Liverani 1988b: 86.
65. Postgate 1992: 255–56.
66. Parker 2001.
67. Postgate 1995.
68. Brinkman 1990: 96–97, 107–11, for the treaty imposed on Shamshi-Adad by Marduk-zakir-shumi I of Babylon.
69. Fitzmyer 1995; Fales 1990.
70. Ikeda 1999: 287.
71. Lemaire and Durand 1984; Dalley 2000.
72. Lamprichs1995.

73. On Assyria and Syria-Palestine see Hawkins 1982, Parpola 2003; on Assyria in the Zagros, see Lanfranchi 2003; on Assyria and Urartu, see Barnett 1982: 333–65, Zimansky 1985, Dinçol 1994; on Assyria and Elam, see Potts 1999: 263–88.

74. See Bär 1996 for types of tribute and its ideological significance; Aubet 2001: 85–95 on Assyrian relations with Phoenician cities.

75. Spalinger 1974a, 1974b.

76. Barnett 1982: 333–65.

77. Hallo and Simpson 1998: 137.

78. Hallo and Simpson 1998: 134.

79. Wiseman 1958; Watanabe 1987; Parpola and Watanabe 1988.

80. Parpola 1980.

81. Zawadski 1988; Oates 1991; Machinist 1997.

82. Liverani 1979; Cifarelli 1998.

83. Tadmor 1999: 55–56.

84. Maul 1999.

85. Oded 1992: 163–76.

86. Liverani 1990.

87. Harrak 1987.

88. Postgate 1969; appendix, text no. 4.

89. Howe 2002: 15–16.

90. Frankenstein 1979; Sherratt and Sherratt 1993; Aubet 2001.

91. Cogan 1974: 42–110; McKay 1973: 60–66; Cogan 1993; Holloway 2002; against Spieckermann 1982.

92. Cogan 1974: 33–34.

93. Cogan 1974: 9–41; Holloway 2002: 123–51 for a discussion of the character and purpose of the destruction of shrines and the spoliation of divine images in the Neo-Assyrian Empire.

94. Sometimes marked with an inscription "as a visible reminder of the overlordship of Assyria"; Cogan 1974: 36.

95. Donner 1977: 418–21.

96. Bedford 2001: 137–38; Holloway 2002: 238–319.

97. Borger 1956: §27 esp. 3, 24–25.

98. Postgate 1979; Diakonoff 1974.

99. Machinist 1993.

100. Smith 1986.

101. Grosby 2002.

102. Frame 1992: 64–65, 67–78, 104–8, 111–13; Porter 1993.

103. Kuhrt 1987: 40–46.

104. Kuhrt 1995: 610–17; Holloway 2002: 293–302.

105. Mann 1986: 130–78.

3

The Achaemenid Empire

Josef Wiesehöfer

1. Introduction

The Achaemenid[1] (Persian) Empire was the largest of all ancient Near Eastern "world empires," spanning from Egypt to Central Asia and the Indus region. Its formation began after 550 B.C.E., when the petty king Cyrus of Anshan/Fars in southwestern Iran and his son Cambyses conquered the mighty Medes and the empires of Lydia, Babylonia, and Egypt. These territories were incorporated into the new "state." For more than two hundred years, the Achaemenids faced no serious opponents. Only the conquests of Alexander the Great, between 334 and 323 B.C.E., terminated Achaemenid rule over Asia. Even then, the prevalent Persian models of governing and administration did not come to an end but heavily influenced later empire building by Alexander, the Seleucids, and the Mauryas in India.[2]

This chapter focuses on the following questions: What were the geographic and demographic parameters of the Persian Empire? How can we best describe the expansionist and postexpansionist phases of the history of this empire, and when and why did the hegemony of the Achaemenids end? How did the empire, at its inception and during its lifespan, affect the inhabitants in the various regions of this kingdom? How did the rulers intend integration to work? What were the structural parameters of this realm, and how did the imperial state maintain its power? Last but not least: what can a comparison with the most important preceding empire, that of the Assyrians, add to our understanding of the Achaemenids?

2. Evidence

The history of the Achaemenid Empire is documented by a variety of sources.[3] Their regrettable lack of explanatory power is caused by several factors. First, the testimonies that do not originate in and around the central areas of royal ideology, such as royal inscriptions and reliefs, are the product of frequently hostile foreign countries, as can be seen in Greek literature and art. Both categories reflect inherent and specific biases. Second, the Iranian historical tradition was predominantly oral in character; thus, its Achaemenid traits can be traced only rudimentarily today.[4] Third, quantifiable material is rare. This evidence includes Babylonian cuneiform tablets, mostly from Mesopotamian archives of the late sixth and early fifth centuries and the second half of the fifth century B.C.E.; Elamite cuneiform tablets of the provincial administration of southwestern Iran of the first half of the fifth century B.C.E.; papyri and ostraca from fifth-century Egypt; and other similar sources. Not only is the actual amount of this material relatively limited, but it is also chronologically and geographically imbalanced. It is therefore difficult to write a history of events from a Persian perspective or to measure the economic performance of the Achaemenid Empire in any meaningful way and to base demographic, social, and economic statements on statistically sound material.

The multilingual royal inscriptions that were set up throughout the empire, the coins and the fine arts of the residences and burial places with their characteristic harmonious mixture of indigenous, modified Near Eastern, and newly designed elements,[5] provide insight into the ideology of rule and government: First, they reminded the royal subjects of the rulers' extraordinary qualities and achievements, as well as their duty of loyalty to these kings. Second, both the inscriptions and the palace and tomb reliefs emphasize the royal idea of the *pax Achaemenidica*, that is, the god-given and universal state of peace that was guaranteed by the kings and desired by their subjects. Opposition to this arrangement, in terms of the Great Kings' announcements, would have seemed nothing short of irresponsible.

Greek literary accounts of the Achaemenids, on the other hand, stand in stark contrast to the royal perspective. The Greek descriptions are varied and partly of high literary quality. All are characterized by the fact that the Persian universal monarchy was never presented as an alternative model to that of the Greek ideal of the autonomous *polis*.[6] In the fifth century, the Greek view of the Persians oscillated between fascination and aversion, between attraction and the need for distance—attitudes typical for social interaction with powerful foreign cultures.[7] Herodotus, who in his *Histories* (second half of the fifth century B.C.E.) tries to set forth "the great and marvellous deeds done by Greeks and barbarians and especially the reason why they warred against each other" (1.1), is even inclined to grant bravery and dignity to the opponents and to present their defeat, which is described as a consequence of the Persian kings' *hybris*, as a warning example to his fellow Athenians. In the course of time, however, not the least because of the experience of political disunity both within and among the city states, Greek tradition became increasingly biased and uniform: we end up with the image of the decadent barbarian "counter-world" with despotic rulers and slave-like subjects—an idea that was certainly also meant to emphasize the Greeks' superior culture and to establish Greek unity by presenting a common foe and an easy prey.[8] But, despite its bias, the Hellenic literary tradition provides an extraordinary amount of relevant and useful information—information, however, that has to be analyzed and evaluated with care. For a long time, the original idea of a succession of world empires ("*translatio imperii*") has been regarded as part of Achaemenid royal ideology; however, much speaks in favor of it being a Herodotean model.[9]

Another less distorted but regionally and chronologically rather restricted perspective on the structures and determining factors of the Achaemenid Empire and the degree of its subjects' loyalty to the king derives from other sources from different parts of the empire, such as collections of clay tablets from Babylonia and Persis. The Babylonian tablets are mostly private archive records, documenting legal and economic transactions. The tablets from Persis are records of the regional administration. These texts provide insight into the administration, social structure, and economy of these two provinces. Other categories include the papyri from the Jewish military colony of Elephantine, which illustrate Jewish life in the Egyptian diaspora; the inscriptions of Egyptian officials in Persian service, which hint at the degree of local elite cooperation; and the Greek inscriptions from Asia Minor, which document the relations between satraps (provincial governors), cities, and temples. The ostraca and coins from Judaea also belong to this group of evidence, whereas the books of the so-called Old Testament, which make reference to Achaemenid times, not only give less information on the Persians than on the special relation between Jahwe and God's own people in post-Exile times but also exaggerate the province's importance for the Great Kings. At the same time, they illustrate an important step in the formation of Jewishness.

Apart from the material from Persis, the archaeological evidence comes predominantly from Syria-Palestine and Anatolia. The multicultural dimension of the Achaemenid Empire is represented particularly well in regional and local art, as well as in the Persian emulation ("*Perserie*") of young aristocrats in late-fifth-century Athens. While the former, however motivated, illustrate the provincial elites' orientation toward examples set by the Great King, indigenous perseverance and rich cultural contacts both within the empire and with the outer world at the same time,[10] the latter give an idea both of Athens' fascination with the enemy's lifestyle and of the great variety of Greco-Persian relations.[11]

3. Beginnings of Persian Rule

Our picture of Persian rule and empire formation has been influenced mainly by the writings of Herodotus.[12] He assigns the earliest dominion over Asia to the Lydians and Assyrians. The Medes then enter the sphere of Assyrian control. Herodotus elevates the Medes, encroaching later on the Assyrian sphere of influence, to a level of definitive power by comparing them to the Lydian kings (Mermnads) in western Asia Minor and to the Babylonians, the heirs of the Assyrians.[13] The Persians finally lose their anonymity under Cyrus (550–530 B.C.E.), who first conquers Astyages, king of the Medes, and then the Lydian king Croesus and later puts an end to Babylonian rule. This account is supported by the legend of Cyrus's life: his

exposure, childhood, and ultimate revelation of his true royal identity. In this legend, Herodotus identifies Cyrus—fancifully—as the grandson of Astyages. Cyrus is
firmly convinced that Tyche—the personification of divine fortune—who granted
him sovereignty over formerly Median and Lydian territories (Herodotus 1.126)
will assist him during his attempts to subdue the Bactrians, Babylon, the Sacas, and
the Egyptians (1.153)—almost the entire continent opposite Europe. With his ford-
ing of the Araxes on the borders of Asia during the battle against the Scythian queen
Tomyris, Cyrus transgresses the boundaries set for him by the gods. According to
Herodotus, Xerxes repeats this mistake later when he crosses the Hellespont. The
story of Cyrus, the admirable founder of this great empire, ends in tragedy, even
though the Persian conquests within the borders of Asia remain in place. Cyrus's
son, Cambyses, even extends the empire significantly through the conquest of Egypt
(525 B.C.E.). But, while Cyrus's downfall was his transgression of the divinely set
borders, his son's were his phantasmagoric military ambitions against Carthage
and Ethiopia (3.17 & 25). These setbacks exacerbate his inclination toward brutality, irascibility, and despotic tendencies. The atrocities committed by him in Egypt,
which transform the more gentle, patriarchal monarchy of his father, Cyrus, into a
despotic and barbarous one, eventually cause the demise of Cyrus's dynasty and a
temporary return of Median rule, as well as the beginnings of Darius's royal line.

Herodotus portrays Darius (521–486 B.C.E.) as a king who falls between the
opposites of paternal, benign ruler and despot. After he has consolidated his empire,
he launches attempts to enlarge it. His campaign against the Scythians, which begins
with the crossing of the Danube (another literal and symbolical "transgression" of
a border), is a failure, saved only by Darius's late decision to retreat. Because of his
politics concerning Macedonia and Thrace, the borders of his empire now about
those of Hellas. The real confrontation between Persians and Greeks begins with
the "Ionian Revolt," especially with Athens' and Eretria's participation (500–494
B.C.E.). Darius initially desires both revenge on those two cities and the subjugation
of all other Greek states. This campaign of vengeance, which Darius's son Xerxes
(486–465 B.C.E.) continues, explodes into a campaign for world domination. The
ensuing personal and military catastrophes of Xerxes and his army are caused both
by the transgression of divinely ordained borders[14] and the fact that the Persians
have long given up their freedom to the command of the king. In the end, Persian
rule is again limited to Asia.

This is Herodotus's view of Persian empire building. Numerous scholars have
relied on his report, explaining that the quest for world domination was part and
parcel of Persian ruling ideology, reflected as such in the royal inscriptions.[15] According to this view, Darius planned to conquer and incorporate all of Hellas, and Xerxes
aimed toward the domination of all of western Europe. The true motivations and
intentions of the Persian kings during the formation of their empire are, of course,
very difficult to nail down in their exact historical sequence. More recent investi-
gations have shown that one essential prerequisite for Persian empire formation

was the existence of a sustainable Elamite, post-Assyrian kingdom in southwest Iran. This was also important for the extent of acculturation and transculturation between the Elamites and the Persians.[16] The Elamite traditions, unsurprisingly, did not remain unchanged in a partly semipastoral (Iranian) milieu but were influenced by Iranian traditions and institutions. Simultaneously, the ethnogenesis of the Persians has to be interpreted as a mixture of "Iranian" and "Elamite" population groups.[17] As a result of Elamite influence, the Persians were imbued with more potential for empire formation than, for example, the Medes. Median rule might best be described as a "loosely unifying leadership."[18] In the end, the Persians under Cyrus were successful in their conflicts against the Medes and the Lydians, integrating the territory of their enemies into their own empire.[19] How the incorporation of new territories was organized in the political and administrative sphere is unknown; we have no sources for any areas except the Lydian western territories.

Babylon, ruled by King Nabonidus at the time, could not have remained unaffected by the defeats of its Median neighbors and its Lydian allies, nor by the Persian control of Susa. But the events leading up to the fatal confrontation with Cyrus are impossible to determine because of the lack of sources. It is clear, however, that tensions must have increased steadily, fueled, among other factors, by Cyrus's alliance with Babylonian population groups that were dissatisfied with the rule of Nabonidus (such as the Priests of Marduk). After his victory at Opis, the subsequent massacre of the Babylonian soldiers, and the conquest of Sippar, Cyrus sent his commander Ugbaru ahead to Babylon. The city opened the doors willingly to the representative of the king; Babylon was thus taken and King Nabonidus captured. Cyrus's triumphal procession into Babylon at the end of October 539 B.C.E. (commemorated as recently as 1971 by the Shah),[20] was held according to the Babylonian tradition, as were his first administrative actions in the city and country. The "Cyrus Cylinder" inscription, for example, was carved by a skilled Babylonian craftsperson and portrays the king as the legitimate ruler of Babylon. Under the divine protection of Marduk, he is shown as fulfilling his civic, public, and political duties toward both gods and people in the best interest of the country and its inhabitants.

With his actions, Cyrus made it possible for the local elite to accept and cooperate with the foreign ruler. After Nabonidus's defeat, the former Neo-Babylonian territories stretching from Palestine in the southwest to the Zagros Mountains in the east had all changed ownership. It is impossible to determine to what extent Cyrus was guided by the Babylonian example in the political annexation of those territories to his realm and how much he was able to change politics during his nine-year rule. The Jewish texts assign Cyrus a major role in the repatriation of the Judaeans after their deportation by Nebukadnezzar and in the rebuilding of the Temple in Jerusalem. But this should be understood as a theologically influenced reconstruction of events, which included the attribution of measures much later approved or begun to this long-awaited emancipator. Although Cyrus would certainly have been concerned about Syria-Palestine,[21] significant changes did not occur until the reigns of his successors.

Cyrus obviously attributed great importance to the annexation of the well-populated and geographically expansive Neo-Babylonian kingdom. We can see this both from the king's ideological efforts and from his concrete policies. Nabonidus's upper-level officials were allowed to remain in their offices; the crown prince Cambyses was made "viceroy" for one year in 538–537 B.C.E., after which he resigned as "King of Babylon" and was replaced by the new provincial governor, Gobryas. In contrast to Lydia, our sources for Babylonia do not give any hint of local rebellion. This conspicuous absence can be seen as an indication of the success of early Persian governance. This success is also confirmed by the fact that in the 530s B.C.E., Cyrus apparently brought large parts of Eastern Iran under his control. The details of how he did this—his strategies, the progression of his campaigns, and his methods for securing the northeast and eastern borders—remain unknown.

After Cyrus's victory over Nabonidus, the Persians shared a border with the Egyptians. The latter were the last remaining major power in the Near East. Their king, Amasis, who found himself without allies, attempted to meet the Persian danger by building up a powerful navy. He enlisted the support of the Greek tyrant Polycrates of Samos, who was a potential threat to the Persians in the East Aegean, and chose Cyprus as an important base for his fleet. Cambyses, son of Cyrus, retaliated by launching his own navy, staffed with experienced sailors from his own subjects under Persian command. This was not his only time-consuming and costly enterprise. Cambyses also constructed and enlarged harbors, conquered Cyprus, and forged alliances with the Arabic tribes whose assistance would be invaluable for the crossing of the Sinai desert. The Persian victory at Pelusium (525 B.C.E.) and the conquest of Memphis and capture of King Psammetichus III signaled the end of the Persian campaign against Egypt. The neighbors to the west capitulated, the southern border was secured through diplomacy, and the large oases in the west came under Persian control. Following his father's example, Cambyses attempted to secure the loyalty and support of the local elite by adapting his politics and royal ideology to the Egyptian tradition. That these measures were at least partially successful can be seen in the inscription of the official Udjahorresnet. The more negative version of Cambyses's conquest of Egypt that appears in Herodotus was influenced by cutbacks in temple funding and later futile Egyptian revolts against the Persians in 486–485 and 460–454 B.C.E.

The causes of the political crisis in the empire that occurred during Cambyses's sojourn at the Nile were manifold. They must have included financial and military exploitation of the subjects in the campaign against Egypt, mounting tensions between the Great King and the powerful Persian aristocracy, and a conflict of succession with his brother Bardiya. The empire found itself in significant political upheaval, recorded both in the Bisutun inscription of Darius I and in Herodotus. The exact sequence of events remains unclear. The Bisutun version of the story involves an official appointed by Cambyses, a Median magus by the name of Gaumata. He took advantage of the discontent of Cambyses's subjects and the murder of Bardiya, which had been ordered by the king himself, and posed as the brother of the king. Under this guise, he ascended the throne and won public approval through a number of popular measures such as canceling taxes and abolishing mandatory military service. However, many scholars assume that Bardiya himself rose up against his brother. Regardless of whether Darius I, who removed Gaumata/Bardiya with his co-conspirators after Cambyses's death, should be considered a regicide and a liar, he was at the very least a usurper, lacking any familial claim to the throne.[22] Darius actively promoted a link between his own Achaemenid clan and Cyrus's Teispid lineage, which is recorded both in the Bisutun inscription and by Herodotus. This constructed genealogy was meant to legitimize his claim to the throne.

The political caesura following Cambyses's death was a huge shift for the empire. Darius contained numerous revolts only with great effort and brutality (522–521 B.C.E.). He would not have been able to achieve even these victories without the assistance of a large proportion of the Persian aristocracy that had been dissatisfied with both Cambyses and Gaumata/Bardiya. The process of empire formation and territorial expansion and the necessary military, political, and fiscal efforts had apparently created dissent among the Great King, the Persian population, and the Persian aristocracy with regard to the development of the respective roles of ruler, aristocracy, and subjects. It is testimony to Darius's considerable political and diplomatic skills that he was still able to maintain the unity of the empire, to tie the alliance of the aristocracy to himself, and to secure his claim to the throne. It is equally an example of his military aptitude and his unscrupulousness. The monument of Bisutun, with its depiction of Darius's triumph over the opposing "Liar-Kings" (as he calls them), is the ultimate expression of these abilities.

Darius's rule was an important chapter in the history of the Achaemenid Empire. Under his sovereignty, the empire reached its greatest territorial expansion, the fiscal policies and administrative bodies underwent major reforms, and a royal ideology was developed. Unfortunately, the historical events of the period following Darius's rule are barely documented; and when they are they are extremely one-sided in their point of view. Our main sources come from the Greek historians and the Old Testament, which are concerned mainly with Greek-Persian or Judaean-Persian relations and the western provinces of the empire. The Bisutun inscription records Darius's campaigns in the second and third years of his rule, against Elam and the Scythians in Central Asia, but this is all that the Persian sources relate. Two chronicles of the latest phase of the empire (345–344 B.C.E. and the time of Alexander)—survive from Babylonia. In addition, some brief historical information can be found in the "Astronomical Diaries," which is not always easy to interpret.[23] Almost all other accounts are not indigenous and often carry a distinct anti-Persian bias.

Darius I expanded his empire to the north, the west, and the east. He secured its borders and strengthened its economy. In the west, the territories integrated into the empire included the Cyrenaica in 513 B.C.E., Thrace, rich in natural resources, and the strategic straits and Aegean islands opposite the coast of Asia Minor. Most important was the acquisition of Samos around 519 B.C.E. Darius made Macedonia tributary to his empire (510 and after 492 B.C.E.).[24] He also made a treaty with Athens in 507–506 B.C.E.[25] In the East, the Persians successfully conquered "Indian" territories. They considered the northern border of their empire to be the Danube, and the failed campaign against the Scythians (c. 513 B.C.E.) proved that their limits in this area of the border lay in defending it against attacks of the nomads. These policies of consolidation and securing of the outer territories suffered a significant setback around 500 B.C.E., when the Ionian cities revolted under the leadership of the tyrant Aristagoras of Miletus; Caria and parts of Cyprus joined the revolt against the Persians. The rebels even conquered and burned Sardis with the help of their Athenian and Eretrian allies. The revolts could be suppressed only by an enormous effort on the Persian side that was aided by some dissent among the Ionians. The Persians spent the following years establishing different types of political institutions in those reconquered cities that promised to remain loyal to the Persian crown. They also mapped each city's territory in order to recalculate the tribute to be handed over and to prevent border disputes between subject cities. Last but not least, the Persians prepared for revenge against Athens and Eretria. Not only had these cities supported the revolt, but Athens, in doing so, had broken its treaty with Persia.[26] While the Persian defeat at Marathon was the inglorious end to an otherwise successful Aegean campaign, it should certainly not be considered a failed attempt to conquer all of Greece. What proved most important for the Persians was not their defeat but its consequences for the political system of Athens (such as the removal of sympathizers with Persians or tyrants) and the creation of an Athenian political identity.

Darius was also more involved in Egypt, as the brief reign of Cambyses had not successfully established any kind of stability. Just as Darius assumed his reign, the Persian satrap there was replaced and a number of measures were designed to secure the king's sovereignty. Some of the most significant of these included the retraction of Cambyses's fiscal measures, the reaffirmation of the old privileges of the temples and the priesthood, the completion of the Necho Canal, and the launching of naval expeditions to and from Egypt. These maritime campaigns were undertaken less for the sake of economic improvement than in a conscious attempt to emulate Pharaonic deeds.

Darius also initiated the construction of the two most important Achaemenid residences, Susa and Persepolis. The Elamite tablets from Persepolis and the foundation inscription ("Foundation Charter") from Susa (*DSf*) record the far-reaching importance of these projects. The king successfully mobilized manpower, raw materials, and artistic templates from all over the empire to realize his idea of Achaemenid rule through the media of architecture, imagery, and text. Even Darius's tomb, in Naqsh-i Rustam, in the new form of a cruciform cliff tomb, is a symbol of this tradition with its inscriptions (*DNa, DNb*) and its reliefs. Gaumata's revolt, as well as those during the early years of Darius's reign, had a significant effect on politics. Darius reformed the administration, the infrastructure, and the security of the empire. He also reworked the ideology of Persian kingship. Both art and text under his reign reflect the idea of a *pax Achaemenidica*, which Darius must have considered more likely to further the integration of the empire than an ideology that portrayed the king as the conqueror and the subjects as the vanquished.

Darius's son and successor, Xerxes (486–65 B.C.E.), was faced with a difficult situation upon assumption of the throne. He had to secure and preserve Persian rule, founded by Cyrus and reformed and legitimized by his father. Recent studies on the Achaemenids have shown that he was more successful as a ruler than the Greek sources would have us believe. Such more recent studies, which have not been favorably received by everyone in the academic community, show that Xerxes had no part in the destruction of Babylonian temples and the abduction of Marduk's statue. It is equally unlikely that the wholesale adoption of his father's royal ideology was a result of his lack of creativity or that his behavior during battles in Greece was marked by cowardice, brutality, and ignorance of proper strategy. Xerxes had learned from his father how to prevent revolts. In case prevention of a revolt proved impossible, as in Egypt or Babylon, he knew how to suppress it. He also knew how to consolidate the most recently conquered territories, integrate them into the empire (such as in the division of the provinces Lydia and Babylonia), and secure them militarily.[27]

Xerxes' only real failure was his attempt to force the Greeks to recognize Persian sovereignty, which he presumably hoped to achieve by setting up a system of Persian-friendly Greek hegemonic powers. This would have brought the entire Aegean under the control of the Great King. His alleged plan to bring all of western Europe under Persian rule is highly unlikely.[28] Some important Greek *poleis* and *ethne*, such as Thebes and Thessaly, did negotiate treaties with the Persians. Depending on the military situation, others stuck to tactical agreements (Delphi) or remained neutral (Argos). Some, such as Messenia, would gladly have traded their dependence on other Greek *poleis* for an alliance with the Persians. In spite of the partial support of the Persians by Greek *poleis*, the anti-Persian members of the "Hellenic League," after a number of failed attempts, managed to secure a series of great victories against the Persian army and navy (Salamis 480, Plataea 479). Athens, Sparta, Plataea, Corinth, Eretria, and Aegina did not have a wider agenda; they were not fighting for Europe in opposition to Asia or in favor of democracy and humanity as opposed to barbarism and despotism. They were simply defending their political independence. But the consequences were formidable. In the years leading up to the Battle of the Eurymedon (460s B.C.E.), Persia found itself pushed back to the eastern Mediterranean and the interior of Asia Minor. Athens advanced to become a hegemonic power in Greece, in fierce rivalry with Sparta, and the Persian wars created pan-Hellenic identities that stood in opposition to the notion of the "barbarian."

In sum, the first phase of Persian empire formation under Cyrus and Cambyses was not achieved through lineage, diplomatic marriages, or voluntary annexations of other states. Instead, the empire was formed through the conquest and incorporation of previously independent kingdoms (Lydia, Babylonia, Egypt) and federations (the federation of the Medes). During the early phases of the conflicts with the Medes and Lydians, it seems as though the Persians provoked their neighbors to military action. But these reactions also appear to have been less a direct result of the Persians' own military initiative than of the gradual geographic expansion of their empire from Persis into the Zagros and into northwestern Iran.

The motives for the war against Babylonia and the overall political situation in eastern Iran are unknown. Presumably, the Persians simply adopted local, traditional administrative and socioeconomic institutions (probably except in the territory of the Medes) in the beginning stages of their sovereignty. They probably also collected taxes or tribute at irregular intervals, added military service requirements, and replaced the local dynasties. The Persians reordered regional political institutions only in the event of a revolt, as in Lydia and Ionia. It is not clear whether the Egyptian war was caused by the formidable Persian supremacy in the Near East or whether Cambyses—in the Assyrian-Babylonian tradition—was actively trying to dispose of his last remaining powerful neighbor. Deliberate territorial expansion of the empire seems to have ended after the subjugation of Samos, the Cyrenaica, Thrace, and the region of the Indus. The continuing "vassal"-type relationship with Macedonia and the likely alliances with some Scythian tribes beyond Sogdia, Arab tribes, and possibly even Ethiopia, should not be considered a continuation of territorial expansion. These regions, which were loyal to Persia, formed an additional protective ring of territories adjacent to the empire. The part that the Athenians and Eretrians played during the Ionian Revolt drove the Persians to the—ultimately unsuccessful—attempt to extend this buffer zone into the Aegean and even (under Xerxes) into mainland Greece. An incorporation of the whole region into the ensemble of the imperial territories was hardly the intent.

This reconsideration of Persian empire formation explains, for one, the repeated attempts of the subjugated elites to dispose of the Persian rule in the early phase of Persian rule. Such uprisings, which continuously reappeared up until the early years of Xerxes' reign, include the revolt of Pactyes in Lydia under Cyrus. Following Darius's ascension to the throne, rebels challenged the crown in Babylonia, eastern Iran, and other areas, some of them even claiming dynastic lineage. Further revolts occurred in Ionia and Cyprus under Darius and in Egypt and Babylonia under Xerxes. For another, this reconsideration facilitates our understanding of the character of empire formation under Darius and Xerxes. These rulers provided the Iranian elite with important roles in the administration of the empire, especially in the form of provincial "top" offices—often at the expense of the local elite. They also reorganized the tributary and fiscal relations between the center of the empire and the provinces and strengthened political and military supervision. The local and regional elites were still allowed to retain their political positions with the exception of the highest-ranking ones. This policy apparently left them with enough prestige not only to tolerate Persian rule but even to adopt the new ideological and practical framework (see later discussion). The royal *pax Achaemenidica* not only ensured peace and order and rewarded its loyal subjects but also threatened harsh punishment of insurgents and rebelling subjects (*bandaka*) (discussed later). The combination of political concepts and measures was very effective in spite of the numerous structural problems that plagued the empire even up to the highest level of government (see later discussion).

The territorial expansion after Darius I not only served the interest of the members of the royal house. The family members of the six co-conspirators against Gaumata/Bardiya, as well as other members of the Persian aristocracy, were rewarded with important political offices throughout the empire and at court and received substantial financial benefits. Even Median aristocrats appear relatively early in leading military and administrative positions. In regional and local contexts, members of the indigenous elites, such as the Greek exiles, also played an important role in politics under Persian rule, as long as they had proved their loyalty to the Great King or gained the status of "friends" or "benefactors." Herodotus mentions individuals of the most diverse backgrounds and even describes former opponents such as Croesus as "warners" (Artabanus) or "warmongers" (Mardonius). His account should be interpreted as a direct result of the author's worldview, not as historical reality. It is impossible to tell who truly was able to exert of influence on the king and his decisions. It remains most likely, however, that such influence would have occurred within the immediate vicinity of the king: at court, in the service of the empire, and in marriage alliances to the royal house.

4. Basic Parameters

4.1. Demography

Information on the demographic parameters of the Achaemenid Empire is rudimentary at best.[29] What we have comes from a variety of different sources, and the numbers they provide us with are highly controversial. As far as the total population of the Achaemenid Empire is concerned, a presentation of two different demographic tables reveals the problems of such calculations (table 3.1).

The methodology employed in extracting figures from literary and archaeological material is highly problematic. This is true for the use of settlement surveys, concentrated almost exclusively on Syria and Mesopotamia, that have produced data that are not only of debatable value but also quantitatively insufficient, as well as literary evidence, which has often been interpreted without regard to its time and place of origin and its specific use of numbers. Herodotus's (3.89) accounts of Achaemenid tributes and the size of the Persian army and fleet during the Persian Wars (490–79

Table 3.1. Modern Estimates of the Population of the
Achaemenid Empire

Area	Region Population
High estimates	
Mesopotamia	c. 5–6,000,000
Bactria/Sogdiana	c. 2,000,000
Margiana	c. 500,000
Central and Eastern Persis	c. 500,000
Susiana and Western Persis	c. 1,000,000
Northern Syria	c. 500,000
Cilicia	c. 2,000,000
Western and Southern Asia Minor	c. 5,000,000
Syria/Palestine	c. 1,500,000–2,000,000
Egypt	c. 5–6,000,000
Eastern regions of the empire	At least c. 7,000,000
Whole empire	c. 30–35,000,000
Low estimates	
Egypt	c. 3,500,000
Near East (without Arabia)	c. 12,000,000
Central Asia and India	c. 1,500,000
Whole empire	c. 17,000,000

B.C.E.) imply a very large population. More detailed analysis, however, proves that his figures are unreliable. Both Herodotus's list of provinces and the figures he gives for the tribute are not based on Persian sources.[30] His description of the size of the army is based on both Homer's epics and Hecataeus's ethnographical work,[31] and the figures he lists for the number of soldiers and ships are based on patterns that express nothing but relations of magnitude. Finally, by exaggerating the size of the Persian army throughout Greek history, authors such as Herodotus, Xenophon, and the historians of Alexander the Great magnify the Greeks' military achievements to make them seem exceptionally glorious. The authors of the fourth century in particular succeeded in making the Persian opponent appear extremely daunting, but only because of the sheer size of its army (whose members had been coerced by the Great King to serve and fight) and not because of any bravery on the part of the soldiers or the tactical skills of their commanders.

The numbers of the workers mentioned in the Elamite "Fortification Tablets" from Persepolis that have been published so far (21,576 in all) are equally problematic; not even in combination with later historians' praise of the fertility and population density of Persis do they enable us to estimate of the size of the population of the core province of the empire. The manual workers and craftsmen employed there were actually members of a special labor force, recruited from all over the empire to serve the king in Fars. The well-balanced proportion of men to women (8,138 men, 8,564 women, 2,687 boys, 2,142 girls) indicates no more than that some of these workers must have lived in family groups. The ratio of different generations does not match other ancient demographic patterns, and an assessment of living and work spaces minimizes the numerical data's meaningfulness. But by looking at a special case (special rations for mothers)[32] and at Greek testimonies of the royal policy of reproduction,[33] it becomes obvious that Persian rulers were interested in the greatest possible number of potential soldiers, officials, and workers.[34] Both the Greek and the indigenous evidence assign much relevance to Achaemenid "forced migration" as a demographic factor. Apart from the workers (*kurtash*) mentioned earlier, working in the treasuries and working houses of Fars and Elymais, one has to remember the *hatru* collectives in Babylonia, organized in terms of their duties, customers or place of origin (see later discussion), and the deported elites of conquered cities and communities (Eretria, Miletus). The royal distribution of land and property to Iranian and non-Iranian officials and officers in newly acquired territories and the service of Achaemenid garrison troops in places far away from their homes also influenced demographic conditions. After all, both of these migratory measures led to the development of an Iranian cultural "diaspora," especially in Hellenistic and Roman Asia Minor.

Persian imperialism led not to the development of new mega-towns (like Babylon) but rather to the adjustment of existing royal centers such as Babylon, Susa, Sardis, and Ecbatana to Persian needs.[35] Still, the Achaemenids contributed significantly to the process of urbanization in the Ancient Near East by promoting satrapal capitals as regional centers (thereby following an Assyrian program) and by investing revenues in constructing new royal cities in their home province of Fars (Persepolis, Pasargadae, Matezzish). Since the "traveling ruler" was a particular feature of Achaemenid kingship,[36] Persian residences (note the kings' self-portrayal as master builders, hunters, and gardeners) were marked by special architectural and landscaped constituents (palaces, fortifications, administrative buildings—open spaces for tents, gardens, and game parks [*paradeisoi*]).[37]

4.2. Economic Institutional Framework and Standards of Living

The enormous wealth of the kings, the members of the Achaemenid clan, and the Iranian and indigenous elites has often been presented and commented on by Greek authors in terms of effeminate *tryphe* ("luxury"). The rich treasuries that Alexander the Great found in the royal residences show that the largest part of the resources was concentrated at court and in the center of the empire. This proverbial "royal gold" had often enough helped to preemptively ward off potential dangers to the empire at its western border and had become a constant nuisance to those Greeks who were Persian enemies. Among the characteristic acts of a good ruler, however, as shown in both Achaemenid inscriptions and the Greek sources, were the systematic punishment of miscreants and rebels and the generous rewarding of benefactors and loyal subjects.[38] These personalities, called *euergetai* or *orosangai* by the Greek authors (< Median *ˇvarusanha-*), were listed at court with their achievements, privileges, and distinctions. The reward they received could be in the form of tax exemption (Greek *ateleia*), special proximity to the king, or gifts such as landed property (or its proceeds or incomes), valuable objects, horses with golden bridles, or merely a seat at the royal banquets.[39] The honored persons were represented on Achaemenid reliefs and elsewhere, and there is reason to believe that such distinctions were granted at public ceremonies (for instance at a royal meal [Greek *tykta*, < Iranian *ˇtaug-*]). Occasions for granting them might be the king's birthday, the designation of the heir to the throne, or an accession.[40] On the other hand, it appears that previously honored subjects who later proved disloyal might be publicly deprived of their privileges and gifts and, at worst, even publicly tortured and executed. Greek tradition equally includes the type of the magnanimous and forgiving ruler.[41]

Along with the Great King's *polydoria* ("open-handedness") which, in the Iranian context, is always to be understood as the mark and privilege of a highly superior sovereign, rather than as a royal gesture within a reciprocal system of gift exchange, one may also recognize something like the ruler's obligation to show particular generosity. This is expressed by what the Greeks describe as the *nomos* of the king's obligation to fulfil his subjects' wishes on certain occasions.[42]

As far as the economic institutional framework and the common people's economic situation are concerned,[43] we have mostly Babylonian and Jewish evidence, both, however, once again only in rudimentary form.[44] On the whole, the economy of the Persian Near East was characterized by continuities with the preceding Neo-Assyrian and Neo-Babylonian empires, but—for Babylonia—with special developments in land tenure, business practices, and legal instruments.

The sources we have for Babylonia under Persian rule do not divulge much information on the contemporary economic circumstances. We can tell, however, that there were "winners" and "losers." The textual and archaeological evidence shows that most of the old cities were served as legal and economic centers; the temples, on the other hand, remained centers of cult and trade, the latter partially regulated by the state. The texts from the early Achaemenid period, the Murashu texts, and texts of other late-fifth-century archives definitively place large landholders, the highest ranking political officials, the so-called business houses/firms, and the royal treasury (thanks to measures intensifying agricultural production and extracting taxes and revenues) among the "winners." The "losers" that emerge from these texts are the temple workers and the smaller landholders organized into *hatrus* (see later discussion). In the course of time, these smaller landholders, to whom the king had leased out land in exchange for services and taxes, came under heavy financial and working pressure.[45]

The political importance of Babylonia as the center of a formerly powerful empire and its agricultural resources provided clear personal benefits for the king.

These factors were certainly among the reasons why Achaemenid kings increasingly amassed property in this province. The Babylonian texts record royal domains, and, more important, royal control over most of the irrigation systems and canals—an essential part of the Tigris and Euphrates river valley. Some Babylonian large land-holders with Iranian or Babylonian names who drew a direct profit from the taxes and services of their "dependents" formed a type of local "landed gentry," which was subordinate to the Persian aristocrats, the "Friends of the King," and the male and female members of the royal house in terms of political importance, prestige, and economic power. The latter mostly left the administration of their estates in the hands of Babylonian stewards and agents. Their control over these properties was very much contingent on their relationship with the king and could be lost very quickly: one need only make the mistake of being loyal to the "wrong" contender for the throne. Other domains were provided to officials in their capacity as officials. It has been noted that there were several good reasons behind this generous allocation of properties by the king to persons who were either related to him or politically close: not merely a reward for special loyalty, these grants were also a means of monitoring and controlling potential political rivals, such as the satrap of Babylonia.

In addition to the large and medium-size estates and temples as land-holding organizations, cuneiform texts also document royal grants of small land parcels to individuals in return for (military) service; these parcels were often part of larger corporate institutions (*hatrus*). The military "fiefs" were of three different types, according to the kind of military service and equipment expected and the basic fighting units of the Persian army: "horse-land," "bow-land," and "chariot-land."[46] The grantees and their obligations were registered in a royal census, kept by officers at the main mustering points of the satrapy to ensure military call-ups in case of need. Apart from the "military" *hatrus*, there were others named for the artisanal, agricultural, or administrative occupations of their members, for the estates or administrative institutions to which their members were attached, or for the geographic or ethnic origins of their members. Land held in such corporate groups was not alienable, but it could be inherited, passed on in dowries, or used as a pledge in exchange for a loan. On the whole, the kings' settlement policy in Babylonia served the empire's needs by both expanding the amount of cultivated land (increasing agricultural production and taxation) and creating a population obliged to perform military service. As the empire stabilized during the reign of Xerxes I and territorial expansion came to a halt, the descendants of the original grantees were asked to pay a silver tax in lieu of performing military service. Like temples and large estate holders, who contracted with family "firms" (e.g., the Murashus) to place the land under cultivation by renting the land on portions to various farmers, the members of the *hatrus* leased their parcels out to those "entrepreneurs," who sublet them to tenants. Other contracts between the two parties were concluded to meet the tax payments of the farmers through exchanging produce on their behalf for a fee. The "Murashu documents" of the second half of the fifth century testify not only to the geographical location of the parcels but also to their administrative integration into the *hatru* organization and to the company's role as financial mediator among those tenants, the original grantees, and the king.

The Egibis, another family "firm," also managed large tracts of crown land and were further involved in business partnerships in which both parties drew up contracts to share both profits and losses on a commercial agricultural venture (*harranu* partnerships). The close relationship among the state, the temples (as "economic engines"), and the "entrepreneurs" was mutually advantageous economically. The family "firms" of the Egibis and the Murashus were the most important mediators between landholders and the crown. With this function they ensured the economic power of the province and its fiscal productivity, even as the gap dividing rich and poor grew ever wider. Nothing indicates a total economic stagnation or economic decline in Babylonia during late Achaemenid rule. In fact, the opposite seems to be the case; everything indicates that Mazaeus handed over to Alexander a well-ordered, politically secure, and extremely lucrative province.

In post-Exile Judaea, a party of lay leaders and priests had established a political organization with the consent of the Persian administration and in exchange for absolute loyalty that guaranteed them a maximum level of sociopolitical participation. It was probably those "nobles and councillors" about whom the traditional class of peasants, already burdened with famine and the "royal tax," complained to Nehemiah. Those rich lenders had tried to take advantage of the debtors' property and families if the latter were unable to pay.[47] However, it was this social crisis that led to a particularly harsh questioning of the theological legitimacy of wealth within the framework of the official Jahwe religion.[48]

Unfortunately, no Persian source exists that offers reflection on the strengths and weaknesses of Achaemenid rule over time. The Greek texts (such as Xenophon's *Education of Cyrus* 8) represent not Persian but uniquely Greek opinions (see earlier discussion). In the Greek sources, the rule of Xerxes is the turning point in Iranian history, a period that initiated the inevitable and unstoppable decline of the Persian Empire. It has been widely accepted that this does not reflect historical reality (see earlier discussion). Near Eastern archaeology, in fact, suggests the exact opposite: the time of Xerxes archaeologically represents the apex of Persian artistic creativity (without wishing to imply that art from the following period of the empire was marked by "cultural conformity"). Reliefs and inscriptions of Darius's time were copied by Xerxes and his successors not out of lack of creativity but to emphasize the continuing validity of his royal maxims. As far as provincial culture is concerned, Caria under Maussolus testifies both to the continuing artistic and cultural influence of the center and to the self-confidence of local dynasties in service of the Persians.

4.3. Exploitation

The Great King seemed to consider himself the ultimate owner of all of the empire's territories, which he administered by order of the gods for the benefit of all inhabitants. However, sources also present the ruler as the master of his own *oikia/oikos*, a household, which consists both of inherited and newly gained property. This property generates rents for the head of the household and allows him to be generous. The households (*oikoi*) of the Persian nobility can be described in a similar way; they differ from the king's *oikia* not so much in terms of structure as in size. The Persians only very rarely modified the social and economic structures of the newly conquered territories.

Although local modes of agricultural production necessarily remained basically the same, the imperial grip on productive resources was tightened in comparison with conditions in the preceding Near Eastern empires. For one, the king, members of the royal family and of the new Iranian administrative elite, garrison officers, and other decision makers, as well as individual "friends" and "benefactors" of the king, had to be endowed with their own *oikoi*.[49] As far as Achaemenid Babylonia is concerned, the reorganization of agricultural production (exploitation by institutional landowners [e.g., the temples] or the crown; *hatru* system) reinforced the dependency of agriculturalists (formerly "free" peasants, "fief" holders, and tenants) on these large landowners and on the mediating entrepreneurial "firms." Also, villagers within satrapies were assigned special duties (e.g., provisioning the satrapal court,[50] the garrisons, the traveling king); those duties were imposed in addition to the regular taxes and services. Finally, the king controlled the access to water.[51] Another important part of Near Eastern economy in Achaemenid times was pastoralism, rendering the reciprocal exchange between the (semi-)nomadic mountain peoples and the sedentary populations profitable to both sides.[52]

According to our sources, the skilled labor in Phoenicia, North Syria, and Babylonia took the form of manufacture for the temples and production of both luxury goods and regular household crafts. The volume of both of these industries is difficult to quantify. Presumably, trade increased significantly during the Persian period.[53] Yet, the sources leave many questions unanswered. There is little evidence for long-distance trade and merchants. Written sources of this period—when they do mention transregional interactions—focus mainly on political and military actions, such as the use of roads and waterways by troops, messengers, and diplomats. The Elamite tablets from Persepolis and the archives of the Egibis and Murashus from Mesopotamia, on the other hand, show a distinctively regional focus. Archaeological material, another important source, requires confirmation through textual evidence to be interpreted as trade objects, instead of diplomatic presents, war booty, or "souvenirs."

What evidence is there to demonstrate an increasing importance of long-distance trade during the Achaemenid period? It has been argued that any political integration of this degree necessarily promotes the exchange of goods. Agreements are reached much more readily, transaction costs are lowered, and any specialized regional agriculture and industry have a better chance to boost sales when political borders are eliminated and the infrastructure is expanded, as was the case with the

Achaemenid system of roads. Unfortunately, we have very little source material to verify these assumptions. Arguments in favor of political integration and the control measures instituted to ensure its success are linked to the idea that the long, stable *pax Achaemenidica* had a beneficial effect on regional and superregional trade. Moreover, the hitherto unfamiliar sophistication and exclusiveness of the royal and aristocratic lifestyle during the Persian period may have sped along long-distance trade, as much of it involved the exchange of strategic or luxury goods. Finally, the importance of the introduction of coinage and its role as a stimulant to trade should be considered. Neither correspondence between traders nor archives documenting superregional trade exist, however, and what evidence there is is not readily susceptible to statistical analysis. In order to test modern theses, one must rely on alternative evidence and methods such as detailed examinations of individual texts, any casual references in Greek literature, or the results of local excavations. As had been common in previous centuries, some of the long-distance trade remained in the hands of agents who were hired by the state or larger organizations such as the Babylonian temples. Another part of the trade network (such as in the Levant) was in private hands, which was likewise not a recent development.[54] The state was not only an important final recipient of merchandise and raw materials that had been acquired by the Phoenician traders in the open market and that often finally flowed into the coffers of the Great King. It also played a pivotal role in the organization of the exchange of raw materials and rations for precious metals or even coins, therefore promoting the development of local markets. Further, it should be noted that Persian mechanisms of exchange, distribution, and social integration were not intended primarily for the benefit of a state-regulated market exchange. Instead, they played a larger role in reciprocal and redistributive exchanges, which are mentioned in the sources as a common feature of this period.

The tribute (*phoros*)[55] was charged and collected at the provincial level; thereby, the Achaemenids followed the traditions of pre-Persian times and used old land registers wherever this was possible and there was no need for reform.[56] *Hyparchs* at the middle level and *chiliarchs* and civic self-governing bodies at the lower level were at the satraps' service in western Asia Minor; they were also familiar with the tax privileges or special duties of people, estates, villages, cities or holy shrines. Part of the taxes—in the form of precious metals—was transported to the empire's centers, while the remainder stayed in the province to be used by the satrap in accordance with royal orders. Contributions in kind, stored in warehouses and granaries, served for the provisioning of garrisons and workers. It is impossible to determine the amount of the king's revenue and the size of the treasures hoarded in the treasuries of the empire. Although Alexander's enormous booty might cause amazement, one must take into consideration the fact that those treasures had been assembled over a period of many decades. Apart from that, they served to maintain the redistributive exchange system between the king and his subjects and, in a broader sense, helped secure the ruler's preeminent political position. The theory that Alexander, with the help of the Great Kings' hoarded treasures, might have planned a systematic and consciously rapid increase of the money supply and a monetary boost to the economy anachronistically seeks to ascribe modern economic knowledge to ancient actors. Alexander's main motives were clearly more pragmatic: he was in urgent need of huge amounts of minted coins for the campaigns he had planned for the following years and to pay off the soldiers who were sent back to Greece and Macedonia after 324 B.C.E. Alexander might also have been aware of the effect of his name on the coins, but the strong economic consequences of his minting policy were more or less unintentional.

In contrast, the royal Achaemenid coinage seemed to serve a single purpose: that of displaying the "royal hero" in a variety of warlike postures. The limited circulation of these coins (the Tigris and Euphrates river valley, for example, continued its use of silver ingots as the most important medium of exchange, while the central Iranian regions relied on the exchange of natural produce and other premonetary forms of currency) shows that in most parts of the empire there was no real connection between coinage and the exaction of tribute. *Sigloi* (silver coins) do not appear in Babylonia and Persia until the fourth century. There is also no evidence that the Persians ever attempted to enforce the exclusive use of royal currency in any region of the empire. In fact, in most regions that used coins as currency, the royal stamp was less commonly used than currency issued by the satraps, local dynasties, or cities. The Great Kings may well have agreed to the minting of any coins that would return to them in the form of tribute. For many "foreign" transactions, "Greek money" was considered more appropriate. It is therefore not surprising that the Persians did not even attempt to standardize weights and measures. The policy on coinage represents the economic, cultural, and administrative diversity of the kingdom in the same way that the hoarding of treasures for political purposes was suited to the character of Persian kingship.

The surviving sources are limited in number and not well distributed in terms of time, geography, and social context, and significant regional variation exists among the four major areas of southern Mesopotamia, northern Mesopotamia, Syria-Palestine, and Iran. Apart from that, it is difficult to quantify economic developments. Population growth, increase of agricultural activity, developments in the "institutional sector," and an increasing volume of trade transactions point to some measure of economic growth in the Achaemenid period. It is clear that the royal house as well as the major Persian and local landowners mostly benefited from this trend, but their improved standard of living is hardly representative of the economic situation of the rest of the inhabitants of the empire, especially during periods of population growth and given significant regional variation in economic development. It is impossible to determine from the available sources to what extent the stability of the kingdom and the increased economic role of the royal house and the large landholders fostered an even more intensive exploitation of the dependants and of "public" resources. Equally, we cannot learn from the sources to what extent, if at all, investments were made toward a more developed infrastructure and social welfare. However, the ideology of the royal "benefactor" and of the "collaboration" of ruler and ruled as a mutually beneficial relationship was unlikely to have worked and the empire might not have enjoyed stability if official claims and reality had diverged and if many imperial subjects had experienced economic and social developments as a clear change for the worse.

4.4. Basic Political Institutions of Rule

"The land of the King," as the Persian Empire is called in Persian treaties with the Greeks, was subdivided into provinces ("satrapies"),[57] which were governed by satraps ("protectors of the empire"), who were installed for an indefinite period and thus could become very influential.[58] But administrative structures cannot easily be identified. First, the royal inscriptions present the empire as an ensemble not of administrative units but of "lands" or "peoples." Second, the highest functionaries' Greek titles and the administrative districts' Greek names are not always clear and uniform. And, third, the borders of the provinces were drawn up afresh from time to time and can rarely be defined with precision. But it is quite clear that full uniformity of the administrative structures on a provincial level and of the relations between the official authorities and the subjects never existed. Depending on tradition, members of royal houses, Persian aristocrats, local dynasts, or city kings acted differently at or below the satrapy level, united only in their common responsibility to the Great King or the satrap. If necessary, supra-regional officeholders were installed (e.g., Cyrus the Younger, the *karanos* of western Anatolia), and, according to political calculation and/or because of particular merits, certain populations enjoyed special privileges. Thus, the leaders of the peoples of the Zagros Mountains, who could be controlled only with great difficulties, were rewarded with presents from the Great King for their promise to respect the royal right of passage, to keep the peace, and to lend the kings their military support in cases of need. The Palestinian Arabs, for example, were exempt from any contributions in exchange for their acknowledgment of sovereignty. Mardonius's politically farsighted reorganization of the West after 494 B.C.E., as well as Artaxerxes II's measures against Euagoras of Salamis and his disturbance of the balance of power on Cyprus in the first half of the fourth century, give us another idea of the variety and unorthodoxy of royal ruling maxims.

A similar flexibility also determined the kings' relations with their neighbors beyond the borders. In the west, for instance, they tried to make the Macedonian king or Athens in the time of Cleisthenes accept Persian orders in foreign affairs (and to symbolically reinforce these treaties by giving "earth and water") in exchange for military or financial support. Although we are only poorly informed about the situation on the northeastern front, there is every reason to believe that the Persian kings and the Scythian "tribes" agreed on an arrangement (economic exchange versus military service) that was profitable for both sides.

Although basically "composite" in character, the Achaemenid Empire was not simply an ensemble of countries and peoples or a "confederation" of political entities with only loose ties among them; institutional variety does not exclude political unity. On the contrary, as has rightly been pointed out,[59] the Achaemenids were able to make cultural diversity serve the needs of imperial unity. Their ability to reconcile the ideology of universal empire with that of regional kingship left its mark on Alexander, the Seleucids, and even the Parthians. The great variety of traditions regarding the relationship between the ruler and his subjects had provided the Persian kings—as followers of their Near Eastern and Egyptian predecessors—with a big repertoire of tested means of rule. Advised by indigenous specialists, they could benefit from the former kings' mistakes and experiment with new strategies.

Wherever possible, the Persian kings took over well-established institutions and functionaries who promised to be loyal. Wherever possible, they asked local authorities and committees to find solutions to and to make decisions on problems on the spot and promoted institutions such as holy shrines, as long as they helped to bring about peace and unity and did not stir up anti-Persian resentment. Wherever possible, they granted new or confirmed old privileges, proved themselves to be generous and grateful rulers, and even abstained from personal revenge on former enemies if they, like Themistocles, changed over to the Persian side. To their subjects they applied a clear and simple standard: loyalty (i.e., the acknowledgment of Persian rule through the payment of tribute and military service) was rewarded, disloyalty severely punished (see later discussion). In general, the Persians fostered good relations with organizations and elites in subjugated territories as a means of pacification and of lowering the costs of running the empire. Respect for the cults of subjugated peoples, the use of local elites as administrators of subjugated territories, and the fostering of an imperial ideology that encouraged a view of mutual benefit all created favorable preconditions for enhanced economic and political performance.[60]

Apart from those composite elements, there are others that might be called "fractal," aiming at uniformity: this includes positioning the royal garrisons at strategically important locations, supported by the respective satrap but controlled by the Great King. And the attendants and informants at the satrapal courts ("the Eyes and Ears" of the Greek sources), whom the Greeks falsely thought of as members of a royal intelligence agency, might be called fractal elements of Persian rule, as well. Whenever former local potentates and officials who had supported the Persian conquerors were able to maintain their political or social positions, they were dependent on the Persian authorities.[61] Others (such as the former tyrant Histiaeus of Miletus and the former Egyptian naval commander Udjahorresnet), who retained honored social positions within their own society, were recruited into the Great King's entourage, thereby losing their former political or military power. Similar modifications of traditional usage can be discerned within the sphere of religious policy: while acknowledging local traditions in order to secure the loyalty of the conquered people and the staff of their holy shrines and to ensure control of the latter's wealth, the Great Kings at times asserted their control of religious affairs through the destruction of the shrines of rebellious people, through the reinforcement of the cohesion of the Persian communities in the provinces with the help of Iranian cults,[62] or through minor but meaningful changes within rituals or ceremonies. The adoption of Aramaic as a *lingua franca* changed local linguistic behavior insofar as it created a new sphere of "official" imperial statements.

The practice of uprooting single persons or groups and transplanting them to distant lands is well attested in Achaemenid times,[63] although there are no examples of real mass deportations (in the Assyrian sense). Besides, not all of the examples given by the Greek historians appear trustworthy down to the last detail. With regard to subjugated Greek cities, it is also not quite clear whether punitive deportations affected whole communities or only their political and military elites (given that rebel cities of the Ionian Revolt and their supporters, such as Miletus or Eretria, do not seem to have been completely abandoned after their subjugation in 494 and 490 B.C.E., respectively).[64] It is also difficult to determine the social and political status of the deportees: Greeks are attested on graffiti and on tablets at Persepolis,[65] but we cannot be sure that all of them were deportees. The same problem applies to the *hatru* communities of Babylonia, whose members were not all deportees or their descendants. Nevertheless, it was this combination of granted autonomy and strict supervision that contributed to the success of the Persian way of empire building.

It has rightly been pointed out that the adoption of Iranian terms in the ideological, administrative, and socioeconomic spheres in different regional languages does not mean that the corresponding institutions themselves had to be identical (unlike, for example, the system of Persian measures and weights, whose impact can be detected in many parts of the empire).[66] On the other hand, the spread of the Persian word *data-* ("law," "order") into almost all languages of the Ancient Near East is a good example of the effectiveness of an elementary "ideological" vocabulary, propagated by the center to underline the authority of the Great King. *Data-* must, of course, not be misunderstood as a kind of "imperial law" or an imperial collection of royally authorised local regulations but has to be taken as a term for every royal decision, every order published by the king.[67] The personal character of this royal law or ordinance is stressed time and again,[68] and it even seems to replace the concept of a divine law.[69]

The idea of a universal empire propagated and symbolically promulgated by the king was present in the Achaemenid Empire; and a significant amount of imitation of kingly behavior and royal virtues by the provincial and local elites also occurred. But there was never a process of "Persianization" (along the lines of its equivalent "Romanization").[70] First, the Old Persian language, Persian culture, and Persian religion did not play a role comparable to that of their Roman counterparts (Persian culture was itself a highly eclectic culture). Apart from that, Achaemenid (i.e., royal Persian) culture and art were strictly connected to the idea of the strong, generous, and rightful king as the gods' representative on Earth, and therefore both came to an abrupt end with the end of the empire. Second, in contrast to the Romans, the Persians never fully developed an ideological system that might have replaced regionally or locally constructed solidarities by fostering empire-wide internal coherence. That is why many of the lasting effects of Persian rule became visible only long after the fall of the empire. Third, the Persians had neither the manpower nor the ideological resources to impose a new political and ideological system on all their subjects, although Persian ideology, court art, and practices surely had an impact on conquered people, and especially their elites. What is normally called Persian "tolerance" was just a way to keep the conquered peoples quiet; although necessity inspired his policies, Darius's way of consolidating the empire is nevertheless proof of the king's farsightedness. Fourth, there was no such Persian sense of mission as we can find, for example, in Roman literary works. Fifth, although Darius I and his successors seem to have been deeply influenced by Zoroastrian (Avestan) terminology and ideas (which they modified to serve their political needs, however), Zoroastrianism never became an important factor for the coherence of the empire,[71] unlike Christianity in late antiquity.

4.5. Principles of Legitimacy and Identity

The ideological traits of Persian kingship, heralded empire-wide in images and inscriptions, are the following. First, kingship is firmly rooted in Persia, or more precisely Persis, as well as in the Aryan ethnic and cultural community, and it requires descent from the family of Achaemenes.[72] The Persians, at the same time, stand out among all peoples on account of their abilities and their special relationship to the ruler. Persian kingship differs from that of the neighbors and predecessors because it exceeds them in power ("king of kings"), not the least thanks to the fact that an unprecedented number of "lands" or "peoples" now acknowledges the rule of the Persian king. Second, Persian kingship is characterized by a special relationship between the ruler and the gods, although no divine descent or godlike qualities are attributed to the king. Auramazda "and the other gods that are" bestowed the kingdom on Darius (or Xerxes); "by the favor of Auramazda" he has been elected and installed, and—successfully—rules the empire. As his "representative" on Earth, he is vested with a kind of royal charisma (*farnah*). Third, as his kingship is owed to the favor of Auramazda, the king is obliged to protect the god's good creation. He is capable of doing so because the god has given him the ability to tell right from wrong and because he has special qualities that are conducive to the promotion of justice and the protection of order. Although an absolute monarch, he is capable of impartiality and self-control, he judges, rewards, and punishes not at whim but steadily and fairly; as a superb horseman, warrior, and farmer, he is able to ward off the dangers threatening his empire. This is why the violent death of a king (his murder or his death on the battlefield) endangers the God-given imperial order just as the disloyalty of the king's subjects (*bandaka*) does. Order, not chaos, peace, not tension, and good conduct of the subjects and royal generosity, not disloyalty and kingly misbehavior, dominate the inscriptions and the imagery of the royal residences. The Persian kings had no trouble adapting their behavior to the royal ideologies of foreign cultures. They were, in fact, keen to gain advantage from them: thus, Cyrus shows himself to be the tool of Marduk in his cylinder inscription from Babylon, and Darius calls himself "king by the favor of Bel" in the copy of the Bisutun inscription from the same place. In the context of his official and social functions both in the palace and as a traveling king, the ruler on the one hand emphasizes the *magister-minister*-relationship between himself and all his subjects (e.g., when distributing gifts or arranging banquets). On the other hand, he gives the impression of being accessible and concerned with the worries of his subjects.

Unlike in the later stages of the Roman Empire, only a few non-Persians were allowed to reach the highest political and military positions (e.g., Belesys, Memnon, and Mentor). Nevertheless, the kings entrusted members of the provincial elites or even foreigners with important honors or tasks. They let them benefit from privileges and gifts, invited them to collaborate, to imitate Achaemenid royal virtues and royal behavior, and to take over Persian customs and traditions and thereby turned them into their followers. Metiochus, the son of Miltiades, the victor of Marathon, was honored with house and home, a Persian wife, and "Persian" children;[73] the same applies to the former Spartan king Demaratus,[74] to the victor at Salamis Themistocles,[75] and to the Egyptian collaborator Udjahorresnet,[76] to name only a few of many examples. On the other hand, political and personal relations on a regional or even local level were much more decisive for the cohesion of an empire than those on the highest decision levels. And it is there, below the satrapal level, that we can detect a great amount not only of autonomy but also of Persian-indigenous cooperation and indigenous imitation of Persian models. We know of numerous examples of marital connections between Persian officers and functionaries and female members of important provincial families; Darius II and his half-sister and wife Parysatis, offspring of Artaxerxes I and his Babylonian wives, show that even half-provincials could ascend to the throne. At the satrapal level, locals occupied leading positions, like the Hecatomnids in Caria, Jewish or Samaritan governors in Jehud or Samaria, or the city kings of Phoenicia and Cyprus. Archaeology has proven that as far as palace architecture, style of home décor, dress, jewelery, and public appearance were concerned, those indigenous elites followed not only local but also royal models.

In other words, although something akin to a "Persian national identity" can be noticed in the royal inscriptions, imperial ideology at the same time aimed at integrating the elites of the provinces within an empire-wide ruling class culture, even at integrating subjugated peoples into a kind of imperial "symbolic universe." No inhabitant of the empire was forced to choose between an "imperial" and a "local" identity; for example, an inhabitant of Smyrna was allowed to keep his own civic (and Greek cultural) identity, but, at the same time, he was invited to regard himself as—and to be proud of being—a member of the most successful and prosperous political entity of his own time, the Persian Empire. However, he was not granted the possibility of rejecting this second identity by rebelling against Persian rule.

4.6. Technology and Scientific Advance

The infrastructural and agricultural measures (the extension of the road system, the maintenance of river traffic and irrigation, and the provision of drinking water and new crops), modeled on Near Eastern examples, facilitated the rapid transfer of troops and improved the diet of royal subjects.[77] The success of these measures is underlined by the Greco-Roman conceptual and practical orientation toward the Persian *angaros*-system ("royal post") and the Persian institution of the *paradeisos*. The adoption of Aramaic as the *lingua franca* of the empire, which had strong effects on the development of Near Eastern languages and scripts, as well as the influence of Persian political and cultural institutions on both that of their neighbors in the west and of the Achaemenids' successors as rulers of western Asia, bear further witness to the impact of Persian rule. The development of new forms of agricultural relations and legal instruments in Achaemenid Babylonia has already been addressed.

5. The End of Achaemenid Rule

Three ideal-typical explanations have been advanced to account for the decline of Persian sovereignty.[78] The first of these views the end of the Persian Empire as the result of the moral and physical shortcomings of the Persians themselves. The second explanation blames insurmountable difficulties inherent in Persian rule, which were present either from the very beginning or from a certain later point in time. The third and most recent theory tends to emphasize the astonishing vitality and wealth of the realm immediately prior to its fall and therefore regards this collapse as sudden and unprecedented. These three explanations could be called, respectively, the "decadence"- or "decline" model, the "crisis" model, and the "catastrophe" model.

The first model, of decadence and decline, has its roots in antiquity. It is commonly present in the self-conception of the classical Greeks as well as their conception of the Foreign/Other.[79] Where did this Greek concept of "Persian decadence" originate? In part a poor understanding of foreign customs and traditions is to be blamed, such as Persian gift-exchange rituals, the role of opulent banquets, or the hoarding of lavish treasures. Greek agenda also played a role. Some authors emphasized the biases and clichés of the Greeks (Ctesias, Isocrates); other texts demonstrated the political theories of their authors (Plato, Xenophon) or issued a call for military action (Isocrates). These texts conform to topical templates that persist far beyond antiquity and even into our own time.

Recent scholarship has increasingly advanced explanations for the collapse of the empire that reach beyond ethical and moral decrepitude. Such theories point to political, military, economic, and social crises that supposedly began during Xerxes' reign and could not be eradicated by subsequent rulers. These crises are thought to have included a number of characteristics, of which the most commonly mentioned are the inability of the Persian kings to unite the empire into an organic whole entity, preventing separatist tendencies in some areas of the empire; the tensions within the royal house; the tensions between the kings and provincial governors (satrap revolts); the increasing dependence on mercenaries while the Persian armies shrank; and economic stagnation resulting from the massive hoarding of precious metal resources, the depletion of the arable land, excessive tax burdens, and the growing rift between social classes. Some classical literary evidence for the control mechanisms employed by the Great Kings (garrisons, fortresses, and even the supposed spy network of the "Eyes and Ears of the king") or for the significant power of the satraps has been used to argue for a "centralized" organization and a "weak sovereignty." Some scholars emphasize the heterogeneity of the realm (described earlier), the surprising amount of local autonomy, and the high levels of governmental tolerance, all of which are often mentioned in the royal inscriptions and reliefs. They—correctly—assume that this was the intended, normal state of affairs but argue that these factors simultaneously indicate weakness in the central authority. The "weak empire" would therefore have been a result of a well-intended but ultimately disastrous concept of rule. A major piece of evidence allegedly supporting this theory is the conspicuous absence of visible Achaemenid traits in the material culture of the provinces.

In reality, the—never existential—crises of the empire at the end of the fifth and fourth centuries were a result of structural problems, which emerged only at certain times. These crises stemmed from the insecurities surrounding successions to the throne[80] and tensions between central and provincial governors or among the latter.[81] Before Alexander, these crises were not caused by revolts among the subjects or by major threats from the outside (this is true also for Agesilaus's and Philip II's campaigns in western Asia Minor). Most subjects—with the possible exception of the Egyptians—had accommodated themselves to this larger empire that provided them with protection from outside and inside threats and with a secure subsistence base.

Only in light of this tendency is it possible to understand how Artaxerxes III was able to reincorporate Egypt into the empire in 343 B.C.E., even though it had been independent for sixty years. Alexander's achievements were not so much the result of the structural weaknesses of Achaemenid rule. He succeeded thanks to his outstanding strategic abilities: his troops were also superior in training, tactics, and military technology, especially when it came to laying sieges, and Alexander knew how to capitalize on the traditions and expectations of his new Persian subjects. His victories at the Granicus and at Issus (334–333 B.C.E.) and the almost simultaneous triumphs of Antigonus in Asia Minor and those of the king himself at Tyre and Gaza were essential for his success. He conquered the Persian Empire after eleven years of hard campaigning. Only in retrospect, from the perspective of later Greek authors, did his victory against the doomed Persians appear easy.

With the exception of a few Greek *poleis* in the west, Alexander did not portray himself as a liberator from the Persian yoke. The Lydians, Egyptians, and Babylonians received him as their new ruler according to the traditions that even the Achaemenid rulers had respected. At the same time that Darius III was rehabilitated as a thoroughly competent ruler, the extent to which Alexander himself had already adopted Achaemenid manners was recognized, even before the death of his rival (as whose avenger and heir he subsequently fashioned himself). He upheld Achaemenid traditions, not to his own Macedonian army or the Greeks, but vis-à-vis the subjects and officials of the king, as well as Darius himself.[82] Intimately familiar with the requirements of Persian kingship, he had attempted to outstrip his opponent in terms of royal virtues by basking in the glow of Cyrus's successes and gathering the Persian dignitaries on his side. Alexander could offer all those who defected to his side the retention of their previous honors and positions. He gained the necessary popularity for himself and his politics through his victories. In cases where he was not successful—where his endeavors did not impress (as in eastern Iran), where his understanding of the peculiarities of Achaemenid politics was insufficient (as in the case of the mountain dwellers), or where irrational actions prevailed over sober deliberation—he broke all opposition with extreme brutality. Where his politics of communication and cooperation were respected, on the other hand, he remained generous. Both of these sides of the Macedonian conqueror of Iran are reflected in later Iranian tradition.

6. Conclusion

The inscriptions of the Achaemenid kings take the loyalty of the subjects for granted; they even present this loyalty as the natural result of divine justice and the royal pursuit of justice, "truth," and the well-being of all subjects of the empire. These conditions are desired by the gods themselves and are meant to be a part of the kings' duties on Earth enjoined by the gods, in particular Auramazda.[83] At the same time, these inscriptions clearly carry the threat of sanctions against anyone who does not follow these divine and royal commandments.[84] Both the Greek sources and the royal inscriptions (viz., *DB*) announce the merciless prosecution and punishment of rebels and insurgents. However, the allegedly biggest offenders in this sense, the "remorseless" kings Cambyses and Xerxes, must be absolved of many of their alleged crimes; their actions did not differ much from those of their popular fathers, Cyrus and Darius. The *pax Achaemenidica* was dependent at all times on both the carrot *and* the stick, on both the guarantee of well-being (within, of course, the framework of traditionally unbalanced economic and social relations) *and* "graveyard peace" following the squashing of revolts.

The victims of Achaemenid empire building and regency rarely have a voice in the known sources, with the exception of some insurgents, otherwise known in the royal policy as "liar kings." Still, we should not fail to recognize those who stood in the way of the Persians' success or those who were not at all inclined to appreciate the actual blessings of Persian rule. We should be less concerned with the princes who lost their lives in dynastic quarrels or with the "liar kings," who mostly had an eye on their own interests; we should be much more interested in those who preferred autonomy in foreign affairs to Persian "vassalage" and in those who were deported or drafted to forcibly work for the profit of the king. It is necessary to think carefully in this respect and to draw the "landscapes of imperialism" anew.

In light of recent scholarship on Augustan culture in Rome,[85] the significance of the emulation of the royal ideology, the royal lifestyle, and the royal art and texts by the Persian elite ought to be reevaluated. Did this "semantic" and "pragmatic" system "of great extent" not also preclude possible alternatives or conflicting concepts? Is its encroachment into the private sphere explicable only as representing its wholesale, eager adoption by the recipients, or could it not also—at least in part— be understood as "noncommittal political applause," that is, the expression of an opportunistic spirit? Along the same lines, could the ubiquitous, repetitive, and all-encompassing presence of royal propaganda in art and formulaic inscriptions, even if their emphasis on peace and order and their lack of warlike scenes might have seemed "congenial," not have resulted in their audiences' weariness? After all, one problem with the messages promoted was that they were not always a true reflection of the political reality—which was not nearly as peaceful as it was made out to be.

The positive image that the Persian kings projected of themselves and their politics has endured until this day, with the exception of the (equally "imagined") occidental version of the story of the Persian Wars between the empire and the Greeks. Especially in contrast to the practices of their immediate predecessors, the Assyrians, the "tolerance" of Persian rule has repeatedly been emphasized—a tolerance that has been said to stand in sharp contrast to the harshness, severity, even brutality of Sargon, Senacherib, or Assurbanipal. This judgment is based to a large extent on the different tone of Assyrian and Achaemenid royal communiqués, be they visual or epigraphic. But this interpretation overlooks at least three important issues. For one, the Achaemenids must have been aware of the Assyrian precedent of the foundation, sustenance, and collapse of an empire at the time when they founded, expanded, and secured their own. For another, Cyrus and his successors did present themselves in accordance with the Assyrian tradition[86] in word (e.g., the "Cyrus Cylinder" from Babylon, which mentions Assurbanipal), image (e.g., royal art, which was strongly influenced by Assyrian motifs[87]), and deed (relentless crushing of rebellions, occasional deportations). They left no doubt that their empire was won by war.[88] Finally, the Achaemenid "minor arts" (e.g., glyptics) often depict nonpeaceful scenes. Moreover, the Persian images of imperial peace are placed on the exterior facades of the palaces, while the Assyrian pictures of conquest and subjugation were situated in the interior of palace suites.[89]

The evidence supports the idea that the Persians learned from Assyrian royal ideology and royal practice—and also from the (Neo-)Babylonian example.[90] Their royal ideology placed more emphasis on the reciprocal relationship between royal patronage and the loyalty of the subjects. It also was more flexible in the administrative aspects of the imperial order through its greater acceptance of local autonomy and avoidance of uniform provincialization. The Persian kings also did not try to create and enforce a divine hierarchy: local gods were never seen as subordinate to Auramazda. Finally, the Persian crown turned away from drastic "pacification" measures such as frequent mass deportation in order to secure their rule.

We can never know for certain the extent of the royal subjects' support, acceptance, or rejection of the Achaemenid "order of peace." In the end, the Achaemenid Empire fell because of the tactical skills of its military opponent, Alexander of Macedon, not because of a lack of interior cohesion or because of administrative or economic crises. Its longevity and success had been the result both of the royal concern with the welfare of the subjects and of the considerable degree of local autonomy and structural "tolerance" that they had been granted; also, however, to the stringent and sometimes merciless control exerted by the central authorities of the empire. Alexander the Great thought these policies worth emulating and consequently gained the title of the "last Achaemenid" (Pierre Briant's term). He was not the last: later Near Eastern empires continued to carry on the legacy of the Persian kings.

NOTES

For extended discussion of this chapter, I would like to thank all of the participants of the colloquia at Stanford and in Perth, especially Peter Bedford and Walter Scheidel. Further, I would like to acknowledge Robert Rollinger for his helpful input. This chapter was translated by Ulrike Krotscheck, with revisions by Walter Scheidel and the author.

1. Cyrus and his sons are conventionally counted among the Achaemenids, although the evidence lists only Darius I and his descendants. It is likely that the union of the lineage of Cyrus and the Achaemenids was achieved only by the marriage of Darius I and Cyrus's daughter Atossa. On a clay cylinder from Bablyon, Cyrus identifies himself as being of the house of Teispes (cf. Rollinger 1998). For the purposes of this chapter, however, I will assign the term "Achaemenid" to all Persian kings.

2. The history of the Achaemenid Empire is treated extensively by Briant 2002a; Allen 2005; Kuhrt 1995 (as part of a history of the Ancient Near East); Wiesehöfer 2001a, Huyse 2005, and Brosius 2006 (as part of a history of ancient Iran); Kuhrt 2001a (as part of a series of empire studies).

3. A broad survey of the sources may be found in Wiesehöfer 2001a: 7–28, 252–57. A collection of (translated) sources is provided by Kuhrt 2007.

4. For the Iranian oral tradition cf. Huyse in press.

5. For the ideology of rule and kingship in Achaemenid art cf. Root 1979; Jacobs 2002.

6. Although Xenophon (*Education of Cyrus*) is doing exactly this while considering the ideal form of government, he nevertheless comes to a clearly negative conclusion as far as the contemporary Persian monarchy is concerned (book 8).

7. For the Greek view of the barbarians (Persians) see generally Schmal 1995; Gehrke 2000; Harrison 2002; the literary view is treated in Hall 1989; Georges 1994; Tuplin 1996: 132–77; Hutzfeld 1999; Bichler 2000; Bichler and Rollinger 2003; the view of Greek art in Raeck 1981; Miller 1997; Bäbler 1998; Hölscher 2000; Miller 2003.

8. Cf. Hutzfeld 1999.

9. Wiesehöfer 2003.

10. Boardman 2000 (with a slightly Grecocentric impact).

11. Miller 1997.

12. On Herodotus's worldview and cultural criticism cf. the excellent work of Bichler (2000). On Herodotus's assessment of the Persians, see Rollinger 2004b; on the "foreign policy" of the Persians see Wiesehöfer 2004a.

13. Rollinger 2003.

14. The dream sequences recounted by Herodotus show that the "higher powers" intervened only after Xerxes' hubristic decisions had already been made (Bichler 2000: 322).

15. Cf., e.g., *XPh* 6–13: "I am Xerxes, the great king, King of Kings, king of the countries containing many races, king on this great earth even far off, the son of Darius the King, an Achaemenid, a Persian, the son of a Persian, an Aryan, of Aryan lineage" (transl. R. Schmitt).

16. Vallat 1996; Liverani 2003; Henkelman 2003.

17. Rollinger 1999.

18. Liverani 2003.

19. Rollinger 1999. There is little reason to believe that the Medes ever ruled over the Persians.

20. Wiesehöfer 1999.

21. On the tolerance of Cyrus, see Kuhrt 1983.

22. On the confusion of succession after the death of Cambyses see Rollinger 1998.

23. See van der Spek 1993, 1998.

24. Zahrnt 1992.

25. Kuhrt 1988; Zahrnt 1992: 256 n.53.

26. Wiesehöfer 2004a describes how much our understanding of Persian politics is influenced by Herodotus's writings and how uncritically and selectively these tend to be interpreted.

27. Sancisi-Weerdenburg 1989 is fundamental for a reinterpretation of Xerxes.

28. Wiesehöfer 2004a.

29. Since the author has already presented his ideas of the features of the Achaemenid Empire in detail elsewhere (Wiesehöfer 2001a), he limits this presentation to the essentials here and omits from earlier scholarship. Pierre Briant's survey (Briant 2002a) has been especially influential thanks to the richness of information and insights it contains.

30. Cf. Jacobs 1994: 93–97; Klinkott 2005: 87–109.

31. Armayor 1978; Klinkott 2005: 96–109.

32. Brosius 1996: 171–78.

33. Herodotus 1.135–36; Strabo 15.3.17.

34. Briant 2002a: 277 ff.

35. Cf. Darius I's trilingual inscription on the building of the palace in Susa [*DSf*]). On the impact of Persian imperialism on Lydian Sardis, see the excellent study of Dusinberre 2003.

36. Briant 1988; Tuplin 1998.

37. Wiesehöfer and Rollinger (forthcoming).
38. Cf. *DNb* 16–17; Herodotus 7.27 ff.
39. Wiesehöfer 2001b.
40. Herodotus 9.110; Plutarch, *Artaxerxes* 26.3; Ctesias *FGrHist* 688 F 15.49.
41. Cf. Aelianus, *Miscellaneous Histories* 6.14. In most cases, in reality, those acts of mercy were politically opportune or even wise, as demonstrated by the cases of Xerxes' opponent Themistocles and the Salaminian king Euagoras, who was granted his former position and status despite his rebellion. At the same time, both cases testify to the flexibility of the Great Kings' policy.
42. Cf. Plutarch, *Artaxerxes* 26.5 ff., an episode that, at the same time, emphasizes the king's full scope of action; or Herodotus 9.108 ff., a novella in which this custom cryptically alludes to a struggle for the throne.
43. For a comprehensive assessment of the economy of the Persian Near East see now Bedford 2007. Cf. also Aperghis 2004.
44. For Achaemenid Babylonia cf. Wiesehöfer 2002. For the most important archives (Egibi, Murashu) cf. Wunsch 1999, 2000a, b; Stolper 1985; Donbaz/Stolper 1997. For the importance of Xerxes' reign, see Waerzeggers 2003/4.
45. For debt bondage around the Ebabbar of Sippar in the time of Cyrus, compare MacGinnis 2003; on the economic problems of smaller landholders and leaseholders in the second half of the fifth century, see Stolper 1985.
46. The initial stages of this system precede Achaemenid rule. "Bow-land," for example, is already known under Nebukadnezzar II (Jursa 1998), and even during the Neo-Assyrian period (evidence: *State Archives of Assyria* V, 16 [*ABL* 201], Z. 6 [during Sargons II's rule]).
47. Nehemiah 5.1–5.
48. Albertz 2001: 102–16.
49. Xenophon, Anabasis 7.8.
50. Cf. Nehemiah 5.14 f.; Herodotus 1.192.
51. Herdotus 3.117.
52. Briant 1982.
53. Wiesehöfer 2004b.
54. Sherratt/Sherratt 1993.
55. Tuplin 1987; Briant 2002a: 388–421.
56. Although very often stated otherwise, Herodotus's so-called tribute list (3.89) does not mirror Achaemenid conditions and is thus relevant only for a study of the author's world view.
57. This and the following section focus on practices following the reforms of Darius I.
58. Klinkott 2005.
59. Briant 1999a.
60. Dusinberre's study on Persian imperialism and Achaemenid Sardis (2003) succeeds in demonstrating that the co-option of loyalties and the incorporation of the local elite into the Achaemenid elite also strengthened the political and ideological allegiance of the local population to the imperial administration. On the other hand, she is able to distinguish a top-down introduction of imperial ideology (internalized by the polyethnic elite of the city and partly even by the entire population) from a bottom-up ideology as a local reaction against this top-down intervention (the elite adapting or reviving local traditions in a conscious or symbolic emphasis on a particular cultural identity). However, the elite's "very sharing of material culture demonstrates that ethnicity was less important to signal than wealth" (207). As far as resistance to Achaemenid ideology is concerned, Dusinberre rightly complains about the insufficiency of the source material.

61. Cf. Xenophon, *Hellenica* 3.1.10 ff.

62. Berossus, *FGrHist* 680 F 11.

63. References in Briant 2002a, s.v. deportations.

64. Ehrhardt 2003.

65. Cf. *Persepolis Fortification Tablets* nos. 1224; 1942; 1965; 2072.

66. Stolper 1999: 1118 f.

67. Wiesehöfer 1995; Kuhrt 2001b.

68. Cf. Darius's tomb inscription (*DNa* 15–22): "Proclaims Darius, the king: By the favour of Auramazda these [are] the countries which I seized outside Persia; I ruled them; to me they brought tribute. What has been said to them by me, that they did. The law that [was] mine, that held them [stable]" (transl. R. Schmitt).

69. Lecoq 1997: 167.

70. Cf. Sancisi-Weerdenburg 2001: 333–38.

71. This is wrongly postulated in Mann 1986a: 241 f.

72. Huyse in press is able to show how Darius I and his successors successfully used Avestan (Zoroastrian) and secular (oral) Iranian folk traditions (about legendary Iranian kings) to make their rule part of an Iranian "historical" continuum.

73. Herodotus 6.41.

74. Whitby 1998.

75. Nollé and Wenninger 1998/99; Cagnazzi 2001; Keaveney 2003.

76. Lloyd 1982.

77. Briant 1994; Wiesehöfer 2004c.

78. Wiesehöfer 1997.

79. Briant 2002b.

80. Briant 1991. In contrast to what happened in the Roman Empire, the numerous assassination attempts on rulers or crown princes led not to dynastic discontinuity but merely to the replacement of one pretender with another from the same royal line.

81. The kings responded to the "Satraps' Revolts" in the fourth century with a number of measures that included military action and the exploitation of the rivalries among the satraps themselves.

82. Briant 2003.

83. Cf. *DPd* 12–24: "Proclaims Darius, the king: May Auramazda bring me aid together with all the gods; and may Auramazda protect this country from the [enemy] army, from crop failure [and] from Falsehood!"; cf. 56–60: "O man, the commandment of Auramazda—let not that seem evil to you! Do not leave the right path! Do not be disobedient!"; and *XPh* 1–6.46–56: "A great god [is] Auramazda, who created this earth, who created yonder heaven, who created man, who created blissful happiness for man, who made Xerxes king, the one king of many, the one master of many... You, whosoever [shall be] hereafter, if you shall think: 'Blissful may I be [while] living and [when] dead may I be blessed,' obey the law, which Auramazda has established! Worship Auramazda at the proper time and in the proper ceremonial style!" (transl. R. Schmitt).

84. Cf. *DB* IV 61–67: "Proclaims Darius, the king: For that reason Auramazda brought me aid and the other gods who are, because I was not disloyal, I was no follower of Falsehood, I was no evil-doer, neither I nor my family, [but] I acted according to righteousness, neither to the powerless not to the powerful did I do wrong, [and] the man who strove for my [royal] house, him I treated well, who did harm, him I punished severely" (transl. R. Schmitt).

85. Here I refer especially to the contribution made by Hölscher 1999.

86. Van der Spek 1983; and P. Bedford in chapter 2.

87. Matthiae 1999: 209–63; Roaf 2003. In contrast to the more dynamic Assyrian art, Achaemenid art seems to be much more fixed, reserved, and lacking major stylistic developments. On the other hand, this type of iconography correlates with the "timeless" nature of inscriptions.

88. Briant 1999b.

89. Kuhrt 2001b: 168.

90. Jursa 2003. Schaudig 2001 demonstrates that Achaemenid royal inscriptions were borrowed from their Assyrian and Babylonian predecessors.

4

The Greater Athenian State

Ian Morris

1. Introduction

If it were worth taking the time to calculate such things, we would probably find that more books and articles have been written on the Athenian Empire of 478–404 B.C.E. than on any ancient empire except the Roman. And if we worked out how much scholarship has been served up per subject of each empire, square mile of territory, or year of the empire's existence, Athens would surely win hands down. Every schoolchild gets to hear about its leaders, poets, and monuments.

Yet despite Athens' renown, this was a decidedly odd ancient empire. Most obviously, it was tiny (fig. 4.1), covering just a couple of thousand square miles. It was barely big enough to make a respectable Assyrian or Roman province, let alone a Persian satrapy. Its total revenues were just 1 or 2 percent of those of the early Roman Empire.[1] Fewer than a million people lived in it, as against 35 million in the Persian Empire and 50 to 60 million in the Roman or Han Chinese. In comparison to the subjects of Assyria, Persia, Rome, or (in most periods) Byzantium, these people were ethnically and culturally remarkably homogeneous; not only were they overwhelmingly Greek, but almost all of them were Greeks who self-identified as Ionians, descendants of the shared ancestor Ion. The other empires discussed in this book dwarfed the Athenian in almost every sense and lasted much longer.

Athens was a quirky empire—so quirky, I suggest in this chapter, that we would do better not to think of it as an empire at all. I make this claim and do it in this context not just to be contrary but because the claim exemplifies two of this book's central propositions: that we should study imperialism as a subset of the larger process of state formation, and that state formation was one of the major dynamics in ancient history. By "state formation" I mean the centralization of political power in officeholders' hands and officeholders' attempts to extend that power, both deeper into civil society and outward by enlarging the units they governed. State formation generated conflict and competition among officeholders, between officeholders and those they administered, and between competing states. These dynamics were among the most important forces in generating not only violence and exploitation

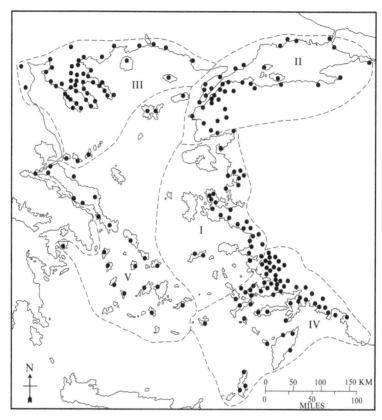

FIGURE 4.1. *The tiny Athenian "Empire." Each dot represents a tribute-paying city in 441 BCE; the Roman numerals represent Athens' administrative subdivisions*

Table 4.1. Standard Periodization of Ancient Greek History

Name	Years BCE
Mycenaean period/Late Bronze Age	c. 1600–1200
Dark Age/Early Iron Age	c. 1200–750
Archaic	c. 750–480
Classical	480–323
Hellenistic	323–30

but also the organizational advances that made possible small but lasting improvements in ordinary people's standards of living.[2]

Greek historians have not normally treated state formation as the central dynamic of the classical period (table 4.1), preferring instead to look at fifth-century Athens as an example of imperialism comparable to the more successful examples of Rome or Persia, and generally presenting Athens' defeat in 404 as the end of the Greek imperial experiment, ushering in an age of interstate anarchy. This can certainly be a useful way to look at Greek history, and it clarifies certain trends, but it also has the great disadvantage of obscuring the differences between classical Greece and genuinely imperial ancient states like Assyria, Persia, Rome, and Byzantium. In comparative terms, I believe that this disadvantage outweighs the benefits of the traditional perspective: it muddies our understanding both of classical Greece itself and of the larger history of the ancient state. It therefore seems worth taking a chapter in this book to examine these differences.

I argue in this chapter that in the fifth century B.C.E. the tempo of state formation in Greece increased sharply. Both internal and external dynamics were at work. Competition for resources and honor between Greek states and fear of and resistance to Persian and (to a lesser extent) Carthaginian power combined to push the three strongest Greek cities—Sparta, Syracuse, and Athens (fig. 4.2a)—down distinct paths of state formation, shaped by local histories, institutional and environmental differences, and specific decisions. Borrowing the terminology of the historical sociologist Charles Tilly,[3] we might say that the Athenian and Syracusan paths were capital-intensive, commercial, and urban, while the Spartan path was coercion-intensive, militaristic, and rural. The Athenian path differed from both the Spartan and the Syracusan, though, in deepening state capacity by creating a centralized tax base and bureaucratic administration. International relations theorists often take it for granted that competition inevitably forces states to deepen institutional capacity,[4] but fifth-century Syracuse and particularly Sparta show that this is not the only possible outcome. Economic historians have recognized that state leaders often choose inefficient solutions to problems because of the prohibitive transaction costs involved in implementing efficient ones and that such inefficient

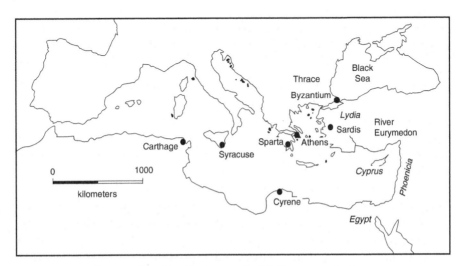

FIGURE 4.2a. *Sites mentioned in this chapter: the Mediterranean basin*

FIGURE 4.2b. *Sites mentioned in this chapter: the Aegean basin. 1 = Coronea; 2 = Thes-piae; 3 = Leuctra; 4 = Plataea; 5 = Megara; 6 = Thebes; 7 = Eleusis; 8 = Tanagra*

solutions create groups with vested interests, whose members will struggle to pre-serve an inefficient (but for them profitable) system.[5] Syracusan tyranny and Spartan *oliganthropia* nicely exemplify these tendencies, but the most interesting fact about interstate competition in fifth-century Greece may be that the Spartan and Syra-cusan "inefficient solutions" did not just persist; they actually defeated Athens' more modern, capital-intensive, bureaucratic state.

I argue that we will make most sense of the political organization we convention-ally call the Athenian Empire not by treating it as a unique experiment in imperial-ism but by seeing it as just one of a variety of routes toward state formation within contemporary Greece. Athenians', Spartans', and Syracusans' fear of and resistance to each other drove their distinct modes of state formation ever faster, and the con-flicts between these three formative states caught up other smaller cities in similar

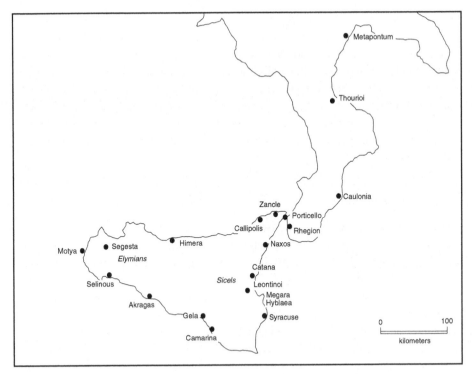

FIGURE 4.2c. *Sites mentioned in this chapter: Sicily and southern Italy*

processes of transformation. The processes came to a head in the Peloponnesian War (or Athenian War, as Spartans and Syracusans must have called it) of 431–404 B.C.E., which permanently closed off the Athens' capital-intensive path, pushed Syracuse back onto an authoritarian path, cruelly exposed the limits of Sparta's coercion-intensive path, and shifted the balance of power away from Greek states in favor of Persia and Carthage. I suggest that translating the Greek word *archê* (which Thucydides used to describe Athens' political system) as "empire" and treating the *archê* as distinct from the processes of state formation going on in other classical Greek cities makes it hard to explain the larger patterns. The Athenians did not create an empire like those that fill the other chapters in this book; their *archê* did not even qualify as a "young empire" in the sense that Jack Goldstone and John Haldon use that term (this vol.). Throughout this chapter I will translate *archê* as "Greater Athenian state"—not a very elegant turn of phrase, perhaps, but one that captures both the similarities and the differences between what the Athenians and their rivals were doing, the processes of state formation that had been going on in Greece for the preceding three hundred years, and how state formation affected the traditional structures of the city-state.

In keeping with this book's general goal of providing a foundation for systematic comparisons between ancient political organizations, I begin in section 2 by describing the sources available for studying fifth-century-B.C.E. state formation, then in section 3 offer a bare-bones narrative of the fifth century to orient readers more familiar with other historical periods. Section 4, describing the basic parameters (environmental, demographic, economic, technological, social, political, and religious) of this world, completes the background treatment. In section 5, I discuss the main concepts we need to understand the shape of fifth-century history, particularly "state formation" and "empire." Sections 6 and 7 form the core of the chapter, reviewing respectively the political, military, economic, administrative, and cultural consequences of Athenian state formation and parallel processes in other Greek states.

2. EVIDENCE

We can divide the evidence into two categories, the written and the nonwritten. Nonwritten evidence, gathered chiefly through archaeological excavations and surveys, does much to fill in the background of demography, living standards, technology, and so on that the written sources generally neglect. It has its own complex problems, but, although these are no more daunting than those surrounding the written sources,[6] historians of ancient Greece have made little use of unwritten evidence. This may be because so many historians of the Athenian Empire emplot their stories as political rather than socioeconomic narratives, and so the archaeological evidence seems less relevant to them.[7] Most attempts to bring nonwritten evidence into the story have consisted of using painted pottery to try to document Athenian economic policies and have had rather mixed success.[8]

The written sources contain far more information about fifth-century state formation but have two main shortcomings—the primary sources were overwhelmingly produced by and about Athenians, while many of the secondary sources were written several centuries later. Most general accounts of the Athenian Empire review the written sources, so I will keep my comments brief.[9]

Herodotus of Halicarnassus (probably 484-c. 420 B.C.E.) was an eyewitness to the growth of the Greater Athenian State but said little about it. Some classicists suggest that the moral of his *History* of the Greco-Persian War of 480–479 was that Athens could, like Persia, become a victim of its own hubris, but he never explicitly said this. Herodotus is useful on Athens' takeover of the anti-Persian alliance in 478–477 but tells us little thereafter.

Thucydides of Athens wrote a long account of the first twenty years of the Peloponnesian War of 431–404 B.C.E., prefaced by a brief review of the period 478–431. He was probably born in the 450s and says that he started writing his *History* in 431, because he saw that this was the greatest war ever. He was still writing in 404, though the *History* breaks off midsentence during the events of 411. Thucydides probably died around 400.

Thucydides' account of his methods[10] sets him apart from other classical historians, and his text commands unique respect today, but interpreting it remains highly problematic. Many of the questions, such as how he composed his text or how we should read the speeches he put in the mouths of the principal actors, have only a marginal impact on the arguments in this chapter, but others, such as his silence about the increase in tribute demands in 425 or his basic perspective on Athenian growth, are more relevant.

In addition to several shorter historical works, Xenophon of Athens (c. 430–350 B.C.E.) wrote a narrative called the *Hellenica* ("Greek Affairs"), picking up where Thucydides left off in 411 and continuing to 362. Xenophon's naïve prose and awkward storytelling have encouraged many classicists to see him as a plodder, but since the 1990s literary critics have claimed to detect artful irony and humor where others had found only incompetence. That said, the *Hellenica* seems far less incisive than Thucydides and has some remarkable omissions.

Fragments survive from other contemporary historians, such as Ion of Chios, Hellanicus of Lesbos, and Ctesias, but these are more often frustrating than enlightening. Important comments also crop up in fifth-century tragedy and in Aristophanes' comedies, and the work of fourth-century orators and philosophers (notably the *Constitution of Athens*, probably written in the 320s B.C.E. by Aristotle or one of his students) often mentions episodes from fifth-century history. But for detailed narratives to set alongside Thucydides, we must rely on much later sources. Diodorus of Sicily (c. 80–20 B.C.E.) offers a continuous survey. His method was generally to find a narrative account such as that of Thucydides or the lost work of the fourth-century writer Ephorus and to follow it as far as possible. He sometimes includes details missing from Thucydides, but in transferring information to his annalistic framework he made many mistakes and rationalized the stories. When Diodorus clashes with Thucydides, few scholars side with him.

Later still, soon after 100 C.E., Plutarch wrote a series of *Parallel Lives* of Greek and Roman statesmen, including the fifth-century Athenian politicians Aristides, Themistocles, Cimon, Pericles, Nicias, and Alcibiades, and Lysander of Sparta. Plutarch makes it clear that his main concern was the reader's moral improvement, not factual accuracy, and his interpretations of Athenian culture often seem colored by the Roman Empire in his own age. But he also had access to sources that no longer survive and clearly read widely and carefully. He can be a major source.

Finally, inscriptions recovered by more than a century of excavation have transformed our narrative.[11] Changes in Athenian democracy led to a boom in record-keeping on stone after 462, and with the transfer of the empire's treasury from the sacred island of Delos to Athens itself in 454, records of the *aparchê* (the one-sixtieth of the tribute given to the goddess Athena) allow us to reconstruct the tribute paid by the subject cities. Unfortunately, few inscriptions contain precise dating information before the very end of the fifth century, and we rely largely on letterforms to date the stones. Until the 1980s there was general agreement on the results, but in the 1990s this collapsed. This calls for an important digression.

Most epigraphers had agreed since the 1930s that any inscription using the three-barred sigma ſ must date before about 445 B.C.E., at which point carvers started using the four-barred version of that letter (Σ). Consequently, historians dated a number of texts describing major Athenian interventions in the internal government of subject cities or Athenian efforts to impose uniform policies on the entire Greater Athenian State to the 450s and early 440s. Harold Mattingly, however, argued in a series of essays beginning in 1961 that the paleographic dogma must be wrong and that most or all of these measures were taken in the 420s or later.[12] He suggested that some carvers carried on using older letter forms and that when we have no date for a decree, we should put more weight on the general historical context than on letter-carving conventions.

For thirty years, most professional historians rejected Mattingly's thesis, but in 1989 a combination of computer-enhanced photography and laser imagery shattered the consensus. An inscription recording a treaty between Athens and Segesta, in western Sicily,[13] is highly unusual in having both "old-fashioned" letters—the three-barred sigma and the rounded-and-tailed rho—and the name of an archon. Unfortunately, the stone was used for many years as a threshold slab, and the movement of the door over the inscription's surface erased all of the archon's name except the final letters –ON. Mattingly, swayed by the fact that including the archon's name is normally a late fifth-century phenomenon, restored the name as Antiphon, archon in 418–417; most historians, swayed by the assumption that the forms of sigma and rho must predate 445, preferred Habron, archon in 458–457. In a landmark essay, Mortimer Chambers, Ralph Gallucci, and P. Spanos showed that Mattingly was almost certainly right.[14] Debate goes on, but the case for 418–417 now seems virtually certain.

We can be confident that one inscription with three-barred sigmas dates well after 446, so there is no reason why others might not do so too. Mattingly argued that, given the financial crisis facing Athens early in the Peloponnesian War, most inscriptions with three-barred sigmas in which Athens takes a tough line with the cities should date to the 420s. He accepted that this argument was highly subjective, and Moses Finley famously mocked it as a "harshness-of-Cleon trap," according to which any assertive decree must come late in the fifth century.[15]

Like every development in source analysis, though, the Mattingly thesis creates new problems as well as solving old ones. For example, there were other occasions earlier in the fifth century when Athens' extensive commitments also created severe financial problems. In the 450s, for instance, Athens was fighting simultaneously in Egypt, Cyprus, the north Aegean, and the Peloponnese, and this could well have brought on a financial crisis in the early 440s.[16] No source covers the 440s in the detail that Thucydides and Aristophanes provide for the 420s, so we might be overlooking an equally plausible context for Athens' financial and administrative interventions. However, the evidence that we do have—the story that when the treasury was moved to Athens in 454 it contained either 8,000 or 10,000 talents; the relatively small tribute sums recorded for 454–453 and subsequent years; the lavish building campaign begun at Athens in the early 440s; and Thucydides' comment that 428 was the first time the Athenians felt the need to impose a direct tax on themselves—suggests that Mattingly probably was right to pinpoint the 420s as the first period of really severe financial constraints.[17]

Another issue is that we do not have to assume that Athens' tougher line was a passive response to financial problems; it could have been driven by ideological concerns. If so, then the early 440s could once again be as plausible a date for many inscriptions as the 420s, particularly if we believe that Callias negotiated a peace treaty between Athens and Persia around 449 and that this called the whole raison d'être of the Greater Athenian State into question.

If we find more examples of Athenian interventions with secure archon dates, a pattern may start to emerge, but for the moment we must live with uncertainty. The Segesta decree shows not all inscriptions with three-barred sigmas date before 445, but the fact that this letterform was still being used in 418–417 does not mean that every inscription with it must date so late. In the case of the regulations for Eretria and Chalcis, for instance, the traditional date of 446–445—immediately after their revolt in 447–446—strikes me as more plausible than Mattingly's suggestion of 424–423.[18] Overall, though, I follow Mattingly's dates in this chapter. It would be foolish to suppose that before Pericles' death Athens never intervened in subject cities' domestic affairs, but, on the other hand, all the circumstantial evidence suggests that the 420s saw a significant acceleration of the tempo of state formation.

In sum, the written record is substantial but has systematic biases. Most of the sources date after 430; every scrap of literary evidence relating to the Greater Athenian State in the period 478–431 can fit into a single book;[19] and downdating most of the inscriptions to the 420s just increases this imbalance. The sources also focus on individuals and politics, and we hear very little from non-Athenians.

For state formation outside Athens we rely overwhelmingly on casual asides in these same sources. Herodotus, Thucydides, Xenophon, Diodorus, and Plutarch all treat Sparta in some detail, but their accounts also suffer from the notorious "Spartan mirage," a tendency either to idealize Sparta or vilify it as an "anti-Athens." The Spartans produced almost no inscriptions to balance the stories that non-Spartans told about them.

Our evidence for Syracuse, the third major state of the fifth century, is even poorer. Herodotus briefly describes Geloan and Syracusan state building in the 490s–480s, and Thucydides goes into more detail about Athens' Sicilian wars in 427–424 and 415–413, but for all else we rely on Diodorus. The western Greeks produced very few inscriptions.[20]

3. BASIC NARRATIVE

In this section I summarize the basic background to fifth-century Greek state formation for readers not familiar with its details. For the sake of clarity I separate the story into Aegean and western stories, although in reality the two regions interacted on multiple levels. I end both stories in 404, with the fall of Athens and Syracuse's treaty with Carthage.

3.1. The Aegean

The first centralized, complex societies that archaeologists call states took shape in Crete around 2100 B.C.E. Like the earlier complex societies of southwest Asia, they were palace-centered monarchies with redistributive economies run by literate bureaucrats. Somewhat similar societies developed in mainland Greece before 1600, but, when migrations, destructions, and depopulation swept the East Mediterranean in the twelfth century, the Aegean palaces collapsed completely. Much simpler societies developed in the eleventh century, with only weak overseas links. Population growth drove recovery in the eighth century, and hundreds of small city-states formed, carried by colonists to Sicily, south Italy, and the shores of the Black Sea.

At first, these weak, relatively egalitarian city-states flourished in something of a power vacuum. The few Assyrians who knew of the Greeks saw them as mercenaries, pirates, and traders, but, as competition over the carcass of the Assyrian Empire mounted in the early sixth century, the Lydians brought the Greek cities of western Turkey into their empire and imposed tribute on them. Herodotus says that King Croesus of Lydia decided against incorporating the Aegean islands into his empire into the 550s;[21] when Cyrus of Persia overthrew the Lydian Empire in 546, he followed the same strategy.

By 546, Sparta was the strongest state in Greece. Spartan power rested ultimately on the city-state's eighth-century conquest of neighboring Messenia and

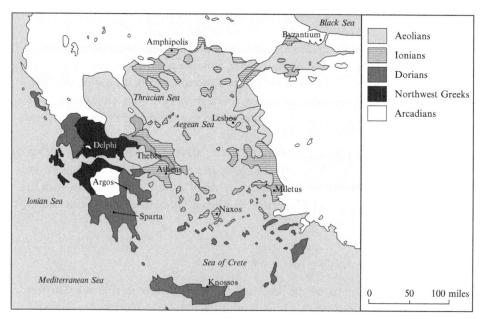

FIGURE 4.3. *Dialect groups in classical Greece (after Morris and Powell 2005: map 4.1)*

the reduction of the Messenians to serf laborers called helots, whose labor allowed Spartan citizens (Spartiates) to devote themselves to full-time training for war. In the early sixth century, Sparta tried to extend helotage into Arcadia but after a defeat around 560 altered course, giving up further annexations and instead creating an alliance known as the Peloponnesian League. Nearly all the allied cities considered themselves Dorians, an ethnic subgroup within the larger Greek population (see fig. 4.3). The allies paid no tribute but did provide troops, creating by far the biggest army in Greece. The Spartans sent an embassy to meet Cyrus on the west coast of Turkey in 546 and warn him not to trouble the Greeks. He reportedly laughed at them but had apparently already decided to turn eastward and to treat the Aegean as the natural northwest frontier for his empire. This remained the case until the late 520s, when Darius took the throne, built a fleet, and approved a series of adventures against Greek cities and Balkan tribes.

In the same years, some Aegean cities were constructing the first Greek fleets. The Peloponnesian League remained unchallenged on land, though, and continued to expand. In 511, Sparta made the rather unusual decision to intervene in a non-Dorian city, sending a small force by sea to overthrow the tyrant rulers of the Ionian Greek city Athens. This failed dismally, so in 510 the Spartans tried again. This time they went by land and expelled the tyrants, but the venture had mixed results. A third Spartan intervention in 508 or 507 to support their chosen candidate in Athens' aristocratic politics fared even worse, ending with an Athenian popular uprising, an undignified Spartan retreat, and the establishment of democracy at Athens. In 506, the Athenians, fearing Spartan revenge, offered submission to Persia. The Athenian assembly subsequently repudiated this, but in Persian eyes Athens was always thereafter a rebellious vassal.

Aegean history took a decisive turn in 499 when the Ionian Greeks of western Turkey revolted against Persia. Athens and Eretria, which were both Ionian cities (Athens in fact considered itself the Ionians' mother city), sent ships to support them. After crushing the Ionians in 494, Darius apparently decided that the only way to secure his northwest frontier was to incorporate mainland Greece too. Several cities submitted in 492. Storms destroyed the punitive force Darius sent against Athens and Eretria in 491, but in 490 a second force sacked Eretria and deported its population. Athens seemed about to meet the same fate but, to general surprise, defeated the Persians at Marathon. Sparta put aside its hostility with Athens in the face of the Persian threat, but the Athenians won the battle before the Spartan force had even set off.

Darius began assembling a much larger force to conquer Greece, but when he died, in 486, Egypt revolted. After crushing the uprising, the new Persian king, Xerxes, apparently decided that Greece was a low strategic priority, but under pressure from his advisers returned to Darius's plan. Recognizing the danger, the Athenians built the biggest warfleet yet seen, in 483, and in 481 they formed an anti-Persian alliance with Sparta. Sparta's Peloponnesian League provided the bulk of the land forces and Athens the bulk of the navy. An embassy to Syracuse that year failed to enlist Sicilian help, and in the end only thirty-one cities resisted Persia. Despite major tensions—which Xerxes tried hard to exploit—the Greek alliance defeated huge Persian forces at Salamis in 480 and Plataea in 479.

In 478, Sparta suggested that the Ionian Greeks relocate to the mainland, obviating the need for a long-term naval war against Persia, for which Sparta was poorly equipped. When this plan fell through, Athens and the Ionians squeezed Sparta out of its leadership role and formed a joint anti-Persian alliance (usually known as the Delian League), made up almost entirely of Ionians. In 477, Aristides of Athens designed a system of tribute through which the allies jointly paid into a fund on the sacred island of Delos, and this fund paid for a fleet to protect them and plunder Persian territory. The system was popular, but the fleet was under Athenian control, and most of the tribute went to pay Athenian rowers. By 470, Athens was using the fleet to stop free-riders leaving the League, and through the 460s hostility toward the organization mounted.

In the 470s and 460s, the League's leading politician was Cimon of Athens, who saw its goal as collaboration with Sparta and hostility to Persia. Paradoxically, Cimon's victory over a major Persian force at the River Eurymedon in or around 466 may have strengthened the feeling that the League was no longer necessary, and when in 465 the League besieged Thasos (one of its major members) to enforce Athenian designs on Thasian mines, Sparta decided to attack Athens. Only an earthquake and a helot uprising in Sparta averted war. Cimon persuaded the Athenians to help Sparta, but in 462 the Spartans rejected their aid. Cimon was discredited and exiled, and a new radical leadership turned Athens against Sparta while simultaneously stepping up the anti-Persian war. From 460 through 446, Athens and Sparta fought the on-again, off-again First Peloponnesian War, much of it waged through proxies, and in 459 Athens also invaded the Persian province of Egypt, only to suffer complete defeat in 454. Fearing that Persian ships might raid Delos and seize the treasury there, Athens now moved the League's silver to the Athenian acropolis. Most historians treat this as marking the shift from a Delian League to an Athenian Empire. Cimon, who returned from exile in 452, led an expedition to Cyprus that stabilized the war with Persia, and Athens and Persia may have signed a peace treaty (what those modern historians who believe in its reality call the "Peace of Callias") in 449; even if they did not, Athenian-Persian hostilities virtually ceased at this point,[22] increasing the sense that the original motivation for consensual submission to Athens, which marked the first steps toward a Greater Athenian State, no longer applied.

In the early 440s, Athens suffered a series of defeats at the hands of Sparta's allies, and in 446 revolts seriously undermined the Greater State. Pericles—now the leading Athenian statesman—restored the situation, signed the Thirty Years' Peace with Sparta, and began a policy of consolidating Athenian power while avoiding overseas entanglements. This held until 433, when Athens concluded alliances with Rhegion, in southern Italy, and Corcyra, which dominated sea routes to the west, and imposed trade sanctions on Megara, an important Spartan ally. Fearing the growth of Athenian power, Sparta declared war in 431, beginning the (Great) Peloponnesian War. Most historians call the first phase of fighting, from 431 through 421, the Archidamian War. Initially, Athens followed Pericles' strategy of avoiding land battles and staying within the city's fortifications while the fleet guaranteed grain imports and raided Sparta's allies, with the goal of wearing Sparta down till it accepted the status quo ante and the fact of Athenian power. Pericles died in 429 in a great plague that struck the besieged city of Athens, and competition for influence in the democratic Assembly drove rival politicians to formulate ever more ambitious plans actually to defeat Sparta on land. In 427, one of these schemes led Athens to intervene in Sicily. It (and several other stratagems) collapsed in 424, and in 421 Athens and Sparta, exhausted, made peace.

Historians usually call the period from 421 through 413 the Peace of Nicias, but the war continued by other means. In a covert operation, the Athenian aristocrat Alcibiades assembled an alliance that forced Sparta to risk everything in a single battle in 418; then, in 415, he persuaded the Assembly to launch a massive invasion of Sicily. Internal conflicts destabilized the attack before it even began, and a two-year siege of Syracuse ended in disaster. Sparta then renewed the war, only to find that even in its final phase (the Ionian War, 412–404), Athens could not be defeated so long as it maintained even a tenuous command of the sea, protecting its grain supply and enforcing tribute payments from its subject cities. In 412, Sparta therefore made a deal with Persia, surrendering the Ionian Greeks in return for enough money to build a fleet that could cut Athens' grain supply. Intrigues between Persian satraps prevented the gold from getting through till the dynamic admiral Lysander took charge of Spartan efforts in 407; even then, Athens kept the grain routes open till 405, when a catastrophic tactical blunder allowed Lysander to capture the Athenian fleet at Aegospotamoi. Athens surrendered the next year, and Sparta took over what remained of the Greater Athenian State.

3.2. The West

Greeks began settling in Sicily in the 730s B.C.E., and, by the sixth century, western cities like Syracuse and Akragas were wealthier than any in the Aegean. They faced no expansionist empire like Lydia or Persia to drive state formation; instead, most cities had open frontiers with indigenous societies that, while often fighting bravely, were less developed than the Greeks and usually lost out. A combination of wars with the Sicels and internal dynamics probably explain the tyrant Hippocrates of Gela's conquest of several neighboring cities in eastern Sicily in the 490s. We do not know whether these cities paid tribute to Gela or provided troops, but one way or another Hippocrates assembled a formidable army. When he died, in 491, his cavalry commander Gelon took over the small kingdom, then, after defeating Syracuse in 485, transferred his throne to that city and put his brother Hieron in charge of Gela. Gelon built up Syracuse's power by relocating the populations of defeated cities to his capital and by making a marriage alliance with Theron, tyrant of Akragas. Both these strategies had more in common with the practices of Near Eastern kings than with those of Aegean Greek cities. Gelon also relied heavily on mercenaries.

Tyrants ruled all the main Greek cities in Sicily and Italy in the early fifth century. Marriage alliances were one of their major tools of international relations, while fallings-out within and between tyrannical families and tensions between tyrants and their own citizens were the main threats to stability. In 483, Gelon's closest ally (and father-in-law), Theron of Akragas, expelled Terillos, tyrant of Himera. Terillos had strong personal ties in Carthage, and his guest-friends there decided to intervene to restore him. This threat was probably one of the main reasons why Gelon rejected the Spartan and Athenian request for help against Persia in 481. The Carthaginians invaded in 480, but Gelon decisively defeated them. Carthage then stayed out of Sicilian politics for two generations, and Syracuse became the dominant western city. The "tyrants' club" led by Syracuse was at its zenith in the 470s, intervening in Italy and fighting the Etruscans, but by 465 the delicate balance between the chiefs had collapsed and civil wars between citizens, "new" citizens who had been transferred by tyrants from one city to another, and the tyrants' mercenaries tore many cities apart. By 461, all the tyrants had fallen. The cities signed a Common Resolution to maintain peace, and many adopted democracy. Syracuse's dominance collapsed, though it remained the largest and richest Greek city in the west.

An indigenous Sicel state emerged in the 450s in the posttyrannical power vacuum, but the Syracusan democracy smashed it in 440, and in 439 Syracuse greatly expanded its army and navy. Over the next few years, Syracuse bullied all its Dorian neighbors into accepting its lead (again, we do not know whether they paid tribute or provided troops) and began threatening Sicily's Ionian Greeks too. Concerned by Syracuse's creation of a second Dorian power bloc, Athens made alliances with Ionian Rhegion and Leontini in 433, committing some ten thousand men and sixty ships on the Ionian side when war broke out in Sicily in 427. In 424, though, the Sicilian Greeks decided that they feared Athens more than one another and signed a general peace.

Syracuse's strength continued to worry the other Sicilian cities, and in 415 Alcibiades of Athens gambled that the Ionians would rally to a new Athenian invasion. He exploited a war between the Greek city of Selinous and the indigenous city of Segesta to attack Syracuse, but by 413 Syracuse had defeated Athens' finest armada and was once again the undisputed leader of Sicily, albeit severely weakened by the struggle. Events then took an unexpected turn. The Segestans, who had drawn Athens in to Sicily, understandably now felt vulnerable, and in 410 they put themselves under Carthaginian protection. Armed with new siege techniques, between 409 and 406 Carthage destroyed Selinous, Himera, Akragas, Gela, and Camarina. In a panic, the Syracusans appointed one Dionysius as sole general, with complete authority and a bodyguard. In 405, Syracuse once again found itself under siege, and once again it survived. Racked by plague, the Carthaginian army withdrew in 404, by which time Dionysius had established himself as tyrant of the greatly weakened city, but since the war had weakened the other Greek cities much more, Dionysius now dominated Greek Sicily in a way that even Gelon had not managed.

4. BASIC PARAMETERS

4.1. Natural Environment and Ecology

Most geographers classify Greece as part of a "Mediterranean" climate zone, with hot dry summers and cool wet winters, but there is much variation within this category. Northwest Greece is mountainous and forested, with some fertile upland valleys, while southern Greece is far drier, with small plains divided by hills and some significant mountains. Thessaly and Macedonia have larger and better-watered plains. The "Mediterranean triad" of cereals, vines, and olives was established almost everywhere before 2000 b.c.e., although because olives will not grow at altitudes above eight hundred meters, mountain dwellers always had to import oil. Some historians add pulses to the triad as a fourth staple. For most people, meat—particularly beef—was a luxury, although sheep and goat were certainly eaten in frequent religious festivals. Fish, too, were considered delicacies. They were not available in sufficient quantity to be a staple but even in small amounts could be an important protein source. Overall, the diet was healthy and serious famines were rare, but skeletal and textual evidence alike suggest that periodic food shortages were common.[23]

Many economic historians believe that long-term trends in age-specific height correlate tightly with nutritional status to provide a predictor of standards of living.[24] Robert Fogel suggested using 1.68 meters as the upper limit for speaking of "short" (i.e., poorly nourished) men,[25] and estimates for Greek heights derived from the long bones fall right around this figure.[26] Ancient Greeks were poorly nourished by modern standards but fare much better when compared with Greeks from just forty years ago; the men buried at Metapontum and in the Athenian Kerameikos cemetery were typically taller than Cypriot Greek military recruits in 1949, who averaged just 1.65 meters.[27]

Greek agriculture was mostly rain-fed, and the major challenge facing Greek farmers was less overall shortages of rain than its unpredictability. Interannual variation was high, requiring farmers to develop storage, friendship, and exchange as risk-buffering mechanisms. Barley, which is more drought-resistant than wheat, was probably the staple food. Between 1931 and 1960, rainfall around Athens varied so much that the barley crop failed one year in twenty, wheat one year in four, and legumes three years in four, and these statistics are probably broadly applicable to classical antiquity.[28] Yields probably rarely exceeded 650 kg per hectare.[29]

4.2. Demography

Population began growing rapidly in Greece in the eighth century b.c.e. Until about 400, growth was fastest around the Aegean Sea and in the western colonies, with northern Greece catching up in the fourth century and western parts of the mainland in the third.[30]

Although infants and children are generally underrepresented in the archaeological record, several cemeteries—including the fifth-century Kerameikos burial ground at Athens—show that infant mortality was high, as we would expect in a predemographic transition society. From a sample of 425 skeletons, Lawrence Angel concluded that the average adult age at death for women rose from 30.9 years in the Early Iron Age (1100–700 B.C.E.) to 36.8 in classical times (c. 480–323 B.C.E.).[31] Physical anthropologists are now more skeptical about being able to age adult skeletons accurately than they were when Angel compiled his data, and recent studies have produced younger adult female ages at death.[32] Nevertheless, Angel's data and more recent studies all show the same diachronic trend of substantial increases in adult ages at death between the ninth century and the fourth.[33] The typical woman's reproductive life was at least five years (or 15–20 percent) longer in the fifth century than it had been in the tenth or ninth.

Comparative demography suggests that population change is normally mortality-led, with the result that if female adult age at death increases within the years of fertility, total fertility rates also increase.[34] With more children being born and/or more of those born surviving to adulthood, population grows until people respond by artificially controlling their fertility, emigrating, or starving. If disease rates increase, the reverse happens. Since it takes time for people to recognize changes in mortality and to recalibrate the relationship between the private and social costs of children or—in the absence of such changes—for Malthusian "positive" checks to increase mortality, periods of rapid growth or decline can occur. Both population growth and decline tend to disrupt premodern states massively.[35] In ancient Greece, periods of population growth correlate strongly with economic growth and state formation, while demographic decline correlates with economic and state collapse.[36]

The literary sources for epidemics are well known,[37] and DNA evidence suggests that the famous plague that broke out at Athens in 430 was a form of typhoid fever. It recurred in 427–426, but since Aegean population as a whole continued to climb for another century, we should probably conclude that it had little long-term effect on the local disease pool.[38] However, Diodorus says that terrible plagues broke out in the Carthaginian army in Sicily in 405 and 396.[39] He does not say these plagues affected the Greeks, too, but they may have been connected to the Sicilian population decline that reached crisis proportions by the 340s.

The textual evidence for absolute population sizes is much disputed, but Mogens Hansen has convincingly argued that there were at least six to seven million Greeks in the fourth century.[40] It is harder to document changes between the fifth and fourth centuries, but my own guess (based largely on survey data, densities in excavated settlements, and the scanty literary sources) is that total Greek population was between 5.5 and 6 million around 450 B.C.E. Hansen has firmly restated the case that the population of Attica—the roughly 2,500 km² of territory that made up the city-state of Athens—peaked at around 350,000 in the 430s.[41] This was a huge population for a city-state, and means that about 6 percent of all Greeks lived in Attica (i.e., the city of Athens plus its traditional hinterland) and about 15 percent of all Greeks in the Greater Athenian State. Most of the more than one thousand known Greek city-states, by contrast, had populations of just a few thousand.

About 40,000 of the 350,000 residents in Attica were adult male citizens. Judging from the settled area of the city of Athens, about 10 percent of the population lived in the urban center, and perhaps another 10 percent in the harbor town of Piraeus. Hansen's figures would mean a density of 139 people/km² in Attica, while the carrying capacity was in the region of 35–42 people/km².[42] Even in the best years for rainfall, Attica had to import two-thirds to three-quarters of its food in the 430s B.C.E. Hence the strategic importance of Athens' defeat at Aegospotamoi in 405; absent a powerful Athenian fleet, Sparta could simply cut off the grain supply and starve the city into submission. The Peloponnesian War caused serious population losses, especially among the poorer men who rowed in the fleet,[43] and at the lowest point in the fourth century there were probably 30,000 citizens and a total population of about 250,000.[44] Athens' population was about 30 percent lower in the 350s than it had been in the 430s and had probably been lower still the early fourth century. Archaeological surveys, on the other hand, suggest that in much of the rest of Greece population was 10 to 20 percent higher in the fourth century than in the fifth. The Peloponnesian War was a demographic disaster for Athens, whose population fell from a little over 6 percent of the Greek total in the 430s to under 4 percent by 350 B.C.E.

Fifth-century Athens' main rival for populousness was Syracuse.[45] Thucydides says Syracuse was no smaller than Athens in 413[46] and its fifth-century walls encircled 120 hectares. As early as the 470s, though, settlement had spread beyond them, and the city's population probably was much the same size as Athens'. The population of Syracusan territory was probably around 250,000 in 415, a density of 53–75/km²—just one-third to one-half of Attica's but still high by preindustrial standards. Franco De Angelis estimates that twice as much land in Greek Sicily was arable as in mainland Greece (perhaps 77 percent, much higher than Garnsey's estimate of 35–40 percent for Attica). At least half a dozen Sicilian states probably had fifth-century populations of forty to fifty thousand.[47] Syracusans may have made up about 4 percent of all Greeks throughout the fifth and fourth centuries, and Sicilian Greeks as a whole about 10 percent in the fifth and rather less in the fourth.

Sparta's demographic situation was very different. Most estimates put the total population of fifth-century Laconia and Messenia, the regions Sparta controlled, in the 200,000–250,000 range, with unfree helots in dispersed settlements making up the great majority, a substantial group of semifree *perioikoi* ("dwellers around") in more nucleated towns, and the small number of fully free Spartiates concentrated at Sparta.[48] Richard Catling extrapolates from survey data to a total population of between 210,000 and 255,000 in the mid-fifth century (a very low density of 14.6/ km² [one-tenth of Attica's density] across Laconia and Messenia as a whole, much lower than the density of 54/km² in the survey area in the city of Sparta's immediate hinterland), falling by about 15 percent by 350 B.C.E.[49] Most text-based historians assume that the helot and perioikic populations grew through the archaic and classical periods while the population of full-citizen Spartiates fell steadily because of Sparta's peculiar citizenship rules. There were about 8,000 Spartiates in 480, but only 2,400 to 4,200 in 418, fewer than a thousand in the mid-fourth century, and no more than 700 in the 240s.[50] Attempts to broaden the citizen body in the 230s and 220s and again in 207 B.C.E. created revolutionary ferments that triggered violent repression by conservative elements within Sparta, then by Macedon, and finally by Rome. The resident population of Laconia may have stood around 3 percent of the total population of the Greek world in the 430s, but by the 360s Sparta was incapable of providing military leadership.

Overall, no one city dominated fifth-century Greece demographically. About 6 percent of all Greeks lived in Attica, roughly 4 percent in Syracuse's territory, and 3 percent in Sparta's. Another dozen or so city-states each contained 1 percent or more of the population. Roughly 15 percent of Greeks lived in the Greater Athenian State, between 5 and 10 percent in the cities under Syracusan control (depending on the exact moment), and perhaps another 10 to 15 percent in Sparta's Peloponnesian League.

4.3. Economic Structures

During the Dark Age, probably 80 to 90 percent of all production was consumed by the primary producers or exchanged over relatively short distances to even out the effects of interannual variability in rainfall. The small residue went to support a not particularly wealthy elite and to small-scale commodity production.[51] Even in the fourth century, we must agree with Paul Cartledge that "The ancient Greek world was massively and unalterably rural";[52] but the proportion of household production mobilized for exchange nevertheless grew strongly between the eighth century and the fourth. The fourth-century Athenian literary sources give the impression that any occupation other than being a farmer, a politician, or a warrior was frowned upon, but speakers tried to avoid mentioning what they called the "invisible economy" of banking, finance, and the market. To have generated the kind of incomes that we know that the Athenian aristocracy had, this sector of the economy must have been substantial. By some estimates, nearly one-third of fourth-century Athens' income must have been in the form of gains from trade.[53]

The growth of Athens and Syracuse as urban markets for food, metals, building, etc., and of organized marketplaces like the Piraeus to supply them speeded up the circulation of goods. Some regions had clear comparative advantages in production: we hear about Athenian silver, olive oil, and fine pottery, Thasian wine, Thessalian and Sicilian grain, Cycladic marble, and Macedonian timber, to name but a few. Coinage was introduced to Greece around 600 B.C.E., and small change was in use before 500,[54] lowering transaction costs.

Surface surveys reveal a partial but important shift in settlement patterns in Greece in the fifth and particularly the fourth centuries. Prior to 500 B.C.E., probably 90 to 95 percent of the population lived in villages of just a few dozen or hundred inhabitants. Most regions had a handful of towns of 1,000 or 2,000 people, and Athens, Corinth, Argos, and Knossos may have had more than 5,000 (but fewer than 10,000) inhabitants. But after 500, increasing numbers of Greeks started living in rural farmsteads. Although debates about population size continue,[55] in the southern Argolid, the ratio of third-order (probably farmstead) sites to second-order (village) sites rose from 3:1 in the archaic period to 6:1 in the classical (c. 500–350 B.C.E.) and 10:1 in the late classical/early Hellenistic period (c. 350–250 B.C.E.).[56]

The shifts were partial. On Kea, even at the height of dispersion three-quarters of the population lived in the main town (population 900–1,200).[57] That said, a shift of 10 to 15 percent of the population still had major economic effects. Historians have formulated a "new model" of classical agriculture, seeing farmers as working contiguous fields, pasturing animals on them, and using manure to reduce fallow.[58] In several regions of Greece, the dense concentrations of surface artifacts that represent ancient settlements are surrounded by lower-density "haloes" of classical sherds, which seem very likely to be domestic debris dispersed by manuring. No such haloes are known from earlier or later periods, strongly suggesting that manuring reached its premodern peak in classical times.[59] Similarly, around Pylos "The palynological data argue for a dense population and a high level of agricultural production during the Classical/Hellenistic period. Human control of the landscape seems to have reached its maximum at that time."[60]

Standards of living rose sharply across the archaic and classical periods. I already mentioned evidence for increasing stature and average age at death; all over Greece, the roofed space in the floor plan of typical house sizes was also increasing, from about 55 m² in the eighth century to 230 m² in the fourth. Since the proportion of houses with second floors also increased, the typical house size probably grew seven- or eightfold. There were similar improvements in the sophistication of house construction and comparable increases in the scale of domestic assemblages.[61] Classical houses (particularly those of the fourth century) were generally comfortable places to live.[62] All the evidence indicates sustained per capita as well as aggregate economic growth in archaic and classical Greece. I have suggested that per capita consumption increased by about 50 percent between 800 and 300 B.C.E.[63]

4.4. Technology

Most Greek technology was fairly basic.[64] We should not imagine a monolithic "traditional" agricultural regime in premodern Greece,[65] but (except for the introduction of iron around 1100 B.C.E.) in many spheres classical technology was much like what had been available a thousand years earlier. There is no good evidence for improvements in seeds or processing techniques, and, so far as we know, agriculture continued to depend entirely on muscle power. New finds have shown that water mills were commoner in the Roman Empire than had been thought,[66] but there is no evidence for extensive use of wind or water power in classical Greece.

Both theoretical and applied science were well developed in classical Greece, and medicine also saw major advances. However, there were few attempts to apply scientific knowledge or principles systematically to solving problems in the real world, and doctors could do little to change basic patterns of mortality. In this, of course, the Greeks were anything but unusual; eighteenth-century England seems to have been the first place in the world to develop a culture that integrated science and technology.[67]

As noted earlier, house building improved sharply, particularly from 550 onward, and to some extent the same was true of public hygiene and water supplies. Late-sixth-century Athens already had public fountain houses, adequate drainage, and piped water. On Samos, Eupalinos cut a broad tunnel for a mile through a hill to bring water to the city in the sixth century, and in the early fifth Phaeax built massive underground stone conduits to drain water away from Syracuse.[68]

Land transportation was primitive. There were a few exceptional feats, such as the construction around 600 B.C.E. of the *diolkos*, a road on which ships could be dragged overland across the Isthmus of Corinth,[69] but generally roads were not well paved. Herodotus was amazed by Persia's Royal Road from Susa to Sardis,[70] and moving large objects was particularly slow work.[71] Strabo explicitly contrasted the high quality of Roman roads with the low standards in Greece.[72]

Sea transport was more developed. Shipbuilding improved in the late eighth century, probably influenced by Phoenician innovations, and the first purpose-built merchant vessels were built on Samos, probably in the late sixth century.[73] Most Greek trading vessels were small, probably about twenty meters long. The stone bases for a ship dedicated in the sanctuary of Hera on Samos around 600 suggest a ship 21.9 meters long and 2.1 meters in the beam,[74] and a late fifth-century wreck from Porticello in the Straits of Messina was about seventeen meters long, with a thirty-ton burden. Another wreck of the same date off Alonnisos, though, seems to be at least twenty-five meters long with a burden of 126 tons, which compares well with many Roman merchantmen.[75] Hull construction had changed little since the Bronze Age, and fore-and-aft rigging was unknown. Harbors were crude by later standards, but sixth-century Samos was again a pioneer, and fifth-century Piraeus boasted substantial facilities.[76] Athens also developed quite sophisticated financial institutions for capital-intensive seaborne trade, although even the largest "firms" in maritime trade seem to have involved just a handful of people.[77]

The Greeks made some notable advances in military technology. By the seventh century, battles were being decided by phalanxes of heavy infantry (hoplites) in bronze armor. On the right terrain, these were devastatingly effective, and between the mid-seventh century and 371, Sparta dominated this form of warfare.[78] Hoplite warfare was capital-intensive, above all in human capital, since discipline and train-ing were all-important. However, since citizen-warriors normally received little or no pay for training or fighting, armies put little strain on the state. Soldiers nor-mally provided their own armor and often settled campaigns with a single battle.[79] On the negative side, hoplites moved slowly, were predictable, and were ineffec-tive against fortifications. Most Greek cities had walls, which in the fifth century deterred direct assaults. Beginning in 409, however, the Carthaginians used new offensive techniques to destroy half a dozen major Greek cities in Sicily. The Greeks rapidly adopted and improved their methods, causing costs to spiral as both offen-sive and defensive siege techniques advanced rapidly.[80] Light troops and cavalry were little used in Aegean Greece until the late fifth century, although cavalry were more numerous and important in Sicily.

The most important developments in fifth-century military technology, though, were at sea. Thucydides seems to say that triremes, fast warships with three decks of oars, were invented in the late eighth century, but there is some evidence that they became common only in the late sixth century.[81] In the fifth century, a trireme cost about a talent to build and rig and probably about another talent per month to sup-port the crew of more than 180 men.[82] This meant a spectacular increase in the costs of war, particularly after Athens used a lucky strike of silver to build the first large fleet, of 200 triremes, in 483.[83] This completely changed the nature of war and state formation. Navies could project state power in ways that had been unimaginable in the sixth century. Thucydides had Pericles remind the Athenians that "With your navy as it is today there is no power on earth—not the King of Persia nor any people under the sun—that can stop you from sailing where you wish. This power of yours is something in an altogether different category from all the advantages of houses and cultivated land."[84] Athens struck with impunity in Egypt, Cyprus, the Black Sea region, and Sicily, as well as all over the Aegean, and naval tactics and training developed even faster than terrestrial ones.[85] As Sparta discovered, the only way to compete with Athenian naval power was to create a similar fleet, but a full summer campaign for such a force would cost at least 600 talents, well beyond the revenue of any normal city-state. The spiraling costs of naval warfare and the need to hire the best rowers were even more important than the rising costs of sieges in speed-ing up the tempo of state formation. In the 390s, Syracuse began using four-decked quadriremes and perhaps invented five-decked quinqueremes, and in 294 Deme-trius the Besieger was using fifteen- and sixteen-banked ships in battle.[86]

4.5. Social Structures

The most unusual feature of classical Greek social structures was male citizen egali-tarianism. An idea of the city-state as a community of equal, local-born men—what I have elsewhere called "the middling ideology"—took hold in the eighth century. It was strongly contested across the seventh and sixth centuries but by 500 had emerged as the only legitimate basis for authority.[87] Most citizen men (probably one-quarter to one-third of the adult resident population in most city-states) considered themselves fundamentally equal, regardless of differences in wealth, education, or lineage. This belief system was accompanied by unusually strong gender and ethnic distinctions. In the fifth century, large numbers of non-Greeks were imported as chattel slaves into those *poleis* where male egalitarianism flourished most strongly. In Attica, there were probably at least 60,000 slaves out of a total resident population of 350,000. Slaves could be found in virtually every walk of life, including war, although there is controversy over the scale of their use in agriculture.[88]

Some city-states, most notably Sparta, made little use of chattel slaves, instead exploiting unfree local populations. The Spartans believed themselves to have invaded Laconia in prehistoric times and to have a right to rule over the local non-Dorian population as a warrior elite. In the eighth century, they conquered neighboring Messenia and reduced its whole population to serfdom. They fought a great war to secure control of Messenia in the mid-seventh century and in the sixth tried to extend this system to Arcadia but were defeated at Tegea in the 560s. The need to control the helots dominated Spartan policy and thought until the Thebans won the battle of Leuctra in 371 and liberated Messenia.[89] Syracuse also had a dependent population called the Killyrioi, although this seems to have been less threatening than the Spartan helots.

The distribution of landed wealth across citizen families, at least in Athens, was comparatively even. The Gini coefficient for landholding in fourth-century Athens is lower than that for all but two of the 1970s agrarian Mediterranean communities studied by the anthropologist John Davis or any of the Roman communities studied by the historian Richard Duncan-Jones.[90] The largest documented fourth-century Athenian estate is Phainippos's, which included just 0.1 percent of the arable land in Attica,[91] much less than the 7.6 to 21.6 percent of arable encompassed within single estates in various provinces in Duncan-Jones's Roman studies. Landholding was ideologically charged, however, and this pattern probably understates the overall degree of wealth inequality. We know of fifth-century Athenians who held very large estates overseas, and differential access to the "invisible economy" of urban, financial, and industrial property must have skewed the distribution of wealth.

We lack comparable data for Syracuse, but the sources agree that the rich were much richer in Sicily than in the Aegean. Diodorus waxed enthusiastic about the richest men in fifth-century Akragas,[92] and some Syracusans were probably wealthier still. When the exiled Syracusan aristocrat Dion fled to the Aegean, in the fourth century, he seemed more like a king than a private citizen.[93]

The Spartiates, by contrast, prided themselves on their economic equality, even calling themselves *homoioi*, "those who are alike." But Hodkinson[94] shows that, on careful reading, the sources reveal real differences in economic power, partly masked by an egalitarian ideology that restrained overt displays of wealth. Discomfort with displays of personal wealth increased all over Greece around 500 B.C.E., but after 425 we can see clear movement back toward more lavish elite behavior in housing, dress, burial, and personalized monuments.[95] Greek culture changed in significant ways in the fourth century to accommodate the growing importance of the rich.[96]

Overall, wealth was apparently more evenly distributed in Greece than in most other complex societies in Mediterranean history, although not so evenly distributed as the Greeks themselves liked to proclaim. The pressures to conform to "middling" norms built steadily across the seventh and sixth centuries, peaked in the fifth century, and then began to weaken. They were strongest in the Aegean and probably weakest in Sicily. In the fourth century, economic power shifted back toward the upper class.

4.6. Political Structures

From the seventh century on, oligarchies of relatively wealthy men ruled most city-states. Sometimes these were narrow; other times, they incorporated the majority of citizens. There was, however, always a strong sense that the ruling elite was answerable to the ordinary citizens, and (particularly in times of war) popular opposition could depose incompetent or corrupt leaders. Normally, oligarchs who were overthrown would be replaced by similar but hopefully more competent noblemen, but sometimes a sole ruler (*tyrannos*) would emerge. By classical times, and probably since the seventh or even eighth century, there was general agreement that tyranny could never be truly legitimate. The difficulty of balancing all the competing factions meant that few lasted more than two generations. Tyrants had all but disappeared by 500 in the Aegean, although they became much more important in the early fifth century in Sicily and again in the fourth. The Syracusan tyrants relied heavily on mercenaries to keep the population under control. Beginning in the later sixth century, though, we see a third response to political failure, with the ordinary male citizens taking over direct rule for themselves—what the Greeks called *demokratia*, or "power of the people."

Within these broad trends, the constitutions of individual Greek states were enormously varied, and I limit myself to brief observations on Athens, Sparta, and Syracuse.

4.6.1. *Athens.* The major institution in the Athenian democracy of 508–322 B.C.E. was an Assembly open to all male citizens over eighteen. They voted directly on all major issues, with only a minimal bureaucracy, no political parties, and weakly institutionalized offices.[97] Usually 6,000 or more citizens attended meetings, which, in the fourth century, took place at least forty times each year. A handful of offices, particularly financial ones, had wealth qualifications, and the Assembly elected the holders of these and military offices. Most offices were open to all citizens, though, or all citizens over thirty, and positions were filled by lot. All officeholders were subject to public scrutiny at the end of their year in office, and these reviews were one of the major arenas for pursuing politics.

Elite political networking was always important, but by the 440s direct appeals to the assembled citizens were normally decisive.[98] Thucydides claimed that until Pericles' death, in 429, Athens was a democracy in name but was in fact ruled by this one man, whose charismatic authority allowed him to guide the people:

> Pericles, by his rank, ability, and his known integrity, was able to exercise an independent control over the multitude—in short, to lead them instead of being led by them; for as he never sought power by improper means, he was never compelled to flatter them, but, on the contrary, enjoyed so high an estimation that he could afford to anger them by contradiction.[99]

Thucydides concedes that in 430 many Athenians were so angry over the loss of their property in the war that they voted Pericles out of his generalship and fined him, but "not long after," Thucydides continues, "according to the way of the multitude, they again elected him general and committed all their affairs to his hands."

The *boulê*, a Council of five hundred men selected largely by lottery from all citizens over thirty years of age, prepared the Assembly's agenda. The term of office on the *boulê* was one year, and no citizen could serve more than twice, which meant that, given the demographic facts of Athens, virtually every citizen would serve. The cumbersome procedures of the *boulê* democratized decision making, severely limiting the ability of any faction to get control of this key institution.[100] The desire to incorporate as many citizens as possible led to the introduction of pay for citizens who attended the jury in the 440s and the extension of this principle to the Assembly in 403.

The overwhelming emphasis on the politician's ability to persuade a mass audience at a single meeting through his powers of speech created enormous pressures. One rhetorical misstep could lead not just to the failure of a carefully planned policy but to the responsible politician's fall from grace, exile, or death.

> [Athens'] leaders had *no* respite...they had to lead in person, and they had also to bear, in person, the brunt of the opposition's attacks. More than that, they walked alone....A man was a leader solely as a function of his personal, and in the literal sense, unofficial status within the Assembly itself. The test of whether or not he held that status was simply whether the Assembly did or did not vote as he wished, and therefore the test was repeated with each proposal.[101]

This was "deep play," as the anthropologist Clifford Geertz called it:[102] politicians were always in over their heads, playing for enormous stakes. On the one hand, the Assembly was full of connoisseurs of rhetoric,[103] ready to pounce on speakers' blunders; on the other, there was real fear that speakers would pander to the people, saying whatever would get votes. The Sausage-Seller in Aristophanes' comedy *The Knights* (424 B.C.E.) was the perfect caricature, but Thucydides insisted in all seriousness that Athens lost the Peloponnesian War because its leaders after Pericles' death "adopted methods of demagogy which resulted in their losing control over the actual conduct of affairs."[104] Many historians have concurred: "Athens lost the war at [the battle of] Aegospotami [in 405], but the disarray of Athenian politics for several years previously had made something like Aegospotami all but inevitable."[105]

While some educated Athenians were eager to form a political elite, others went along with democracy only because they profited from it,[106] and others still resisted it. In 457, critics plotted with Sparta to launch an oligarchic coup,[107] and in 411 opponents of democracy actually seized control in the wake of demoralization caused by the Sicilian expedition's failure. On the whole, though, the democracy was remarkably stable, and the major legacy of the critics—including Plato, Aristophanes, the Old Oligarch, and Thucydides himself—was a sophisticated analysis of popular power.[108] These oppositional texts have been massively influential in modern times, portraying the democracy as willful, irresponsible, and ignorant. They often have a point; yet Finley was surely right to conclude that

> Much of the credit for the Athenian achievement must go to the political leadership of the state. That, it seems to me, is beyond dispute. It certainly would not have been disputed by the average Athenian. Despite all the tension and uncertainties, the occasional snap judgment and unreasonable shift in opinion, the people supported Pericles for more than two decades....These men, and others like them (less well-known now) were able to carry through a more or less consistent and successful programme over long stretches of time. It is altogether perverse to ignore this fact, or to ignore the structure of political life by which Athens became what she was, while one follows the lead of Aristophanes or Plato and looks only at the personalities of the politicians, or at the crooks and failures among them, or at some ethical norms of an ideal existence.[109]

4.6.2. Sparta. Sparta governed itself very differently, through four main institutions:[110]

1. Two kings, one each from the Agiad and the Eurypontid families. These were the chief religious and military officers of the state, although, following problems in 506 B.C.E., only one of them was sent with the army on each campaign.
2. A council of five *ephors*, elected from all Spartiate full citizens over thirty years of age for one year at a time. The *ephors* were chosen by acclamation; whichever five nominees got the loudest cheers when they appeared before the citizen Assembly won the office. The *ephors* policed the kings. Two *ephors* accompanied the king on campaign, and the *ephors* could depose the kings. However, they were also subject to scrutiny by the next group of *ephors* at the end of their year of service. A man could be an *ephor* only once.

3. A *gerousia*, or Council of Elders, consisting of the two kings plus twenty-eight men over the age of sixty elected from the Spartiates. The Assembly could vote only on measures that the *gerousia* had approved. The *gerousia* further had the right to dissolve the Assembly if it took a decision that the *gerousia* disapproved of and sat in judgment on any cases involving penalties of disenfranchisement, exile, or death.

4. An Assembly of all male Spartiates over thirty years of age. No decision was official state policy until the Assembly had approved it, but, unlike the Athenian Assembly, the Spartans rarely discussed proposals: they normally only voted (by shouting).

The Spartan system was widely idealized in antiquity as a "mixed constitution," perfectly blending monarchical, aristocratic, and democratic elements. In practice, however, politics was more complicated. From the age of seven until they married after thirty (and often still then), Spartan men spent most of their time in male-only age sets and dining groups. These created strong crosscutting ties, reinforced and complicated by institutionalized pederasty.[111] Patronage played a larger role in decision making than at Athens,[112] and Aristotle described election to the *gerousia* as *dynasteutikê*, "on dynastic principles."[113]

The fluidity of Spartan institutions and the importance of extraconstitutional powers created situations in which it was never clear where exactly the buck stopped. Energetic kings like Agesilaos (reigned 401–360 B.C.E.) or even the regent Pausanias (c. 480–471) could wield far more influence than the formal division of powers would suggest, while others—like Pleistoanax (458–408)—were outmaneuvered by aggressive *ephors*. When the dynamics were more balanced, power was dispersed across several institutional contexts. This could lead to paralysis if no consensus could be reached but also left room for exceptional men from outside the establishment, like Brasidas in the 420s, Lysander between 410 and 400, and Antalcidas in the 380s, to achieve prominence. Hodkinson concludes that

> for all the uniqueness of the Spartiate upbringing and way of life [the political system] perpetuated the existence of a typical Greek aristocracy. Fragmentation of authority and some freedom of decision for the assembly ensured the sharing of influence among the leading lineages which made up this aristocracy. This was threatened by the excessive influence of outstanding individuals and, like all normal aristocracies, the Spartiate aristocracy did its best to control such men.[114]

The very institutions that fostered the obedience and respect for authority that made Sparta's hoplites the firmest and most reliable in Greece perhaps also restricted the scope for effective and imaginative leadership. Herodotus and Thucydides both emphasized the Spartans' slowness,[115] and, once removed from the checks and balances of the political arena at home, Spartan leaders tended to behave erratically and to be unusually open to corruption. Thucydides concluded that "the Spartans proved to be quite the most remarkably helpful enemies that the Athenians could have had."[116]

4.6.3. Syracuse. The sources are very thin: barely half a dozen chapters in Herodotus on the Deinomenid tyrants (485–465 B.C.E.), a scattering of anecdotes in Diodorus and a few passing comments in Thucydides on Syracuse's democracy (465–405), and an extremely hostile tradition about Dionysius I (405–367).

All our anecdotes imply that the tyrants acted solely in pursuit of their own goals, but we have few clues about how they worked with, or around, other institutions in Syracuse. For what it is worth, Gelon was apparently staunchly antidemocratic. He took power in 485 by supporting landed *gamoroi* against the poorer citizens, and Herodotus attributes to him the remark that "the masses are very disagreeable to live with."[117] Some historians think Gelon was less consistently hostile toward the poor than this implies, but the sources they appeal to are not impressive.[118] It is commonly said that Diodorus attests to the survival of the Assembly under Gelon in the 480s because the tyrant appealed to the masses by appearing before them unarmed, but what Diodorus actually says is that Gelon called an assembly of his troops as part of his plan to keep them loyal to him.[119] If anything, the story emphasizes Gelon's dependence on military rather than popular institutions. His use of mercenaries and his willingness to enroll them as citizens suggests that he saw himself as outside Syracusan civil society, as perhaps befitted an interloper from Gela. The much-discussed thank-offerings he and his brother Hieron sent to Delphi and Olympia for their victories in 480 and 474 are ambiguous. Gelon styled himself a Syacusan, while Hieron distinguished between "Hieron, the son of Deinomenes, and the Syracusans."[120] Diodorus (11.38, 66) calls Gelon and Hieron *basileis*, but there is no way to know exactly what constitutional implications this description has. Pindar three times called Hieron a *basileus*, meaning constitutional king, and once a *tyrannos*, or unconstitutional ruler. Herodotus also used both terms, and the fact that Pindar used both titles in a single poem suggests that we should not seek legal niceties here.[121]

Syracuse's relations with its subject cities were very different from Athens' or Sparta's; in fact, we can only call them dynastic. Gelon began as tyrant of Gela, then moved to Syracuse in 485 and put Gela under his brother Hieron. Gelon then cemented an alliance with Theron, tyrant of Sicily's second-strongest city, Akragas, by marrying Theron's daughter Demarete. When Gelon died, Hieron promoted himself from Gela to Syracuse, married both the daughter of Anaxilas (the tyrant of Rhegion) and Theron's niece, put his surviving brother Polyzelus in charge of Gela, married the widowed Demarete to him, and married Polyzelus's daughter off to Theron. Gelon and Hieron created a web of royal kinship worthy of early modern Europe and utterly unlike Aegean politics.

Aristotle described the regime set up in Syracuse after the fall of the tyrants in 465 as a *politeia*, or middle ground between aristocracy and democracy. There has been much debate over whether we should consider it democratic.[122] Most historians stress its differences from Athens. Consolo Langher, for instance, emphasizes the influence of the *chariestatoi*, or "best men,"[123] although Diodorus's descriptions do not really justify this. Diodorus's most significant comment on the *chariestatoi* is at 11.92, where he speaks of disagreements in 451 B.C.E. over what to do with the Sicel leader Ducetius when he surrendered. Diodorus says that the mass of citizens favored a hard line and that the *chariestatoi* were more lenient. In other passages, Diodorus emphasizes demagogic elements in the 450s, the brief establishment of an equivalent to the Athenian ostracism, and threats of tyranny.[124] Diodorus's perceptions may have been colored by his knowledge of Athenian democracy, though, and there are hints that elected officers did hold more power at Syracuse than Athens. Thucydides makes the board of generals sound important in 415, and even after the reforms of Diocles gave new powers to the people in 412, Diodorus says that in 406 a group of *archontes* fined Dionysius for speaking out against the generals.[125] But overall, while there were clear differences between Athenian and Syracusan political systems in the mid-fifth century, both seem to be variants on the same underlying set of principles, with great power vested in popular assemblies.

Our understanding of Dionysius I's constitutional position and methods of ruling is no better. He used the title *strategos autokrator*, "sole-ruling general," and an office of admiral is attested. His treaty with Athens in 368 definitely refers to civic institutions other than the tyrant himself but is broken at the crucial point.[126]

4.7. Religion

Greek religion was polytheistic.[127] At its core were a dozen Olympian gods, who had come to power through a great struggle with Kronos, the Titans, and Typhoeus. Greek origin stories have much in common with Near Eastern examples from the Bronze Age on.[128] Zeus and Hera, who behaved much like a human couple, headed the pantheon. There was general agreement on its structure, although gods were worshipped with different epithets in different cities. Alongside the Olympians was a host of semidivine heroes, nature spirits, and chthonic powers known only from curse inscriptions, most of them peculiar to one location. These too have strong parallels in the Near East.[129]

In comparison with most ancient Mediterranean societies, though, and especially those in the Near East, religious authority was remarkably weak in classical Greece. At Athens, there were a few priesthoods reserved to specific families or descent groups, but most were open to all citizens and filled by lot.[130] Isocrates even said that "they believe that the office of ... priest is one that anyone can fill."[131] Herodotus was amazed that in Persia a religious specialist was required before an offering could be made to the gods; in Greece, anyone could sacrifice.[132] The Delphic oracle had considerable prestige, but even this could be challenged. When the Athenians sent to Delphi to ask whether they should resist Persia in 480, the answer they got seemed to be saying no, so they sent back for another and got a more satisfactory response.[133] In Sparta, oracles carried more weight, which Hodkinson ascribes to a constant search for sources of authority in a fragmented political structure.[134] It certainly earned the Spartans a reputation for being foolishly superstitious.

In Athens, religion seems to have been carefully circumscribed. Attempts to link religion and politics were always disastrous, as when Themistocles built a small shrine of Artemis Aristoboule (i.e., Artemis of the Wise Counsel, referring to his own advising role at the battle of Salamis in 480) next to his house in the 470s. The temple is unassuming enough, but Plutarch says that it outraged the Athenians and played a part in Themistocles' fall from favor and flight from the city.[135]

In striking contrast to its role in most ancient societies, religion did little to legitimize or stimulate Greek state formation. Assyrian kings claimed to feel driven to make war to force their earthly rivals to recognize Ashur's supremacy in the divine hierarchy; Cyrus announced that he had to take over Babylon to restore the religious order that Nabonidus had neglected; and his Achaemenid successors represented themselves as fighting to ensure the victory of the Truth over the Lie.[136] Athenians, Spartans, and Syracusans, however, made no such claims. The most explicit discussion of the relationship between divine and interstate power relations comes in Thucydides' Melian Dialogue, when Thucydides has the Athenians say

> So far as the favor of the gods is concerned, we think we have as much right to that as you have. Our aims and our actions are perfectly consistent with the beliefs that men hold about the gods and with the principles that govern their own conduct. Our opinion of the gods and our knowledge of men lead us to conclude that it is a general and necessary law of nature to rule whatever one can. This is not a law that we made ourselves, nor were we the first to act upon it when it was made. We found it already in existence, and we shall leave it to exist forever among those who come after us. We are merely acting in accordance with it, and we know that you or anybody else with the same power as ours would be acting in precisely the same way. And therefore, so far as the gods are concerned, we see no good reason why we should fear to be at a disadvantage.[137]

Athenian justifications of power never appeal to special relationships with the gods; they are ruthlessly secular, either stating rational principles, as at Melos in 416, or claiming that Athens' service in the Persian Wars justifies power over other states, as at Sparta in 432.[138] Temples played a part in war and state building, but more as repositories of wealth than as dispensers of divine favor. The Athenian state borrowed heavily from the goddess Athena, and Thucydides had Pericles worry that the Spartans might plunder the treasuries of Olympia and Delphi to hire mercenary sailors, but there is no sign that Athenians thought the gods required them to extend their state.[139]

5. Key Concepts

5.1. Archê, *Empire, Foreignness, and State*

Greek historians conventionally divide the history of the Athenian "Empire" into two phases: an early one, when the organization was largely consensual and aimed at common action against Persia, and a later one, when the Athenians ruled more harshly and in their own interests. Historians often call the first phase the Delian League (a purely modern term, with no basis in the sources) after the sacred island of Delos, where the organization's treasury was kept, and the second phase the Athenian Empire.

The obvious starting point is Thucydides' terminology. He normally calls the political unit led by Athens an *archê*, literally "rule." He seems to have carefully distinguished between *archê* and *hêgemonia*, "hegemony," which denoted a looser form of alliance or control.[140] At 1.97 he described the fairly consensual anti-Persian alliance of 478 as *hêgemonia* and Athens' unpopular control in 431 as *archê*. He said that *archê* was based on overwhelming *dynamis*, or "power," and that those over whom the Athenians wielded their *archê* could be said to be enslaved.[141]

Historians normally translate *archê* as "empire," but, despite their careful philological analyses of Thucydides' Greek, they seem not to worry much about specifying what "empire" means in English. For example, not once in his 620-page classic *The Athenian Empire* did Russell Meiggs say what he thought an empire was. But this hardly made him unusual among classical historians. In introducing a collection of essays titled *Imperialism in the Ancient World*, Peter Garnsey and Dick Whittaker noted that most of the contributors shied away from defining "empire" or "imperialism." Garnsey and Whittaker suggested that the contributors' largely implicit models broke down into two types. They called these definitions "restricted" (i.e., very historically specific and grounded in the ancient actors' own terminology) and "abstract" (i.e., drawing on generalized, cross-culturally applicable models of "empire").[142] In the chapter looking at fifth-century Athens, Finley quite rightly noted that the former practice "give[s] excessive weight to purely formal considerations, which, if adopted rigorously, would fragment the category 'empire' so much as to render it empty and useless," ruling out comparative analysis.[143] For example, some historians feel that "empire" is too strong a word for what the Athenians created, presumably (though they rarely spell this out) because they are making implicit comparisons with other imperial systems, finding the Athenian *archê* wanting in some crucial respect(s). Rather than specifying an analytical framework that would work for the particular case of Athens while also clarifying the comparisons that must underlie their unease with the word "empire," some classicists suggest that (despite Thucydides' usage) we should translate *archê* as "hegemony" or else refuse to translate the Greek at all, speaking only of *archê* or *symmachia*.[144] Wolfgang Schuller made a more promising start by beginning his study of the Athenian "Empire" with Weber's distinction between *direkte* and *indirekte Herrschaft*, but, instead of making this the basis for a typology of forms of *Herrschaft* that could clarify what kind of organization the Athenians created and its significance for Greek history, Schuller used Weber's categories to redescribe Thucydides' diachronic *hêgemonia-archê* development: Athens began with *indirekte Herrschaft*, then moved toward *direkte Herrschaft*.[145]

Finley suggested that we should begin instead by recognizing that "Common sense is right...there have been throughout history structures that belong within a single class on substantive grounds, namely, the exercise of authority (or power or control) by one state over one or more other states (or communities or peoples) for an extended period of time."[146] If we limit defining empire to a philological exercise, with the central question being whether we translate *archê* as "hegemony," "empire," or *direkte Herrschaft* or—worse still—just transliterate it, we are ducking the analytical challenge.

We must therefore look outside classicists' analyses for useful tools. We might begin with the political scientist Michael Doyle's suggestion, in his influential book *Empires*, that

> Empire...is a relationship, formal or informal, in which one state controls the effective political sovereignty of another political society. It can be achieved by force, by political collaboration, by economic, social, or cultural dependence. Imperialism is simply the process of establishing or maintaining an empire.
>
> These definitions...distinguish empires from the rest of world politics by the actual foreign control of who rules and what rules a subordinate polity.[147]

Doyle emphasizes political boundaries: an imperial power is "a foreign state" that imposes political control or effective sovereignty over another state. Thus, the study of empires is primarily a matter of international relations. Doyle traces this perspective back to Thucydides himself.[148]

Doyle's definition of empire makes an interesting contrast with the historical sociologist Michael Mann's summary of the mainstream Weberian definition of the state as:

1. a *differentiated* set of institutions and personnel, embodying
2. *centrality*, in the sense that political relations radiate outwards from a centre to cover a
3. *territorially demarcated area*, over which it exercises
4. a monopoly of *authoritative binding rule-making*, backed up by a monopoly of the means of physical violence.[149]

We should immediately note major overlaps between Doyle's empire and Mann's state: both are territorially extensive hierarchical political organizations, through which one group of people exercises control over others. Charles Tilly, another historical sociologist, makes this explicit, defining the state in such a way that it includes empires and city-states as subtypes:

> Let us define states as coercion-wielding organizations that are distinct from households and kinship groups and exercise clear priority in some respects over all other organizations within substantial territories. The term therefore includes city-states, empires, theocracies, and many other forms of government, but excludes tribes, lineages, firms, and churches as such.[150]

Borrowing one of Finley's favorite analytical tools, we might envision a spectrum of territorially extensive coercion-wielding organizations. At one end are empires; at the other, states. The empire end of the spectrum would be characterized by a strong sense of foreignness between rulers and ruled. In the extreme case, all people in all regions incorporated into the empire would consider themselves to be ethnically, religiously, and/or culturally distinct from the rulers, belonging "naturally" to autonomous units. The nineteenth-century Ottoman and the early twentieth-century Austro-Hungarian empires tended toward this end of the spectrum. On the whole, the more recently the territorially extensive organization has been created, the stronger this sense will be and the closer the organization will stand to the empire end of the spectrum. With the passage of time, and with institutional and cultural change, the sense of difference may decline, and the "empire" will move toward the "state" end of the spectrum. Most of today's well-established, legitimate nation-states were at one time much nearer to the empire end of the spectrum and over time moved toward statehood. In Benedict Anderson's famous phrase, the state is an imagined community.[151] The case of France, united now for the best part of a millennium, illustrates this well. In the fourteenth and fifteenth centuries, the English king's claim that parts of what we now call France belonged to him seemed plausible enough that the two countries spent more than a hundred years at war; whereas by the late nineteenth century there was such consensus around Frenchness and the idea of a French state that detaching regions was unthinkable and Germany's annexation of Alsace and Lorraine in 1871 could be considered a *casus belli*. By contrast, the former Soviet Union, created in 1917 on the ruins of the Russian Empire, and Yugoslavia, manufactured in 1919 out of peoples who had until recently been subjects of the Habsburg and Ottoman empires, arguably never moved far from the imperial end of the spectrum (though we might feel that Yugoslavia was territorially not extensive enough to count as a proper empire, whatever its ethnic, religious, and cultural diversity).[152]

Fifth-century Athens was not an empire. In fact, we might even debate whether Athens was on the spectrum from statehood to empire at all before the fifth century. Borrowing now an analytical tool from Charles Tilly, we can broaden our model from a Finleyan one-dimensional spectrum to a two-dimensional space, with a scale from state-ness to empire-ness along the horizontal axis and power (some combination of military force, revenue, and organizational capacity) on the vertical

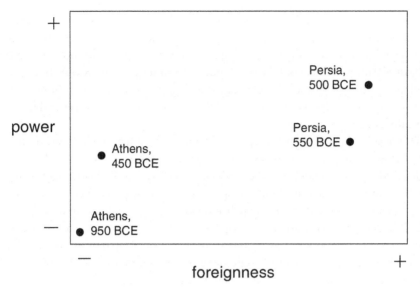

FIGURE 4.4. *A schematic representation of state power and the sense of foreignness between rulers and ruled in Athens and Persia*

(fig. 4.4). We could represent Athens' history from the tenth century B.C.E. through the fifth largely as one of the efforts of some men to create and monopolize offices through which they could command the obedience and resources of others and the efforts of some of those others to grab these offices from them and/or to resist this process. Athens always scored low on empire-ness, so its history played out at the left-hand side of this box. Persian history, by contrast, all happened on the right hand side of figure 4.4. Cyrus I's kingdom in 550 was almost as much an empire as Darius I's in 500, in the sense of being large, hierarchical, and characterized by a strong sense of foreignness between rulers and ruled; what changed—particularly with Darius's reforms in the 510s—was that the empire's military, financial, and administrative strength increased. As the diagram shows, I believe that already in 550 the Persian Empire had more state power than Athens ever mustered, but, thanks to bad luck, poor judgment, and tactical weaknesses, even by 480 it could not project its power well enough to defeat the Greeks.

Overall, the would-be rulers in Athens and most other Greek cities did not do very well. Classical democracy was a compromise between the need to have state institutions and the mass of ordinary citizens' desire to prevent anyone from controlling them. The Assembly and lawcourts were the scenes of endless negotiations over these conflicting principles.[153] The victory over Persia in 480 and the particular way the Ionians constituted postwar resistance in 477 gave the Athenians a chance to expand their state power greatly. They pursued this ruthlessly for the next fifty years, so that in the 420s the Greater Athenian State was vastly more powerful than

Athens had been before the Persian War. But Athens was scarcely more of an empire in 425 than it had been in 485; it continued to rule an ethnically, culturally, and religiously homogeneous organization of Ionian Greeks. The story most relevant to classical Athens is not about the development from state to empire but about the development from a very small and loose form of state—not so different from what the historical sociologist Gary Runciman calls a proto-state—to a larger and more centralized one.[154]

This observation has four consequences. First, while Athens might have become a multiethnic empire in time (had it, say, permanently taken over Egypt in the 450s or defeated Syracuse, then captured Carthage in the 410s, as Alcibiades apparently hoped),[155] in reality the transition to empire never even began, and any possibility was permanently aborted by Athens' defeat in 404 B.C.E. Second, the kinds of questions historians normally ask about empires—particularly postcolonial questions about hybridity, mimicry, or the creation of third spaces inspired by humanists like Edward Said and Homi Bhabha[156]—are just not very appropriate to the Athenian case. Third, the organization we normally call the Athenian Empire was simply the most capital-intensive of several paths toward state formation being pursued by fifth-century Greeks (and their neighbors). Fourth, state formation, by which I mean the process of expanding central power, was the most important developmental force in the fifth-century Greek world.

Doyle's international-relations approach, focusing on the imperial end of the state-empire spectrum, certainly helps us think about some aspects of the Greater Athenian State, but Thucydides himself is clear that it cannot explain everything. In a famous pair of passages, he has Pericles and Cleon characterize Athenian power over other cities as being like that of a *tyrannos*, or sole ruler within a city-state.[157] Thucydides may have invented this metaphor himself, or it may have been common coinage in the late fifth century. Either way, some Athenians saw what Athens was doing to the Aegean in terms of a model of state powers. We should also remember that Thucydides begins his account not with an analysis of imperialism in the sense that Doyle defines it but with the "Archaeology," a review of the history of increasing levels of state control over financial and military resources and the ability of rulers to project power. As Robert Connor and Lisa Kallet-Marx insist, Thucydides' decision to begin this way shows that this was how he thought about the Athenian *archê*—in terms quite similar to Mann's definition of statehood.[158]

5.2. Foreignness

I am suggesting, like many comparativists in the past twenty years, that we think of empires as a type of state, characterized by a strong sense of foreignness between rulers and ruled. I believe that calling the Athenians' fifth-century *archê* an empire is a mistake because the sense of foreignness was, by the standards of the other ancient empires described in this volume, very weak. Since so much depends on this distinction, I should say a few words about what I mean by "foreignness."

I am not claiming that there was *no* sense of foreignness within the Greater Athenian State. Naxians and Chians knew they were not Athenians. Yet, we can also be certain that they felt less different from Athenians than they did from Persians, Egyptians, or Macedonians. People commonly measure foreignness along multiple axes, but, any way we look at the Greek evidence, we have to conclude that the sense of difference was very limited in the fifth-century Athenian *archê*.

First, I take ethnicity, normally defined in the social sciences as a discursively constituted identity built around putative descent from a common ancestor.[159] There is often disagreement within a community over categorization: Rome, Carthage, and Athens all had multiple origin stories, allowing people to select the version that worked best for them at a particular moment. The idea that all Greeks were *Hellênes*, sharing descent from Hellen, goes back at least to the seventh century.[160] Many cultural historians think it was merely one among many stories in archaic Greece and gained general acceptance only after the Persian War of 480–479;[161] whether that is correct or not, Hellen certainly seems to have dominated Greek ethnic thought in the mid- and late fifth century.

Rulers and subjects alike in the Greater Athenian State overwhelmingly considered themselves Hellenes; in fact, they overwhelmingly considered themselves Ionic Hellenes, descendants (in Hesiod's version) of Hellen's grandson Ion, son of Xouthos. Other Greeks, such as the Spartans and the Syracusans, saw themselves as Dorians, descendants of Xouthos's brother Doros; others still traced their roots back to Hellen's third son, Aeolus, or to his grandson (Ion's brother) Achaios. We hear of competing genealogies within several "Ionian" cities, including Athens,[162] but as early as about 600 B.C.E. the Athenian statesman Solon could call his city "the oldest land of Ionia,"[163] from which all other Ionian cities had been founded. In the fifth century, this version seems to have dominated Athenian thought.[164] The Greater Athenian State was, then, not just an organization of people belonging to a single ethnic group, the Greeks; it was an organization of people belonging to a single ethnic subgroup, the Ionians. The sense of ethnic difference between rulers and ruled within the Greater Athenian State was tiny, unlike that in Assyria, Persia, Rome, and Byzantium.

Some scholars treat language as a central issue in ethnicity. Ionic, Doric, and other dialects of Greek definitely sounded different, and individual cities often had their own variants of the common alphabet. Greeks were aware of these differences, but they do not seem to have posed major barriers to communication or—by themselves—to have been a basis for constructing distinct identities;[165] in any case, since nearly all members of the Greater Athenian State used the Ionic dialect, we have to conclude that the sense of linguistic difference between rulers and ruled within the Greater Athenian State was as tiny as the sense of ethnic difference and much less than that found in Assyria, Persia, Rome, and Byzantium.

So too their religious differences. Divine epithets, sacred calendars, and even the members of the pantheon did vary from city to city, and Greek and non-Greek gods could be equated with one another; yet, in the fifth century, there was clearly a recognizably Greek religious system.[166] Indeed, Herodotus could have the Athenians cite shared gods, temples, and sacrifices as one of the main defining features of "Greekness" (*to Hellênikon*).[167] Again unlike in Assyria, Persia, Rome, and Byzantium, the sense of religious difference between rulers and ruled within the Greater Athenian State was tiny.

We get the same results if we look for cultural differences more loosely defined. Greek culture was not monolithic,[168] but its variations seem very small by comparison with those in other empires. I suggested in an earlier study[169] that four broad regional material culture groups developed in Greece in the eleventh century B.C.E. The Greater Athenian State lay almost entirely within the central (Aegean) group, and by the late sixth century the differences between the four groups were rapidly disappearing, as courtyard houses, temples in the canonical styles, *kouros* and *korê* statues, and black-glaze pottery drove out archaic variations. Again unlike Assyria, Persia, Rome, and Byzantium, the sense of cultural difference between rulers and ruled within the Greater Athenian State was tiny.

For all these reasons, I conclude that lumping fifth-century Athens in with the genuine multiethnic empires discussed in this book's other chapters would be a mistake. Residents in the subject cities often did feel different from the Athenians, but their differences were political, rather than ethnic, linguistic, religious, or cultural. We will understand the fifth-century transformation of the Aegean most fully if we look at it through the lens of state formation.

5.3. State Formation

"The state" has been a central concept in social scientific and humanistic thought for centuries and means many things to many people. According to Oswyn Murray, among Greek historians "To the Germans the *polis* [city-state] can only be described in a handbook of constitutional law; the French *polis* is a form of Holy Communion; the English *polis* is a historical accident; while the American *polis* combines the practices of a Mafia convention with the principles of justice and individual freedom."[170]

Murray is right to emphasize the weight of national schools of thought, but we should not overlook the way that the empiricist, philological German-language tradition provided a shared framework uniting the diverse national schools until well into the twentieth century. Intellectual historians normally see Jakob Burckhardt's 1890 classic, *Griechische Kulturgeschichte*, as the linchpin. Burckhardt argued that the city-state both expressed the Greek *Geist* and provided the framework for its development, acting as a kind of hothouse in which freedom and rationality could grow. As scholars came to terms with Schliemann's discovery of Greek Bronze Age civilization in the 1870s, they generally concluded that the Greek state, in Burckhardt's sense, evolved out of tribal societies left behind by the fall of Mycenae and reached its paradigmatic form between the eighth and the fourth century B.C.E.[171]

In the 1970s and 1980s, this model came under severe attack for its idealism and lack of fit with the facts,[172] but by then a new approach, coming out of Anglo-American archaeology and evolutionary anthropology, was gaining ground. This tradition thought about "the state" not as a *Geist* but as a cross-culturally applicable level of socioeconomic complexity normally defined in terms of social differentiation and hierarchy, recognized archaeologically through settlement patterns, monuments, and forms of display.[173] Anthony Snodgrass's *Archaeology and the Rise of the Greek State*[174] was the crucial contribution to this line of thought. From this perspective, "state formation" tends to be seen as a point of transition from simple, pre-state structures, to more complex, state-level ones, including permanent social stratification and centralized monopolies on resources.[175] Like the idealist approach, the neo-evolutionist tradition tends to conceive state formation as a one-time transition, normally placing it in the eighth century.

Historians and archaeologists often decide to borrow social-scientific concepts just at the moment they lose credibility in their donor disciplines, and state formation is no exception. The most influential neo-evolutionary theoretical statements appeared in the 1960s,[176] even though political scientists (particularly in the United States) had already begun retreating from "the state" as an analytical category in the 1950s, on the grounds that it could not be separated adequately from cognate concepts.[177] In the 1980s, neo-evolutionary approaches to state formation became firmly established in Greek history and archaeology, just as prehistorians in other fields started to abandon them; by this time, however, political scientists had rediscovered the concept and were busy "bringing the state back in."[178]

Political scientists' new approaches to state formation in 1980s and 1990s differed strongly from older ones, particularly in emphasizing state formation as an ongoing process rather than a one-time transition. George Steinmetz argued that

> The study of state-formation is inherently historical, because it focuses on the creation of durable states and the transformation of basic structural features of these states. Sometimes state-formation is understood as a mythic initial moment in which centralized, coercion-wielding, hegemonic organizations are created within a given territory. All activities that follow this original era are then described as "policy-making" rather than "state-formation." But states are never formed once and for all. It is more fruitful to view state-formation as an ongoing process of structural change and not as a one-time event.[179]

This, I suggest, is the most fruitful way to think about classical Greece. The eighth century was a turning point in the history of Greek state formation, with a sharp increase in the power of central authorities, which began building monumental temples, waging wars, and enforcing codified laws,[180] but while the city-states of the eighth through sixth centuries were more powerful than the communities of the preceding "Dark Age," and while they boasted many more remarkable cultural achievements than did many ancient states—and particularly the other empires discussed in this book—they were strikingly weak. They had tiny revenues and minimal coercive powers. Most states relied on harbor and market dues, rent from state properties, and (where available) income from mines. There was virtually no direct taxation; land taxes and poll taxes were considered tyrannical, and income taxes were unimaginable. Normally states spent most of their minuscule income on cult activity. War was capital-intensive but (as noted in section 4) in archaic times made few demands on state revenues: the wealthier citizens who made up the hoplite phalanx normally supplied their own arms and armor and received no pay for whatever time they put into training. A single battle in the agricultural off-season settled most campaigns. Most big cities made substantial investments in a defensive wall, but we know of few sustained sieges (the mythological ten-year case of Troy aside), and logistical support for armies on campaign was virtually nonexistent.[181]

This began to change in the late sixth century.[182] Sparta's hoplites must have been better trained than others since at least the seventh century, but in the sixth the whole structure of the state was deformed to allow them to train full time. Revenue transfers were in kind and from helots to Spartiates, rather than involving centralized taxation and administration, but the Spartan army nevertheless represented heavy investment in human capital. In a few states, particularly those that relied on imports and therefore had a large pool of sailors (e.g., Corinth, Samos, Aegina, Chios, Corcyra, Syracuse, and Athens), state navies began to be a significant factor after 550. From Song-dynasty China to Habsburg Spain, states have consistently financed their fleets privately as far as they could,[183] and we should probably assume that archaic Greek *poleis* operated the same way, commandeering or hiring merchants' *pentekonters* when they needed to fight. In the late sixth and early fifth centuries, though, population growth increased the quantities of food being traded and therefore the revenue generated by indirect taxes, giving some states the possibility of spending more lavishly. The Athenians' decision to spend the income from the silver strike of 483 on a fleet produced a quantum leap in the costs of war and, presumably, the sophistication of administration.[184] Athens, Syracuse, and a few other cities then began concentrating much greater powers at the center, threatening to transform old ways of life. To make sense of this we need to move beyond thinking of state formation as a one-time transition toward thinking of it historically.

5.4. *Forms of the State in Greece*

In several earlier essays, I have suggested that the social structures of archaic and classical Greek city-states do not fit well into the now-conventional evolutionary thinking about complex society.[185] I tried to make this point by comparing an ideal type of classical city-state organization with Ernest Gellner's hugely influential model of the "agro-literate state" (fig. 4.5). Gellner based this on Emile Durkheim's century-old theory of mechanical solidarity, suggesting that

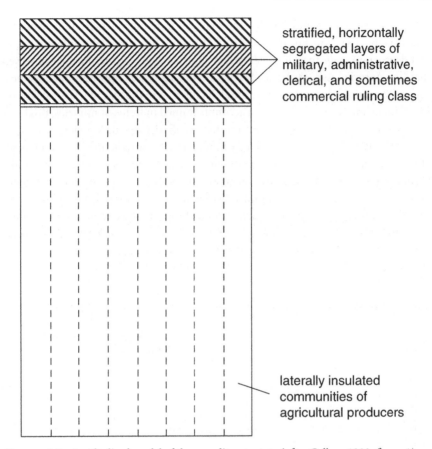

stratified, horizontally
segregated layers of
military, administrative,
clerical, and sometimes
commercial ruling class

laterally insulated
communities of
agricultural producers

FIGURE 4.5. *An idealized model of the agro-literate state (after Gellner 1983: figure 1)*

In the characteristic agro-literate polity, the ruling class forms a small minority of the population, rigidly separate from the great majority of direct agricultural producers, or peasants. Generally speaking, its ideology exaggerates rather than underplays the inequality of classes and the degree of separation of the ruling stratum.... Below the world of the horizontally stratified minority at the top, there is another world, that of the laterally separated petty communities of the lay members of society.... The state is interested in extracting taxes, maintaining the peace, and not much else, and has no interest in promoting lateral communication between its subject communities.[186]

Fig. 4.5 is not a good representation of classical or archaic Greek city-states. These city-states knew no rigidly separated ruling class lording it over a downtrodden peasantry. Insofar as they had military, priestly, and administrative elites, these were only very loosely defined. Fig. 4.5 has no room for the free citizens who formed the core of the city-states. Because Greek city-states were so small and had so few legal barriers between town and country, their villages were much less laterally insulated than in Gellner's vision. Freedom and equality meant fundamentally different things in a democratic *polis* than in a Gellnerian agrarian state. Gellner himself observed that "the Agrarian Age was basically a period of stagnation, oppression, and superstition. Exceptions do occur, but we are all inclined, as in the case of Classical Greece, to call them 'miracles.'"[187] Like most accounts framed in terms of miracles, this lacks explanatory power, but it does bring out the peculiarity of Greek society.

The Greater Athenian State created a fundamental contradiction. Figure 4.6 is my attempt to represent the social structure of classical Athens as seen from the inside. It differs radically from Gellner's generalized social structure of agrarian states in figure 4.5. Athens actively promoted democratic structures in other city-states in the fifth century, nudging them further toward the structure represented in figure 4.6. But, when we take a broader geographical perspective, looking at Athens and other city-states from the outside, we see that the Athenian *archê*—which indirectly

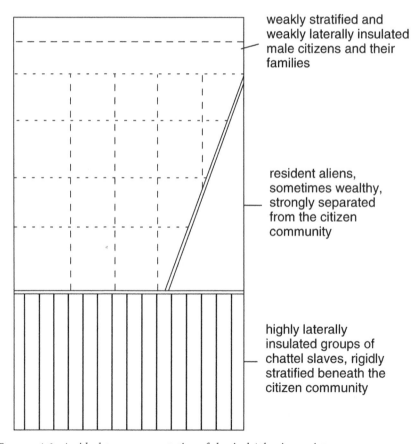

weakly stratified and weakly laterally insulated male citizens and their families

resident aliens, sometimes wealthy, strongly separated from the citizen community

highly laterally insulated groups of chattel slaves, rigidly stratified beneath the citizen community

FIGURE 4.6. *An ideal-type representation of classical Athenian society*

created many of the revenues that underwrote the structure of figure 4.6—was gradually converting the Aegean *as a whole* into something very like figure 4.5. The Athenians were turning themselves from an egalitarian citizen community into the stratified, horizontally segregated layers of a military and administrative ruling class, standing above the laterally insulated communities of subjected *poleis*. In effect, figure 4.6 was becoming the top part of figure 4.5. Athens imposed a single foreign policy and carried it out with a single, Aegean-wide armed force. Fixed, annual contributions from each city—basically the same thing as taxes—paid for this armed force. Athenian administrators collected these payments and intervened on a regular basis in local politics. They sent out administrators to the subject cities and judged many of these cities' most important lawsuits, sometimes requiring the defendants to come to Athens for trial. Athens became the Aegean's economic central place and imposed its own weights, measures, and coinage on the other cities. Contrary to traditional practice in the Aegean, Athenians seized or bought land in the territories of other cities. Not content with all this, Athens tried to turn the Aegean into an imagined Athenian community, pressing old claims to be the ancestral homeland of all Ionian Greeks and integrating the subject cities into Athenian rituals. The overall effect of these changes in the fifth century was to begin relegating the subject cities to the status of Gellner's laterally separated communities of primary producers and promoting Athens itself to the status of capital city of a territorial, national state of Ionian Greeks. Athens was becoming home to a ruling elite interested in extracting taxes, maintaining the peace, and defending itself—that is, something Gellner would have immediately recognized as an agro-literate state.

The Greater Athenian State was an unusual formation, to be sure. It combined male democracy within the metropolis with the self-interested objectives of security, raw materials, manpower, rents, and taxation, while providing peace and trade as public goods. It ruled through a combination of bureaucracy and delegation to local elites, integrating the cities economically through market exchange. Probably most free men in the Greater Athenian State benefited from it to some degree, though Athenian citizens (and, according to Thucydides,[188] rich Athenian citizens above all) surely reaped the greatest rewards. Its social character was hierarchical, with Athenians at the top.

Probably no other state in history has had exactly this combination of traits, although some (particularly, I think, medieval Venice and Genoa) come quite close. More important than looking for precise analogies, though, is the fact that every element in my brief description is drawn from the historian Niall Ferguson's simple typology of forms of power (table 4.2). Ferguson says his table "should be read as a menu rather than a grid":[189] each historical case mixes and matches features from each column, creating a unique variation on the broadly shared theme of state and imperial power.

By 421 b.c.e., the Aegean as a whole looked something like figure 4.5. Had Athens won the Peloponnesian War (whether by defeating Sparta outright or just

Table 4.2. Niall Ferguson's "Menu" of Variations on the Theme of State and Imperial Power (Ferguson 2004: Table 1)

Metropolitan System	Self-interested Objectives	Public Goods	Methods of Rule	Economic System	Cui Bono?	Social Character
Tyranny	Security	Peace	Military	Plantation	Ruling elite	Genocidal
Aristocracy	Communications	Trade	Bureaucracy	Feudal	Metropolitan populace	Hierarchical
Oligarchy	Land	Investment	Settlement	Mercantilist	Settlers	Converting
Democracy	Raw materials	Law	NGOs	Market	Local elites	Assimilative
	Treasure	Governance	Firms	Mixed	All inhabitants	
	Manpower	Education	Delegation to local elites	Planned		
	Rents	Conversion				
	Taxation	Health				

achieving Pericles' goal of avoiding defeat), this process of state formation would have continued. This, I suggest, is one of the most important changes that the Greater Athenian State wrought. The second major change is that—as Thucydides insisted[190]—the growth of Athenian power was significant not just as a fact in its own right but because it also generated fear in other city-states, putting pressure on them either to submit, accelerating the process, or to react, accelerating a process of secondary state formation. In the language of international relations theorists, they had to bandwagon with Athens or balance it. Whichever they did, though, the result was that state formation accelerated. This was the most important social, economic, and cultural process in classical Greece, and the Athenian Empire, as we conventionally but misleadingly call it, can be understood only in the context of a larger process of state formation embracing the whole Greek world and even the non-Greek world beyond it.

6. The Greater Athenian State

In this section I attempt to document my claim that, beginning with the creation of the so-called Delian League in 478–477, Athens moved the Aegean toward a social structure like that in figure 4.5. I hope to show that, far from creating an empire—defined, as above, as a territorially extensive, hierarchical, multiethnic political organization with a strong sense of foreignness between rulers and ruled—fifth-century Athens tried to develop an Ionian Greek territorial state with Athens as its capital city. This structure cannot meaningfully be compared with the Assyrian, Persian, Roman, and Byzantine empires discussed in the rest of the book; rather, it was the first stage in the transformation of a city-state into a Greater Athenian State.

I review the surviving evidence under four broad headings of political/military, economic, administrative, and cultural changes. All the data I present are already well known to classical scholars, but, I believe, their significance has been obscured by the lack of clearly focused questions. I conclude (1) that Athens was in the process of becoming the capital of a larger territorial state; (2) that this process began immediately in 478–477 but accelerated sharply after 431; (3) that war and preparation for war were its primary motors; and (4) that there is every reason to assume that the process would have continued had Athens not been defeated in 404. One implication is that the most profitable comparison for fifth-century-B.C.E. Greece might be fifth-century-B.C.E. Rome, and the most useful question to ask about such a comparison might be why Rome succeeded in breaking out of the city-state framework to become first a territorial state and then a genuine multiethnic empire, while Athens did not.

In section 7, I look outside the Greater Athenian State at other examples of state formation in fifth-century Greece (particularly Sparta and Syracuse). I review the surviving evidence and argue that in most cases state formation either began or speeded up in response to Athenian state formation. The one case where this is not exactly true, Sparta, is also the most important; and, in a rather interesting way, the exception that really does prove the rule.

6.1. Political/Military Institutions

Athens took three major political/military steps, creating an Aegean-wide foreign policy, an Aegean-wide military force that monopolized legitimate violence, and general peace within the Greater Athenian State.

6.1.1. Foreign Policy. Even a casual reading of Herodotus reveals how common wars were in the sixth-century Aegean. The Persian threat encouraged some cities to set aside their rivalries in 481, and, after Sparta's withdrawal in 478–477, those Greeks who gathered at Delos were eager to continue this unity against Persia. Thucydides says that the *proschêma* ("pretext" or "announced intention") of the alliance was to plunder Persian territory in compensation for their losses in the war of 480–479. Later, though, he has various critics of Athens say that the goal was to defend Ionia against Persia or to defend the freedom of the Greeks.[191] There has been intense debate over what the "original policy" was.[192] The evidence is insufficient to resolve them, but, since the main activities in the 470s and 460s were clearly directed against Persia, we do not need to go into details here.[193] Andocides, writing ninety years later, claims that Athens was interested only in gaining power over the other cities, but Thucydides—hardly an Athenian apologist—presents the story less cynically.[194]

Thucydides and Diodorus both say that policy was decided in a general assembly (*synodos*) set up on Delos.[195] We do not know whether it was unicameral, with all cities having one vote, or bicameral, with a chamber of allies balancing decisions made in the Assembly at Athens, but Thucydides' comments at 3.10 make most sense if there was a unicameral assembly. By 415 the Athenians were acting without consulting the other cities, even when they provided troops,[196] and Thucydides' silence about the assembly of cities in his detailed account of the events of leading to the outbreak of the Peloponnesian War strongly suggests that Athens had taken complete control by 432. Meiggs argued that the transition came during the 440s.[197]

All the cities swore to have the same friends and enemies for all time,[198] and Athens did not tolerate departures from the Aegean-wide policy. Diodorus says that by 464 some cities found Athenian control oppressive and took to plotting among themselves, scorning the general assembly.[199] When Naxos tried to leave the association, probably some time around 470, Athens used the fleet to prevent this, and, Thucydides adds, "later the same thing also happened to each of the other cities as circumstances arose."[200] Athens fought major wars to keep Thasos (465–463), Euboea (447–446), Samos (440–439), and Lesbos (428–427) under control. On the whole, the other cities supported Athens in these endeavors. After 413, there was more general resistance to Athens, although some cities remained very loyal.[201]

6.1.2. Armed Forces. This unitary foreign policy depended on united armed forces under central control. In 477, the cities appointed Aristides "the Just," a prominent Athenian statesman, to work out what each of them would contribute to such a force. Some provided ships and crews (above all Athens, which had two hundred triremes, but also Samos, Chios, and Lesbos), while others made cash contributions. Aristides' assessments won unanimous approval,[202] and he appointed Athenian treasurers (*hellenotamiai*) to oversee the finances.[203]

Most of the contributions recorded in the tribute lists from 454 on are much smaller than the two or three talents that it cost to keep a trireme at sea for a summer campaign. United armed forces provided economies of scale; even the tiniest cities could contribute, and, by pooling its resources, the organization could muster greater forces than the individual cities could ever assemble. In effect, the cities bought security from Persian attack very cheaply, and this must be the main reason that the organization was initially so popular. Returning to the calculations I made in note 2, subjects of the Greater Athenian state were paying about half to two-thirds as much for security as subjects of the Roman Empire under Augustus.

The two hundred Athenian triremes dominated the fleet, and an Athenian, Cimon, quickly established himself as the alliance's main military leader. There is no evidence for any significant debates within the fleet over whether it should follow Athenian directions. This stands in sharp contrast to the arguments over strategy among the Greeks in 480,[204] although it may partly reflect the interests of our sources. The only serious challenge to unity came from the unwillingness of some cities to submit to the rigors of discipline and training in pursuit of the common goal. The same problem had led to the breakup of the united Ionian fleet facing Persia in the 490s.[205] Thucydides and Plutarch say some cities were reluctant to face the strains of war and agreed to pay cash instead of providing the ships and crews they had originally been assessed for.[206]

There are two sides to this story. On the one hand, Athens was apparently happy for Lesbos, Chios, and Samos to provide ships, calling them the guardians of Athenian power.[207] Athens disbanded the Samian and Lesbian armed forces only in 439 and 427, respectively, after failed revolts, and Chios went on contributing ships till its own revolt in 412. A whole variety of cities contributed ground troops throughout the fifth century.[208] Provided these forces served effectively under Athenian command, they functioned as a cheap way to outsource some of the fighting.

On the other hand, it also suited Athens to have the cities pay cash. To remain a great power in the Aegean, Athens would need a larger fleet than any other city; substituting tribute for military service effectively had the other cities pay for the Athenian fleet. While Athens hired all comers as rowers, much of the tribute ended up in the pockets of the poorer Athenian citizens as pay for service in the fleet. As Thucydides explains, "The result was that the Athenian navy grew strong at the cities' expense, and when they revolted they always found themselves inadequately armed and inexperienced in war."[209]

The compromise that ensued was perhaps the perfect result for Athens: Samos, Chios, and Lesbos shared some of the human costs of war with Athens but could not begin to challenge Athens for leadership of the united fleet. Athens not only controlled the association's foreign policy but also monopolized the major instrument of coercion within the Aegean. With this, they compelled would-be free-riders to pay tribute, imposed democracies, and prevented other cities from backing out of their obligations.

6.1.3. General Peace. Writing a century after the events, Isocrates noted that the political system created in 477 provided general peace in the Aegean.[210] As so often, he had a polemical point, but the only time we hear of Athens' subject cities fighting one another is a war between Samos and Miletus in 440, over control of the small city of Priene, which lay between them. Athens ordered them to stop and to refer Priene's fate to Athenian judgment. Miletus apparently accepted this instruction, but Samos refused. Athens then imposed peace and set up a democratic government in Samos. The Samians overthrew this and rebelled, with support from Byzantium and the Persian satrap Pissuthnes. It took Pericles nine months to crush the uprising.[211]

In 440, Samos was one of just three cities still contributing ships to the centralized fleet rather than paying tribute, and its proud aristocrats clearly resented being treated as mere provincial burghers in the Greater Athenian State. So far as we can tell, though, the leaders of other cities were less haughty and in any case had few or no armed forces to use in quarrels with their neighbors. If they did find ways to make war rather than submitting their complaints to Athens, we can only assume that they complied with Athenian demands to stop. This fifth-century peace stands in marked contrast to the situation in the sixth century, when, even though our sources are meager, they record many wars between these same cities. Athens intervened regularly in civil strife within the cities, almost always in support of pro-democratic factions.[212] Before 431, this must have kept civil wars to a minimum, although, once the Peloponnesian War broke out, anti-democratic factions could rely on Spartan assistance, and the level of violence escalated.[213]

6.2. Economic Institutions

Athens took four major steps, creating centralized taxation on a much larger scale than had ever been seen in Greece, setting up a central market, introducing a single coinage, and opening up the physical resources of the Aegean to central exploitation.

6.2.1. Centralized Taxation. Greek states famously avoided regular direct taxation. Athens, however, created two kinds of tax, producing greater and more reliable revenue flows than any Greek state had enjoyed before.[214] The most important new revenue source was the tribute (*phoros*) assessed by Aristides and his successors, controlled by Athenian *hellenotamiai*. As noted earlier, a few cities paid in kind, providing military services, but most exchanged cash for security. Much remains obscure about these funds,[215] and our sources never call the tribute tax, but this was how it functioned. The second form was taxes on the use of harbors, and particularly on goods passing through the Hellespont.[216]

We do not know exactly what it cost to build triremes. Augustus Boeckh assembled the relevant sources and estimated perhaps one talent for the hull and another for the equipment, with prices rising through time. Vincent Gabrielsen has emphasized the problems with this calculation but offers no alternatives, so, as a rough rule of thumb, Boeckh's best guess must stand.[217] At different points during the fifth century, depending on rates of pay,[218] it probably cost between half a talent and a full talent to keep a trireme at sea for a month. The Athenians built one or two hundred triremes in 483 B.C.E. from the state's share of the proceeds of a huge silver strike.[219] Even after this initial outlay, keeping a fleet of two hundred ships at sea for a three-month summer campaign must have cost something like 500 to 1,000 talents, by the time we have figured in repairs and replacements (if each ship lasted around twenty years, as seems likely, even without losses in battle an average of ten new triremes would be needed each year). Plutarch says Pericles kept sixty ships at sea for eight months each year in the 440s, which would have cost at least 250 to 300 talents per annum in wages in peacetime.[220]

The exact size of the tribute in the years before 454 is no clearer. Thucydides says that the *phoros* came to 460 talents in 477 B.C.E.[221] The tribute lists beginning in 454 B.C.E. generally record revenues closer to 400 talents. Given that Athens controlled more cities in and after 454 than in 477, some historians conclude that the number in Thucydides' text is wrong or includes the cash equivalent of ships and their crews as well as the money actually paid, even though Plutarch accepted Thucydides' figure and Diodorus put it even higher, at 560 talents.[222] Whatever the correct sum, little would have been left over after covering the fleet's expenses, even in years without major wars. On the other side of the balance sheet, campaigns against Persia in the 470s through the 450s were highly profitable,[223] and other forms of tax augmented the tribute, so that Athens built up a large cash reserve. In 431, the treasury held 6,000 talents and at one point had reached 9,700 talents.[224]

When Athens had to fight serious wars, though, the tax base proved inadequate. The Samian war in 440–439 cost either 1,200 or 1,400 talents and the siege of Potidaea in 431–430 at least 2,000 talents.[225] Athens imposed an indemnity on Samos[226] and probably did so on other rebels but then had to reduce their tribute while they were paying off the costs of wars against them. Estimates of the total cost to Athens of the twenty-seven years of the Peloponnesian War range from 35,000 to 47,500 talents.[227] Despite Athens' financial strength in 431,[228] the costs of war shocked everyone. In 428, Athens was supporting larger armed forces than ever before,[229] and Thucydides has the Mytileneans cite Athenian financial exhaustion as one reason for rebelling that year.[230]

The war against Persia had been the impetus for the original creation of the tribute in 477, and the war against Sparta forced a major escalation in the 420s. Plutarch[231] says that the tribute grew from 460 talents in 477 B.C.E. to 600 in 431 B.C.E. and to 1,300 talents in the 420s.[232] The Thoudippos Decree of 425 B.C.E. expressly says that the "tribute...has become too little"[233] and imposes an exceptional reassessment, increasing the revenue demanded to between 1,460 and 1,500 talents (although Athens probably received less). Increasing the tribute also increased the transaction costs of its collection. The number of officials involved proliferated, and Thucydides repeatedly refers to Athens sending out special ships to extract payment.[234] A scholiast on Aristophanes' *Knights* (line 1,070) adds that the men commanding these ships "made great profits." Athens took drastic steps to tighten up collection procedures in the early 420s, and some cities fell behind on their payments.[235] Between 433 and 423 B.C.E., Athens also took out new loans from Athena that added up to nearly 6,000 talents,[236] and in 428 the Athenians voted to impose a direct tax, or *eisphora*, on themselves. Thucydides says that this was the first time Athens had done this and that it brought in 200 talents.[237] An inscription also refers to an *eisphora* in Miletus, probably in 426–425, although we do not know whether this was imposed by Athens or by the Milesians themselves.[238]

The burden of taxation via tribute grew sharply in the 420s. The greatest gap in our knowledge, though, is precisely who paid the tribute in each city. No source ever tells us. Finley suggested that "If the normal Greek system of taxation prevailed—and there is no reason to believe that it did not—then the tribute for Athens was paid by the rich, not the common people."[239] In fact, city-states normally tried to cover public expenditures by combining regular liturgies on the rich (*enkyklioi*) with income derived from the sale or leasing of public property and indirect taxes on harbors and markets.[240] We know that for some cities this easily covered the tribute. Herodotus[241] says that Thasos's public revenue from mines and other properties was 200 to 300 talents per year, while its normal tribute payment, starting probably in 443 B.C.E., was 30 talents per year. Given the cities' unanimous approval of Aristides' assessment, we should assume that the tribute was based on the size of the regular public revenues, not on population or private wealth, and that the payment was normally less than the city would have spent for its own security. This means that before 431 the tribute was in effect a direct tax that Athens imposed on the cities, which they covered largely from their public property and local indirect taxes. The sharp increase in tribute in the 420s may have strained public resources, forcing cities to turn more often to irregular liturgies (*prostaktai*), "donations" (*epidoseis*), and even special direct taxes (*eisphorai*). If so, then the pressure of war partially converted the tribute into a direct tax on local elites.

In 413, Athens suspended the tribute and instead imposed a tax of 5 percent on all goods passing through the harbors of the subject cities.[242] Thucydides suggests that this was an attempt to increase revenues. Many historians assume that the tribute brought in roughly 900 talents each year between 418 and 414, so the 5 percent figure might mean that the Athenians expected to be able to tax more than 18,000 talents worth of seaborne trade per annum; alternatively, they may have felt in the wake of the Sicilian disaster that, despite the costs of collecting it, an indirect tax would be more popular with the cities and produce a higher yield than trying to enforce the hated tribute. Whatever their thinking, the shift to an indirect tax on trade was apparently less successful than the Athenians had hoped, because tribute collection had resumed by 410. Xenophon says that in the same year Athens established a 10 percent tax on all goods passing through the Hellespont,[243] although the "10 percent tax" mentioned in Callias's financial decree (probably passed in 422–421)[244] may be the same one.

6.2.2. Central Market. Money flowed into Athens, which rapidly became one of the leading marketplaces in the Mediterranean. The Old Oligarch recognized the financial side effects,[245] not least the revenues raised by a 1 percent tax on all imports and exports through the Piraeus. Perhaps even more important, Athenian spending power linked trade networks over large areas. Writing probably in the 420s, the comic poet Hermippos described in mock-Homeric language the goods that flowed into the harbor:

> From Cyrene silphium-stalks and ox-hides, from the Hellespont mackerel and all kinds of salt-dried fish, from Thessaly salt and sides of beef, from Sitalkes an itch to plague the Spartans, from Perdikkas lies by the shipload. Syracuse provides hogs and cheese—while as for the Corcyreans, may Poseidon destroy them in their hollow ships, because they are of divided loyalty. These things then come from those places; but from Egypt we get rigged sails and papyrus, from Syria frankincense, while fair Crete sends cypress for the gods, and Libya provides plenty of ivory to buy. Rhodes provides raisins and dried figs, while pears and fat apples come from Euboea, slaves from Phrygia, mercenaries from Arcadia. Pagasai furnishes slaves, and branded rascals at that. The acorns of Zeus and glossy almonds come from the Paphlagonians, and are the ornaments of a feast. Phoenicia provides the fruit of the palm and the finest wheat flour, Carthage supplies carpets and cushions of many colors.[246]

Piraeus became the Aegean's clearinghouse and remained so even after 404.[247]

6.2.3. Single Coinage, Weights, and Measures. Probably in 425–424, Klearchos moved a decree stipulating that all mints for local silver coinages in the cities would be closed and that henceforth the entire Greater Athenian State would use Athenian weights, measures, and coinage.[248] There has been much argument over the causes and consequences of this decree. Many historians have imagined cynical Athenian attempts to profit by increasing demand for silver mined in Attica or to gain on the exchange rate offered on local coinages. On the whole, these arguments are not very convincing.[249] Thomas Martin's suggestion that the switch to Attic standards made the collecting tribute and the Eleusinian First Fruits easier is a far more convincing explanation of Klearchos's intentions.[250] That said, operating with a single currency must also have facilitated trade. Numismatists have not detected any sharp metrological boundary (either in the early 440s or mid-420s) indicating a switch to Athenians standards, which may mean that the decree had little immediate impact; but there was nevertheless a general drift in this direction during the fifth century.[251] Whether through this decree or through countless individual decisions, Athenian standards gradually came to provide a single system of weights and measures within the Aegean, lowering the transaction costs of trade.

6.2.4. Centralization of Resources. Nearly all city-states jealously guarded access to the basic source of wealth, the land, by restricting ownership to citizens. Athens systematically undermined this, opening land ownership in the subject cities to Athenians. This was done partly through official seizures of land and partly through private initiative.

Official seizures took two forms, colonies (*apoikiai*) and clerouchies (*klerouchiai*). Colonies were founded as self-governing cities in supposedly empty territory. They could take several forms. The oldest, going back to the eighth century, involved the occupation of what seemed to the Greeks to be unclaimed lands outside the Aegean, as when Athenians and other Greeks resettled the abandoned territory of Sybaris in Italy as the new colony of Thourioi in 444–443.[252] The seizure of Ennea Hodoi from the non-Greek Thracians in 465[253] was a similar operation, although in this case the Thracians fought back and massacred the Greeks. Athens also developed a new kind of colonization, however, forcibly expelling the population of hostile cities and replacing them with Athenian citizens, as at Aegina in 431, Potidaea in 430, and Melos in 416.[254]

Clerouchies, by contrast, involved Athenians taking over some of the territory of other cities while their original occupants remained in place. There is some ambiguity in the sources over whether Athenians actually relocated to their new lands or stayed in Athens and extracted rents.[255] Like the colony, the clerouchy was an old institution. Athens had settled 4,000 men in Chalcis after winning the war of 506 and an unrecorded number on Salamis around the same time.[256] During the fifth century, at least 15,000 Athenians (and perhaps closer to 20,000) out of a citizen population peaking around 40,000 in the 430s obtained land in colonies or clerouchies.

Isocrates claimed that the Athenians did all this "for the protection of the cities' territories, not for our aggrandizement,"[257] but Plutarch had a very different view. Focusing on the demographic and political consequences, he suggested that Pericles "relieved the city of a large number of idlers and agitators, raised the standards of the poorest classes, and, by installing garrisons among the allies, implanted at the same time a healthy fear of rebellion."[258] Some historians think Plutarch's view was colored by Roman colonial practices, but it does seem that clerouchs and colonists came largely from the poorer citizens, and there is other evidence of Pericles' concern to limit the number of Athenians.[259]

Whatever its other results, the Athenian landgrab opened the basic economic resources of the empire to centralized exploitation. In taking control of land all over the Aegean, Athenians made the most serious assault on the principle of city-state autonomy since Sparta annexed Messenia in the eighth century. The Athenians could, of course, claim that colonies and clerouchies were traditional institutions, but alongside this "official" landgrab we also hear of individual Athenians obtaining land in the subject cities. No source systematically discusses this, but several refer in passing to Athenians owning such land.[260] The most surprising evidence comes from inscriptions recording the state auction of property belonging to men involved in the mutilation of the herms and profanation of the Eleusinian Mysteries in 415 B.C.E. The otherwise unknown Oionias held land in Euboea valued at 81 talents and 2,000 drachmas, while Nicides also held land in Euboea, Adeimantos had a farm on Thasos, and there is a reference to the sale of unharvested crops in the Troad.[261] Oionias's property is worth far more than that of any other known Athenian, and Finley suggested that Thucydides' well-known comment that the *kaloikagathoi*, the Athenian upper class, were the main beneficiaries of the empire must be referring to such acquisitions of property.[262]

The Athenians did not create an Aegean-wide land market, since (other than Lysias's reference[263] to rights of intermarriage [*epigamia*] between Athens and Euboea) there is no sign that non-Athenians could buy property in Attica. Demosthenes comments that Pasion owned much land in Attica before he became a citizen and that Phormion did the same through a citizen intermediary,[264] but everything about these cases suggests that they were strange exceptions. The anger of the subject cities about Athenians taking over their land[265] also suggests that this was a one-way process. The Athenians wanted to break down the centuries-old boundaries around individual cities, but only in their own favor. We should see their seizure of Thasos's mines on the Thracian mainland in 465 in this light and perhaps also Thucydides' reference to his own family having mining interests in this area.[266] These were blatantly exploitative steps.

6.3. *Administration*

In this sphere Athens took three major steps, creating an intercity ruling class of Athenian administrators, interfering in the constitutions of the subject cities, and centralizing legal processes.

6.3.1. Central Ruling Elite. Athens set up a network of what are usually called "imperial magistrates" across the Aegean.[267] [Aristotle] refers to seven hundred *archai* (offices) at Athens itself and a further seven hundred outside Athens. The Old Oligarch claimed that these *archai* were so ubiquitous that the Athenians learned how to row without realizing it by going out to the cities to fill them, and Aristophanes made jokes about them.[268] We know little about what these Athenian officers did, but they functioned to tie the cities more closely to Athens and made sure Athenian needs were implemented on the ground.

Like the landgrab, these Athenian magistrates broke with city-state traditions. One category, the *proxenoi* (local men who represented Athenian interests to their fellow citizens),[269] went back well into archaic times, but others were new, such as the *archontes*, Athenians resident in the cities, clearly with some significant power;[270] the *episkopoi*, overseers of some kind, probably traveling from city to city;[271] and the *phrouroi* and *phrourarchoi*, some kind of military establishment in the cities.[272]

6.3.2. Constitutional Interference. The sources agree that Athens generally tried to have democratic institutions run the cities.[273] The Old Oligarch says that Athens once supported an oligarchy because it was convenient but that this soon revolted and massacred the commoners.[274] Historians working from the Tribute Lists have proposed a variety of scenarios for what happened, but Athens definitely restored democracy quickly.[275] Athens had a clear ideological preference for popular government and a sense that citizens of democracies would be more loyal than citizens of oligarchies.[276] A handful of inscriptions from the 450s onward attest to Athens insisting on democracies after suppressing revolts.[277]

6.3.3. Centralization of Legal Process. This was one of the most important administrative dimensions of Athenian state building. City-states guarded their legal processes as jealously as their land, but Athens centralized several key dimensions of the law. Thucydides had the Athenians in Sparta in 432 defend themselves against complaints that it was wrong to make members of the subject cities come to Athens for trial. The Old Oligarch agreed with critics that it was wrong to make other Greeks sail to Athens for trials but also recognized the advantages this brought Athens.[278] Isocrates noted that the Spartans had severely criticized Athens for this practice but defended it, adding that "we governed all the cities under the same laws, deliberating about them in the spirit of allies, not of masters."[279] Regulations for cities that had revolted supply some specific details. In a decree probably passed in 446, the Athenians swore that they would neither deprive Chalcidians of citizenship nor exile, arrest, kill, or confiscate the property of any of them without a trial and the consent of the Athenian people; the Chalcidians agreed that in cases involving penalties of exile, death, or loss of citizen rights, defendants would have the right of appeal to Athens.[280] At Erythrae, in 453–452, the Athenians tied local and Athenian law together in another way, ruling that anyone exiled from the city for murder would also be exiled from the entire Greater Athenian State.[281] Antiphon even claimed that "it is not permitted—even for a city—to punish anyone by death without the consent of the Athenians."[282] These interventions in local law in the interests of a generalized Athenian justice mark a sharp break with earlier Greek practices.

6.4. Culture

The Athenians took three major steps, turning Athens into the cultural capital of the Aegean, uniting the cities through the shared symbolism of Athenian coinage, and making ritual claims to be the ancestral home and religious center of all Ionian Greeks.

6.4.1. Athens as Cultural Capital. Something like 6 percent of all Greeks lived in Attica in the fifth century, so, other things being equal, we might expect about the same percentage of famous artists and writers to have lived there. However, as table 4.3 shows, this was not the case. Nearly nine times as many of the cultural figures whose names have survived were born in Athens as this null hypothesis predicts, and nearly twelve times as many spent all or substantial parts of their careers there. Unless we assume that Athenians were just naturally more talented than other Greeks, we have to conclude that Athens drew in so many artists, writers, and thinkers that it became a cultural hothouse, in which native Athenians were disproportionately likely to excel.[283]

The obvious explanation is that the wealth that flowed into Athens made it the most important center of artistic patronage. There is even some evidence that Pericles promoted Athens' role as a cultural capital. Thucydides had him claim that "our city is the School of Hellas," the cultural center toward which all Greeks had to look.[284] In Plutarch's account of the decision to build new temples on the acropolis providing public pay for poor Athenians was a major motive, but Plutarch also had

Table 4.3. Fifth-Century Cultural Figures

	Number	Percentage
Birthplace		
Athens	76	52
Outside Athens	71	48
Total	147	100
Main workplace		
Athens	99	70
Outside Athens	42	30
Total	141	100

Sources: Hornblower and Spawforth 1996; Pollitt 1965

The totals for birthplace and main workplace differ because several figures only have one type of information preserved, or there is debate (particularly over where they spent their careers).

Pericles begin his justification by insisting that the buildings "will bring Athens glory for all time."[285] Whether or not Pericles self-consciously sought to make Athens the eye of Greece, mother of arts and eloquence,[286] this was what the city had become by the 420s. Artists, authors, scholars, and philosophers flocked there to take advantage of the wealth and patronage it afforded. Plato's *Protagoras* and *Ion* give a sense of the cosmopolitan intellectual climate this created. Everyone who was anyone had to come to Athens, and Hegemon of Thasos even wrote a comedy about how it felt to go back to his hometown after making good in the big city.[287] The result was an extraordinary cultural efflorescence, arguably unparalleled until Florence in the fifteenth century. Once this cultural dominance had been established, it proved durable, surviving the defeats of 404 and 338 to last into Roman times.[288]

I briefly want to consider (and reject) two alternative explanations. The first is that Athens' cultural dominance predated the empire and had no causal connection to it. After all, Athenian vase painters produced much of the finest work in Greece for five centuries before the establishment of the empire or the democracy, particularly the Late Geometric Ia "Dipylon style" in the mid-eighth century. But, from the seventh century on, the most innovative vase painters came from Corinth and Miletus, and their craft was in any case a minor art when compared with sculpture and architecture, the best archaic examples of which were also non-Athenian.[289] Only one out of the twenty to twenty-five archaic poets whose work survives was Athenian. The rise of Athenian cultural dominance was sudden and happened in the early fifth century.

Boedeker and Raaflaub present a second possibility, noting that, while fifth-century Athens was certainly a rich imperial city, it was also a rich *democratic* city.[290] Only a little Athenian art directly celebrated the empire and even less celebrated the democracy,[291] but they must be correct that democratic institutions and openness gave greater scope for the multitude of talented people in Athens to push artistic and intellectual expression in directions that would not have been possible elsewhere. The dramatic festivals of the Great Dionysia and the opportunities for rhetoric, both of them specifically democratic phenomena, gave Athens overwhelming dominance in tragedy, comedy, and oratory (although Syracuse produced, and retained, notable figures in all these fields).[292] Andrea Nightingale and Josiah Ober have also argued that opposition to democracy was a major factor in pushing the intellectual circles around Plato and Thucydides to develop such sophisticated positions.[293]

Overall, the Athenian cultural miracle seems to have owed most to the combination of high investment in cultural innovation all over archaic Greece, an unprecedented concentration of resources in fifth-century Athens, and a handful of prominent men (particularly Pericles) who self-consciously strove to make Athens a center of patronage. The fact that Athens had democratic institutions doubtless influenced the particular direction the artistic, literary, and intellectual communities took as they formed. The result was a heady brew, giving Athens an unparalleled amount of what the political scientist Joseph Nye calls "soft power," an attractive culture that—whatever they might think of Athens' political ambitions—made people want to be part of the Athenian world.[294]

6.4.2. Shared Coinage. Finley emphasized the political dimensions of Klearchos's Coinage Decree over the economic, seeing it largely as an ideological statement of the subjection of the cities.[295] Recent scholarship has sharply criticized this view.[296] The debate has been polarized; while Finley may have minimized the economic dimensions of the decree as part of his critique of formalist models, Figueira perhaps goes to the opposite extreme in entirely rejecting substantivism. Leslie Kurke has underlined the symbolic importance of coinage in Greek thought in the age of Herodotus, and it might be simplistic to assume that, because the shift toward Attic standards facilitated the collection of tribute and the activities of traders (as it clearly did), it did not also make a huge political statement about Athens' claims for the unity of the Aegean.[297]

6.4.3. Ionian Center. Athens seems to have been at least as self-conscious about "religious politics" as about becoming a cultural center.[298] I argued earlier in this chapter that the sense of religious difference between Athens and the subject cities was tiny compared to that between the Assyrians, Persians, Romans, Byzantines, and many of their subjects, but the Athenians nonetheless worked hard to reduce it even further. Their best-known measure was the requirement that subject cities send a cow and a panoply of armor to Athens for the Great Panathenaea festival, symbolically recognizing Athens as their mother city. This is first documented in the regulations for Erythrae in 453–452,[299] when it may have been a special provision, but by the time of Thoudippos's decree in 425 it was required of all the cities. A highly probable restoration of the fragmentary inscription adds the significant detail that the cities' representatives are to walk in the procession "like colonists."[300]

If Mattingly is right in down-dating to the 420s many of the inscriptions formerly placed in the 440s, it begins to look as if Athens started pushing its genealogical claims over the cities much harder once the Peloponnesian War broke out.[301] A mother-city could expect a degree of respect from its colonies, and successful Ionianism was potentially a force for cohesion within the Aegean. In 425, Athens also revived religious competitions at Delos, the Ionians' most important sanctuary, and purified the island.[302] Nicias put on a magnificent display, even if it ended badly.[303]

Thucydides has Hermocrates of Syracuse say in 415 that shared heritage had been important in persuading the Ionian cities of Sicily to accept Athenian leadership in 427 but that Athens had then deprived them of full independence.[304] In response, Euphemos, the Athenian representative, pointed to the fact that the Ionians were the Athenians' kinsmen, who "willingly accepted servitude"; he added to this the facts that Athens was stronger than the other Ionians and that it had stood up against Persia while they had submitted.[305] Thucydides himself seems not to have taken Ionian descent very seriously as an argument for Athenian dominance over the cities, and, in his catalogue of the Athenian allies at Syracuse, he emphasized the complexity of factors involved, some ethnic, and some pragmatic.[306]

Thucydides may not have thought religious ideology important, but the epigraphic record suggests that at least some of Athens' leaders put great emphasis on it. A series of inscriptions records Athens setting up sacred enclosures for Athena Mistress of the Athenians (*Athena Athenon medeousa*) at Chalcis, on Samos, and on Aegina, and, when Athens sent a clerouchy to Mytilene in 427, the income of three hundred of the three thousand plots of land taken over was given to the support of Athena.[307] In a decree probably dating to the 420s, the Athenians required all subject cities to offer First Fruits in Eleusis (equivalent to a small tax in kind, of 0.17 percent on barley and 0.08 percent on wheat) and invited all cities in Greece to follow suit.[308] As late as 380 B.C.E., Isocrates says that this practice was still common, which makes it sounds as if numerous cities responded and thought of it as a serious religious obligation.[309]

6.5. Athenian State Formation

The Aegean world changed rapidly between 478 and 431 and the pace of change accelerated further between 431 and 404. Athens emerged as the Aegean's cultural and economic center, controlled its foreign policy and armed forces, and intervened frequently in other cities' internal affairs. This was a period of rapid state formation; by 404, Aegean society looked more like figure 4.5 than it had since the collapse of the Mycenaean palaces eight hundred years earlier. War and preparation for war drove this process of state formation. Fear of Persia lay behind Athens' creation of a large fleet in 483 and its acceptance of Spartan leadership in 481. It lay behind the Ionians' switch to Athenian leadership in 478 and their acceptance of Aristides' proposal in 477. We have no direct evidence for why the cities generally supported Athens' use of force to prevent would-be free-riders from leaving the organization between the 470s and the 430s and acquiesced in Athens' interference in local constitutions, but, in addition to the fear factor, a general model of the decision-making process would need to include mass-elite tensions, pay for rowing, plunder from the Persian wars in the 470s through the 450s, rivalries between the subject cities, Athenian support for local democracy, and financial and psychological benefits the Greater Athenian State may have offered to local elites in the subject cities. After 431, the costs of war drove Athens to increase the tempo of state formation; as Tilly famously said about early modern Europe, "states made war, and war made states."[310]

7. SECONDARY STATE FORMATION

Thucydides says that "What made [the Peloponnesian] war inevitable was the growth of Athenian power and the fear which this caused in Sparta."[311] We can broaden his conclusion: Athenian state formation and the fear it inspired in other

Greeks stimulated defensive state formation all over the Greek world, which in turn drove Athens to new efforts. The one apparent exception to this generalization—remarkably—is Sparta. The Spartans managed to defeat Athens in 404 despite having fiercely resisted the very capacity-building reforms that most political scientists would assume they had to make; only to reveal that the exception proved the rule, because defeating Athens created opportunities for radicals to challenge everything about Spartan traditions. I describe developments at Sparta and Syracuse and more briefly discuss those at Olynthus, Thebes, Mytilene, and Argos. Numerous other examples could be added.

7.1. Sparta

To understand Spartan state formation in the fifth century, we must go back at least to the ninth. The Spartans, who saw themselves as invading conquerors, had reduced the Laconians to serfdom by this time and did the same to the Messenians in the eighth and seventh centuries. By 600 B.C.E., the most important geopolitical fact about Sparta was firmly in place: its prosperity and power depended on controlling the helots.

In the early sixth century, Sparta tried to extend helotage into Arcadia, but defeat at Tegea in the 560s produced a sense that this form of state formation had reached its limits. Over the next twenty years, Sparta created a network of bilateral treaties with most of the cities of the Peloponnese, which historians conventionally refer to as the Peloponnesian League.[312] Sparta's allies apparently agreed to help it against helot revolts and to follow it in war against any enemies it chose. The League was a protection racket: pro-Spartan oligarchs got protection not only from rivals and democratic elements within their cities but also from the Spartans' own menaces.[313] They did not pay tribute or provide regular levies; nor, apparently, did they forgo the right to make war against other members of the League. The League cost Sparta very little so long as its allies believed it could and would punish defectors, and gave it massive military strength. By 540, it was the greatest power in Greece,[314] and Herodotus simply took Spartan dominance for granted in his account of the 490s and 480s.

That said, the Peloponnesian League had limitations. It did include non-Dorian states and did act outside the Peloponnese (e.g., Samos [525], Phocis [510s], Athens [510–505]), but its primarily Dorian and Peloponnesian members often hesitated to follow Sparta in these directions. When Sparta pushed the League to attack Athens in 506, Corinth balked,[315] and probably over the next half-dozen years Sparta gave League members the right to vote on whether to follow it into wars.

In creating the Peloponnesian League, the Spartans chose a low-cost way to concentrate coercive power, outsourcing war rather than building state capacity, then spent the next century and a half quarreling over whether to accept its limitations or to restructure their society to build state capacity and overcome them. The two key issues were the relationship between citizens and helots and *oliganthropia*, the decline in citizen numbers (see section 3).

The Spartans' famous secrecy means that we know little about their debates, but, judging from their actions, we may deduce that most of the leading men were willing to accept the limitations that the Peloponnesian League imposed on state power if the alternatives risked breaking up helotage and/or redistributing property. It is easy to see why they felt this way. By 500, the Greek state system had reached an equilibrium in which Sparta was the greatest power and the distribution of property within Laconia and Messenia put its leading families among the richest in Greece. Maintaining this balance was a full-time job; why risk everything to extend state power when the adventures in Samos, Phocis, and Athens seemed to suggest that the marginal returns to growth were already declining? Ste. Croix even speaks of a "natural" Spartan foreign policy: "to concentrate on keeping her League together, and to avoid foreign adventures and above all the sending of any large armies of Spartiates outside the Peloponnese."[316]

Only an existential threat could make the Spartan elite consider state-strengthening reforms, and even then they were divided and hesitant. Although it was clear by 483 that Xerxes aimed to conquer all of Greece and would probably annihilate Sparta, some of Sparta's leading men remained obsessed by the fact that the Athenians had not consulted them before dragging Greece into war with Persia.[317] Not until 481 did Sparta invite other cities to join the Peloponnesian League in fighting Xerxes, and even then it rejected aid from Argos and Syracuse if it meant sharing leadership.[318]

Fearing for its very survival, Sparta may have modified army recruitment in 480 (Thermopylae and Plataea are the first times we hear of helots and *perioikoi* fighting alongside the Spartiates),[319] but the events of 478 reveal how ferociously Sparta's leaders resisted state-strengthening reforms. Defending Ionia would require a permanent navy; either Sparta would have to cede control to maritime states with large revenue flows, like Athens, Aegina, and Corinth, or it would have to raise money on its own account. When Sparta's attempt to sidestep the question by moving the Ionians to the mainland failed, Pausanias, the Spartan regent who had won the battle of Plataea, may have emerged as the main champion of state-strengthening reforms. He took over the fleet in 478, only to be rejected by Athens and the other Ionians because of his arrogance. He then set up in Byzantium on his own account before being charged with intriguing with Xerxes and plotting to free the helots and make them citizens. Much is obscure, but Pausanias apparently recognized that Sparta had to become a naval power and could do this only by transforming its social structure. Cartledge even links Pausanias to an abortive helot uprising in the late 470s and ties this to troubles within the Peloponnesian League, including battles against Tegea, Argos, the Arcadians, and Messenian rebels.[320] If he is right, Sparta went through a fierce struggle in the 470s between radicals like Pausanias, ready to overturn the helot system to create a modern naval state, and conservatives who wanted to preserve the status quo at home by supporting a "dual hegemony" in which Sparta dominated on land and Athens on sea. Thucydides says that the

Spartans were happy to hand naval control to Athens in 478, but Herodotus sees the Athenians pushing them aside, and Diodorus tells a story that Sparta split over the issue, with the younger citizens wanting to go to war to remain the single dominant power in Greece.[321]

After this crisis, Sparta's conservatives retained control for fifty years. So far as we can tell, the decision to assist Thasos against Athens in 465 produced no upheavals like those surrounding Pausanias in the 470s, and the disastrous earthquake and helot uprising of 464 reinforced the "dual hegemony" policy, culminating in a request for Athenian assistance against the rebels. The ensuing break with Athens in 462 indirectly exposed the weaknesses of the Peloponnesian League structure. Sparta could not prevent Corinth and Megara going to war with each other, and the angry Athenians were able to detach Megara from the Spartan alliance.[322] Throughout the "First Peloponnesian War" that followed, Sparta made only one foray outside the Peloponnese and instead fought through proxies whenever possible. Even the decisive victory over Athens at Coronea in 447 was won not by Sparta but by Boeotian exiles and Locrians.[323]

Sparta determinedly avoided entanglements that might endanger its comfortable position at the head of the Peloponnesian League, its control over the helots, and the increasing concentration of wealth in just a few hands. Thucydides says that the Spartans had to fight repeatedly to keep their allies in line but that by the 430s it had finally recognized that the growth of Athenian power was undermining the Peloponnesian League and making this position untenable.[324] Sparta had to do something.

Some Spartans, at least, recognized by 432 that they would need a fleet, but, sticking to their traditional strategy of avoiding state-strengthening reforms that would endanger the status quo, they tried to persuade either the Dorian Greeks of Italy and Sicily or the Persians to pay for it.[325] The first of these options was a nonstarter, and the second involved making Persia an attractive offer. Ste. Croix suggests that Thucydides' comment that as late as 424 the Persians could not work out what exactly Sparta was asking for reflects deep divisions among Sparta's leaders over whether they were willing to pay Persia's price.[326]

The war strained Spartan social structure, and when Athens took Pylos in 425 the collapse of helotage seemed possible.[327] Sparta took extreme steps, creating regular patrols,[328] freeing helots who helped supply the trapped Spartan garrison at Pylos, massacring 2,000 helots who seemed threatening, and sending another 700 off to Thrace with Brasidas in 424.[329] Brasidas's force is the first time we hear of helots being armed as hoplites, and it may be that the notoriously innovative Brasidas was ready to make state-strengthening moves regardless of the risks (he also put Spartan governors in the cities he captured). He certainly aroused jealousy and resistance from other Spartans.[330]

Fighting Athens without reforming the state was leading to disaster, and by 422 the Peloponnesian League was in serious trouble, with Mantineia waging its own war against Tegea.[331] It then became clear that even thinking about reforms was equally dangerous. The treaty Athens and Sparta signed in 421 eased the helot problem[332] but the Corinthians saw it as the beginning of a Spartan attempt to reduce the allies to slavery.[333] Mantineia, Elis, and Corinth all left the League, and Corinth expected its collapse if Tegea joined them.[334] But this was not to be: however inappropriate its weak state structures were to fighting a complicated war with Athens, Sparta could still beat all comers in a straightforward hoplite battle, and when it did so at Mantineia in 418 it trumped all Sparta's other problems and restored its prestige.

If Mantineia saved Sparta from collapse, the Athenian disaster in Sicily in 413 reopened the possibility of victory. Again, the Spartans tried to obtain this without deepening state capacities, hoping that the Syracusans would provide a fleet or that Persia would pay for one. As in the 420s, the Spartan leadership went back and forth in 412 and 411 over whether to pay Persia's price—the surrender of Ionia—before finally caving in.[335] Even then, though, Persians found it all too easy to manipulate Sparta's clumsy institutions, and it was not until the ambitious Lysander forged a personal friendship with Cyrus in 407 that adequate money came through. It now became clear that there was simply no way to win the war without seriously challenging Sparta's state structures, and the struggle within Sparta's leadership intensified. Lysander's formal power came from his position as admiral, but he could hold this for only one year. When forced to give up the position, in 406, Lysander returned all the unspent funds to Cyrus. The new admiral, Callicratidas, was a conservative who, apparently, would make peace with Athens before he would bend Spartan traditions.[336] Sparta now learned the lesson the Romans would rediscover in the Second Punic War: fighting a great war requires a great leader. The Spartans came up with a legal fiction, *de iure* appointing Lysander as secretary to the admiral in 405 but *de facto* giving him full naval power.[337] According to Andocides and Isocrates, his personal ties to Cyrus brought in 5,000 talents by 404.[338] He made himself the richest man in Greece, received cult honors on Samos in 403, and imposed pro-Spartan (in fact, pro-Lysander) oligarchies all over the Aegean.[339] Xenophon says that, thanks to Lysander, just four hundred Spartans ruled over all the Greeks.[340]

To defeat Athens, Sparta's leaders risked creating a man who could overturn all they held dear, but in 403 they struck back. King Pausanias confronted Lysander over his settlement at Athens, and the Persian satrap Tissaphernes helped Pausanias to dismantle Lysander's system of oligarchies in other cities.[341] The conservatives apparently recognized that victory had changed Sparta forever and anticipated that they would have to maintain Lysander's system of governors over subject cities that paid tribute and perhaps even send out Spartan colonists.[342] Lysander, however, was unwilling to compromise and fought back, manipulating the royal succession in 400 B.C.E. in favor of his friend Agesilaos. We do not know whether Lysander had any connection to a planned uprising by helots and other noncitizens, thwarted in 399,[343] but he may have planned to turn the kingship into an elected position so that he could take it himself.[344] In the end, Agesilaos got the better of Lysander, who was killed in 395, but even King Pausanias, Lysander's bitter enemy in 403, ended up proposing the abolition of the *ephors*.[345]

Classical Sparta is a fascinating case for the political scientist. By the late sixth century, the Spartan elite had everything it could want, and it spent the fifth century trying to preserve this. In the 480s and 420s, many of Sparta's leaders preferred risking destruction to undertaking capacity-deepening reforms that would jeopardize their social system; in 479, in 446, and again in 404 their anachronistic state did defeat apparently more powerful and modern rivals, albeit by getting others to do the heavy lifting. Paradoxically, it was victory that came closest to revolutionizing Sparta. The men who saw how to defeat Persia and Athens—the regent Pausanias in the 470s and the admiral Lysander in 407–395—also saw that massive reforms would concentrate power in their own hands. Once again, the state made war and war made the state—just not in ways that standard theory would predict.

7.2. Syracuse

Greeks began settling in Sicily in the late eighth century. Nearly all the new communities remembered a specific founder, date of foundation, and city of origin, but their formation normally seems to have been a messy process, drawn out across several generations and involving people from many different places.[346] Not surprisingly, state formation followed different paths in the west than in the older communities of the Aegean.

Most obviously, western Greeks settled among non-Greek communities and expanded geographically at their expense. Some, including Syracuse, reduced their neighbors to serfdom. By the sixth century, most western cities had more, and more fertile, territory than Aegean communities.[347]

Their internal structures were as open as their frontiers. In a famous speech set in 415 Thucydides had Alcibiades say that

> The Sicilian cities have swollen populations made out of all sorts of mixtures, and there are constant changes and rearrangements in their citizen bodies. The result is that they lack the feeling that they are fighting for the own fatherland; no one has adequate armor for his own person, or a proper establishment on the land. What each man spends his time on is in trying to get from the public whatever he thinks he can get either by clever speeches or by open sedition—always with the intention of going off to live in another country, if things go badly with him. Such a crowd as this is scarcely likely either to pay attention to one consistent policy or to join together in concerted action.[348]

Alcibiades's prediction, of course, turned out to be disastrously wrong, but Thucydides presents the speech as being one the Athenians found plausible. There is also some archaeological evidence that Sicilian cities were sociologically fragmented. Starting around 700 B.C.E., Aegean Greeks tended to represent their cities in their death rituals as single, homogeneous communities, each sharing a unified symbolic system to which all buriers adhered. Sicilian buriers, by contrast, often deployed multiple symbolic systems, suggesting strongly that the kind of fragmentation Thucydides' Alcibiades described was a long-term structural feature of western Greek cities.[349] The varied origins of settlers and the open frontier with native populations probably had a lot to do with this; the weakness of civic solidarity (in comparison to that among the Aegean cities, at least) may have made it easier for some men to become very rich (again, by Aegean standards).

The general fluidity of colonial life may at first have made it harder to build state power. Typically, monumental public architecture appears only a century or so after a city's foundation. Before 500, though, Sicilian states like Akragas and Selinous were building rows of temples more imposing than anything in the Aegean, suggesting a sharp increase in state revenue, most likely from taxes on trade in agricultural staples. The combination of social fluidity and abundant private and public wealth may also explain why tyranny was so successful in late-sixth- and early-fifth-century Sicily. Thucydides comments that it was only in Sicily that tyrants managed to look beyond securing their own positions and rose to great power.[350]

Three variables—fluidity, wealth, and tyranny—pushed western Greek state formation down somewhat different paths from those open in the Aegean. Intercity conflicts were often highly personal feuds between tyrant families and easily fed into struggles within each city between the tyrant and civil society (meaning both wealthy aristocrats and the poorer mass of citizens). Some historians have suggested that fear of Carthage was as important in Sicilian state formation around 500 B.C.E. as fear of Persia was in the Aegean: Herodotus has Gelon of Syracuse say in 481 that he had fought an earlier war against Carthage, which Justin sets before 489,[351] and our sources also mention a conflict around 510 between the Spartan adventurer Dorieus and the Elymian city Segesta, perhaps in alliance with Carthage.[352] The balance of evidence, though, suggests that Carthage had no military ambitions in Sicily until 480 and that Syracuse's tyrants exaggerated or fabricated stories of early conflicts with Carthage.[353]

Sicilian state formation took a dramatic turn in the 490s when Hippocrates of Gela rapidly captured Callipolis, Naxos, Zancle, and Leontinoi, simultaneously fighting the Sicels. Our evidence is a single chapter in Herodotus, which may not even list the victories in chronological order.[354] He does, though, make it clear that Hippocrates defeated his neighbors on the battlefield and that cavalry were important. Luraghi suggests that Hippocrates gained a temporary tactical advantage, perhaps by using increasing state wealth to hire Sicel and Arcadian mercenaries.[355] We are equally ignorant of what kind of political structure Hippocrates created and how grand his ambitions were. The fact that Corinth and Corcyra intervened in 492 may mean that mainland Greeks perceived Gela as a destabilizing threat, or it may just reflect the traditional relationship between Syracuse and its founders, in which case the most important detail of the story would be that Hippocrates gave up Syracuse for possession of Leontinoi, suggesting that he had no ambitions beyond being a regional east Sicilian power.

By the time Gelon transferred the seat of the tyranny to Syracuse, in 485, his power definitely rested on mercenaries, which he used against his subjects as well as against his external enemies. To some extent, Gelon pioneered the path Athens would follow after 478 by converting capital into coercive power rather than taking the Spartan path of outsourcing warfare to allies to avoid having to build state capacity. We have very little evidence, though, about Syracusan fiscal structures, and what we do know is highly ambiguous. Our sources' silence could be significant; if Syracuse had ever introduced tribute or taxation anything like the Athenian type, it is hard to believe that neither Herodotus, nor Thucydides, nor Diodorus would ever have mentioned it. [Aristotle]'s silence in *Oeconomica* 2.20 is most significant, since this chapter is a series of stories of Dionysius I's underhanded expedients to raise cash. Dionysius may have imposed direct taxes on the Syracusans themselves: [Aristotle] says he taxed animal husbandry so heavily that Syracusans gave it up (leading, of course, to another money-grubbing trick by the tyrant), and Diodorus says that when Dionysius transplanted the Caulonians to Syracuse, in 389, he gave them five years' exemption from taxation.[356] However, we do not know whether this refers to direct taxes that Syracusan citizens otherwise had to pay or to the kind of indirect taxes found in every Greek state.

The sources are not clear, then, whether Dionysius established direct taxation at Syracuse; even if he did, that need not mean that the Deinomenid tyrants did the same from the 480s through the 460s. My guess, though, is that direct taxation was a source of regular Syracusan state revenue and that the wish to increase the tax base partly explains the tyrants' eagerness to relocate defeated people to Syracuse. Gelon moved all the citizens of Camarina, half those of Gela, and the rich from Megara Hyblaea and Euboea to Syracuse, selling the poor from the latter two cities into slavery. His brother Hieron moved people around even more freely, depopulating Catana in 476 and resettling it with ten thousand immigrants from Syracuse and the Peloponnese.[357] Dionysius I renewed these policies and also planted no fewer than fourteen settlements of former mercenaries to control potentially or actively hostile Greek and Sicel populations.

As well as regular revenues, Syracuse's tyrants also raised vast sums for particular wars or building projects, but apparently they had difficulty sustaining these efforts, leading to boom-and-bust cycles. Between 401 and 398, Dionysius conscripted sixty thousand men to extend Syracuse's walls, built 160 new ships sheds, refitted his 110 triremes, built 200 new ships, including quadriremes, and paid technicians to develop quinqueremes and new kinds of catapults. He then scoured the west Mediterranean for mercenaries, paying top rates and providing superb equipment, before sacking Motya with an army of eighty-three thousand men in 397.[358] The very next year, though, when Carthage sent an army to Sicily, Dionysius's forces had evaporated. Similarly, after defeating the Athenian armada in 413, Syracuse had only the resources to send a tiny force to the Aegean.[359] The picture under the Deinomenids is less clear, but after their offer to send huge forces to fight Persia in 481 and actually putting them into the field against Carthage in 480,[360] we hear little more of Syracusan military power, but much about unpaid mercenaries. It sounds as if the Syracusan state could raise large sums in *ad hoc* ways for specific crises—particularly under the tyrants—but could not maintain these revenue flows over the long run. This could produce great triumphs like those over Carthage in 480 and 397 and over Athens 413 but also generated abrupt collapses like those against Carthage in 409–405 and again in 396. Fiscal instability perhaps had something to do with the sudden collapses of the entire tyrannical governance system in the 460s and 350s.

The fall of the tyrants in 465 clearly weakened the Syracusan state, which lost its subjects and presumably stopped taxing its citizens directly. Diodorus refers to taxes on the Sicels in this period, with a sharp increase in 439 to fund larger armed forces,[361] but we know little about this. Diodorus says that Syracuse planned "to subdue all Sicily little by little" and by 427 was putting such severe pressure on its neighbors that Leontinoi invited Athens to come to its aid. Thucydides' brief account of the war makes it sound like Syracuse was leading an alliance of Dorian states that had more in common with the Peloponnesian League than with the Greater Athenian State, and in 424 it required a congress of all the warring states to bring the conflict to a close, rather than the Syracusans speaking for the Dorians.[362] With just a minor exception, this Congress of Gela left each city in possession of what it held, but in 415 Syracuse clearly had no automatic claim to support from other Sicilian cities, again suggesting that democratic Syracuse built its power in the 430s through the 410s through loose military alliances rather than by deepening state capacity.[363] The Athenians gambled that most Sicilian Greeks feared and hated Syracuse enough that they would bandwagon with Athens, whereas the Syracusans hoped that the other Sicilians would join them to balance against the Athenian threat.[364] The Syracusans were right and the Athenians wrong in 424, but in 415 both were wrong, and most Sicilians remained neutral until the outcome was clear.[365]

The Athenian threat in 415 encouraged some of Syracuse's leaders to increase state power dramatically. Hermocrates persuaded the Assembly to reduce the board of generals from fifteen to three members, to give the generals unrestricted power, and to swear obedience to them, simultaneously decreeing compulsory military training for all men and arming hoplites at state expense. Despite the dire military situation, though, the Assembly retained control and threw the original three generals (including Hermocrates) out of office in 414.[366] The last years of the fifth century saw struggles between democratic, "small state" elements and state builders who, to perhaps varying degrees, had tyrannical leanings. In 412, the Assembly largely undid Hermocrates' centralization,[367] only for Carthage's astonishing military victories in 409–406 to renew the pressures favoring state growth. Dionysius apparently openly associated himself with Hermocrates' agenda, marrying Hermocrates' daughter, marrying his own sister to Hermocrates' brother-in-law, and executing one of Hermocrates' rivals. After making his name in thoroughly Hermocratean style by prosecuting the sitting generals, he persuaded the Assembly to double military pay and arm one thousand citizens at state expense. He then took the younger soldiers outside the city before marching back to the dockyards with them, proclaiming himself tyrant, and redistributing land on a huge scale in 406.[368] Once in power, Dionysius reverted to the state-building strategies of the Deinomenids. Helped enormously by the fact that Carthage had destroyed all the main Greek cities except Syracuse, he could by 394–393 be called *archon*, or leader, of Sicily.[369]

State formation was every bit as important at Syracuse as at Athens or Sparta, but the city followed its own path. Syracuse pursued capital-intensive state formation, relying on mercenaries and fleets, but it never developed bureaucratic and financial institutions on anything like the Athenian scale. I have suggested that the fluidity of western Greece, which fragmented citizen communities and made tyranny viable throughout the classical period, was the main reason for this. Syracusan tyrants could generate tremendous power through direct taxes on their own subjects, expropriations from the aristocracy, population relocations, the hiring of temporary mercenary forces, and dynastic marriages—all without creating Athenian-type institutions that might be turned against them. Nontyrants, by contrast, were generally more concerned with preventing any of their rivals from becoming a tyrant than with building state capacities. Syracuse must have developed some bureaucratic structures to fund its expansion from the 430s through the 410s, but in the 460s and again in 412 its citizens were apparently more than willing to surrender state power rather than risk renewed tyranny. They kept their leaders on a tight leash even in 415–414, but, when the still-deeper crisis struck in 406, efforts to strengthen the state led straight to the rise of a new tyrant. Despite all the differences in social structure, local history, and external threats that divided Athens, Sparta, and Syracuse, once again war made the state and the state made war.

7.3. Olynthus, Thebes, Mytilene, and Argos

While the big three formative states inevitably dominate fifth-century history, their processes of expansion generated defensive state formation all around them. I present brief accounts of four examples of this.

7.3.1. Olynthus.

In 432, as tensions mounted with Corinth, the Athenians decided to make a preemptive strike by ordering Potidaea, one of their subject cities, to pull down its city walls and cut ties with Corinth, its mother city. At the same time, Athens planned to attack King Perdiccas of Macedon and ordered the invasion fleet to reduce Potidaea on its way to Macedon. This played into Perdiccas's hands; for some time he had been urging the Greeks of Chalcidice to abandon their home towns and form one big city at Olynthus. Trapped between a potentially hostile Macedon and Thrace[370] and a definitely hostile Athens, the latter intent on extending its power over Potidaea, the Chalcidians now formed a union and prepared for war.[371] We know few details of the state-building activities of the Chalcidian League, but they were clearly successful, since they proved a major thorn in the Athenians' flesh. After 404, the League engaged in long struggles with both Sparta and Macedon, before its dissolution by the former in 386 and the destruction of Olynthus by the latter in 346.[372]

7.3.2. Thebes. There is some debate over whether there was a Boeotian federal league dominated by Thebes as early as 500 B.C.E.,[373] but, if so, this structure was broken up after 479 in retaliation for Thebes' support of Persia. In 458, a Spartan army fought a small war in Doris and on its way home passed through Boeotia. Diodorus says that the Thebans persuaded Sparta to restore their city's walls and to force the other Boeotians to accept Theban leadership, in return for a Theban commitment to Sparta to take a lead against Athens.[374] Thucydides has a completely different explanation for why Sparta and Athens fought the battle of Tanagra in 457.[375] Nancy Demand argues the case for Diodorus,[376] but even if Diodorus's account is correct, Athens' domination of Boeotia between 457 and 447[377] again reduced Thebes to a weak, isolated city-state. After 447, the Thebans created a new Boeotian League, which gave them substantial control over the foreign policies of other cities and for the next sixty years Thebes was the only Boeotian city to mint coins.[378] According to speakers in Thucydides,[379] Thebes could draw other Boeotian cities into its orbit largely because they were always fighting each other. Just as Athens did in the Aegean, Thebes imposed order in Boeotia, centralizing its policies and armed forces.

The first act of the Peloponnesian War was a surprise attack by Thebes on Plataea, in an attempt to use the general war with Athens to expand the Boeotian League.[380] Thebes pressed ahead with this policy in the war's first few years, persuading and/or compelling the populations of the smaller, unwalled Boeotian cities to move to Thebes.[381] Thucydides says that when Plataea fell, in 426, Theban citizens took its land on ten-year leases—rather as Athenians had done on Lesbos a year earlier.[382] Fear of Athens and fighting against Athens seem to have been central to Theban state formation. Theban fears had some substance; Demosthenes was planning an attack as early as 426, and, when he launched it in 424, he did so in the hope that the Boeotians might feel so oppressed by Thebes that they would revolt.[383] Thebes took the lead in resistance, helping Tanagra in 426 and holding the place of honor on right wing at Delion,[384] but it combined example with coercion, taking advantage of heavy Thespian losses in this battle to force that city to dismantle its walls.[385] By 404, Thebes was a major power, negotiating on equal terms with Sparta, and owed much of this to its resistance to Athenian designs on Boeotia.

7.3.3. Mytilene. In 428, Thucydides tells us, "the Mytileneans were forcibly making the whole of Lesbos into one state under the control of the Mytileneans." The Mytileneans had intended to revolt later, after strengthening their fortifications, and were caught by surprise when Athens got wind of the plot in 428, but they refused to give up the union (*xynoikesis*) of Lesbos.[386] We have no details of exactly what the Mytileneans were doing to unify Lesbos,[387] since Athens immediately besieged the city, which fell in 427, but once again, state formation was a response to Athenian power.

7.3.4. Argos. Argos had probably controlled most of the Argive plain since the late eighth century, but, after it took terrible casualties in the battle of Sepeia, around 494, even such tiny neighbors as Mycenae and Tiryns had escaped from its domination. The close alliance between Athens and Argos's traditional enemy Sparta in the 470s created an alarming situation, and in the 460s Argos rapidly reincorporated the rest of the plain into a larger Argive state.[388] Athens' breach with Sparta after 462 gave Argos insurance but, when Athens and Sparta moved back together after 421, the Argives renewed their campaign of alliance making and state building.[389] Argos was driven not by fear of Athens but by fear that Athens would fail to balance Sparta. By contrast with those states that centralized power to defend themselves against Athenian expansion (and in some cases used fear of Athens as an excuse to swallow up smaller neighbors), Argos centralized when Athens was not acting powerfully enough. But this was apparently the exception: Athens never had any designs on Argos and saw it chiefly as a potential ally against Sparta. The general pattern throughout the Aegean between 478 and 404 was secondary state formation in response to the increasing power of the Greater Athenian State.

8. Conclusion

I have argued that if, like most comparative historians, we define an empire as a subtype of state characterized by a strong sense of foreignness, we must see fifth-century Athens as an example of state formation rather than an example of imperialism. The Athenian case does not cast much light on the dynamics of mature ancient empires like those whose stories fill the other chapters in this book. It does, though, cast a great deal of light on the early stages of state formation, in which one city starts to break out from of a network of similar cities to become a territorial state, absorbing much or all of the rest of the network. There is good reason to think that this was how most of the great states of antiquity originally formed,[390] but so few primary written sources survive from most ancient examples that the student of state formation has to rely heavily on much less informative archaeological evidence.

Thinking in terms of a Greater Athenian State rather than an Athenian Empire requires us to work on a broader geographical scale, setting Athens more firmly in the context of competitor states, and on a longer chronological scale, seeing fifth-century state formation as merely one phase of a process extending back at least as far the end of the Bronze Age and forward to the Greeks' incorporation into the Roman Empire.

The broader geographical scale reveals the Greater Athenian State as one among several paths of state formation, unusual only in being more capital-intensive and bureaucratic than other Greek paths. Syracuse's path also relied on converting capital into coercion, but Syracuse did not build as much state capacity as Athens because the success of tyranny made strong administrative institutions dangerous. Sparta, by contrast, moved along a coercion-intensive path, avoiding building state administrative capacity in the name of preserving specific property relations. Other cities—Olynthus, Thebes, Mytilene, Argos—developed their own variations on these paths. Each city was unique, but all shared not only in the general acceleration of the tempo of state formation in the fifth century (and particularly after 431) but also in the timeless formula that war made states and states made war. Competition—between state officeholders, between nonstate associations, between state officeholders and civil society, between states—was the central dynamic. To make sense of fifth-century Athens, we have to place its particular conflicts within the broader set of conflicts that made up Greek society.

The longer chronological scale reveals how state formation transformed society. Archaic Greek states had developed in a rather peculiar direction, putting great power in the hands of ordinary male citizens, but the very success of these states undermined their egalitarian structures. The Spartan *homoioi*, "those who are alike," were in some ways the most equal citizens in the Greek world, but conquering and holding down the helots in Laconia and Messenia effectively converted an egalitarian community into a tiny aristocracy ruling over a much larger subject population and sharply increased wealth differences within the Spartiate group. Despite lurching from crisis to crisis, the Spartans held their system together through the fifth century, only to see it unravel in the fourth. And, for all the obvious differences between Athens and Sparta in the fifth century, their long-term histories were in some ways rather similar. Athens' citizens created an aggressively democratic political structure after 508–507 B.C.E., only for their success in state building after 477 to start turning this too into an aristocracy ruling subject cities. The Spartans and the Athenians both defined membership in these ruling aristocracies in very unusual ways, and both would have been horrified to be told that they were turning into aristocratic rulers; yet, that was indeed what was happening. Syracusan state formation, by contrast, was much more conventional by ancient Old World standards. Sole rulers provided the most effective leadership, treated cities as their personal possessions, and looked on the people around them as subjects, not fellow citizens. In Sparta, Athens, and Syracuse alike, though, the fifth century saw conflict between state formation and the egalitarian structures of civil society. The failure of all three states to resolve this problem was decisive for the long-term history of Greece.

In spite of this chapter's length, it has only scratched the surface of fifth-century state formation, and, rather than closing questions down with definitive answers, I feel that it has only served to open new ones. Two seem particularly pressing. First, why did the tempo of state formation accelerate so dramatically in the fifth century?

That is, was this a purely Greek development or part of a larger trend? And was it driven by the conscious decisions of political actors, or was it a response to deeper forces? Answering this question will mean relating the narrative of political, military, and administrative history to demography and economics in new ways, and understanding better the Greeks' relationships to the societies around them. Second, why did Athens, the most modern Greek state with the biggest population, most advanced technology, most meritocratic administration, and deepest state capacity, fail to break through to become first a territorial Greek state and then a multiethnic empire like those described in the other chapters of this book?

NOTES

I want to thank everyone who took part in the Ancient Empires conferences at Stanford and Perth in 2000, 2001, and 2002 for their comments on earlier versions of this chapter, and particularly the other contributors to this volume, plus Alan Bosworth, Lance Davis, Steve Haber, David Laitine, and Meg Butler. In a conference on military participation ratios at Yale in 2005, John Ferejohn, Emily Mackil, Josh Ober, Frances Rosenbluth, and Barry Strauss also gave me helpful feedback on these ideas. In May 2007, I had the honor to be named as the Blackwell Lecturer at Bristol University, where I gave four lectures on this theme. I received invaluable comments from the audience, the many friends I made there, and the respondents (Tom Harrison, Stephen Howe, and Robin Osborne). In April 2008 Josh Ober and Joe Manning invited me to discuss the chapter with their "Political economies in late classical Greece" seminar at Stanford. Meg Butler, David Konstan, Josh Ober, and Oxford University Press's anonymous reader also made insightful suggestions on earlier versions of the chapter. Like all the contributors to this volume, I thank Steve Haber and the Social Science History Institute for the support and commitment that made this work possible. Finally, I want to offer long-overdue thanks to Richard Tomlinson, who first taught me about the Athenian Empire in an undergraduate seminar at Birmingham University more than a quarter of a century ago. The errors of fact and fancy that no doubt clutter this chapter are there despite the input of so many friends.

1. Xenophon (*Anabasis* 7.1.27) says that the Athenian Empire brought in 1,000 talents per year, which, despite all the controversy over the "normal" tribute level, seems to be in the right area (e.g., Meiggs 1972: 258–59). I assume an average wheat equivalent intake of 250 kg/person/year (c. 2,000 calories/person/day) and an average cost of 2–3 obols/adult/day in 400 B.C.E. prices (Loomis 1998: 35; 1 talent = 6,000 drachmas = 36,000 obols). Keith Hopkins (1980: 118–19) plausibly estimated the annual revenue of the Roman Empire in the early first century C.E. as >824 million sesterces. If one *modius* of what (6.55 kg) cost about 3 sesterces, we get a conversion rate of 1 drachma (Athenian 400 B.C.E. value) = 1.6 sesterces (Roman early first century C.E. value). The Roman income of, say, 830 million sesterces would then be worth about 86,500 talents; the Athenian income of 1,000 talents, about 9.6 million sesterces (i.e., Athens brought in about 1.2 percent of the Roman figure). Even the inflated demands of 425 B.C.E. (tribute of 1,460 talents, plus perhaps 500 talents in indirect taxes) would have been worth only a little under 20 million sesterces, or 2.3 percent of the Roman income.
2. Morris et al. 2007.
3. Tilly 1992.
4. E.g., Waltz 1979: 118.

5. E.g., North and Thomas 1973: 7; Arthur 1989: 116–17; Mahoney 2000: 521.

6. Morris 2005a; Hedrick 2006.

7. Osborne (1999) suggests some ways to combine the written and nonwritten sources.

8. E.g., B. R. MacDonald 1982; Erickson 2005. The distribution of wine amphoras may have more potential (Lawall 1998; 2000).

9. To some extent coins blur the written/nonwritten distinction. They have their own problems but can be important sources (Figueira 1998).

10. Thucydides 1.20–22.

11. Meiggs and Lewis (1969) collect many of the key texts, and Fornara (1983) and Hornblower and Greenstock (1984) translate them.

12. The essays are collected in Mattingly 1996.

13. *IG* i³ 11 (Lewis 1984).

14. Chambers et al. 1990, with Matthaiou 2004.

15. Mattingly 1996: 10–11; Finley 1978.

16. Meiggs 1972: 129–74.

17. 8,000 talents, Diodorus 12.38; 10,000 talents, Diodorus 12.54; 13.21; 454–453 B.C.E., *IG* i³ 259 (Lewis 1984); 428 B.C.E., Thucydides 3.19.

18. Regulations, *IG* i³ 39, 40 (Lewis 1984); revolt, Thucydides 1.114.

19. G. Hill 1951.

20. Hodkinson 2000: 9–64 discusses the Spartan sources and De Angelis, forthcoming, those from western Greece.

21. Herodotus 1.27.

22. The main exception came in 440 B.C.E., when the satrap Pissuthnes sent a fleet to support Samos's rebellion (Thucydides 1.116).

23. Generally, see Garnsey 1999.

24. E.g., Floud et al. 1990; Steckel and Rose 2002; Fogel 2004.

25. Fogel 1993: 14.

26. Morris 2004.

27. Angel 1972.

28. Garnsey 1988: 8–16.

29. Sallares 1991: 372–89; Garnsey 1992.

30. Bintliff 1997.

31. Bisel and Angel 1985: tab. 4.

32. E.g., Bisel 1990; Henneberg and Henneberg 1998.

33. Morris 2007.

34. See, e.g., Livi-Bacci 1997.

35. Goldstone 1991: 27–37.

36. Morris 2004; Scheidel 2004a.

37. Grmek 1989.

38. Thucydides 2.47–54, with Papagrigorakis et al. 2006. Recurrence in 427–426: Thucydides 3.27.

39. Diodorus 13.114; 14.63, 70–71.

40. Hansen 2006a. Hansen offers an even higher figure, including millions of "Hellenized" peoples in the west Mediterranean and Balkans. This strikes me as overlooking the complexity of ethnic identity in antiquity (see J. Hall 1997). My own excavations in Sicily, like several other recent projects in the west Mediterranean, suggest that, as late as 500 B.C.E., Hellenization was a very limited phenomenon (Morris and Tusa 2004).

41. Hansen 1985.
42. Garnsey 1988: 90; Sallares 1991: 72.
43. Strauss 1986: 70–86.
44. Hansen 2006b: 19–60.
45. Morris 2006: 43–46.
46. Thucydides 7.28.
47. De Angelis 2000; Garnsey 1988: 92; Hansen 2006a.
48. Cartledge (1987: 174) estimates the number of helots at 175,000–200,000, while Hodkinson (2000: 134–35) suggests 162,000–187,000. The range suggested by Scheidel (2003a) may favor slightly lower numbers.
49. Catling 2002: 209.
50. Hodkinson 2000: 421; Aristotle, *Politics* 1270a29–31; Plutarch, *Agis* 5.
51. Morris 2004; 2007.
52. Cartledge 1998: 6.
53. E. Cohen 1992; Jew 1999.
54. Howgego 1995; Kim 2001.
55. E.g., Pettegrew 2001, with associated comments.
56. Morris 2006.
57. Cherry et al. 1991: 337.
58. Burford (1993) summarizes the arguments evenhandedly.
59. Snodgrass 1994; Ault 1999.
60. Zangger et al. 1997: 594.
61. Morris 2005a.
62. Hoepfner and Schwandner 1994; Hoepfner 1999; Nevett 1999; Ault 2006.
63. Morris 2004. Saller (2005) suggested a similar increase across the western Mediterranean during the early Roman Empire.
64. Mokyr 1990: 20–30, 193–99; Meijer and van Nijf 1992; and Humphrey et al. 1998 collect the evidence.
65. Halstead 1987.
66. Greene 2000; Wilson 2002.
67. Mokyr 2002; Landes 2003.
68. Thompson and Wycherley 1972; Herodotus 3.60; Diodorus 11.25.
69. Verdelis 1956; Strabo 8.2.1.
70. Herodotus 5.52–53.
71. *IG* II² 1673 = Meijer and van Nijf 1992: no. 173.
72. Strabo 5.3.8.
73. Plutarch, *Pericles* 26; Casson 1986.
74. Walter and Vierneisel 1959: 11–13.
75. Eiseman and Ridgway 1987; Hadjidaki 1996.
76. E.g., Strabo 17.1.6–10; Appian, *Punic Wars* 8.14.96; Josephus, *Jewish War* 1.408–414. Samos: Herodotus 3.60. Piraeus: Garland 1987.
77. See Demosthenes 35.10–11; Isager and Hansen 1975; Reed 2003.
78. See now Hodkinson and Powell 2006.
79. Hanson 2000. Van Wees (2004) suggests that hoplite warfare developed more gradually.
80. Garlan 1974.
81. Thucydides 1.13, 14; Herodotus 1.166; 3.39; Wallinga 1993.
82. Morrison et al. 2000.

83. Herodotus 7.144.
84. Thucydides 2.62.
85. Strauss 2000.
86. Diodorus 14.51–44; Plutarch, *Demetrius* 43.
87. Morris 1998a; 2000: 109–91; cf. Hanson 1995; Kurke 1999; Balot 2001. Foxhall (2001) and Hammer (2005) have raised some interesting objections.
88. Hunt 1998; Wood 1988; Jameson 1992.
89. Hodkinson 2000: 113–50. Revisionists (e.g., Ducat 1990; Luraghi 2003) have challenged this traditional interpretation of the history of helotage, but their arguments remain rather speculative.
90. Davis 1977, scoring .22 to .87; Duncan-Jones 1990: 129–42, scoring .39–.86.
91. [Demosthenes] 42, with Ste. Croix 1966.
92. Diodorus 13.81, 84.
93. Plutarch, *Dion* 15.
94. Hodkinson 2000.
95. Morris 1992: 108–55; 1998b.
96. Morris and Powell 2005: 370–99.
97. Hansen 1991.
98. Connor 1971.
99. Thucydides 2.65.
100. Rhodes 1972.
101. Finley 1985: 61–62.
102. Geertz 1973: 412–53.
103. Thucydides 3.38.
104. Thucydides 2.65.
105. Strauss and Ober 1990: 72.
106. Thucydides 8.48.
107. Thucydides 1.107.
108. Ober 1998.
109. Finley 1985: 74–75.
110. Andrewes (1966), Ste. Croix (1972: 124–51), and Hodkinson (1983) remain the fundamental treatments of fifth-century Spartan politics.
111. Cartledge 1981.
112. Hodkinson 1983: 263–65; Cartledge 1987: 139–59.
113. Aristotle, *Politics* 1306a18–19.
114. Hodkinson 1983: 280.
115. Herodotus 8.4–5, 49–83; Thucydides 1.68–71.
116. Thucydides 8.96.
117. Herodotus 7.156.
118. Luraghi 1994: 369; Consolo Langher 1996: 286–88.
119. Diodorus 11.26.
120. Meiggs and Lewis 1969: nos. 28, 29.
121. Pindar, *basileus*: *Olympian* 2.23; *Pythian* 2.60; 3.70; *tyrannos*: *Pythian* 3.85. Herodotus 7.156, 161.
122. Aristotle, *Politics* 1304 a 27; debate, see Rutter 2000; Robinson 2004: 123–51.
123. Consolo Langher 1996: 288–95.
124. Diodorus 11.86–87.

125. Thucydides 6.35, 38; Diodorus 13.34–35, 91.

126. Tod 1948: no. 136 = Harding 1985: no. 52.

127. Generally, see Burkert 1985; Zaidman and Schmitt-Pantel 1992.

128. Hesiod, *Theogony* 453–885, with commentary in West 1966.

129. Faraone 1992.

130. Garland 1984.

131. Isocrates 2.6.

132. Herodotus 1.132.

133. Herodotus 7.140–43.

134. Herodotus 5.90–91; Thucydides 5.16; Hodkinson 1983: 273–77.

135. Vanderpool 1964; Plutarch, *Themistocles* 22.

136. Kuhrt 1995: 509–518, 676–86; Bedford, this vol.; Wiesehöfer, this vol.

137. Thucydides 5.105.

138. Thucydides 1.73–77.

139. *IG* i³ 369, 375, 377 (Lewis 1984) = Meiggs and Lewis 1969: nos. 72, 84 = Fornara 1983: nos. 134, 154, 158; Thucydides 1.143; see Davies 2001.

140. Wickersham 1994: 31–34.

141. Thucydides 1.99, 98.

142. Garnsey and Whittaker 1978.

143. Finley 1978: 104.

144. E.g., Kolbe 1938; Schäfer 1939.

145. Schuller 1974: 2–3.

146. Finley 1978: 104.

147. Doyle 1986: 45.

148. Doyle 1986: 30.

149. M. Mann 1986b: 112.

150. Tilly 1992: 1–2.

151. Anderson 1991; Hobsbawm 1990.

152. Thinking of empires as a subtype of state, characterized by a sense of difference between rulers and ruled, is a well-established principle among social scientists and modern historians: see, e.g., Howe 2002: 9–34; Ferguson 2004: 7–13.

153. Ober 1989.

154. Runciman 1989: 152–53.

155. Thucydides 6.15.

156. Particularly Said 1993; Bhabha 1994.

157. Thucydides 2.63; 3.37.

158. Thucydides 1.1–19; Connor 1984: 20–32; Kallet-Marx 1993: 23–36.

159. See J. Hall 1997: 17–33.

160. Hesiod fragment 9 (Merkelbach and West, eds., 1967).

161. See particularly E. Hall 1989.

162. J. Hall 1997: 51–56 summarizes the traditions.

163. Solon fragment 4 (West, ed., 1991–92).

164. E.g., Herodotus 1.56, 143; Thucydides 7.57. Euripides' tragedy *Ion* offers a different genealogy, apparently trying to reconcile Athenians' Ionian descent with the tradition of their autochthonous origins.

165. See particularly J. Hall 1997: 176–77.

166. See Burkert 1985; Polinskaya 2000.

167. Herodotus 8.144.
168. Dougherty and Kurke, eds., 2003.
169. Morris 1998b.
170. Murray 1990: 3.
171. E.g., Ehrenberg 1969: 3–25.
172. Gawantka 1985.
173. Johnson and Earle 2000 and Trigger 2003 are excellent recent examples.
174. Snodgrass 1977, extended in Snodgrass 2006.
175. Hansen (2006c) provides a good overview of the new consensus.
176. Sahlins and Service 1960; Service 1962; Fried 1967.
177. Mitchell 1991.
178. E.g., Rueschemeyer et al. 1985; Block 1988; Jessop 1990; Tilly 1992.
179. Steinmetz 1999: 8–9.
180. Morris 2003; forthcoming.
181. Morris and Powell 2005: 148–70.
182. See van Wees 2004.
183. E.g., Lo 1969; Kamen 2003: 167–72, 184–86. On the transformation of British naval funding after 1688, which broke the early-modern mold as dramatically as Athens broke the archaic Greek mold in 477 B.C.E., see Brewer 1988.
184. Morris 2005b.
185. Morris 1991; 1997; 2003.
186. Gellner 1983: 9–10.
187. Gellner 1988: 22.
188. Thucydides 8.48.
189. Ferguson 2004: 11.
190. Thucydides 1.23.
191. Thucydides 1.96; 3.10; 6.76.
192. E.g., Rawlings 1977; Raaflaub 1979; Giovannini and Gottlieb 1980; Robertson 1980.
193. Thucydides 1.98–100.
194. Andocides 3.37–38; Thucydides 1.96.
195. Thucydides 1.96; Diodorus 11.47.
196. E.g., Thucydides 6.8–26; 7.57.
197. Meiggs 1972: 173 n. 1.
198. [Aristotle], *Constitution of Athens* 23.5; Plutarch, *Aristides* 25. Rhodes (2006: 15) is skeptical about such oaths.
199. Diodorus 11.70.
200. Thucydides 1.99.
201. There is a large literature on the loyalty of the cities; see Rhodes 2006: 178–88.
202. Thucydides 5.18; Diodorus 11.46; Plutarch, *Aristides* 24.
203. Thucydides 1.96.
204. Herodotus 8.40–64.
205. Herodotus 6.12.
206. Thucydides 1.99; Plutarch, *Cimon* 11.
207. [Aristotle], *Constitution of Athens* 24.2; cf. scholiast on Aristophanes, *Birds* 880, citing Theopompus and Eupolis.
208. Thucydides 2.9; 7.57; Diodorus 12.42; Pausanias 5.10.4; Meiggs and Lewis 1969: no. 34.
209. Thucydides 1.99.

210. Isocrates 4.104.
211. Thucydides 1.115–17; Plutarch, *Pericles* 24–25.
212. Old Oligarch 1.14; 3.10; Plato, *Seventh Letter* 332b-c; Aristotle, *Politics* 1307b22.
213. Thucydides 3.82.
214. See Thucydides 1.80; Demosthenes 23.209; Andreades 1933: 3–193.
215. See Samons 2000.
216. The Hellespont tax may have begun by 426–425 (Rubel 2001).
217. Boeckh 1840: 196–210, with Eddy 1968: 189–92; Gabrielsen 1994: 139–42.
218. Loomis 1998: 36–45.
219. Herodotus 7.144.
220. Plutarch, *Pericles* 11.
221. Thucydides 1.96.
222. Plutarch, *Aristides* 24; Diodorus 11.47.
223. Plutarch, *Cimon* 9–13.
224. Thucydides 2.13; Samons 2000.
225. Diodorus 12.28; *IG* i^3 363 (Lewis 1984); Thucydides 2.70.
226. Thucydides 1.117.
227. Andreades 1933: 222.
228. Thucydides 2.13.
229. Thucydides 3.17; on the authenticity of the passage, Kallet-Marx 1993: 130–34.
230. Thucydides 3.13.
231. Plutarch, *Aristides* 24.
232. Cf. [Andocides] 4.11.
233. *IG* i^3 71.16–17 (Lewis 1984).
234. Thucydides 2.69; 3.19; 4.60, 75.
235. *IG* i^3 34, 52, 61, 68 (Lewis 1984).
236. *IG* i^3 369 (Lewis 1984), with Samons 2000.
237. Thucydides 3.19.
238. *IG* i^3 21 (Lewis 1984).
239. Finley 1978: 125.
240. Andreades 1933: 126–61.
241. Herodotus 6.46.
242. Thucydides 7.28.
243. Xenophon, *Hellenica* 1.1.22.
244. *IG* i^3 52.7 (Lewis 1984); see Rubel 2001; Eich 2005: 155–56.
245. Old Oligarch 1.18. Andreyev (1990) and Eich (2005: 150–55) emphasize Athens' "Über-akkumulation."
246. Hermippos, *The Porters* frag. 63, trs. J. K. Davies 1978: 110–11; cf. Old Oligarch 2.7; Thucydides 2.38.
247. Isocrates 4.52.
248. *IG* i^3 1,453 (Lewis 1984).
249. See Figueira 1998: 227–47.
250. T. Martin 1984: 196–207; cf. D. M. Lewis 1987: 60–63; Figueira 1998: 259–95.
251. Figueira 1998: 296–315.
252. Diodorus 10.3–7; Plutarch, *Nicias* 5; Fornara 1983: no. 108.
253. Thucydides 1.100.
254. Thucydides 2.27, 70; 5.116; Figueira 1991.

255. A. H. M. Jones 1954: 168–74; Brunt 1966; Erxleben 1975.

256. Herodotus 5.77; *IG* i³ 1 (Lewis 1984).

257. Isocrates 4.107.

258. Plutarch, *Pericles* 11.

259. See *IG* i³ 46.40 (Lewis 1984), [Aristotle], *Constitution of Athens* 26, Plutarch, *Pericles* 37.

260. E.g., Plato, *Euthyphro* 4c; Xenophon, *Memorabilia* 2.8.1; Andocides 3.15; *IG* i³ 118.20–22 (Lewis 1984).

261. Oionias, *IG* i³ 422.177, 311; 424.15, 17, 150; 426.53; Nicides, *IG* i³ 430.1 (Lewis 1984).

262. Finley 1978: 123; Thucydides 8.48.

263. Lysias 34.4.

264. Demosthenes 36.5–6.

265. Diodorus 15.23, 29.

266. Thucydides 1.100, 105.

267. Balcer 1976; 1977.

268. [Aristotle] *Constitution of Athens* 24.4; Old Oligarch 1.19; Aristophanes, *Birds* 1021–52.

269. Reiter 1991.

270. E.g., *IG* i³ 21.77–80; 34.6–7; 156; 1453 (Lewis 1984); Antiphon 5.47.

271. *IG* i³ 14.13–14; 34.7 (Lewis 1984); Aristophanes, *Birds* 1021–34; Harpocration, s.v. *episkopos*.

272. *IG* i³ .14–15, 38–39, 52, 55; 21.77 (Lewis 1984); Aristophanes, *Wasps* 235–37; Eupolis, *Cities*, fragment 233; Isocrates 7.65; Plutarch, *Pericles* 12.

273. Thucydides 3.82; Old Oligarch 1.14; 3.10; Plato, *Seventh Letter* 332b-c; Aristotle, *Politics* 1307b22.

274. Old Oligarch 3.11.

275. Gehrke 1980; Robertson 1987; Piérart 1983–85.

276. Thucydides 3.47.

277. *IG* i³ 14; 37; 48 (Lewis 1984).

278. Thucydides 1.77; Old Oligarch 1.16.

279. Isocrates 4.113; 12.66; quotation from 4.104.

280. *IG* i³ 40.5–10, 71–76 (Lewis 1984); Balcer 1978.

281. *IG* i³ 14.40–33 (Lewis 1984).

282. Antiphon 5.47.

283. In contrast to the seventh and sixth centuries, where leading cultural figures were widely distributed across Greek cities, in the fifth century Athens and, to a lesser extent, Syracuse were the only places to be: Boedeker and Raaflaub, eds., 1998; Morris and Powell 2005: 289–311.

284. Thucydides 2.41.

285. Plutarch, *Pericles* 12–14.

286. Milton's expression, in *Paradise Regained* (1671) book 4, line 240.

287. Athenaeus 15.698d–99c.

288. Ostwald 1992.

289. Hurwit 1985.

290. Boedeker and Raaflaub 1998: 322–25.

291. Castriota 1992; Boedeker and Raaflaub, eds., 1998.

292. Cole (1991) and Schiappa (1999) dispute the significance of Tisias and Corax, the Syracusans said to have been the first systematic theorists of rhetoric, but the links among rhetoric, Syracuse, and democracy remain strong (Robinson, ed., 2004: 147).

293. Nightingale 1995; Ober 1998.

294. Nye 2005.

295. Finley 1978: 309 n. 47; 1985: 168–69; *IG* i³ 1453 (Lewis 1984).

296. E.g., T. Martin 1984: 196–207; Figueira 1998: 245–58.

297. Kurke 1999. von Reden (1997) and Seaford (2004) develop related ideas.

298. Schuller 1974: 112–24; Fehr 1979–81; Smarczyk 1990.

299. *IG* i³ 14 (Lewis 1984).

300. *IG* i³ 71.57–58 (Lewis 1984).

301. E.g., *IG* i³ 34.51–43; 46.11–12 (Lewis 1984).

302. Thucydides 1.118.

303. Plutarch, *Nicias* 3.

304. Thucydides 6.76.

305. Thucydides 6.82–83.

306. E.g., Thucydides 1.75–76; 5.89; 7.57.

307. Chalcis, *IG* xii.9.934; Samos, *SEG* 1.375; Aegina, Figueira 1991: 115–20; Mytilene, Thucydides 3.50.

308. *IG* i³ 78 (Lewis 1984).

309. Isocrates 4.41.

310. Tilly 1975: 73.

311. Thucydides 1.23.

312. Herodotus 1.65–68.

313. Thucydides 1.19, 144.

314. Herodotus 1.69, 141, 152; 5.49.

315. Herodotus 5.92.

316. Ste. Croix 1972: 100.

317. Herodotus 8.142.

318. Herodotus 7.133–36, 148–62; cf. 8.3 on Athenian involvement.

319. Diodorus 11.4; Isocrates 4.90; Herodotus 9.10, 11, 28, 29, 61, with Hunt 1997; van Wees 2004: 181.

320. Cartledge 1979: 213–16, with Herodotus 9.35.

321. Thucydides 1.95; Herodotus 8.3; Diodorus 11.50.

322. Thucydides 1.103.

323. Thucydides 1.113.

324. Thucydides 1.118.

325. Thucydides 1.81; 2.7, 67; Herodotus 7.137; Diodorus 12.41.

326. Ste. Croix 1972: 155; Thucydides 4.60.

327. Thucydides 4.51, 55.

328. Thucydides 4.65, with van Wees 2004: 238.

329. Thucydides 4.26, 80, 108; Plutarch, *Lycurgus* 28.

330. Thucydides 4.108, 132.

331. Thucydides 4.134; 5.33.

332. Thucydides 5.23.

333. Thucydides 5.27, 29, 30.

334. Thucydides 5.32.

335. Thucydides 8.18, 37, 58.

336. Xenophon, *Hellenica* 1.6.7; Plutarch, *Lysander* 6.

337. Xenophon, *Hellenica* 2.1.6–7; Diodorus 13.100; Plutarch, *Lysander* 7.

338. Andocides 3.29; Isocrates 8.97. Diodorus (14.10) says just 1,000 talents. Pritchett (1974: 47–48) tabulates and discusses the sources.

339. Xenophon, *Hellenica* 1.6.4; Diodorus 13.70; Plutarch, *Lysander* 5–6.
340. Xenophon, *Anabasis* 6.6.9.
341. Xenophon, *Hellenica* 3.4.2, 7.
342. Xenophon, *Hellenica* 3.2.8; 4.8.7.
343. Xenophon, *Hellenica* 3.3.4–11; Aristotle, *Politics* 1306b34–36.
344. Diodorus 14.13; Plutarch, *Lysander* 24–26.
345. By this time Pausanias was in exile. Unfortunately, the crucial passage in Strabo (8.5.5) is corrupt, and it is not clear whether Pausanias wanted to defend or to overthrow the Lycurgan system (Cartledge 1987: 163; cf. Aristotle, *Politics* 1301b19–21).
346. See Osborne 1998; De Angelis 2003.
347. De Angelis 2000.
348. Thucydides 6.17.
349. Jackman 2005.
350. Thucydides 1.13.
351. Herodotus 7.158; Justin 14.1.
352. Herodotus 5.46; Diodorus 4.23; Pausanias 3.16. See Maffoda 1996: 46–55 on the general context.
353. Anello 1986.
354. Herodotus 7.154.
355. Luraghi 1994: 165–69.
356. [Aristotle], *Oeconomica* 2.2.20; Diodorus 14.106. Andreades (1933: 122) concluded from [Aristotle] that Dionysius established a 2-stater poll tax, but in fact the passage speaks only of a ruse through which the tyrant tricked each citizen out of 2 staters.
357. Herodotus 7.156; Diodorus 11.49.
358. Diodorus 14.51–44.
359. Thucydides 8.26, 28, 84; Xenophon, *Hellenica* 1.2.8, 10; Diodorus 13.34.
360. Herodotus 7.158.
361. Diodorus 12.30.
362. Thucydides 3.86–90; 4.68–65; Giangiulio 1997. The Syracusan alliance was itself allied to the Peloponnesian League (3.86).
363. The transfer of the leading men of Leontinoi to Syracuse before 422 (Thucydides 5.4) shows that Syracuse continued to pursue tyrannical-style state formation, but this example seems to be unique.
364. Thucydides 4.60; 6.33, 34, 76–88.
365. Thucydides 7.33.
366. Thucydides 6.72, 103.
367. Diodorus 13.93.
368. Diodorus 13.91–96; Plato, *Seventh Letter* 347b; Plutarch, *Dion* 37.
369. Tod 1948: no. 148 = Harding 1985: no. 20. Lysias (6.6) called him *basileus*, "king," probably also in the 390s.
370. Thucydides 2.101.
371. Thucydides 1.56–58.
372. Zahrnt 1971.
373. Buck 1979: 107–120.
374. Diodorus 11.81.
375. Thucydides 1.107.
376. Demand 1982: 31–33.

377. Thucydides 1.108.
378. Salmon 1978; 1994; Maffoda 1999: 89–100.
379. Thucydides 3.62; 4.92; cf. Aristotle, *Rhetoric* 1470a2.
380. Thucydides 2.2.
381. *Hellenica Oxyrhynchia* 17.3.
382. Thucydides 3.68.
383. Thucydides 3.95; 4.76.
384. Thucydides 3.91; 4.93.
385. Thucydides 4.133.
386. Thucydides 3.2–3.
387. Quinn 1981: 25–33.
388. Herodotus 6.83; Diodorus 11.65; Strabo 8.6.10–11.
389. Thucydides 6.7.
390. Yoffee 2005.

wealth was more important than numbering allies

5

The Political Economy of the Roman Empire

Keith Hopkins[†]

1. Introduction

The Roman Empire lasted as a single political system for five centuries and more. At its height, it stretched from the Black Sea to the Red Sea to the Atlantic Ocean. This essay explores how the empire was governed, how its wealth was created, and how that wealth was distributed among competing elements of the population: the central government, the emperor, the aristocracy, the army, the city of Rome, municipal elites, peasants, and slaves.

2. Origins and Evolution

By origin, the Roman Empire was an empire of conquest, one of a handful of empires which developed throughout the world in the golden millennium of empire formation and religious innovation (c. 550 B.C.E.–650 C.E.). This world-wide evolution of large preindustrial states depended crucially on three material innovations: the effective use of iron weapons and tools, writing, and money. Iron was used to conquer and plough. Writing was used to organize collectives of humans toward common objectives, both instrumentally and symbolically in spite of distances in space and time (for example, via written religious texts and law codes). Coinage (first introduced in large quantities into Rome in the third century B.C.E.) was used to store value and to reward, motivate and exploit subjects.

In this perspective, the Roman Empire represented only one further stage in the gradual evolution of states from tribes to kingdoms and from kingdoms to larger and larger empires. Rome was thus the grandchild of Mycenae and Troy and the heir of countless and now unknown warring tribes, which have left no epics or histories. Rome was also the immediate heir and beneficiary of important empires, such as Carthage (conquered in 202 B.C.E.), Macedon (conquered in 168 B.C.E.), Syria (63 B.C.E.), and Egypt (30 B.C.E.). Symptomatically, the first Roman emperor, Augustus (31 B.C.E.–14 C.E.), wore the image of that other great empire builder Alexander on his signet ring but then later changed his seal to his own image.[1]

One secret of successful empire lay in frequent and sometimes radical innovations. Politically, for example, Rome changed from an early monarchy of allegedly Etruscan kings (traditional dates 753–509 B.C.E.) to a native oligarchic aristocracy. And then, much later, Rome changed again, from a primarily aristocratic form of government back to monarchy (31 B.C.E.–476 C.E. in the west, and for much longer in the eastern empire). But even this oligarchic aristocracy (509–31 B.C.E., in a period conventionally labeled the Republic) was itself significantly restrained by a powerful combination of participatory democracy and the widespread obligation of citizens to military service. So aristocratic leaders had to solicit election to high political office from their social inferiors. And laws were passed by a mass electorate. In disputed votes on the passage of laws, and in disputed elections for high office—and most elections were disputed—the plebs had effective political power, even though the collective power of the people was constitutionally manipulated in an elaborate block-voting system, which repeatedly gave disproportionate weight to the more prosperous citizens.[2]

Aristocratic exploitation of the poor was also limited by the collective power of the Roman citizen army. Once drawn up in military formation, the armed citizens had irresistible power; their repeated withdrawal from cooperation with the rich was celebrated in historical myth, as the "secessions of the Plebs." The aristocracy had little choice but to give way and concede privileges to the people. These populist movements, enshrined constitutionally in the prestige and powers of the ten Tribunes of the People and in the Roman sense of collective identity, were historically and symbolically important. They performed perhaps the same function in Roman cultural self-perception as the English charter myth of the Magna Carta or the American individualistic dream of Abraham Lincoln or the self-made millionaire, from rags to riches.

The threat of using military force to resolve political issues recurred, and civil wars broke out toward the end of the period of rapid imperial expansion (225–30 B.C.E.).[3] Social tensions were exacerbated because the rewards of empire were very unequally distributed. For example, in this period, a huge number, well over 1 million, perhaps even 2 million slaves were imported from conquered provinces into Italy. And these imported slaves displaced even larger numbers of free peasants in central and southern Italy. Tens of thousands of these slaves were subsequently freed and absorbed into the Roman citizen body. The ejected peasants, in their turn, created wave upon wave of migrants to different areas. Many of them were recruited into the Roman army; others went to the city of Rome, where they were tempted by the prospect of state-subsidized and later free wheat doles; others migrated to other growing Italian towns. Yet more peasants and ex-peasant soldiers emigrated to colonies, where they were granted land by victorious generals, at first in southern and northern Italy and later also in the conquered provinces.[4]

This process of overseas colonization (49–13 B.C.E.), especially during and in the aftermath of bitter civil wars, served multiple functions. It removed literally tens of thousands of Italian peasants from the crowded Italian land market and gave them bigger individual plots overseas, which were useful as bulwarks of Roman power in the conquered provinces. So imported slaves and Roman colonists moved in opposite and complementary directions: slaves to Italy and free Romans to the provinces. And, at the same time, the mass emigration of free citizens from Italy freed more land for ownership by the newly enriched and land-hungry aristocrats, who in this period of expansion and insecurity wanted their large estates in Italy worked by imported slaves. There was no other investment opportunity that offered the same security and status. Together, mass overseas colonization and the regular provision of free wheat doles to a large number of citizens (more than 200,000 adult males) in the city of Rome provided the economic underpinning of Augustus's political settlement.

Augustus was the victorious leader of one faction in the long civil wars that followed Julius Caesar's assassination, in 44 B.C.E. He successfully turned his military power into a quasi-constitutional but autocratic monarchy (the so-called Principate or High Empire [31 B.C.E.–235 C.E.]). Augustus and his immediate successors transformed the governance of the Roman state. Familiarity with their long-lasting success should not blind us to the brilliant inventiveness of their reforms.[5]

First, the army was recruited decreasingly from among Roman citizens living in Italy and increasingly from among citizens living in the provinces and from provincials (see section 6.3). The army was no longer recruited ad hoc for particular campaigns but was recruited long-term for from sixteen to twenty-five years, with a very large terminal bonus (equal to almost thirteen years' pay), which helped ensure loyalty. The army (except for the small elite palace guard and metropolitan police force) was not stationed in Italy but strung out defensively along the distant frontiers. In short, the citizen army that had so threatened the central polity during the last century of the Republic was demilitarized and disempowered. The army was well paid but dispersed so that it could not easily unite to rebel. Few modern third-world countries have managed to control their military so effectively. (Admittedly, the palace guard played a hand in choosing and dismissing emperors—but the selection of emperors rarely had consequences for the efficiency of government.)

Second, under the emperors, the old aristocrats who had survived the murderous civil wars of the Late Republic were apparently seduced by their individual chances of success in a superficially restored oligarchy. But now there was an emperor in charge to ensure that all the traditional oligarchic rules about power-sharing were strictly enforced (such as short tenure of offices and long gaps between offices). So, politically successful aristocrats spent about fifteen or twenty long years competing with one another, under the skeptical and supervisory eyes of a less-than-generous emperor (or his heir), who repeatedly used capricious cruelty (if we are to believe aristocratic commentaries), confiscations, and executions as techniques of control.

The end result was that the Roman aristocracy became, much more than it had ever been before, an aristocracy of office with extremely low rates of hereditary succession (see section 6.1 for more details). As in the army, elite vacancies were increasingly filled by provincials. So the elite of the conquerors merged with the elite of the conquered.

Third, the emperors at Rome effectively changed the nature of Roman citizenship. The plebs at Rome were disfranchised and no longer constituted the electorate for competing aristocrats; for that task the emperors probably considered that they were too volatile and corruptible. So the emperors enlarged on republican tradition and bought off the plebs with bread and circuses. Not that the metropolitan crowd was completely depoliticized. After all, it still remained each emperor's biggest captive audience. That was where he knew he was king and god; the people in circus or amphitheater were his personal claque, mostly conned into servile flattery, bought by lavish gifts and shows, but from time to time, as both sides must have known, the crowd could turn nasty and bayed for blood.

The disfranchisement and demilitarization of the citizens at Rome allowed citizenship itself to become a status symbol. Here the emperors built on what had long been a radical Roman tradition. After all, Rome had begun as a city-state. It had conquered the surrounding towns and tribes and, as it expanded, had incorporated its successive neighbors into partial and then full citizenship.[6] It was a stroke of generous and self-interested genius. Julius Caesar, Augustus, and their successors followed this absorptive tradition and increasingly rewarded first Italians, then leading provincials with the symbolic status of citizens. In the reign of Augustus, citizens numbered about 4 to 5 million people (about 7–10% of the empire's population).[7] Thereafter, the number of citizens steadily increased, until in 212 c.e. practically all the inhabitants of the empire were awarded full citizenship. It was now time, the emperors apparently considered, for the traditional divide between conquerors and conquered to be forgotten. All inhabitants of the empire were now both citizens and subjects. But they were by no means all equal. A new empire-wide stratification of respectables (*honestiores*) and mean folk (*humiliores*) now separated the privileged from the exploited.[8] And, needless to say, several exquisite gradings (e.g., "most perfect," "most egregious," "illustrious") differentiated the elite.[9]

3. THE FISCAL SYSTEM

Early Rome was, and for long remained, a warrior state. In order to survive and flourish, Rome had to exploit not only its enemies and allies but also its own citizens. Initially, it exploited its own citizens primarily by exacting military service, civil obedience, and a small proportional tax on property (0.1% of capital value each year).[10] All citizens (adult males) were liable to military service, up to ten years in the cavalry and sixteen years in the infantry, although even in the infantry, obligations were graded according to wealth. For example, the very poorest citizens (*proletarii*) were considered capable of contributing only children (*proles*) to the state. At the very least, this rudimentary system implied that the Romans state from early times kept lists of all its citizens and recorded the value of each citizen's property so that each could be allocated with rough justice to one of seven classes (knights, classes I–V, proletarians). Seen another way, the Roman system of obligation, whether to fight or pay taxes, differentiated and reinforced various layers of the status pyramid. But overall the state did not require much money, because most administrative jobs, even the highest, were undertaken by volunteers, that is, by those who could afford them. This ancient parsimony molded the Roman state's expectations for centuries.

In retrospect, one central problem of the Roman state during this period of rapid growth was how to reward the beneficiaries of empire differentially (e.g., how to let the rich and powerful get richer and more powerful) without alienating the support and compliance of the various strata at the bottom of the social pile. Even the richest Romans needed the obedience of the Roman free poor, slaves, allies, and conquered subjects. And that dependency of the rich on the poor constrained exploitation. The problem was all the more intractable because, as the empire expanded, relative positions, even at the bottom of the social scale, shifted.

The allies provide a neat case in point. As Rome defeated its neighbors, they were successively embraced as Latins or allies, as almost like Romans. The sole obligation of the allies in return was to provide Rome with soldiers, annually or as requested. The more Rome expanded territorially within Italy, the more generous Rome became in extending allied status to its defeated Italian enemies. Again, in retrospect, it seems that Rome's continuous drive to territorial expansion derived partly from Romans' own warrior ambitions and greed and partly from the repeated need to reinforce the allies' military obligations by getting them once again to provide troops. By the end of the second century b.c.e., allies were regularly contributing perhaps two-thirds of the Roman field armies without sharing significantly in the profits of empire.[11] Small wonder, then, that the allies eventually rebelled. Surprisingly, their dominant collective objective (at least in the Roman records) was not secession but overt equality, with full Roman citizens. Rome, after a considerable struggle, adroitly surrendered.[12] At one stroke, then, in the eighties b.c.e., the number of adult male Roman citizens trebled to close to 1 million.[13] Once again, the Roman state had managed to restore the delicate balance between beneficiaries of empire and its exploited subjects.

Defeated enemies understandably paid most of the costs of empire. At first, Roman conquerors compensated themselves handsomely for the trouble of overcoming resistance, with booty, comprising stored treasure in gold and silver, or captured humans, who were either ransomed or sold as slaves. Ideally, this booty was originally handed over to the Roman state, though victorious generals occasionally dedicated a portion to a god to whom they had made a solemn vow in the the heat of the battle in return for securing victory. Gradually, generals also took an increasing share for themselves and their lieutenants and distributed relatively modest sums to their lesser officers and soldiers. By the end of the period of rapid imperial expansion, conquering generals and administrators of pacified provinces routinely expected to make substantial personal profits with which to cover the costs of their political careers and their social ostentation at Rome. They shared some of these profits of office with their entourage and occasionally secured land grants for their retiring vererans. Also in the growing empire, defeated enemies paid huge indemnities to recompense Rome for the costs of defeating them. Carthage, for example, paid an indemnity over fifty years after its second defeat, in 202 B.C.E.. But gradually these indemnities were transformed into routine taxation, only some of which went to pay and feed occupying troops. The substantial rest was remitted to Rome.

4. Taxation and the Central Government

The Roman Empire began as an empire of conquest, which gradually and disjoint-edly moved along an axis from booty to indemnities to taxation. Some sense of the scale of Roman taxation would be helpful. Unfortunately, reliable statistics are scarce. In the third century B.C.E., before its expansion overseas, the Roman state subsisted on low and fluctuating taxation, which reflected its own unpre-dictable needs and its reliance on the voluntary services of its citizens. A generous estimate puts its revenues then at 4–8 million HS (= *sestertii*) per year. By 150 B.C.E., state revenues had risen sevenfold to 50–60 million HS per year (at roughly constant prices); before the middle of the last century B.C.E., revenues had risen again sixfold, to 340 million HS, as Rome conquered the wealthiest kingdoms accessible. By the middle of the first century C.E., again at near constant prices, revenues had more than doubled to about 800 million HS per year.[14] In sum, tax revenues had risen at least one hundredfold in three centuries.

But Roman taxes were low as a proportion of probable gross product. Per capita taxes amounted to only 13 HS per person per year, or, at a standard (and arbitrary) farm gate price (3 HS per *modius* of 6.55 kg), 28 kg wheat equivalent per person/year, 11 percent of minimum subsistence.[15] This tax load in wheat terms was more than the English or French governments raised regularly in the seventeenth century but very much less than they raised in the eighteenth century.[16] Since many inhabit-ants of the Roman Empire produced and consumed significantly more than mini-mum subsistence, the actual rate of taxation was significantly less than 10 percent, probably closer to 5 percent of gross product.[17] Of course, the tax burden was prob-ably not evenly distributed. And taxes transmitted to the central government were probably less than the total of taxes exacted by greedy and corrupt tax collectors. It seems clear that, at least in Egypt, the Roman state operated a pervasive and inva-sive apparatus, even at these levels of tax extraction.[18] When I say that taxes were low, I do not mean to imply that Roman peasants, paying for benefits they could not see, typically experienced them as low. Indeed, there is significant evidence that many Egyptian peasants struggled to pay their poll tax in cash by splitting it into several instalments.[19]

Why were Roman taxes so low? Two immediate answers come to mind: one genetic (in the *Genesis* sense), the other structural. Genetically, the Roman state had set its tax targets only by the need to recover the costs of war and defense. Since it was an empire of conquest, taxpayers were defeated subjects (after 167 B.C.E. until the fourth century C.E., the citizen inhabitants of Italy paid no land tax). And, since it was an empire of conquest, the state did not offer its subjects much service: rudimentary justice to prevent violence, roads for speedy military communications, and defense. Tax collection was the main job of provincial governors. But even by the second century C.E., there was only one Roman elite administrator for every 400,000 inhabitants of empire, whereas in twelfth-century China there was one elite administrator per 15,000 people.[20] Roman administrators levied their taxes and by and large provided only peace in return.[21]

Structurally, the Roman state always operated a binary system of beneficiaries. The state shared the profits from conquest with its leaders and, to a lesser extent, with its soldiers. Public taxes were low so that private incomes of the rich, primarily rents from estates, could be higher. Rents and taxes were in competition for a limited surplus. And, at the same time, they were complementary. The profits of the rich bound them into supporting the state, of which they were the prime beneficiaries. The aggregate wealth and income of the aristocracy, broadly understood, was probably as great as, or greater than, the tax income of the central government.[22] That is why emperors in need repeatedly confiscated the estates of the superrich, both as an expression of their autocratic power and because these were the biggest assets available in the Roman economy. But, even if these stolen estates were incorporated into the private property of the emperors, their management had to be delegated back to an aristocrat (in the broad definition of the term). In sum, aristocratic wealth seriously constrained the central government's tax-raising powers. And, in the Later Empire, rich landowners' capacity to resist the central government's attempts to raise taxes was the rock on which the western empire foundered.

5. THE STEADY STATE

The Roman Empire was one of the largest political systems ever created, and one of the longest lasting. Only the Chinese empire lasted longer. At its height, in the second century C.E., the Roman Empire stretched from the Atlantic coast of north Africa to the Black Sea and from Hadrian's Wall, in the north of England, to the Red Sea. Its land mass was equal to more than half that of the continental United States. The territory once occupied by the Roman Empire is now split among forty different countries. Its population totaled perhaps 60 million people, or between one-fourth and one-sixth of the whole world's population at the time.[23]

Size matters; it was an important source and index of the power that Rome exercised. In a preindustrial economy, land and labor are the two primary ingredients of wealth. The larger the Roman Empire became, the more people it subjected and the more taxes it exacted. The more wealth the Roman state controlled, the more territory it was able to acquire and defend. For example, between 225 and 25 B.C.E., the period of Rome's striking imperial expansion, the population subject to Roman rule increased perhaps fifteenfold, from about 4 to 60 million people. But the government's tax revenues rose by at least a hundredfold (from about 4–8 million HS in 250 B.C.E. to more than 800 million HS in 25 B.C.E., at roughly constant prices: see section 4). Rome had conquered and absorbed several mini-empires (Macedon, Syria, Egypt) and numerous tribes. It had total control of the Mediterranean basin and beyond.

The huge size of the Roman Empire was a symptom of the fanatical dedication at all levels of Roman society to fighting wars and to military discipline and of the desire both for immediate victory and for long-term conquest. "No human force could resist Roman might" (Livy 1.16). Some Romans even imagined that they could, if they wished, rule or had already "subjugated the whole world" (*Res Gestae*, preamble). As it was, they absorbed all that (or more than what) was then worth conquering, with the giant exception of the Parthian empire, on its eastern borders. Further expansion, as the first emperor, Augustus, was reported to have said, would have been like fishing with a golden hook (Suetonius, *Augustus* 25). The prize was not worth the risk. A Roman historian in the second century, looking back over more than a century of "long and stable peace and the empire's secure prosperity," wrote:

> Since they [the emperors] control the best regions of the earth and sea, they wisely wish to preserve what they have rather than to extend the empire endlessly by including barbarian tribes, which are poor and unprofitable. (Appian, *Roman History*, Preface 7)

Appian commented that he had himself seen some of these barbarian ambassadors at court in Rome, offering themselves up as subjects. But their petitions had been refused, as they would have been "of no use."

The empire's persistence was a symptom of the thoroughness with which Romans destroyed previous political systems and overrode the separate cultural identities of the kingdoms and tribes which they had conquered. Or, rather, the Romans, particularly in areas of already established polities and high culture, left their victims with a semitransparent veil of self-respect that allowed them an illusion of local autonomy. This partial autonomy was limited to individual towns (not groups of towns). And it was restricted by Roman provincial governors' expectation of subservience and, reciprocally, by the local elites' own desire for assimilation—whether that meant assuming Roman culture and Roman-style rank or borrowing Roman power in order to resolve local power struggles. Either way, as elite and subelite provincials became more like Romans, and filled Roman administrative posts, local independence was systematically undermined. And provincial cultures all over the empire, at least in outward veneer, became ostensibly Romanized.[24]

For example, by the end of the second century, half of the central Roman senate was of provincial origin.[25] In western Europe, the language of the conquerors percolated to all levels and effectively displaced native local languages as the *lingua franca*. Latin became the common root of modern Romance languages. But, in the eastern half of the empire, Greek remained the accepted language of Roman government. Even there, it was an instrument of change; for example, in the ancient culture of Egypt, writing in Greek letters (Coptic) displaced native Egyptian demotic script.[26] And many Romans, to establish their credentials as people of high culture, learned Greek. Assimilation was a two-way process, by which the ideal of what it meant to be Roman itself gradually changed. That said, the impact of Roman rule is still visible in the ruins of Roman towns from all over the empire: temples to Roman Jupiter and to the Capitoline gods, statues of emperors (in some towns by the dozen), triumphal arches, colonnaded town squares, and steam baths. To be Roman was to be sweaty and clean. The Roman Empire was an empire of conquest but also a unitary symbolic system.

A modern map gives only a slight indication of Roman achievements. Rome's huge empire was created when the fastest means of land transport was the horse-drawn chariot, the pack-donkey, and the ox-cart. So the Roman Empire was in effect several months wide—and larger in winter than in summer. But the modern map shows up the empire's single salient feature: the centrality of the Mediterranean Sea. The Mediterranean Sea was at the center of Roman power, if only because transport by land, in Roman conditions, cost fifty or sixty times as much (per ton/km) as transport by sea and about ten times as much as transport by river.[27]

So the Roman Empire was at heart a fusion of coastal cultures, bound together by cheap sea transport, except in winter, when ships usually did not sail. The suppression of piracy during the last century b.c.e. made the Mediterranean into the empire's internal sea. Cheap transport gave the Roman Empire a geopolitical advantage, which in its economic impact was the equivalent of the highly productive irrigation agriculture at the core of other pre-industrial empires. The city of Rome could profit from and enjoy the surplus produce imported from all its coastal provinces. Rome stood at the center of a network of major cities (Alexandria, Antioch, Carthage, Cadiz, Ephesus, Aquileia), all of which were on the seacoast or rivers.

The city of Rome was by far the richest market in the whole empire, by volume and by value. Prices there were highest. It was there that merchants could make (or lose) their fortunes. It was there that the emperor and high aristocrats had their palaces. Rome was where emperors and aristocrats spent a large part of their taxes and rents. Rome was the prime engine of long-distance trade. The principle behind this assertion is simple. Whatever was imported into Rome from the provinces as money taxes and money rents, provincial towns had to earn back (taking one year with another) by the manufacture and sale of goods. In order to be able to pay money taxes again in subsequent years, provincial towns (villages, peasants) had to earn back the money that they had paid and sent overseas in taxes and rents. This simple equation—taxes plus rents exported roughly equaled in value exported and traded goods—however oversimplified it is, highlights the lines of trade and the volume of traffic that criss-crossed the Mediterranean, through a network of coastal or riverine towns centered on, and fueled primarily by, consumption in the city of Rome.[28]

The centrality of the Mediterranean should not blind us to the huge landmass of Roman conquests. Julius Caesar, in pursuit of military glory, advanced Roman power to Gaul and Britain. Under Augustus, armies and administrators incorporated large territories in northwestern Spain, western Germany, Switzerland, and the Balkans. In sum, the Romans had advanced the boundaries of empire as far as the ocean in the west and the Sahara desert in the south. To the northwest, the rivers Rhine and Danube (eventually supplemented by a long line of forts) roughly demarcated the comfortable limits of Roman power and also served as convenient lines of supply to the frontier armies.[29]

The considerable distance between the city of Rome and its land frontiers had far-reaching but diverse, even contradictory, implications. Distance and slow travel overland effectively insulated Rome and its political leaders from attack by marauding barbarians (until 410 c.e.) or by rebellious generals, whose collaboration was in any case hindered by fragmented commands split along an extended frontier and among rival aristocrats. Frontier armies intervened effectively only twice in central politics (in 69 and 193 c.e.) in more than two centuries. The Roman military was depoliticized—an achievement all the more remarkable if we compare it with the frequency of coups d'état in contemporary third-world states. Complementarily, sheer size and slowness of communications also prevented close control and swift reaction by the central government to crises on the periphery. Even in an emergency, for example, it took nine days for a messenger on a series of horses to ride from Mainz, Germany, to Rome.[30] Routine messages about the death of rulers took very much longer, and the time of their arrival was unpredictable.[31] In the late third century c.e., in an effort to resolve these problems, emperors split the empire into four parts, each with its capital closer to the frontiers. But there was another and seemingly insuperable problem. The northern territories were economically less developed, less urbanized, and less densely populated than the southern coastal regions of the Mediterranean. These northern regions could only with difficulty in Roman (as against postmedieval) times produce sufficient taxes to pay for their own extensive defense.

6. Configurations of Power

6.1. Emperors and Aristocrats

For emperors, too, the maintenance of control was (it seems reasonable to imagine) a central objective. If it was, they were not very good at it. Of the first eleven emperors, only four died (or were reputed to have died), naturally. The basic problem was the founding ideology of the Principate. Monarchy was made more acceptable to the traditional senatorial aristocracy by the fiction that the emperor was only first among equals (*princeps*). The clear implication was, therefore, that any Roman aristocrat of distinguished descent could himself become emperor. Hence, there was a long-term structural tension between emperors and aristocrats. That was a basic feature of Roman politics. Emperors in the first century killed dozens of aristocrats. They repeatedly created a reign of terror that would have made Ivan the Terrible seem mild.

The Roman aristocracy was remarkably different from any feudal or postfeudal European aristocracy. At its core was a political elite of six hundred senators. They were chosen in each generation both from among the sons of senators and from a politically inactive, much larger land-owning elite, originally based in Italy but increasingly derived from all over the empire. Ideologically, the image usually represented by Roman elite writers (and by modern historians suckered to think that ideology represents reality instead of disguising it) is that the Roman senatorial aristocracy was hereditary. But, in fact, intergenerational succession rates in the Roman aristocracy were remarkably low. The basic reason was that, unlike European feudal and postfeudal aristocracies, which were aristocracies based on land ownership and hereditary title, the Roman senatorial aristocracy was a competitive aristocracy of office. And, in order to be a top official (ordinary consul or supplementary [*suffect*] consul), the successful contestant had to have held a whole series of administrative posts; this demand was sometimes relaxed for claimants of very distinguished descent, who were promoted quickly without any qualifying military experience. In short, the successful Roman political aristocrat had to have been a successful administrator and to remain in favor for years, sometimes under different emperors or influential advisors at court.

The net effect, as I have indicated, was an extraordinarily low rate of succession in the Roman political elite. Roughly speaking, in the first two centuries C.E. and beyond, far fewer than half of top consuls had a consular son(s); among the second rank of supplementary consuls, overall far fewer than a quarter had a consular son, grandson, or great-grandson. The number of consuls after 70 C.E. varied between eight and ten per year, far fewer than the usual cohort of twenty entrants to the senate at age about twenty-five; allowing for death, between half and two-thirds of entrants to the senate achieved a consulship. By extension, it is reasonable to assume that among the third-ranking senators who never became consul, succession rates were even lower than for first- or second-ranking consuls. Overall, the succession rate among all known senators in the second century was less than half that of British barons in the fourteenth or fifteenth centuries.[32]

The great majority of senators were newcomers to the political aristocracy. Looked at from another perspective, and as in modern political elites, most Roman politicians came from families that sent representatives into politics for only one generation. Complementarily, and this for our present purposes is most important, there was a rather large pool of rich landowners spread across the empire, some of whom occasionally sent a son as its representative into central politics. These provincial families subsequently profited for generations in their home localities from the hereditary honorary status that their exceptional representative's political success had secured through senatorial membership or consular status, without incurring, again, the huge expense, risk—or profits—that a political career involved. The Roman aristocracy, broadly understood, had a small semihereditary core, a fluid and porous outer ring of politically and administratively active representatives (albeit with no explicit representative functions), and a broader pool of potential senators who were politically active, if at all, only at the local level.

By tradition, senatorial aristocrats were the wealthiest men at Rome. Under the Republic (until 31 B.C.E.), they were the generals and governors who benefited most from the booty and plunder of wars and provincial administration.[33] Under the Principate, emperors controlled senatorial aristocrats (at least according to history books written by senators and their allies) by a whole array of divisive tactics. I list them without being able to assign them relative weights:

- capricious and terrorizing persecution, imprisonment, murder
- strict adherence to the old-fashioned rules of oligarchic power sharing (short tenure of office, collegiality, gaps between offices, age-related promotion, prosecutions for corruption)
- cutting of the ties between political careers and popular election (the Roman plebs were disfranchised early in the first century C.E.)
- supplementing of collective senatorial decisions (*senatus consulta*) with individual decisions made by the emperor himself (*decreta*), sometimes in consultation with friends (*consilium*)
- denial of military experience to the most prestigious aristocrats - an increase in the status costs of being an aristocrat at court in Rome (many were bankrupted)
- promotion of provincial newcomers to senatorial rank (which diluted hereditary hold)

The cumulative impact of all these devices was to weaken the collective and institutional power of the senate as a consultative, policy-making body. The court, and its corridors, displaced the senate as the powerhouse of the Roman state.[34]

Nevertheless, the monarchy, for all the aristocratic complaints, provided a carapace for aristocratic enrichment. The landowning aristocracy, broadly understood, increased in aggregate prosperity.[35] The basic reason for this is clear. In Republican times, nearly all senatorial wealth was concentrated in Italian landholdings and investment in in-town housing, supplemented by investment through agents in collective enterprises, such as overseas trade and tax collection. Expert scholars will know the slender evidential base for generalizations of this type, but my reasoning is simple enough. The larger the investment needed (for example, in Roman housing or in overseas trade), the more likely was senatorial involvement. After all, a single four-hundred-ton ship laden with wheat arriving in a port near Rome was worth up to 1 million HS, the minimum qualifying fortune for a senator; one luxury cargo arriving in Alexandria from India is known from a recently discovered papyrus fragment to have been valued at seven million HS.[36] If no senators were involved in such ventures (to say nothing of silver mines, of which more later), we have to posit the existence of a class of equally wealthy nonsenators. These were presumably the ascendants of future senators. And I have already argued for the existence of a wider group of basically land-owning senatorands – that is, families capable of sending a representative into aristocratic politics occasionally. Under the emperors, aristocratic wealth was no longer concentrated in Italy.

Under the emperors, aristocrats increasingly owned estates spread over the whole empire. In the second century, they were legally required to own first one-third, later reduced to one-quarter, of their estates in Italy—in itself an index of their continuing provincialization.[37] Over time, aristocrats collectively owned a significant share not just of Italy but of the whole Mediterranean basin. In the middle of the first century C.E., six senators were reputed (of course it was an exaggeration, but a straw in the right wind) to own all Tunisia.[38] Aristocrats' aggregate wealth increased, as did the fortunes of individual aristocrats. A few illustrative figures will suffice. Cicero in the middle of the last century B.C.E. wrote that a rich Roman needed an annual income of 100,000 to 600,000 HS; in the late first century, Pliny, a middling senator, had an annual income of about 1.1 million HS per year. In the fourth century, middling senators in the city of Rome were said to enjoy incomes of 1,333 to 2,000 Roman pounds of gold a year, equivalent to 6–9 million HS per year.[39] In sum, aristocratic fortunes, on these admittedly vulnerable figures, had doubled or trebled in the first century of the Principate and had again risen more than sixfold between 100 and 400 C.E. Monarchy and the politico-economic integration of the whole empire, however superficial, had enabled aristocrats to become very much richer.

6.2. The City of Rome

The city of Rome was by far the largest city in the Roman world. By the end of the first century B.C.E., it had a population of about 1 million people.[40] It was as large as London in 1800, when London was the largest city in the West. Rome could be so large because it was the capital not just of Italy (population c. 7 million) but of a Mediterranean empire. Rome's population had grown rapidly by more than six times from an estimated 150,000 in 225 B.C.E..[41] The capital's growth was fed by three streams of immigrants:

- free citizens and allied rural emigrants from Italy (as small peasant families were displaced by fewer slaves working on larger farms)
- slaves, adult males particularly, who were forced to migrate by Rome's conquest of the Mediterranean basin in the last two centuries B.C.E.

- free craftsmen and traders, particularly from coastal towns in the Mediterranean

The city of Rome grew, and its huge size was maintained only by a steady stream of immigrants.

Rome could be so large, partly because the Roman state (from 58 B.C.E.) continually subvented and guaranteed (with occasional glitches) a basic supply of wheat to its registered free citizen population. The reported number of recipients varied, but in the reign of Augustus seems to have stabilized at around 200,000–250,000 adult males. Each received 33 kg wheat (5 *modii* of 6.55 kg) per month, which was more than enough for one adult (if he did not live on bread alone), but not enough for a family. In the fourth century C.E., state handouts were supplemented by rations of wine and pork.[42]

The state supply of free wheat to a fixed number of adult male citizens had significant political, economic, and demographic implications. Free distributions symbolized citizens' right to benefit collectively from the fruits of conquest. Romans were now the chosen people. The first emperor, Augustus, reportedly wondered whether to abolish the wheat dole but wisely decided against it, allegedly on the grounds that the issue might become a political football and others might seek or gain kudos from the dole's restoration.[43] Augustus's successor, Tiberius, (14–37 C.E.) preserved the dole but abolished the people's participation in elections. Citizens at Rome had become state pensioners, bribed into quiescent dependence by bread and circuses. The emperors' generosity underwrote their continued popularity. Rome was, after all, the main stage on which emperors acted their role as rulers of the world.

Economically, the exaction, storage, transport, and distribution of 100,000 tons of wheat per year to Rome was a sizable task. The wheat came primarily from Sicily, north Africa, and Egypt.[44] The volume itself was not the problem, though at peak periods Rome's port at Ostia and the short stretch of the Tiber (21 km) along which barges were hauled must have been jammed. Egypt alone yielded in wheat tax more than the city of Rome and the frontier armies needed together.[45] It was more a problem of organization, consistency of supply, and price. On the private market (since state supplies had to be supplemented), wheat prices in Rome were four times higher than they were in Egypt and two two three times as high as they were in Sicily and the rest of Italy.[46] The city of Rome stood at the peak of a pyramid of rising prices. The total cost of supplying state wheat to Rome amounted to more than 15 percent of state revenues (100,000 tons at 9 HS per modius = 135 million HS). But the supply of free wheat to citizens at Rome presumably also helped the labor force buy wine and oil produced on the estates of the rich and/or held down the price of labor in the capital. The free wheat dole subsidized the rich as well as the poor.

Demographically, the attractions of the free wheat dole and the huge consumer market that Rome constituted must have helped stimulate a continuous flow of immigrants to the city of Rome. In outsiders' imagination, the streets of Rome were paved with gold. For the Christian writer of *Revelation*, Rome was a scarlet harlot adorned with gold and jewels, sitting astride its seven hills, sucking the blood of countless nations, and drinking from a golden cup full of abominations and the impurites of fornication; Rome was the "great city that holds sway over the kings of the earth."[47] In a Jewish writer's imagination, Rome had 365 streets; in each street there were 365 palaces; each palace had 365 stories; and each storey contained enough food to feed the whole world.[48] Rome, with its huge baths, its temple roofs glistening with gilded bronze, beckoned as a city of opportunity even to those who had little chance of ever going there.

But in pre-industrial societies, larger cities have higher death rates than smaller cities, and smaller cities have higher death rates than the surrounding countryside. The city of Rome was a deathtrap, which sucked people in and killed them off with infectious diseases. Even the baths, which cleansed the relatively prosperous, may have helped concentrate diseases (like modern hospitals); Roman doctors recommended baths for people suffering from malaria, cholera, dysentery, infestation by worms, diarrhea, and gonorrhea, and the emperor Hadrian allowed the sick to use baths in the morning before the healthy.[49]

So Rome could maintain its huge population only by constant influx of immigrants, both from its Italian hinterland and from overseas. If death rates in Rome were only ten per thousand higher in Rome than in the rest of Italy—and Wrigley thinks that in London in the eighteenth century, the difference may have been significantly greater than that—then Rome, with a population of 1 million people, needed 10,000 migrants a year.[50] If the difference in mortality between metropolis and countryside was fifteen per thousand, then just to maintain its population, Rome needed 15,000 fresh migrants per year.[51] Immigration to Rome took place at double the rate of migration to the army (see section 6.3). It must have prevented any natural increase in Italian population and/or contributed, like military recruitment, to Italy's depopulation.[52] On the other hand, migration had a triply beneficial impact. It allowed an effective increase in agricultural productivity (the remaining peasants, fewer in number, could each work more land); it provided migrants who were lucky enough to return to their home town or village an image of metropolitan lifestyles (classy pots and silk underwear); and it either increased or maintained the market for agricultural and manufactured (handmade) exports.

6.3. The Army

The army was the biggest (typically 300,000 soldiers) and by far the most effectively organized power grouping in Roman politics. It combined hierarchy, training, a clear command structure, discipline, regular pay, flexibility in unit size (from small maniple to army-size groups of several legions), and aggressive persistence in the pursuit of fixed objectives. It had no similarly effective rival or imitator in civilian politics. During the late Republican period of imperial expansion, soldiers, in search of bounty and security, had repeatedly intervened in central Italian politics. But, under the emperors, as part of the Augustan settlement, the army was effectively depoliticized. This was an amazing political achievement.

After 31 B.C.E., frontier armies intervened directly in central politics only twice in more than two centuries: in 69 C.E. (after the death of Nero), and in 193 C.E. (after the assassination of Commodus and the auctioning of the imperial thone by the palace guards). The Roman peace meant both an end to imperial expansion (with the exception of Britain and Dacia [modern Romania] and the absorption of marginal client kingdoms such as Mauretania [modern Morocco]) and the internal pacification of conquered provinces. As a result, for almost two centuries, most inhabitants of the Roman Empire never or rarely saw a soldier. Rome had become a civil society.

This radical shift toward depoliticizing the military was (?purposefully) engineered by a whole series of evolutionary changes.[53] The great bulk of the army was eventually dispersed along distant frontiers, in garrisons that usually held only one legion (of 5,000–6000 soldiers), so that cooperation between rival commanders that might threaten the center became very difficult to achieve. Governors of provinces in which legions were stationed were typically chosen only after years of loyal service and almost never from among the top echelons of the senatorial elite; that is, army commanders by social rank were not regarded as potential claimants to the throne.[54] They held office for only shortish terms (typically three years). Under-officers—tribunes, prefects, and centurions—also either held office for short terms and/or were shifted to different legions on promotion so that no long-term loyalty could build up between under-officers and men.[55]

Soldiers serving in legions (about 150,000 men), on the expiry of their service of twenty-five to twenty-six years were paid a loyalty bonus equal to thirteen years' pay. The length of soldiers' service was increased from an unsustainable sixteen years, first to twenty and then to twenty-five years; this extension of military service both reduced costs, because a large proportion of soldiers died during these extra years, and mitigated problems of recruitment. This new system of cash bonuses to veterans on retirement, inaugurated in 6 C.E., helped divert Roman legionaries from their traditional ambition to end their days owning Italian land—a process that had contributed so much to land seizures and the consequent political instability of the Late Republic. Instead, veterans, increasingly of provincial origin, typically settled in the provinces, along the frontiers where they had already lived the bulk of their lives.[56] The depoliticization of the army under the emperors was based on long service along distant frontiers, on the regular grant of a large bounty on retirement, on the increasingly provincial origin of the army, and on the severance of the link between citizens at Rome (soon disfranchised) and their empowerment by military service. There were fewer citizen soldiers and effectively no citizen voters.

Locating the new imperial army along the distant frontiers contributed significantly to the rural depopulation of Italy, even though the imperial army was necessarily, substantially, and increasingly of provincial (i.e., not Italian) origin.

A simple calculation illustrates probabilities. At twenty years of service, a legionary (i.e., citizen) army of 150,000 soldiers needs on average 9,500 recruits per year; it may seem, as it has seemed to some scholars, a smallish number from a free population of 5 million people. But if soldiers were recruited at age twenty, they would have equalled 20 percent of all Italian citizen twenty-year-olds (if Italy's free citizen population equaled 5 million, then, in ancient conditions of mortality ($e_0 \sim 25$), there were only 47,500 male survivors to age twenty).[57] If the soldiers then spent their army service in the provinces and settled there, Italy would be rapidly depopulated by emigration at this rate. I must stress that this calculation is a statement not of fact but of parametric probability. Fertility obviously depends on the females left behind as much as on the soldiers who emigrated, and about that we know nothing. But at first sight it seems that an unforeseen consequence of Augustus's and his successors' policy of locating citizen troops along the frontiers was an immediate and significant depopulation of Italy.

Surviving evidence of burial inscriptions, which may or may not be statistically representative, suggests that during the reign of Augustus, 68 percent of legionaries were of Italian origin. By the middle of the first century, this proportion had fallen to less than half (48%), and by the end of the century to 22 percent; in the second century, apparently, only 2 percent of citizen soldiers were of Italian origin.[58] No wonder that in 9 c.e., after the crushing defeat of a Roman army (three legions each nominally of 6,000 soldiers were killed in north Germany), Augustus, who feared that the Germans would invade Italy, had great difficulty in raising recruits and resorted against all tradition to recruiting ex-slaves.[59]

Military costs remained by far the largest element in the Roman state budget; in the first century c.e., they accounted for more than half the total (c. 450 ?? out of a budget of more than 800 million sesterces).[60] And, although, with hindsight, we know that the Roman army did not often intervene in central politics, Roman emperors must always have feared that it might. The army had to be placated. What is surprising, then, is that, given the army's potential for disruption, soldiers' pay in terms of silver never surpassed the level reached in the reign of Augustus. Put another way, every time that the nominal pay of soldiers was subsequently raised (in c. 83?, 193, and 212 c.e.), the silver coinage was soon debased so that the cost in precious metal to the treasury was held roughly constant.[61] Soldiers collectively did not exercise their armed might to increase their sector share of total wealth. For whatever reason, it looks as though total army costs had reached the limit of what Roman financial administrators could raise or allocate to the army within the state budget.

The dispersion of the legionary armies and their auxiliary (noncitizen) counterparts, hundreds of miles from Rome along the frontiers, left a power vacuum at the center. It was filled partially by the palace (praetorian) guard. This palace guard was a small elite troop, a few thousand strong, of highly paid soldiers, garrisoned in Rome. It was commanded by usually two prefects, each of whose powers were

designed to balance those of the other. They were considered to be extremely influential within palace politics, but they were also only knights (albeit with the rank of
consuls) and so socially disbarred from becoming emperor (until Macrinus in 217
C.E., but he reigned for only one year). On several occasions, the palace played a key
role in securing the throne for a particular candidate. And, for historians of Rome,
ancient and modern, individual successions to the throne have often seemed to be
the very stuff of politics.

7. ECONOMIC GROWTH

Over the past few years, there have been several attempts to locate economic growth
in antiquity.[62] Of course, some scholars have denied that it occurred. Certainly, there
was never in antiquity the steep curve of economic growth that marks the modern
world.[63] Perhaps the very search is an attempt to find the roots of modern experience in classical antiquity, which forged so many aspects of Western culture.

All that said, I still think the Roman Empire provided conditions for modest economic growth (a growth that was minuscule by modern standards but significant
for the experience of some Romans):

- by extending the area of cultivated land, especially in northwestern Europe
  and the Balkans
- by increasing the size of agricultural units to achieve economies of scale
- by using systematic accounting methods to control costs or measure relative rates of return from different crops
- by allowing and encouraging the growth or persistence of towns, with
  their relatively sophisticated division of labor
- by achieving significant increases in productivity, but only in very limited
  spheres, which had only a superficial impact on the total economy

Under Roman rule, the northern provinces adopted some of the superior farming
techniques, first tried out in the southeast, such as crop rotation, selective breeding
(for example, to produce larger oxen), and new crops (for example, peas and cab-
bage were first introduced into Britain under Roman rule—with long-term effects
on British cooking). Even if some of the extra land brought into cultivation was
marginal, with lower productivity, nevertheless the total impact of Roman conquest
was both to increase average agricultural productivity and to aggregate product.[64]

We have exiguous but significant evidence in Roman agricultural handbooks
that at least some landowners were thinking (however inexpertly) about relative
rates of return from different crops and the most effective use of labor and draught
animals. The Heroninus archive from Roman Egypt in the third century C.E. shows
systematic attempts to control draught-animal costs by the unified management of
the scattered farms that made up a large estate.[65] Perhaps what is most surprising
is that the central Roman government, at the end of the third century and in the

fourth, actually tried to increase agricultural productivity (and its own tax returns) by encouraging farmers to cultivate extra land (emphyteutic leases) and to use innovative techniques.[66] Alas, we have no idea how successful or isolated these initiatives were. But at least Roman rulers tried, and that is quite unexpected.

Successive empires that came under Roman control, and the Roman Empire in particular, encouraged the growth of towns and so of nonagricultural occupations. Towns, even pre-industrial towns, make possible a relatively sophisticated division of labor and concentrate higher value production. There are 85 different occupations recorded in stone inscriptions and painted slogans on the street walls of the small town of Pompeii (population c. 12,000?), 110 in the small town of Korykos in southern Turkey, and 268 occupations named on stone inscriptions found in the city of Rome.[67] All these lists are likely to be incomplete, and besides, having separate names for slightly different occupations or hierarchical gradings within occupations may reflect cultural differences as well as differences in occupational specialization. That said, relative numbers can serve as a crude index of economic development. Compare, for example, the Roman number with the more than 350 occupations found in London in the eighteenth century.[68]

What is particularly striking about the towns of the Roman Empire is their number, their location mainly in the coastal regions around the Mediterranean Sea, and the size of the largest cities. Rome, as we have seen, had a population (if our ancient evidence is to be trusted) of about 1 million people; Alexandria is thought to have had a population of half a million people.[69] Antioch and Carthage had populations of well over 100,000. Although each of these secondary but major cities began as the capital of a mini-empire later conquered by Romans, they maintained or even expanded their populations even after they ceased to be the seats of kings. Unlike Rome, their populations were not subsidised by free distributions of basic food. They had to support themselves by the services that they provided, by manufacture and by trade. Only to a limited extent can they be envisaged as "consumer" cities, that is, unproductive cities, living off the expenditure of agricultural rents by their richest inhabitants.[70] That said, it seems doubtful that the population of all the towns in the Roman Empire exceeded 20 percent of the total population.[71]

The Roman Empire was huge, and large enough to effect important economies of scale. One obvious saving was in military expenditure. The Roman army at about 300,000 soldiers in the first century c.e., and fewer than 400,000 in the second century, was significantly smaller than the aggregate armies of the mini-empires, kingdoms, and tribes that the Roman Empire conquered. The Roman imperial army in the first century constituted barely 2 percent of all adult males in the empire, whereas average military participation among Romans in the last two centuries b.c.e. was 13 percent of adult males. That was one part of the peace dividend. But the cut in overall military expenditure (Ptolemaic Egypt alone had been credited with an army of 240,000 soldiers[72]) indicates that the apparent wealth of Rome in the first two centuries c.e. was not so much the product of economic growth as it was the product of piling up into Rome (and, to a lesser extent, other cities), the transferred savings from the taxes previously spent in the conquered kingdoms.

Another arena for massive growth was in the production of coinage. Duncan-Jones reckoned that by the middle of the second century C.E. there were 7 billion HS of silver coins in circulation, which is roughly four times my estimate of the volume of Roman coins in circulation in the middle of the last century B.C.E..[73] And the volume of Roman coinage had already grown ten times in the century before that.[74] But more of that in a moment. Confirmation of the huge volume of Roman silver-lead mining (silver was produced by cupellation as a by-product of lead mining) comes impressively from an apparently incontrovertible source.

I refer to the Greenland icecap and the peat bogs or lake sediments of France, Germany, Ireland, Spain, Sweden, and Switzerland. A whole series of recent studies from a variety of sites has shown with remarkable concordance that the volume of wind-borne contaminants from smelting mineral ores reached a significant peak in the Roman period.[75] Hong and associates showed that lead pollution from systematic samples of the Greenland icecap, datable to between 500 B.C.E. and 300 C.E., reached densities four times the natural (i.e., prehistoric) levels. Renberg and associates showed that lead contamination in a wide assortment of sediments from southern Swedish lakes reached a peak in or around the first century C.E.. Shotyk and associates showed, in a study of a Swiss peat bog, that there was a huge upsurge in lead pollution from the first century B.C.E. to the third century C.E., when pollution (and presumably production) began to decline.[76]

There seems little doubt among these investigators that the main source of contamination in this period was lead smelting and cupellation for silver and copper in the Roman Empire, and particularly Spain. Hong and associates showed that copper production in the world rose sevenfold in the last five centuries B.C.E., continued at a high but reducing level in the first five centuries C.E., and then fell sevenfold to reach a trough in the thirteenth century. Once again, they are convinced that classical civilizations, and in particular the Roman Empire, were the major source of this wind-borne pollution.[77]

Ancient methods of smelting were so inefficient that in the period 500 B.C.E. to 500 C.E., according to these estimates, some 800 metric tons of copper were carried in the high atmosphere to Greenland. Lead pollution in antiquity reached levels not reached again until the eighteenth century. And lead production in the Roman period averaged at least three times the level reached in the first half of the last millennium B.C.E..[78] If air-borne pollutants constituted 10 percent of lead smelted, total production in the Roman period can be estimated as on average 32,000 tons per year, reaching a peak of about 50,000 tons. This may be compared with an average world production of only 4,000–7,000 tons per year in the period 1000–1500 C.E.. In sum, Roman levels of metal production (lead, copper, silver) were very much higher than the levels in either earlier or immediately subsequent periods.

These scientific estimates of ancient pollution and total production give us an unprecedented vision of economic growth and inefficiency in classical antiquity.

Of course, the scientific conclusions may be both speculative and subsequently disputed. And they do relate to only one small sector of the Roman economy. Perhaps tens of thousands of Roman miners, woodcutters, charcoal burners, and donkey-drivers slaved in harsh conditions to produce these metals for consumption as coins and divine statues. And, perhaps, their mining activity was made possible by rich men (or emperors) investing fortunes in some mines that burrowed deep underground.[79] But the basic productivity of each worker was probably low, and tens of thousands of miners is but a tiny fraction of the millions of peasants working in agriculture. As so often in Roman economic history, we confront a Janus image: on the one hand mass low productivity, and on the other hand seemingly impressive advance, but in a narrow sector.

We can approach the implications of a massive growth in money supply more conservatively. The most important product of the Spanish mines was silver, which was used from the third century B.C.E. onward principally for minting coins. As the Roman Empire grew in size, the money supply increased dramatically. And the money supply grew, even more dramatically, once peace had been established throughout the empire under successive emperors (31 B.C.E.–235 C.E.). Peace and stable government helped mold the whole of the Mediterranean basin and beyond into a single (relatively) integrated monetary economy. Table 5.1 illustrates this process of growth in the money supply.

In the mid-second century B.C.E., when the Roman Empire included parts of Spain, southern France, Italy, northern Africa, and Greece, according to a crude and inevitably fallible estimate, the gross number of Roman silver coins in circulation was only 50 million *denarii*. A century later, in about 50 B.C.E., when the Roman Empire included virtually the whole of the Mediterranean basin (except Egypt), the volume of silver money in circulation had increased eightfold, to about 410 million *denarii*.[80] The biggest known stimulus to this growth was increased expenditure on paying soldiers and on fighting wars and the correspondingly increased income from taxation. Soldiers and tax-paying subjects needed coins. In the same period, taxes rose more than sixfold, from about 13 million *denarii* per year in the mid-second

Table 5.1. Crude Estimates of Growth in the Roman Money Supply (Total Amount in Circulation, in Millions of *Denarii*)

Date	Gold	Silver	Tax Revenues	Price Index
150 BCE	v. low	50	13	33
100 BCE	v. low	320	—	—
50 BCE	low	410	85	100
27 BCE–14 CE	?1,000	750	?200	—
c. 160 CE	3,000[a]	1,716[b]	?250	200
c. 230 CE	—	—	—	300/400

Dash indicates data not available. [a]120 million gold coins (*aurei*) weighing c.880 tons. [b]Total weight 5,766 tons.

century B.C.E. to 85 million *denarii* per year in 62 B.C.E.[81] Please note that money supply (as estimated here) was several times (much more than five times, if we include the silver coinage minted in the cities of the eastern Mediterranean) as large as the tax flow. Does this indicate that money transactions were servicing much more than the payment of taxes and the reciprocal flow of trade that taxes stimulated?

By the mid-second century C.E., when the Roman Empire was at its greatest territorial extent, the volume of silver coinage in circulation had again grown. By a similarly fallible estimate, the volume of silver coinage in circulation was roughly four times greater than it had been in 50 B.C.E. (1.716 billion instead of 410 million *denarii*, excluding Egypt).[82] The earlier figures cover only the silver coins minted in Rome and circulating principally in the western half of the empire (including Italy). The later figures comprise silver coins circulating in the whole of the Mediterranean basin and beyond. But it is doubtful that the whole increase in the number of silver coins circulating can be attributed to this extension of the geographical area covered.[83] It seems more probable that this huge increase in the volume and value of silver coins circulating throughout the whole Roman Empire reflected a rise in the volume and value of goods bought and sold for money.

The huge growth in the Roman money supply under the emperors is corroborated by the radical restructuring and unification of the coinage system that the Roman emperors instituted and maintained. Julius Caesar, Augustus, and their successors minted huge volumes of gold coins (well over 1 million gold coins a year on average).[84] By the middle of the second century C.E., according to Duncan-Jones's admittedly speculative estimates, the value of gold coins amounted to twice the value of all silver coins in circulation.[85] The whole configuration of the Roman monetary economy had been revolutionized. The total value of the coinage system (gold plus silver) had, by these estimates, grown twelve times since the middle of the last century B.C.E. (table 5.1). But prices had perhaps only doubled (table 5.1).

Of course, gold coins constituted only the top tier of the money market. A single gold coin perhaps supported a poor citizen family in the city of Rome for a month. Even so, gold coins were not out-of-reach rarities. Young soldiers, for example, typically received three gold coins when they were recruited.[86] Emperors gave regular, though smaller, bonuses in gold to their troops and to the citizens registered for the free wheat dole in the city of Rome on accession, on announcing an heir, or to commemorate an anniversary. Complementarily, subjects paid a special tax in gold (*aurum coronarium*) on precisely the same occasions. The emperors had diversified the Roman monetary system out of silver and bronze into a three-tiered system of gold, silver, and bronze.

By the mid-second century C.E., the Roman monetary system (outside Egypt, which had its own rather inferior coinage but again one that expanded enormously under Roman rule),[87] again according to Duncan-Jones's innovative and speculative estimates, consisted of 120 million gold coins (*aurei* struck at forty-five to the Roman pound) worth 3 billion *denarii* and about 1.7 billion silver *denarii*.[88] All the gold coins and the great majority of the silver coins (perhaps three-quarters of the total) were minted at Rome itself; the rest were minted in Syria and Asia Minor, but to a compatible standard and purity.[89] Bronze coinage (with perhaps more than 5 billion coins in circulation) was mostly produced locally and circulated locally. It represented only about 5 percent to 10 percent of total value.[90]

By these estimates, in the mid-second century, Roman gold coinage in total weighed 880 tons and by recent values (c. $400–600 per troy oz. in 2005–2006) was worth $11–17 billion, not much for a modern industrial economy but a huge investment for a pre-industrial state. The silver coinage also constituted a huge investment. It weighed in total something over 5,000 tons at a time when producing a ton of silver cost up to 1,000 man-years of labor (mining, draining, carting, felling timber, making charcoal, smelting, refining, guarding, transporting, minting).[91] From 1530 to 1630, by comparison, Europe imported from America about 140 tons of silver a year.[92] The Roman silver coinage system would have absorbed only about fifty tons per year for more than a century.

How was it possible for the Roman coinage system to grow so much without hyperinflation? I assume here that classical economic principles, and in particular Fisher's price equation, $P = (M \times V)/Q$, holds where P = the price level, M = the money supply, V = the speed of circulation, and Q = the quantity of goods bought and sold. We know nothing or very little about the speed at which money circulated in Roman conditions. For the moment, let us assume that V was constant. So if money supply increased twelvefold (albeit over a considerably greater geographical area) and if prices only doubled (though the database for any such conclusion is dangerously, even recklessly, thin), then it must be that the quantity of goods traded in the market increased hugely between 50 B.C.E. and 150 C.E.

But does Fisher's price equation apply in Roman conditions? I am inclined to think that this is a nonsensical question. But I do still have colleagues (as well as the ghost of my teacher Moses Finley in my conscience) who believe that it is impossible or at least unprofitable to use modern economic concepts in order to analyse a pre-industrial embedded economy. For them, the ancient economy was a cultural system, which was dominated by nonrational considerations of status and ritual and

Table 5.2. Growth in Military Expenditure (in Millions of *Denarii*)

Date	Actual	Standardized to 50 BCE Prices
218–201 BCE	31	10
200–188 BCE	14	5
187–168 BCE	9	3
6–70 CE	123	92
83–170 CE	179	90
195 CE	287	?200
215–230 CE	434	217

Table 5.3. Annual Rates of Coin Production, Purity Index, and Price Index

Date	Coins Produced per Year in Millions of *Denarii*		Purity Index (27 BCE = 100)		Price Index (50 BCE = 100)
	Gold	Silver	Gold[a]	Silver[b]	
200–158 BCE	—	1	—	—	33
119–80 BCE	—	14	—	—	—
73–59 BCE	—	4	—	—	—
50 BCE	—	—	—	—	100 (base)
43 BCE	>7	—	103	—	—
27 BCE	>14	—	100 (base)	100 (base)	—
64–68 CE	202	8	93	84	133
69–79 CE	90	38	—	82	—
88–96 CE	—	23	97	88	—
98–117 CE	31	19	93	83	—
117–138 CE	28	16	—	81	—
138–161 CE	35	19	—	79	—
161–180 CE	31	16	—	71	200
193–211 CE	—	30	—	50	—
215 CE	—	20	82	44	—
222–235 CE	—	22	—	37	300/400

Sources: Hopkins 1980; Duncan-Jones 1994; Harl 1996

Dash indicates data not available. [a]Gold content in percentage. [b]*Denarii* per pound of silver.

so was immune to cold rational analysis or reconstruction. So let us pursue the question for a minute. At the end of the second century and at the beginning of the third century C.E., successive emperors raised soldiers' pay significantly, so total annual military expenditure over forty years (190–230 C.E.) more than doubled (the increase was 142%: see table 5.2). The average volume of silver coins minted per year rose in roughly the same period (180–235 C.E.) by 40 percent, and the silver content of the dominant coin the *denarius* was almost halved (from 71% to 37%) (table 5.3). Prices (again, unfortunately, on exiguous evidence) apparently rose in the same period by 50 or 100 percent (table 5.3). This chain of cause and consequence does make it seem that the Roman monetary economy is analyzable in terms of classic price theory.

It may seem tempting to regard such a massive increase in the money supply and in the probable volume of traded goods as an unequivocal index of economic growth. But I suspect that the huge volume of money minted is explicable only if a large proportion was exported in return for Eastern luxuries or if a large proportion, especially of gold coins, were kept inert as treasure, with practically nil velocity. As I reconstruct it, Roman emperors competitively produced silver and gold as a virtual state monopoly, without much regard for the costs of production. They produced coins as economic objects for the facilitation of trade and taxation but above all as symbolic objects of ostentation and political authority. In short, Roman money did not match completely its modern equivalents. Roman money was part real money and part a monument to political ambition. It cannot therefore be readily used as an index of growth.

Notes

Keith Hopkins died in March 2004, before he was able to revise this chapter for publication. With very minor adjustments, the text of this chapter represents the final version of his manuscript, dated August 13, 2002. Walter Scheidel supplied almost all of the footnotes and bibliographical references in April 2006. Only the references in the main text and elements of footnotes 21, 47–49, 57, 66–67, 71, 76–78, 83, 87, and 89 are derived from Hopkins's own manuscript. We are grateful to Christopher Kelly for helpful comments on these editorial revisions.

1. Suetonius, *Augustus* 50.
2. The role of the people in the political system of the Republic continues to be much debated: see most recently Millar 1998; Mouritsen 2001; Morstein-Marx 2004.
3. Brunt 1971b: 74–147 for an overview of the period of instability from 133–27 B.C.E.
4. This model has been developed in detail in Hopkins 1978a: 1–98, esp. 1–74. For recent qualifications, cf. Jongman 2003. For the scale of colonization, see Brunt 1971a: 190–98, 234–265, 294–344. For a higher estimate of slave imports in the last two centuries B.C.E. (2–4 million), cf. Scheidel 2005.
5. On Augustus' regime and reforms, see, e.g., Zanker 1988 and Raaflaub and Toher 1990, and most recently Eck 2003 and Galinsky 2005.
6. Cornell 1995: 293–398 for a full survey.
7. Augustus, *Res Gestae* 8. Brunt 1971a: 116 reckons with five to six million, allowing for some underregistration.
8. Garnsey 1970; Rilinger 1988.
9. Eck 2000: 262.
10. Cf. Frank 1933: 75, 79.
11. Velleius 2.15, with Brunt 1971a: 677–86.
12. Cf. Mouritsen 1998 for a revisionist account.
13. Brunt 1971a: 91–99.
14. Frank 1933: 66, 141, 322–23; Hopkins 1980: 119, with Duncan-Jones 1994: 46 and Hopkins 1995/96: 46.
15. Hopkins 1995/96: 45–46, slightly modifying earlier estimates in 1980: 120.
16. Hopkins 1980: 120 n.56.
17. Cf. Hopkins 1995/96: 47, for taxes at 5 percent to 7 percent of actual GDP.
18. Wallace 1938.
19. Wallace 116–34.
20. Hopkins 1983a: 186. Even if we allow for perhaps up to 10,000 support staff (slaves and seconded soldiers) in this period, total numbers increased several times in the following centuries: Kelly 2004: 111.
21. This may be a misleading generalization. One mid-second century administrator in Egypt received nearly 2,000 petitions submitted in fewer than three days (P. Yale 61). He had answers publicly posted for the petitioners to read.
22. Hopkins 1995/96: 50. See now also Jongman 2007: section IV.i.

23. Frier 2000: 814 (Roman Empire); Cohen 1995: 400 (world).

24. For recent perspectives on the complex process of culture change in the Roman Empire, see Woolf 1998; MacMullen 2000; Keay and Terrenato 2001; Cooley 2002; Hingley 2005.

25. Hopkins 1983a: 200, based on Hammond 1957: 77.

26. Hopkins 1991: 144–48.

27. Hopkins 1983b: 104.

28. This model was first developed in Hopkins 1980 and revised in Hopkins 1995/96 = 2002.

29. On the imperial frontiers, see esp. Dyson 1985; Whittaker 1994.

30. Tacitus, *Histories* 1.12 and 56, with Ramsay 1925: 63–65; cf. Plutarch, *Caesar* 17 (from Rome to the Rhone in seven days).

31. Duncan-Jones 1990: 7–29.

32. Hopkins 1983: 120–200.

33. Shatzman 1975.

34. Winterling 1999.

35. Mratschek-Halfmann 1993.

36. Rome: Hopkins 1983b: 101 (for a value of 400,000–600,000 HS, which must be adjusted upwards to account for higher wheat prices in the capital). Alexandria: Hopkins 1995/96: 59 with 73 n.75.

37. Pliny the Younger, *Letters* 6.19; *Historia Augusta, Marcus Aurelius* 11.

38. Pliny the Elder, *Natural History*, 18.35.

39. Hopkins 1995/96: 50 with 69 n.37.

40. Hopkins 1978a: 96–98.

41. Cf. Morley 1996: 39 (?200,000 in 200 B.C.E.).

42. Rickman 1980: 156–209.

43. Suetonius, *Augustus* 42.

44. Garnsey 1988: 231–32.

45. Hopkins 1995/96: 55–56.

46. Hopkins 1995/86: 58 with 73 n.68. On the grain market in the Roman Empire in general, see now Erdkamp 2005.

47. *New Testament, Revelation of St John* 17.

48. *Babylonian Talmud, Pesahim* 118b.

49. Celsus, *On Medicine* 4.2–28; *Historia Augusta, Hadrian* 22. On disease in the city of Rome in particular, see Scheidel 2003.

50. Wrigley 1967: 46 = 1987: 135; cf. Morley 1996: 44.

51. Cf. Scheidel 2003: 175 (?20 per 1,000).

52. See also Morley 1996: 33–54.

53. See esp. Campbell 1984 and 2002: 106–21.

54. Hopkins 1983a: 173.

55. Domaszewski 1967: 97 and n.2.

56. E.g., Mann 1983.

57. Accurate calculation is more complex than this. Crucially, we do not know what happened to the fertility of the women whom the soldiers would have married if they had stayed in Italy. The estimate for annual recruitment has been extrapolated from Scheidel 1996a: 122 table 3.15. For similar intake requirements (15–20% of Italian twenty-year-old males) under the early emperors, cf. ibid. 93–94, 96 n.18.

58. Derived from Forni 1953: 159–212, with Forni 1974: 366–80.

59. Suetonius, *Augustus* 25.

60. Hopkins 1995/96: 46.

61. Duncan-Jones 1994: 227 tab. 15.6 summarizes the data on silver fineness.
62. E.g., Millett 2001; Morris 2004, 2005; Saller 2002 = 2005; Hitchner 2005; Jongman 2007; Scheidel 2007b.
63. Cf. Saller 2002: 259 fig. 12.1 = 2005: 230 fig. 11.1.
64. Extension: e.g., Drexhage et al. 2002: 72–84. Intensification: e.g., Kron 2000, 2002.
65. Rathbone 1991.
66. E.g., P. Panop. Beatty 2 lines 211–14, discussed in Kelly 2004: 118.
67. Hopkins 1978b: 72; Joshel 1992: 176–82.
68. Hopkins 1978b: 71.
69. Rome: see n. 40. Alexandria: Delia 1988, esp. 284.
70. On this concept, see most recently Erdkamp 2001.
71. The major cities (Rome, Alexandria, Antioch, and Carthage) had a total population of less than 2 million, or 3 percent of the empire's total population. I suspect the rest of the urban population in the empire totaled more than 10 percent but less than 15 percent of the total. At the moment, I have no idea how to calculate the proportion of villagers engaged primarily in nonagricultural occupations.
72. Appian, *Roman History, Preface* 10.
73. Duncan-Jones 1994: 170 (mid-second century c.e.); Hopkins 1980: 109 fig. 2 (mid-first century b.c.e.).
74. Hopkins 1980: 107–9. See now also Backendorf 1998 and Lockyear 1999, for a five- to tenfold increase in that period.
75. Hong et al. 1994; Renberg et al. 1994; Hong et al. 1996a, b; Cortizas et al. 1997; Weiss et al. 1997; Rosman et al. 1997; Shotyk et al. 1998; Brannvall et al. 1999; Renberg et al. 2000; Kempter and Frenzel 2000; Brannvall et al. 2001; Alfonso et al. 2001; Cortizas et al. 2002; Boutron et al. 2004; Kylander et al. 2005; Schettler and Romer 2006. For surveys of some of these case studies, see Weiss et al. 1999 and Makra and Brimblecombe 2004; cf. also Nriagu 1998. Among ancient historians, a few of these findings have been utilized by Wilson 2002: 25–27 and de Callatay 2005.
76. Hong et al. 1994: 1841; Renberg et al. 1994: 323, 326; Shotyk et al. 1998: 1637.
77. Hong et al. 1996a: 246.
78. Hong et al. 1994: 1841; Nriagu 1998: 1622.
79. On the scale of the imperial mining economy, see now Wilson 2002: 17–29.
80. Hopkins 1980: 107–9, esp. 108 and n.23.
81. See n. 14.
82. See n. 73.
83. Duncan-Jones reckons that the volume of silver coinage minted in the eastern towns totaled roughly one-quarter of all the silver coinage in circulation (1994: 170).
84. Duncan-Jones 1994: 168. Note that 1 gold coin (*aureus*) = 25 denarii = 100 HS.
85. Duncan-Jones 1994: 168–70.
86. Davies 1989: 20.
87. See Christiansen 1988.
88. Duncan-Jones 1994: 168–70.
89. For the latter, see Harl 1996: 97–124. Eastern silver coins were tariffed at 3 or 4 *denarii*. Under Nero, debasement was tried out on Egyptian, then on other eastern coins before being introduced at Rome. Similarly, in the second century c.e., eastern silver coins were debased sooner than central Roman coins.
90. Duncan-Jones 1994: 170.
91. Patterson 1972: 231.
92. Fischer 1996: 336 n.37.

6

The Byzantine Empire

John F. Haldon

1. INTRODUCTION

In the context of the other "empires" being discussed in this volume, the Byzantine example is something of an anomaly. First, it was for most of its existence—from the seventh to the fifteenth century c.e.—territorially rather small (restricted largely to the southern Balkans and Asia Minor); second, although historians from the seventeenth century have called it an empire, its "emperor" increasingly came to be described by the Greek word *basileus*, king. Third, it was an "empire" the history of which is largely one of contraction, with occasional efforts to recover lost territories followed by further contractions, so that imperialist exploitation of foreign conquests is the exception rather than the rule. Exploitation is thus meaningful only in terms of the ways in which the state and society of Byzantium functioned—who exploited whom and how, in economic and political terms—and with respect to the cultural impact of Byzantine civilization on the outside world. In this chapter I shall be concerned for the most part with the former.

In spite of the fact that it represents one of the most interesting examples of a late ancient state formation that survived, with substantial modifications, well into the medieval period, the Byzantine (or medieval East Roman) Empire has received remarkably little attention from either comparative historians or state theorists, certainly when compared with the treatment afforded Rome, out of which Byzantium evolved. This situation seems to me to reflect the fact that historians and specialists of the Byzantine world have themselves been very reluctant to generalize from their work or to draw broader conclusions within a comparative context, so their subject has remained fairly difficult of access to the nonspecialist. It is worth bearing in mind that the study of the Byzantine world and its culture, economy, and society evolved directly out of classical philology, and classical philology, with its earlier empirical and positivist emphasis, bequeathed to Byzantine Studies a similar tendency. This seems today somewhat paradoxical, insofar as classical philology has more recently been strongly affected by developments in structural linguistics, comparative literary theory, and, more recently, poststructuralist critiques of traditional approaches to notions of author, reader, and intertextuality, while the study of Roman history, society, and institutions has likewise been transformed since the 1950s by similar developments, as well as by exciting advances in archaeology and related sciences. In contrast, and in spite of some changes that have become apparent only in the past few years, the study of the Byzantine world remains firmly embedded in the traditional pattern.

There have been some important exceptions, however, and significant innovative perspectives have now opened up, especially in the study of Byzantine literature[1] but also, under the influence of Western medieval and Roman archaeology, in the study of Byzantine material culture, urbanism, and related phenomena. Recent work has raised issues of resource appropriation and distribution, and related issues of logistics, both in military and other aspects, have now been broached.[2] But the lack of synthesizing works by specialists in the field, which would put Byzantium into a longer-term comparative perspective, means that outsiders have tended, and still tend, to pass over this state and society with little or no comment. Work by scholars such as Peter Brown and Alexander Kazhdan on aspects of the social-cultural history of the late Roman, Byzantine, and Western medieval worlds; by Michael McCormick on the ways in which the Islamic and East Roman, and the medieval Italian and Frankish worlds, were connected through patterns of travel and communication; by Chris Wickham on the evolution of society and economy across the European and Mediterranean worlds after the fifth century C.E.; and Alan Harvey and Michel Kaplan on the agrarian economics of Byzantium in their wider context have begun to address the issues from a broader, comparative perspective.[3] But Byzantium still appears frequently, especially in general histories and more popular literature, as some sort of uniquely privileged survival, a haven of Orthodox spirituality, Roman law, and oriental despotism, taken as a special case rather than in its natural Balkan and Anatolian context. Those working from a broader comparative standpoint have only recently begun, and mostly fairly superficially, to integrate the Byzantine world into their syntheses. The first volume of Michael Mann's admirable survey, *The Sources of Social Power*, mentions it briefly and problematically; the treatment in the second volume of Runciman's *A Treatise on Social Theory* is just as brief, although better with respect to the conclusions it draws; most other comparativist surveys—for example, Tainter's *The Collapse of Complex Societies*—barely pay lip service to the Byzantine case.[4] Perry Anderson's *Passages from Antiquity to Feudalism* pays serious attention to the East Roman context, but his very able treatment is vitiated for today's reader in part by the fact that since the time of writing, in the early 1970s, a number of important advances in understanding how the East Roman state evolved have been made.[5] Anderson was also working within an Anglo-Marxist framework in which he wanted to retain traditional notions of "mode of production" and demonstrate that, whereas Western feudalism was the result of a synthesis of slave and primitive-communal ("Germanic") modes, no such synthesis took place in the East and in the Balkans because of the conservatism of the eastern Roman state superstructure. As we will see, this conclusion is not entirely incorrect, although it needs to be expressed in different terms to be of heuristic value. But the main difficulty is that the framework of the discussion, which tends toward an illustration of the uniqueness of Western social-economic evolution, does not really contribute to a discussion of exploitation and power relationships, the more so since Anderson does not really give adequate space to the internal dynamism of Byzantine culture and political-economic development. In addition, most of these debates are vitiated still by a perspective that tends, even if unintentionally, to present medieval eastern Roman culture as stagnant and fossilized, thus further inhibiting any possibility of seeing the dynamic structures that underlay the apparently slow rates of change evident in some of the sources. In fact, as soon as one takes the full range of source materials into account, and most particularly the now rapidly increasing volume of archaeological data, such views become manifestly untenable.[6] My own *The State and the Tributary Mode* represents an attempt to correct this general picture by placing the late Roman and Byzantine social formations firmly in a comparative historical and social-economic context and foregrounding the state and the nature of state power.[7] But it is perhaps indicative of the situation that work of this sort, while it has been taken up by outside specialists and comparativists, has met with little response from inside the field. A recent exception is the attempt to place Byzantine culture in a comparative and "civilizational" context as part of a critique of work on the "Byzantine" background to Balkan and eastern European history.[8]

Apart from these debates, the Byzantine world has attracted "outside" attention in two specific connections: the first is in relation to the evolution of the so-called Byzantine commonwealth, that is to say, the development of a distinctly "Byzantinizing" cultural zone in eastern and southeastern Europe and western Russia. Here, Byzantine traditions, predominantly with respect to Orthodox Christianity and ecclesiastical organization, and in the associated culture of an imperial court with ecumenical pretensions, became firmly established and influenced the development of those cultures thereafter, and until the present day in certain respects. This influence was not restricted to the level of popular piety and Church structures or to palace culture and religious art; it affected also attitudes toward and definitions of power and the relationships between ruler and elite and between center and periphery. Although there have been few broadly comparative treatments from outside the specialist field (again, Mann and Runciman deserve mention as well as Skocpol and Gellner, all of whom approach the issue from very different perspectives and none of whom says very much on the question of Byzantine influence), a useful descriptive account of the issues by a specialist has appeared that serves as a good starting point for further comparative work.[9]

The second case has to do with transition or transformation: where the Byzantine world impinges directly on the outside world, and especially upon the history of western medieval Europe, it has attracted greater attention. Thus, the period from the late fourth to the seventh century, during which the western Roman world was transformed into the various "Germanic" successor kingdoms and during which the Roman Empire in its supposedly traditional form finally disappeared, has attracted some comparative historical discussion, in which broader issues are raised.[10] Even more explicitly, the period of the Crusades, and in particular the first to fourth crusades (c. 1097–1204) during which Byzantine and western Christian cultures came into direct and sometimes hostile contact, has been an important stimulus to comparative work, both with respect to cultural history and in terms of political structures and the social relationships underlying them. This has been most apparent in the debate about whether or not Byzantium was ever "feudal" in the Western sense, even if that sense has now also been challenged,[11] but it has also affected other aspects of the history of the Byzantine world.[12]

Yet, in spite of these points of contact and areas of common interest, it is only with some difficulty that I can present a critique of the preexisting literature on the comparative situation and evolution of the Byzantine state, since there is so little to discuss. Few specialists, for example, have attempted to look at the Byzantine state either in the context of wider discussion of state formation and power[13] or in terms of its "dynamic," in the way that, for example, Luttwak has attempted to do for the Roman Empire in the period of the early Principate.[14] In the present chapter, therefore, I will attempt to sketch in what I think are the main structural features of the development of the Byzantine state and the societies or social subsystems that supported it, the relationship between "the state" as a set of institutions and a social elite or elites, and the methods and degree of "exploitation" involved in their maintenance, and how these structures evolved and were transformed over time.

2. WHAT WAS "BYZANTIUM"?

The name "Byzantium" is a convenient convention, coined by French scholars during the seventeenth century to describe the Roman Empire in the East after the fifth and sixth centuries C.E. The western Roman Empire was already in the process of transformation that was to produce the various barbarian successor kingdoms of the Franks, Visigoths and Ostrogoths, Burgundi, and so forth. When exactly "Byzantine" began and "late Roman" ended is a moot point. Some prefer to use the term "Byzantine" for the eastern part of the Roman Empire from the time of Constantine I, that is to say, from the 320s and 330s; others apply it to the eastern empire from the late fifth or sixth century, especially from the reign of Justinian (527–565). In either case, the term "Byzantine" legitimately covers the period commencing with the late Roman era and is used to describe the history of the politics, society, and culture of the medieval East Roman Empire until its demise at the hands of the Ottomans in the fifteenth century.

It was a society of contrasts—a mass of rural and provincial peasant producers, constituting perhaps 90 percent of the total population for most of its history, and a few major urban centers, of which Constantinople itself—the Queen of Cities, the second Rome—was by far the largest and the wealthiest, the seat of emperors, the focal point of literacy and elite culture. It was a sophisticated state, with a complex fiscal system supporting an army, navy, and administrative bureaucracy that was able to preserve the basic forms of the late ancient state well into the high middle ages. It was also the heartland of the Orthodox Church, and from the ninth century it became the center of a far-flung Christian cultural commonwealth and of a network of imitative polities stretching from the Balkans to the Russian principalities. It is represented in the sources, especially the written sources, and in the monuments and art it generated, through a complex political-theological system, in which the emperor was an autocratic ruler whose power derived directly from God and whose task it was on Earth to maintain order and harmony in imitation of the heavenly sphere. In consequence, ceremony and ritual were fundamental components both of court life, which itself was felt to act as an exemplar for the rest of society and the barbarian world, and of the Byzantine understanding of the world. Emperors were appointed by God, but emperors could be overthrown, and a successful usurper must, it was reasoned, have the support of God—even if men were unable at first to grasp the logic of His choice—otherwise he could not have met with success. God's choice of a bad ruler and, by the same token, the occurrence of natural calamities and phenomena of all kinds, including defeats in battle or enemy attacks, were, as in the rest of the medieval world, interpreted as signs from God, usually of his displeasure. A seventh-century story records that the abbot of a monastery near Constantinople had a dream in which he was able to ask God if all rulers and tyrants were appointed by divine choice. The answer was in the affirmative. "Then why, O Lord," replied the abbot, "did you send the wicked tyrant Phocas to rule over the Romans?" "Because I could find no one worse," came the reply.[15]

Plagues, earthquakes, comets, wars, and other such phenomena were thus part of the relationship between the human and the divine and were acted upon accordingly. Disasters or political calamities were frequently taken as warnings that the Chosen People—the Christian Romans—had strayed from the path of righteousness and were to be brought back to it by appropriate action, so the search for a reason, or a scapegoat, usually followed. Such a logic underlay many important imperial initiatives, even if there were longer-term social and economic factors at work that determined the choice of a particular form of action or response. Such motives also lay behind the stress on Orthodoxy, "correct belief," that is, correct interpretation of the Scriptures and the writings of the Fathers of the Church, so that many of the ecclesiastical-political conflicts within the Byzantine world, and thus between the Byzantine Church or government and the papacy, for example, were set off by conflicts begun over the issue of whether or not a particular imperial policy was accepted as Orthodox or not.

Given the length of its existence, it is clear that considerable changes in state organization, as well as in social and cultural values, took place over that time, so that, while there are enough constants and continuities to make the use of one term for the whole social formation entirely legitimate, it is also true to say that in several respects the state and society of the fifteenth century bore little relationship to those of the sixth. This is particularly true of the social and economic relationships in Byzantine society and the vocabulary through which they were understood; it is even more so in the case of many of the state's key administrative apparatuses.

The "Byzantines" actually called themselves Romans—*Romaioi*—and if they did use the words "Byzantium" or "Byzantine," they were used (illustrative of the connections that learned Byzantines drew between their own culture and that of the ancient world) to describe the capital city of their empire, Constantinople, ancient Byzantion. The hallmarks of this culture were that it was Christian, that the language of the state and the dominant elite was Greek, and that its political ideology was founded on its identity with the Christian Roman empire of Constantine the Great. Much more important from the perspective of cultural self-identity, the literate Byzantine elite from the late eighth and ninth centuries located its roots in the late Roman world and regarded the classical inheritance in learning and literature—in a suitably Christian guise, naturally—as its own. The elite used this cultural capital to differentiate itself from the foreigner, barbarian, or outsider, as well as within Byzantine society to distinguish itself from the semiliterate or illiterate masses of rural and townsfolk.

In 1869, the historian William Lecky wrote:

> Of that Byzantine empire, the universal verdict of history is that it constitutes, without a single exception, the most thoroughly base and despicable form that civilisation has yet assumed. There has been no other enduring civilisation so absolutely destitute of all forms and elements of greatness, and none to which the epithet *mean* may be so emphatically applied....The history of the empire is a monotonous story of the intrigues of priests, eunuchs, and women, of poisonings, of conspiracies, of uniform ingratitude.[16]

This image, which nicely reflects the morality and prejudices of the mid-Victorian world, has been remarkably resilient. Indeed, it lives on in some popular ideas about the Byzantine world, a combination of Victorian moralizing and Crusaders' prejudices, and in the use of the adjective "Byzantine" in a pejorative sense. And there are some modern writers—for the most part, not professional historians—who have, consciously or not, transferred these prejudices to the world of contemporary scholarship, if not with respect to the "corrupt" Byzantine court, then in terms of a romantic, "orientalist" image of Byzantium that merely contributes to the continued obfuscation of the nature of Byzantine society and civilization. In the light of the evidence in the written sources, the Byzantine court was certainly no more corrupt, venal, or conspiracy ridden than any other medieval court in West or East. But it has taken a long time to deconstruct these attitudes. Historians working within the western European tradition in particular have been victims, in this respect, of the nationalist and Eurocentric propaganda that arose in the seventeenth and eighteenth centuries and afterward and in the context of the evolving nationalist and rationalist attiitudes of the age, by which northern and western European culture was credited with an integrity, sense of honor, and straightforwardness that the corrupt "orientalized" medieval Byzantine world (and also the Islamic world, consigned to the same fate) had lost.

Like any other political system, the East Roman Empire struggled throughout its existence to maintain its territorial integrity. Its greatest problem was posed by its geographical situation, always surrounded by potential or actual enemies: in the east, the Sasanid Persian Empire until the 620s, then the Islamic caliphates, and finally the Seljuk and Ottoman Turks; in the north, various groups of immigrant Slavs (6th–7th centuries), along with nomadic peoples such as the Avars, Bulgars, Chazars, Hungarians [Magyars], and Pechenegs; and, in Italy and the western coastal region of the Balkans, the Lombards and Franks and, later, both Saracens (from North Africa and Spain) and Normans (late 10th to mid-12th century). Finally, from the twelfth century, various Italian maritime powers vied in competing to maximize their influence over Byzantine emperors and territory. Overambitious (although sometimes initially very successful) plans to recover former imperial lands and a limited and relatively inflexible budgetary system were key structural constraints that affected the history of the empire. From the eleventh century, and especially from the late twelfth century, the empire's economy was gradually overtaken by the rapidly expanding economies of western Europe and the Italian peninsula. The capture and sack of Constantinople by the Fourth Crusade in 1204 and the partition of its territory among a variety of Latin principalities and a Latin "empire," a rump of the former Byzantine state, spelled the end of Byzantium as a serious international power. In spite of the re-establishment of an imperial state at Constantinople from 1261, the growth of Balkan powers such as the Serbian empire in the fourteenth century and the Ottomans in both Anatolia and the Balkans thereafter were to prevent any reassertion of Byzantine power in the region. By the time of its final absorption into the Ottoman state, the "empire" consisted of little more than Constantinople, some Aegean islands, and parts of the southern Peloponnese in Greece.

The history of Byzantium is not just the history of its political fortunes, of course. The evolution of Byzantine society, transformations in economic life, the relationship between urban centers and rural hinterlands, the constantly shifting apparatuses of the state's fiscal and administrative machinery, the nature and development of Byzantine (Roman) law, the growth of ecclesiastical and monastic power, both in economic as well as in ideological terms, developments in forms and styles of visual representation, literature, architecture, and the sciences—all these elements are but part of a complex whole described by the term "Byzantine," which this brief survey will introduce.[17]

3. Evidence

The nature of the evidential base necessarily means that the student of the Byzantine world must exploit all types of available source material, from narrative histories written in the mould of Thucydides, via archaeology and a range of specialist-related disciplines such as epigraphy and sigillography (the study of lead seals, a particularly important source for the middle Byzantine period), to theological, liturgical, and dogmatic texts, state documents, official treatises, tax registers, private and public letters, diplomatic texts, acts and records of ecclesiastical councils, legal texts and laws, and so forth. Historians of the Byzantine world tend thus to become experts in many fields apart from that in which they are specifically interested, simply in order to extract the maximum benefit from the many varied types of source material, the use of each of which brings with its own specific methodological problems.

Apart from the chronicle literature and historiography of the period, which contains a great deal of relevant information—narrative accounts of battles and campaigns, occasionally by eyewitnessess or those who had spoke with or had access to eyewitnesses and their reports—there are several classes of evidence for the administration and organization of the state and government at its many levels of activity. Lead seals provide a particularly rich source of information for the administrative structures of the Byzantine state, since, between the seventh and the eleventh century especially, most officials, even quite humble ones, had seals bearing their name and/or their title(s) and rank, which they attached to official documents or correspondence. Equally important are the semi-official lists of court precedence of the ninth and tenth centuries, drawn up by palace officers to determine who sat where at imperial receptions and including fairly elaborate descriptions of the various administrative departments of central and provincial administration. Specialist texts dealing with military organization, taxation, and the law and justice also exist, as well as texts on imperial and religious ceremony and ritual. Hagiographical and related writings represent a particularly important source, since they can reflect popular and unofficial views and attitudes in a way less open to works that are conceived as belonging to the genre of historiography and chronography. Saints' lives and related collections of miracles have regularly been used by historians to shed light on Byzantine society and institutions, as well as beliefs and everyday life. But they are also a dangerous source, since they are always informed by a clear ideological program—representing the saint or chief character in the best possible light, encouraging the reader or listener to imitate the piety and spiritual purity of the protagonists as far as they were able, and imbued in consequence with sets of values, implicit and explicit, which invariably meant the introduction of a strongly interpretative element by the writer or compiler. Hagiographies were a widely used type of literature, both read by individuals and groups and listened to by even larger numbers of people, in churches or monasteries, for example. Nevertheless, used with caution, they can be of great value in helping to answer some of the questions in which we are interested in this volume.

There are many other types of written source material, of course. Theological writings, the letters of churchmen or monks, and the acts of Church councils provide valuable insights into attitudes as well as structures, and private letters and diplomatic documents all are essential to understanding how Byzantine state and society worked on a day-to-day basis. Beyond written sources, the evidence of archaeology is crucial in the development of an understanding of Byzantine material culture, urbanism, and village and rural life, as well as issues of settlement pattern, land use and demography, and other issues. Indeed, the archaeology of settlement has proved vital in challenging the picture of urban and rural development to be read from the written sources, since it offers evidence of a diversity of levels of development, of function, and of regional variation that provides a much more complex but at the same time much more helpful insight into social, cultural, and economic evolution. Numismatics, not strictly "archaeological," is a crucial aspect of the study of material culture and the economy, of course, and can tell us a great deal about such diverse matters as symbolism and iconography, market and commercial exchange, the government's fiscal system, and the process of wealth accumulation and redistribution, and so forth. The range of sources is, therefore, very broad, and the historian needs always to work with a broad range of materials if any meaningful composite picture of Byzantine society and culture is to be developed. In the essay that follows, I have drawn on as wide a range of materials as possible through the relevant modern literature. Those who wish to pursue specific issues of source analysis and use should pursue those questions through the works I have cited.[18]

4. PHYSICAL CONTEXT

The Byzantine Empire straddled the Balkan peninsula and Asia Minor. After the collapse of Roman power following the Arab attacks and conquests of the years 634—650, it was an empire reduced to a rump of its former self. By the year 700, all its North African and western Mediterranean provinces had also been lost, with the possible exception of a tenuous Roman presence in the Balearics. Yet, the regions it retained were among the least wealthy of its former provinces, among which Egypt had contributed as the most productive, the main source of grain for Constantinople, and a major source of the state's tax income. From figures given by a range of late Roman sources for the eastern half of the empire (thus excluding Italy and Africa, which anyway contributed only one-eighth or so of the total), it has been calculated that Egypt contributed something like one-third of the state income (both gold and grain) derived from the prefectures of Oriens and Illyricum together; that the dioceses of Asiana, Pontica, Macedonia, and Oriens together contributed about four-fifths of the gold revenue, with Pontica and Oriens (which included the frontier regions and their hinterlands) providing a further proportion—more than 50 percent—of the grain levied for the army. Comparing these figures with more detailed budgetary details from the sixteenth-century Ottoman records, one observes that the income of the Balkan region up to the Danube and that of Ottoman Anatolia were very approximately equal. While there are some disparities in coverage between these regions in their late Roman and Ottoman forms, this gives a crude idea of the relative economic value of the two regions. In the late Roman period, however, the bulk of the state's income outside Egypt had been derived from the rich provinces of Syria, Mesopotamia, Euphratensis, Osrhoene, Phoenicia, Palestine, and Cilicia, all lost after the 640s and only partially, in their northern perimeter, recovered in the tenth century. With the loss of Egypt and these eastern provinces, therefore, and with effective control over all but the coastal periphery of much of the southern Balkans lost during the late sixth and first half of the seventh centuries, the overall income of the state collapsed to a fraction of the sixth-century figure: one figure plausibly suggested is that it was reduced to a quarter.[19] In order fully to appreciate the economic and political history of the Byzantine world, some knowledge of its physical geography is necessary; the following descriptive section is intended to summarize the main points.

4.1. Anatolia

During the late Roman period (fourth to early seventh centuries), Anatolia was divided into some twenty-four provinces. These provinces were in turn grouped into dioceses under *vicarii*, those of Asia Minor belonging chiefly to the dioceses of Pontica and Asiana, partly to that of Oriens. The whole formed part of the praetorian prefecture of the East, with its headquarters at Constantinople, a massive administrative circumscription that included all of the Middle Eastern districts of the empire with Egypt and parts of North Africa, as well as the European provinces of Thrace, Haemimontus, and Rhodope (modern Turkey in Europe, with parts of southeastern Bulgaria and northeastern Greece).

The most densely settled regions were the narrow coastal plains in the north and south and the much broader plains of the Aegean region, dissected by the western foothills of the central plateau, which run from east to west. Urban settlements were concentrated in these areas, although there were other groups of cities in certain inland regions with more sheltered climatic conditions than the central plateau and the eastern mountains usually afforded. Land use throughout the medieval period and into modern times was predominantly pastoral on the plateau, with the cultivation of cereals, vegetables, vines, and olives dominating the fertile coastal regions. All cities depended upon their agricultural hinterlands for their economic survival, although those with good harbor facilities or other access to the coast were also centers of long-distance as well as local trade and exchange.

Politically and militarily, Anatolia was at peace throughout the Roman period and until the beginning of the seventh century, except for the existence of brigandage in less accessible regions such as Isauria and the brief civil wars of the late fifth century, which involved both this region and parts of western Anatolia.

Culturally, Anatolia remained always a region of diversity. By the late sixth century, most of the non-Greek indigenous languages had died out (e.g., Isaurian,

Galatian, Lycian), except for Armenian and some related dialects in the northeast, although there is some slight evidence that certain languages survived for longer in the more isolated regions. Greek dominated, although a wide range of dialect forms seems to have developed, some of which still survive (although no longer in Turkey: Pontic Greek, for example, which moved with its refugee speakers, expelled during the 1923 exchange of populations between Greece and Turkey).

In theory, a uniform Christian faith dominated, but in practice local variations, often bordering on the heretical, marked out many districts. There is evidence from the late seventh century for the existence of several heretical sects of a dualist nature, most important among which were the Paulicians of the eastern mountain region (centered around modern Divri), who, in the ninth century, and with military and financial assistance from the caliphate, posed a serious threat to the unity of the state until they were crushed by the emperor Basil I (867–886). During the iconoclastic period (eighth–ninth centuries), the various regions took different sides, although this represents local vested interests and political opportunism, rather than religious affiliations.

In its efforts both to cope with demographic and fiscal problems and to eradicate religious opposition, the state often transferred populations from one area to another. Anatolia thus gained from the import of Slav and other Balkan groups, while southeast Europe received heretical groups that brought with them dualist ideas and stimulated the growth of heterodox beliefs such as Bogomilism in Bulgaria during the tenth and eleventh centuries. During the eleventh century and after, there was a large-scale migration of Syrians and especially Armenians into southwestern Asia Minor, partly a result of imperial expansion eastward in the tenth century, partly a result of the Seljuq threat in the middle of the eleventh century.

With the arrival of the Seljuq Turks in the 1060s, the defeat of the imperial army at the battle of Mantzikert in 1071, and the ensuing internal factionalism and dissension, much of eastern and central Asia Minor fell under Turkish sway; although imperial efforts to recover some of the lost regions met with partial success during the reigns of Alexios I (1081–1118) (and with the assistance of the armies of the First Crusade) and his successors John II and Manuel I—up to 1180—lack of resources and the strength of Turk resistance meant that by the end of the twelfth century the empire was effectively confined to the northern and southern littorals and the western coastal plains of the region. During the period of the Latin empire (1204–1261), the successor empire of Nicaea was able to reassert imperial control to a degree, in western Anatolia; but after the restoration of an imperial Byzantine state at Constantinople in 1261, priorities shifted away from this frontier, and Turkish groups under the leadership of a variety of warlords and clans reduced imperial possessions to a few coastal enclaves and fortified centers. By the early fourteenth century, Byantine control over Asia Minor had effectively withered away.

4.2. The Balkans

The Balkan peninsula is a region dominated by mountain systems, and, although not particularly high, these cover some 66 percent of the surface area. The main formations are those of the Dinaric Alps, which push down from the western Balkan region in a southeasterly direction and which, in the Pindos range, dominate western and central Greece. Extensions and spurs of these mountains dominate southern Greece and the Peloponnese. The Balkan range itself (Turk. *balqan*, "densely wooded mountain"; Gk. Haimos) lies north of Greece, extending east from the Morava for about 550 km as far as the Black Sea coast, but the Rhodope range forms an arc running down from this range through Macedonia toward the plain of Thrace. The coastal and riverine plains are in consequence relatively limited in extent, and, together with the very marked climatic variations between coastal, Mediterranean-type conditions and inland/highland, continental-type conditions, present a very accentuated settlement pattern consisting in a series of fragmented geopolitical entities, separated by ridges of highlands, fanning out along river valleys toward the coastal areas.

The history of the region has been heavily marked by this structure; in spite of the administrative unity and the relatively effective fiscal and military administration of the late Roman and Byzantine states, they still had to function in a geophysical context in which communications were particularly difficult and economic relationships were of a specific type. In particular, the southern Balkan peninsula has no obvious geographical focal point. The main cities in the medieval period were Thessaloniki and Constantinople, yet these were peripheral to the peninsula and its fragmented landscape. The degree and depth of Byzantine political control during the middle ages is clearly reflected in this. In the Rhodope mountains, perhaps the most inaccessible of those mentioned, as well as in the Pindus range, state authority, whether Byzantine or Ottoman, always remained a rather distant factor in the lives of the inhabitants. These were regions in which paganism and heresy could survive with little interference or control from a central government or Church establishment.

This geophysical structure also affects land use. The highland regions are dominated by forest and woodland; the lower foothills are dominated by woodland, scrub, and rough pasturage. Only the plains of Thessaly and Macedonia offer the possibility of extensive arable exploitation; the riverine plains and the coastal strips associated with them (such as the region about the Gulfs of Argos and Corinth, much more limited in extent) present a similar but more restricted potential. These are the regions where orchards, as well as viticulture and oleoculture, are chiefly located. Inevitably, the pattern of settlement, of both large urban centers and rural communities, is largely determined by these features.

Finally, the relationship between this landscape of mountains, gulfs, and valleys on the one hand and the sea on the other is fundamental to the cultural, as well as the political and military, history of Greece. The sea surrounds Greece except along its northern bounds, and the extended coastline, including gulfs such as those of Corinth or Thessaloniki, which penetrate deep into the interior, serves as a means of communication with surrounding areas such that even interior districts of the Balkans often share in the Mediterranean cultural world outside. The sea was also a source of danger: seaborne access from the west, from the south, or from the northeast via the Black Sea made Greece and the Peloponnese particularly vulnerable to invasion and dislocation. Once again, the political geography of this part of the Byzantine world plays a very specific role in its general historical evolution.

5. Introductory Description

The Roman state from the late fourth to the mid-seventh century was structured as a hierarchy of administrative levels, headed by the emperor. The latter was both a figurehead of great symbolic importance, since he was perceived as God's representative on Earth, and a practical ruler actively involved in every aspect of government, surrounded by a palatine and household apparatus that was the center of imperial administration. Civil and fiscal power was delegated from the emperor to progressively lower levels of this pyramidal system, first to the so-called praetorian prefects, whose prefectures were the largest territorial circumscriptions in the state; then on to the *dioecesae* or dioceses, into which each prefecture was further divided and which had a predominantly fiscal aspect. The dioceses were divided into *provinciae* or provinces, territorial units of fiscal and judicial administration, and these were further divided into self-governing *poleis* or *civitates*, the cities, each with its *territorium* or hinterland. Cities were the basic tax-collecting units, and the leading landowners of the cities were responsible for collecting taxes of varying sorts, assessed on a yearly basis according to estimates of state budgetary requirements for the year ahead. This pattern was slowly transformed after the third century, and, by the middle of the sixth century, the state intervened directly to ensure that taxes were properly assessed and collected. The late Roman state was thus a complex bureaucracy, rooted in and imposed upon a series of overlapping social formations structured by local variations on essentially the same economic basis across the whole central and east Mediterranean and Balkan world. Social and political tensions were exacerbated by several factors: religious divisions between different Christian creeds, which had also a regional pattern; local economic conditions, especially in the poorer regions of the Balkans; and the burden placed upon the tax-paying population—again varying strongly by region—as a result of the state's needs with respect to its administrative apparatus and, in particular, its armies. All these elements were in turn affected by periodic shifts in imperial religious policy, which reflected both the power politics of the court and the convictions of individual rulers.[20]

While agrarian production dominated the economy, the cities were the homes of a literate elite of landowners (although, in the less heavily urbanized regions, ranch-like country estates with fortified villas could be found), many of whom were members of what is loosely dubbed the "senatorial aristocracy." Social status was largely determined by whether one had held an active post in the imperial bureaucracy and at what level, that is, by one's relationship to the system of imperial titles and precedence, access to which was determined largely, but not exclusively, by family wealth and kinship, although regional variations were marked.

The Church and the theological system it represented (from the late fourth century the official religion of the Roman state and, probably by the mid-sixth century, the majority religion within the empire) played a central role in the economy of the Roman world—it was a major landowner—as well as in imperial politics, in influencing the moral and ethical system of the Roman world, and in directing imperial religious policy. Emperors were inextricably involved in the conflicts generated by theological disagreements, given the prevailing view that the emperor was chosen by God, that he had to be Orthodox, and that his role was to defend the interests of Orthodoxy and the Roman, that is, Christian, *oikoumenê* (the inhabited, civilized —Roman—world). Yet there were a number of paradoxes in the ways in which the role of the Christian Church affected East Roman culture, for there was no single and universally agreed theology; fundamental differences emerged during the fourth and fifth centuries that led to real splits in interpretation and liturgical practice, and, since these also took on a regional aspect, the result was a geographical regionalization of creed and belief. Two opposed interpretative theologies dominated: monophysitism (the doctrine of a single divine nature), which understood the Trinity as entirely divine, so that Christ could not be understood as being in any way human, thus could not have died on the cross and been resurrected, and dyophisitism (the doctrine of a dual nature, human and divine), according to which the Trinity could indeed be all things at all times, in a combination of essences beyond human understanding. Egypt, much of Syria, and Armenia became predominantly "monophysite" (although with substantial pools of dyophisitism in Palestine and the Lebanon, for example), while Asia Minor, the Balkans, and the west were dyophysite. And while these divisions were not responsible for the geopolitical divisions that developed thereafter within the empire, they certainly played an important role and contributed to the religious as well as the political map of the Near and Middle East thereafter.

All these structures underwent a series of important transformations between the late sixth and the early ninth century. In spite of the problems faced by the eastern half of the empire in the middle and late fifth century, its greater structural cohesiveness and flexibility enabled it to survive both external attacks and the disruption of economic and trading patterns. It was also able during the sixth century to take the offensive and to recover large regions that had been lost to invaders or settlers. Thus, the East Roman state in the early 630s still embraced North Africa, Egypt, modern Syria, western Iraq, and western Jordan, along with the Lebanon and Palestine, Anatolia, much of the Balkans, Sicily, Sardinia, and considerable areas of

Italy, although its Italian holdings had been reduced by the Lombards. Most of the Balkans was out of effective central control and was dominated by Slav or other invaders. The cost of this sixth-century imperialism was very great, however, and when, in the 630s, the Arabs emerged from the Arabian peninsula under the banner of Islam and the holy war, imperial resistance was little more than token. By 642, all of Egypt and the Middle Eastern provinces had been lost, Arab forces had penetrated deep into Asia Minor and Libya, and imperial forces had been withdrawn into Asia Minor, to be settled across the provinces of the region as the only available means of supporting them. Within a relatively short period, the East Roman state lost some 50 percent of its area and 75 percent of its resources. This induced radical changes on an administrative system and government that still had to maintain and equip a considerable army and an effective fiscal organization if it was to survive.[21] While many of the developments that led to this transformation were in train long before the seventh-century crisis, it was these developments that brought things to a head.

All areas of social, cultural, and economic life were affected. The devastation, abandonment, shrinkage, or displacement of many cities in Asia Minor as a result of invasions and raids, especially from the 640s but also during the period of the Persian wars (602–626), combined with the fact that, by the late sixth century, the function of cities in the state fiscal system was already changing, encouraged the state to move its fiscal attention to the village community, which became the main unit of assessment by the late seventh century. There occurred a "ruralization" of society.[22] This picture was further affected by the preeminent position taken by Constantinople in these changed conditions. The establishment of the new imperial capital in the year 330, on the site of the ancient city of Byzantion, with the imperial court, a senate, and all the social, economic, and administrative consequences, had far-reaching consequences for the pattern of exchange and movement of goods in the Aegean and east Mediterranean basin.[23]

The social elite was transformed. The so-called senatorial aristocracy of the late Roman period, itself only recently formed from the ranks of the imperial bureaucracy and service aristocracy brought into existence during the fourth century,[24] was replaced by a narrower elite of what appear at first glance to be largely "new men" selected by the emperors on a more obviously meritocratic basis. But this group undoubtedly included substantial numbers of the older elite, especially in the central departments of state and fiscal administration in and around the capital, although the sources tell us very little on this point. And, by the same token, many of the provincial establishment who now became prominent derived from the less well-known middling ranks of provincial landowners and officials of the preceding centuries. Whatever their origins, however, members of the imperial administrative and military hierarchy of the state were initially heavily dependent upon the emperor and upon imperially sponsored positions.[25] But, as a result of its increasing grip on state positions and the lands it accrued through the rewards attached to such service, this elite soon turned into an aristocracy. During the eighth and ninth centuries, it was still very dependent on the state; during the tenth and especially the eleventh centuries, it became both increasingly independent and more self-aware as a social elite. The state had to compete directly with a social class whose enormous landed wealth and entrenched position in the apparatuses of the state meant that it posed a real threat to central control of fiscal resources.[26]

The events of the seventh century had two further results. In the first place, there took place a reassertion of central state power over late Roman tendencies to decentralization. The hierarchy of administrative levels remained but was simplified and leveled somewhat, with the emperors exercising more direct control over the appointment of senior posts and the management of key areas of state policy, especially fiscal and military affairs. The state was both limited by, and in its turn partly defined, the nature of key economic relationships. This is exemplified in the issue and circulation of coin, the basic mechanism through which the state converted agricultural produce into transferable fiscal resources. Coin was issued chiefly to oil the wheels of the state machinery and to reward the imperial bureaucracy and senior military cadres; wealth was appropriated and consumed through a redistributive fiscal mechanism. The state issued gold in the form of salaries and largesse to its bureaucracy and armies, which exchanged a substantial portion thereof for goods and services in maintaining themselves. The state could thus collect much of the coin it put into circulation through tax, the more so since fiscal policy generally demanded tax in gold and offered change in bronze. Considerable sums of gold coin remained in private hands, however, thus contributing to the continuance of a substantially monetized economy even in periods of considerable financial and economic dislocation. There were periods when this system was constrained by circumstances, resulting in ad hoc arrangements for supplying soldiers and raising tax in kind, for example (as in the late seventh century), and it also varied by region. But in a society in which social status and advancement (including the self-identity of the aristocracy) were connected with the state, these arrangements considerably hindered economic activity not directly connected with the state's activities. The continued power and attraction of the imperial establishment at Constantinople, with its court and hierarchical system of precedence, as well as the highly centralized fiscal administrative structure, consumed the whole attention of the Byzantine elite, hindering the evolution of a more highly localized aristocracy that might otherwise have invested in the economy and society of its own localities and towns, rather than in the imperial system.[27]

In the second place, the empire was confined almost entirely to its "dyophysite" regions. The subjects of the Byzantine Empire were henceforth the Orthodox; the majority of eastern Christians outside the political bounds of the empire—with some exceptions in Palestine, for example—were seen either as heretics or dangerously close to heresy (and the same applied in reverse, of course; indeed, the monophysite view within the former eastern provinces was that the empire had been punished for its lack of Orthodoxy by the Islamic conquests). But this also had the effect of consolidating the "imperial church" within the empire and increasing the identification—completed by the late Byzantine period—of imperial with Orthodox (and eventually with Greek and what was later to evolve as a form of Greek nationalism). There evolved an eastern "Orthodox" identity with empire that served as an important focus for resistance to outside cultural as well as political influence and that became a crucial factor in the way Byzantines responded to the economic as well as the cultural influence of the West from the eighth century on.

6. Resources and Competition

The evolution of the Byzantine state was determined by many interlinking factors. One way to approach its history is to look at the issue of resources and power, in other words, in particular, how were resources exploited and controlled, and by whom, and how were the products of those resources distributed across the social formation as a whole at different times? How much of the wealth produced in the different sectors of the economy—agrarian, pastoral, commercial—could be taken in the form of rent and tax or indirectly, in skills, services, and labor?

Resources consisted of agricultural and pastoral produce, ores and other raw materials, labor, and skills and knowledge. The crucial issue for the central government was maintaining enough control over those resources to ensure its own continued existence; the structural evolution of taxation and the apparatus of fiscal exploitation illustrates this quite clearly, and from this standpoint, the history of the empire as a political entity can be summed up in terms of the ways through which this aim was achieved. In particular, this means a discussion of the fact that, throughout its long history, the central government had always to compete with others—the senatorial landowning elite, the middle and late Byzantine aristocracy, foreign merchants—over these resources, which were, of course, finite. The importance of that tension reveals itself very clearly in the internal political history of the empire, and the instrumental means by which one set of interests or another within the leading elements of East Roman society gained or lost its predominance are reflected in the history of both fiscal policies and civil conflict.

Looking at the conflicts that thus arose offers particularly useful insights into the ways in which the Byzantine state actually worked and under what conditions centralized state power and authority are likely to break down. In modern industrialized societies, for example, taxation is the means whereby the state redistributes surplus value that has already been produced and distributed across society among both the owners or controllers of productive resources in land and labor power and those who sell their labor power in return for a wage or salary. In premodern societies, in contrast, surplus appropriation can take place only through rent or tax, in their various forms; the processes involved necessarily reflect the direct contact between state or dominant elite and tax- or rent-payers. In both cases, the nature of the social and economic tensions between those who do the appropriating and those who do the producing is determined by two features: competition over the distribution of resources between the potentially antagonistic elements in this equation and the forms taken by tax and rent, through which surplus is appropriated in the first place.

Both state centers and ruling elites in premodern formations thus have an equally powerful vested interest in the maintenance of those social and economic relations to which they owe their position. The state (as embodied in a central or ruling establishment) must appropriate any surplus itself or ensure that an adequate portion of such a surplus is passed on to it to be certain of survival. But there has historically always been a tendency for the functionaries entrusted with these duties to evolve, however gradually, their own independent power bases, thus representing a competitor with the state for resources. The relationship between the ruler or ruling elite and those who actually appropriate a surplus on their behalf is, in consequence, always contradictory and potentially antagonistic because, as indicated, dominant socioeconomic groups and states function at the same level of primary appropriation, since there is no real difference, except in scale and administrative organization, between the extraction of tax and that of rent, whatever the form it takes. The "antagonism" was, of course, a structural antagonism; it need not necessarily be expressed through any awareness on the part of the individuals or groups in question. Furthermore, this relationship is generally not a simple one-to-one equation; the state may be embodied in a particular power elite, which may or may not originate in a dominant social class or aristocracy, for example, so that a whole complex of interwoven social, economic, and political vested interests is involved. But the ability of the state to extract surplus depends ultimately upon its power to limit the economic and political strength of such potentially competing groups. The only real way to achieve this has been to create, or attempt to create, a totally loyal, because totally dependent, administrative group, a bureaucracy that is identified entirely with the interests of the central establishment, such as the Ottoman *kapikullari* or the earlier *Mamluk* elite. Byzantine emperors were able to achieve this for a while (although they may not have had this intention) by the circumstances peculiar to the second half of the seventh century. But, in the longer term, this structured relationship was central both to the failure of the Byzantine state to resist economic challenges from elsewhere and to the success of the Italian commercial republics with respect to their own social and economic organization.[28]

But the history of the structures of the state—taxation, military organization, justice, the palatine administration, and so forth—represent only one aspect of a more complex whole, and we must not forget that the individuals who in groups or by themselves acted as agents in this scheme of things also functioned within a field of cultural activities, through which they expressed themselves in language and through which they established and defended their own individual identities as members of a wider society. Literature and visual representation of all types, religious and secular buildings, all contributed to the perceived environment inhabited by the subjects of the Byzantine emperor, as well as of the emperor himself. The importance of this becomes apparent when such perceptions directly impinge on political actions and cultural responses to change. In this respect, Runciman's theory of the competitive selection of social practices can usefully inform explanations of change over time. In essence, the approach he has outlined is intended to enable discussion of general social evolution within the context of detailed conclusions reached by specialists across a wide range of historical cultures. The essence of this approach is, quite simply, that it is social practices, which are themselves constitutive of the roles through which social formations are defined, that are adopted—selected—according to circumstances. These social practices, and hence the modes of social and political organization that they represent, survive or not according to their functional effectiveness in competition with other sets of practices. Social practices evolve in response to specific internal and external pressures or other structural tensions, and those practices that evolve in ways that confer on their bearers an advantage at one or more levels of social organization will, should they compete with less functionally effective modes of social organization, contribute to the eradication or extinction of the latter. It is the historian's task to determine explanations for the development and transformation of such sets of practices, for how and why they bestow differential competitive advantages in different historical contexts. Microhistorical analysis can thus inform macrohistorical explanation in a fruitful collaboration.[29]

For resources can also be reckoned in terms of cultural attitudes and "ideologies," since these too have an instrumental input into the ways in which a culture appropriates its physical environment and responds to political situations. As the empire's political situation stabilized following the nadir of the seventh and early eighth centuries, for example, so a more diverse culture began to evolve, as various genres of late Roman and Hellenistic literature were revived, albeit in a clearly Byzantine form, while "classical" motifs in visual art also made their appearance. And, together with this revival of learning and literature, there evolved also a heightened consciousness of the differences between the educated and literate and those who were not, a consciousness that was represented especially strongly within the bureaucratic and ecclesiastical establishment at Constantinople. The educated writers of the ninth century were only beginning to grapple with this heritage and to make it their own again. By the middle of the eleventh century, the revival of interest in classical literature and style was characteristic of the Byzantine social elite. The diglossy that had haunted the Greek-speaking world from the first century B.C.E. by which the spoken demotic Greek of ordinary everyday life was distinguished from a literary and somewhat artificial and archaizing form of the language was reinforced by this process, of course. An accurate use of archaic Attic Greek when writing, combined with a thorough knowledge of classical mythology and rhetorical methods as well as the established canon of Christian writers, was the hallmark of the educated Byzantine, through which she or he was differentiated from the functionally literate clerk or village priest as well as the illiterate mass of the population. Choice of theme and topic reflected not just the writer's educational attainment and classical knowledge, however, but also a strategy for reinforcing the point of the topic about which the author was writing. The deliberate exploitation by historians and chroniclers of material from ancient texts, often incorporated almost verbatim, was part of this picture, for the selection of material was dictated also by what was considered appropriate as much as by what actually happened. Choice of language in speaking or in writing thus became a matter of cultural politics. It is no coincidence that the highly educated composer of a group of twelfth-century satirical poems set in Constantinople, chose to set his verse down in a demotic form of the language, rather than in the classical form with which he was thoroughly familiar.[30]

But political expansion, military success, and the confidence engendered by the empire's dominant position in the east Mediterranean region in the first half of the eleventh century also led to an increasing cultural arrogance about Byzantine superiority, in which the culture and character of non-Byzantines were treated with an increasing element of contempt. This is not universally so, but it is clear enough in a substantial amount of the writing of the period. This is especially true of attitudes toward the "Latins," attitudes that had an instrumental effect on Byzantines' abilities to comprehend and respond to Western economic and military growth. Until the ninth and early tenth centuries, and in spite of the power of the Frankish empire, there had been no serious rivals either to Byzantine ideological claims or to Byzantine cultural achievements. As the tenth century drew on, it became clear that the medieval West was in fact a region of great economic, social, and, above all, military dynamism, a dynamism that the Byzantines had to confront in the eleventh century in the form of the Normans in particular but equally, in terms of both economic and political power, in the shape of the Italian merchant cities. Stereotypes of the barbarous Westerner became common. The political and military success of these "barbarians" began to be seen as a serious threat to imperial power, and, as Western cultural attitudes challenged the assumptions of the Greek-speaking Byzantine elite and their values, so fear gave such caricatures an added edge. Traditional suspicion of Western liturgical and other religious practices, of the papacy and its claims, all now combined to blind most Byzantines to the political realities of "Latin" power and potential and to encourage a xenophobia and hostility that were, through the direct confrontation of these two halves of the Christian world in the events of the Crusades, to lead to massive and irreversible mutual misunderstandings and hatred. The sack of Constantinople and the fourth crusade in 1203–1204 were symptoms as well as results of these developments.[31]

7. Modes of Exploitation

A fundamental principle of late Roman and Byzantine taxation was to ensure the maximization of exploitation and hence of revenues. Tax was assessed according to a formula tying land, determined by area, quality, and type of crop, to labor power, a formula referred to as the *capitatio-iugatio* system. Land that was not exploited, either by agriculture or for pasturage, was not taxed directly. The tax burden was reassessed at intervals, originally in cycles of five, then of fifteen years, although in practice it took place far more irregularly. Maximization of income was achieved in the late Roman period by a system under which land registered for taxation but not cultivated was attributed for assessment to neighboring landlords, a process known as *adiectio sterilium*. From the seventh or eighth centuries, a number of changes were introduced. Each tax unit was expected to produce a fixed revenue, distributed across the taxpayers, who were as a body responsible for deficits, which they shared. The tax unit—the community, in effect—was jointly responsible for the payments due from lands that belonged to their tax unit but were not farmed, for whatever reason. Remissions of tax could be requested or bestowed to compensate for such burdens, but if the community took over and farmed the land for which it had been responsible, it had also to pay the deficits incurred by the remission. As noted already, the cities lost their role as crucial intermediaries in the levying of taxation, which was now devolved for the most part upon imperial officials of the provinces and upon the village community.[32]

Money in the form of coin had always played a central role in the economy of the Roman world. But its function and centrality varied across time. The financial crisis faced by the Roman government in the late third and early fourth centuries had forced the state to introduce alternative and more effective means of paying its armies and administration, and payment in kind, or rations, became a standard means of achieving this. During the late fifth and sixth centuries, in the East, the preeminent position of coinage was reasserted, following a series of important minting reforms, but the seventh-century changes saw this position challenged once more. Coinage was issued to oil the wheels of the state machinery and to pay the considerable salaries of the state administration and army, and, as noted earlier, wealth was appropriated and consumed through a redistributive fiscal mechanism. The state collected as much of its revenue as it could in gold coin; fiscal policy generally demanded tax in gold and offered change in bronze.[33] Vast amounts of gold remained in nonstate hands, however, as the evidence of coin hoards, on the one hand, and the continued payment of the state administration with gold throughout the period demonstrate. During the second half of the seventh and the first half of the eighth centuries, this system was constrained by circumstances, so that a large proportion of the state's requirements for its army and administration was raised chiefly but by no means exclusively (since the administrative and military hierarchy continued to receive substantial salaries in gold coin) in kind. There always remained strong regional as well as chronological variations: areas in which urban or rural markets existed and were secure from hostile attack, such as the metropolitan regions around Constantinople, were generally supplied not only with gold but also with bronze coinage, for example, in contrast to what appears to have been the situation in the provinces away from the capital. Such constraints had always operated in remoter localities or areas where the activities of the state did not promote such monetized activity, as in Anatolia after the cutting back of the state postal and transport service in the 530s, for example, and they continued to operate thereafter, affected from time to time by the particular historical situation. By the same token, the pressure exerted by the state elite in the use of this coinage for investment and purchases at all levels meant an extremely high degree of monetization across the empire's territories, although the extent of the availability of the non-precious-metal coinage on the one hand and its value against gold (and silver) on the other determined the extent to which the less wealthy in society could access market relations without resorting to means such as credit or barter; indeed, it has been argued that extensive credit arrangements were also in place, permitting the transfer of values without the direct transfer of coin. Even if the pattern was in places uneven, fluctuating dramatically at times according to local circumstances, the presence of the army, and local patterns of agrarian production and levels of output, economic life was generally highly monetized.[34]

The Roman and Byzantine system worked as it did because it was a plurimetallic system: a base metal coinage of account was available through which day-to-day exchanges could be carried out, which functioned because it usually had a stable rate of exchange with the precious metal coinage. When this broke down, price inflation usually followed, accompanied by a move from the extraction of taxes in cash to one in kind (with all the implications for economic relations and activity which that entails); this was the case in the third and into the fourth centuries and in the late seventh and part of the eighth centuries.

The government faced two main problems. To begin with, it had to estimate how much gold coinage should be produced to maintain the cycle of redistribution through taxation. In the second place, it needed to know how much bronze coinage was required to facilitate this cycle at the lower level. In the first case, there are several historical examples showing the effects of a shortage of gold: Procopius and John Lydus note that the closure of the postal stations on many of the routes operated by the *cursus publicus* deprived local producers of a market for their goods and thus of the gold with which to pay their taxes. A situation similar to that described by Lydus and Procopius affected the rural population of the provinces during the 760s, when the emperor Constantine V seems deliberately to have restricted the circulation of gold but demanded tax payments in coin, thus forcing the producers to sell their crops at artificially deflated prices, and there are other examples from the following centuries.[35] And the fate of the base metal coinage contrasts with the relatively constant rate of production and gold content of the precious-metal coinage from the middle of the seventh to the ninth century and beyond. The history of the Byzantine coinage during this period is certainly complex, involving considerable variations in the weight and style of the bronze issues, with several changes introduced by successive rulers, the (re)introduction of a silver coinage linking the gold and bronze denominations under Leo III (which adversely affected the production of fractional gold denominations), and substantial reforms and stabilization of the bronze under Leo IV and, later, as noted earlier, under Michael II and Theophilos.

The most important change in fiscal arrangements that took place after the seventh century seems to have been the introduction of a distributive tax assessment, according to which the annual assessment was based on the capacity of the producers to pay, rather than on a flat rate determined by the demands of the state budget. This involved, of course, accurate records and statements of property, and one important result was that the Byzantine Empire evolved one of the most advanced land-registration and fiscal-assessment systems of the medieval world, as well as one of the most sophisticated bureaucracies for administering it. It also appears to have been associated with the ending of the connection between the land tax and the poll tax; instead of a combined *captatio-iugatio* assessment, the land tax, or *kanon*, was now assessed as a separate item, with the replacement for the poll tax, known as the *kapnikon*, or "hearth" tax, raised on each household. These changes may not have happened overnight, and there is no imperial legislation to give us a clue as to when and how they occurred, but they had been completed by the middle of the ninth century, and probably long before.

The regular taxation of land was supplemented by a wide range of extraordinary taxes and corvées, noted already, including obligations to provide hospitality for soldiers and officials, maintain roads, bridges, fortifications; and deliver and/or produce a wide range of requirements such as charcoal or wood. These continued unbroken into the middle and late Byzantine periods, although their Latin names were mostly replaced with Greek or Hellenized equivalents. But certain types of landed property were always exempt from many of these extra taxes, in particular the land owned or held by soldiers and that held by persons registered in the service of the public post, in both cases because of traditional favored conditions of service and because they depended to a degree on their property for the carrying out of their duties (see later discussion of soldiers). Although the basic land tax and the accompanying hearth tax now became the fundamental elements of the tax system, it was complicated by the addition of a vast range of extra and incidental impositions; quite apart from the extraordinary taxes in kind or services mentioned already, government tax officials began to add more and more extras to their demands, in the form of fees for their services and demands for hospitality (which could then be commuted for money), so that the system became immensely ramified. During the second half of the eleventh century, depreciation of the precious-metal coinage combined with bureaucratic corruption led to the near-collapse of the system.[36]

Fundamental changes were not made until the early twelfth century, when inflationary pressures and the complexity and ad hoc nature of the old system forced the emperors to introduce important changes. The older charges were rationalized, standard rates were established, and the bureaucracy was trimmed. But, increasingly, as the wealthy and powerful managed to extract exemptions for themselves and their lands from many fiscal burdens, the weight of the state's demands fell upon an increasingly hard-pressed peasantry, and the social divisions within the empire, which had grown with the evolution of the new, middle Byzantine elite as it gradually turned itself into an aristocracy of office and birth, became more and more apparent. During the late ninth century, the system of communal responsibility for untilled lands was transformed into a system whereby land could be temporarily exempted from taxation, removed from the fiscal district to which it originally belonged and administered separately, or granted special reductions in taxation. Such interventionist measures seem to have been intended to maintain as close a degree of control as possible over fiscal resources in land. Yet, over the same period, and in order to retain control over its fiscal base and to compete with the elite and the powerful, the government itself began to transform fiscal land into state lands, so that rents to the government in its capacity as a landlord now became indistinguishable in many respects from taxation. There is some evidence from the eleventh century that some landlords invested in "improvements" in their estates, including the construction of mills, for example, which were leased out or exploited directly, but the extent to which this resulted in increased agrarian output is not clear. And whether the state's estate managers followed suit is entirely unknown, although more research remains to be done in this field.

The evolution of *pronoia* represented an alternative means of redistributing resources by the government but also encouraged this overlap.[37] This institution represented a major change in the ways in which resources were administered. Meaning literally "care" or "forethought," the term referred to the concession by the state of the right to receive the revenues from certain public (i.e., fiscal, or taxed) districts or of certain imperial estates and their tenants, along with part or all of the rents and taxes raised from them. Such grants were made to individuals by the emperors for a variety of reasons. They took the form of personal grants from the ruler, who represented the state in the institutional sense; while there was also a more general meaning of the term *pronoia*, the most important involves *pronoia* grants in return for military service. This was a new departure, and, involving as it did, for the first time, the temporary alienation of state revenues to private individuals, it marks a further move along the line from absolute to devolved state power. It is important to emphasise that *pronoia* grants were at first limited to members of the extended family of the imperial clan, the Comneni, and that, although the emperor Manuel I appears to have employed them a little more liberally, they first appear on a wider scale after the events of 1204 and the introduction into many areas of the Byzantine world of Western, feudal arrangements. These no doubt had an influence on the Byzantine way of doing things and may have speeded up the development of *pronoia* on a more generalized basis. But such grants were given not only on a large scale to individuals but also to groups and sometimes on a very small scale, while the government, at least in theory, always retained the right to revoke such a grant. They rarely became hereditary in the proper sense.[38] And there is no evidence, either, that holders of such grants of revenue intervened in the process of production, except insofar as demands for tax and rent might promote an increase in the rate of exploitation of peasant labor.

Until the end of the twelfth century, the government was able to retain a fairly effective control over fiscal resources. But the growth of the aristocracy, which had first challenged the state in the tenth century, had continued; it was from members of that elite that the emperors after the late eleventh century were drawn and whose hold on power was determined largely by their ability to maintain a series of family alliances, through marriage, governorships, and so on, with their peers. After 1204 in particular, the devolution of imperial authority became the chief means by which emperors governed and administered and through which imperial resources were mobilized. Central taxation—the land tax and its associated impositions—remained the basis of government finance, but, as the empire shrank territorially, so commerce came to play a more important role, yet one that was already limited by the strength and dominant position in the carrying trade of Italian merchants and maritime power. The fact that the *kommerkion* on trade was, by the end of the empire, more important as a source of income than the land tax illustrates the insoluble problem faced by the emperors of the last century of Byzantium.

By the late thirteenth century, the land tax was raised on the basis of a flat rate, assessed at regular intervals, but modified in accordance with local conditions and other factors, while the tax on labor power had reappeared as an imposition on individual peasant tenants and their households. Supplementary taxes and impositions continued to be raised; some of them devolved onto landlords, for example, and many of them were designated for specific types of government expenditure or to cover the expenses of particular state requirements, such as the hiring of mercenary forces or the paying of tribute to foreign powers. In one case, in the Peloponnese during the first half of the fifteenth century, taxes introduced by the Ottomans, who had controlled the region for some sixteen years after 1404, were retained by the Byzantine administration that took over, so Islamic taxation terms appear in a Byzantine context: *ushr* (tithe) and *haradj* (land tax), for example.[39] What is worth stressing in all this is the relative degree of flexibility exhibited by the state's fiscal machinery over a long period of time, perhaps an indication of the direct appreciation of what was at stake—control over vital resources—on the part of successive generations of rulers and fiscal administrators. In fiscal practice, more than in any other area of Byzantine state activity, ideology seems not to have masked or obfuscated the realities of the situation, with the single exception of the state's approach to trade and commerce, of which more follows.

8. A Brief Account of the Dynamics of the Byzantine State: Economics and Ideology

There existed a fundamental contradiction in the Byzantine world between the fiscal interests of the state and the nonstate sector of private merchants, bankers, shipping, and so on. The state represented a particular set of ways and means of regulating the extraction, distribution, and consumption of resources, embodying a strongly autarkic relationship between consumption and agricultural production. The export of finished goods, the flow of internal commerce between provincial centers, as well as between the provinces and Constantinople, and the movement of raw materials and livestock were determined to a large extent by three closely connected factors: the demands of the state apparatus (army and treasury) for raw and finished materials and provisions; the state's need for cash revenues to support mercenary forces and the imperial court; and the demands of the imperial capital itself, which dominated regional trade in the western Black Sea and northwest Asia Minor, the north Aegean, and the south Balkans. The pattern of supply and demand was already heavily slanted toward Constantinople, as we have seen, and this pattern became even more accentuated after the loss of central Anatolia to the Turks in the 1070s and 1080s. Trade in the Byzantine world was mostly inward-looking, from the provinces and from the empire's neighbors to Constantinople and between the provinces. Such trade represented after the late ninth century a flourishing aspect of the internal economy of Byzantine society, and large numbers of traders and entrepreneurs were associated with it. But the exploitative state apparatus still dominated, although, as in the late Roman world, while state-dominated trade may have had an inhibiting effect in some respects, it may also have encouraged trade and commerce along the routes most exploited by the state itself, precisely because private entrepreneurial activity can take advantage of state shipping and transportation.

But this essentially late Roman pattern left little room at the level of production and distribution of wealth for outwardly directed commercial activity or enterprise. Even when the state farmed fiscal contracts, the opportunities for private entrepreneurial activity were limited, not just by state intervention but by social convention. What one did with newly acquired wealth was to invest not in independent commercial enterprise but rather in the state: titles, imperial sinecures or actual offices, and court positions were first on the list of priorities. And, although land and the rent accruing from landed property (in addition to the ideologically positive realization of self-sufficiency) were important considerations, it is clear that imperial titles and pensions were just as fundamental to the economic position of the power elite. Investment in commerce was ideologically marginalized, even though the developing group of *archontes*, the local middling and small-scale landed elites of the provincial towns and cities, had in many regions of the empire an active involvement in small-scale commodity production and manufacturing, and the associated movement of goods that resulted; the best-documented examples come from the south Balkan silk industry, but there is no reason to doubt that other regions witnessed similar activity.[40] Such ideological structures or practices can be traced back to the late Roman period and before, associated with aristocratic ideals of culture, the use of time, notions of leisure, and so forth; they reflected the desired self-image of a social elite, and the socioeconomic context of the Byzantine world up to the tenth and early eleventh century offered no challenge to them, since they had no damaging results for the status and position of the elite.

For most wealthy Byzantines, resources were derived predominantly from rents and market sales (depending on area and period) from agricultural production and membership of the state establishment and the considerable salaries in gold that were associated with it. The wealth that the members of this elite could expect to derive from trade and commerce, both during the early period of its evolution and in the tenth and eleventh centuries, appears to have been of far less significance than that derived through rents and state positions, even if it may at times have been considerable. Thus, while merchants were an active element in urban economies by the eleventh century, playing an important role in the distribution of locally produced commodities, they appear have occupied a relatively subordinate position in the process of wealth redistribution as a whole. In particular, they played no role in the perceptions of the society in general in the maintenance of the empire and in the social order as it was understood. The social elite had no interest in their activities, except as suppliers of luxury items on the one hand and as a means of selling off the surpluses from their own estates at local towns or fairs or in the capital on the other. At the same time, the government exercised a somewhat inhibiting control over entrepreneurial enterprise, insofar as it carefully supervised the relationship between traders selling goods to the capital and those who bought those goods and sold them on or worked them into other commodities. In view of the fact that such control was exercised also over the import and export of other goods, such as grain, between the empire and its neighbors, trade offered only minimal inducements, except where a particular loophole in these arrangements could be exploited or where a hitherto unregulated commodity was involved. Even foreign traders were subject to these controls, at least until their power and economic influence became too powerful, in the late twelfth century. Groups of foreign merchants were thus normally resident in a specific quarter and had to be accompanied by imperial officials when they did business.[41]

This contrasts very clearly with the situation in the Italian merchant cities with which the Byzantines did business in the late eleventh and twelfth centuries, especially Venice, Genoa, and Pisa. To begin with, while the major trading cities possessed an agricultural hinterland from which most members of the urban elite derived an income, leading elements of the elites of these cities were at the same time businessmen whose wealth and political power were often dependent as much on commerce as on rents. As they evolved during the eleventh and into the twelfth century, the city-states themselves, increasingly dominated by merchant aristocrats and their clients, came to have a vested interest in the maintenance and promotion of as lucrative and advantageous a commerce as possible, so that the economic and political interests of the leading and middling elements were identical with the interests of the city, its political identity, and its independence of outside interference. State/communal and private enterprise were inseparable. The economic and political well-being of the city as a state was thus to a large extent coterminous with that of the social elite and its dependents. The Byzantine state, in contrast, played no role at all in promoting indigenous enterprise, as far as we can see from the sources, whether for political or economic reasons, and viewed commerce as simply another minor source of state income; commercial activity was regarded as, and was with respect to how the state worked, peripheral to the social values and political system in which it was rooted.[42]

This difference is not a reflection of the failure of an archaic and statist political-economic system to respond to new conditions, with respect to either international commercial relations or internal economic growth. There did exist a relatively active, albeit more or less entirely inwardly directed, commerce, and a merchant "class" to conduct it. But the interests of commerce were subordinate to the relationship between the political and ideological structure of the imperial state on the one hand and the perceived interests of the dominant social-economic elite on the other. I emphasize the word *perceived*. Commerce was seen as neither economically nor politically relevant, an apathy conditioned by the way in which state and society had evolved over the centuries. For those at the top of the social scale, it was viewed as both economically unimportant and socially and culturally demeaning; while for those who were involved in trade it brought no social advancement and, for the most part, no great social wealth.

This combination of practices, rooted in the value system of the world of ancient elites, was reinforced by the relative economic superiority of the Byzantine over the early medieval Western world until the tenth century. It is important to stress that these modes of social practice were the result of sets of positive choices made in respect of perceptions and understanding of how the world worked, that is, they were made with the subjects' vested interests and social identities firmly in mind. While it may be that the ultimate effect of such patterns of social practice was to lead to the demise of the broader political framework within which the social and economic position and status of the elite was embedded and thus ensured, "rationality" in arriving at choices and courses of action must be seen as culturally determined in respect of the possibilities of the members of any given culture to perceive different "realities." What may appear with historical hindsight as an evolutionary dead-end (albeit one that it took a further three centuries to reach) must not of necessity have been understood at the time. Indeed, it is usually the case that social groups, in responding to shifts or transformations in their conditions of existence—insofar as they become aware of them and in respect of which aspects of the changes they are able to perceive—adopt reactionary or conservative responses, attempting to reinforce the patterns and structures with which they are familiar. The results of such responses are not usually, of course, those intended or predicted. But if we ignore the socially determined nature of perception and explanation, and, thus, of choice, we risk falling into a naïve methodological individualism or "rational choice theory" paradigm that obliterates difference and variation in the generation of motives, intentions, and action and thus also the possibility of explaining change, both in space and across time. In this respect, Runciman's theory of social selection, which allows for both competitive selection and the cultural determination of perception, seems much more satisfactory from an explanatory perspective.

Given these preconditions, and the rise of the Italian maritime cities, especially Venice and Genoa, in the eleventh and twelfth centuries, the longer-term results for the Byzantine economy and state were unfortunate. Internal conflicts, military failures, and the political collapse of the late eleventh century, the establishment of a series of hostile Turkish states in Anatolia, and the need for the Byzantines to call upon allies with military and especially naval resources that they could themselves no longer mobilize pointed the way. The naval weakness of the imperial government throughout the twelfth century, particularly with respect to the threat from the Normans in Sicily, directly promoted reliance upon Venetian assistance, purchased through commercial concessions. Together with the role played by Venice, Pisa, and Genoa, among several cities, during the period following the First Crusade (and the competition between Venice and Genoa in particular), this paved the way for Italian commercial infiltration of the Byzantine economic and exchange sphere during the twelfth century, culminating in the concessions achieved under the emperors of the late twelfth century. Indeed, it was because Italian commerce was on a small scale and was regarded as unimportant to the economic priorities of both state and aristocracy that it was enabled to prosper. Demographic expansion in Italy stimulated the demand for Byzantine grain and other agrarian produce, which meant that Venetian and other traders slowly built up an established network of routes, ports, and market bases, originally based on carrying Byzantine bulk as well as luxury goods and Italian or Western imports to Constantinople, later expanding to a longer-distance commerce to meet the needs of an expanding Italian market. Commerce and merchant or banking activity were no less marginal to the Byzantine elite in the twelfth century than they had been before the eleventh century. Yet, while Byzantine society appeared to be solidly based within the traditional framework, a new and much more complex Mediterranean-wide market was evolving, linking East and West, a market upon which cities such as Venice and Genoa depended very heavily for their political existence and the relatively newfound power and wealth of their ruling elites.[43]

Coinage reforms in the early twelfth century, necessitated by the collapse of the traditional but (from the point of view of market activities) very inflexible monetary system from the 1060s through the 1080s, made day-to-day money transactions easier. But greater commercial exchange and commodity production, stimulated by the economic expansion of the eleventh century, combined with the greater flexibility of the reformed coinage, also facilitated an increasing involvement of outsiders in internal Byzantine commerce and investment. This was seen chiefly as an irritant and as a political problem by Byzantine commentators, although some bemoaned also the fate of Byzantine merchants. But the observation was itself made possible because of the successful exploitation by Italians of an expanding market that had not impinged upon Byzantine consciousness a century earlier, although the presence of Italians in Constantinople certainly appears to have stimulated local services, such as the production and supply of naval equipment of all sorts. The real expansion of Venetian and Genoese activity within the empire began toward the end of the twelfth century, when improved relations between the Byzantine government and the Venetians, Genoese, and Pisans reflect Byzantine concerns about the political designs of the emperor Frederick Barbarossa and the need to win friends and allies with naval potential as well as political power in Frederick's geopolitical backyard. The concessions granted by Byzantine rulers reflect the notion that trade still occupied a marginal place in the economy of the state. They also reflect both the fact that Byzantine rulers could still effectively exploit the hostile relations between Venice and Genoa and the overwhelmingly noncommercial, political emphasis placed by the imperial government on these matters.[44]

The fourth crusade, which sacked Constantinople in 1204 and carved up the empire, destroyed the traditional order. When a reconstituted central imperial state was revived, in 1261, it inhabited a very different world, not simply in terms of the well-established political presence of Western powers in the east Mediterranean and Aegean regions but also in terms of the state's ability to maintain itself. The reduced income derived from the appropriation of surplus through tax on a much smaller, and constantly shrinking, territorial base, the fragmentation of territory and political authorit, and the lack of a serious naval power with which to defend its interests were fundamental. Income derived from taxes on commerce played a proportionately larger role in real terms as well as in the eyes of the central government. Yet, the traditional elite, with few exceptions, was still based on the income from land, while the state itself was unable to compete with Italian and other commercial capital and shipping. In the mid-fourteenth century, the emperors attempted to exploit the political situation in the Black Sea at the expense of the Genoese and to bolster the position of Byzantine merchants by reducing dues payable at the port of Constantinople so that they could compete equally with those imposed upon the majority of Italian traders and thus promote an increase in imperial revenue. Genoese coercion soon restored the situation. Nevertheless, the emperor's plan reveals the importance of revenues of this sort to the much-reduced empire, but by this time it was too late effectively to change the pattern that had evolved, although a number of Byzantine aristocrats had begun to take an active interest in commerce. With a few exceptions, "Byzantines" or "Greeks" played a generally subordinate role to Italians, sometimes as business partners, often as small-time entrepreneurs, as middlemen, and as wholesalers; frequently they acted as small-scale moneylenders or bankers, rarely as large-scale bankers (although there were some) or major investors, still more rarely in major commercial contracts. Indeed, the market demands of Italian-borne commerce began also to influence the patterns of production within the empire, with the result that the state itself no longer had any effective role in managing or directing the production of wealth.[45]

In the context of the economic growth that affected the whole European and middle eastern world from the tenth and eleventh centuries, the preeminence of Italian shipping in trade and commerce within the formerly relatively closed Byzantine sphere had unforeseen effects. First, it contributed to the economic growth of those Italian merchant cities most involved and resulted in turn in an increase in their dependency on that trade for their own internal stability. Second, it deprived the various Byzantine successor states and their elites of any possibility of successfully responding and adjusting to the economic and political conditions that prevailed after 1204 and especially after 1261, since by the time they showed an interest in commerce and shipping on a large scale, Italian merchants, bankers, and shippers already had a long-established dominance, together with a network of markets and a system of business and managerial practices with which Greek enterprise, whether or not supported by a state, could not hope to compete.

Yet commerce became increasingly essential to the growth of local economies within the Byzantine world, at the same time impinging to an ever greater extent on the traditional means of state-directed redistribution of wealth. Its untrammelled operation contradicted the essence of imperial state control and threatened also the traditional mode of operation of aristocratic landholding and consumption. Byzantine entrepreneurial activity thus not only posed a threat to the state's efforts to maintain a position of dominance with regard to the appropriation and distribution of social wealth but also presented a direct challenge to the preeminent position of the landed aristocracy within the state. The operation of the traditional fiscal establishment, together with the ideological and cultural devaluation of commerce, prevented indigenous commerce from taking advantage of expanding markets. Inadequate investment in a context already dominated by Italian shipping in respect of external trade meant that Byzantine merchants were never in a position to mount an effective challenge.

Neither foreign merchants nor commerce caused the political breakdown of central imperial power, however much they undercut the efforts of the state to retain central control over its resources and, more important, the process by which those resources were distributed, especially during the second half of the twelfth century. On the contrary, it was the structural relationship between the centralized bureaucratic state and its fiscal machinery on the one hand and the dominant social elite on the other that were determinant. This relationship, and the practices through which it was expressed, underlay the political and fiscal collapse of the state in the years immediately prior to the Fourth Crusade, after which the movement of goods in the Aegean and in the east Mediterranean basin was firmly in the hands of Italian commerce and investors, however important the role of Byzantine and Greek middlemen and petty traders may have been within this network. As the empire shrank, so commerce and trade, rather than land, came to be the main source of state income. But, by the end of the empire, the government shared only minimally in this resource.

9. IMPERIALISM AND EXPLOITATION: THE CULTURAL DIMENSION

So far, I have surveyed some aspects of the ways in which the imperial government and the social elite of the empire exploited the productive resources of the empire's territories to maintain their own existence, in other words, economic exploitation. These methods of exploitation were, of course, supported by a legal and institutional framework of property relations and state rights, which were themselves important in the realization and maintenance of such structures. But, at certain periods, exploitation took on a more externalized aspect, when the empire went onto the offensive, both militarily as well as culturally. In the former case, conquest—justified always on the grounds that the conquered lands were "really" Roman—involved the reabsorption of new territories into the fiscal-administrative apparatus of the state. Conflict arose over who reaped the benefits, the central government or the provincial elites whose attempts to convert new territories into private estates challenged state fiscal dominance, and thus form part of the picture already painted. Such exploitation had also a cultural political aspect, insofar as Byzantines, and in particular the Constantinopolitan cultural elite, while siphoning off physical resources from such lands, generally looked down upon the conquered populations as inferior provincials, attitudes sometimes tinged with a racist bias with regard to assumed characteristics of different population groups, which were dismissed as "barbaric" or uncultured (although it should be stressed that such views prevailed also with respect to the "indigenous" provincials of the empire, so there was no real distinction between the two groups of exploited populations).[46]

In the latter case, Byzantine cultural imperialism tended to take the form of missionary activities to convert conquered populations to the Christianity of the Constantinopolitan patriarchate, and in the period from the middle of the ninth century until the eleventh century there was a conscious policy directed from the capital to establish a Byzantine cultural protectorate in the Balkans in particular, spreading to Kievan Russia through diplomatic and military alliances in the late tenth century.[47] In the central and western Balkans, however, conflict between Rome and Constantinople developed, for the papacy was equally interested in expanding its own ecclesiastical-political and, therefore, cultural power in these regions. One of the reasons for the sharpening of tensions between Byzantium and the West lies in this conflict over cultural power in neighboring territories, which served also as political-military as well as cultural buffers between the East Roman world and the barbarian lands beyond them.[48]

Cultural identity is, obviously, a crucial element in both attitudes to "outsider" as well as internal social-cultural differentiation. With its roots ultimately in the

Roman Republic, and with its elite at least consciously aware of its Roman imperial heritage, the Byzantine Empire was in truth the last of the ancient empires to survive beyond the great transformative movements of the period from the fifth to the seventh centuries. In particular, its history illustrates the ways in which a political ideological system such as that of the Christian eastern Roman Empire possessed the capacity to respond to the very difficult and constantly evolving circumstances in which it found itself. From within the context of the particular prevailing social, economic, and cultural conditions, this system of beliefs was able subtly to shift the angle from which the world was perceived, understood, and hence acted upon, by focusing on aspects of the "symbolic universe," the "thought-world" of the Christian East Roman world, which were better suited to bear new interpretations and alternative ways of thinking about the changed conditions in which people found themselves—although, in its final years, and in spite of the intellectual dynamism shown by Plethon or Palamas, no corresponding explanation emerged for the massive divergence between the political realities of the rapidly dwindling Byzantine state and the ideological claims pretensions to which it was heir.[49]

Through much of its history, the Byzantine symbolic universe was able to absorb the challenges thrown up by the transformed circumstances of its existence and, indeed, in the end, to outgrow and outlast even the state that had nurtured it. Yet, this flexibility was founded on a solid footing. Byzantines' identity as Roman and Orthodox, together with the Hellenistic and classical Greek cultural heritage in literature in particular, which Byzantines cherished as a key symbol of their cultural identity, provided them with a certainty that nothing could shake. And this was true even if educated Byzantines in the ninth and tenth centuries spent a great deal of time pondering the questions raised by their recent history and searching for the historical roots they needed in order to furnish themselves with a clear image of the purpose of the events that had affected them.

It is a paradox that the relative social flexibility and openness of Byzantine society was founded in its late Roman social and political order, for it contrasts in this respect, at least until the fifteenth century and beyond, very strongly with the medieval West. Here, a group of successor states and principalities had sprung up on Roman ground, intermixing and integrating quite rapidly with the original elites and, more gradually, with the mass of the ordinary indigenous population. The social relations that eventually evolved out of this produced by the twelfth century a society that was increasingly rigidly hierarchized, in which movement from one social level to another was achieved with great difficulty, if at all. In the Byzantine world, in contrast, it was possible to move from very humble status to that of mighty lord, and, although the possibilities varied across time and according to the situation and, especially, the situation and power of the magnate elite, there are examples of several such characters throughout the period.

Identity was essential to survival. Byzantine identities were shaped not in a vacuum but in the context of the relations both between different elements within society and between neighboring cultures and peoples. There were two strains or tendencies in particular within Byzantine culture that made a particular contribution to the Byzantine identity, elements that had been combined, not always comfortably, through much of the empire's history and that finally came into open opposition in the last century or so of the empire's existence. Hellenistic rationalism, and the classical literary and philosophical heritage that accompanied it, had always lived in uneasy coexistence with the religious antirationalism and piety of the "fundamentalist" strain of Christianity. In the seventh century, as noted already, this conflict or tension had revealed itself in the debates over issues of causation and faith, resulting in an uneasy compromise. The empire had no serious rivals in the "barbarian" West until the late tenth and eleventh centuries; while in the East the Islamic caliphate replaced the Sasanid Persian Empire as the other major power. The difference between the two was that while the latter was Muslim, it was also civilized; the West was a barbarous region. But when Western military and economic strength began to affect this comfortable view of things, the Byzantines coped only with difficulty. Already in the late ninth century, Pope Nicholas I had humiliated the emperor and his advisers by demonstrating that they were relatively ignorant of their Roman heritage and its traditions, contributing at least in part to an imperially sponsored revival of interest in Roman law, among other things. Western Christianity and its different ways on the one hand and the existence of Christian neighbors in the Balkans with whom the empire was often at war on the other made a simple identity of Roman Empire with (orthodox) Christianity difficult, if not impossible. Rival political formations that could effectively challenge Byzantine power on land and at sea and the very public rejection by Western powers of Byzantine claims to hegemony heightened the tensions and brought home the contradictions in the imperial ideological claims to universal imperial authority. And the simple fact was that, as a result of the missonary activity noted already, after the ninth century the Orthodox Church exercised effective authority over a far wider territory than the Roman emperors themselves. As the empire shrank territorially and politically after 1204, this became even more marked.[50]

The result was, beginning already in the eleventh and twelfth centuries, a retreat into "hellenism," the search for the Greek roots of East Roman culture. Yet, ironically, this conceded just the point that had in the first place so outraged Byzantine sensibilities, when in the ninth century Western rulers began to refer to the Byzantine emperor as ruler "of the Greeks." To an extent, the flowering of Greek literature and classicism that marks the period from the twelfth century signals a retreat toward a form of cultural isolationism through which Byzantines could continue to believe in their own superiority and differentness, in their right to be the Chosen People, and in their destiny as the true representatives of God's kingdom on Earth, regardless of the political realities.

These tendencies, both in their metropolitan and their provincial forms, became even more marked as the empire shrank and fragmented. After 1204, the patronage of an imperial court disappeared, to be replaced by the much less generous support, for a more limited range of cultural activities, of the various small successor states, and even after the restoration of the empire in 1261, the provincialization of much cultural production as well as the reduction in expenditure is apparent. But, by this time, the realities of Byzantine politics and economic life and the formal ideology of the empire could no longer be comfortably matched. The empire became a small and dependent state, its rulers impoverished, its treasury empty, its defenses dependent upon foreign goodwill or hired soldiers. At the same time, the power and authority of the Church, which, of course, now exercised authority over more territory than the imperial government, grew in proportion as imperial authority declined. In the last century of the empire's life, indeed, it was often the Church, with its greater resources and greater authority, that paid for or maintained defensive structures and the soldiers to serve on them. And as the Byzantine state declined, so the retreat into a Greek and Orthodox identity independent of the earthly empire became an increasingly prominent feature of late Byzantine thought.

It was in this context that a clash of ideas took place between the Hellenistic rationalist tradition, so recently revitalized, and the so-called hesychastic movement, with its antirationalist emphasis on personal sanctity, contemplation, and the power of prayer. There had long been a tradition of mysticism in the eastern Church, in which it was open to any Christian to attain a momentary union with the divinity through meditation and spiritual devotion. This tradition had coexisted alongside the Hellenistic elements of Byzantine culture, and a substantial theological literature evolved around the issue of contemplation. But the advent of hesychasm, with its alien modes of posture and meditative practices, caused both concern and ridicule among many traditional thinkers. The two perspectives were embodied in the politics of the time, with the hesychasts able to dominate the imperial court during the period of civil war of the 1340s and to retain considerable authority thereafter. To what extent the hesychastic movement reflected also a response to the political decline of the empire and a flight from the concerns of a secular and religious tradition that appeared to be doomed to extinction is impossible to say. But the effects of this influence in cultural terms is not hard to see: a real reduction in the study of the natural and physical sciences (mathematics, astronomy, music), as well as of history and classical literature, and a corresponding rise in the amount of virulent anti-Latin polemic. There continued to be scholars of this classical heritage, but they were far fewer in number and worked in a more isolated cultural environment.

Yet an extreme version of the alternative, Hellenistic, tradition also found its protagonists, most notably at Mistra, in the southern Peloponnese, in the person of George Gemistus Plethon, who moved to the opposite extreme by rejecting Christianity and proposing a Hellenic religion in which the moral precepts of Plato would predominate and in which an ideal state, ruled by a philosopher-king and guided by the rule of law modeled on Plato's *Laws* would provide the Greeks with a new future. But his more extreme ideas were never taken up, while his more moderate notions on reforming the state could not have worked in view of the inevitable opposition they aroused from the land-owning and ecclesiastical elite.

The appearance of these two variant aspects of the Byzantine tradition nicely illustrate the ways in which Byzantines tried to come to terms with the dramatic changes their society was undergoing in its final years. It is ironic that, in the end, the last Byzantines, who increasingly had begun to call themselves *Hellenes*, Greeks, rather than *Romaioi*, Romans, turned their back on the Roman part of their heritage in order to maintain their delusion of superiority and to preserve the force of the imperial ideology. They sought to preserve their identity through a quest for a lost Hellenic—a classical Greek—identity on the one hand or a mystical spiritualism that largely ignored the realities of contemporary politics on the other. Political leaders retreated into literary and artistic pursuits and interests. From the point of view of Hellenic culture and imperial ideology, it was the Church that became the heir to the Roman Empire in the East.

Although the secular state of Byzantium disappeared, the culture it had nurtured and represented for so long continued to exist through the study of patristic and Byzantine theological literature within the Orthodox world, particularly in monastic contexts and in the study of the classics and history, especially in Italy, to which many learned Byzantines removed prior to or shortly after the fall of Constantinople in 1453. The influence of Byzantine learning in all fields, as well as of the classical tradition in Byzantine painting, was fundamental to the shaping of the Italian Renaissance thereafter. And, even within the new Ottoman world, a number of Greek historians were able to chronicle the last years of the empire, some espousing a pro-Ottoman perspective, others remaining studiously neutral in their account of the disappearance of what had been the foremost power in the east Mediterranean and Balkan region. This historiographical inheritance, along with many other facets of Byzantine civilization, was then transmitted to the European Enlightenment scholars of the seventeenth and eighteenth centuries, and so on to our own time. But it is an inheritance that concerns not simply the transmission of a culture and its forms to our own forbears. It has had a direct impact both on western European responses to the history of the Balkans and the Levant up to the present day, and it has even more directly (through the school syllabus, the structures and traditions of the modern Orthodox Church, the political agendas of politicians from the late eighteenth century into the twenty-first century) affected the political and cultural evolution of Greece, Turkey, and their neighbors.

10. ALTERNATIVES: THE FORMATION OF THE FIRST ISLAMIC STATES

The early Islamic conquests, the extinction of the Sasanid Persian state, and the loss to the East Roman state of its Middle Eastern and North African territories mark a dramatic change in the historical evolution of the regions affected, as well as those around them. More important from our perspective, they provide us with the opportunity to study the creation *ab initio* of a new "imperial" state and political formation, partly derived from those that preceded it, partly inspired by radically new ideological imperatives and their social and economic implications. This was an empire of conquest, and whether or not the Islamic historical record can be relied upon (all the historical accounts date from the late eighth century or after), and whether or not the initial expansion of Islam was the result of a coordinated strategy, the fact remains that by the 670 s a major new political formation had been established, supported by a ruling elite that drew its legitimacy from a combination of success in conquest, its kinship relations and identities, and the maintenance of an army supported by a combination of state salaries and grants and private enterprise.[51]

The question of the distribution of resources and revenues, and the degree to which the caliphs had access to the revenues from a given area, was from the beginning a fundamental problem in the new polity. There is little doubt that already by the 670 s, and certainly by the 690 s, a tax system and fiscal apparatus, a centrally controlled army, and a judiciary existed, administered at least in theory from Damascus; in other words, all the key elements for a state were present. Yet, the degree of control over resources exercised by the caliphs remains unclear; in the case of Egypt, where a considerable amount of detailed evidence for fiscal practices survives, it seems that the Islamic administration, based at al-Fustat, was more or less autonomous with respect to the financing and administration of its army and its fiscal system.

Two institutions, and the practices and traditions that came to be associated with them, were central to the fiscal administration and to the distribution of resources in the early Islamic state. The first was the so-called *dîwân*, the list of names of soldiers (and their dependents), accompanied by the amount of the salary ("*atâ*") owed to each on a monthly basis. Originally established by the caliph 'Umar in response to the results of the first wave of conquests in the late 630 s, the principle upon which the *dîwân* functioned was that Muslims would not settle on the land but remain rather as a separate caste of hereditary dependents upon the Islamic community (in effect, the state), established in specially founded garrison settlements or towns. These garrisons would then derive their incomes from the revenues of the conquered territories in their neighborhood. There were differential rates, determined by seniority of association with the Prophet, acceptance of Islam, and the first conquests. The income for this was thus raised within the province where the soldiers or their dependents dwelled, and both collection and distribution were administered by the provincial governor, appointed in theory by the caliph.

The second institution was that of *fay'*, literally "booty," the land and other immovables acquired through conquest. Following the conquests, all such booty came to be regarded as divisible, to be distributed among the conquerors, so that the revenues from such lands would thereafter simply be divided up, under local provincial supervision, without caliphal interference. The caliphs attempted from the beginning, however, to obtain control of some of these revenues for their own administrative purposes, without which they would neither be able to support a central governmental apparatus nor expand or recruit for their military forces. From the beginning, this tension caused problems. One of the earliest political assassinations in Islamic history, that of the caliph 'Uthmân, has been connected with such a dispute, originating in al-Kûfa.

This conflict over resources and the functioning of the two institutions of *dîwân* and *fay'* constituted the single most important issue around which political struggle was focused in the early Islamic period.[52] By the time of Marwân I (683–4 CE) the *dîwân* was in theory closed; no more additions could be made, although, in a series of appeals for support, various contenders for caliphal power did thereafter add the names of their supporters. But the relative fiscal autonomy of the provinces, even those quite near the central lands of the state, is underlined by the fact that the income for the *dîwân* was collected at provincial level, rather than organized from Damascus. The localization of collection and redistribution of resources to the army is apparent when it is remembered that military salaries could frequently be paid in kind, as seems to have been the case in late-seventh-century Egypt and, probably, in Palestine at the same period.[53] Efforts on the part of caliphal administrative officials to intervene directly in the collection and distribution of resources for military pay were seen as detrimental to the local military.

Armies were supported by other means in addition to the salaries derived to those listed on the *dîwân*. In some cases, tribute from neighboring vassal peoples was paid directly to the army of a particular province or region; in others, resources from provinces where no soldiers were based but that could produce an appropriate revenue were ascribed to a specific army, as was certainly the case in parts of Iraq. Armies on campaign were often raised on the basis of a promise of booty following expected success, while provincial governors or caliphs could raise forces on a temporary basis for specific campaigns, using revenue reserves or income from other sources for the purpose. But, as a general rule, all the historical evidence points to the assumption on the part of those registered in the *dîwân* of each province that their pay—*'atâ'*— was drawn from the revenues of their own province, in turn extracted from the conquered territories and other resources—*fay'*—and therefore belonging to those so registered by right of conquest, not to the caliph or any other central institution.

11. The Politics of Redistribution

The surplus remaining after the salaries to the army had been paid was thus a major bone of contention between provinces and center. A proportion was forwarded to Damascus, but the evidence for Egypt shows that it was tiny—an estimate of 5 percent has been made. Given the proximity of Egypt to Damascus and the relative ease with which cash could be moved over such a distance, the assumption that more distant provinces forwarded the same amount of revenue or even less seems justified.[54] Individual governors who had different attitudes to their province and to the caliph of the time undoubtedly behaved differently according to the context, and there is some evidence to suggest that certain governors were much more efficient than others at extracting surplus for the caliphs or, in contrast, in retaining it for use in the province.

The limitations on revenues that could be extracted from the provinces by the caliphs encouraged the development of caliphal estates, obtained though conquest, confiscation, or family inheritance, from which substantial rents could be extracted. The Marwânids in the late seventh and first half of the eighth century possessed substantial estates in Iraq and Arabia, and probably in Syria, as well, and the income from these was employed both in maintaining the court and in hiring mercenary armies that would be loyal to the caliphs themselves and not be swayed by provincial loyalties. The development of such estates affected patterns of agricultural exploitation and land settlement, so that "state" intervention had an important impact on the economy of such regions.[55]

One of the results of this localization of resource extraction and consumption— in contrast to the East Roman state at the same period—was the attempt by the caliphal authorities to settle Syrian troops in Iraq, in the garrison town of Wâsit. The transfer of soldiers, as major consumers of resources, from areas that could maintain them with difficulty to areas whose revenues were more substantial was in itself not new (troops from Iraq had been sent to Khurasan in the 670s for the same reasons), but in view of the importance of the Syrian army to the government at Damascus, and the fact that the move provided the Syrians with opportunities they could not find in Syria, it heightened tensions between the armies of the two regions, the Iraqis claiming, of course, that the Syrians were wrongly trespassing on the *fay'* of the men of Iraq.[56]

Conflict over revenues was thus a central and systemic aspect of the first Islamic state formation. But this tension was moderated by a series of other considerations, in particular the dynastic politics of the caliphate, and the regional and "tribal" loyalties that came with, or evolved out of, the conquests in the 630s and 640s.[57]

A sketch of the power-relationships in the caliphate from the period of the first Umayyads through the Abbasid revolution of the late 740s and into the tenth century illustrates a complex, constantly fluctuating pattern woven from the vested interests, both economic and ideological, of a whole range of different social, ethnic, and religious groupings, interests that rendered it impossible for much of this period to assert and realize an effective central authority. Several factors contributed. In the first place, the authority of the caliphs as well as their chief advisers rested on interpretations of the Qur'an and the Sunna, the traditions of the Prophet, and there existed a number of different and sometimes conflicting interpretations, most obviously the disagreements among the the fragmented, localized, but still dangerous Kharidjite groups that first appeared in the late 650 s. The term refers originally to those tribesmen who rejected both Ali and Mu'âwiya, preferring to fight for their independence as conquerors in the territories they had won, free from any central régime. During the late seventh century, it was applied more widely to other politically as well as ideologically motivated movements hostile to the Damascus régime. In the second place, the intensely regionalized identities of the conquerors, in turn overlaid by the growth in the number of converts to Islam from among the conquered populations (*mawali*), added a second layer of complexity to local politics and their connections with the caliphs and their court. "Tribal" conflicts based on what were often vague kin identities and vested local economic interests related to *fay'* and other revenues and rights meant that the caliphate was a vast sea of competing and potentially conflicting loyalties in which warfare and violence could occur over apparently minor changes of policy at the center, most notably the tension between Syrian and Iraqi interests during the Umayyad period or between the interests of Khurasan and Iraq or Jazîra under the 'Abbâsids, for example. And, in the third place, the dynastic politics of the Umayyad-Marwânid clan from the 680 s and those who opposed their power provided further opportunities for conflict within the widely dispersed and multifactional Arab elite.[58]

The regionalization of politics was reinforced by the reliance of the Umayyads upon their Syrian soldiers for the maintenance of their authority elsewhere. This had specially unfortunate repercussions in Iraq. The identity of the *ahl al-shâm*—the "men of Syria"—can be seen to have a been a factor of major importance in the life of the Umayyad caliphate. It is clear that from 'Abd al-Malik's reign until the break up of the Umayyad state after the death of Hisham, in 743, a process completed by the Abbasid revolution in 749–750, tribal solidarities had largely been replaced, or at least overlain, by regional ones. To what extent the Syrians saw themselves as distinct, except in direct contrast with Iraqis or other clearly regional groups, is difficult to say, since most of the sources that describe this Syrian identity do so from an outsider's perspective. What needs perhaps to be emphasized is not that regional identities replaced traditional ascribed "tribal" affiliations (for example, Qaysi-Yemeni, northerners and southerners) but rather that, from the late seventh century, regional identity became as important as kinship (real or imagined) as a marker. At the same time, however, we must also recognize that these two sets of identities were not mutually exclusive and that the identity brought out for a particular group by the members of that group, by their opponents, or in the sources depended very much on both the political and the cultural context, as well as the perspective from which the writers of sources recorded and interpreted the events in question and the political and military context of the events themselves. Those who wished to arouse popular opinion against the Umayyad government sought to exploit regional loyalties that, at the time, had a particular ideological valence.[59] Yet, the opportunistic revival of Qaysi-Yemeni identities in other contexts illustrates the fact that, throughout the early period and well into late medieval times, traditional nonregional identities lived on.

Given the context-bound nature of the use of these new regional identities and the loyalties and traditions they invoked or inspired, it is not surprising that in the second and third generations after the Muslim conquest, even the new settlers from Arabia began to acquire such local patriotisms, and this naturally developed earlier among the Yamaniya (those whose origins lay in, or were thought to lie in, southern Arabia) of Syria, most of whose ancestors had in fact been living there before the coming of Islam. The *ahl al-shâm* clearly emerged as a military elite, with their disciplined fighting techniques and higher salary levels. The Syrians were, however, more than just one regional pressure group among many. By the reign of Hishâm (724–743), they had come, in a real sense, to form a professional army apart from the bulk of Muslims. There seems to be no parallel for the role of the Syrian army in the contemporary Byzantine state, where the evidence suggests that the military in each area was composed of locally recruited troops with local roots, although the role of the *Opsikion* forces provides a distant parallel, and regional identities and loyalties certainly played an important role. Much more important, the military in the Umayyad caliphate, unlike the Byzantine military, never had any distinct legal status, though it did enjoy a privileged financial position. By the late Umayyad period—the 730 s and 740 s—the Muslim community, the *umma*, was divided into military and nonmilitary sections, a development that was to remain strikingly true of Muslim communities in the Near East throughout pre-Ottoman times.

Caliphal politics came to depend upon the need to compromise between these various and opposed factions and interests, the need to raise sufficient revenues to maintain some sort of centrally controlled army, and the need to maintain a sufficient degree of religious orthodoxy to retain the ideological loyalty of the dominant interest groups within the Islamic world. Even with the Abbasid revolution in 750 and the attempts of caliphs from al-Saffâh (750–754) to Hârûn ar-Rashîd (786–809) and his sons to reconcile some of these tensions (in particular between converts and Arabs), an effective central administration with an effective long-term purchase on resources away from the central lands failed to maintain its power for more than a couple of generations before successive caliphs needed to discover new ways of re-establishing their power. Beginning with the establishment of an independent Hispanic province under the last Umayyads in the 750 s and 760 s, followed by the increasing independence of the more far-flung territories under régimes of sometimes hostile ideological hues, especially in western North Africa, the caliphate begins during the late ninth century to lose any semblance of political unity and to become a congeries of regional powers owing ideological loyalty to Baghdad (where they were Sunni) or having none at all (where varying forms of Shi'ism prevailed).

The unity represented by the concept of a caliphate, therefore, in spite of brief periods under particular caliphs when it was almost a political reality, became by the late ninth century merely notional: it retained to a considerable extent its ideological-religious authority in the regions from Syria-Palestine across to eastern Iran and Khurasan, but in North Africa the success of Isma'ili Shi'ism in the early tenth century, the expansion of the Fatimids into Egypt by the 960s, their occupation of much of Syria, and their direct challenge to Baghdad thereafter illustrates the fragmentation of the Islamic world both ideologically and territorially.

In the course of these developments, several features should be noted. First, although Islamic forms of justice and regional government were introduced into the comquered territories, and despite the administrative reforms of caliphs such as 'Abd al-Malik (685–705) in the late seventh century, the underlying socioeconomic relations between peasant agriculturalists and those who expropriated surpluses remained much as it had been before. Caliphal policies affected agrarian production in various ways, of course, attracting considerable numbers of agrarian producers to urban centers and fostering an increase in raiding and caravan-robbing when taxes and related impositions became too heavy.

In this highly regionalized, multifactional social-political context, no single elite evolved. In contrast to the (geographically far smaller) neighboring East Roman state, a much more complex series of overlapping and intersecting regional and ideological elements existed in a constantly shifting pattern of alliances and conflicts. At one level, that of the "religious institution" or *'úlamâ'*—religious personnel and associated structures[60]—a fundamental antipathy toward government and government service evolved in parallel with the tension between the secular administrative (fiscal and military) needs of the caliphs on the one hand and the Qur'ânic traditions in which the Islamic community, the *umma*, was based. Combined with views such as those of the first and second generations of tribal warriors in Syria, Jazira, and Iraq, resentful of caliphal efforts to obtain a share of the revenues from the conquests, this dislike provided fertile ground for religiously justified political opposition to any central or centralizing régime.

At another level, the various ways that the Alid and Shi'ite traditions evolved similarly provided ideological, political, and geographical lines of demarcation, involving successive caliphs in major military expenditures, accompanied by the search for new means of attracting revenues, and short-term, opportunistic political alliances in an effort to retain a real political authority. Complicating this situation were the tribal and ethnic identities and divisions, producing a constantly fluctuating recombination of ideological, geographical, and political aspects that rendered ineffective the attempts by, for example, the first Abbasid caliphs, from Mansur (754–775) to Harun ar-Rashid and his sons, to establish an administrative structure that was effective over more than the central lands.[61]

The failure of the rulers in Baghdad in this respect is highlighted by the evolution of the so-called *iqtâ'*, or revenue-grant. Unlike in the twelfth-century East Roman context, where the similar *pronoia* was introduced as one element in a gradual restructuring of central power, the *iqtâ'* represents the inability of the central authority to do more than recognize a situation that was out of its hands. *Iqtâ'* refers to an endowment of revenues from land, originally granted before the reign of Mutawakkil (847–861), usually to members of the ruling family and their favorites for services rendered, and always on a short-term basis. Under Mutawakkil, however, *iqtâ'* grants were made to the leaders of the main military corps based at Samarra in an effort to entice them to accept the transfer of their forces to districts away from the politically central regions around the capital; similar grants were made to members of the Tâhirid clan, whose power had extended well beyond their political control of the eastern Iranian provinces into Baghdad, Fars, and Samarra and whose loss of positions (through various political intrigues inspired by the caliph) was thus compensated. There were two main results of Mutawakkil's policies: first, while the chief military commander and the chief fiscal administrative official of major provincial groupings were in charge of their regions under central government supervision, the potentially autonomous position they occupied brought into being a military-bureaucratic alliance that became a major challenge to the government thereafter; second, the granting of *iqtâ'* connected with the exercise of their duties to officers in the provinces was the first step in a process through which the center would lose effective control over both fiscal and military resources in its own central lands. By the time of the caliph Mu'tamid (870–892), central politics had resolved into two multifaceted but clearly opposed factions: those who were for the exploitation of the regions to the advantage of the central government but who, in order to maintain firm control there, favored at the same time the use of military-administrative *iqtâ'* throughout the empire in order to achieve this (through the loyalty of the officers thus appointed) and those who wished to avoid the extension of *iqtâ'* precisely because of the possible dangers inhering in them and who thus attempted to assure the military of regular and acceptable stipends, to maintain a clear division between military and administrative functions and appointments, and to accept the different fiscal interests of the provinces and the center.

The military-administrative *iqtâ'* that was evolving thus entailed the appointment of military commanders to many regions in which they had complete authority over all matters, including fiscal affairs, in exchange for which they undertook to forward from the revenues that the regions produced a fixed sum to the central treasury. By the 880s, and in order to ensure that he had the resources to oppose a series of rebellions in Iraq as well as further east, Muwaffaq (the brother of the caliph al-Mu'tamid and effective ruler of the empire) extended and formalized the application of major military-administrative *iqtâ'*. Perhaps the clearest example is that of Ahmad b. Tûlûn, who was given complete authority over Egypt in return for a regular contribution from Egyptian revenues to Baghdad. Ibn Tûlûn's administration was so effective that southern Syria and Palestine were added to his domains, with the result that he soon had ambitions to bring the *thughûr*, or frontier regions in North Syria and Iraq, under his control, also, the better to have access to the immensely profitable trade routes of the east Mediterranean basin. While the Baghdad government was still attempting to suppress the Zanj rebellion in southern Iraq[62] and to deal with the Saffarid rebels in the east, Tûlûnid forces attempted to compel the regions of the *thughûr*, including Tarsus, to accept their dominion (partly with

Byzantine encouragement), but without success. In fact, while the Tûlûnid interests in trade could be met by exploiting the potential of the Syrian ports, the economic interests of the regions of the *thughûr* were bound in with the overland trade routes from the East, thus with the central government at Baghdad. After some fighting, a compromise was reached in the mid-880s, by which the Tûlûnids were confirmed in their authority over Syria and Palestine and agreed in return to pay the central treasury a relatively modest revenue each year. Muwaffaq attempted toward the end of his rule to reverse the policy that he had been forced to adopt, restricting the concession of *iqtâ'* where possible, although against considerable opposition. A coup shortly after his death, in 892, replaced the faction that had supported this policy with one that wished to reassert the earlier approach.

12. CENTER AND PERIPHERY

In effect, the central government had maintained a precarious hold on affairs by adopting ad hoc policies appropriate to the needs of the moment, then attempting to reverse them when they were found to be disadvantageous. The religious leadership nominally exercised by the caliphs served at first to cement an admittedly fragile, but still real, caliphal political hegemony; but the internal opposition to the Umayyads in the period from the 720s to their fall in 750 and, later, the semi-autonomy granted by the Baghdad rulers to their secular representatives in most provinces pushed what might have been an important unifying element into the background, even if it was severely compromised long before this by a range of oppositional movements. The long-term policies introduced in the second half of the ninth and the first half of the tenth centuries tended to have a single purpose, to strengthen central authority (and revenues), but without regard for the ideological and economic vested interests of the regions that were affected. The increasing tendency of these regions to assert their own economic interests had a direct impact on central revenues, of course, which in turn affected the central state's ability to mobilize effective forces through which its control could be maintained. When Mu'tadid came to power, in 892, the central treasury is reported to have been exhausted. Military-administrative *iqtâ'* were the only means left to the new ruler, either to maintain a semblance of centrral authority or to extract some revenues, and the wholesale adoption of this means of supporting provincial administration and military force rapidly led to the appearance of provincial commanders in possession of an *iqtâ'* who were able to rule more or less independently, defying both demands for revenues and central foreign policy. In a further effort to avoid the fiscal implications, tax-farming of the central lands was introduced, with initially beneficial results. But the military leaders stationed in the provinces demanded similar concessions, while local dignitaries, tribal leaders, wealthy merchants, and landowners instigated a flood of minor and major uprisings in their efforts to obtain similar concessions and privileges. Many, especially those with a revenue-farming contract, raised their own armies, to the extent that the overlap in personnel between military commanders and tax-farmers meant that the real distinction between tax-farming and *iqtâ'* was obscured and began to vanish.

It was in this context that the growth of the numerous independent emirs in the middling and outlying provinces took place. In frontier regions, especially the *thughûr* between Byzantium and Islam, local warlords could establish semi-independent regimes with relative ease, obtaining recognition of their authority from Baghdad by having their territories granted to them as *iqtâ'*. This occurred in Armenia and Azerbaijan in the 890s, while local Arab clans such as the Hamda-nids entrenched themselves on a similar basis to the south and west. While a strong caliph such as Mu'tadid (892–902) was able, through vigorous campaigning, to recover a degree of central control, however, this was short lived. Even the remark-able success of Muktafî (902–908) in deposing the Tûlûnids of Egypt and restoring central authority (by cleverly exploiting the political-military situation arising from the so-called Qaramite rebellion in the Syrian-Iraqi desert zone) was nullified by the constant drain on central resources brought about by the frequent necessity of imposing authority on clans such as the Hamdanids of Jazira and their clients. Efforts at tax reform foundered when central demands clashed with the willing-ness of either the producing population or local leaders and military commanders to pay. The Fâtimid attacks on Egypt from their base in Cyrenaica represented a similar drain, and it was not long before the caliph had to recognize Egyptian auton-omy in order to combat such inroads, although Egyptian revenues continued to flow toward Baghdad. Caliphal inability to deal with the civil strife of the 920s and 930s, brigandage and local secession in southern Iraq, and the failure of tax reforms ultimately led to the creation of a secular government, under an official known as the *Amîr al-Umarâ'*—supreme commander—in charge of both military and fiscal affairs, but this slowed the process of dissolution down hardly at all, since differ-ent military officers fought each other for the supreme command. The "provinces" by this time, of course, referred in effect only to the regions immediately around Baghdad. The Daylamite rebellions in northern Iran and the widespread localized warfare that accompanied them from the 920s, directed largely at seizure of the trade routes that passed from the Volga, via Bukhara, through eastern and central Iran to Baghdad, ushered in a period of general lawlessness and central government ineffectiveness. It ended only when a Daylamite clan, the Bûyids, and its followers succeeded in taking Baghdad, from which a loose confederation, the different parts of which were ruled by various members of the Bûyid family, was established. While the position of caliph was maintained, the caliphate was effectively broken up into its constituent elements in the East, based respectively in northern Iran, Fars and Kirman, and Iraq. The capture of Baghdad by the Bûyids in 945 marked the real end of the caliphate as a politically unified state. The caliphate was henceforth a single identity only by virtue of the claims of the caliphs and of the very notional common identity of Muslims throughout the territory over which he exercised his religious authority. But even here the various schismatic groups, especially in Spain, north Africa, and Egypt, acted as an effective challenge to such a common Islamic identity.

13. STATES, RESOURCES, AND THE FORMS OF REDISTRIBUTION

The history of the major Islamic state formations from the beginnings through to the Ottoman period, and as exemplified very partially here, is in effect the history of a three-cornered struggle between central government (or the various factions that vied for power at the center), local vested interests (urban, tribal, mercantile, or a combination), and provincial rulers who were often the nominal representatives of the rulers but who represented in effect a fragmented but still semi-autonomous political elite. Each made short-term alliances, often determined also by religious-ideological identities and political-religious ambitions (especially in the case of the various Isma'ili sects from the ninth century on), in order to attain short-term ends. None was able to gain mastery without the other; yet the structural tensions between the perceived values as well as the objective economic interests of the other groups (in terms of their position in the political structures of appropriation and redistribution of surplus wealth) meant that a constant struggle was waged among them, resolved for different regions only on a relatively short-term basis by their incorporation into a differently accented political formation (the Fatimid polity, for example or, more lasting, the Ottoman). Of course, and as has been observed by others, this reflects factors such as the impact of Islamic law and tradition on both political life and economic relationships. Equally, it reflects the highly fragmented structures of local power and the tensions among urban and rural production, tribalism, and the interests of the major political center. What it does not reflect is any fundamental structural difference between the ways in which agrarian wealth was produced and appropriated in different parts of the Islamic world and in the Balkan and Anatolian regions of the East Roman world.

14. CONCLUSIONS: MODELS AND METHODS

I have approached the evolution of the structures that made up "Byzantium" from two perspectives, although they have remained more or less implicit. On the one hand, I have chosen to foreground purely "economic" categories, looking chiefly at patterns of resource use: how were resources appropriated, distributed, and consumed, and what were the points of conflict between different social-economic groups, or classes, generated by these relationships? Naturally, one must begin by defining "the economic." But, from this point of view, any explanation of the course of Byzantine history and the fate of its state and social institutions must recognize and give explanatory priority less to any tension or contradiction between the interests of "exploiters" and "exploited" than to those between the two chief elements of the social-political elite, that is, the power elite that dominated the central government at any given moment, and the provincial elite that derived its power from land and the resources it provided (and bearing in mind that the two were rarely clearly separable, frequently overlapped, and depended for their constitution on very short-term vested political-ideological interests, including kinship). Such tensions are systemic, that is to say, they are unavoidable aspects of the ways in which elites extract resources from producers, and they can be found without exception in all premodern state systems. The comparison with early Islamic state formative processes highlights this.

The different fiscal institutional arrangements that evolved in the Byzantine Empire over the period from the fourth to the fifteenth century reflect both the government's need to maintain control over enough resources to ensure its economic and political dominance and such conflicts of interests. They also reflect the international situation with respect to changing degrees of competition for natural and created resources, including people and territory. I have also built into this model all the cultural factors outlined earlier, so political praxis as well as notions of "efficiency" are obviously to be understood as culturally circumscribed by the "common sense" of the culture. Thus, it is possible to resolve the issue of whether or not Byzantine society was "feudal" at some periods first by redefining what this term is meant to imply from the point of view of economic relationships and second by seeing shifts in the social and political relations of surplus distribution, which produce changes in the institutional arrangements of state and society, as one aspect of this tension. It is thus tensions and contradictions in the basic economic structures that play the fundamental role in determining how the society evolves and responds to shifts in its external circumstances and its internal constitution.[63]

On the other hand, I have also employed a more explicitly Darwinian approach, following Runciman, for example, seeing the history of the empire as determined by the results of the competitive selection of social, ideological, and political-institutional practices. This again helps to locate those points within the social structure and across time at which certain developments, including developments within the ideological sphere, began to generate effects that can be seen (from the historian's perspective) to have led to specific negative or positive results, why they were originally "selected," and how that process occurred. The combination of practices that generated Byzantine attitudes toward the production of wealth, for example, and the resultant responses of both individuals and ruling or governing elites to the issues of commerce and trade can be shown to have had important positive consequences for the survival of the empire in the period up to the ninth century. But, in the context of a somewhat different international economic and political situation, after the tenth century especially, it is their negative results for both ruling elite and imperial government that become apparent. In the late period, it is true, and under the influence of different circumstances, certain groups were able successfully to challenge these practices, but by then the economic context had already altered sufficiently for the resultant changes to be ineffectual. By the same token, the statist or dirigist fiscal and monetary régime that the empire inherited from the late Roman world and which it refined during the seventh to the ninth centuries clearly contributed to the survival of the empire and its ability to consolidate and even expand thereafter. Yet, it was these very institutional patterns that led to the collapse of the monetary and fiscal system in the middle and late eleventh century, paradoxically at a time when the nonstate economic sector was flourishing.[64] One of the most valuable aspects of Runciman's theorization of the competitive selection of social practices and the emergence of systactic structures is that it automatically assumes the instrumentality of beliefs, which traditional materialist approaches frequently neglect.

Neither approach excludes the other. On the contrary, I would argue that, while the first provides a framework or metatheory within which to ask general questions about dynamics and evolutionary potentials, the second offers a valuable model for the microstructural analysis of these dynamics and their evolution. Together, they help to make some sense of an extremely complex array of sources, including textual, archaeological, and representational materials. This explicit methodological pluralism may thus appear to abandon a single metatheory in favor of a more particularist heuristic framework; in fact, I would argue that it is possible still to work within a single overarching theoretical strategy and employ second-order theories to tackle specific issues, as long as the two share a common philosophical basis (in this case, epistemologically realist and materialist).[65] Since the questions we ask must inevitably determine the shape of the theories we generate to provide answers, this seems to me a reasonable way to avoid both methodological relativism and monocausal determinism.

NOTES

1. E.g., Cameron 1991; Mullett 1997.
2. Haldon 1999.
3. Brown 1971, 1981; Kazhdan 1974; McCormick 1998, 2001; Wickham 2005; Harvey 1989; Kaplan 1992.
4. Mann 1986a; Runciman 1989; Tainter 1988.
5. Anderson 1974.
6. See, for example, Arnason 2000 for discussion of these tendencies.
7. Haldon 1993.
8. Arnason 2000.
9. Mann 1986; Runciman 1989; Skopcol 1979; Gellner 1988. Specialist: Obolensky 1971.
10. E.g., de Ste Croix 1981; Cameron 1993; Haldon 1993, 1995.
11. See Reynolds 1994.
12. E.g., Jacoby 1993.
13. Garnsey and Whittaker, eds. 1978; Claessen and Skalník, eds. 1981; Kautsky 1982; Mann 1986; Carneiro 1987; Runciman 1989; Khoury and Kostiner, eds. 1990.
14. Luttwack 1976.

15. See Haldon 1992: 135 and n.52.

16. Lecky 1869: 2, 13–14.

17. For a short survey of Byzantine landscape, communications, and political history, see Haldon 2005.

18. Brubaker and Haldon 2001.

19. Jones 1964: 462–64; Hendy 1985: 164 ff., 616–20.

20. Brown 1971; Jones 1964; Haldon 1997.

21. Haldon 1997.

22. Brandes 1989; Haldon 1997.

23. Brandes 1989; Spieser 1989; Kaplan 1986.

24. Kelly 2004; Banaji 2001.

25. Haldon 2004.

26. Haldon 1997: 153–72, 395–99; Cheynet 1990.

27. Angold, 1985; Harvey, 1989.

28. Haldon 1993.

29. Runciman 1989.

30. Cameron 1991, 1992; Mullett, 1997; Kazhdan and Epstein 1985.

31. Angold 1995; Brand 1968; Nicol 1972; Lilie 1993.

32. Jones 1964, 1967; Hendy 1985; Haldon 1997.

33. Hendy 1985: 602 ff., 662 ff.; Hendy 1989; Morrisson 1991.

34. Garnsey and Whittaker 1998: 316–17, 326–37; Liebeschütz 2001: 45; Hendy 1985: 289–96, 602–7; Morrisson and Sodini 2002: 214–19; Banaji 2001: 39–88.

35. Hendy 1985.

36. Harvey 1989; Haldon 1997; Oikonomides 1996.

37. Angold 1984; Hendy 1985; Harvey 1989.

38. Harvey 1989; Bartusis 1992, 156–89; Magdalino 1993.

39. Angold 1984; Laiou-Thomadakis 1977; Oikonomides 1969.

40. Harvey 1989; Hendy 1985; Mango and Dagron 1995; Laiou 1980/81, 1982.

41. Angold 1984; Hendy 1989; Jacoby 1991/92.

42. Abulafia 1987; Balard 1989; Nicol 1988; Martin 1988.

43. Laiou 1981/82.

44. Hendy 1985, 1989.

45. Laiou 1981/82; 1982; Angold 1975.

46. Whittow 1996; Obolensky 1971; Mango 1994; Dvornik 1970.

47. Ivanov 2003.

48. Dvornik 1948, 1970.

49. Dvornik 1966; Haldon 1997.

50. Angold 1984; Magdalino 1993; Nicol 1972, 1979.

51. Noth 1994; Donner 1981, 1995.

52. Tritton 1954; Simonsen 1988; Puin 1970; Hinds 1972.

53. Donner 1986.

54. Dennett 1950.

55. Kennedy 1992.

56. Shaban 1971: 111, 115.

57. Shaban 1971: 60–164.

58. Shaban 1971, 1976; Kennedy 1981.

59. Compare for example a series of rebellions in 700–702, 714–715, and 740, respectively: see Shaban 1971: 110 ff., 128, 143–44, 179.

60. Lybyber 1913.
61. See Shaban 1976: 20–70 for a clear account of the period c. 770–840 in which these different elements played a role.
62. Not a slave rebellion, however, as is popularly assumed: Shaban 1976: 100 ff..
63. Haldon 1993.
64. Harvey 1989; Hendy 1989.
65. Bhaskar 1978, 1987; Hillel-Rubin 1979; McLennan 1989.

7

Sex and Empire

A Darwinian Perspective

Walter Scheidel

For the end of a policy would not be, in the eyes of the actors or their historians, simply to conquer others and bring all into subjection. Nor does any man of sense go to war with his neighbors for the mere purpose of mastering his opponents; nor go to sea for the mere sake of the voyage; nor engage in professions and trades for the sole purpose of learning them. In all these cases the objects are invariably the pleasure, honor, or profit resulting from these undertakings. (Polybius 3.4)

It is certain that with almost all animals there is a struggle between the males for the possession of the female. This fact is so notorious that it would be superfluous to give instances. (Darwin 1871: 259)

1. HUMAN NATURE AND ANCIENT EMPIRES

1.1. Power and Fitness

Why empires? Or, more generally, why power? In his landmark study of the sources of social power—the first part of which is largely dedicated to the subject of our volume, ancient empires—Michael Mann steers clear of motivational models of human behavior. "We can take for granted the motivational drive of humans to seek to increase their means of subsistence. That is a constant."[1] But why do humans seek to increase their means of subsistence? Is that a goal in itself? To Mann, it does not matter: one seeks power as a "generalized means" (Talcott Parsons's phrase) "for attaining whatever goals one wants to achieve." The nature of these goals does not require further analysis: "If I talk sometimes of 'human beings pursuing their goals,' this should be taken not as a voluntaristic or psychological statement but as a given, a constant into which I will inquire no further because it has no further social force." No attempt is made to identify ultimate causes underlying proximate motivation. In my view, this approach not only impoverishes our vision of human behavior but effectively prevents us from understanding and explaining the recent history of our species.[2]

This volume focuses on empire, power, and exploitation. From Mann's perspective, exploitation is a way of pursuing the unquestioned goal of increasing the means of subsistence by exercising power. But why should exploiters want to increase their means of subsistence? This question is not nearly as pointless as it has been made to seem. From an evolutionary perspective, resources are of no value in and of themselves. They acquire intrinsic utility only in as much as they are instrumentalized in enhancing inclusive fitness, defined as "the reproductive success of individual genes, including that of identical copies which are present in near kin."[3]

Humans, like all other complex organisms on this planet, are hydraulic vehicles generated by self-replicating molecules linked up in genes, the basic particulate units of inheritance that are passed intact from one generation to the next. These vehicles, the phenotypic expression of the underlying genotype, have evolved for the purpose of protecting those biomolecules from environmental hazards and have come to facilitate their interaction with the outside world, primarily for the sake of energy consumption, and—in sexually reproducing species—for the purpose of replication. In the latter case, the phenotypical (i.e., physical and behavioral) properties of these vehicles determine the replicating germ cells' chances of meeting others in order to reproduce. Since genetic survival (i.e., successful replication) is contingent on scarce energy resources, reproductive processes inevitably involve competition, which in turn drives evolution in response to natural selection. Natural selection, equivalent to the differential reproduction of genotypes, ultimately selects for reproductive success. As a result, the behavior of organisms is adaptive if it increases the chances of reproductive success. Because genetic survival is by definition the only raison d'être of organisms, their evolved behavior has been conditioned by this reproductive imperative. Thus, organisms can be said to have been designed by natural selection to operate successfully in a competitive environment in ways that contribute to the replication of their genes.[4]

In sexually reproducing species, competition for resources is ultimately equivalent to competition for mates. Owing to sexual asymmetries in gamete size and reproductive physiology, females and males in diploid species differ markedly in terms of their reproductive strategies. Female lifetime reproductive success is constrained by a fixed number of gametes and by prolonged gestation and placental nurture and subsequent lactation. All these features constitute very considerable parental investment of energy resources. By contrast, males are limited in their reproductive performance not so much by physiological features as by competitors. Whereas the mean reproductive success of all males in a generation must equal the reproductive success of all females, variance in reproductive success may greatly differ between the sexes. Unlike females, males may increase their reproductive success significantly by depriving competitors of mating opportunities. This difference is crucial in determining reproductive behavior. In all species, the sex that invests less will compete more for mating opportunities,[5] because the sex allocating a smaller proportion of reproductive effort as parental effort benefits more from competing for mate quantity. Therefore, males gain more reproductively from gathering a harem of females than females would gain from gathering a harem of males. This is why polygyny is so common in mammals, where females are high obligate investors.[6] In about 95 percent of mammalian species, some males monopolize sexual access to more than one female, usually through intensive intermale competition. In polygynous species, variance in reproductive success is much higher for males than for females. Thus, while male resources increase fertility at the "high" end of reproductive variation—resource-rich males mate with more and/or more fecund females—females' resources avert failure at the "low" end, as they require only sufficient resources to raise viable offspring.[7]

Typically, resources, status, and power co-vary with reproductive success for males. Because male variance in reproductive success is high, great expenditure and risk may be profitable. Among humans, where men use resources to gain reproductive advantage, this merely increases variance in male reproductive success.[8] Male fitness differentials range from differences in mating success, such as the number of wives and their reproductive value (above all, age), the frequency of extramarital matings, and the incidence of remarriage, to differential marital fertility, differential child survivorship, and the differential allocation of reproductive chances to offspring. Dominance, status, and wealth have all been positively associated with a variety of mechanisms promoting male reproductive success, including the number of serial or simultaneous conjugal unions, the number of extramarital liaisons, age at first marriage or reproduction, spouse's age at first reproduction, interbirth intervals, and probability of cuckoldry.[9] Thus, a growing number of studies have established a strong correlation between cultural and reproductive success. In general, the acquisition of symbolic capital—honor, prestige, power—translates to the accumulation of material capital, which enhances reproductive success.[10] As E. O. Wilson put it in his seminal work, "to dominate is to possess priority of access to the necessities of life and reproduction. This is not a circular definition; it is a statement of a strong correlation observed in nature."[11] Chagnon is right to remind us that in evolutionary time, struggles among humans were more likely over the means of reproduction than over the means of production.[12] However, with the rise of sedentary agriculture, these two tend to converge.

1.2. Human History and Primate Models

In human history, we would expect customs and institutions to reflect these underlying mechanisms. At the same time, it would be difficult to appreciate the impact of this biological infrastructure except within an explicitly Darwinian conceptual framework. An evolutionary perspective provides the only comprehensive model of the behavior of all organic beings, including Homo sapiens.[13] And, in fact, evolutionary approaches have made considerable headway in a variety of disciplines.[14] Perhaps unsurprisingly, acceptance and success have varied with the proximity of different fields to the life sciences.[15] Hence, the more an academic field has traditionally been governed by modes of discourse that are hostile or oblivious to science and reductive reasoning, the slower progress has been.[16] In the social sciences, anthropologists have more readily embraced Darwinian concepts than historians have been willing to do.[17] In view of established traditions, this may hardly occasion surprise, but is nevertheless impossible to justify. No one will want to claim that simple, "primitive," "tribal" societies—the "savages" of yesteryear—are somehow closer to the animal kingdom and therefore more suitable for the application of evolutionary concepts than "civilized" complex societies. All people are animals, regardless of their cultural environment. As a consequence, there is no obvious reason why an evolutionary perspective should not be of comparable utility (or lack thereof) in either field. The explanation must doubtless be sought in the institutional structure of academic production that favors certain modes of enquiry in some compartments but discourages them in others. History, post-historic turn, is now surely one of the least receptive areas.[18] Ancient history, conventionally chained to literary criticism, is no exception, even though the 1990s witnessed the publication of a fair amount of pioneering work.[19] In any event, arbitrary firewalls cannot fail to narrow the horizon of historical research:

> To break this seamless matrix of causation—to attempt to dismember the individual into "biological" versus "nonbiological" aspects—is to embrace and perpetuate an ancient dualism endemic in western cultural tradition: material/spiritual, body/mind, physical/mental, natural/human, animal/human, biological/social, biological/cultural. This dualistic view expresses only a premodern version of biology, whose intellectual warranty has vanished.[20]

For Gellner, logical coherence is a sign of conceptual progress: "the failure to bring findings from diverse fields together into one unified picture is in our society a sign of insufficient advance in one field or the other or both, but not of some inherent insulation of diverse phenomena."[21] In our case, "insufficient advance" will be encountered primarily in the humanities.

There is no more immediate form of exploitation of humans than that which directly involves their bodies, and, given the nature of bodies as agents of reproduction, sexual exploitation can reasonably be defined as the ultimate and quintessential form of human exploitation. If ancient imperialism facilitated exploitation, we must address the question of whether or how it faciliated the exploitation of reproductive capacity. How might the beneficiaries of empire increase their mating success in order to enhance their inclusive fitness? We may crudely distinguish between two complementary and overlapping ways of achieving this goal: by direct appropriation of the means of reproduction—that is, by obtaining or monopolizing access to fecund females, controlling their bodies by means of marriage or purchase—or indirectly, by appropriating the means of production so as to acquire symbolic and material resources that facilitate access to mates whose bodies are not subject to permanent control, as in the case of prostitution or extramarital liaisons. It will be immediately apparent that this distinction is one of degree rather than substance, in that the means of ensuring direct control are similar to or identical with those conducive of occasional matings, namely status, wealth, and power.

These links between access to resources and access to females can be traced back to our primate ancestors:

> In intermale reproductive competition, males seek to monopolize either females or resources that are crucial to female reproduction. The spatiotemporal distribution of resources should determine which of these strategies is most effective, partly through its effect on resource defensibility, which is considered a key influence on patterns of aggressive competition. In line with this argument, we suggest that the object of intergroup aggression should be predictable by resource alienability—i.e., the extent to which resources can be profitably seized. Thus, fruit trees used by territorial monkeys are alienable, because territorial boundaries can shift.... Again, individual females are not alienable from a female-bonded nonhuman primate troop, because females are unwilling to leave their female kin. They are alienable, however, in species in which females transfer. This framework accounts for the association between male-male cooperation and female transfer, and it suggests that if material resources of sufficient value (i.e., importance to reproduction) are alienable, competition over females should give way to competition over material resources.[22]

The same mechanisms are encountered among humans.[23] Manson and Wrangham test their hypothesis by comparing human societies with few or no alienable resources with those that have valuable objects or land that can be seized. They find that in forty-two foraging societies, the presence of alienable resources was significantly associated with conflict over resources. At the same time, polygyny and wealth are strongly correlated in societies where alienable resources are available.[24]

Applied to the theme of this volume, this scenario suggests that males cooperate in hazardous ventures because, ultimately, they stand to improve their reproductive success and inclusive fitness. Since humans in complex, sedentary societies are able to control territory and storable surplus, we expect them to compete primarily over territory and material resources because these will facilitate access to mates.[25] In these societies, females are highly transferable, both in the context of consensual virilocal marriage (the most common pattern of animal dispersal in primate and other mammalian species) and in cases of forcible seizure and claustration (for marriage, concubinage, and slavery). It is clear that competition over females and competition over resources are not mutually exclusive; rather, capture of females remains an option on top of seizure of resources, especially at the initial, often violently disruptive stage of conquest.[26] This model is universally applicable and guarantees that the basic behavioral preconditions for territorial expansion are automatically present in any human society.[27]

By contrast, the actual incidence of corresponding activities, such as offensive intergroup aggression and imperialist expansion, as well as success and failure, are determined by unrelated environmental factors. In his pathbreaking survey of human development since the inception of agriculture, Diamond demonstrates that geographical divergence in ecological conditions (such as the availability of domesticable plants and animals), as well as geomorphological features (such as the relative isolation or openness of different regions), ultimately account for the most fundamental variations in human social and cultural development.[28] Thus, complex exploitative systems first arose in the ecologically most favored parts of the planet, such as the Near East, India, and China, only belatedly in the Americas, and not at all in marginal zones such as Australia. In this way, ecological constraints have mediated the universal drift of human social organization toward increasing complexity.[29] This emerging consensus on the nature of the ultimate determinants of human cultural diversity permits us to relate a phylogenetic constant, such as evolved behavioral propensities, to behavioral variables, such as the specific *style* of differential reproduction and sexual exploitation in a given ecological niche at a particular stage of civilizational accomplishment—in this case, ancient empires.[30]

1.3. Proximate Mechanisms and Ultimate Causation

At this point, perhaps belatedly, it may be expedient to address the common objection that sexual urges are not known to prompt humans to engage in warfare or exploitation of resources. Immanuel Kant distinguished three passions—for possession, for power, and for honor—but not for offspring. The tempting question to what extent this omission is explicable in terms of his personal psychology would miss the point, since his observation is in any event irrelevant to the issue of adaptation. As Robin Dunbar puts it,

> Individuals may be persuaded to engage in warfare by any number of motives.... Which (if any) of these mutually incompatible explanations is the case is irrelevant to whether or not warfare is functional in biological terms. That question is answered solely in terms of whether or not warfare increases or decreases the actor's inclusive fitness (or, as a proximate measure, gives the actor access to resources that will influence his/her ability to reproduce).... Non-biologists thus fall into the common trap of assuming that explanations in terms of "selfish genes" have something to do with motivations. In practice, the same functional effect can be produced by many different motivations in as many different cases.[31]

This is an important clarification, especially for historians used to probing representations and teasing out meanings. It is unnecessary and unhelpful to examine claims and ideologies associated with imperialism and exploitation when we are interested in ultimate causation.[32] The crucial difference lies between proximate causation (the mechanism that brings something about) and ultimate causation, which concerns adaptive significance entailing reproductive consequences. In other words, it does not matter whichever motives ostensibly determine behavior, given that the consequences of this behavior for inclusive fitness are subject to natural selection and that natural selection favors adaptive behavior. Irons suggests "as a hypothesis that in most human societies cultural success consists in accomplishing those things which make biological success (that is, a high inclusive fitness) probable. While cultural success is by definition something people are conscious of, they may often be unaware of the biological consequences of their behavior."[33]

This is not to say that perceived motivation is wholly irrelevant; if the claim that contemporary American men on average think of sex every five minutes during their waking hours is valid cross-culturally, the average man (depending on mean life expectancy) will think of sex between 2.5 and 5 million times in his postpubescent lifetime. By implication, all men who ever lived on earth must have thought of sex approximately 50 quadrillion times. It is hard to imagine that this persistent reflex (which squares superbly with evolutionary theory) has been of no importance to conscious motivation. Even so, Darwinian theory can be empirically corroborated only by observed or attested behavior.

Needless to say, this is inevitably a tall order for the student of ancient history: in this case, human behavior cannot be directly observed but must be tenuously reconstructed from invariably highly fragmentary and often biased sources. For this reason alone, it is essential to concentrate on broad patterns of behavior rather than discrete events or phenomena. For much of ancient history, sweeping cross-cultural surveys are the only way to identify such patterns.[34] This explains the format of the following sections of this chapter.

Yet, before I move on to ancient imperialism, one further potential source of confusion merits comment. Darwinian theory predicts that natural selection favors the evolution of behavioral traits that tend to create opportunities for increasing inclusive fitness. The wording is crucial: opportunities do not necessarily lead to the desired results. By the standards of recorded human history, evolution moves at a glacial pace; thus, favored behavioral traits can be adaptive only in the context of the "environment of evolutionary adaptedness" (EEA). They do not necessarily have the same effect in the fast-changing conditions of the recent past. Therefore, what we are looking for is not merely evidence that imperial success increased the reproductive success and inclusive fitness of primary beneficiaries (although studies of contemporary populations have of course repeatedly shown that such evidence does exist in abundance[35]) but also evidence of the fact that imperial success enabled these beneficiaries to engage in behavior that would ordinarily promote reproductive success. Male competitors for fecund females are conditioned to seek out sexual gratification rather than children per se, but, because procreation is positively correlated with sexual intercourse, the net effects on reproductive success tend to be similar. Even so, the distinction between sex and reproduction is of considerable importance. This is best brought out by the observation that in modern Western societies, social status is frequently (though not invariably) unrelated to reproductive success.[36] Using proxy measures for cultural success (education, though not income), Vining even argues for a negative correlation between wealth and fertility.[37]

Looked at more closely, however, this apparent lack of fit between theory and data is easy to explain.[38] For example, it has been shown that extremely wealthy men are still in the habit of boosting lifetime reproductive success by means of higher rates of remarriage, thus outreproducing the general male population.[39] More important, Pérusse finds that, while social status may now often be dissociated from *actual* male fertility, it is still significantly related to *potential* fertility, as estimated from copulation frequency: in fact, status is by far the most important factor accounting for variance in this proximate determinant of reproductive success and inclusive fitness. This suggests that in the absence of modern means of fertility control, paternity tests, and socially imposed monogamy, cultural success would on average still translate to higher reproductive success.[40] Moreover, lifetime fertility is an imperfect measure of inclusive fitness. Allowing for long-term effects, low fertility in high-status environments need not be indicative of low fitness; cultural success may well serve to enhance inclusive fitness in the long run.[41] Thus, Rogers devises a model that stresses that heritable wealth has reproductive value independent of fertility as long as it increases the reproductive chances of offspring and suggests that wealth and fertility may be of roughly equal value in estimating inclusive fitness.[42] This observation goes a long way in explaining low fertility in privileged groups.[43] Harpending and Rogers consider the possibility that under conditions of density-dependent population regulation, such as might exist in a stratified society in which the lowest social stratum constitutes a demographic sink, a strategy favoring offspring quality might result in higher long-term fitness. Most recently, Boone and Kessler have proposed an alternative model that seeks to explain reduced fertility as part of an evolved strategy to maximize long-term fitness in the face of periodic ecological crises.[44] As I show in section 1.5, these attempts to account for reproductive restraint are of particular interest in the present context.

1.4. Determinants of Polygyny

For men, polygyny has traditionally been the most commonly desired mating pattern in human history. In two samples of cultures from the Human Relations Area Files (HRAF), 77 percent (n = 250) and 76 percent (n = 563) practiced some form of polygyny, respectively, whereas only 17 and 21 percent were strictly monogamous.[45] However, in polygynous societies, the majority of all unions are monogamous; plural marriage is usually limited to high-status individuals (i.e., those with wealth and/or of advanced age). According to a recent survey of published work, the actual incidence of plural marriage in polygynous societies has ranged from 2 to 50 percent in various twentieth-century African and Asian populations.[46] A rate of 25 to 35 percent appears to have been a common upper limit. Marital data for fifteen African countries from 1966 to 1977 show that the average plural family included 2 to 2.5 wives, with only a small proportion of unions involving three or more wives.[47] Comparable stratification can be observed in Mormon polygamy: 15 to 20 percent of marriages in a sample of six thousand prominent Mormon families were polygamous; of 1,784 polygamous men, 66.3 percent had two wives, 21.2 percent had three wives, 6.7 percent had four wives, and fewer than 6 percent had five or more. However, leaders benefited disproportionately from this practice; the founder of the sect, Joseph Smith, has been credited with twenty-seven, forty-eight, or eighty-four wives.[48] Socioeconomic status is a major determinant of Mormon polygamy.[49] The same pattern can be found at the opposite end of the developmental spectrum: in one Melanesian sample, 9 percent of 663 men had more than one wife, but only 1 percent had more than two.[50]

Polygamy rates for men and women differ. The proportion of all married women married polygamously is usually significantly higher than the corresponding proportion of all men; at the very least, there will always be twice as many polygamously married women in a given group as there are polygamously married men. This imbalance can be illustrated with reference to a group of Australian Aborigines in which ninety-four men were monogamously married and fifty-eight (or 38.2 per cent) were polygamous. However, 170 of 264 married women lived in polygamous unions, or 64.4 per cent.[51] Under these circumstances, in populations with a balanced adult sex ratio, many adult men would be deprived of spouses. Offensive warfare serves to alleviate this problem: not only may casualties skew the adult sex ratio in favor of women, but military success enables the victors to transfer additional women to their own group. Both mechanisms help reduce the social tensions arising from inequalities in access to mates and foster in-group cohesion and cooperation. Thus, imperial success that renders possible the appropriation of out-group women (either directly by capture or indirectly via the appropriation of mate-attracting resources) simultaneously favors polygyny among the male beneficiaries of this success and reinforces their imperialist motivations.

Polygyny cannot be seen as a single syndrome "but is produced by diverse strategies under a range of different conditions and comprises different systems of meaning and function."[52] Even so, it is possible to identify the most critical variables underpinning polygynous practices. White and Burton relate the occurrence and intensity of polygyny to warfare for plunder, the taking of (female) captives, and male labor migration.[53] In an ambitious study designed to test these and alternative assumptions and to assess the relative importance of different explanatory variables, Bretschneider codes data from 186 societies of the Standard Cross-Cultural Sample (SCCS). While White and Burton maintain that warfare for plunder and the capture of women are positively correlated with levels of polygyny, Bretschneider introduces military success as a further variable, predicting that it will amplify this effect. He also predicts that population size is positively correlated with offensive external warfare, and thus polygyny.[54] The data strongly support these assumptions.[55] It deserves notice that in the cluster of warfare/demography predictors, Bretschneider finds no significant correlation between male mortality in warfare or difference in marriage age and polygyny. Hence, it seems that military aggression alone does not favor polygyny; success is an essential ingredient. Although Bretschneider is concerned with multiple marriage—"when war for plunder/captives is present and militarily successful, female captives tend to be integrated in the winning society through marriage"—the observed correlations can logically be expected to hold for the seizure of territory and resources (as opposed to mere plunder) and the enslavement of women (as opposed to marriage), as well.[56] In fact, White and Burton regard all conditions that increase access to resources needed for supporting large households as facilitating polygyny; these include expansion into new territory through success in war and migration to unoccupied lands. Bretschneider argues that this argument is supported by the finding that militarily successful war for plunder and captives is a good predictor of polygyny.[57]

White and Burton hold that warfare for plunder increases wealth differentiation among men and thus raises polygyny rates among the wealthy.[58] They also note that if social differentiation among men is associated with higher levels of polygyny, plunder should increase polygyny even in the absence of captured wives. In apparent contrast, Bretschneider finds that "when war for plunder and captives is frequent, wealth differences among men will level out, more than a few wealthy men may be able to marry polygynously and a pattern of 'general' polygyny is likely to exist."[59] These two positions are not as contradictory as it might seem. In small and weakly differentiated—often "tribal"—groups, universal participation in communal warfare will result in widespread polygyny in the event of substantial military success. In highly stratified complex large-scale systems, such as ancient empires, however, participant-beneficiaries are unlikely to constitute more than a fairly small minority of the total population, and strong hierarchical privileges may skew the distribution of resources and captives even further in favor of rulers and elites.

According to a popular view, polygyny may under certain circumstances create household wealth. However, Bretschneider finds little support for White's concept of "Wealth-Increasing Polygyny" (or "Polygyny with Autonomous Co-Wives"), according to which residential autonomy of multiple wives predicts a polygyny pattern in which the addition of each wife increases the likelihood of the acquisition of another, given that added co-wives augment wealth.[60] The other main category, "Male Ranked Polygyny with Related Co-Wives," requires husbands to generate the wealth to support one or more wives, and husbands and wives co-reside.[61] With this type, the requirements are mostly on the husband to attract and support additional wives, and polygyny does not vary positively with female contribution to subsistence. This latter scenario was clearly dominant in ancient imperial societies that practiced polygamy.[62] Moreover, plow agriculture is negatively correlated with polygyny,[63] which helps explain why polygyny was more widespread in the African savannah than in the Mediterranean or the Near East, where only the wealthy could afford to adopt this custom. This model does not logically require co-wives to be related (cf. earlier discussion), nor is it contingent on the existence of formal marital unions; any form of accumulation of dependent women in a household will be "male ranked," that is, correlated with male status and resources. In important respects, "Male Ranked Polygyny" is equivalent to "resource-defense polygyny," a concept used in the study of animal species in which males monopolize resource-rich sites that attract aggregations of females.[64]

1.5. Ancient Empires and Darwinian Predictions

The main question is, How do ancient empires conform to the predictions of the primate model of competition over females and/or alienable resources? Imperialism is an extension of intergroup aggression in general, implying a more elaborate and formalized system of operations and control but ultimately serving the same objective. If all groups can be expected to compete for reproductive success, empires differ only in terms of scale. Crudely put, success and attendant power should result in improved reproductive success for those who are heavily invested in the imperialist project. The establishment and exploitation of empires require a high level of social cooperation and hierarchical stratification. Hence, the reproductive benefits of successful imperialism can be expected to vary with the degree of involvement—de facto or symbolic—of the beneficiaries in the building, maintenance, and exploitation of empires.

In highly hierarchical and despotic societies, benefits are most likely to be concentrated at the top. Imperial expansion affects both the size and the complexity of successful states: growth in size favors the creation of new layers of hierarchy, which are likely to add to reproductive inequality.[65] This may create tensions between elite monopolization of resources and sex partners and the need for cooperation in maintaining the imperial system. In these societies, we would expect imperialism to benefit primarily rulers and aristocracy and secondarily essential maintenance personnel, such as soldiers and officials. We would expect increases in reproductive success to be correlated with the social and political hierarchy and cultural success to translate directly to inclusive fitness. In hierarchical societies in which the large majority of the population is regularly excluded from political or even military participation, we would expect such benefits to be limited to a relatively small segment of the total population. Under these circumstances, imperial exploitation would tend to increase inequality in reproductive success by privileging groups closely involved in the system, and even within the population of all beneficiaries a disproportionately large share of resources and mating opportunities would accrue to those at the very top of the social pyramid. All these predictions are corroborated by empirical evidence from ancient Near Eastern empires and comparable political entities from around the world. This correlation between despotism and reproductive inequality is explored in section 2.

In more egalitarian societies, by contrast, we would expect the concentration of resources and females in elite circles to be attenuated or at the very least concealed in order to promote social cohesion and participation of the citizenry in imperialist activities. Nevertheless, resource inequality would still predict differential reproductive success. In the context of socially imposed monogamy, a characteristic feature of egalitarian societies, differential mating success needs to be achieved by a variety of extramarital mating mechanisms from concubinage to slavery and prostitution. Relevant evidence from the Greco-Roman world is analyzed in section 3.

In sum, I hope to show that, in terms of differential reproduction, these two types of ancient empires differ more in style than in substance. Differences in social and political organization shape the institutions that mediate between cultural and reproductive success: royal and aristocratic harems and lawful polygamy in the Near East, concubinage and chattel slavery in the classical Mediterranean. In each case, however, their ultimate function was the same: to convert imperial power into inclusive fitness.

In humans, owing to singularly protracted childcare, a premium has been placed on postpartum parental investment. As a consequence, female mate choice is governed by the desire to obtain resources from long-term mates, an objective that conflicts with the desire for multiple fertilization in males.[66] While it is in the interest of fathers to invest in their offspring, primarily in the context of stable pair-bonds, it is likewise in their interest to maximize reproductive output. We may therefore predict that, ideally, human males should seek to have it both ways, that is, to limit the number of children receiving parental investment in accordance with paternal resources and simultaneously to seek out opportunities for further fertilization without corresponding long-term investment, enhancing what I propose to call "marginal reproductive success." In this, shifting balances of effort, risk and outcome play a crucial role.

I will argue that mixed strategies along these lines are very much in evidence in the ancient societies under review. These empires developed cultural institutions and legal norms that not only facilitated the sexual exploitation of women but at the same time allowed beneficiaries—above all, high-status men—to strike a balance between lifetime reproductive success (i.e., the desire to maximize offspring quantity) and estate preservation in the interest of inclusive fitness (i.e., the desire to maximize offspring quality by limiting paternal investment in acknowledged offspring and the number of heirs).[67] As for the latter, privileged groups have long been known to reduce their marital fertility out of status anxiety, defined as "a strong commitment among married couples to the preservation of the material basis for their own high social status and to the transmission of that status to their children."[68] Since differential reproductive success regularly co-varies with social status and heritable wealth facilitates intergenerational status preservation, from an evolutionary perspective, "strong commitment" of this kind is only to be expected among high-status families.[69]

Again, the question of conscious motivation does not strictly speaking enter the equation. It would be unnecessary to ask whether Assyrians or Persians or Romans deliberately waged wars or organized their households or devised laws in ways aiming to maximize their reproductive benefits from imperial success and thus increase inclusive fitness. All that needs to be shown in this context is that such institutions and norms were adaptive in the sense that they successfully mediated between cultural and reproductive success. I will show that in the major ancient empires, this was regularly the case. Even apparent constraints, such as Greco-Roman monogamy, can readily be accommodated within this explanatory framework.[70]

2. Despotic Empires

2.1. *Despotism and Differential Reproduction*

As we have seen in section 1.4, the incidence of polygyny is strongly correlated with successful warfare and appropriation of resources. In principle, two basic conditions are necessary for polygyny to arise: females must be "economically defendable," and polygyny is more feasible—and sensible in Darwinian terms—when female sexual cycles are asynchronous.[71] Both conditions are particularly well met in highly stratified human societies. Levels of polygyny vary with population size: in small foraging groups, like the Inuit, good hunters and fighters may gain primary sexual access to two or three women; local leaders, like Yanomamö headmen, to as many as ten; supralocal leaders, like Trobriand chiefs, to as many as a hundred; and heads of complex states, like the Inca, perhaps thousands. Dickemann notes "the capacity of human groups to control the labor of other, unrelated, individuals allows the development of harem polygyny far beyond the bounds that any individual family, however extended, could support."[72] As a consequence, "the bigger a polygynist's harem, the more likely he is to depend on exploitation."[73] This association between hierarchy, despotism and polygyny is very strong in a world sample of 104 politically autonomous societies studied by Betzig.[74] This linkage is easy to understand in Darwinian terms:

> Darwinian theory predicts that to the extent that conflicts of interest among individuals are not overridden by common interest, or by an overpowering force, they will be manifested, and they will, ultimately, be reproductively motivated. Where such conflicts exist, men and women are expected to exploit positions of strength in resolving them to their own advantage, and they are expected to turn that advantage to proportionate means to reproduction. *Hierarchical power should predict a biased outcome in conflict resolution, which should in turn predict size of the winner's harem*, for men, a measure of success in reproduction.[75]

As noted before, the ruling elites will have to strike a balance between their desire to monopolize resources and the need to maintain sufficient levels of cooperation. In Betzig's summary, "exploitation will exist to the extent that subordinates are constrained by ecological benefits, whereas cooperation will exist to the extent that dominants are constrained by social benefits."[76] When individuals group to take advantage of high-quality territory, differences in fighting ability will emerge as dominance hierarchies, and dominants will be free to extract fitness benefits from subordinates.[77] Human societies are notable for their division of labor: subordinates raise dominants' fitness directly, as workers but also—or above all—as procurers and defenders of resources (i.e., soldiers and administrators). If a dominant's fitness increases with the mean fitness of the group, then a subordinate's service in resource acquisition or defense should be rewarded accordingly, if not proportionally. Where a subordinate's services are essential and irreplaceable, dominants will be impelled to concede fitness benefits, such as access to resources and mates. In this case, fitness benefits conceded are most likely to translate into reproductive success.[78] Imperial systems inevitably depend on the participation and collusion of different groups from elite commanders and local mediators or intermediaries (such as local elites) to soldiers and officials. The burden of providing fitness benefits to these varied strata falls on out-groups, both members of ethnic-core populations whose services are less essential for the imperial project and members of subject populations.

In humans, owing to a variety of physiological and social checks (such as concealed ovulation, infertility, the incidence of conception and implantation, miscarriage, and infidelity), even successfully polygynous men are severely constrained in their reproductive success by the fertility of their mates. Thus, regardless of socioeconomic status, only men with extensive and well-guarded harems are able to raise their average lifetime fertility beyond a score or so.[79] For this reason, progressive accumulation and monopolization of sex partners is bound to pay off in reproductive terms, and cultural and legal institutions that put no numerical limit on the number of women under the control of individual men are therefore most adaptive, but only insofar as inequality in reproductive success does not interfere with the requirement to share resources with subordinates, as noted above.[80] Here, the exploitation of outsiders rendered feasible by successful imperial expansion offers unique opportunities for reconciling the conflicting goals of accumulation and redistribution of fitness benefits: enabling rulers and nobles to monopolize women on a grand scale, it also leaves room for the rewarding of essential subordinates that is commensurate to the real or perceived value of their contribution.[81]

2.2. Comparative Historical Evidence

In her cross-cultural study of despotism and differential reproduction, Betzig attempts "to determine how often power has been used to the end of reproduction...throughout the course of history and before." Her subsequent work revisits this issue in considerable detail.[82] These substantial surveys of pertinent evidence could easily be extended by numerous additional sources. In this context, a few telling instances will suffice.

Dahomey, a powerful African empire of the nineteenth century, is in many ways a typical case.[83] The royal harem allegedly consisted of thousands of "wives," constantly replenished by war captives selected by the king. Even allowing for some hyperbole, the genetic consequences of royal privilege were perceived to be considerable; as Herskovits notes concerning the capital, "it had seemed as though in the city of Abomey at least, it would be difficult to find Dahomeans who were not descended from royalty." In general, the reproductive hierarchy paralleled the social hierarchy: village chiefs had more wives and children than commoners.[84] In the kingdom of Asante, at the end of the nineteenth century, the number of wives in multiple marriages would range from two to a thousand. The king himself was credited with 3,333 spouses, a symbolic figure that is nevertheless suggestive of the order of magnitude and of the unquestioned association of cultural with reproductive success.[85] In 1848, a missionary recounted a tour of the palace of the Asante king: "During our progress through the harem, one lady was introduced to us by the king as his favorite wife, his declared standard of estimation being, much to our amusement, the large number of children she had borne him."[86] Kings of Uganda and Loango would be credited with 7,000 wives each.[87] In Yoruba society, concubinage drew on thousands of female slaves. Influential men—landowners and warlords—always had multiple wives, some hundreds; this caused an extremely uneven distribution of the female population in society.[88] Among the Azande in Nilotic Sudan around 1900, only a minority of men were bigamists, and fewer still married to more than two women. However, village chiefs would boast thirty, forty, or one hundred wives, and the king more than five hundred.[89]

The medieval Khmer kings were endowed with five wives and several thousand concubines, the latter subdivided into several classes. Physical attractiveness was noted as a selection criterion.[90] Elaborate ranking systems of this kind are typical of particularly large and centralistic empires with intensive ruler worship. Under the Western Zhou dynasty in ancient China, the emperor had access to one queen, three consorts, nine wives of second rank, twenty-seven wives of third rank, and eighty-one concubines.[91] The sexual purpose of this arrangement is thrown into sharp relief by the fact that the court ladies recorded the menstrual cycle of these women and scheduled their congress with the emperor. In the upper classes, men had only a single principal wife (without the option of remarriage), but the bride would introduce her maids into her husband's household as his future secondary wives or concubines.[92] In this case, the nexus between wealth and polygyny and likewise between dependent service and sexual exploitation is crystal clear. The latter is further underlined by the example of Huan, the Duke of Qi in the seventh century B.C.E., who supposedly established a private brothel with thousands of women in his own palace.[93] More power invariably translated into bigger harems. The harem of the Han emperors grew to 6,000 in the second century C.E.[94] According to the *Dalofu*, a sex manual of the Tang period, the recent restoration and expansion of imperial might had increased the scale of sexual exploitation at the top:

Nine ordinary consorts every night, and the Empress two nights at full moon, this was the ancient rule, and the Ladies-in-waiting kept a careful record of this with their vermilion brushes. But at present the women in the seraglio of the Nan-mei Palace, three thousand in number, all together approach the Emperor displaying their charms. Is this not because the bodies of all these myriad women are reserved for this one man?[95]

Commercial prostitution is traced back to either the seventh or the third centuries B.C.E., coinciding in any event with imperial expansion and the increasing prosperity of a middle class insufficiently wealthy to keep additional women on a permanent basis.[96] The trickle-down effect of imperial wealth and its impact on sexual behavior are readily discernible behind this development.

In the Inca empire, the Inca's women were kept in depots scattered across the country. When they reached the age of eight to ten years, large numbers of girls, known as *manacona*, were taken from their places of origin to live and serve in the *aclla huasi*, or "Houses of the Chosen Women." They were reviewed in the capital, Cusco, and divided into various categories according to their social origins, physical attractiveness, and aptitudes. The *yura aclla*, blood relatives of the Inca, were consecrated to the cult of the Sun and were expected to remain chaste. The next-highest layer was made up of the *huayrur aclla*, the most beautiful girls, from whom the Inca selected his secondary wives. Those virgins passed their time in textile manufacturing and food processing. Once called by the king to serve their reproductive function, they worked in the palace as servants until they were allowed to return home. The *paco aclla* were earmarked for the chiefs whom the Inca wished to reward, while the *yana aclla*, lacking background or beauty, became the servants of the others.[97]

This system is noteworthy for three reasons. First, it highlights with almost brutal clarity the direct connection between political power and reproductive privilege. Second, it illustrates the principle that the privileged sought to preserve their status for future generations while maximizing their genetic contribution to the next generation; whereas the queen, usually a close relative (sometimes even a sister) of the king, produced legitimate heirs and the children of concubines related to him up to the fourth degree enjoyed special privileges, all other concubines produced bastards who followed the status of their mothers. Thus, status privileges and hence material resources were reserved for a minority within the Inca's offspring. And, third, the gradated redistribution of *paco aclla* among different strata of the elite exemplifies the need of rulers to bestow fitness benefits upon essential subordinates in accordance with their contribution to the management of the exploitative structure. In 1613, Felipe Guaman de Ayala reported that under the Incas, principal nobles had been allotted fifty women each; leaders of vassal nations had been allowed thirty; provincial governors, twenty; lower-level chiefs (depending on the number of their subordinates), from three to fifteen.[98]

The contemporaneous Aztec Empire generated similar modes of sexual exploitation and hierarchies of reproductive privilege. While royal harems reputedly contained thousands of women and top aristocrats accumulated hundreds of concubines, lesser nobles had to make do with correspondingly fewer consorts. Not surprisingly, several Aztec emperors were credited with more than one hundred children each.[99] Provincial tributes included young women to be impregnated by elite males, and imperial revenue enabled the state to provide wet-nurses who took care of the offspring of nobles for the first five years of life.[100] Later on, a Franciscan observer would claim that "since the lords and chiefs stole all the women for themselves, an ordinary Indian could scarcely find a woman when he wished to marry."[101]

Fitness benefits usually bunched at the very top. Ismail the Bloodthirsty, king of Morocco (b. 1672, d. 1727), is reputed to have fathered at least 888 children. This total may seem hard to believe, since in forty years of reproductive history, owing to the various physiological constraints noted earlier, Ismail is unlikely to have been responsible for more than two hundred to four hundred live births.[102] This calculation also casts doubt on the claim that the Nizam of Hyderabad became father four times in the space of eight days, with nine more expected the following week.[103] Nevertheless, there can be no doubt that large harems provided unique mating prospects for individual men. Dickemann observes that "given nine-month pregnancies and two- to three-year lactations, it is not inconceivable that a hardworking Emperor might manage to service a thousand women."[104] Islam allows four legitimate wives but puts no limit on the number of concubines. Consequently, the caliph Al-Mutawakkil (847–861) could be credited with 4,000 concubines and the emir Abd Ar-Rahman II (822–852) with 6,300. Ottoman harems are said to have ranged from 200 to 1,200 women.[105] I have already referred to some comparable African examples. Sources from India from the fifth century B.C.E. to the sixteenth century C.E. talk of royal harems holding up to 12,000 or 16,000 women.[106] In all these cases, even if concubines were put to economically productive work, they were more likely to be a drain on resources than profitable assets, especially since they had to be maintained in some style.[107] Moreover, claustration was deemed necessary to ensure paternity.[108]

It is worth noting that despotic polygyny is not exclusively confined to highly stratified societies of a relatively remote past. By the early 1990s, the North Korean dictator Kim Il-sung and his son and successor Kim Jong-il had reputedly acquired around one hundred mansions and villas. These residences hosted the so-called Mansion Special Volunteer Corps, a retinue of young women selected for their physical attributes. Supposedly numbering in the thousands, these women were organized in the *kippeunjo* ("Happy Corps"), composed of actresses and singers, and the *manjokjo* ("Satisfaction Corps") and *haengbokjo* ("Felicity Corps"), which were more straightforwardly charged with the provision of sexual favors. A special party unit was said to scour schools all over the country for beautiful girls and to persuade parents to volunteer their daughters' services. Officials might offer up potential concubines as gifts to their supreme leaders. Women were discharged after their early twenties. In addition, the *kwabu-jo*, a corps division made up of attractive widows, was established to extend sexual services to senior associates of the regime.[109]

2.3. Comparative Scientific Evidence

A recent survey of Y-chromosomal DNA in sixteen contemporary Central Asian populations provides the most dramatic example to date of the covariance of political power and reproductive success. About 8 percent of all men in this region (or 16 million individuals) belong to a Y-chromosome lineage that originated in Mongolia approximately one millennium ago and can plausibly be linked to the paternal ancestors of Genghis Khan (b. c.1162, d. 1227), a ruler who established control over a vast terrority stretching from the Caspian Sea to the Pacific Coast. This is consistent with historical references to massive predatory polygyny at Genghis' court and those of his male-line descendants (known as the "Golden Family"), who continued to dominate the region for generations.[110] In addition, an analogous study discovered another unusually common Y-chromosomal lineage in northeastern China and Mongolia that may arguably be associated with the Manchu Qing dynasty, which ruled China from 1644 to 1912.[111] These, however, are merely the most extreme instances of a broader trend that has repeatedly been documented in studies of Y-chromosomal and mitochondrial patterns in present populations: for instance, it can now be shown that while the majority of male Icelanders descend from Scandinavian settlers, the majority of Icelandic women have Gaelic ancestry, which reflects the privileged access to the women of medieval Ireland enjoyed by Viking raiders and conquerors. Similarly, in the same period, successive waves of male invaders from Germany and Scandinavia created new Y-chromosomal lineages in the most affected parts of Britain that reduced the odds of genetic survival of the indigenous male population.[112] Sex-specific surveys of genetic descent thus confirm the premise that, on average, males experience greater variance in reproductive success (i.e., inclusive fitness) than women and allow us to link this phenomenon to competition over power and resources.

2.4. Ancient Near Eastern Empires

2.4.1. Mesopotamia, Syria, and Palestine. The major complex societies of the Fertile Crescent and Iran fit the same mold. Owing to the vagaries of source preservation, some of the most detailed and evocative evidence comes from two of the lesser powers in the region. The archive of King Zimri-Lim of Mari reveals that, in addition to his principal queen, the ruler had several secondary wives (one for each of his five palaces), as well as numerous concubines, who shared common quarters separated from the regular wives. Many of the latter appear to have been of foreign origin, particularly war captives. In a letter to his principal queen, Zimri-Lim asked her to select new women for his harem: "choose thirty female-weavers—or however many who are choice and attractive, who from their toe nails to the hair of their heads have no blemish." Having changed his mind, he announced in a subsequent missive that he himself was going to pick the right "girls for the veil."[113] As Lerner aptly notes, "the wife's cooperation in the matter is taken for granted, and her husband's sexual use of the captive women…is assumed as a routine matter."[114] Other letters show that "singers" served as "girl-friends" of the king, competing with his queen for his attention. The scale of royal polygyny appears to have been a function of the kingdom's power: thus, the number of palace women rose from 44 under Yasmah-Addu to 232 under Zimri-Lim, in part thanks to human booty from the conquest of the city of Kahat.[115]

A few centuries later, in the kingdom of Arrapha, the kings maintained palaces in several cities. For the palace in Zizza, thirty-one and thirty-five concubines are attested, while as many as forty-eight may have present at one point.[116] Further harems are known from the capital, Nuzi, and from the city of Anzukallim. At Nuzi, one prince is known to have kept a principal wife plus seven to nine further women in one household and two to four in another, several of them together with their children. Private citizens, by contrast, would have a second wife only if they could afford to do so.[117] Unfortunately, nothing seems to be known about the mating opportunities of soldiers and bureaucrats.

Resource polygyny can be traced back to Sumerian culture. That there is no evidence of harems in pre-Sargonic Sumer but only from the Ur III period on highlights the correlation between imperial expansion and the accumulation of women in the hands of the powerful.[118] For the Ur III empire, many royal consorts are known by name. While the legal texts of that period know only of monogamous relationships, terms for secondary wives and concubines are attested in literary texts, pointing to more varied social practice, presumably in elite circles.[119] The law already recognized the possibility that a slave woman could lawfully be raised to the status of wife.[120] Informal sexual relations with slave women—slavery had become widespread in the Ur III period[121]—are not mentioned in these texts; we may assume that they were of no relevance in a legal context. Sexual access to slave women had been an unquestioned prerogative of their owners since from the very beginning.[122]

Harem-like institutions are repeatedly attested in Mesopotamian sources.[123] Unfortunately, a group of Middle Assyrian documents known as "harem edicts" are badly broken.[124] Harem size was sensitive to military success and imperial expansion. In the twelfth century B.C.E., King Shilhak-Inshushinak of Elam, having taken the city of Karindash, proclaimed that "all the descendants of the king of Karindash, his wives, concubines and relatives were rounded up and taken into exile." In 671 B.C.E., following the conquest of Egypt, the Assyrian king Asarhaddon transferred the harem of the Ethiopian king Taharka to Assyria.[125] Similar activities were attributed to Pharaohs and Persian kings (see sections 2.3.2–3).

The Old Testament highlights the same link between imperial growth and royal polygyny. In a long line of biblical characters, beginning with Abraham, his wife, Sarah, and her maid, Hagar, in Genesis 16, parallel relationships are invariably attributed to men in leadership positions.[126] In fact, the biblical tradition traces a gradual upscaling process parallel to increasing stratification, from moderately promiscuous patriarchs to more polygynous judges and on to kings with their substantial harems. Monarchs in particular were thought to have operated on a novel scale: Deuteronomy 17.14, 17, warns the Israelites that a king might take too many wives (and amass too much gold and silver). David, even when his authority was limited to Hebron, had six wives and later added others; the sources grant him eight named wives and additional unknown ones, plus concubines.[127] Solomon supposedly accumulated a huge harem of seven hundred wives and three hundred concubines.[128] This expansion was clearly imagined to have been a function of imperial success: "now king Solomon loved many foreign women, together with the daughter of Pharaoh, women of the Moabites, Ammonites, Edomites, Sidonians, and Hittites."[129] The eighteen wives and sixty concubines of Rehoboam, Solomon's less powerful son—responsible for twenty-eight sons and sixty daughters—seem modest in comparison.[130] In this context, the historical reliability of these passages is of secondary importance; what matters here is that the biblical tradition faithfully mirrors the Near Eastern model of royal polygyny and the almost mechanical quantitative relationship between power, resources, and reproductive success. Religious language cast royal polygyny as a divine reward that could be as easily withdrawn as it had been bestowed: "I anointed you king over Israel, ... and I gave you ... your master's wives into your bosom. ... I will take your wives before your eyes, and give them to your neighbor, and he shall lie with your wives in the sight of this sun."[131]

Among commoners, polygamous relationships were the subject of several Old Babylonian marriage contracts.[132] On these occasions, however, we never find more than two women involved.[133] The Codex Hammurabi protected a wife against a second co-wife, and the latter was to be accepted only if the former proved barren, while still considered inferior.[134] Otherwise, in the absence of special circumstances (such as infertility, sickness, or misconduct of the first wife), the existing wife first had to agree to the second union. The sources reflect multiple status differentiation, between wives and slave concubines, or between a slave-wife as second wife and a slave concubine in lieu of a second wife.[135] Slave women may have been encouraged to establish sexual relations with their owners by stipulations of the Codex Hammurabi providing for their freedom, along with that of their children, upon the owner's death. However, such children needed to be adopted first.[136]

In Assyrian law, by contrast, the wife had no explicit rights vis-à-vis her husband; only the wife was capable of committing adultery, never the husband.[137] Wives were not entitled to inherit from their husbands.[138] Slave women were sharply differentiated from proper wive; in public, wives were veiled, a practice that was strictly forbidden to slaves.[139] Concubines were often chosen from slaves.[140] It has been suggested that the term for concubine, *esirtu*, is etymologically derived from the term for "captive woman."[141] Attitudes toward polygyny appear to have changed over time, in step with growing imperial success; while Old Assyrian marriage contracts occasionally envisage the possibility of a second wife only to rule it out, Middle Assyrian law considers the presence of two wives normal practice, one "in front" and one "behind."[142] Later on, Assyrian merchants active in Kanesh in Anatolia were allowed to take local women—so-called slave girls—as secondary wives while their regular wives stayed at home.[143] This provision affords us an all too rare glimpse of the fringe benefits of imperial success for subordinates: as members of the dominant group, Assyrian merchants commanded the clout or resources to acquire mates from among less privileged populations in peripheral regions. In this way, mating opportunities were transferred from the male population of these areas to the Assyrian visitors. We will come across similar mechanisms in the case of Greek colonists and Roman soldiers (see section 3).

In her study of Neo-Babylonian marriage contracts, Roth finds that the introduction of a second wife was repeatedly deemed a cause for divorce. Even so, the presence of a co-wife did not always result in the dissolution of the previous union: in one case, in keeping with the tradition set by the Codex Hammurabi (see earlier discussion), a married but childless man was allowed to take a second wife. Outside the sphere of formal unions, married men had considerably more leeway. These marriage contracts contain no adultery clauses for husbands, only for wives.[144] In this period, cohabitation of a married man with a slave woman was acceptable as long as it did not reduce the share of property inherited by the wife. The owner's children with a slave woman, unless adopted, remained slaves. Thus, no legal obligations arose from sexual relations with one's own slaves. Many slave women were hired out either to brothels or to individuals as personal concubines.[145] Brothels were known as "the place where they know slave women." Documented pay scales allow us to gauge the socioeconomic status of the patrons. Rent for a slave concubine amounted to eighteen liters of barley per day, a considerable outlay compared to the daily remuneration of an adult worker of six liters. A monthly fee of 10 shekels of silver would have been forbiddingly high for an adult worker with an annual income of 12 shekels. The leasing of concubines was clearly an upper-class pleasure.[146] Once more, resource polygyny was a correlate of wealth and status. We can only speculate that Persian domination may have reduced the ability of Babylonians to acquire surplus women, thereby driving up the cost of polygyny.

2.4.2. Egypt. In Egypt, most of the evidence of resource polygyny dates from the period of imperial expansion during the New Kingdom. Royal polygamy is attested only from the New Kingdom on but may, of course, have existed before. In that period, the consorts of the pharaoh were divided into the "principal wife" and the supplementary "king's wives," the latter differentiated into royal and nonroyal spouses.[147] Again, imperial success promoted polygyny. The practice of diplomatic marriages with foreign noblewomen peaked in the New Kingdom; thus, in addition to his principal wife, Amenophis III kept two princesses from Syria, two from Babylonia, one from Arzawa; and two from Mitanni (one of the last two having being accompanied by no fewer than 317 ladies-in-waiting).[148] Amenophis II brought from Palestine to Egypt 232 sons but 323 daughters of princes, plus 270 female court singers.[149] In an extant letter, Amenophis III informs a vassal prince in Palestine that he has dispatched an officer "to fetch beautiful women" for the pharaonic court, urging him to "send very beautiful women, but none with shrill voices."[150] The most conspicuous case by far is that of Ramses II, who is known to have fathered approximately ninety sons and daughters.[151] However, the recent discovery of the labyrinthine tombs of the sons of Ramses may raise this tally even further. The royal women were housed in harems, an institution attested since the Old Kingdom.[152]

The spread of polygyny beneath the royal level is difficult to determine. Many documents are ambiguous, making it hard to decide whether multiple wives associated with individual men were held simultaneously or serially. Pertinent evidence is available from the Old Kingdom on.[153] In a survey of twelve cases from the Middle Kingdom, one scholar concludes that "it is likely that we should recognize the limited existence of polygamy in the official classes of the Middle Kingdom."[154] Although some of these wives may have been partners in consecutive monogamous unions, examples such as the tomb of Mery-'aa from the First Intermediate Period, which identifies his six wives, make it hard to accept that this interpretation should always be preferable to the view that some unions were in fact polygamous in nature.[155] Robins cautiously suggests that "it seems possible that among the elite at least, the taking of more than one wife may have occurred but was not particularly common."[156] Commoners, as usual, must ordinarily have been monogamous.[157]

In any event, formal polygamy was not the only option. Though concubines are difficult to identify terminologically, they undoubtedly existed in upper-class circles.[158] In some tomb chapels of the Eighteenth Dynasty, children appear who were borne by women other than the wife. Slave women were available for sexual relations. In one text, a son specifically asserts that he did not have sexual intercourse with the female servants of his father; it appears to have been his respect for the prerogatives of his father that made his restraint noteworthy. Even in the absence of clearcut evidence, it seems plausible to conclude that illegitimate children arising from such unions did not normally inherit.[159]

2.4.3. Persia. The Persian Empire of the Achaemenid dynasty (sixth to fourth centuries B.C.E.) exceeded all previous Near Eastern empires in terms of size and power (see chapter 3). In later centuries, the Parthian Arsacid dynasty (third century B.C.E to third century C.E) and the Persian Sasanid dynasty (third to seventh centuries C.E) managed to maintain significantly smaller but nevertheless far-flung supra-ethnic polities. These three successive "Persian empires" (not counting the interlude of the Macedonian-run Seleucid kingdom) provide ample evidence of the traditional link among imperialism, despotism, and differential reproduction. Cultural institutions favored polygyny: Mazdean ("Zoroastrian") religion was not opposed to multiple marriage or concubinage.[160] Late Pahlavi texts picture polygynous elite households, "great houses bustling with women and fast chariots, with spread-out rugs and piled-up cushion heaps."[161] According to *Yasht* 17.10, "the women are sitting on the lovely couch with the cushions; they adorn themselves with clips, with square ear-rings and a necklace decorated with gold: 'When will the master come to us? When will we have the pleasure of experiencing love with our bodies?'"[162] Late traditions even credited Zardusht/Zoroaster himself with three wives.[163]

The polygynous marriage and mating customs of the Achaemenid kings are particularly well attested.[164] The multiple marriages of Darius I may primarily have served political purposes.[165] Later on, Artaxerxes I had seventeen sons, five of whom are known by name; we also know the names of his queen and of three secondary wives.[166] Artaxerxes II was credited with no fewer than 115 sons by concubines in addition to his 3 legitimate sons.[167] Artaxerxes III was said to have killed fifty or eighty of his brothers when his father died.[168] According to various Greek authors, large numbers of concubines, supposedly numbering into the hundreds, lived at the royal court.[169] The sexual component of their duties was no secret; described as the most beautiful women of Asia, they participated in feasts and hunts and guarded the king's sleep at night. According to one source, every night the king chose one of them as his consort.[170] These harems were considered considerable assets, and physical proximity was valued: thus, after Darius III's defeat at Issos, Alexander was able to capture large numbers of royal women who had accompanied the king on his campaign.[171] Similar retinues are attested for Sasanian kings: Odaenathus of Palmyra was said to have captured the "concubines" of Shapur, and Galerius the "wives" of Narses.[172]

Briant and Brosius argue that many of these women, of foreign descent but apparently of high social rank, had been captured during military campaigns and transferred to the palaces.[173] After the defeat of the Ionian uprising, "the most beautiful girls were dragged from their homes and sent to Darius's court."[174] What might otherwise be dismissed as Greek fabrication is corroborated by a report in a Babylonian chronicle that after the sack of Sidon in 345–344 B.C.E., Artaxerxes III transferred to Babylon large numbers of captive women, who "entered the palace of the king."[175] The romantic tale of Esther, set under Xerxes I, is also premised on the notion that imperial power and despotism translates to reproductive opportunities:

> Let beautiful virgins be selected for the king, and let the king appoint commissioners in all the provinces of his kingdom to gather together every beautiful young virgin to the acropolis of Susa, to the house of the women under the authority of Hegai, the king's eunuch who is in charge of the women; and let him give them their beauty treatment. (Esther 2.2–3)

While this may seem like a fairy-tale out of *The Thousand and One Nights*, Briant reminds us of the equivalent practice of the Chinese Tang emperors, who levied levy tribute in the form of young women and had attractive candidates gathered by their agents throughout the empire.[176] The collection of *manacona* in the Inca Empire provides another parallel (see section 2.2). The correlation between harem size and imperial power still obtained in the late Sasanian period: Xusraw II, arguably the wealthiest Sasanid king, could be credited with 12,000 women or, alternatively, with 3,000 concubines and thousands of female servants and musicians.[177] The historical tradition also reflects the considerable demand for eunuchs created by huge royal harems. Thus, five hundred castrated boys were reportedly included in Babylonia's annual tribute to the early Achaemenid court.[178] At the end of the fifth century B.C.E., when the rebellious city of Calchedon on the Bosporus was punished by mass castration of the local boys, the victims were subsequently sent to King Darius II.[179]

From the Achaemenid to the Sasanian periods, polygyny was practiced on a proportionately smaller scale among the ruling elites. According to Herodotus, "every man has a number of wives, and a much greater number of concubines," a claim later echoed by Strabo concerning the Parthians, who "marry many wives and keep at the same time a number of concubines, for the sake of having many children."[180] While this scenario of universal polygyny cannot be taken at face value, it may well be representative of privileged members of Iranian society.[181] Persian nobles, especially satraps, imitated royal polygynous custom.[182] Surenas, the victor of Carrhae, was said to have been accompanied by two hundred carts for his concubines.[183] Most of the evidence comes from the Sasanian period. Ammianus offers a slightly less indiscriminate account: while the Persians of his day had numerous concubines, they contracted few or many marriages "according to their means" (Amm. 23.6.76).[184] In reality, resource inequality must have prevented most Persians from establishing polygynous households. The critical variable of wealth appears to be alluded to in a passage in the *Frahang i Oim*, envisaging someone "with a co-wife, he who has a fortune."[185] Only Sasanian nobles were probably regularly polygamous,[186] even keeping their own harems (*shabestan*). Technically, polygamy was legal in the Sasanid period.[187] Sasanian law reckons with one or two principal wives (the latter in separate households) and secondary wives.[188] As usual, only the principal wife or wives and their children could inherit. The lesser co-wives included slaves and war captives. This nexus between military success and polygyny is already in evidence in the Achaemenid period: a woman from Kos who defected to the Greeks after the Persian defeat at Plataea had reportedly been turned "by force" into the concubine of the Persian noble Pherendates, and the Persian Autophradates was said to have acquired a Macedonian woman in a similar way.[189]

Literary critics and cultural historians weaned on deconstructions of "othering" and diatribes against the perils of "orientalism" will be skeptical of my ostensibly uncritical use of Greek references to Persian polygyny as evidence for social history. It is true that the archetypal motif of the woman-grabbing enemy goes well with the caricature of debauched despots surrounded by harems and slavish courtiers. These features are indeed familiar ingredients of the "orientalist" vision, which can be traced back to Ktesias and his tales about the Achaemenid court.[190] As I will show (section 3), for the Greeks of the classical period, not only despotism but also polygyny were marks of the "barbarian." According to a recent critic, the Roman literary tradition of the Parthians—aligned with the Medes/Persians of the Greek sources—constructed the Orient as a "märchenhafte Gegenwelt," pervaded by oriental despotism, fabulous wealth, extravagant luxury, effeminate lifestyle, and unbridled sexuality, as expressed in polygamy.[191] And, indeed, we would be ill advised to accept any of the passages of classical literature referred to earlier as unbiased or reliable. Likewise, it does not matter that the ancient tradition is consistent over space and time: after all, this might simply reflect the persistence of successful clichés. What does matter, however, is the match between the Greco-Roman sources and primary Near Eastern evidence on the one hand (sections 2.4.1–3) and the former and comparative evidence from other despotic empires on the other (sections 2.2–3). These convergences suggest that significant structural properties of the putative oriental counterworld constructed by Mediterranean authors coincide far too closely with information transmitted from within these and comparable societies to have been "constructed" from scratch or distorted beyond recognition.[192] Rather, Greek and Roman authors are likely to have situated their accounts within a real-world framework of Near Eastern despotism, rigid hierarchy and social stratification, and concentration of material and sexual resources at the top of the social pyramid, which could then be embellished for increased entertainment value and harvested for moralizing or xenophobic value judgments.[193] Therefore, "outside" literary references to differential reproduction in the Persian empires are of illustrative value inasmuch as they are compatible with independent "inside" evidence, even if individual episodes or details are distorted or invented.

Incidentally, the Sasanian evidence casts light on the social tensions associated with reproductive inequality. It seems that despite the ongoing appropriation of foreign women, elite polygyny skewed reproductive opportunities to such an extent that marriageable women were lacking in the lower classes.[194] Poor Persians must have been traditionally monogamous,[195] but sometimes not even that. In the 490s C.E., King Kavadh, then an inexperienced teenager, tried to enforce communal access to women. His efforts appear to have been directed against the aristocracy, seeking to dilute aristocratic lineages.[196] In this context, he may also have passed a law limiting the accumulation of women in noble harems (excluding his own).[197] As a result, he was deposed by his nobles and restored only with foreign help. In the 530s, Mazdak, a religious and social reformer, went a step further by preaching community of women and property in general.[198] The tradition, confused as it is, suggests that Mazdak did not aim for abolition of private property or the family, only for redistribution, claiming that "whoever had a surplus in respect of landed property, women or goods had no better right to it than anyone else."[199] Women were clearly seen as property, unjustly concentrated in the hands of the few. Crone may be right to hold that Mazdak's goal was "not simply that women hoarded in princely harems should be redistributed,"[200] but this demand provided a starting point that proved appealing to the underprivileged masses. King Xusraw I had to crush the resulting popular movement with great bloodshed. This episode highlights the precarious nature of the balance between fertility maximization among the ruling class and the need to share fitness benefits with subordinates. In the case of the late Sasanian Empire, reproductive benefits accruing from imperial expansion and exploitation appear to have been monopolized by the elite and, one suspects (though no evidence is available), essential helpers, such as the military, whereas even in Persian society proper, commoners found themselves at the wrong end of transfers of reproductive capacity.

2.4.4. Imperialism and Differential Reproduction. All the major states reviewed in section 2.4 shared cultural and legal institutions that facilitated the translation of cultural success—imperial power and wealth—into reproductive success. One might be tempted to argue that these institutions enabled elites to engage in polygyny regardless of imperial success. However, imperialism clearly affected the scale of reproductive inequality. While in the twelfth century B.C.E., long before the apogee of the Assyrian empire, the Assyrian king Ninurta-tukul-Ashur controlled about forty wives, the Sasanian king of kings Xusraw II could be credited with up to twelve thousand consorts.[201] As noted earlier, successful expansion increased the number of palace women in Mari from 44 to 232, whereas the rulers of the less powerful kingdom of Arrapha had to make do with a few dozen per palace. The most prolific Pharaoh, Ramses II, ruled at a time of almost unprecedented imperial expansion. The kings of Israel could be portrayed as moving from seven-plus wives under David to seven hundred under Solomon and back down to eighteen after the division of the realm. Similarly, the number of concubines attributed to Khmer rulers dropped from three to five thousand under the Angkorian empire to two to three hundred in the more modest postclassical period.[202]

This correlation between imperial and reproductive success is only dimly reflected in sources concerning the general population. Thus, it may or may not be coincidence that polygynous relationships are not attested for the smallish Sumerian city-states of the first half of the third millennium B.C.E. but emerge in the Ur III period. It is also interesting to observe that in Old Babylonian and Old Assyrian law, as well as in Nuzi, bigamy is usually rejected in marriage contracts, unless justified by special circumstances, whereas documents from the more powerful Middle Assyrian Empire take the presence of two wives as a given, and that large numbers of wives and concubines could be ascribed to wealthy members of the still more powerful Persian, Parthian, and Sasanian empires.

Slavery was a major means of facilitating fitness transfers. Large-scale seizures of out-group women most immediately benefited the rulers, as with Zimri-Lim's request to his wife to select new inmates for his harem and the growth of his harem after the taking of Kahat; Shilhak-Inshushinak's appropriation of the wives and concubines of the king of Karindash; Asarhaddon's transfer of the Egyptian ruler's harem; Amenophis III's capture of Palestinian princesses and singers; and Darius I's and Artaxerxes III's seizure of the women of Miletus and Sidon, respectively. At the same time, and perhaps more important, slavery likewise enabled less exalted circles to partake in the sexual exploitation of empire. Regardless of constraints on the number of legitimate wives, the number of slave concubines was limited only by the resources of their owner (or lessee, as in Neo-Babylonian society). From the perspective of the owner, sexual relations with slave women had the advantage of leaving the heritable estate untouched; the offspring of such unions was not normally entitled to an inheritance. Thus, the sexual exploitation of slave women is consistent with the two-tier model of reproduction proposed in section 1.5: while the number of potential heirs and successors was limited through monogamous or bigamous marriage norms, congress with slave women ensured "marginal reproductive success" that was characterized by the dissociation of intergenerational gene and resource flows.

The observed association between the growth of disposable surplus among the beneficiaries of empire and the concomitant increase in reproductive opportunities is perfectly in keeping with Darwinian predictions. In view of the constraints put on male lifetime fertility by female reproductive physiology,[203] reproductive self-restraint in the face of growing resources would not have made sense for the beneficiaries of imperial exploitation. Rather, they needed to seek to increase their reproductive chances by balancing the requirements of long-term fitness preservation (by means of channeling heritable resources into a small number of "legitimate" children by one or a few principal wives) with the desire to maximize "marginal reproductive success" (by accumulating concubines as/or domestic slaves).

Mazdak's agitation illustrates the adverse consequences of disparities in the transfer flows of females and material resources. Thus, if privileged groups derive material benefits from imperial exploitation that are not fully matched by the centripetal transfer of dependent women from subject populations, increased elite wealth is likely to exacerbate reproductive inequality even within the imperial core population. Drawing on transferred resources, elites will then attract additional women from within the lower strata of their own society, thereby depriving low-status men of the in-group of mating opportunities. It appears that, in some cases at least, the availability of highly mobile mates, such as female slaves, was insufficient to relieve competitive pressures within the in-group. A fortiori, this unresolved tension between political factors favoring differential reproduction and the social need for cooperation was a particularly sensitive issue in less despotic and more egalitarian societies, to which I now turn.

3. Mediterranean Empires

3.1. Socially Imposed Monogamy

"Until the spread of Christianity, prescriptively monogamous societies were exotic exceptions."[204] From the onset of reasonably reliable written documentation, the citizens of Greek city-states and the Roman *res publica* are known to have contracted strictly monogamous marriages. The fact that, despite the recent surge of scholarly interest in Greek and Roman family history, this extraordinary circumstance is still taken as a given rather than recognized as a significant phenomenon in need of enquiry and explanation will best be taken as powerful evidence of the abiding conceptual and analytical isolation of ancient history as an academic subject.[205] It is equally striking that modern attempts to understand the unusually egalitarian nature of the early Greek *polis* or the strong cohesion of Roman Republican society appear completely oblivious to the social implications of monogamy. In actual fact, Greco-Roman monogamy was highly unusual. Greeks and Romans were not only surrounded by polygynous cultures—from the Celts, Germans, Thracians, and Macedonians to the Persians, Egyptians, and various North African peoples[206]—but eventually succumbed to the pressure of polygynous neighbors—the Macedonians in the case of classical Greece, the Germans in the case of the Western Roman empire, and the Arabs in the case of much of the Byzantine Empire.[207] In the Homeric epics, the Greeks even celebrated the feats of polygynous heroes set in their own past (see section 3.3).[208]

Whence monogamy? In general, we may distinguish between "ecologically imposed" and "socially imposed" monogamy, depending on whether it is ecological conditions or customs and laws that do or do not permit polygamy. Alexander and associates speculate that, even allowing for concubinage and extramarital sex, "the net effect of rules prescribing monogamy is almost certainly a significant depression in the variance of male reproductive success relative to that in stratified societies which do not prescribe monogamy."[209] In other words, socially imposed monogamy (SIM) interferes with the translation of cultural into reproductive success and therefore requires explanation. For instance, SIM has been argued to be an adaptive response to the increased importance of competition between coalitions, leveling the reproductive opportunities for men and thereby reducing competitiveness and increasing the likelihood of cooperation in the face of extrinsic challenges.[210] However, MacDonald rejects the assumption that complexity and success of states are predicated upon SIM; China is one of the most obvious examples to the contrary.[211] Unfortunately, his own survey of Greco-Roman SIM is descriptive rather than explanatory in nature. With respect to post-Mycenaean Greece, the evidence indicates "a rather sudden change to an egalitarian social system based on monogamy, endogamy, misogyny, and a deemphasis on heterosexual relationships," which had the effect of "deemphasizing sexual competition among males and promoting political cohesion and high levels of altruism."[212] It remains doubtful to what extent the loss of complexity in the

Dark Ages, commonly associated with the subsequent formation of the *polis*, can account for SIM: after all, even small and undifferentiated groups (such as Inuit or Yanomamö) are known to have practiced resource polygyny.[213] If anything, Roman SIM is even more difficult to explain, given that it survived major political, economic, and social change. Greeks and—for all we can tell—Etruscans were monogamous, but even if we allowed for significant formative Greco-Etruscan influences on early Rome, this would merely shift the question back in time.[214]

On a theoretical level, MacDonald contemplates "a role for coercive processes in which wealthy males are prevented by social controls from optimizing their reproductive success." Other factors may also have come into play: "In light of the preponderance of intensive polygyny among the stratified societies of the world, SIM must be seen as a low-probability outcome of social conflict in these societies, but one whose probability may well have been increased by ecological circumstances such as the diffuse, highly fragmented structure of the ancient Mediterranean city-states."[215] The question of whether SIM may have been adaptive in terms of inclusive fitness must remain open.[216] At any rate, this is not the place to explore this problem in any detail; I hope to return to this issue in a future study of Greco-Roman monogamy. For our present purposes, MacDonald's most relevant point is that, given abiding resource inequalities in Greek and Roman society, "from an evolutionary perspective, this acceptance of economic and social inequality is facilitated by sexual egalitarianism. Indeed, from an evolutionary perspective, economic inequalities that are not translated into reproductive advantages are of relatively little importance."[217] In other words, the strong principle of SIM *among citizens* may have fostered social cohesion in the absence of significant resource redistribution.[218] Herlihy also believes that SIM permitted "a paradoxical combination of principles, sexual equality and social inequality."[219] For that reason, it was essential for privileged segments of the population to be seen to be honoring this principle, even if it was only a façade.

In fact, from an evolutionary perspective, we would expect it to have been just that, a façade. Prescriptively monogamous societies are not necessarily effectively monogamous.[220] The concept of "effective monogamy" allows a distinction between the socially imposed marital pattern and the actual breeding pattern, which may be different.[221] Any union that is not based on "a prolonged and essentially exclusive mating relationship between one male and one female" is not "effectively monogamous."[222] "Effective monogamy" is now known to be uncommon in primate species.[223] It is generally assumed that extramarital sex (including concubinage) and remarriage would also skew reproductive success in prescriptively monogamous societies, albeit less so than in openly polygynous systems.[224] In view of the difference between monogamy as a sociographic unit, indicating the togetherness of two heterosexual individuals, and monogamy as the individual's mating strategy, indicating an exclusivity in reproduction, "partner-restricted behavior, if it is non-sexual, and especially parental roles, should not be used to identify mating systems (understood as procreation strategies)."[225] In either very simple or very modern societies with prescriptive monogamy, differential reproductive success is primarily a function of extramarital sex, often in the form of sperm competition between a long-term partner/provider and a casual mate.[226] As a consequence of the latter, "paternal discrepancy" (i.e., the frequency with which children are not the genetic offspring of their putative fathers) is conventionally put at 10 percent, and nonpaternity is now the leading cause of failure of genetic screenings. Published estimates of "paternal discrepancy" range from 1.4 percent for Caucasians in postwar Michigan and 2 percent for the !Kung bushmen to 30 percent in deprived urban areas of Britain.[227] In societies with socially and legally condoned mechanisms of extramarital fertilization by married men, by contrast, we may reasonably expect variance in male reproductive success to be significantly greater—and correlated with socioeconomic status—than in societies that effectively penalize extramarital sex by a variety of means (from the recognition of universal human rights and the suppression of slavery to legal obligations providing for paternity tests and alimonies). Hence, societies that benefit from the material exploitation of imperial possessions and accept various mechanisms of sexual exploitation outside marriage are the ones that are most likely to be effectively polygynous while upholding the principle of SIM. As I show in the following sections, Athens, Sparta, and Rome belong in this category of intensively polygynous imperialist powers.[228]

3.2. Monogamous Marriage and Polygynous Slavery

Greek and Roman laws envisaged severe punishment for sexual relations with someone else's wife. At the same time, concubinage with free or slave women (the former usually of noncitizen status) was commonly condoned. Sexual relations with one's own slaves, however, constituted the most convenient means of enhancing "marginal reproductive success." In prescriptively monogamous societies, the sexual exploitation of slaves takes on added importance. MacDonald accepts Hopkins's view that Roman slavery "allowed the elite to increase the discrepancy between rich and poor without alienating the free citizen peasantry from their willingness to fight in wars for the further expansion of the empire."[229] What neither of them considers, however, is that slavery was instrumental in stratifying reproductive success without violating the socially desirable principle of SIM. It has long been argued that in archaic Greece, and to a lesser degree in Rome, the development of slavery and freedom went hand in hand, in that the import of foreign labor in the form of chattel slaves reinforced notions of political and legal (if not economic) equality.[230] At the same time, the probable contribution of chattel slavery to formal (i.e., marital) sexual egalitarianism and thus to egalitarianism and social cohesion in general has been ignored. This is particularly surprising considering Finley's apt reference to "free sexual access to slaves which is a fundamental condition of all slavery."[231] In reality, chattel slavery was the answer not only to the cultural preference of elites for exploiting labor but also to their innate desire to convert the resultant surplus into reproductive advantage.[232]

Pertinent evidence of sexual relations between Greek and Roman masters and their female slaves will be reviewed later (sections 3.3 and 3.5). Here, I hope to reinforce my general point about the pervasiveness of this phenomenon with the help of comparative evidence from a more recent slave society in which racial prejudice, religious injunctions, and norms of social propriety made the sexual exploitation of slave women *less likely* than in any other major slave system on record: the antebellum South. Yet, despite these apparent constraints, the scale of this practice in the southern slave states can hardly be exaggerated. Gutman and Sutch estimate that in the 1850s, more than 4 and perhaps as many as 8 percent of black slaves had been fathered by whites. Miscegenation flourished despite racist contempt and the contemporary assertion that only lower-class whites engaged in sex with black slaves.[233] Steckel 1980 finds that miscegenation with slaves was positively correlated with the proportion of free men ages 15 to 49 in the county, with urbanism, and with city size; slave women without separate dwellings were more exposed to sexual advances than others. Thus, the incidence of sexual relations rose with increasing physical proximity of slaves and free men, especially their owners.

On his tour of Louisiana, Frederick Law Olmsted was told by a planter that "there is not a likely-looking black girl in this State that is not the concubine of a white man. There is not an old plantation in which the grandchildren of the owner are not whipped in the field by the overseer."[234] From the slave's perspective, "if God has bestowed beauty upon her, it will prove her greatest curse. That which commands admiration in the white woman only hastens the degradation of the female slave."[235] The results of Thomas Jefferson's relationship with Sally Hemings are now well known; van Buren's vice president, Richard Johnson, openly supported two children by Julia Chinn, a black slave.[236] The slaveowners' wives, while largely condemned to silence, were painfully aware of the situation.[237] As Mary Boykin Chesnut wrote in her famous diary on March 14, 1861,

> Like the patriarchs of old, our men live all in one house with their wives and their concubines; and the mulattoes one sees in every family partly resemble the white children. Any lady is ready to tell you who is the father of all the mulatto children in everybody's household but her own. Those, she seems to think, drop from the clouds.[238]

Looking back on her youth, Felton observed that "the crime that made slavery a curse, lies in the fact that unbridled lust placed the children of bad white men in slave pens, on auction blocks, and no regard was shown to parentage or parental responsibility in such matters." She also remembered planters who "defied the marriage law of the state by keeping up two households on the same plantation, one white and the other colored, and both women were afraid to make public outcry."[239] Well before that, a sister of the U.S. president James Madison is supposed to have said that "we southern ladies are complimented with the name of wives, but we are only the mistresses of seraglios."[240]

These sources confirm that in a slave society in which manumission had become extremely rare, the children of slaves by their owners were not normally freed or otherwise cared for. Even in Louisiana, a state with a stronger Romance tradition, owners only infrequently sought to provide for such offspring, and heirs usually opposed such attempts.[241] Finkelman argues that the fact that a slave woman's child followed her status may have been an incentive for men to have sex with her: "by predetermining the status of a possible offspring, white men might have been *less* concerned about the outcome of their sexual adventures."[242] This assumption is fully consistent with the principle of "marginal reproductive success" (section 1.5): sex with slave women increased inclusive fitness without attendant costs; on the contrary, slave-born children even augmented the father's estate. Hence, it is hardly surprising that more permissive slave societies witnessed sexual relations of this kind on an even grander scale. Genovese contrasts the comparative *restraint* of North American slaveholders, attributed to northern puritanism, with the behavior of their Portuguese counterparts in Brazil, who had a reputation for openly flaunting colored mistresses while married and where sons who had not sampled their fathers' slave girls found their masculinity called into question. Corresponding evidence from other slave systems could be added *ad libitum*.[243]

Greece and Rome were two of the very few genuine "slave societies" in history.[244] While slave ownership was disproportionately concentrated among the elites, it also spread into considerable parts of the general population. Hence, slavery served the double purpose of allowing privileged groups—the primary beneficiaries of empire—to accumulate human resources for the exploitation of labor and sexual capacity and of enabling subordinates to participate in this process in accordance with their personal means. Since in historical times Greek and Roman slaves were usually outsiders—members of other *poleis* or, more commonly, non-Greeks in the case of Greece, noncitizens and, increasingly, non-Italians in the case of Rome—large-scale slave ownership was to a large extent a function of imperial success.[245] In Spartan society, the wholesale de facto enslavement (or enserfment) of entire ethnic groups, classified as helots, served the same purpose (see section 3.3.3). In all those cases, whenever imperial success was contingent on cooperation among the citizenry and associated with the acquisition of slaves, we would expect reproductive inequality to have been shifted from the marital sphere into the grey area of "marginal reproductive success" predicated on the sexual exploitation of slave women.

3.3. The Greek World

3.3.1. Early Traditions: Women, War, and Colonization. With regard to the association between rank and military aggression on the one hand and reproductive success on the other, the social universe of the Homeric epics conforms extremely closely to Darwinian predictions. This is scarcely surprising, given that grand tales of this kind commonly focus on evolutionarily significant patterns of human interaction.[246] In the *Iliad*, the Trojans are portrayed as defending their city for the sake of their wives and children, while their women are targeted as booty by the Greek invaders. There is no reference to the actual or prospective sale of captured women; rather, they are earmarked for private use by their captors. Female rank is to be preserved even in bondage: while noblewomen are distributed among the Greek war leaders and turned into concubines (and are repeatedly assigned children by their new partners in the later mythological tradition), commoners keep on serving these ladies as before.[247] Access to reproductive capacity is invariably a function of rank, that is, cultural success: in the scene that triggers the central conflict of the *Iliad*, Agamemnon lets Achilles know that "I shall take the fair-cheeked Briseis, your prize, I myself going to your shelter, that you may learn well how much greater I am than you, and another man may shrink from likening himself to me and contending against me" (1.184–7). Later on, trying to lure Achilles back into action—that is, to ensure the cooperation of an indispensable subordinate—Agamemnon promises him "seven women of Lesbos... who in their beauty surpassed the races of women" (9.128–9) and, after the fall of Troy, will "let him choose for himself twenty of the Trojan women who are loveliest of all after Helen of Argos" (9.139–40). Meanwhile, Achilles already has other captive women at his disposal: "and a woman lay beside him, one he had taken from Lesbos, Phorbas's daughter, Diomede of the fair coloring; and in the corner, Patroklos went to bed; with him also was a girl, Iphis the fair-girdled, whom brilliant Achilles gave him, when he took sheer Skyros, Enyeus's citadel" (9.664–8).

Two features merit attention: these sex partners are invariably obtained through military success, and their allocation is governed by a redistributive system in which superiors, that is, high-status men, make use of their seemingly automatic, a priori claim to such captives in order to reward subordinates, that is, lower-status men whose cooperation is desired or required. Multiple layers of hierarchy are discernible (Agamemnon/Achilles, Achilles/Patroklos); women are assigned according to the status of their male recipients.[248] This rank-based prerogative is challenged by Thersites, reminding Agamemnon that "your huts are filled with bronze, and many women are in your huts, chosen spoils that we Achaeans give you first of all, whenever we take a citadel" (2.227–8). His reproach not only confirms the posited principle of a priori high-status privilege but also casts light on the tension between the leaders' desire to increase their inclusive fitness and the reluctance of subordinates to forgo fitness benefits.

As a consequence, it is only logical that individual leaders are endowed with multiple mates. Next to their *alochos* (the commonest term for the legitimate wife), several of them keep one or more additional women as wives; examples include the Trojan king Priamos, with three wives, and Telamon and Oileus. In addition, concubines (*pallakes*) produce illegitimate children.[249] In the *Odyssey*, Odysseus makes up a story that he is the son of a rich man who had sons with his legitimate wife, while Odysseus was borne by a bought *pallakis*, and that, after the father's death, the sons kept most of the estate, giving him just "a house and little else" (14.199–214). Once more, we encounter the familiar motifs of the association of wealth and polygyny and of the concurrent desires to improve inclusive fitness through estate preservation and to branch out into "marginal reproductive success." Slave women are freely accessible to their owners: Laertes refrained from sexual congress with his female slave "for he shunned his wife's wrath."[250]

Considering the considerable difficulties of explaining the emergence of SIM in the Greek *polis* (discussed in section 3.1), it would be helpful if we were able to determine whether or in which ways "Homeric society" reflects historical conditions.[251] The same is true for quasi-mythological traditions concerning early Greek colonization. According to what appear to be two aitiological myths handed down by Herodotus, early Greek migrants operated in a "Homeric" mode. In one case, the Ionians, when they took over Miletus, killed the native Carian men but took their women to wives; in another, the Lemnians raided Attica, seized Athenian women, and kept them as concubines, producing rich progeny.[252] Stories like these raise genuine historical questions: did Greek colonization entail the violent appropriation of non-Greek women and/or contribute to reproductive inequality in the target regions, and did it increase the reproductive success of the migrants? If, as we must assume, founding expeditions were skewed in favor of men, where did their future wives come from? Jean Rougé, one of the few to address this important issue, argues that intermarriage with locals must have been common all over the Mediterranean during the archaic period.[253] However, it is far from obvious that local women were readily available, especially since some—probably most or all—populations in the target areas would have practiced some form of resource polygyny. In a highly fragmentary passage, Archilochos seems to claim that when the Parians wrested control of Thasos from the native Thracians, they took native women as their wives.[254] The reproductive implications of the subjugation of native populations by Greek settlers are worth considering.[255] And, even in cases of peaceful interaction or fusion, the occupation of fertile land by Greek settlers and their other resources may have attracted local women at the expense of low-status local men, heightening existing reproductive inequality.[256] Thus, even in the absence of imperial structures, once Greek settlements had been firmly established, male colonists were likely to have enjoyed an edge in competition for local sex partners. The slave trade could only have widened this inequality.

It may not be entirely coincidental that the archaizing motif of "tribal-style" military action for the express purpose of forcibly obtaining female mates repeatedly resurfaces in both Greek and Roman historiography. Herodotus treats his audience to the tale of how soldiers from Chios, retreating after a defeat at the hands of the Persians, entered the territory of Ephesos after dark when the local women were celebrating a religious holiday in the fields and were attacked and killed by the Ephesians, who "at once supposed them to be brigands who were after their women."[257] The most famous incident of this kind is the mythical "Rape of the Sabine Women," when the all-male citizens of newly founded Rome staged a festival to lure young women from the surrounding communities into their city, then seized and turned them into their wives.[258] Ancient authors even fabricated a mirror image of this momentous "event": thus, after the Gallic sack of Rome several centuries later, their Latin neighbors are made to attack the weakened city, demanding the surrender of a substantial number of women for marriage in return for peace.[259] In view of the unquestioned real-life custom of appropriating the female members of defeated populations, the male anxieties and desires reflected in all the accounts surveyed in this section may well be grounded in subliminal appreciation of the fitness implications of territorial conflict.

3.3.2. Athens. In historical times, Athenian citizens married monogamously. By the fifth century, monogamy had come to be considered a quintessentially Greek custom. Monogamy among an alien culture merited notice (as for instance with Herodotus's questionable claim that the Egyptians practiced monogamy, "as the Greeks do"), whereas polygamy was regarded as unhellenic.[260] Euripides ascribes bigamy to the Thracians, rejecting it as a "barbarian" custom: "we count it shame that over two wives one man hold wedlock's reins."[261] Overt polygamy was not only un-Greek but also inequitable, the mark of tyranny: Dionysios I had multiple wives.[262] Tyranny is portrayed as sexual as well as political in nature; nonconsensual intercourse in particular was seen as hybristic, a dishonoring act if performed among citizens.[263] The imperial Roman biographical tradition was to produce a plethora of variations on that irresistible theme (see section 3.5.3).

However, Athenian men were expected only to marry, not to mate, monogamously. Husbands were not required to be faithful to their wives. Just as in Assyria or Rome, married men were incapable of committing adultery vis-à-vis their wives. In keeping with the axiom of estate preservation through the limitation of legitimate heirs, only proper wives were ordinarily capable of producing legitimate children. Marital monogamy made this principle easier to uphold than in polygamous societies.[264] The only known exception to this rule dates from the late fifth century B.C.E., when male citizens were temporarily permitted to father legitimate offspring with a second woman in addition to with their own wives. This procedure, which may well have entailed bigamous marriage, was probably an emergency measure prompted by the catastrophic casualties of the Peloponnesian War.[265] It deserves attention that the only men reputed to have availed themselves of this concession were celebrities who moved in elite circles, from the super-wealthy Kallias to Euripides and Socrates. From a Darwinian perspective, it would not be surprising if men of means were the main beneficiaries of this exceptional relaxation of SIM.

Extramarital sexual relations resulting in illegitimate offspring permitted propertied Athenian to enhance their "marginal reproductive success." This could be achieved in any of three overlapping legally and socially condoned ways: concubinage, prostitution, and domestic slavery.[266] The best-known passage on this subject may well engage in special pleading (and eschews reference to sexual intercourse with those domestic slaves who are not subsumed under concubines) but nevertheless suggests the simultaneous presence of different layers of sexual relations in the lives of married men: "*Hetairai* we keep for pleasure, concubines (*pallakai*) for the daily care of our bodies, and wives (*gynaikes*) to procreate children legitimately and to have a trusty guardian of the things inside."[267] A citizen could have a concubine (*pallake*)—a loosely defined category perhaps best summed up as "kept women"—instead of or in addition to a wife.[268] Men associated with free concubines "with a view to free children."[269] Free women of this kind would be either citizens or resident aliens (metics). Concubinage normally implies co-residence.[270] Some—a few, many?—concubines were slaves, and sometimes war captives.[271]

Evidence of stable polygynous relationships involving a man, his wife, and one or more concubines is scarce. As is to be expected in a prescriptively monogamous society, and even more so in a participatory democracy wary of upper-class rule bending, it was considered socially desirable to keep up appearances. Married Athenian citizens could maintain sexual relations inside and outside the household as long as some basic rules of social propriety were observed with respect to the feelings and standing of the legitimate wife. Thus, wives and courtesans were expected to be kept physically apart, as with Mantitheus's two partners in separate households in Demosthenes 39 and 40. According to another speech, Lysias refrained from bringing two *hetairai* to his own house "out of respect for his wife" and other coresident female kin but lodged them with an unmarried friend of his.[272] A very wealthy old man abandoned his family for one of his slaves, a former prostitute, who managed a tenement block for him.[273] Even in the absence of a legitimate wife, plural relationships called for physical separation: the successful orator Hyperides (then apparently widowed) reportedly kept three mistresses in separate homes in different parts of Attica.[274] Failure to show a minimum of consideration invited censure: thus, Alcibiades' wife was alleged to have tried to divorce him for bringing free and slave *hetairai* into their house.[275] In Sophocles' *Trachinian Women*, Deianeira allows her husband license outside the home but finds cohabitation with other women in the marital household unbearable.[276] It was the violation of etiquette, not the fact of polygyny as such, that constituted transgressive behavior, and it is primarily in regard to social protocol that Athenian polygyny differed from resource polygyny in other societies.[277]

For wealthy Athenians, this must have been a small price to pay, all the more so as these norms of propriety did not necessarily impair "marginal reproductive success." The passages cited in the previous paragraph confirm that in the same way as in all other cultures under review, and in keeping with the Darwinian correlation of cultural with reproductive success, men of property were most likely to engage in this kind of resource polygyny. Further evidence could be added: in one speech, for instance, another wealthy man was reputed to have freed one *hetaira* and given another one away while he was married.[278] Davidson is surely right to conclude that "it was considered a mark of prosperity or of extravagance to keep more than one woman."[279]

Moreover, while open concubinage in the joint household of a married couple was deemed inappropriate, casual sex with domestic slaves did not occasion similar opprobrium.[280] It is unremarkable that these relations hardly ever surface in Athenian oratory: relationships with slaves were of no consequence. Even so, Lysias once hints at the tensions in a household where the wife suspected her husband of having sex with a domestic slave woman: "so that you may have a try here at the little maid (*paidiske*)—once before, too, when you were drunk, you pulled her about."[281] The jealousy of wives who suspect the existence of sexual relations between husbands and slaves is a recurrent motif.[282] On the stage, Aristophanes could present this kind of affair as an ordinary occurrence.[283] Only comparative evidence (see section 3.2) is capable of conveying an impression of the probable scale of this practice. Incidentally, one of the numerous divergent theories seeking to explain Pericles's citizenship law of 451–450 B.C.E. reckons with significant transfers of the offspring of masters and slave women into the citizen population. From that time on, only the children of an Athenian father and anAthenian mother were admitted to citizenship.[284] Walters speculates that previously, sons of masters by slaves had been presented as legitimate and enrolled as citizens.[285] In this connection, it may be relevant that Aristotle knew of the enfranchisement of mixed citizen-slave offspring in other Greek *poleis*.[286] If citizens had once indeed had the option of selectively legitimizing children fathered with slave women, this would merely have given them more leeway in defining the boundaries between "official" and "marginal" reproductive success.[287] Slaveowners had no obligations to such progeny. Dio of Prusa regaled his audience with the story of one of Kallias's sons, who was accompanied on a military campaign by a slave his age who looked so much like him that when the slave returned to report the son's death, he could claim to be the son himself and lay claim to his estate. The logical implication that this doppelgänger slave was in fact likewise Kallias's son did not have to be made explicit: in the same speech, Dio observed that many Athenians had sexual relations with their slave women, some secretly, others openly.[288]

To a large extent, commercial prostitution also relied on slavery.[289] Davidson describes the archaeological remains of an Athenian brothel with at least twenty rooms, inhabited by what appear to have been foreign slaves from Thrace, Anatolia, and Syria. The discovery of more than one hundred loom-weights in the same building shows that sexual exploitation and forced manual labor went hand in hand; the combination of prostitution and weaving must have increased overall productivity.[290] *Ergasterion*, factory, was also a word for brothel. Outside brothels and the streets, prostitutes, *hetairai*, were also available at upper-class symposia. Although Plato and Xenophon, our main sources for the Greek symposion, "take great pains to avoid intimations of fornication" (though rather clumsily in the case of the latter author) and never mention *hetairai* among the dinner guests, in other sources the presence of hired women was commonly associated with those events.[291] In Dover's words,

> No danger attended the sexual use of women of servile or foreign status, whether they were prostitutes owned by a brothel-keeper, *hetairai* who were looking for long-term dependence on agreeable and well-to-do men, concubines owned by the user himself or lent by a relative or friend, or dancers, singers, or musicians whose presence at men's drinking parties exposed them to importuning, mauling, kidnapping (an occasion for fighting between rival males), temporary hire, or straightforward seduction enjoyed by both partners.[292]

Just observes that, while "the evidence for all manner of sexual licence outside the home with women of non-citizen status is overwhelming," "if chastity was a virtue, it was a virtue reserved for the wives and daughters of Athenian citizens."[293] Thus, extramarital sex was contingent upon access to noncitizen women. At the same time, it required financial resources: multiple concubinage and attendance at symposia in particular must have been privileges of elites. In other words, polygyny-bearing structures were firmly entrenched in Athenian society, and the proximate determinants of reproductive success (i.e., mating opportunities) were, as usual, correlated with cultural success (i.e., socioeconomic status).

This raises the question of whether differential reproduction was facilitated by imperial expansion and exploitation. Kurke links the emergence of the *hetaira* (as opposed to the common prostitute) to the generation of new wealth through long-distance trade and monetization in the sixth century B.C.E.[294] Further economic expansion would likely have increased the scale of polygynous relationships. There can be no doubt that in the fifth century B.C.E., Athens benefited, in material terms, from its naval empire.[295] The concentration of imperial revenues served to attract foreigners, who took up residence in Attica as metics, and enabled the acquisition of slaves. Prostitution had an urban bias,[296] and imperial success advanced Athens' development as a major city. War captives often ended up in brothels.[297] Moreover, successful warfare provided additional mating opportunities even for subelite men; apart from rape, soldiers must often have been able to obtain slaves they could not otherwise have afforded.[298] Even so, leaders may again have benefited more than others.[299] The seizure of land from defeated enemies or rebellious allies and the foundation of substantial colonies of citizens in such territories[300] provided both direct access to the female members of subordinate or, at any rate, comparatively less privileged populations and enhanced indirect access to mates by way of the assignation of new resources, such as land (allowing lower-class citizens to join the hoplite class). On all these issues, our sources are virtually silent. The main exception is Aeschines' claim that his opponent Timarchos, as *archon* of Andros (an island under Athenian control), "in his treatment of the wives of free men showed such licentiousness as no other man ever did."[301] While the truth of this allegation perforce remains doubtful, it suggests that Aeschines—and his audience—appear to have regarded sexual exploitation as a credible instance of maltreatment of Athens' subjects. One late and expressly fictitious character, the Athenian citizen in Terence's comedy *Phormio* who is married in Athens but takes another legitimate wife in Lemnos, gives us an idea of the presumably more impressive opportunities afforded to the mobile and aggressive Athenian citizenry of the bygone imperial period.

As we have seen in section 2, in premodern societies, imperial success commonly increases reproductive success among the main beneficiaries of imperial exploitation. In the case of despotic societies, these benefits are to a large extent monopolized by rulers and nobles and only to varying but invariably limited degrees percolate into society at large. As a result, imperial success tends to raise variance in male reproductive success. In democratic Athens, we might expect the resultant inequalities to have been less pronounced than in more traditional sociopolitical formations. SIM had the effect of channeling the resources of high-status men into relations with out-group women of free alien or unfree status. At the same time, ordinary citizens would have expected to partake in extramarital reproductive opportunities. While this relationship is impossible to substantiate on the basis of primary evidence, it seems reasonable to assume that, on average, Athenian citizens enjoyed fitness benefits they would have lacked in the absence of successful imperial exploitation. The allocation of land in subject territories must have raised the marriage prospects of previously underprivileged members of the citizen community, while the transformation of tribute into compensation for services must have raised the purchasing power of the citizen population of Attica, and especially of those residing in Athens, facilitating concubinage for married and unmarried men alike and supporting immigration-based professional prostitution. Last but not least, the spoils of empire may have been instrumental in preserving abiding inequalities in wealth in the face of political egalitarianism: as long as wide sections of the citizenry benefited from the exploitative opportunities of the Athenian empire, the elites were guaranteed enjoyment of their riches old and new, together with the attendant fitness advantages. Thus, in the final analysis, the principal beneficiaries of imperial success may have been high-status men who were able to maintain, or even raise, reproductive variance in an environment that was hostile to traditional modes of monopolization of political power.

3.3.3. Sparta. For many generations, Sparta had been the only major hegemonic power in Greece. Just like other Greeks, the Spartans practiced monogamous marriage.[302] Indeed, until King Anaxandrides was allowed to supplement his infertile wife with a second spouse, bigamy had supposedly been "unheard of in Sparta."[303] However, domination of the helot populations of Laconia and Messenia gave Spartan citizens sexual access to comparatively huge numbers of powerless subordinates.

Nothoi, bastards born "(out) of helot women," were presumably the illegitimate sons of Spartan citizens.[304] These children appear to have been identical with the *mothakes*, non-Spartiates reared together with legitimate citizen sons: Aelianus describes them as foster brothers of the sons of wealthy families, while Phylarchus claims that "the boys of citizen status each... make some boys their foster-brothers—some one, other two, and some more."[305] Of course, not all of these foster brothers need have been the biological half-brothers of the Spartiates' sons; even so, as Ogden points out, "systematic mass-generation of *nothoi* should not be ruled out."[306] Foster care along these lines was inevitably correlated with wealth, something that is made explicit by Aelian and also implied by Phylarchus. Hodkinson, while disputing the conventional identification of *nothoi* with *mothakes*, argues nevertheless that since *nothoi* could be reared in style only by propertied fathers, "the presence or absence of *nothoi* will have been a visible mark of differentiation among Spartiate families." This suggests that, to some extent, the prestige of citizen households was based on sexual relations between the household head and his female servants.[307]

Under those circumstances, the sexual exploitation of subject women facilitated resource polygyny,[308] deprived subject men of mating opportunities, and helped strengthen the system at the same time, given that these foster sons would perform military service alongside legitimate citizen offspring. Access to helot women enabled individual Spartiates to translate cultural success (i.e., material resources) into reproductive success, and, by inducting select bastard sons into the in-group, helped Spartan society as a whole to maintain control over its helot population and its network of foreign allies.

3.4. Hellenistic Empires

The polygamous habits of the kings of Macedon and several of the Diadoch empires highlight the fragility of SIM even in culturally "hellenized" environments. There can no more be serious doubt that the Argead kings of Macedon were traditionally polygamous but failed to establish clear hierarchies of wives and their sons.[309] In the light of comparative evidence, Ogden's suspicion that Macedonian rulers married many wives "'simply because they could" seems by far the most obvious explanation.[310] As we have seen, it is monogamy, not polygamy, that requires explication.

Philip II is known to have had eight wives.[311] In this regard, he could be distinguished from the Persian king Darius III only in that, unlike the latter, he "did not take his women to war with him."[312] His son Alexander eventually acquired four parallel wives: Barsine, the hellenized daughter of a Persian noble, in 332 B.C.E.; Roxane, a captive Bactrian noblewoman, in 327 B.C.E.; and Stateira, the eldest daughter of Darius III, and Parysatis, the youngest daughter of Artaxerxes III, in 324 B.C.E. In addition, he reputedly kept Darius III's 360 royal concubines for his own personal use.[313]

A number of the Macedonian rulers of the hellenistic successor kingdoms followed the example of Philip and his son.[314] Lysimachus was married to four women, and to at least two of them simultaneously. Ptolemy I had four known wives and was likewise known as a polygamist, as was Demetrius I Poliorcetes, with his eight known wives. Demetrius II Aetolicus also practiced polygamy; four of his wives are known, one of them a Thessalian war captive.[315]

Besides, more casual relations also resulted in offspring: Eumenes II may have fathered at least two sons with two different concubines.[316] Ancient source coverage of royal concubines is extremely uneven, and most remain unknown.[317] Even so, Ptolemy II is credited with eleven courtesans known by name, and Demetrius I with nine.[318] Problems of definition arise from the fact that "there were few absolute distinctions of status or profile between queens, wives, concubines and courtesans." Whenever the origin of royal consorts is known, it is almost always a city in Greece, and not normally Macedon itself. In the case of hellenistic kings, imperial wealth and success appear to have attracted high-status concubines.[319] That native women are hardly ever mentioned in this connection may be a result of the fact that only the most privileged partners of hellenistic kings came to be mentioned in the sources, and those were usually Greek. Moreover, local populations would probably satisfy demand at the lower rungs of the new ruling class.

Whether or to what extent Macedonian and Greek commoners from Egypt to Bactria sought to emulate the polygynous habits of their rulers remains unknown. Marriage contracts from the Egyptian chora forbid the husband to bring other women into his household or to keep a concubine, have children with another woman, or keep a separate household that his wife will not manage (presumably for a concubine; cf. section 3.3.2).[320] Since the state was unable to enforce legitimacy limitations, restrictions of this kind had to be stipulated in formal contracts.[321] The fact that, according to early Ptolemaic census documents studied by Clarysse and Thompson, immigrant families of Greek and Macedonian origin were more likely to own slaves than native Egyptian families underlines the superior socioeconomic status of many of these newcomers.[322] In view of the general correlation between resources and mating advantages, it is hard to imagine that these inequalities—which must largely have been the result of privileges conferred upon these immigrants whose presence was crucial in maintaining imperial control—did not translate to differential reproductive success.

3.5. The Roman Empire

3.5.1. Marriage and Concubinage. In Roman society, from the earliest recorded times, monogamy was mandatory.[323] In fact, polygamy appears to have been impossible even in theory: marriage with someone other than an existing wife caused the cessation of any existing relationship because it implied that the requisite marital consensus had come to an end.[324] Roman law and custom acknowledged quasi-marital relationships that did not legally count as marriage, that is, concubinage.[325] For us, the principal question is whether married Romans could also keep concubines during their marriages. Modern scholars have repeatedly affirmed as well as rejected this notion: in purely quantitative terms, the literature is split right down the middle.[326] There is no compelling reason to think that it was impossible, or unheard of, to take a concubine without repudiating the current wife.[327] Some legal provisions suggest that, at the very least, parallel relationships were considered an option that had to be reckoned with. According to the grammatician Festus, "the ancients rightly labeled her a *paelex* who married a man who [already] had a wife," apparently envisioning her as the Roman equivalent of the long-term Greek concubine (*pallake/pallax*).[328] In the third century c.e., Papinian referred to a marriage contract that obligated one husband to pay his wife a penalty if he resumed relations with a former concubine,[329] an arrangement that is reminiscent of the Ptolemaic texts mentioned earlier (section 3.4). Although in the sixth century c.e. Justinian held that, in keeping with "ancient law," husbands were forbidden to keep wives and concubines simultaneously,[330] we cannot be sure just how "ancient" this prohibition actually was, and if it predated the third century c.e.. In any event, for all we can tell, parallel relationships with wives and concubines do not seem to have been common or socially acceptable.[331] Literary allegations of polygyny among married men or multiple concubinage are now usually rejected as hostile rhetoric.[332] Epigraphically attested quasi-marital unions between one man and different wives that could be interpreted as polygynous may well have been successive rather than parallel relationships, even if this is not made explicit in these texts.[333] In most cases, a formal association with a concubine was established instead of, and not in addition to, a legitimate union.[334] For wealthy Romans, concubinage served as a means of avoiding the fragmentation of estates and of preserving social disparity: concubines were not expected to produce legitimate children and heirs.[335] Thus, in Darwinian terms, Roman concubinage was designed to contribute to "marginal reproductive success" by creating offspring that was excluded from primary paternal investment. While concubinage facilitated the continued exploitation of former slaves—as concubines—it did not normally create polygynous relationships outside the sphere of slavery.[336]

3.5.2. Sex and Slavery. In the absence of polygamy or habitual polygynous relationships with wives and concubines, sexual access to chattel slaves constituted the principal means of increasing male reproductive variance. In Gardner's pithy summary of the legal situation since Augustus, "sex with a slave counted, for a married woman, as adultery under the terms of the Julian law. For a man, sex with slave girls did not count." Various types of evidence leave little doubt that this situation was exploited widely.[337]

It is undeniably true that many of the literary references are satirical or moralizing in nature. Some make fun of it the practice: well-known examples include Horace ("When your organ is stiff, and a slave girl or young boy from your household is near at hand and you know you can make an immediate assault, would you sooner burst with tension? Not me. I like sex to be there and easy to get."), Juvenal

("I'll wager that you are one hundred percent a man. It's a bet. So will you confess, or must the torturer rack the truth from your slave girls?"), and Martial ("You know you were begotten by a slave, and you blandly confess it, Sosibianus, when you address your father as 'master,'" or, more extreme (1.84), "Quirinalis does not think he should take a wife, meanwhile he wishes to have sons; and he has discovered how to secure that object: he fucks slave girls, and fills his town-house and his rural estates with home-born slave-knights. A genuine *pater familias* is Quirinalis.").[338] Others simply take it for granted, as in Petronius ("what a master orders is not shameful") or in the Elder Seneca, according to whom unchastity was "a necessity" for slaves.[339] Plutarch stands out for his advice to the wives of slaveowners: "If a man in private life, who is incontinent and dissolute in regard to his pleasures, commits some peccadillo with a paramour or a slave girl, his wedded wife ought not to be indignant or angry, but she should reason that it is respect for her which leads him to share his debauchery, licentiousness, and wantonness with another woman."[340] Unique among the pre-Christian sources is a fragment of the mid-first-century C.E. Stoic philosopher Musonius Rufus criticizing the lack of restraint of "the man who has relations with his own slave girl, a thing which some people consider quite without blame, since every master is held to have it in his power to use his slaves as he wishes."[341] Much later, the Christian Salvian chastized provincial landowners for their sexual relations with their slave women: "When the head of the household behaves like the husband of the slave girls, his wife is not far removed from the status of a slave. And was there any wealthy Aquitanian who did not behave like that? Was there any whose promiscuous slave girls did not have a right to look on him as their lover—or their husband?"[342]

I quote these texts for three reasons. First, spin (and therefore critical literary exegesis) matters little, for, whatever the spin, the message is always the same: owners have sex with female slaves. Second, this message is highly consistent with comparative evidence from better documented slaveowning societies.[343] And, third, it is likewise highly consistent with less loaded statements in other Roman sources. When the slaveowner Larcius Macedo was thought dead, his apparent demise was noisily lamented by his slave *concubinae*.[344] Slaves had no legal recourse against the adulterous disruption of their quasi-marital unions with other slaves, presumably perpetrated by their owners.[345] The intention to marry one's own former slave justified her manumission before age 30 (the minimum age-limit set by the *lex Aelia Sentia*); the fact that a slave was the owner's biological child (*filius/filia naturalis*) activated the same exemption.[346] And, indeed, in some inscriptions, the owner of a slave is also the father.[347] *Filii naturales* of this kind are frequently referred to in Roman law: blood ties between owner and slave become a factor in legal discussions of manumission, damage assessment, and inheritance.[348] The legal anomaly that a slave woman's children were not included among her fruits (unlike in the case of livestock) made it easier for a putative owner/father to retain a child even if the mother was sold.[349] According to Ulpian, one might happen to inherit an estate comprising one's own biological father, mother, or brothers.[350] Such heirs must have have been the children of testators by their slave women. In his study of Roman wills, Champlin speculates that slaves instituted as heirs "may have had a sexual liaison with the testator" or "may have been an illegitimate child of the testator."[351] However, even though slaves and ex-slaves could be made heirs, this often involved adoption.[352] Slaveowners had no legal obligations to children they fathered with their own slaves. At the same time, they were free to choose to acknowledge, manumit, institute as heir, and adopt any of these children. In this way, Roman slaveowners retained the greatest possible degree of control over the allocation of their material resources: while they were unconstrained in disseminating their genes among their slaves, it was also left to them to decide whether or to what extent to match gene flow with the flow of paternal investment: in this regard, their options ranged from the sale of such offspring on one end of the scale to adoption on the other. In short, the Roman slave system optimized "marginal reproductive success." Syme notes the "singular dearth of evidence about aristocratic bastards," which he attributes to a pervasive code of silence.[353] This silence is best taken as powerful testimony to the masterful efficiency of the Roman elite in separating acknowledged from marginal progeny and in regulating paternal investment accordingly.

In her study of Roman polygyny, Betzig suggests that "slave women were kept to breed their masters' bastards." She also considers it possible that the Romans frequently freed slaves because they were often related to them and suspects biological ties behind owners' care for *vernae*, homeborn slaves.[354] Taken at face value, these may seem tall claims, and ones that are not testable against quantifiable evidence. Even so, the proposed link between freedom and consanguinity undoubtedly improves on earlier accounts of Roman manumission that take absolutely no account of the latter; Hopkins's narrow functionalist analysis is an obvious example.[355] As for Betzig's more far-reaching assumption that female slaves were owned for the purpose of procreation, it deserves notice that scholars have long been puzzled by the apparent paucity of activities performed by slave women, as opposed to their ostensibly more productive male counterparts.[356] Since female slaves cannot have been much less numerous than male slaves,[357] their sexual capacities may well have been of greater importance than is usually believed. Even so, the implication that slaves were purposely acquired as breeders, and in particular as breeders of their owners' illegitimate children, is impossible to substantiate. At any rate, the question of conscious motivation does not even have to enter the equation (cf. section 1.3). For that reason, I propose to restructure Betzig's hypothesis and rephrase it as follows: in Roman society, certain women bred their masters' bastards because they were slaves.

Owing to the mechanisms of the slave supply—producing balanced sex ratios for unfree births and low sex ratios for war captives and foundlings—many slaves were female; slave ownership was a function of wealth, that is, cultural success; in a society that prohibited polygamy and apparently discouraged polygynous concubinage, sexual access to slaves offered the quantitatively most important opportunity to increase male reproductive success; therefore, wealthy Roman men must have found it feasible to acquire substantial numbers of female slaves and intrinsically desirable to involve them in sexual relations. In elite households, where husband and wife were served by separate slave staffs, sexual encounters were easy both to engineer and to conceal. Once again, cultural success can reasonably be assumed to have raised variance in male reproductive success, in that "marginal reproductive success" was contingent on, and must have correlated with, the availability of material resources.

The sexual exploitation of female slaves in the context of domestic slavery was complemented by commercial prostitution, which was to a significant extent sustained by slavery.[358] Flemming argues that the clientele of brothels belonged to less privileged strata of society, often those who could not afford to keep slaves of their own. Urbanization facilitates prostitution: hence, the unusually high levels of urbanization in Roman Italy—triggered by imperial success—must have favored the spread of prostitution and enabled growing segments of the general population to participate. Unfortunately, the actual scale of urban prostitution has proven difficult to measure: estimates of the number of brothels in Pompeii, the only Roman city that is sufficiently well preserved to permit detailed examination, have recently dropped from several dozen to nine.[359] In principle, the growth of Roman slavery and Italian urbanization were both functions of imperial exploitation; thus, inasmuch as slavery and urbanization facilitated prostitution, Roman imperialism can be said to have boosted prostitution.

3.5.3. Despotism and Differential Reproduction. In the Roman literary imagination, one-man rule and despotic power are intimately associated with polygyny and the forcible accumulation of sex partners. A few salient examples will suffice to illustrate this point. Caesar had a reputation as a major womanizer; Augustus even "as an elderly man is said to have harboured a passion for deflowering girls, who were collected for him from every quarter, even by his wife"; Tiberius comes across as hopelessly debauched, abducting freeborn girls to corrupt them; Caligula reportedly likewise spoiled married matrons; Claudius is credited with insatiable sex drive and many affairs, and again, his wife, Messalina, procured mistresses for him; Nero put married women into brothels; Vespasian, in his role as a more restrained "good" emperor, kept several mistresses after the death of his principal freedwoman concubine, whereas his son Domitian, designated one of the "bad" emperors, constantly engaged in sexual activities, which he referred to as "bed-wrestling."[360] Commodus, also "bad," "herded together women of unusual beauty, keeping them like purchased prostitutes in a sort of brothel for the violation of their chastity"; in this way, he acquired three hundred concubines, "gathered for their beauty and chosen from both matrons and harlots."[361] Even the "good" emperor Pertinax, having at first dismissed Commodus's entourage, had many of them brought back "to administer to the pleasures of the old man." Elagabalus, beyond the pale even by the standards of "bad" rulers, "never had intercourse with the same woman twice except with his wife" and installed a palace brothel. In a more exotic flourish, he is also made to hitch chariots to women of the greatest beauty, driving them "usually himself naked."[362]

Asking "how much was the economic and political inequality in the Roman empire matched by reproductive inequality, or polygyny," Betzig makes much of these stories.[363] At first sight, her willingness to accept them as reliable evidence will seem naïve to the literary critic. Strictly speaking, her suggestion that the internal consistency of such anecdotes confirms their credibility remains a non sequitur: the reverse interpretation—that sexual conduct of this kind was a topos that could indiscriminately be ascribed to different individuals—seems at least as plausible. Then again, her point that the Roman biographical tradition tallies well with what is more reliably known about other premodern kings and emperors may carry greater force. The one thing we can be sure of is that Roman upper-class authors consistently associated the despotic use—for them, abuse—of monarchical power with promiscuity in general and with transgressive sexual behavior in particular. Thus, while reasonably "good" rulers (such as Caesar, Augustus, and Vespasian) are merely credited with strong sexual appetites and polygynous affairs, their "bad" counterparts are portrayed as violating social norms by compelling sex from nonconsenting free or even married women. From a Darwinian perspective, this explicit link between political inequality in its most extreme form and reproductive potential is in itself of considerable interest, given that it mirrors faithfully a fundamental principle of differential male reproductive success.[364] The close match between what Romans thought, or found expedient to claim, their rulers did and what we know rulers in more overtly polygynous cultures actually did is similarly striking (see sections 2.2–3).

Even so, it remains difficult to resolve the tension between these underlying realities and the creative power of literary representation.[365] For a literary critic, the actual conduct of Roman emperors may be of secondary importance or even irrelevant, and it is perfectly feasible to dissect the biographical tradition as a patchwork of complementary stereotypes that could be rearranged in a limited number of constellations in keeping with the biases of the observer. Intertextual relationships also come into play: when the Roman aristocrat Fabius Valens is said to have advanced "with a long and luxurious train of harlots and eunuchs" when he campaigned for Vitellius,[366] we are immediately reminded of such quintessentially "oriental" characters as Darius III or Surenas, the victor of Carrhae (see section 2.4.3). By contrast, the student of reproductive variance must address a more intractable—and less fashionable—question: does the literary tradition reflect existing mechanisms of creating mating opportunities for powerful Romans? Are we to believe that the Romans would have created lurid images of the reproductive consequences of despotic power that are both perfectly plausible in Darwinian terms and compatible with comparative evidence if they had lacked any practical experience with these consequences? Without proper contextualization, this common-sense "no smoke without fire" approach will seem simpleminded; when judged against the background of evolutionary theory and comparative data, it may become more respectable. However that may be, Roman elite authors inhabited a world of habitual sexual coercion; they were men for whom the sexual availability of disempowered women—slaves—was a given. In their search for a definition of the "tyrant," it seems to have been attractive to model the relationship between disempowered citizen/subject and ruler/master (*dominus*) on their own relationship with their slaves. Reducing respectable—that is, free and/or married women—to the status of sexually available slaves, the tyrant-emperor overturns the social order by restaging in the sphere of the free (and upper-class) citizenry patterns of interaction that are unquestioningly accepted between owners and slaves.

Given their immense wealth and the correspondingly large number of women at their disposal, from female slaves and freedwomen to women who would have been attracted by their status, Roman emperors cannot have found it difficult to mate with as many women as they wished.[367] Whether certain emperors chose to display their power by interfering with the reproductive rights of their subordinates—a central theme of the biographical tradition (and a motif also found in other cultures[368])—remains open to debate. In my view, this tradition is instructive for two different reasons. First, it shows that, with regard to the correlation between cultural success and the proximate determinants of reproductive variance, the literary imagination operates within a conceptual framework that puts heightened emphasis on critical evolved behavioral mechanisms. In this regard, Roman biography (just like Greek stories about tyrants) resembles Homeric myth (see section 3.3.1). And, second, by likening the sexual conduct of emperors to that of slaveowners, this particular strand of the literary tradition helps corroborate our model of chattel slavery as the primary means of translating cultural into reproductive success in societies that upheld SIM (see sections 3.2–3 and 3.5.2).

3.5.4. Imperialism and Mate Choice: The Roman Army. Besides the ruling elites and the metropolitan population, soldiers were the only substantial group of primary beneficiaries of Roman imperial success. We would expect their privileged position as essential subordinates to have enhanced their chances of reproductive success. Rape, prostitution, and access to newly enslaved women may count as obvious means to this end. Successful campaigning would inevitably have provided ample opportunity for sexual coercion.[369] For our present purposes, the crucial question is whether, thanks to successful imperialist ventures, Roman soldiers enjoyed higher reproductive success than they would have without joining up and/or than the male population of the subject regions in which these soldiers were active. While the first half of this question is impervious to empirical examination, the second merits further scrutiny. For the year 171 B.C.E., Livy reports that Roman soldiers on duty in

Spain had produced four thousand children with local women who had to be settled in a Latin colony.[370] In later centuries, when Roman soldiers served for extended periods of time, received regular pay, and were stationed mostly in the frontier zones of various provinces, inequalities in material resources and legal status were likely to benefit these soldiers in the competition for mates.

On a conventional estimate, the military absorbed between two-thirds and three-quarters of the imperial budget during the Principate.[371] Thus, in what must have been the single largest systematic transfer of resources in Western history prior to the modern period, much of the revenue extracted from a taxpayer base of maybe 60 to 70 million people was redistributed to some 350,000 to 400,000 professional soldiers. Annual average per capita GDP probably did not exceed HS 250, and many people were poorer than this; minimum per capita subsistence in the provinces may have been as low as HS 100 annually. By comparison, the base wage of a legionary stood at HS 900 in the first century c.e. and rose to HS 1,200 for much of the second century c.e.and more rapidly in the early third century c.e.. Officers were paid in fractional or full multiples of this base stipend; moreover, upon discharge, veterans could expect to receive a bonus equivalent to ten times their annual compensation in cash or land. In general, there can be little doubt that Roman soldiers were significantly better off than the commoner population of their areas of deployment.[372] Widespread slave ownership is indicative of the relative affluence of Roman soldiers.[373] The Roman military also generated significant demand for prostitutes.[374]

The prediction that this privileged access to material resources—as well as their citizenship status, which could eventually be passed on to their children—was likely to translate into reproductive success is consistent with primary evidence. Literary evidence adopts the usual moralizing slant, associating contacts between soldiers and local women with luxury and corruption, inevitably with dire consequences: the train of women, children, and slaves that supposedly slowed down Varus's doomed legions and the mingling of the proverbially spoiled Syrian army with the local population are just two examples.[375] Even so, these sources merely put a particular spin on what appears to have been common practice. Although from Augustus to Septimius Severus, soldiers could not legally be married, inscriptions document de facto unions, albeit to a much smaller degree than for civilians: fellow soldiers and freedwomen were more likely to dedicate epitaphs for active soldiers than freeborn (quasi) spouses.[376] Soldiers were able to designate their partners and children heirs in the same way as lawfully married men.[377] Even polygynous relationships may not have been unknown.[378] Three papyri from the late second century c.e. record the parallel presence of de facto wives and *focariae*, apparently additional concubines, of Roman soldiers.[379] Military diplomas for auxiliary soldiers took pains to prevent polygamy; some scholars have suggested that they may have reacted to actual attempts.[380] Polygyny is at least a possibility in the case of the will of a Roman naval veteran who gave freedom to two female slaves who also, together with the daughter of one of them, became his heirs; in the absence of a wife, it is tempting to identify these women as his concubines and the child as his own.[381]

More than half of all wives of auxiliary soldiers who are known from discharge diplomas had been acquired in the province of service.[382] The unions of legionary soldiers, who later on usually settled in the provinces where they had been on active duty, would have followed a similar pattern. Congress with Roman soldiers—be it as concubines or lawful wives—was a means of social mobility for native women, who benefited from their husbands' superior material resources and produced children who could themselves attain citizen status.[383] Such unions exemplify the Darwinian principle that female mate choice, governed by the desire to increase inclusive fitness, favors mates with above-average resources and the ability to improve the status of joint offspring, thereby contributing to inclusive fitness rather than merely raising lifetime reproductive success. In some cases, the resultant variance in male reproductive success—privileging Roman soldiers over local competitors—may have had a significant impact on the mating opportunities of the native male population.[384] There are two ways in which a hypergamous mating system may deprive a significant number of low-status men of reproductive opportunities: either the polygynous concentration of women in the hands of an elite reaches such a scale that it creates an absolute numerical lack of mates for low-status men or the introduction of additional high-status men into a given population is sufficiently massive to produce the same effect among locals. Even though slavery, sustained by long-range transfers of human chattels, will have attenuated the impact of the demands of soldiers on the local marriage market, in heavily militarized regions the presence of garrisons that were of substantial size in comparison to the civilian population may nevertheless have created serious imbalances. In Britain, for example, some 40,000 soldiers in their twenties and thirties would have faced between 200,000 and 300,000 women ages fifteen to thirty-five years. Even if some of these soldiers had been of local origin, perhaps one woman in ten had the option to choose a foreign soldier over a native mate or spouse. The potential for competitive pressure would have reached a comparable scale in other frontier zones, above all the valleys of the Rhine and the Danube.[385] These sexual repercussions of Roman imperialism have yet to be acknowledged in modern studies of provincial "Romanization."

3.5.5. Conclusion. Roman imperialism entailed the transfer of people and resources on a scale unprecedented in Mediterranean history. Millions of women were uprooted, enslaved, and moved, above all to Rome or to central Italy, to satisfy the demand of the slave markets. Hundreds of thousands of settlers and veterans were assigned agricultural land that had been taken away from its previous owners. During the imperial period, millions of recipients of public revenue were distributed across the empire as professional soldiers. These movements greatly enriched the ruling elite, known for concentrating in its hands ever larger amounts of cash, real estate, and slaves. The attendant inequalities in cultural success provided this elite with an enormous potential for reproductive success. Cultural institutions, primarily chattel slavery and secondarily concubinage, enabled the elite to convert this potential into tangible fitness benefits. Other segments of Roman society participated on a correspondingly smaller scale: while colonists, soldiers, and veterans had the chance to exploit their privileged access to resources at the local level for reproductive purposes, city-bound migrants gained access to extramarital sexual relations provided by prostitutes. The sexual exploitation of slaves—as concubines, domestic servants, or prostitutes—was pivotal to the transmutation of cultural into reproductive success. In turn, widespread availability of these slaves, staggered depending on status, was guaranteed by successful imperialism; not only were slaves obtained through warfare, but the transfer of material resources enabled the recipients, through their purchasing power, to maintain, expand, or even create market mechanisms that continued to provide new slaves and likewise enabled them to keep female slaves even when it may have been economically irrational to do so.

4. CONCLUSION: THEORY AND EVIDENCE

The central predictions generated by an evolutionary approach to ancient imperialism have been outlined in section 1.5 and need not be repeated here. By and large, the empirical evidence gathered and discussed in sections 2 and 3 tends to support these predictions. In all imperial systems under review, regardless of their marriage customs and constitutional properties, the appropriation of resources facilitated reproductive success. "Facilitated" is the critical term: for Darwinian theory to hold, it is behavior that is *by nature* associated with reproductive success—that is, heterosexual intercourse—that matters, not reproductive outcome as such. This definition has allowed us to include mechanisms such as prostitution in our discussion of fitness-enhancing mechanisms, regardless of whether congress with prostitutes (who may routinely have used contraceptives and abortifacients) actually resulted in conceptions or live births. Moreover, the crucial variable is inclusive fitness rather than lifetime reproductive success. Inasmuch as the future reproductive success of offspring is contingent on socioeconomic status, estate preservation is as important as offspring quantity. In all societies surveyed in this chapter, legal institutions permitted male beneficiaries of imperial success to strike a balance between these two critical variables. In polygamous systems, the designation of one or more wives as "principal" spouses made it easier to focus paternal investment on a fraction of one's gross legitimate offspring. Concubinage served the same purpose. Kautsky notes that in what he terms "aristocratic empires," the involvement of aristocrats with nonaristocratic women was the result of interclass marriage prohibitions that limited men's choices and encouraged them to seek sex without formal commitment.[386] Similar restrictions in Athens and Rome also had the effect of steering upper-class men toward informal relationships that helped them preserve their material resource base. Moreover, since the amount of time spent in stable heterosexual relationships is an important determinant of male reproductive success,[387] concubinage of not-yet-married, divorced, or widowed men (or of husbands physically separated from their wives, such as the Assyrian merchants mentioned in section 2.4.1) tended to increase their genetic contribution to the next generation. The sexual exploitation of female slaves offered mating opportunities outside the sphere of marriage or stable concubinage that were inevitably strongly correlated with economic status. In this context, the number of potential mates—that is, wealth—constituted the only real constraint on reproductive success. Slavery had the added advantage of allowing the primary beneficiaries of imperialism to shift the cost of increasing reproductive success—that is, decreasing mating opportunities for others—to subject or enemy out-groups. This mechanism, which helped foster social cohesion within the in-group even beyond the circle of primary beneficiaries, was more strongly developed in nondespotic societies (such as Greek *poleis* or Republican Rome) than in traditional monarchies. Even so, this difference appears to have been largely a matter of degree.

As I have already pointed out in section 1.5, questions of conscious motivation are of limited relevance here. In the case of domestic slavery, for example, male owners may have acquired female property for any number of reasons. In his discussion of the sexual exploitation of slaves in nineteenth-century Africa, Lovejoy argues that, "for some aristocrats, sexual domination was probably a substitute or an expression of political power."[388] The first reason may well have held for wealthy Athenians or Romans of the imperial period, who, constricted in their ambitions by democratic ideology or monarchical rule, derived vicarious pleasure from the penetration of powerless subordinates. However, regardless of such proximate factors, only ultimate consequences are of genuine significance for our understanding of human behavior. In this regard, the convergence between (1) imperial expansion, (2) the exploitation of imperial success in the form of forced transfers of resources and humans, (3) cultural norms and legal institutions that facilitated both the conversion of cultural into reproductive success and the balancing of the complementary aims of maximizing quantitatively a man's genetic contribution to future generations (by increasing lifetime reproductive success) and of optimizing offspring quality (through the preservation of heritable status) for the sake of enhancing inclusive fitness, ordinarily achieved by raising "marginal reproductive success," and (4) actual behavior (insofar as it can be reconstructed from inadequate ancient sources) merits particular attention. The interplay of these four variables determined the actual consequences of imperial success for reproductive success in general and variance in male reproductive success in particular. It is easy to imagine counterfactual conditions that would have favored different outcomes. For instance, SIM might have been strengthened in substance by an ideology that was hostile to extramarital relations of any kind, as Christianity was to be in later centuries; male infidelity could have been penalized by law; the marriage or adoption of slaves could have been prohibited; slaves could have been granted legal recourse against sexual exploitation in the same way that law and custom sometimes recognized a limited right of excessively brutalized slaves to appeal to the authorities. Any of these measures would have made it more difficult to convert cultural into reproductive success. As it is, and despite the general Darwinian prediction that "the function of laws is to regulate and render finite the reproductive strivings of individuals and subgroups within societies, in the interest of preserving unity in the larger group,"[389] it would seem difficult to devise social and legal norms and institutions that were *more* conducive to the maximization of inclusive fitness of the primary beneficiaries of imperial success than the norms and institutions that actually prevailed across a wide range of ancient empires, from Mesopotamia to Rome.

Were ancient empires established in order to facilitate sexual exploitation? At the most superficial level of conscious deliberation, motivation, and justification, the answer must be no. There is no evidence that the acquisition of new sex partners figured prominently—or at all—in the dominant ideologies of ancient empires. Regarding the most fundamental underlying behavioral mechanisms, the answer must be yes. Since imperialism is ultimately an expression of evolved innate propensities from cooperation to male dominance and intergroup aggression, and since dominance and successful aggression confer status benefits that are positively correlated with reproductive advantages, ancient—or any—empires would not have been established in the absence of behavioral traits that have evolved to promote inclusive fitness. Both approaches leave much to be desired. While the former, "culturalist" perspective fails to relate ideological representation and observed behavior to deeper, subconscious motivational structures, the latter, "geneticist" view is static and almost tautological in its reductionist simplicity and neglects the proximate determinants of human behavior. The challenge lies in amalgamating these approaches into a coherent whole. So far, traditional historical studies have persistently ignored the sexual dimension of imperial exploitation or—not explicitly but by implication—marginalized it as a coincidental side effect of imperialism. As I have tried to show in this essay, evolutionary theory strongly suggests that increased reproductive opportunities or variance in male reproductive success, far from being merely accidental consequences, were ultimately the most significant rewards of empire. Cultural studies of the representation of sexual relations in imperial contexts might therefore benefit from an appreciation of the underlying behavioral predispositions, thereby reconnecting protean language games with the hard surfaces of genetic heritage. At the same time, Darwinian interpreters of historical phenomena would do well to turn their attention to the interplay between ultimate motivation and proximate causation in order to identify the mechanisms that allow evolved behavioral propensities to influence and to be expressed in social and cultural institutions.

In terms of the causal nexus between cultural and reproductive success, the experience of ancient empires appears to have been broadly typical of that of premodern societies in general. For most of human history, competitive and exploitative strategies that were ultimately grounded in evolved fitness-enhancing behavioral propensities would on average tend to increase actual fitness. The dissociation of cultural from aggregate reproductive success (to the extent that traditionally fitness-enhancing traits and accomplishments have begun to fail to translate to actual reproductive success: cf. section 1.3) is a comparatively recent phenomenon, at first limited to Western societies and only gradually disseminated across the world. This development is well outside the remit of the academic field of ancient history. Rather, students of the ancient world need to inquire into the causes of regional and temporal variation in the sociocultural institutions that mediate cultural and reproductive success in an attempt to relate observed differences in the norms and conventions governing sexual competition to specific ecological, economic, or ideological contexts and circumstances.

Notes

1. Mann 1986a 5. Cf. already Mann 1977: 286: "I make two assumptions which I will in no way justify here: that mankind is restless and greedy for more of the good things of life, and that essentially this is a quest for greater material rewards."

2. Mann 1986a: 6. For a striking illustration of the resultant superficiality of sociological and historical attempts to explain the phenomenon of imperialism, see the survey in Doyle 1986: 22–30, 123–28.

3. Badcock 1991: 71.

4. Classic surveys include Wilson 1975; Dawkins 1982, 1989. Badcock 2000 and Buss 1999, 2005 explore the impact of this selection process on human behavior. Genes are not the only replicators that are subject to selective pressures: memes (now defined by the *OED* as "elements of a culture that may be considered to be passed on by non-genetic means"—i.e., learning) compete and proliferate in similar ways. However, while it is true that genetic and memetic fitness need not coincide (e.g., Dawkins 1989: 193–94; Dennett 1995), it has commonly been assumed that memetic reproductive success is contingent upon its consequences for genetic fitness (e.g., Cavalli-Sforza and Feldman 1981; Lumsden and Wilson 1981; Durham 1991), and this principle must necessarily be correct in the long term. For an ambitious discussion of the complementarity of memetic and genetic evolution, see now Blackmore 1999. (For biological alternatives to genetic replication, cf. Woolfson 2000.)

5. Trivers 1972.

6. But cf. Hrdy 1997, 2000, for some qualifications.

7. Access: Borgerhoff Mulder 1992: 353. Variance: Low 2000a: 55 fig. 3.3, 66.

8. Low 1993. For a telling example of the principle of higher male than female variance in reproductive success in a human population, see Daly and Wilson 1983: 89 fig. 5.6. See also section 2.2.

9. Betzig 1988: 5.

10. For quantitative assessments of this positive correlation among successful competition, status, resources, and reproductive success, see esp. Chagnon 1979; Irons 1979; Essock-Vitale 1984; Faux and Miller 1984; Kaplan and Hill 1985; Mealey 1985; Turke and Betzig 1985; Flinn 1986; Hughes 1986; Borgerhoff Mulder 1987, 1988; Hewlett 1988; Voland 1990; Cronk 1991; Roskraft, Wara, and Wiken 1992; Low 1994; Casimir and Rao 1995. For the importance of

fighting prowess, see e.g. Chagnon, Flinn, and Lelancon 1979; Chagnon 1988. See also Kaplan 1985 on Hill 1984. Betzig 1986, 1992b, 1993, 1995 provide qualitative surveys. For theory, cf. Harpending and Rogers 1990.

11. Wilson 1975: 287.

12. Chagnon 1979: 375.

13. I agree with MacDonald 1988: 336 that "at the present time sociobiological theory is the only theory that is powerful enough to provide an explanatory framework for the descriptive data generated by cross-cultural and historical studies of human development." For classic works, see Wilson 1978; Alexander 1979, 1987. Convincing challenges to evolutionary approaches to the study of human behavior in its various manifestations, including culture, have yet to appear; much of the existing work is driven by ideological bias (e.g., Rose, Lewontin, and Kamin 1984; Rose and Rose, eds. 2000; for a rebuttal, see Alcock 2001) and/or fuzzy rhetoric (most recently, Malik 2000). Kitcher 1985 stands out for an incisive critique of inadequate methods but likewise fails to invalidate the underlying interpretive framework. Segerstrale 2000 surveys the debate. Irons and Cronk 2000: 12–13 notice a "tidal shift" from a priori indictments of "sociobiology" in the 1980s to a growing acceptance of Darwinian interpretations in a variety of academic fields in the 1990s. This development is well reflected in the rapidly expanding bibliography of pertinent scholarship at http://www.hbes.com.

14. E.g., Barkow 1989; Buss 1994; Chisholm 1999; Low 2000a.

15. Cf. Liebermann, Reynolds, and Friedrich 1992.

16. See Maxwell, ed. 1991, for a cross-disciplinary survey that is now much in need of updating. Cf. also Betzig 1997a.

17. E.g., Chagnon and Irons, eds. 1979; Betzig, Borgerhoff Mulder, and Turke, eds. 1988. For history, see in general Betzig 1991, 1992a, and Wettlaufer 2002; for individual studies, Betzig 1986, 1992b,c, 1993, 1994, 1995, 2002, 2005; Boone 1988; Kroll and Bachrach 1990; MacDonald 1990, 1995; Weisfeld 1990; Hager 1992; Bergstrom 1994; Johnson and Johnson 1997; Käär et al. 1998; Hill 1999; Wettlaufer 2000; see also Voland, ed. 1992. The only extended debate known to me is Johnson and Johnson 1991, 1993, 1995; Hekala and Buell 1993, 1995. On religion, see Reynolds and Tanner 1995; Boyer 2001; Atran 2002; Wilson 2003; Dennett 2006; on war, van der Dennen and Falger, eds. 1990. In his diatribe against sociobiology and genetic determinism, Lewontin 1992: 90 points out that practitioners in that field mostly draw on evidence from simple and modern cultures but "do not look much at the historical record of European society, of which they seem to be quite ignorant." This charge was valid then, and progress has been slow since. See Herlihy 1995 and Wettlaufer 2000, 2002 for rare contributions by professional historians interested in evolutionary approaches.

18. Irons and Cronk 2000: 13 single out cultural anthropology for its increasingly lonely rejection of evolutionary perspectives, arguing that as "the study of behavior has largely been supplanted in cultural anthropology by the study of meaning," its "continued biophobia . . . is related . . . to the focus on meaning." (Kuper 1999 offers a trenchant critique of the current emphasis on cultural determinism in anthropology. For a first attempt to reconcile cultural relativism with evolutionary theory, see Cronk 1999.) The same is true of postmodernist historiography, largely for the same reason. Cf. more generally Hinde 1987.

19. Betzig 1991: 134–35, 1992b,c, 1993, 2005; Sallares 1991; Scheidel 1996b,c, 2004; Weiler 1993; Burkert 1996. Cf. also MacDonald 1990.

20. Tooby and Cosmides 1992: 21.

21. Gellner 1989: 61–2.

22. Manson and Wrangham 1991: 374 (references omitted).

23. Separate field studies have now established a coherent pattern of raiding behavior among chimpanzees, our closest genetic relatives; it entails furtive incursions of bands of adult males into neighboring ranges for the sole purpose of violent and sometimes fatal attacks on isolated males that, if sufficiently successful and frequent, result in the forcible incorporation of fecund females into the victorious band and may even lead to the dissolution of neighboring groups (Wrangham and Peterson 1996: 5–21). In this context—that is, in the absence of extrasomatic wealth—no exploitative arrangements are feasible, and the growth of aggressive/expansionist bands is constrained by low size thresholds for group fission. Under roughly similar ecological conditions, comparable intragroup cooperation and raiding practices can be observed in simple human groups (ibid., 63–82, and cf. Boehm 1992. Keeley 1996, on the character of primitive warfare in general, is consistent with this model). Thus, human aggression appears to be directly rooted in our evolutionary past (going back to the shared ancestors of hominids and chimpanzees: cf. Wrangham and Peterson 49–62). The earlier notion of a behavioral hiatus (in terms of agressiveness) between great-ape and middle-range human societies—that is, for most of hominid evolution—that interprets observed similarities between the two as homologues rather than the result of uninterrupted evolutionary progression (Knauft 1991) is less economical and suffers from a dearth of reliable information on hominid behavior.

24. Manson and Wrangham 1991: 375.

25. It deserves notice that territorial expansion is already a pervasive feature in *pre-state* warfare: Keeley 1996: 108–12. For a model of early resource competition, see Durham 1976.

26. Cf. Nishida 1991. With regard to low-complexity societies, Keeley 1996: 125–26 stresses the "interchangeable character of exchange and war": "Trade, intermarriage, and war all have the effect of moving goods and people between social units. In warfare, goods move as plunder, and people (especially women) move as captives. In exchange and intermarriage, goods move as reciprocal gifts, trade items, and bride wealth, whereas people move as spouses. In effect, the same desirable acquisitions are thus attained by alternative (but not mutually exclusive) means." I would add that, at the level of complex sociopolitical systems, access to more distant transferable individuals (again, especially women) who would not otherwise have been available (e.g., through marriage) and the ability to extend plunder by means of regular taxation, provide further incentives to imperial expansion.

27. It is possible that socioeconomic changes introduced by the "Agricultural Revolution" have been particularly conducive to male aggression and intergroup conflict: see, *cum grano salis*, McElvaine 2001, a somewhat eccentric "biohistorical" survey of sexual politics in human history that misrepresents contemporary evolutionary thinking (30–32; for a state-of-the-art summary of gene-environment interaction, compare Thornhill and Palmer 2000: 1–30).

28. Diamond 1998.

29. Delineated by Wright 2001.

30. The Diamond/Wright model of differential cultural evolution addresses the problem identified by Sahlins 1976: XI, that "biology, while it is an absolutely necessary condition for culture, is equally and absolutely insufficient: it is completely unable to specify the cultural properties of human behavior or their variations from one human group to another." Their perspective also vindicates the cultural-evolutionist approach to the study of human societies (e.g., White 1959; Johnson and Earle 2000) that is now often considered ideologically undesirable.

31. Dunbar 1991: 378–79. In the same context, he also makes the similarly important point that "that a behaviour pattern can be shown to be adaptive does not mean that it will

necessarily be exhibited by all members of a given species; nor does it imply that it cannot be modified by learning or socialisation. Evolutionary explanations about adaptiveness are always context-specific: they depend on the precise balance between costs and benefits. Since these may differ not only between members of the same social group but also between groups living in different environments, the expression of a given trait will vary ... *even if it does* have a significant genetic basis."

32. Cf., however, Meyer 1990, for the importance of psychocultural processes. The interplay of universal behavioral propensities, ecological variation (see previous section), and memetic evolution (see n.4) that determines levels of endemic aggressiveness and expansionism in different societies still awaits detailed analysis. For a wide-ranging critical survey of modern explanatory models of "primitive" warfare, see van der Dennen 1990.

33. Irons 1979: 258.

34. For problems of evidence, see sections 2.4.3 and 3.5.3.

35. See n.10.

36. Low 1994: 224–25.

37. Vining 1986.

38. Cf. also Low 2000b.

39. Essock-Vitale 1984, on the "Forbes 400" of 1982.

40. Pérusse 1993. Irons 1997: 49 argues that, since human status striving evolved in an environment that featured resource polygyny and inefficient birth control, it was adaptive for men to compete for status per se, since it was bound to pay off reproductively. Only today, as these conditions have changed, status striving per se does not automatically predict reproductive success and might even interfere with it. For sophisticated models of how modern incentives to parental investment and consumption may invert the traditional correlation of status with reproductive success, see now Kaplan 1996; Kaplan and Lancaster 2000. For a different perspective, cf. Abernethy 1999. Foster 2000 considers the limits of modern fertility decline.

41. Rogers 1990; cf. Mace 1998.

42. Rogers 1995: 94.

43. Undocumented extramarital fertility is another significant variable: see discussion of Pérusse 1993 and section 3.1.

44. Harpending and Rogers 1990; Boone and Kessler 1999.

45. Murdock 1967, 1981. On how to measure polygyny, see Low 1988. Westermarck 1921: 1–51 gives a rich if dated survey of polygamous practices around the globe.

46. Altman and Ginat 1996: 482–83 n.7.

47. Welch and Glick 1981.

48. Foster 1984: 210 (stratification), 151 (Smith).

49. Faux and Miller 1984; Mealey 1985.

50. Westermarck 1921: 19.

51. Badock 1991: 133.

52. White 1988: 558.

53. White and Burton 1988.

54. Bretschneider 1995: 40–41.

55. Ibid. 121–24; cf. 128.

56. Ibid. 120–21 (lack of correlation), 124 (quote).

57. Ibid. 171.

58. White and Burton 1988: 875.

59. Bretschneider 1995: 124.

60. Bretschneider 1995: 177–79; White 1988: 549–50.

61. White 1988: 550–52.

62. This model does not logically require that co-wives are related, not is it predicated on the existence of formal marital unions.

63. Bretschneider 1995: 171.

64. Emlen and Oring 1977. Bretschneider 1992 shows why the two other main concepts of polygyny ("male dominance polygyny" and "female defense polygyny") are not applicable to humans. By contrast, his criticism of the "polygyny threshold" model (187–89) merely raises procedural issues.

65. Cf., e.g., Betzig 1993: 53.

66. Buss 1994.

67. For cross-cultural correlation of male inheritance bias with polygyny, see Hartung 1982, confirmed by Cowlishaw and Mace 1996: 89.

68. Johansson 1987: 463.

69. For an earlier discussion of the difference between gene transmission and the social creation of heirs and successors, see Betzig 1993: 57–67.

70. The following analysis of empirical evidence is strictly reductionist; I focus on factors that I consider to be of crucial significance from an evolutionary perspective and exclude all features and implications that I do not consider essential to my argument. As a result, only men are envisaged as actors pursuing their reproductive goals, while the consequences of their actions for the reproductive success and inclusive fitness of their female mating partners—though of considerable interest in principle (cf., e.g., Hartung 1982; Clutton-Brock 1988: 472–73)—will not receive further consideration; this is one of the topics that would merit attention in a more expansive discussion of my subject. The issue of female mate choice is already subsumed within the standard correlation of cultural and reproductive success; in other scenarios, when nonconsensual sexual relations suspend female choice, mate choice has no social force. I focus exclusively on heterosexual relationships: homosexual intercourse has no reproductive potential and is therefore irrelevant in the context of this study. Again, a comprehensive account of sexual exploitation would also need to explore the Darwinian dimension of nonreproductive relations. (Cf., e.g., the finding that cross-culturally, polygyny is positively correlated with tolerated male homosexuality at certain ages: Cvorovic 2001.)

71. Dickemann 1979: 173–74.

72. Ibid. 174.

73. Betzig 1991: 135.

74. Betzig 1986, esp. 94–96, 134–36; 1994: 21 table 1. In Betzig's 1997b: 400 curt summary, "despotism explains differential reproduction." For an economic model of the correlation between inequality and polygyny, see Grossbard 1980: 329–30. Summers 2005 surveys research on the evolutionary ecology of despotism.

75. Betzig 1986: 9 (italics in original).

76. Betzig 1994: 28.

77. Cf. Vehrencamp 1983, on animals.

78. Betzig 1994: 30–31.

79. Einon 1998: 423. Moreover, in the absence of substantial extrasomatic wealth and attendant formalised privileges, very high status may adversely affect reproductive success (cf., e.g., Dunbar 1995; Packer et al. 1995; Mueller and Mazur 1998). This problem is unlikely to arise in highly stratified complex societies such as premodern empires.

80. Cf. also Hartung 1999. Elite focus on access to women characterized by youth and/or physical attractiveness—attributes correlated with high fecundability—enhances the fitness

benefits of differential reproduction (on cross-cultural uniformity in standards of beauty, see, e.g., Kenrick and Keefe 1992; Cunningham et al. 1995; Singh and Luis 1995; for variation with regard to body mass, cf. Anderson et al. 1992). This preference is well attested in the record: see Betzig 1993: 54–56, and in the following sections.

81. Needless to say, the distribution of fitness benefits among subordinates need not be envisaged as the direct allocation of mates. Given the correlation between cultural and reproductive success, access to the material benefits accruing from the exploitation of the resources of empire will ultimately have the same effect.

82. Betzig 1986: 4. Later work includes 1992b, 1993, 2002, 2005.

83. Herskovits 1938; cf. Betzig 1986: 70–71.

84. Herskovits 1938: 45 (harem), 38 (quote), 10 (chiefs).

85. Betzig 1986: 75.

86. Klein 1981: 207.

87. Westermarck 1921: 21.

88. Lovejoy 1983: 174–75.

89. Betzig 1986: 74.

90. Zhou Daguan, *The Customs of Cambodia* 6, in Smithies 2001: 31.

91. Van Gulick 1974: 17.

92. Ibid. 20–1. On polygynous concubinage in ancient China, see also Hinsch 2002: 39–40, 85–86.

93. Van Gulick 1974: 65 n.2.

94. Bielenstein 1986: 259.

95. Quoted ibid. 206.

96. Ibid. 65.

97. Garcilasco de la Vega 1871: 297–301; Rostworowski de Diez Canseco 1999: 176.

98. Betzig 1986: 77.

99. Ibid. 42, 46.

100. Durán 1952: 131; Padden 1967: 20. Cf. Carrasco 1999: 203 for another example of elite reproductive privilege in the Aztec Empire.

101. Motolinía 1951: 202.

102. Thus Einon 1998. But cf. Gould 2000.

103. Cooper 1916: 158.

104. Dickemann 1979: 175–76.

105. Ibid. 175.

106. Summarized by Betzig 1993: 41.

107. For a good example of this principle, see Joshi 1995: 38–39, on the multiple wives of the Rajputs, an Indian warrior caste, who not only did not work at all but also required attendance.

108. Betzig 1986: 78–82 and 1993: 48–52.

109. Martin 2004: 196–201. For sexual predation on a smaller scale in comparable regimes, cf. Montefiore 2003: 505–8, on the activities of Lavrenti Beria, head of Stalin's NKVD, and Chang and Halliday 2006: 407, on Mao Zedong.

110. Zerja et al. 2003. For the context, see, e.g., Sailor 2003.

111. Xue et al. 2005. At least 1.6 million men belong to this group. Note that by the beginning of the twentieth century, the officially recognized Qing nobility alone had grown to more than eighty thousand members.

112. Helgason et al. 2000 (Iceland); Capelli et al. 2003 (Britain).

113. Batto 1974: 21–28.

114. Lerner 1986: 71.

115. Stol 1995: 135. On the harem at Mari, see Durand and Margueron 1980; cf. also Durand 1985. Despite some reservations against the application of the Arabic term "harem" to ancient Near Eastern societies, especially regarding the implied severity of female claustration (Westenholz 1990: 513–16), there can be little doubt about the existence of the institution as such. Cf. also Lesko and Ward in Lesko, ed. 1989: 44–45 (on Egypt).

116. Mayer 1978: 112.

117. Morrisson in Lesko, ed. 1989: 183.

118. Cf. Stol 1995: 135.

119. Neumann 1987: 132, 135.

120. *Codex Urnammu* 25–26; Neumann 1987: 135–37.

121. Siegel 1947.

122. Cf. Lerner 1986: 76–100.

123. See Seibert 1974: 41–51, on women in palaces, especially 41–4 and 50–1 on "harems." Cf. n.115.

124. Stol 1995: 135 and n.83.

125. Seibert 1974: 50–1.

126. Hamilton 1992: 565 and Betzig 2005, with reference to Esau (three wives and five sons: Genesis 26.34, 28.9, 36.2), Jacob (two wives, two maids, and twelve sons: Genesis 29.15–30, 35.22–26), Gideon (many wives and seventy sons: Judges 8.30–1), Jair (thirty sons: Judges 10.4), Ibzan (thirty sons and thirty daughters: Judges 12.9), and Abdon (forty sons and thirty daughters: Judges 12.14).

127. 1 Samuel 18.17–30, 25.38–43; 2 Samuel 3.2–5, 5.13. For concubines, see 2 Samuel 5.13, 16. Twenty of his children are known by name: 2 Samuel 5.13–16; 1 Chronicles 3.5–9, 14.3–7.

128. 1 Kings 3.1, 11.3; Proverbs 31.10; Ecclesiastes 2.8.

129. 1 Kings 11.1.

130. 2 Chronicles 11.21. His own son Abijah had to make do with fourteen wives, twenty-two sons, and sixteen daughters: 2 Chronicles 13.21.

131. God to David in 2 Samuel 12.7–8, 11, highlighted by Betzig 2005.

132. Westbrook 1988: 103–11.

133. Ibid. 103; Seibert 1974: 16; Wilcke 1984.

134. Korosec 1938: 281, 284.

135. Westbrook 1988: 109, 111.

136. Seibert 1974: 16–17, 21; Saggs 1995: 106.

137. Korosec 1938: 287, 290.

138. Driver and Miles 1935: 135.

139. On veiling, see ibid. 126–34. Veiled slave women had their ears cut off: ibid. 131, 409.

140. Contenau 1954: 18.

141. Driver and Miles 1935: 127–28, 479.

142. Stol 1995: 130 and n.42–43 (Old Assyrian), 129 (Middle Assyrian). See Driver and Miles 1935: 232–33, for the interpretation of the term *urkittu* as second wife in terms of rank, not in time. It deserves notice that the Assyrian practice of mass deportations of defeated populations appears to have had little to do with this; although the number of deportees may have run into several millions (Oded 1979: 19–22), they were often skilled men or complete families rather than unattached women (ibid. 22–25). Technically the property of the king, captives were distributed among civilian officials and soldiers (ibid. 111–14), though

apparently primarily as laborers. The fact that deportees were not classified as slaves may be of crucial importance here (ibid. 85); one might speculate that women who had lost their husbands were enslaved and transferred separately; these women could then be turned into concubines.

143. Neumann 1987: 136–37; Stol 1995: 129–30.

144. Roth 1989: 12, 41–42, 15.

145. Dandamaev 1984: 133, 411. For examples of lease contracts, see 134–35.

146. Ibid. 135 and n.73. For comparable leases in ancient China, see section 2.2.

147. Robins 1993: 27.

148. Redford 1984: 36, 134. See more generally Robins 1993: 30–6.

149. Seibert 1974: 51.

150. Redford 1984: 36–37. For similar transfers, see sections 2.4.1 and 2.4.3.

151. Kitchen 1982: 252, listed in Gauthier 1914: 80–113; for discussion, see Kitchen 97–112.

152. Reiser 1972; Seipel 1977; Robins 1993: 39–41; Tyldesley 1995: 179–207 (with a dutiful critique of modern projections of images of the Ottoman harem onto Pharaonic Egypt: 179–80; as noted in n.115 and n.192, arguments of this kind are missing the point).

153. Kanawati 1976.

154. Simpson 1974: 104.

155. Ibid. 100–1. Cf. Tyldesley 1995: 49–50.

156. Robins 1993: 65.

157. Allam 1975: 1167.

158. Robins 1993: 61–62. See Manniche 1987: 21, for a governor with concubines and their children.

159. Robins 1993: 65–67.

160. E.g., Mazahéri 1938: 133–43.

161. *Yasht* 10.30; Schwartz 1985: 656.

162. Seibert 1974: 43.

163. Klima 1966: 567–68.

164. Briant 1996: 289–97; Brosius 1996: 36–37.

165. Briant 1996: 144–45.

166. Prásek 1910: 171; Ktesias 44.

167. Prásek 1910: 217; Justin 10.1.1; Curtius Rufus 10.5.23.

168. Prásek 1910: 220; Justin 10.3; Curtius Rufus 10.5.23.

169. The attested numbers may well be symbolic: 300 (Heracleides *FGrHist* 689 F 1) or 360 (Deinon *FGrHist* 690 F 27; Diodorus Siculus 17.77.5; Curtius Rufus 3.3.24, 6.6.8; Plutarch, *Artaxerxes* 27.1; Dikaiarchos *FHG* II p. 240 F 18, in Athenaios 13.557b). Briant 1996: 292 defends the tally of 360 with reference to the calendar of 360 days (plus 5 intercalated days) then in use in Persia. Parmenion was said to have captured 329 royal concubines (Athenaios 13.608a). On the controversy over the location of the harem at Persepolis, see Brosius 1996: 31. For a critical discussion of female claustration in this context, see Briant 1996: 295–97. For the eunuchs of the royal harem, see Llewellyn 2002.

170. Diodorus Siculus 17.77.7. Briant 1996: 294–95 discusses the sex lives of the Persian kings.

171. Arrian 2.12.3–8; Curtius Rufus 3.13.12–4.

172. Historia Augusta, Valerian 7; Eutropius 9.25. Cf. later discussion of Surenas.

173. Briant 1996: 290–1: Brosius 1996: 32.

174. Herodotus 6.32.

175. Briant 1996: 291.

176. Briant 1996: 291–92.

177. Klima 1957: 104.

178. Herodotus 3.92.1.

179. Arrian *FGrHist* 156 F 79–80 as interpreted by Bosworth 1997 (esp. 300).

180. Herodotus 1.135; Strabo 15.3.17.

181. Brosius 1996: 64 n.39 notes that we know very little about nonroyal marriages in Achaemenid Persia from primary sources. Hence, the absence of polygamy in these texts cannot be used as an *argumentum e silentio*.

182. For examples, see Herodotus 9.76.1; Xenophon, *Hellenica* 3.1.10; Plutarch, *Themistocles* 31.2. For satrapial courts as copies of the royal court, see Briant 1996: 357–59.

183. Plutarch, *Crassus* 21. See Brosius 1996: 89–90 for further references (Herodotus 7.83.2, 9.76.1; Xenophon, *Anabasis* 1.10.2; Aelianus, *Miscellaneous Histories* 12.1). Plutarch, *Themistocles* 26 refers to a particular type of closed vehicle used by Persians to move their wives and concubines, who were otherwise locked up at home.

184. Ammianus 23.6.76.

185. Klima 1966: 567.

186. Mazahéri 1938: 135; Klima 1966: 567.

187. E.g., Klima 1966: 567–68; Perikhanian 1983: 647. In Christensen's 1944: 322 somewhat sweeping summary, "la famille etait fondée sur la polygamie."

188. Klima 1957: 95. The later law code *Madigan i Hazar i Dadestan* refers to bigamy with two fully legitimate (and presumably equal) wives (*padixshayiha*): Klima 1966: 567. Christensen 1944: 323 points out that we do not know how many principal wives a man could have; two is the minimum.

189. Herodotus 9.76: Plutarch, *Moralia* 339a.

190. Sancisi-Weerdenburg 1987: 43–44.

191. Schneider 1998: 106–7.

192. The unwillingness to distinguish between actual structural features of Eastern societies and the spin put on them by Western observers undermines fashionable critiques of "orientalism." Kabbani 1994 is a typical example, taking issue with lurid accounts of sexual languor in Ottoman harems. For the historian, it is the existence of this institution (and its implications for social and political structure, as examined in section 2.1) that ought to matter, not the manner in which it is represented in colonialist sources. Cf. also Pierce 1993, "debunking" the image of the Ottoman harem.

193. It merits notice that even the most novelistic scenes in authors like Ktesias, dealing with "harem intrigues," undoubtedly reflect realities of polygynous courts: see Ben-Barak 1987, for the ancient Near East, or Ogden 1999, on Hellenistic monarchies (see section 3.4).

194. Klima 1957: 105.

195. Christensen 1944: 322.

196. Crone 1991: 21–23, 30.

197. Klima 1957: 239, which is however a conjecture.

198. I follow the revisionist chronology proposed by Crone 1991, separating Kavadh's measures from those of Mazdak under Xusraw I.

199. Tabari, quoted by Crone 1991: 24.

200. Crone 1991: 25.

201. Seibert 1974: 51.

202. Coe 2003: 139, 214.

203. Einon 1998.

204. Van den Berghe 1979: 48.

205. The longest discussion of Greek monogamy and polygamy I am aware of is that of Erdmann 1934: 87–103, who likewise fails to consider monogamy a noteworthy institution.

206. Friedl 1996: 28–29 lists references to polygynous societies in the orbit of Greek and Roman culture. For Thrace, see Herodotus 5.5, 5.16, minus his fanciful embellishments; also Euripides, *Andromache* 215; for the Celts, see Caesar, *Gallic War* 6.19.3, with Pelletier 1984: 14; cf. also Markale 1975: 36, for plural marriage with annual contracts.

207. For the Macedonians, see section 3.4. The Visigothic and Merovingian kings were hardly restrained in taking multiple wives; in the upper classes, multiple legal wives supplemented by concubines were the norm (Ross 1985). For the Arabs, see section 2.2.

208. The reverence of monogamous Christians for the polygamous patriarchs and kings of the Old Testament provides an interesting parallel.

209. Alexander et al. 1979: 420.

210. Alexander's position as summarised by Betzig and Weber 1993: 46.

211. MacDonald 1990: 198.

212. Ibid. 204–11.

213. It is true that since, in general, polygyny is positively correlated with male stratification, decreasing resource inequality among men favors the spread of monogamy (Kanazawa and Still 1999). We would therefore expect egalitarian societies to be less polygynous than systems with highly skewed resource allocation. However, SIM is not a matter of degree but an absolute principle: as male mating value varies even in the absence of material resource imbalances, low complexity alone cannot entirely explain the introduction of SIM. The observation that, in principle, SIM benefits the majority of men more than the majority of women (e.g., Wright 1994: 98) is consistent with the view that SIM fosters intermale cooperation.

214. MacDonald 1990: 211–23 only discusses the mechanisms in Roman society favoring SIM without attempting to explain why it arose in the first place (cf. also Betzig 1992c).

215. MacDonald 1995: 5–6.

216. Ibid. 7 entertains the possibility that "because of increased internal solidarity and cohesiveness, groups characterized by SIM and/or socially imposed altruism may exhibit greater reproductive success than groups in which individuals (and especially wealthy, powerful individuals) are free to pursue individually optimal reproductive strategies." This proposition seems virtually untestable.

217. MacDonald 1990: 233.

218. Kanazawa and Still 1999: 37–40 challenge what they call the "male compromise hypothesis" by pointing out that, in a large modern cross-cultural sample, democracy (as opposed to authoritarianism) is not significantly correlated with monogamy (as opposed to polygamy); by contrast, the level of male resource inequality and the extent of women's rights and power are shown to be powerful predictors of the incidence of monogamy.

219. Herlihy 1995: 581.

220. E.g., Brown and Hotra 1988.

221. Daly and Wilson 1983: 152.

222. Wittenberger and Tilson 1980: 198.

223. Fuentes 1998. The extent to which human sociality has been fashioned by monogamous relationships remains doubtful: ibid., 897. Cf., e.g., Hawkes et al. 2000. *Contra* Diamond 1992: 71, human testicle size does not point to habitual monogamy (as defined earlier): see Geary

1998: 89. Moreover, sexual dimorphism may be a better predictor of polygyny (cf. Geary 84–88 for primates).

224. Alexander at al. 1979: 420. But cf. Brown and Hotra 1988 for an effectively monogamous population under unusual environmental conditions (Pitcairn). In a sample of 862 societies, only 16 percent were found to be exclusively monogamous in terms of marriage (Murdock 1967). However, this statistic tells us little about actual mating patterns (Fuentes 1998: 897).

225. Wickler and Seibt 1983: 45.

226. Baker and Bellis 1995.

227. Ibid. 199–200; cf. Mace 2000: 5.

228. Perhaps unsurprisingly, the current wave of cultural-constructivist scholarship on Greco-Roman sexuality pays no attention to this issue; for a recent overview, see Karras 2000. Parker 2001: 330–38 exemplifies the conventional Pavlovian reaction to "biological reductionism" in the study of (ancient) sexuality.

229. MacDonald 1990: 234, with reference to Hopkins 1978a: 14.

230. E.g., Finley 1959/81; Patterson 1991.

231. Finley 1969: 260.

232. In effect, my approach to the emergence of Greco-Roman chattel slavery is as functionalist as the analyses of Finley and Hopkins. It differs from existing accounts in acknowledging the significance of exploitation beyond the economic sphere, that is, with regard to human reproductive capacity.

233. Gutman and Sutch 1976: 152. Genovese 1976: 413–31. See already Stampp 1956: 350–61, esp. 355 for slave concubines.

234. Olmsted 1861: 240.

235. Brent 1973: 27.

236. Betzig and Weber 1993: 50.

237. See, e.g., Gwin 1985; Bleser 1991; Clinton 1991.

238. Chesnut 1951: 21–22.

239. Felton 1919: 93.

240. Betzig and Weber 1993: 49.

241. Schafer 1987. In Dutch South Africa, which was even more strongly influenced by Roman law, children by slave women were rarely acknowledged or freed (Scully 1993: 70–71). Under different circumstances, societies dependent on the Roman legal tradition often favored the integration of such children: e.g., Gaudioso 1992: 67.

242. Finkelman 1997: 209.

243. Genovese 1976: 423. E.g., Bush 1990: 110–15, on sexual slave exploitation in the Caribbean. On slave concubines, see Patterson 1982: 434 n.58.

244. E.g., Hopkins 1978a: 99–102.

245. While this is certainly true of Rome and Sparta (and at least to some extent of classical Athens), and although initially slaves were pictured as captives, the early expansion of chattel slavery in late archaic *poleis*, such as Chios, was not associated with imperial expansion (Finley 1959/81). In those cases, it might be more profitable to consider the introduction of slaves as a means of fostering cohesion among the citizenry by reducing labor exploitation of the free and promoting marital egalitarianism (see preceding discussion).

246. Epics: Fox 1995. For evolutionary perspectives on literature in general, see esp. Carroll 1995, 1999; Cooke 1999; Gottschall et al. 2004. See now Gottschall 2008 for a comprehensive discussion of wars over women in the Homeric tradition.

247. Wickert-Micknat 1983: 21–32, 40–45.

248. Nowag 1983: 37–38.

249. Wickert-Micknat 1982: 83–84; Mauritsch 1992: 92–98; Ogden 1996: 23–24.

250. 1.433. For later examples of jealousy, see Thalmann 1998: 29, and section 3.3.2.

251. The marriage customs of the Minoan and Mycenaean era must have been as unknown to the Greeks of later periods as they are to us; cf. briefly Billigmeier 1985: 14–15 on Linear B material. The Near Eastern evidence discussed earlier raises the possibility that some form of (harem) polygamy may also have existed in Greek Bronze Age palace centers. Hunt forthcoming argues that conflict over women in the Homeric tradition reflects actual conditions in Early Iron Age Greece.

252. Herodotus 1.146; Pausanias 7.2.6 (Miletus); Herodotus 6.138 (Lemnos). Similar stories were placed in a less distant past: see Schaps 1982: 203 and Hunt forthcoming for references.

253. Rougé 1970. Cf. also van Compernolle 1982.

254. Archilochos A IV 23 (Treu 1979: 61): *epeita gynaikas ei*[*chon*]. See Rougé 1970: 314; Graham 1978: 93; Treu 1979: 213. On intermarriage on Thasos, see Graham 92–93; he concludes that, "while there is no evidence and no good argument in favor of peaceable conditions, there is at least some evidence of hostility" (94). Cf. 97 for parallels in the region. For an inversion of this process, cf. Strabo 5.4.4 (native Campani taking over the Greek women of Cumae).

255. For an extreme case, see the enserfment of the Mariandynoi by the Greeks of Heraklea Pontika (Burstein 1976: 28–30). Sicily offers further evidence. Unfortunately, the section on relations between colonists and natives in Descoeudres, ed. 1990: 131–204 does not touch on this issue.

256. For example, the fact that Ptolemy I acknowledged the Cyrenian citizenship of the children of mixed Cyrenian-Libyan unions (*SEG* 9.1 pr. 2–3) points to a long tradition of intermarriage; cf. Hdt. 4.153, with Rougé 1970: 315–16.

257. Herodotus 6.16.

258. Livy 1.9. As usual, the emphasis is on elite privilege: "the larger part were carried off indiscriminately, but some particularly beautiful girls who had been marked out for the leading patricians were carried to their houses by plebeians told off for the task" (1.9). On a different occasion, the mother of the mythical Roman king Servius Tullius, Ocresia, was described a "beautiful" war captive brought to the royal palace (Ovid, *Fasti* 6.628).

259. Plutarch, *Romulus* 29, *Camillus* 33, *Moralia* 313a. For the Romans' equally telling solution to this conundrum, see section 3.5.

260. Herodotus 2.92; Erdmann 1934: 87.

261. Euripides, *Andromache* 215; cf. also 177 ff.

262. Diodorus Siculus 14.44; Plutarch, *Dionysius* 3; Aelianus, *Miscellaneous Histories* 13.10. On the marriages of Greek tyrants, see Gernet 1981: 289–302, who speculates that Peisistratos may also have been bigamous (290–1).

263. Cohen 1993; Doblhofer 1994: 34–40.

264. Cf., e.g., Watson 1980: 240–1.

265. Ogden 1996: 72–75. For a parallel from Germany shortly after the end of the Thirty Years' War, see Westermarck 1921: 51; for nineteenth-century Paraguay, see Becker 1974. Cf. most recently Harford 2006: "After more than a decade of war between separatist rebels and the Russian army, there are not many marriageable men to go around in Chechnya. So, acting Prime Minister Ramzan Kadyrov, probably not a feminist, proposed a radical step: 'Each man who can provide for four wives should do it.'"

266. Cohen 1991 assumes, on the basis of comparative evidence from the Mediterranean, that the seduction of other men's women was a competitive activity that conferred status

upon the successful seducer but simultaneously clashed with the cooperative virtues of Athenian society and thus resulted in moral condemnation. The facticity of this model remains open to debate. Cf., e.g., Carey 1995.

267. Pseudo-Demosthenes 59.122. For discussion, see, e.g., Sealey 1984: 117–19 and now Davidson 1997: 73–77, who stresses that accounts in other sources lack the terminological consistency suggested by this passage (cf. also Kurke 1997: 108). Cox 1998: 170–89 provides a careful discussion of *hetairai* and concubinage in Athens. See also Lape 2002/3: 131–2 for the anti-elite bias inherent of the limitation of legitimacy to the offspring of wives.

268. Sealey 1984: 119; MacDowell 1978: 89–90.

269. Demosthenes 23.53, with reference to a Draconian (i.e., putatively seventh-century B.C.E.) law granting immunity to a man who kills a man caught with a "concubine kept for the production of free children" (e.g., Davidson 1997: 98). Cf. also Lape 2002/3: 125.

270. For Just 1989: 52, any *hetaira* who took up residence with a man counted as a *pallake*.

271. Cox 1998: 174 n.31.

272. Demosthenes 59.22.

273. Isaeus 6.21.

274. Idomeneus *FGrHist* 338 F 14.

275. Pseudo-Andocides 4.14.

276. Sophocles, *Trachinian Women* 435 ff, 456 ff, 536–37. Erdmann 1934: 98–99.

277. When in fourth-century B.C.E. Athens it was made a punishable offense for a citizen (of either sex) to *synoikein* with an alien, this must have referred to formal marriages, not to concubinage (Just 1989: 62–64).

278. Demosthenes 36.45.

279. Davidson 1997: 102. For an analogous pairing of monogamy with concubinage, cf. Westermarck 1921: 46: a century ago, among the Hindus of India, the British authorities counted 1,008 wives per 1,000 husbands, while, at the same time, "the keeping of concubines by wealthy Hindus [was] a recognised usage."

280. On the sexual exploitation of Greek slaves see most recently Klees 1998: 162–66.

281. Lysias 1.12.

282. E.g., Homer, *Odyssey* 1.433; Plutarch, *Moralia* 144b-c, on Gorgias; Menander fr. 402 Edmonds.

283. Aristophanes, *Peace* 1138–39.

284. *Athenian Constitution* 26.4. For recent discussions, see, e.g., Boegehold 1994; Ogden 1996: 59–69.

285. Walters 1983: 332.

286. Aristotles, *Politics* 3.1278a25–34, 6.1319b6–11. The status of the children of slave women fathered by their owners is not actually known, although it is usually assumed to have been that of their mothers (e.g., MacDowell 1978: 80). Erdmann 1934: 105 reports an older view that in pre-Draconian times, slave women could bear free children. Demosthenes 23.53 implies that concubines who were not themselves free would give birth to slave children.

287. Cf. Just 1989: 53 for the view that in pre-democratic Athens, the distinction between legitimate and illegitimate children depended on the father's desire to recognize them rather than on the marital status of the mother. Cox 1998: 172 points out that, by the classical period, "all *nothoi* recognized by their fathers or bastards of other types of slave or free non-citizen mothers were restricted from inheriting." Hence, male gene proliferation would readily coexist with concentration of resources upon legitimate offspring. In his *Laws* (930d), Plato provided for the expatriation of the offspring of masters and slaves (together with the slave parents), presumably in order to maintain the separation of free from slave.

288. Dio Chrysostomus 15.15, 15.5.

289. Herter 1957, 1960 gathers the evidence for Greco-Roman prostitution. For recent discussions of Athenian prostitution, see Keuls 1993: 153–204 and Davidson 1997: 78–91.

290. Davidson 1997: 85–90.

291. Ibid. 91–97.

292. Dover 1974: 210.

293. Just 1989: 138, 170.

294. Kurke 1997: 107.

295. Finley 1978/81; chapter 4 of this volume.

296. Herter 1960: 71–72.

297. Ibid. 79 n.148.

298. In Menander's "Hated Man," the title character is distressed that his slave-mistress, a war captive, does not return his affection. For pertinent references from classical Greece, see Hunt forthcoming (Herodotus 9.81, on the battle of Plataea, Plutarch, Alcibiades 16.5, on Melos, and Demosthenes 19.305–7, on Olynthus).

299. In his description of the Aetolians' sack of Pellene (241–240 B.C.E.), Plutarch, *Aratus* 31, has "the leaders and captains going around grabbing the wives and daughters of the Pellenians, and taking off their own helmets and putting them on [the women's] heads so that no one else would take them," while the common soldiers were busy searching for money. The officer's privilege lends this story a Homeric flavour. As Schaps 1982: 203 points out, it does not matter whether this account is a fabrication: the implied focus on money and women seems perfectly realistic.

300. Graham 1983: 166–210.

301. Aeschines 1.107.

302. Ogden 1996: 238–39.

303. Herodotus 5.40.

304. Teles in Stobaeus, *Anthology* 3.3.40.8; Ogden 1996: 217–18.

305. Aelianus, *Miscellaneous Histories* 12.43; Phylarchus *FGrHist* 81 F 43. Ogden 1996: 218–24.

306. Ogden 1996: 221.

307. Hodkinson 1997: 55–62, esp. 54–55.

308. As so often, gene proliferation and the channeling of resources to legitimate offspring went hand in hand: Hodkinson 1989: 90–2 discusses polyandry with brothers and consanguineous marriage as means of estate preservation. (In this context, polyandry should not be seen as a sign of female empowerment: Millender 1999).

309. Ogden 1999 is now the fundamental study of Macedonian royal polygyny. For Argead polygamy, see esp. IX-X, and XVI with n.16–17 for further literature; for a historical account, see 3–40, and cf. also Carney 2000: 23–27. With reference to earlier debates on whether the Argeads really were polygamous or rather serially monogamous, Ogden XIV-XV notes that "the question of monogamy and polygamy among the Argeads has been further complicated by the debate as to whether the Macedonians were "Greek" (a debate that has recently become savagely politicized), with polygamy considered alien to the "Greeks."

310. Ogden 1996: XVI.

311. Ibid. 17–27.

312. Athenaeus 13.557b.

313. Justin 12.3.10.

314. Plutarch, *Comparison of Demetrius and Antony* 4 observes that their example made it acceptable for Demetrius I Poliorcetes to have multiple wives, whereas it was inappropriate

for the Roman Marcus Antonius to engage in bigamy. Here, polygamy is deemed un-Roman, just as it used to be seen as un-Greek. Carney 2000: 228–32 reckons with a decline of royal polygamy in the third century B.C.E.; however, stronger emphasis on "queenship" may simply have resulted in supplementary consorts keeping a lower profile (cf. 231).

315. Ogden 1996: 57–62 (Lysimachus), 68–73 (Ptolemy I), 173 (Demetrius I), 179–82 (Demetrius II).

316. Ibid. 202–10.

317. Carney 1992; Ogden 1999: 213–72.

318. Ogden 1996: 221–23. It is possible that hellenistic kings kept mobile harems in the form of designated womens' quarters on "floating palaces," that is, outsize ships (cf. Ogden 1999: 275).

319. Ibid. 215 (quote), 243–47.

320. *P. Eleph.* 1; *P. Giss.* 1.2.

321. Ogden 1996: 338–41.

322. Clarysse and Thompson 2006.

323. Speculations about the possibility of "group marriage" in early Rome (Franciosi 1995: 159–81) are impossible to substantiate.

324. Friedl 1996: 47 and n.9. Cf., however, Cicero, *Orator* 1.183, on the question of whether a second marriage would automatically terminate a preexisting union or merely add a *concubina* to the first wife.

325. The standard work of reference on Roman concubinage is now Friedl 1996. Among earlier work, see esp. Rawson 1974; Treggiari 1981. For a rapid survey of concubinage in world history, see Boyer 1986.

326. Friedl 1996: 214–15 n.5–6 produces a hefty bibliography of some seventy contributions, half of them arguing for and half of them against the quasi-polygamous character of Roman concubinage. Most studies in Romance languages favor the former, most anglophone works (and all studies prior to c.1880) the latter position. For discussion, see Friedl 214–28.

327. Rousselle 1984: 81.

328. Festus 248 L.

329. *Digest* 45.1.121.1.

330. *Justinianic Code* 7.15.3.2.

331. Saller 1987: 85 n.43.

332. Friedl 1996: 218–20.

333. Thus Friedl 1996: 220–8, drawing on an exhaustive catalogue pertinent evidence (380–94) that supersedes previous work on this subject.

334. Saller 1987: 73.

335. Friedl 1996: 273; Saller 1987: 74–76.

336. Friedl 1996: 274.

337. Gardner 1986: 221. For the sexual exploitation of Roman slaves, see Garrido-Hory 1981; Kolendo 1981; Gardner 1986: 221–22; Bradley 1987: 116–18; Rawson 1989: 18. Treggiari 1979: 192–94 tends to downplay its extent, cf. also 1982: 20–22. On the sex life of Roman slaves, see also Morabito 1986. Defensive claims by accused rapists that they had mistaken free women for slaves shows that, although the compelling of sex with slaves owned by others was penalized, it counted as a much lesser offense than the rape of free (citizen) women: Doblhofer 1994: 20–1. In general, in both Greece and Rome, perpetrators of sexual violence could be described as men who dealt with free women *as if* they were slaves and/or war captives (the raping of whom would have been acceptable) (ibid. 22).

338. Horace, *Satires* 1.2.16–9; Martial 1.81, 84.

339. Petronius 75.11; Seneca, *Controversies* 4 pr. 10.

340. Plutarch, *Moralia* 140b.

341. Fragment 12. For discussion of this and the previous passage, see, e.g., Saller 1987: 78–79, 1996: 126–27.

342. Salvian, *On the Kingdom of God* 7.4.

343. In Portugal, sex between men and slave girls was regarded as a joke (Saunders 1982: 103). The audience of Roman satirists clearly shared this view. However, Roman elegy may arguably show some appreciation of the helplessness of female slaves in the face of sexual exploitation: e.g., James 1997. For parallels to the more critical statements quoted earlier, see section 3.2.

344. Pliny the Younger, *Letters* 3.14.3.

345. *Justinian Code* 9.9.23.

346. Gaius, *Institutes* 1.19.

347. Herrmann-Otto 1994: 42–46, 88–90.

348. Rawson 1989: 23–29.

349. Watson 1987: 103–4.

350. *Digest* 30.71.3.

351. Champlin 1991: 137.

352. *Digest* 28.2.11; Herrmann-Otto 1994: 85–86 n.179.

353. Syme 1960/79: 511.

354. Betzig 1992b: 323 (quote), 323–42; 1986: 73; 1992b: 339, 334–37.

355. Hopkins 1978a: 115–32. "For the masters, manumission was economically rational" (131).

356. E.g., Treggiari 1979.

357. Scheidel 2005.

358. Flemming 1999: 56–61. On Roman prostitution in general, see Herter 1957, 1960; McGinn 1998a; Stumpp 1998. For the nexus between enslavement in war and prostitution, see Dio Chrys. 7.133 and *Cod. Iust.* 8.50.7.

359. While Evans 1991: 137 still reckoned with 22 *lupanaria*, Laurence 1994: 73 reports only nine purpose-built facilities, of which seven are single *cellae*. Earlier estimates went as high as thirty-five or more. McGinn 2002 is the most recent discussion.

360. Suetonius, *Caesar* 50–2, *Augustus* 71 (cf. section 2.4.1, on the wife of Zimri-Lim of Mari), *Caligula* 36; Cassius Dio 40.2.5–6, 40.18.3; Suetonius, *Nero* 27, *Vespasian* 21, *Domitian* 22.

361. *Historia Augusta, Commodus* 5.8, 5.4.

362. *Historia Augusta, Commodus* 5.8, 5.4, *Pertinax* 7.8–9, *Elagabalus* 24.2–3, 29.2.

363. Betzig 1992b: 310 (quote), 313–20.

364. The association of male high status with female beauty frequently found in Greek and Roman accounts of forced sexual intercourse (Doblhofer 1994: 43–44) underlines this point. If physical attractiveness is an honest signal of reproductive potential (see Thornhill and Grammer 1999: 106–9 for a survey of pertinent scholarship), the status of the exploiter can be expected to be positively correlated with the physical appearance of the exploited. For pertinent references, see n.80. Etcoff 1999 summarizes evolutionary insights into the nature and function of beauty.

365. For an example of the problems involved, see McGinn 1998b.

366. Tacitus, *Histories* 3.40–1.

367. As in the case of the Roman aristocracy in general, it does not really matter that evidence of imperial bastards is extremely rare (Scheidel 1999: 279); cf. section 3.5.2.

368. According to Saletore 1974: 83–84, an Indian king "would forcibly halt all nuptial processions passing through his capital without assigning any reason and, without any sense of shame or guilt, pounce on the bride, take her away to his palace to deflower her and after he had done the foul deed would send her to her husband's house." Again, while the facticity of this account is uncertain, the imagined link between despotism and sexual predation is the same as in Rome.

369. Thus, a Roman officer credited with raping a Galatian queen could be described as "making a soldier's use of his good fortune" (Plutarch, *Moralia* 258d-f). Thus also Livy 38.24, about a centurio "characterized by both the lust and greed of the soldier" who rapes a beautiful war captive; Polybius 21.38 notes that he "used his good fortune as soldiers do." Phang 2001: 254–55 and now esp. Phang 2004 discuss the historical evidence. For a Darwinian study of rape, see Thornhill and Palmer 2000.

370. Livy 43.3.1–4.

371. Duncan-Jones 1994: 33–46, esp. 45.

372. Wierschowski 1984.

373. Speidel 1989.

374. Stumpp 1998: 186–91.

375. Cassius Dio 56.20.1–2; Tacitus, *Histories* 2.80.3. But see also Tacitus, *Histories* 4.65.

376. Friedl 1996: 229–69 and esp. Phang 2001. Unions were never *banned*; rather, the state merely withheld legal acknowledgment.

377. Since the reign of Hadrian, even the children of soldiers who had died intestate were able to claim limited inheritance rights if they were able to document their descent: Phang 2001: 38–40.

378. Friedl 1996: 256–57 discusses possibly polygynous relationships in inscriptions, concluding that they were probably successive rather than simultaneous. Phang 2001: 412–13 concludes that the evidence is ambiguous. Cf. section 3.5.1.

379. Gilliam 1968.

380. Allason-Jones 1989: 63; Friedl 1996: 264.

381. Keenan 1994: 104.

382. Friedl 1996: 264–65.

383. I remain unimpressed by the absence of unions between Roman soldiers and native women recorded on epitaphs in North Africa (Cherry 1998: 101–40). As Cherry makes clear, these texts show not "how often Roman married indigene (which is historically unrecoverable), but the incidence of intermarriage across cultural identities" (ibid. 100). The potential weakness of the epigraphic approach is highlighted by his observation that only 1 out of 185 known unions with soldiers involves a wife with a non-Romanized name (120 table 4.1), an implausibly low frequency of intermarriage (as Cherry himself concedes: cf. 122). It might make more sense to assume that soldiers married local women who had already switched to Roman names or who did so after marriage. This is not to deny the possibility that some of the soldiers' wives were the daughters of other soldiers (e.g., Shaw 1983: 148). In any event, the African garrisons may arguably have been more isolated from the native populations than garrisons in other provinces. Cf. also Pollard 2000: 151–59 for much more meager evidence from Roman soldiers' unions in Syria. In general, about 90 percent of all wives of soldiers and veterans in the epigraphic record bear "Roman" names (*duo nomina* with a Latin *nomen gentile* and a Latin or Greek *cognomen*), leaving little room for indigenous single names or "Roman" names with an indigenous *cognomen*, commonly indicating recent enfranchisement (Phang 2001: 191). Taken at face value, this would seem to suggest

that soldiers overwhelmingly formed unions with women who were either "Roman" (in the narrow sense of citizens who were of Italian origin or descended from other citizen soldiers or enfranchised auxiliary veterans or women who were "Iunian Latins," that is, informally manumitted ex-slaves who had belonged to Roman citizens), or (both legally and culturally) "Romanized" in the sense that they descended from (long?) enfranchised locals. See furthermore Scheidel 2007a.

384. For what may have been a related issue, cf. *Digest* 34.9.14 (with Stumpp 1998: 191 and n.117), on sanctions against (previously honorable) women who committed *stuprum* with soldiers.

385. However, at least in the early stages of occupation, unions with slaves and freedwomen appear to have mitigated this pressure to a considerable extent: cf. Phang 2001: 193–94 (42–50 percent of legionaries' epitaphs at the Danubian frontier in the first century C.E. were set up by freedwomen). Unions with indigenous women may have required a certain amount of social and cultural integration: see n.383.

386. Kautsky 1997: 209.

387. Low 2000a: 66–67 notes that human societies practising serial monomgamy experience greater variance in male than in female reproductive success and are "functionally polygynous."

388. Lovejoy 1990: 179.

389. Alexander 1979: 240.

Bibliography

Abernethy, V. D. (1999) "A Darwinian account of the fertility opportunity hypothesis." *Population and Environment* 21: 119–48.

Abou-Assaf, A., P. Bordreuil, and A. R. Millard (1982) *La statue de Tell Fekherye et son inscription bilingue assyro-araméenne*. Paris.

Abulafia, D. (1987) *Italy, Sicily and the Mediterranean, 1100–1400*. London.

Albertz, R. (2001) *Die Exilszeit: 6. Jahrhundert v.Chr*. Stuttgart.

Alcock, J. (2001) *The triumph of sociobiology*. New York and Oxford.

Alcock, S. E., et al., eds. (2001) *Empires*. Cambridge.

Alexander, R. D. (1979) *Darwinism and human affairs*. Seattle.

Alexander, R. D. (1987) *The biology of moral systems*. Hawthorne.

Alexander, R. D., et al. (1979) "Sexual dimorphisms and breeding systems in pinnipeds, ungulates, primates, and humans," in Chagnon and Irons, eds. (1979): 402–35.

Alfonso, S., et al. (2001) "A European lead isotope signal recorded from 6000 to 300 years B.P. in coastal marshes (SW France)." *Atmospheric Environment* 35: 3595–3605.

Allam, S. (1975) "Ehe," in W. Helck and E. Otto, eds., *Lexikon der Ägyptologie*. Vol. 1. Wiesbaden: 1162–81.

Allason-Jones, L. (1989) *Women in Roman Britain*. London.

Allen, L. (2005) *The Persian Empire*. Chicago

Allen, M. (2005) "Power is in the details: Administrative technology and the growth of Ancient Near Eastern cores," in C. Chase-Dunn and N. E. Anderson, eds., *The historical evolution of world-systems*. Basingstoke: 75–91.

Altman, I., and J. Ginat (1996) *Polygamous families in contemporary society*. Cambridge.

Anderson, B. (1991) *Imagined communities*. 2nd ed. London.

Anderson, J. L., et al. (1992) "Was the Duchess of Windsor right? A cross-cultural review of the sociobiology of ideals of female body shape." *Ethology and Sociobiology* 13: 197–227.

Anderson, P. (1974) *Passages from antiquity to feudalism*. London.

Anderson, P. (1974/79) *Lineages of the absolutist state*. London.

Andrae, W. (1977) *Das wiedererstandene Assur*. 2nd ed. revised by B. Hrouda. Munich.

Andreades, A. M. (1933) *A history of Greek public finance* I. Tr. C. N. Brown. Cambridge, Mass.

Andrewes, A. (1966) "The government of classical Sparta," in Badian, ed. (1966): 1–20.

Andreyev, Y. (1990) "Ausserathenische Quellen der Reichtumsbildung Athens im 5./4. Jhs. v. u. Z." *Jahrbuch für Wirtschaftsgeschichte* 1990.2: 115–75.

Anello, P. (1986) "Il trattato del 405/4 a.C. e la formazione della 'eparchia' punica di Sicilia." *Kokalos* 32: 115–80.

Angel, L. (1972) "Ecology and population in the east Mediterranean." *World Archaeology* 4: 88–105.

Angold, M. (1975) *A Byzantine government in exile: Government and society under the Laskarids of Nicaea (1204–1261).* Oxford.

Angold, M. (1984) *The Byzantine Empire 1025–1204: A political history.* London.

Angold, M. (1985) "The shaping of the medieval Byzantine 'city.'" *Byzantinische Forschungen* 10: 1–37.

Angold, M. (1995) *Church and society in Byzantium under the Comneni, 1081–1261.* Cambridge.

Aperghis, M. (2001) "Population—production—taxation—coinage: A model for the Seleukid economy," in Z. H. Archibald et al., eds. *Hellenistic economies.* London: 69–102.

Aperghis, M. (2004) *The Seleukid royal economy.* Cambridge.

Appadurai, A., and C. Breckenridge (1976) "The South Indian temple: Authority, honour and redistribution." *Contributions to Indian Sociology* 10: 187–211.

Appadurai, C. (1981) "The past as a scarce resource." *Man* 16: 201–19.

Armayor, O. K. (1978) "Herodotus' catalogues of the Persian empire in light of the monuments and the Greek literary tradition." *Transactions and Proceedings of the American Philological Association* 108: 1–9.

Arnason, J. P., S. N. Eisenstadt, and B. Wittrock, eds. (2005) *Axial civilizations and world history.* Leiden.

Arnasson, J. P. (2000) "Approaching Byzantium: Identity, predicament and afterlife." *Thesis Eleven* 62: 39–69.

Arthur, B. (1989) "Competing technologies, increasing returns, and lock-in by historical events." *Economic Journal* 99: 116–31.

Assmann, J. (1992) *Das kulturelle Gedächtnis: Schrift, Erinnerung und politische identität in frühen Hochkulturen.* Munich.

Atran, S. (2002) *In gods we trust: The evolutionary landscape of religion.* New York.

Aubet, M. E. (2001) *The Phoenicians and the West: Politics, colonies, and trade.* 2nd ed. Cambridge.

Ault, B. (1999) "*Koprones* and oil presses at Halieis." *Hesperia* 68: 549–73.

Ault, B. (2006) *Excavations at ancient Halieis* II. *The houses: The organization and use of domestic space.* Bloomington, Ind.

Bäbler, B. (1998) *Fleißige Thrakerinnen und wehrhafte Skythen: Nichtgriechen im klassischen Athen und ihre archäologische Hinterlassenschaft.* Stuttgart.

Backendorf, D. (1998) *Römische Münzschätze des zweiten und ersten Jahrunderts v. Chr. vom italienischen Festland.* Berlin.

Badcock, C. (1991) *Evolution and individual behavior: an introduction to human sociobiology.* Oxford and Cambridge, Mass.

Badcock, C. (2000) *Evolutionary psychology: A critical introduction.* Cambridge and Malden, Mass.

Badian, E., ed. (1966) *Ancient society and institutions.* Oxford.

Baker, R. R., and Bellis, M. A. (1995) *Human sperm competition: Copulation, masturbation and infidelity.* London.

Balard, M. (1989) "The Genoese in the Aegean," in B. Arbel, B. Hamilton, and D. Jacoby, eds., *Latins and Greeks in the Eastern Mediterranean after 1204.* London: 158–74.

Balcer, J. M. (1976) "Imperial magistrates in the Athenian Empire." *Historia* 25: 257–87.

Balcer, J. M. (1977) "The Athenian *episkopos* and the Achaemenid 'King's Eye.'" *American Journal of Philology* 98: 252–63.

Balcer, J. M. (1978) *The Athenian regulations for Chalkis: Studies in Athenian imperial law.* Weisbaden (*Historia* Einzelschrift 33).

Balot, R. (2001) *Greed and injustice in classical Athens.* Princeton.

Banaji, J. (2001) *Agrarian change in late antiquity: Gold, labour, and aristocratic dominance.* Oxford.

Bang, P. F. (2003) "Rome and the comparative study of tributary empires." *Medieval History Journal* 6/2: 189–216.

Bang, P. F., and C. Bayly (2003) "Introduction: comparing pre-modern empires." *Medieval History Journal* 6: 169–87.

Bär, J. (1996) *Der assyrische Tribut und seine Darstellung. Eine Untersuchungen zur imperialen Ideologie im neuassyrischen Reich.* Neukirchener-Vluyn.

Barkey, K. (1997) *Bandits and bureaucrats: The Ottoman route to state centralization.* Ithaca, N.Y.

Barkow, J. H. (1989) *Darwin, sex, and status: Biological approaches to mind and culture.* Toronto, Buffalo, and London.

Barnett, R. D. (1982) "Urartu," in J. Boardman et al., eds. *The Cambridge Ancient History* III.1. 2nd ed. Cambridge: 314–71.

Bartusis, M. C. (1992) *The late Byzantine army: Arms and society, 1204–1453.* Philadelphia.

Batto, B. F. (1974) *Studies on women at Mari.* Baltimore and London.

Beaulieu, P.-A. (2006) "Official and vernacular languages: The shifting sands of imperial and cultural identities in first millennium B.C. Mesopotamia," in S. L. Sanders, ed., *Origins of writing, margins of cultures.* Chicago: 187–216.

Becker, G. S. (1974) "A theory of marriage: Part II." *Journal of Political Economy* 82.2.2: S11-S26 (repr. in R. Febrero and P. S. Schwartz, eds., *The essence of Becker*, Stanford [1995]: 310–28).

Bedford, P. (2007) "The Persian Near East," in Scheidel et al., eds. (2007): 302–29.

Bedford, P. R. (2001) *Temple restoration in early Achaemenid Judah.* Leiden.

Ben-Barak, Z. (1987) "The queen consort and the struggle for succession to the throne," in Durand, ed. (1987): 33–40.

Bergstrom, T. (1994) "Primogeniture, monogamy, and reproductive success in a stratified society." Department of Economics, University of California, Santa Barbara, Paper 1994B.

Betzig, L. (1986) *Despotism and differential reproduction: A Darwinian view of history.* Hawthorne.

Betzig, L. (1988) "Mating and parenting in Darwinian perspective," in Betzig et al., eds. (1988): 3–20

Betzig, L. (1991) "History," in Maxwell, ed. (1991): 131–40.

Betzig, L. (1992a) "A little history of Darwinian history." *Ethology and Sociobiology* 13: 303–7.

Betzig, L. (1992b) "Roman polygyny." *Ethology and Sociobiology* 13: 309–349 (repr. in Betzig, ed. [1997]: 375–98).

Betzig, L. (1992c) "Roman monogamy." *Ethology and Sociobiology* 13: 351–83.

Betzig, L. (1993) "Sex, succession, and stratification in the first six civilizations," in L. Ellis, ed., *Socioeconomic inequality and social stratification.* Vol. I. Westport, Conn.: 37–74.

Betzig, L. (1994) "The point of politics." *Analyse & Kritik* 16: 20–37.

Betzig, L. (1995) "Medieval monogamy." *Journal of Family History* 20: 181–216.

Betzig, L. (1997a) "Introduction: People are animals," in Betzig, ed. 1997: 1–17.

Betzig, L. (1997b) "Why a despot?" in Betzig, ed. 1997: 399–401.

Betzig, L. (2002) "British polygyny," in M. Smith, ed., *Human biology and history*. London and New York: 30–97.

Betzig, L. (2005) "Politics as sex: The Old Testament case." *Evolutionary Psychology* 3: 326–46.

Betzig, L., ed. (1997) *Human nature: A critical reader*. New York and Oxford.

Betzig, L., and S. Weber (1993) "Polygyny in American politics." *Politics and the Life Sciences* 12: 45–52.

Betzig, L., M. Borgerhoff Mulder, and P. Turke, eds. (1988), *Human reproductive behaviour: A Darwinian perspective*. Cambridge.

Bhabha, H. (1994) *The location of culture*. London.

Bhaskar, R. B. (1978) *A realist theory of science*. Brighton.

Bhaskar, R. B. (1987) *Scientific realism and human emancipation*. London.

Bichler, R. (2000) *Herodots Welt*. Berlin.

Bichler, R., and R. Rollinger (2003) "Greece VI: The image of Persia and Persian in Greek literature," in *Encyclopaedia Iranica* 11: 326–29.

Bielenstein, H. (1986) "Wang Mang, the restoration of the Han dynasty, and Later Han," in D. Twitchett and M. Loewe, eds., *The Cambridge History of China, I: The Ch'in and Han empires, 221 B.C.—A.D. 220*. Cambridge: 223–90.

Billigmeier, J.-C. (1985) "Studies on the family in the Aegean Bronze Age and in Homer." *Trends in History* 3, 3–4: 9–18.

Bintliff, J. (1997) "Regional survey, demography, and the rise of complex societies in the ancient Aegean: Core-periphery, neo-malthusian, and other interpretive models." *Journal of Field Archaeology* 24: 1–38.

Bisel, S. (1990) "Anthropologische Untersuchungen," in W. Kovacscovics, ed., *Kerameikos* XIV: *Die Eckterrasse*. Berlin: 151–59.

Bisel, S., and J. L. Angel. (1985) "Health and nutrition in Mycenaean Greece," in N. Wilkie and W. Coulson, eds., *Contributions to Aegean Archaeology*. Minneapolis: 197–210.

Blackmore, S. (1999) *The meme machine*. Oxford and New York.

Bleser, C. K. (1991) "Southern planter wives and slavery," in D. R. Chesnutt and C. N. Wilson, eds., *The meaning of South Carolina history: Essays in honor of George C. Rogers, Jr.*. Columbia, S.C.: 104–20.

Block, F. (1988) *Revising state theory*. Philadelphia.

Boardman, J. (2000) *Persia and the west: An archaeological investigation on the genesis of Achaemenid Persian art*. London.

Boeckh, A. (1840) *Urkunden über das Seewesen des attischen Staates*. Berlin.

Boedeker, D., and K. Raaflaub (1998a) "Reflections and conclusions: democracy, empire, and the arts in fifth-century Athens." In Boedeker and Raaflaub, eds. (1998): 319–44.

Boedeker, D., and K. Raaflaub, eds. (1998b) *Democracy, empire, and the arts in fifth-century Athens*. Cambridge, Mass.

Boegehold, A. L. (1994) "Perikles' citizenship law of 451/0 B.C.," in A. L. Boegehold and A. C. Scafuro, eds., *Athenian identity and civic ideology*. Baltimore: 57–66.

Boehm, C. (1992) "Segmentary "warfare" and the management of conflict: Comparison of East African chimpanzees and patrilineal-patrilocal humans," in A. H. Harcourt and F. B. M. de Waal, eds., *Coalitions and alliances in humans and other animals*. Oxford: 137–73.

Boone, J. L. (1988) "Parental investment, social subordination and population processes among the 15th and 16th century Portuguese nobility," in Betzig et al., eds. (1988): 201–19.

Boone, J. L., and K. L. Kessler (1999) "More status or more children? Social status, fertility reduction, and social long-term fitness." *Evolution and Human Behavior* 20: 257–77.

Borger, R. (1956) *Die Inschriften Asarhaddons, Königs von Assyrie*n. Graz.

Borgerhoff Mulder, M. (1987) "On cultural and reproductive success: Kipsigis evidence." *American Anthropologist* 89: 617–34.

Borgerhoff Mulder, M. (1988) "Reproductive success in three Kipsigis cohorts," in T. H. Clutton-Brock, ed., *Reproductive success: Studies of individual variation in contrasting breeding systems*. Chicago and London: 419–35.

Borgerhoff Mulder, M. (1992) "Reproductive decisions," in E. A. Smith and B. Winterhalder, eds., *Evolutionary ecology and human behavior*. New York: 339–74.

Bosworth, A. B. (1997) "The emasculation of the Calchedonians: A forgotten episode of the Ionian War." *Chiron* 27: 297–313.

Bourdieu, P. (1968) "Structuralism and the theory of sociological knowledge." *Social Research* 35: 682–706.

Boutron, C., et al. (2004) "Anthropogenic lead in polar show and ice archives." *Comptes Rendue Geoscience* 336: 847–67.

Boyer, L. (1986) "Concubinages et concubinats du code d'Hammurabi à la fin du XIXe siècle," in J. Rubellin-Devichi, ed., *Les concubinages: Approche socio-juridique*. Paris: 127–63.

Boyer, P. (2001) *Religion explained: The evolutionary origins of religious thought*. New York.

Bradley, K. R. (1987) *Slaves and masters in the Roman empire: A study in social control*. New York and Oxford.

Brand, C. M. (1968) *Byzantium confronts the West, 1180–1204*. Cambridge, Mass.

Brandes, W. (1989) *Die Städte Kleinasiens im 7. und 8. Jahrhundert*. Berlin.

Brannvall, M. L., et al. (1999) "The medieval metal industry was the cradle of modern large scale atmospheric lead pollution in northern Europe." *Environmental Science and Technology* 33: 4391–95.

Brannvall, M. L., et al. (2001) "Four thousand years of atmospheric lead pollution in northern Europe: A summary from Swedish lake sediments." *Journal of Paleolimnology* 25: 421–35.

Brent, L. (1973) *Incidents in the life of a slave girl*. Ed. L. M. Child. San Diego, New York, and London.

Bretschneider, P. (1992) "Sociobiological models of polygyny: A critical review," *Anthropos* 87: 183–91.

Bretschneider, P. (1995) *Polygyny: A cross-cultural study*. Uppsala.

Brewer, J. (1988) *The sinews of power: War, money and the English state, 1688–1783*. Cambridge, Mass.

Briant, P. (1982) *État et pasteurs au Moyen-Orient ancien*. Paris and Cambridge.

Briant, P. (1988) "Le nomadisme du Grand Roi." *Iranica Antiqua* 23: 253–73.

Briant, P. (1991) "Le roi est mort: Vive le roi! Remarques sur les rites et rituels de succession chez les Achéménides," in J. Kellens, ed., *La religion iranienne à l'époque achéménide*. Ghent: 1–11.

Briant, P. (1994) "L'eau du Grand Roi," in L. Milano, ed., *Drinking in ancient societies: History and culture of drinks in the Ancient Near East*. Padua: 45–65.

Briant, P. (1996) *Histoire de l'empire perse de Cyrus à Alexandre*. Paris.

Briant, P. (1999a) "Histoire de l'empire achéménide aujourd'hui: L'historien et ses documents." *Annales HSS* 1999: 1127–36.

Briant, P. (1999b) "The Achaemenid empire," in K. Raaflaub and N. Rosenstein, eds., *War and society in the ancient and medieval worlds.* Cambridge, Mass.: 102–28.

Briant, P. (2002a) *From Cyrus to Alexander: a history of the Persian Empire.* Winona Lake, IN.

Briant, P. (2002b) "History and ideology: The Greeks and 'Persian decadence,'" in T. Harrison, ed., *Greeks and barbarians.* Edinburgh: 193–210,

Briant, P. (2003) *Darius dans l'ombre d'Alexandre.* Paris,

Brinkman, J. A. (1983) "Through a glass darkly: Esarhaddon's retrospects on the downfall of Babylon." *Journal of the American Oriental Society* 103: 35–42.

Brinkman, J. A. (1984) *Prelude to empire: Babylonian society and politics, 747–626 B.C.* Philadelphia.

Brinkman, J. A. (1990) "Political covenants, treaties, and loyalty oaths in Babylonia and between Assyria and Babylonia," in Canfora, Liverani, and Zaccagnini, eds. (1990): 81–111.

Brinkman, J. A. (1995) "Reflections on the geography of Babylonia (1000–600 B.C.)," in Liverani, ed. (1995), 19–29.

Brinkman, J. A. (1997) "Unfolding the drama of the Assyrian empire," in Parpola and Whiting, eds. (1997): 1–16.

Brinkman, J. A., and D. A. Kennedy (1983) "Documentary evidence for the economic base of early Neo-Babylonian economic texts: A survey of dated Babylonian economic texts, 721–626 B.C." *Journal of Cuneiform Studies* 35: 1–90.

Brosius, M. (1996) *Women in ancient Persia (559–331 B.C.).* Oxford.

Brosius, M. (2006) *The Persians.* London.

Brown, D. E., and D. Hotra (1988) "Are prescriptively monogamous societies effectively monogamous?" in Betzig et al., eds. (1988): 153–59.

Brown, P. R. L. (1971) *The world of late antiquity.* London.

Brown, P. R. L. (1981) *The cult of the saints: Its rise and function in Latin Christianity.* Chicago.

Brubaker, L., and J. F. Haldon (2001) *Byzantium in the iconoclast period (ca. 680–850): The sources. An annotated survey.* Aldershot.

Brunt, P. A. (1966) "Athenian settlements abroad in the fifth century B.C.," in Badian, ed. (1966): 71–92.

Brunt, P. A. (1971a) *Italian manpower 225 B.C.–A.D. 14.* Oxford (repr. 1987).

Brunt, P. A. (1971b) *Social conflicts in the Roman Republic.* London.

Buck, R. J. (1979) *A history of Boeotia.* Edmonton.

Bunnens, G. (1993–94) "Tell Ahmar/Til Barsip, 1988–1992." *Archiv für Orientforschung* 50–51: 221–25.

Bunnens, G., ed. (2000) *Essays on Syria in the Iron Age.* Louvain.

Burford, A. (1993) *Land and labor in the Greek world.* Baltimore.

Burkert, W. (1985) *Greek religion.* Cambridge, Mass.

Burkert, W. (1996) *Creation of the sacred: Tracks of biology in early religions.* Cambridge, Mass., and London.

Burstein, S. M. (1976) *Outpost of Hellenism: The emergence of Heraclea on the Black Sea.* Berkeley.

Bush, B. (1990) *Slave women in Caribbean society 1650–1838.* Kingston.

Buss, D. M. (1994) *The evolution of desire: Strategies of human mating.* New York.

Buss, D. M. (1999) *Evolutionary psychology: The new science of the mind.* Boston.

Buss, D. M., ed. (2005) *The handbook of evolutionary psychology.* Hoboken.

Cagnazzi, S. (2001) *Gli esìli in Persia*. Bari.

Cameron, A. (1991) *Christianity and the rhetoric of empire: The development of Christian discourse*. Berkeley.

Cameron, A. (1993) *The Mediterranean world in late Antiquity, A.D. 395–600*. London.

Cameron, A., and L. Conrad, eds. (1992) *The Byzantine and Early Islamic Near East* I: *Problems in the literary source material*. Princeton.

Cameron, A., ed. (1995) *The Byzantine and Early Islamic Near East* III: *States, resources and armies: Papers of the third workshop on late Antiquity and early Islam*. Princeton.

Campbell, B. (1984) *The emperor and the Roman army 31 B.C.–A.D. 235*. Oxford.

Campbell, B. (2002) *War and society in imperial Rome 31 B.C.–A.D. 284*. London and New York.

Canfora, L., M. Liverani, and C. Zaccagnini, eds. (1990) *I trattati nel mondo antico: Forma, ideologia, funzione*. Rome.

Capelli, C., et al. (2003) "A Y-chromosome census of the British Isles." *Current Biology* 13: 979–84.

Carey, C. (1995) "Rape and adultery in Athenian law." *Classical Quarterly* 45: 407–17.

Carneiro, R. L. (1987) "Cross-currents in the theory of state formation." *American Ethnologist* 14: 756–70.

Carney, E. D. (1992) "The politics of polygamy." *Historia* 41: 169–89.

Carney, E. D. (2000) *Women and monarchy in Macedonia*. Norman, Okla.

Carrasco, D. (1999) *City of sacrifice: The Aztec empire and the role of violence in civilization*. Boston.

Carroll, J. (1995) *Evolution and literary theory*. Columbia, S.C.

Carroll, J. (1999) "The deep structure of literary representation." *Evolution and Human Behavior* 20: 159–73.

Cartledge, P. (1981) "The politics of Spartan pederasty." *Proceedings of the Cambridge Philological Society* 30: 17–36.

Cartledge, P. (1987) *Agesilaos and the crisis of Sparta*. Baltimore.

Cartledge, P. (1998) "The economy (economies) of ancient Greece," *Dialogos* 5: 4–24.

Cartledge, P., E. Cohen, and L. Foxhall, eds. (2001) *Money, labour and land: Approaches to the economies of ancient Greece*. London and New York.

Casimir, M. J., and A. Rao (1995) "Prestige, possessions, and progeny: Cultural goals and reproductive success among the Bakkarwal." *Human Nature* 6: 241–72.

Casson, L. (1986) *Ships and seamanship in the ancient world*. 2nd ed. Princeton.

Castriota, D. (1992) *Myth, ethos, and actuality*. Madison, Wis.

Catling, R. (2002) "The survey area from the Early Iron Age to the classical period," in W. Cavanagh, J. Crouwel, R. Catling, and G. Shipley, *Continuity and change in a Greek rural landscape: The Laconia survey* I. London and Athens: 151–256.

Cavalli-Sforza, L. L., and Feldman, M. W. (1981) *Cultural transmission and evolution: A quantitative approach*. Princeton.

Chagnon, N. (1979) "Is reproductive success equal in egalitarian societies?" in Chagnon and Irons, eds. (1979): 374–401.

Chagnon, N. (1988) "Life histories, blood revenge, and warfare in a tribal population." *Science* 239: 985–92.

Chagnon, N., and W. Irons, eds. (1979) *Evolutionary biology and human social behavior: An anthropological perspective*. North Scituate, Mass.

Chagnon, N., M. V. Flinn, and T. Melancon (1979) "Sex-ratio variation among the Yanomamo," in Chagnon and Irons, eds. (1979): 290–320.

Chambers, M. H., R. Gallucci, and P. Spanos, P. (1990) "Athens' alliance with Egesta in the year of Antiphon." *Zeitschrift für Papyrologie und Epigraphik* 83: 38–63.

Champakalakshmi, R. (1981) "Peasant state and society in medieval South India: A review article." *Indian Economic and Social History Review* 18: 411–26.

Champlin, E. (1991) *Final judgments: Duty and emotion in Roman wills, 200 B.C.–A.D. 250.* Berkeley.

Chang, J. and J. Halliday (2006) *Mao: The unknown story.* London.

Cherry, D. (1998) *Frontier and society in Roman North Africa.* Oxford.

Cherry, J., J. L. Davis, and E. Mantzourani, eds. 1991. *Landscape archaeology as long-term history: Keos in the Northern Cyclades.* Los Angeles.

Chesnut, M. B. C. (1951) *A diary from Dixie.* Boston.

Cheynet, J.-C. (1990) *Pouvoir et contestations à Byzance (963–1210).* Paris.

Chisholm, J. S. (1999) *Death, hope and sex: Steps to an evolutionary ecology of mind and morality.* Cambridge.

Christensen, A. (1944) *L'Iran sous les Sassanides.* 2nd ed. Copenhagen; repr. Osnabrück, 1971.

Christiansen, E. (1988) *The Roman coins of Alexandria: Quantitative studies.* 2 vols. Aarhus.

Cifarelli, M. (1995) "Enmity, alienation and Assyrianization: The role of cultural difference in the visual and verbal expression of Assyrian ideology in the reign of Assurnasiral II (883–859 B.C.)" Unpublished Ph.D. thesis, Columbia University.

Cifarelli, M. (1998) "Gesture and alterity in the art of Ashurnasirpal II." *Art Bulletin* 80: 212–28.

Cipolla, C. M., ed. (1970) *The economic decline of empires.* London.

Claessen, J. M., and P. Skalník, eds. (1978) *The early state.* The Hague.

Claessen, J. M., and P. Skalník, eds. (1981) *The study of the state.* The Hague.

Clarysse, W., and D. Thompson (2006) *Counting the people in Hellenistic Egypt.* Cambridge.

Clinton, C. (1991) "'Southern dishonor': flesh, blood, race, and bondage," in C. Bleser, ed., *In joy and sorrow: Women, family, and marriage in the Victorian South.* New York and Oxford: 52–68.

Clutton-Brock, T. H. (1988) "Reproductive success," in Clutton-Brock, ed. (1988): 472–85.

Clutton-Brock, T. H., ed. (1988) *Reproductive success: Studies of individual variation in contrasting breeding systems.* Chicago and London.

Coale, A. J., and P. Demeny (1983) *Regional model life tables and stable populations.* 2nd ed. New York.

Coe, M. D. (2003) *Angkor and the Khmer civilization.* New York.

Cogan, M. (1974) *Imperialism and religion: Assyria, Judah and Israel in the eighth and seventh centuries B.C.E.* Missoula.

Cogan, M. (1993) "Judah under Assyrian hegemony: A reexamination of imperialism and religion." *Journal of Biblical Literature* 112: 403–14.

Cohen, D. (1991) *Law, sexuality and society: The enforcement of morals in classical Athens.* Cambridge.

Cohen, D. (1993) "Consent and sexual relations in classical Athens," in A. E. Laiou, ed., *Consent and coercion to sex and marriage in ancient and medieval societies.* Washington, D.C.: 5–16.

Cohen, E. (1992) *Athenian economy and society: A banking perspective.* Princeton.

Cohen, J. E. (1995) *How many people can the earth support?* New York and London.

Cohen, R., and E. R. Service (1978) *Origins of the state: The anthropology of political evolution.* Philadelphia.

Cole, S. (1996) *Nippur in Late Assyrian times c. 755–612 B.C.* Helsinki.

Cole, S., and P. Machinist (1998) *Letters from priests to the kings Esarhaddon and Assurbanipal.* Helsinki.

Cole, T. (1991) "Who was Corax?" *Illinois Classical Studies* 16: 65–84.

Connerton, P. (1989) *How societies remember.* Cambridge.

Connor, W. R. (1971) *The new politicians of fifth-century Athens.* Princeton.

Connor, W. R. (1984) *Thucydides.* Princeton.

Consolo Langher, S. N. (1996) *Siracusa e la Sicilia greca.* Messina.

Contenau, G. (1954) *Everyday life in Babylon and Assyria.* London.

Cooke, B. (1999) "The promise of biothematics," in J. B. Bedaux and B. Cooke, eds., *Sociobiology and the arts.* Amsterdam and Atlanta: 43–62.

Cooley, A., ed. (2002) *Becoming Roman, writing Latin? Literacy and epigraphy in the Roman West.* Portsmouth, R.I.

Cooper, E. (1916) *The harim and purdah: Studies of Oriental women.* New York.

Cornell, T. J. (1995) *The beginnings of Rome: Italy and Rome from the Bronze Age to the Punic Wars (c. 1000–264 B.C.).* London and New York.

Cortizas, A. M., et al. (1997) "Four thousand years of atmospheric Pb, Cd and Zn deposition recorded by the ombrotrophic peat bog of Penido Vello (northwestern Spain)." *Water, Air and Soil Pollution* 100: 387–403.

Cortizas, A. M., et al. (2002) "Atmospheric Pb deposition in Spain during the last 4600 years recorded by two ombotropic peat bogs and implications for the use of peat as archive." *Science of the Total Environment* 292: 33–44.

Cowlishaw, G., and R. Mace (1996) "Cross-cultural patterns of marriage ad inheritance: A phylogenetic approach." *Ethology and Sociobiology* 17: 87–97.

Cox, C. A. (1998) *Household interests: Property, marriage strategies, and family dynamics in ancient Athens.* Princeton.

Crone, P. (1991) "Kavad's heresy and Mazdak's revolt." *Iran* 29: 21–42.

Cronk, L. (1991) "Wealth, status, and reproductive success among the Mukogodo of Kenya." *American Anthropologist* 93: 345–60.

Cronk, L. (1999) *That complex whole: Culture and the evolution of human behavior.* Boulder, Colo., and Oxford.

Cronk, L., N. Chagnon, and W. Irons, eds. (2000) *Adaptation and human behavior: An anthropological perspective.* New York.

Cunningham, M. R., et al. (1995) "Their ideas of beauty are, on the whole, the same as ours: Consistency and variability in the cross-cultural perception of female physical attractiveness." *Journal of Personality and Social Psychology* 68: 261–79.

Cvorovic, J. (2001) "Polygyny and tolerated male homosexuality." Paper delivered at the 2001 Human Behavior and Evolution Society Conference, London.

Dalley, S. (2000) "Shamshi-Ilu, language and power in the western Assyrian empire" in Bunnens, ed. (2000): 79–88.

Daly, M., and M. Wilson (1983) *Sex, evolution, and behavior.* 2nd ed. Belmont.

Dandamaev, M. A. (1984) *Slavery in Babylonia: From Nabopolassar to Alexander the Great (626–331 B.C.).* De Kalb, Ill.

Darwin, C. (1871) *The descent of man, and selection in relation to sex.* London.

Davidson, J. (1997) *Courtesans and fishcakes: The consuming passions of classical Athens.* London.

Davies, J. K. (1978) *Democracy and classical Greece.* Glasgow.

Davies, J. K. (2001) "Temples, credit, and the circulation of money," in A. Meadows and K. Shipton, eds., *Money and its uses in ancient Greece*. Oxford: 117–28.

Davies, R. (1989) *Service in the Roman army*. Edinburgh.

Davis, J. (1977) *People of the Mediterranean*. London.

Dawkins, R. (1982) *The extended phenotype*. Oxford and New York.

Dawkins, R. (1989) *The selfish gene*. New ed. Oxford and New York.

De Angelis, F. (2000) "Estimating the agricultural base of Greek Sicily." *Papers of the British School at Rome* 68: 111–148.

De Angelis, F. (2003) *Megara Hyblaia and Selinous*. Oxford.

De Angelis, F. (forthcoming) *A social and economic history of Greek Sicily*. New York.

De Callatay, F. (2005) "The Graeco-Roman economy in the super long run: Lead, copper, and shipwrecks." *Journal of Roman Archaeology* 18: 361–72.

De Ste Croix, G. E. M. (1981) *The class struggle in the ancient Greek world*. London.

Delia, D. (1988) "The population of Roman Alexandria." *Transactions of the American Philological Association* 118: 275–92.

Demand, N. (1982) *Thebes in the fifth century B.C.* London.

Dennett, D. C. (1950) *Conversion and the poll-tax in early Islam*. Cambridge, Mass.

Dennett, D. C. (1995) *Darwin's dangerous idea: Evolution and the meanings of life*. London.

Dennett, D. C. (2006) *Breaking the spell: Religion as a natural phenomenon*. New York.

Descoeudres, J.-P., ed. (1990) *Greek colonists and native populations*. Oxford.

Di Cosmo, N. (1999) "State formation and periodization in Inner Asian history." *Journal of World History* 10: 1–40.

Diakonoff, I. M. (1974) "Slaves, helots and serfs in early antiquity." *Acta Antiqua* 22: 45–78.

Diamond, J. (1992) *The rise and fall of the third chimpanzee*. London.

Diamond, J. (1997) *Guns, germs and steel: The fates of human societies*. New York.

Dickemann, M. (1979) "The ecology of mating systems in hypergynous dowry systems." *Social Science Information* 18: 163–95.

Dietrich, W. (2003) *The Neo-Babylonian correspondence of Sargon and Sennacherib*. Helsinki.

Dinçol, A. M. (1994) "Cultural and political contacts between Assyria and Urartu." *Tel Aviv* 21: 6–21.

Doblhofer, G. (1994) *Vergewaltigung in der Antike*. Stuttgart and Leipzig.

Domaszewski, A. v. (1967) *Die Rangordnung des römischen Heeres*. 2nd ed. Cologne and Graz.

Donbaz, V., and M. W. Stolper (1997) *Istanbul Murašû Texts*. Leiden.

Donner, F. M. (1981) *The early Islamic conquests*. Princeton.

Donner, F. M. (1986) "The formation of the Islamic state." *Journal of the American Oriental Society* 106: 283–95.

Donner, F. M. (1995) "Centralized authority and military autonomy in the early Islamic conquests," in Cameron, ed. (1995): 337–60.

Donner, H. (1977) "The separate states of Israel and Judah: The beginning of the Assyrian period of the history of Israel and Judah," in J. H. Hayes and J. A. Miller, eds., *Israelite and Judean history*, London: 415–21.

Dover, K. J. (1974) *Greek popular morality in the time of Plato and Aristotle*. Oxford.

Doyle, M. (1986) *Empires*. Princeton.

Drexhage, H.-J., H. Konen, and K. Ruffing (2002) *Die Wirtschaft des Römischen Reiches (1.-3. Jahrhundert): Eine Einführung*. Berlin.

Driver, G. R., and J. C. Miles (1935) *The Assyrian laws*. Oxford.

Ducat, J. (1990) *Les hilotes*. Paris.

Dunbar, R. I. M. (1991) "Comment." *Current Anthropology* 32: 378–79.

Dunbar, R. I. M. (1995) "The price of being at the top." *Nature* 373: 22–23.

Duncan-Jones, R. (1990) *Structure and change in the Roman economy*. Cambridge.

Duncan-Jones, R. (1994) *Money and government in the Roman empire*. Cambridge.

Durán, D. (1964) *The Aztecs: The history of the Indies of New Spain*. New York.

Durand, J.-M. (1985) "Les dames du palais de Mari à l'époque du Royaume de Haute Mésopotamie." *Mari* 4: 385–436.

Durand, J.-M., and J. Margueron (1980) "La question du harem royal dans le palais de Mari." *Journal des Savants*: 253–80.

Durand, J.-M., ed. (1987) *La femme dans la Proche-Orient antique*. Paris

Durham, W. H. (1976) "Resource competition and human aggression. Part I: a review of primitive war," *Quarterly Review of Biology* 51: 385–415.

Durham, W. H. (1991) *Coevolution: genes, culture and human diversity*. Stanford.

Durkheim, E. (1961) *The elementary forms of the religious life*. New York.

Durkheim, E. (1976 [1933]) *The division of labor in society*. Trans. G. Simpson. New York.

Dusinberre, E. (2003) *Aspects of empire in Achaemenid Sardis*. Cambridge.

Dvornik, F. (1948) *The Photian schism: History and legend*. Cambridge.

Dvornik, F. (1966) *Early Christian and Byzantine political philosophy*. 2 vols. Washington, D.C.

Dvornik, F. (1970) *Byzantine missions among the Slavs: SS. Constantine-Cyril and Methodius*. New Brunswick, N.J.

Dyson, S. L. (1985) *The creation of the Roman frontier*. Princeton.

Eck, W. (2000) "The growth of administrative posts," in *CAH* XI. 2nd ed. Cambridge: 238–65.

Eck, W. (2003) *The age of Augustus*. Oxford and Malden, Mass.

Eddy, S. K. (1968) "Athens' peacetime navy in the age of Pericles." *Greek, Roman and Byzantine Studies* 9: 141–56.

Edwards, C., and G. Woolf, eds. (2003) *Rome the cosmopolis*. Cambridge.

Ehrenberg, V. (1969) *The Greek state*. London.

Ehrhardt, N. (2003) "Milet nach den Perserkriegen: Ein Neubeginn?" in E. Schwertheim and E. Winter, eds., *Stadt und Stadtentwicklung in Kleinasien*. Bonn: 1–19.

Eich, A. (2005) *Die politische Ökonomie des antiken Griechenlands (6.-3. Jhs. v. Chr.)*. Cologne.

Eich, P. (2005) *Zur Metamorphose des politischen Systems in der römischen Kaiserzeit: Die Entstehung einer "personalen Bürokratie" im langen dritten Jahrhundert*. Berlin.

Einon, D. (1998) "How many children can one man have?" *Evolution and Human Behavior* 19: 413–26.

Eiseman, C., and B. Ridgway (1987) *The Porticello shipwreck: A Mediterranean merchant vessel of 415–385 B.C.* College Station, Texas.

Eisenstadt, S. N. (1969) *The political systems of empires*. New York.

Eisenstadt, S. N. (1986) "The axial age breakthroughs—their characteristics and origins," in Eisenstadt, ed. (1986): 1–25.

Eisenstadt, S. N., ed. (1976) *The decline of empires*. Englewood Cliffs, N.J.

Eisenstadt, S. N., ed. (1986) *The origins and diversity of axial age civilizations*. Albany, N.Y.

Elat, M. (1987) "Der *tamk῀ru* im neuassyrischen Reich." *Journal of the Social and Economic History of the Orient* 30/3: 233–54.

Elias, N. (1967) *Über den Prozeß der Zivilisation. Soziogenetische und psychogenetische Unter-suchungen.* 1: *Wandlungen des Verhaltens in den weltlichen Oberschichten des Abaendlandes*; 2: *Wandlungen der Gesellschaft. Entwurf zu einer Theorie der Zivilisation.* Bern.

Emlen, S. T., and L. W. Oring (1977) "Ecology, sexual selection, and the evolution of mating systems." *Science* 197: 215–23.

Erdkamp, P. (2001) "Beyond the limits of the "consumer city": A model of the urban and rural economy in the Roman world." *Historia* 50: 332–56.

Erdkamp, P. (2005) *The grain market in the Roman empire: A social, political and economic study.* Cambridge.

Erdmann, W. (1934) *Die Ehe im alten Griechenland.* Munich.

Erickson, B. (2005) "Archaeology of empire: Athens and Crete in the fifth century B.C." *American Journal of Archaeology* 109: 619–63.

Ertmann, T. (1997) *Birth of the Leviathan: Building states and regimes in medieval and early modern Europe.* Cambridge.

Erxleben, E. (1975) "Die Kleruchien auf Euböia und Lesbos und die Methoden der attischen Herrschaft im 5. Jh." *Klio* 57: 83–100.

Essock-Vitale, S. M. (1984) "The reproductive success of wealthy Americans." *Ethology and Sociobiology* 5: 45–49.

Etcoff, N. (1999) *Survival of the prettiest: The science of beauty.* New York.

Evans, J. K. (1991) *War, women and children in ancient Rome.* London and New York.

Fabietti, U. (1982) "Sedentarization as a means of detribalisation: Some policies of the Saudi government towards the nomads," in T. Niblock, ed., *State, society and economy in Saudi Arabia.* London: 186–97.

Fales, F. M. (1984a) "The Neo-Assyrian period," in Archi, ed. Circulation of goods in non-palatial context in the ancient Near East. Rome: 207–20.

Fales, (F.) M. (1984b) "A survey of Neo-Assyrian land sales," in Khalidi, ed. (1984), 1–13.

Fales, F. M. (1990) "Istituzioni a confronto tra mondo semitico occidentale e Assiria nel I millennio a.C.: Il trattato di Sefire," in Canfora, Liverani, and Zaccagnini, eds. (1990): 149–73.

Fales, F. M. (2001) *L'impero assiro: Storia e amministrazione (IX–VII secolo A.C.).* Rome.

Fales, F. M., ed. (1981) *Assyrian royal inscriptions: New horizons in literary, ideological and historical analysis.* Rome.

Fales, F. M., and J. N. Postgate (1992, 1995) *Imperial administrative records.* 2 vols. Helsinki.

Faraone, C. (1992) *Talismans and Trojan horses.* Oxford.

Faux, S. F., and H. L. Miller (1984) "Evolutionary speculations on the oligarchic development of Mormon polygyny." *Ethology and Sociobiology* 5: 15–31.

Fehr, B. (1979–81) "Zur religionspolitischen Funktion der Athena Parthenos im Rahmen des delisch-attischen Seebundes." *Hephaistos* 1: 71–91; 2: 113–25; 3: 55–93.

Felton, R. L. (1919) *Country life in Georgia in the days of my youth.* Atlanta.

Fentress, J., and C. J. Wickham (1992) *Social memory.* Oxford.

Ferguson, N. (2004) *Colossus: The price of America's empire.* New York.

Figueira, T. (1981) *Aegina. Society and politics.* Salem, N.H.

Figueira, T. (1991) *Athens and Aigina in the age of imperial colonization.* Baltimore.

Figueira, T. (1998) *The power of money: Coinage and politics in the Athenian Empire.* Philadelphia.

Finkelman, P. (1997) "Crimes of love, misdemeanors of passion: The regulation of sex and race in the Colonial South," in C. Clinton and M. Gillespie, eds., *The devil's lane: Sex and race in the early South.* New York and Oxford: 124–35.

Finley, M. I. (1959) "Was Greek civilisation based on slave labour?" *Historia* 8: 145–64 (repr. in Finley [1981]: 97–115).

Finley, M. I. (1969) "The idea of slavery: Critique of David Brion Davis' *The problem of slavery in western culture*," in L. Foner and E. D. Genovese, eds., *Slavery in the New World: A reader in comparative history*. Englewood Cliffs, N.J.: 256–61.

Finley, M. I. (1978) "The Athenian empire: A balance sheet," in Garnsey and Whittaker, eds. (1978): 101–26 (repr. in Finley [1981]: 41–61).

Finley, M. I. (1981) *Economy and society in ancient Greece*. Ed. B. D. Shaw and R. P. Saller. New York.

Finley, M. I. (1985) *Democracy ancient and modern*. 2nd ed. London.

Fischer, D. H. (1996) *The great wave: Price revolutions and the rhythm of history*. Oxford.

Fitzmyer, J. A. (1995) *The Aramaic inscriptions of Sefire*. Rev. ed. Rome.

Flemming, R. (1999) "*Quae corpore quaestum facit*: The sexual economy of female prostitution in the Roman Empire." *Journal of Roman Studies* 89: 38–61.

Flinn, M. V. (1986) "Correlates of reproductive success in a Caribbean village." *Human Ecology* 14: 225–43.

Floud, R., K. Wachter, and A. Gregory (1990) *Height, health and history*. Cambridge.

Fogel, R. W. (1993) "New sources and new techniques for the study of secular trends in nutritional status, health, mortality, and the process of aging." *Historical Methods* 26: 5–43.

Fogel, R. W. (2004) *The escape from hunger and premature death, 1700–2100*. Cambridge.

Fornara, C. W. (1983) *Translated documents of Greece and Rome* I: *Archaic times to the end of the Peloponnesian War*. 2nd ed. Cambridge.

Forni, G. (1953) *Il reclutamento delle legioni da Augusto a Diocleziano*. Milan and Rome.

Forni, G. (1974) "Estrazione etnica e sociale dei soldati delle legioni nei primi tre secoli dell''impero," in *ANRW* II 1. Berlin and New York: 339–91.

Forrer, E. (1920) *Die Provinzeinteilung Assyriens*. Berlin.

Foster, B. (1993) *Before the muses: An anthology of Akkadian literature*. 2 vols.

Foster, C. (2000) "The limits to low fertility: A biosocial approach." *Population and Development Review* 26: 209–34.

Foster, L. (1984) *Religion and sexuality: The Shakers, the Mormons, and the Oneida community*. Urbana, Ill., and Chicago.

Fox, R. (1995) "Sexual conflict in the epics." *Human Nature* 6: 135–44.

Foxhall, L. (2001) "Access to resources in classical Greece: The egalitarianism of the polis in perspective," in Cartledge et al., eds. (2001): 209–20.

Frahm, E. (1997) *Einleitung in die Sanherib-Inschriften*. Vienna.

Frame, G. (1992) *Babylonia 687–627 B.C.: a political history*. Leiden.

Frame, G. (1995) *Rulers of Babylonia: From the Second Dynasty of Isin to the end of Assyrian domination (1157–612 B.C.)*. Toronto.

Franciosi, G. (1995) *Clan gentilizio e strutture monogamiche: contributo alla storia della famiglia romana*. 5th ed. Naples.

Frank, T. (1933) *An economic survey of ancient Rome* I: *Rome and Italy of the Republic*. Baltimore.

Frankenstein, S. (1979) "The Phoenicians in the Far West: A function of Neo-Assyrian imperialism," in Larsen, ed. (1979), 263–94.

Fried, M. (1967) *The evolution of political society*. New York.

Friedl, R. (1996) *Der Konkubinat im kaiserzeitlichen Rom: Von Augustus bis Septimius Severus*. Stuttgart.

Frier, B. W. (2000) "Demography," in *CAH* XI. 2nd ed. Cambridge: 787–816.

Fuchs, A., and S. Parpola (2001) *The correspondence of Sargon II, Part III: Letters from Babylonia and the eastern provinces.* Helsinki.

Fuentes, A. (1998) "Re-evaluating primate monogamy." *American Anthropologist* 100: 890–907.

Gabrielsen, V. 1994. *Financing the Athenian fleet.* Baltimore.

Galinsky, K. (2005) *The Cambridge companion to the age of Augustus.* Cambridge.

Garcilasco de la Vega, I. (1871) *Royal commentaries of the Yncas.* London.

Gardner, J. F. (1986) *Women in Roman law and society.* London and Sydney.

Garlan, Y. (1974) *Recherches sur la poliorcétique grecque.* Paris.

Garland, R. (1984) "Religious authority in archaic and classical Athens." *Annual of the British School at Athens* 79: 75–123.

Garland, R. (1987) *The Piraeus.* London.

Garnsey, P. (1970) *Social status and legal privilege in the Roman empire.* Oxford.

Garnsey, P. (1988) *Famine and food supply in the Graeco-Roman world: Responses to risk and crisis.* Cambridge.

Garnsey, P. (1992) "Yield of the land," in Wells, ed. (1992): 147–53.

Garnsey, P. (1999) *Food and society in classical antiquity.* Cambridge.

Garnsey, P., and C. R. Whittaker (1978) "Introduction," in Garnsey and Whittaker, eds. (1978): 1–6.

Garnsey, P., and C. R. Whittaker (1998) "Trade, industry and the urban economy," in A. Cameron and P. Garnsey, eds., *The Cambridge ancient history* XIII: *The late empire, A.D. 337–425.* 2nd ed. Cambridge: 312–37.

Garnsey, P., and C. R. Whittaker, eds. (1978) *Imperialism in the ancient world.* Cambridge.

Garrido-Hory, M. (1981) "La vision du dépendant chez Martial à travers les relations sexuelles." *Index* 10: 298–320.

Gaudioso, M. (1992) *La schiavitù domestica in Sicilia dopo i Normanni: Legislazione, dottrina, formule.* Catania.

Gauthier, H. (1914) *Le livre des rois d"Egypte.* Vol. 3. Cairo

Gawantka, W. (1985) *Die sogennante Polis.* Stuttgart.

Geary, D. C. (1998) *Male, female: The evolution of human sex differences.* Washington, D.C.

Geertz, C. (1973) *The interpretation of cultures.* New York.

Gehrke, H-J. (1980) "Zur Geschichte Milets in der Mitte des 5. Jhs. v. Chr." *Historia* 29: 17–31.

Gehrke, H-J. (2000) "Gegenbild und Selbstbild: Das europäische Iran-Bild zwischen Griechen und Mullahs," in T. Hölscher, ed., *Gegenwelten zu den Kulturen Griechenlands und Roms in der Antike.* Munich and Leipzig: 85–109.

Gellner, E. (1983) *Nations and nationalism.* Oxford.

Gellner, E. (1988) *State and society in Soviet thought.* Oxford.

Gellner, E. (1989) *Plough, sword and book: The structure of human history.* Chicago and London.

Genovese, E. D. (1976) *Roll, Jordan, roll: The world the slaves made.* New York.

Georges, P. (1994) *Barbarian Asia and the Greek experience: From the archaic period to the age of Xenophon.* Baltimore and London.

Gernet, L. (1981) *The anthropology of ancient Greece.* Baltimore and London.

Giangiulio, M. (1997) "Atene e la Sicilia occidentale dal 424 al 415." In *Seconde Giornate Internazionali di Studi sull'Area Elima, Atti* II. Pisa and Gibellina: 865–88.

Gibson, J. C. L. (1975) *Textbook of Syrian Semitic inscriptions* II: *Aramaic inscriptions, including inscriptions in the dialect of Zenjirli*. Oxford.

Gibson, J. C. L. (1982) *Textbook of Syrian Semitic inscriptions* III: *Phoenician inscriptions, including inscriptions in the mixed dialect of Arslan Tash*. Oxford.

Giddens, A. (1993) *Sociology*. Cambridge.

Gilliam, J. F. (1968) "P. Wisconsin 14." *Bulletin of the American Society of Papyrologists* 5: 93–98 (repr. in *Roman army papers* [Gieben: Amsterdam, 1986]: 329–34).

Giovannini, A., and G. Gottlieb (1980) *Thukydides und die Anfänge der athenischen Arche*. Heidelberg.

Godelier, M. (1978) "Infrastructures, societies and history." *Current Anthropology* 19: 763–71.

Godelier, M. (1984) "Modes of production, kinship and demographic structures." in M. Bloch, ed., *Marxist analyses and social anthropology*. London: 3–27.

Goffman, D. (1990) *Izmir and the Levantine world, 1550–1650*. Seattle.

Goldstone, J. (1991) *Revolution and rebellion in the early modern world*. Berkeley.

Goldstone, J. (2000) "The state," in E. Borgatta and R. J. V. Montgomery, eds., *The encyclopedia of sociology*. 2nd ed. New York: 2996–3003.

Goldstone, J. A. (1991) *Revolution and rebellion in the early modern world*. Berkeley.

Gottschall, J. (2008) *The rape of Troy: evolution, violence, and the world of Homer*. Cambridge.

Gottschall, J., et al. (2004) "Sex difference in mate choice criteria are reflected in folktales from around the world and in historical European literature." *Evolution and Human Behavior* 25: 102–12.

Gould, R. G. (2000) "How many children could Moulay Ismail have had?" *Evolution and Human Behavior* 21: 295–96.

Graham, A. J. (1978) "The foundation of Thasos." *Annual of the British School at Athens* 73: 61–98.

Graham, A. J. (1983) *Colony and mother city in ancient Greece*. 2nd ed. Chicago.

Grayson, A. K. (1972–1975) *Assyrian royal inscriptions*. 2 vols. Wiesbaden.

Grayson, A. K. (1975) *Assyrian and Babylonian chronicles*. Locust Valley, N.Y.

Grayson, A. K. (1980) "Histories and historians of the Ancient Near East: Assyria and Babylonia." *Orientalia* 49: 140–94.

Grayson, A. K. (1991a) "Assyrian civilization," in J. Boardman et al., eds., *The Cambridge Ancient History* III.2. 2nd ed. Cambridge: 194–228.

Grayson, A. K (1991b) *Assyrian rulers of the early first millennium I (1114–859 B.C.)*. Toronto.

Grayson, A. K (1996) *Assyrian rulers of the early first millennium II (858–745 B.C.)*. Toronto.

Grayson, A. K. (1999) "The struggle for power in Assyria: Challenge to absolute monarchy in the ninth and eighth centuries B.C,." in Watanabe, ed. (1999): 253–270.

Greene, K. (2000) "Technological innovation and economic progress in the ancient world: M. I. Finley reconsidered." *Economic History Review* 53: 29–59.

Grmek, M. (1989) *Diseases in the ancient Greek world*. Tr. M. and L. Muellner. Baltimore.

Grosby, S. (2002) *Biblical ideas of nationality: Ancient and modern*. Winona Lake.

Grossbard, A. S. (1980) "The economics of polygamy." *Research in Population Economics* 2: 321–50.

Gutman, H., and R. Sutch (1976) "Victorians all? The sexual mores and conduct of slaves and their masters," in P. A. David, H. G. Gutman, R. Sutch, P. Temin, and G. Wright, *Reckoning with slavery*. New York and Oxford: 134–62.

Gwin, M. C. (1985) "Green-eyed monsters of the slavocracy: jealous mistresses in two slave narratives," in M. Pryse and H. J. Spillers, eds., *Conjuring: black women, fiction, and literary tradition*. Bloomington, Ind: 39–52.

Hadjidaki, E. 1996. "Underwater excavations of a late 5th century merchant ship at Alonnesos, Greece," *Bulletin de correspondance hellénique* 120: 561–93.

Hager, B. J. (1992) "Get thee to a nunnery: Female religious claustration in medieval Europe." *Ethology and Sociobiology* 13: 385–407.

Haldon, J. F. (1986) "Ideology and social change in the seventh century: Military discontent as a barometer." *Klio* 68: 139–90 (repr. in Haldon, *State, army and society in Byzantium: Approaches to military, social and administrative history, 6th–12th centuries* [London: 1995], ch. 2).

Haldon, J. F. (1992) "The works of Anastasius of Sinai: A key source for the history of seventh-century East Mediterranean society and belief," in Cameron and Conrad, eds. (1992): 107–47.

Haldon, J. F. (1993) *The state and the tributary mode of production*. London.

Haldon, J. F. (1995) "Pre-industrial states and the distribution of resources: The nature of the problem," in Cameron, ed. (1995): 1–25.

Haldon, J. F. (1997) *Byzantium in the seventh century: the transformation of a culture*. 2nd ed. Cambridge.

Haldon, J. F. (1999) *Warfare, state and society in the Byzantine world, 565–1204*. London.

Haldon, J. F. (2004) "The fate of the late Roman senatorial elite: Extinction or transformation?" in Haldon and Conrad, eds. (2004): 179–234.

Haldon, J. F. (2005) *Byzantium: A history*. Stroud.

Haldon, J. F. and L. I. Conrad, eds. (2004) *Elites old and new in the Byzantine and early Islamic Near East: Papers of the Sixth Workshop on Late Antiquity and Early Islam*. Princeton.

Hall, E. (1989) *Inventing the barbarian: Greek self-definition through tragedy*. Oxford.

Hall, J. (1997) *Ethnic identity in Greek antiquity*. Cambridge.

Hallo, W. W., and W. K. Simpson (1998) *The ancient Near East: A history*. 2nd ed. Fort Worth.

Halstead, P. (1987) "Traditional and ancient rural economies in Mediterranean Europe: Plus ça change?" *Journal of Hellenic Studies* 107: 77–87.

Hamilton, V. P. (1992) "Marriage," in D. N. Freedman, ed., *The Anchor bible dictionary*. Vol. 4. New York: 559–69.

Hammer, D. (2005) "Ideology, the symposium, and archaic politics." *American Journal of Philology* 125: 479–512.

Hammond, M. (1957) "Composition of the senate, A.D. 68–235." *Journal of Roman Studies* 47: 74–81.

Hansen, M. (1985) *Demography and democracy*. Copenhagen.

Hansen, M. (1991) *The Athenian democracy in the age of Demosthenes*. Oxford.

Hansen, M. (2006a) *The shotgun method: The demography of the ancient Greek city-state culture*. Oxford.

Hansen, M. (2006b) *Studies in the population of Aigina, Athens and Eretria*. Copenhagen.

Hansen, M. (2006c) *Polis: An introduction to the ancient Greek city-state*. Oxford.

Hanson, V. D. (2000) *The western way of war: Infantry battle in classical Greece*. 2nd ed. New York.

Hanson, V. D. (1995) *The other Greeks*. New York.

Harding, P. (1985) *Translated documents of Greece and Rome* II: *From the end of the Peloponnesian War to the battle of Ipsus*. Cambridge.

Harford, T. (2006) "I do, I do, I do, I do: The economic case for polygamy." *Slate* (February 18) (www.slate.com).

Harl, K. W. (1996) *Coinage in the Roman economy, 300 B.C. to A.D. 700*. Baltimore and London.

Harpending, H., and A. Rogers (1990) "Fitness in stratified societies." *Ethology and Sociobiology* 11: 497–509.

Harrak, A. (1987) *Assyria and Hanigalbat: A historical reconstruction of bilateral relations from the middle of the fourteenth to the end of the twelfth centuries B.C.* New York.

Harris, W. V. (2005) "Morris Keith Hopkins 1934–2004." *Proceedings of the British Academy* 130: 81–105.

Harrison, T., ed. (2002) *Greeks and barbarians*. Edinburgh.

Hartung, J. (1982) "Polygyny and inheritance of wealth." *Current Anthropology* 23: 1–12 (repr. in Betzig, ed. [1997]: 331–43).

Hartung, J. (1999) "The number of losers is more important than the size of the jackpot." *Evolution and Human Behavior* 20: 215.

Harvey, A. (1989) *Economic expansion in the Byzantine Empire 900–1200*. Cambridge.

Hawkes, K., J. F. O'Connell, N. G. Blurton Jones, H. Alvarez, and E. L. Charnow (2000) "The grandmother hypothesis and human evolution," in Cronk et al., eds. (2000): 237–58.

Hawkins, J. D. (1984) "The Neo-Hittite states in Syria and Anatolia," in J. Boardman et al., eds. *The Cambridge Ancient History* III.1. 2nd ed. Cambridge: 388–435.

Hawkins, J. D. (1995) "The political geography of North Syria and South-East Anatolia in the Neo-Assyrian period," in Liverani, ed. (1995), 87–101.

Hedeager, L. (1987) "Empire, frontier and the barbarian hinterland: Rome and Northern Europe from A.D. 1–400," in M. Rowlands, M. Larsen, and K. Kristiansen, eds., *Centre and periphery in the ancient world*. Cambridge:125–40.

Hedrick, C. (2006) *Ancient history: Monuments and documents*. Oxford and Malden, Mass.

Heinzelmann, M. (1975) "L'aristocratie et les évêchés entre Loire et Rhin jusqu'à la fin du VIIe siècle. *Revue d'Histoire de l'église de France* 62: 75–90.

Heitzman, J. (1991) "Ritual polity and economy: The transactional network of an imperial temple in medieval South India." *Journal of the Economic and Social History of the Orient* 34: 23–54.

Hekala, T., and P. D. Buell (1993) "The perils of misunderstood and incomplete information: a reply to Johnson and Johnson." *Ethology and Sociobiology* 14: 271–87.

Hekala, T., and P. D. Buell (1995) "Providing the requested historical consultation: Hekala and Buell's rebuttal to Johnson's reply." *Ethology and Sociobiology* 16: 71–82.

Helgason, A., et al. (2000) "Estimating Scandinavian and Gaelic ancestry in the male settlers of Iceland." *American Journal of Anthropology* 67: 697–717.

Hendy, M. F. (1985) *Studies in the Byzantine monetary economy, c. 300–1450*. Cambridge.

Hendy, M. F. (1989) "Byzantium, 1081–1204: The economy revisited, twenty years on," in Hendy, *The Economy, fiscal administration and coinage of Byzantium*. London: ch. 3.

Henkelman, W. (2004) "Persians, Medes and Elamites: Acculturation in the Neo-Elamite period," in Lanfranchi et al., eds. (2004): 181–232.

Henneberg, R., and M. Henneberg (1998) "Biological characteristics of the population based on analysis of skeletal remains," in J. Carter, ed., *The chora of Metaponto: The necropoleis* II. Austin, Tex.: 503–62.

Herlihy, D. (1995) "Biology and history: The triumph of monogamy." *Journal of Interdisciplinary History* 25: 571–83.

Herrmann-Otto, E. (1994) *Ex ancilla natus: Untersuchungen zu den "hausgeborenen" Sklaven und Sklavinnen im Westen des Römischen Kaiserreiches*. Stuttgart.

Herskovits, M. J. (1938) *Dahomey: An ancient west African kingdom* II: New York.

Herter, H. (1957) "Dirne." *Reallexikon für Antike und Christentum* 3: 1149–1213.

Herter, H. (1960) "Die Soziologie der antiken Prostitution im Lichte des heidnischen und christlichen Schrifttums." *Jahrbuch für Antike und Christentum* 3: 70–111.

Hewlett, B. (1988) "Sexual selection and paternal investment among Aka Pygmies," in Betzig et al., eds. (1988): 263–76.

Hill, E. (1999) "Lineage interests and nonreproductive strategies: An evolutionary approach to medieval religious women." *Human Nature* 10: 109–34.

Hill, G. F. (1951) *Sources for Greek history between the Persian and Peloponnesian Wars*, ed. R. Meiggs and A. Andrewes. Oxford.

Hill, J. (1984) "Prestige and reproductive success in man." *Ethology and Sociobiology* 5: 77–95.

Hillel-Rubin, D. (1979) *Marxism and materialism*. Brighton.

Hinde, R. A. (1987) *Individuals, relationships and culture: Links between ethology and the social sciences*. Cambridge.

Hinds, G. M. (1972) "The murder of the Caliph ʿUthmân." *International Journal of Middle East Studies* 3: 450–69 (repr. in Hinds, *Studies in early Islamic history*, eds. J. Bacharach, L. Conrad, and P. Crone [Princeton]: 29–55).

Hingley, R. (2005) *Globalizing Roman culture: Uunity, diversity and empire*. London and New York.

Hinsch, B. (2002) *Women in early imperial China*. Lanham, Md.

Hitchner, R. B. (2005) "'The advantages of wealth and luxury': The case for economic growth in the Roman empire," in Manning and Morris, eds. (2005): 207–22.

Hobsbawm, E. (1990) *Nations and nationalism*. Cambridge.

Hodkinson, S. (1983) "Social order and the conflict of values in classical Sparta." *Chiron* 13: 239–81.

Hodkinson, S. (1989) "Inheritance, marriage and demography: Perspectives upon the success and decline of classical Sparta," in A. Powell, ed., *Classical Sparta: Techniques behind her success*. London: 79–121.

Hodkinson, S. (1997) "Servile and free dependants of the Spartan 'oikos'," in M. Moggi and G. Cordiano, eds., *Schiavi e dipendenti nell'ambito dell' 'oikos' e della 'familia'*. Pisa: 45–71.

Hodkinson, S. (2000) *Property and wealth in classical Sparta*. London.

Hodkinson, S., and A. Powell, eds. (2006) *Sparta and war*. London.

Hoepfner, W., and E.-L. Schwandner (1994) *Haus und Stadt im klassischen Griechenland*. 2nd ed. Munich.

Hoepfner, W., ed. (1999) *Geschichte des Wohnens* I: *500 v. Chr.-500 n. Chr. Vorgeschichte-Frühgeschichte-Antike*. Stuttgart.

Holloway, S. W. (2002) *Aššur is king! Aššur is king! Religion in the exercise of power in the Neo-Assyrian empire*. Leiden.

Hölscher, T. (1999) "Augustus und die Macht der Archäologie," in *La révolution romaine après Ronald Syme: Bilans et perspectives*. Vandoeuvres and Geneva: 237–73.

Hölscher, T. (2000) "Feindwelten—Glückswelten: Perser, Kentauren und Amazonen," in T. Hölscher, ed., *Gegenwelten zu den Kulturen Griechenlands und Roms in der Antike*. Munich and Leipzig: 287–320.

Hong, S. M., et al. (1994) "Greenland ice evidence of hemispheric lead pollution 2 millennia ago by Greek and Roman civilizations." *Science* 265: 1841–43.

Hong, S. M., et al. (1996a) "History of ancient copper smelting pollution during Roman and medieval times recorded in Greenland Ice." *Science* 272: 246–49.

Hong, S. M., et al. (1996b) "A reconstruction of changes in copper production and copper emissions to the atmospheric during the past 7000 years." *Science of the Total Environment* 188: 183–93.

Hopkins, D. (1997) "Agriculture," in E. M. Meyers, ed., *The Oxford encyclopedia of archaeology in the ancient Near East*. Vol 1. New York and Oxford: 22–30.

Hopkins, K. (1978a) *Conquerors and slaves: Sociological studies in Roman history 1*. Cambridge.

Hopkins, K. (1978b) "Economic growth and towns in classical antiquity," in P. Abrams and E. A. Wrigely, eds., *Towns in societies: essays in economic history and historical sociology*. Cambridge: 35–77.

Hopkins, K. (1980) "Taxes and trade in the Roman empire (200 B.C.–A.D. 400)." *Journal of Roman Studies* 70: 101–25.

Hopkins, K. (1983a) *Death and renewal: Sociological studies in Roman history 2*. Cambridge.

Hopkins, K. (1983b) "Models, ships and staples," in P. Garnsey and C. R. Whittaker, eds., *Trade and famine in classical antiquity*. Cambridge: 84–109.

Hopkins, K. (1991) "Conquest by book," in *Literacy in the Roman world*. Ann Arbor, Mich.: 133–58.

Hopkins, K. (1995/96) = (2002) "Rome, taxes, rents and trade." *Kodai* 6/7: 41–75 (repr. in Scheidel and von Reden, eds. [2002]: 190–230).

Hornblower, S., and M. C. Greenstock, eds. (1984) *The Athenian Empire*. 3rd ed. London Association of Classical Teachers no. 1.

Howard-Johnston, J. D. (1995) "The two great powers in late Antiquity: A comparison," in A. Cameron, ed., *States, resources and armies: Papers of the third workshop on late antiquity and early Islam*. Princeton: 157–226.

Howe, S. (2002) *Empire: A very short introduction*. Oxford.

Howgego, C. (1995) *Ancient history from coins*. London.

Hrdy, S. B. (1997) "Raising Darwin's consciousness: Female sexuality and the prehominid origins of paternity." *Human Nature* 8: 1–49.

Hrdy, S. B. (2000) "The optimal number of fathers: Evolution, demography and history in the shaping of female mate preferences," in D. LeCroy and P. Moller, eds., *Evolutionary perspectives on human reproductive behavior*. New York: 75–96.

Hughes, A. L. (1986) "Reproductive success and occupational class in eighteenth-century Lancashire, England." *Social Biology* 33: 109–15.

Humphrey, J., J. Oleson, and A. Sherwood, eds. (1998) *Greek and Roman technology: A sourcebook*. London.

Hunger, H. (1992) *Astrological reports to Assyrian kings*. Helsinki.

Hunt, P. (1998) *Slaves, warfare, and ideology in the Greek historians*. Cambridge.

Hunt, P. (forthcoming) "Wars over women in early and classical Greece."

Hurwit, J. (1985) *The art and culture of early Greece, 1100–480 B.C.* Ithaca, N.Y.

Hutzfeld, B. (1999) *Das Bild der Perser in der griechischen Dichtung des 5. vorchristlichen Jahrhunderts*. Wiesbaden.

Huyse, P. (2005) *La Perse antique*. Paris.

Huyse, P. (in press) *Histoire orale et écrite en Iran ancien entre mémoire et oubli*. Paris.

Ibn Khaldun (1958) *The Muqaddimah*. 3 vols. Trans. F. Rosenthal. New York.

Ikeda, Y. (1999) "Looking from Til Barsip on the Euphrates: Assyria and the West in the ninth and eighth centuries B.C." in Watanabe, ed. (1999): 271–302.

Irons, W. (1979) "Cultural and biological success," in Chagnon and Irons, eds. (1979): 257–72 (repr. in Betzig, ed. [1997]: 36–45).

Irons, W. (1997) "Looking back two decades," in Betzig, ed. (1997): 46–49.

Irons, W., and L. Cronk (2000) "Two decades of a new paradigm," in Cronk et al., eds. (2000): 3–26.

Isager, S., and M. Hansen (1975) *Aspects of Athenian society in the fourth century B.C.* Odense.

Ivanov, S. A. (2003) *Vizantiiskoe missionerstvo: Mozhno li sdelat' iz "Barbara" khristianina?* Moscow.

Jackman, T. (2005) "Political communities in the Greek colonies of Sicily and southern Italy." Unpublished Ph.D. dissertation, Stanford University.

Jacobs, B. (1994) *Die Satrapienverwaltung im Perserreich zur Zeit Darius III.* Wiesbaden.

Jacobs, B. (2002) "Achämenidische Kunst—Kunst im Achämenidenreich: Zur Rolle der achämenidischen Großplastik als Mittel der herrscherlichen Selbstdarstellung und der Verbreitung politischer Botschaften im Reich." *Archäologische Mitteilungen aus Iran und Turan* 34: 345–95.

Jacoby, D. (1991/92) "Silk in western Byzantium before the Fourth Crusade." *Byzantinische Zeitschrift* 84/85: 452–500.

Jacoby, D. (1993) "The Venetian presence in the Latin Empire of Constantinople (1204–1261): The challenge of feudalism and the Byzantine inheritance." *Jahrbuch der Österreichischen Byzantinistik* 43: 141–201.

James, S. L. (1997) "Slave-rape and female silence in Ovid's love poetry." *Helios* 24: 60–76.

Jameson, M. H. (1992) "Agricultural labor in ancient Greece," in Wells, ed. (1992): 135–46.

Jameson, M. H., C. Runnels, and T. van Andel (1994) *A Greek countryside.* Stanford.

Jas, R. (1996) *Neo-Assyrian judicial procedures.* Helsinki.

Jaspers, K. (1949) *Vom Ursprung und Ziel der Geschichte.* Munich.

Jessop, B. (1990) *State theory: Putting states in their place.* University Park, Pa.

Jew, D. (1999) "Food, silver, trade and liturgies: Modelling the Athenian economy." Unpublished M.Phil. thesis, Cambridge University.

Johansson, S. R. (1987) "Status anxiety and demographic contraction of privileged populations." *Population and Development Review* 13: 349–70.

Johns, C. H. W. (1898–1923) *Assyrian deeds and documents recording the transfer of property, including the so-called private contracts, legal decisions and proclamations preserved in the Kouyunjik collections of the British museum, chiefly of the 7th century B.C.* 4 vols. Cambridge and London.

Johnson, A. W. and T. Earle (2000) *The evolution of human societies: From foraging group to agrarian state.* 2nd ed. Stanford.

Johnson, S. B., and R. C. Johnson (1991) "Support and conflict of kinsmen in Norse earldoms, Icelandic families, and the English royalty." *Ethology and Sociobiology* 12: 211–20.

Johnson, S. B., and R. C. Johnson (1993) "There is, indeed, a misunderstanding: Reply to Hekala and Buell." *Ethology and Sociobiology* 14: 289–91.

Johnson, S. B., and R. C. Johnson (1995) "Support and conflict of kinsmen: A response to Hekala and Buell." *Ethology and Sociobiology* 16: 83–89.

Johnson, S. B., and R. C. Johnson (1997) "Kinship and the quest for wealth and power as influences on conflict in the Punjab, 1839–1846." *Evolution and Human Behavior* 18: 341–48.

Jones, A. H. M. (1954) *Athenian democracy*. Oxford.

Jones, A. H. M. (1964) *The later Roman empire, 284–602: A social, economic and administrative survey*. 3 vols. Oxford.

Jones, A. H. M. (1967) *The Greek city from Alexander to Justinian*. 2nd ed. Oxford.

Jongman, W. M. (2003) "Slavery and the growth of Rome: The transformation of Italy in the second and first centuries B.C.E.," in Edwards and Woolf, eds. (2003): 100–122.

Jongman, W. M. (2007) "The early Roman empire: Consumption," in Scheidel et al., eds. (2007).

Joshi, V. (1995) *Polygamy and purdah: Women and society among the Rajputs*. Jaipur and New Delhi.

Jursa, M. (1998) "Bogenland schon unter Nebukadnezzar II." *Nouvelles assyriologiques brèves et utilitaires*: 116–17.

Jursa, M. (2003) "Observations on the problem of the Median 'empire' on the basis of Babylonian sources," in Lanfranchi et al., eds. (2004): 169–80.

Just, R. (1989) *Women in Athenian law and life*. London and New York.

Käär, P., et al. (1998) "Sexual conflict and remarriage in preindustrial human populations: Causes and fitness consequences." *Evolution and Human Behavior* 19: 139–51.

Kabbani, R. (1994) *Imperial fictions: Europe's myths of Orient*. Rev. ed. London.

Kallet-Marx, L. (1993) *Money, expense, and naval power in Thucydides' History 1–5.24*. Berkeley.

Kamen, H. (2003) *Empire: How Spain became a world power 1492–1763*. New York.

Kanawati, N. (1976) "Polygamy in the Old Kingdom." *Studien zur Altägyptischen Kultur* 4: 149–60.

Kanazawa, S., and M. C. Still (1999) "Why monogamy?" *Social Forces* 78: 25–50.

Kaplan, H. (1985) "Prestige and reproductive success in man: A commentary." *Ethology and Sociobiology* 5: 115–18.

Kaplan, H. (1996) "A theory of fertility and parental investment in traditional and modern human societies." *Yearbook of Physical Anthropology* 39: 91–135.

Kaplan, H., and K. Hill (1985) "Hunting ability and reproductive success among male Ache foragers: Preliminary results." *Current Anthropology* 26: 131–33.

Kaplan, H., and J. B. Lancaster (2000) "The evolutionary economics and psychology of the Demographic Transition to low fertility.," in Cronk, Chagnon, and Irons, eds. (2000): 283–322.

Kaplan, M. (1986) "Quelques aspects des maisons divines du VIe siècle." *Aphieroma ston Niko Sborono*. Rethymno: 70–96.

Kaplan, M. (1992) *Les hommes et la terre à Byzance du VIe au XIe siècle: Propriété et exploitation du sol*. Paris.

Karras, R. M. (2000) "Active/passive, acts/passions: Greek and Roman sexualities." *American Historical Review* 105: 1250–65.

Kataja, L., and R. Whiting (1995) *Grants, decrees and gifts of the Neo-Assyrian period*. Helsinki.

Kautsky, J. H. (1982) *The politics of aristocratic empires*. Chapel Hill, N.C.

Kazhdan, A., and A. Epstein (1985) *Change in Byzantine culture in the eleventh and twelfth centuries*. Berkeley and Los Angeles.

Kazhdan, A. P. (1974) *Social'nyj sostav gospodstvujuscego klassa v Vizantii XI-XII vv.* Moscow.

Keaveney, A. P. (2003) *The life and journey of Athenian statesman Themistocles (524–460 B.C.?) as a refugee in Persia*. Lewiston, Maine.

Keay, S., and N. Terrenato, eds. (2001) *Italy and the west: Comparative issues in Romanization.* Oxford.

Keeley, L. H. (1996) *War before civilization.* New York and Oxford.

Keenan, J. G. (1994) "The will of Gaius Longinus Castor." *Bulletin of the American Society of Papyrologists* 31: 101–7.

Kelly, C. (2004) *Ruling the later Roman Empire.* Cambridge, Mass., and London.

Kempter, H., and B. Frenzel (2000) "The impact of early mining and smelting on the local tropospheric aerosol detected in ombotropic peat bogs in the Harz, Germany." *Water, Air and Soil Pollution* 121: 93–108.

Kennedy, H. (1981) *The early Abbasid Caliphate: A political history.* London.

Kennedy. H. (1992) "The impact of Muslim rule on the pattern of rural settlement in Syria," in P. Canivet and J.-P. Rey-Coquais, eds., *La Syrie de Byzance à l'Islam.* Damascus: 291–97.

Kenrick, D. T., and R. C. Keefe (1992) "Age preferences in mates reflect sex differences in human reproductive strategies." *Behavioral and Brain Sciences* 15: 75–133.

Keuls, E. (1993) *The reign of the phallus: Sexual politics in ancient Athens.* 2nd ed. Berkeley.

Khalidi, T., ed. (1984) *Land tenure and social transformation in the Middle East.* Beirut.

Khoury, P. S.. and J. Kostiner, eds. (1990) *Tribes and state formation in the Middle East.* Berkeley.

Kim, H. (2001). "Small change and the moneyed economy," in Cartledge et al., eds. (2001): 44–51.

Kitchen, K. A. (1982) *Pharaoh triumphant: The life and times of Ramesses II, king of Egypt.* Warminster.

Kitcher, P. (1985) *Vaulting ambition: Sociobiology and the quest for human nature.* Cambridge, Mass., and London.

Klees, H. (1998) *Sklavenleben im klassischen Griechenland.* Stuttgart.

Klein, A. N. (1981) "Inequality in Asante: A study of the forms and meanings of slavery and social servitude in pre- and early colonial Akan-Asante society and culture." Unpublished Ph.D. dissertation, University of Michigan.

Klima, O. (1957) *Mazdak: Geschichte einer sozialen Bewegung im sassanidischen Persien.* Prague.

Klima, O. (1966) "Zur Problematik der Ehe-Institution im alten Iran." *Archiv Orientální* 34: 554–69.

Klinkott, H. (2005) *Der Satrap: Ein achaimenidischer Amtsträger und seine Handlungsspielräume.* Frankfurt.

Knauft, B. M. (1991) "Violence and sociality in human evolution." *Current Anthropology* 32: 391–428.

Kolbe, W. (1938) "Die Anfänge der attischen Arche." *Hermes* 73: 249–68.

Kolendo, J. (1981) "L'esclavage et la vie sexuelle des hommes libres à Rome." *Index* 10: 288–97.

Korosec, V. (1938) "Ehe," in *Reallexikon der Assyriologie.* Vol. 2. Berlin and Leipzig: 281–93.

Kroll, J., and B. S. Bachrach (1990) "Medieval dynastic decisions: Evolutionary biology and historical explanation." *Journal of Interdisciplinary History* 21: 1–28.

Kron, G. (2000) "Roman ley-farming." *Journal of Roman Archaeology* 13: 277–87.

Kron, G. (2002) "Archaezoological evidence for the productivity of Roman livestock farming." *Münstersche Beiträge zur Antiken Handelsgeschichte* 21.2: 53–73.

Kühne, H., ed. (1991) *Die rezente Umwelt von Tall Šeh Hamad und Daten zur Umweltrekonstruktion der assyrischen Stadt Dur-katlimmu.* Berlin.

Kühne, H. (1995) "The Assyrians on the Middle Euphrates and the Hābur," in Liverani, ed. (1995): 69–85.

Kuhrt, A. (1983) "The Cyrus cylinder and Achaemenid imperial policy." *Journal for the Study of the Old Testament* 25: 83–97.

Kuhrt, A. (1987) "Usurpation, conquest and ceremonial: from Babylon to Persia," in D. Cannadine, ed., *Rituals of royalty: Power and ceremonial in traditional societies.* Cambridge: 20–55.

Kuhrt, A. (1988) "Earth and water." *Achaemenid History* 3: 87–99.

Kuhrt, A. (1995) *The ancient Near East c. 3000–330 b.c.* Vol. 2. London and New York.

Kuhrt, A. (2001a) "The Achaemenid Persian empire (c. 550–c. 330 b.c.e.): Continuities, adaptations, transformations," in Alcock et al., eds. (2001): 93–123.

Kuhrt, A. (2001b) "The Persian kings and their subjects: a unique relationship?" *Orientalistische Literaturzeitung* 96: 165–73.

Kuhrt, A. (2007) *The Persian empire: A corpus of sources from the Achaemenid period.* 2 vols. London.

Kulke, H. (1982) "Fragmentation and segmentation versus integration? Reflections on the concept of Indian feudalism and the segmentary state in Indian history." *Studies in History* 4: 237–63.

Kuper, A. (1999) *Culture: The anthropologist's account.* Cambridge, Mass., and London.

Kurke, L. (1997) "Inventing the hetaira: Sex, politics, and discursive conflict in archaic Greece." *Classical Antiquity* 16: 106–50.

Kurke, L. (1999) *Coins, bodies, games, and gold: The politics of meaning in archaic Greece.* Princeton.

Kwasman, T. (1988) *Neo-Assyrian legal documents in the Kouyunjik Collection of the British Museum.* Rome.

Kwasman, T., and S. Parpola (1991) *Legal transactions of the royal court on Nineveh.* Helsinki.

Kylander, M. E., et al. (2005) "Refining the pre-industrial atmospheric Pb isotope evolution curve in Europe using an 8000 year old peat core from NW Spain." *Earth and Planetary Science Letters* 240: 467–85.

Laiou, A. (1980/1) "The Byzantine economy in the Mediterranean trade system: Thirteenth-fifteenth centuries." *Dumbarton Oaks Papers* 34–35: 177–222.

Laiou, A. (1982) "The Greek merchant of the Palaeologan period: a collective portrait." *Praktika tês akademias Athênôn.* Athens: 96–124.

Laiou-Thomadakis, A. (1977) *Peasant society in the late Byzantine Empire: A social and demographic survey.* Princeton.

Lamprichs, R. (1995) *Die Westexpansion des neuassyrischen Reichs: Eine Strukturanalyse.* Neukirchener-Vluyn.

Landes, D. (2003) *The unbound Prometheus: Technological change c. 1750 to the present.* 2nd ed. Cambridge.

Lanfrachi, G. B. (2003) "The Assyrian expansion in the Zagros and the local ruling elites," in Lanfranchi, Roaf, and Rollinger, eds. (2003): 79–118.

Lanfranchi, G., M. Roaf, and R. Rollinger, eds. (2003) *Continuity of empire (?): Assyria, Media, Persia.* Padova.

Lape, S. (2002/3) "Solon and the institution of the "democratic" family form." *Classical Journal* 98: 117–39.

Larsen, M. T., ed. (1979) *Power and propaganda: A symposium on ancient empires.* Copenhagen.

Laurence, R. (1994) *Roman Pompeii: Space and society.* London and New York.

Lawall, M. (1998) "Ceramics and positivism revisited: Greek transport amphoras and history," in H. Parkins and C. Smith, eds., *Trade, traders, and the ancient economy*. London: 75–101.

Lawall, M. (2000) "Graffiti, wine selling, and the reuse of amphoras in the Athenian Agora, ca. 430 to 400 B.C.," *Hesperia* 69: 3–90.

Layard, A. H. (1849) *Nineveh and its remains*. London.

Lecky, W. E. H. (1869) *A history of European morals from Augustus to Charlemagne*. 2 vols. London.

Lecoq, P. (1997) *Les inscriptions de la Perse achéménide*. Paris.

Lemaire, A., and J.-M. Durand (1984) *Les inscriptions araméennes de Sfiré et l'Assyrie de Shamshi-ilu*. Paris.

Lemerle, P. (1979) *The agrarian history of Byzantium from the origins to the twelfth century: the sources and the problems*. Galway.

Lerner, G. (1986) *The creation of patriarchy*. New York and Oxford.

Lesko, B. S., ed. (1989) *Women's earliest records from ancient Egypt and western Asia*. Atlanta.

Lewis, A. R. (1976) "The dukes in the 'Regnum Francorum' A.D. 550–751." *Speculum* 51: 381–410.

Lewis, D. M. (1984) *Inscriptiones Graecae* I. Berlin.

Lewis, D. M. (1987) "The Athenian Coinage Decree," in I. Carradice, ed., *Coinage and administration in the Athenian and Persian Empires*. Oxford: 53–63.

Lewontin, R. C. (1992) *Biology as ideology: The doctrine of DNA*. New York.

Lieberman, L., L. T. Reynolds, and D. Friedrich (1992) "The fitness of human sociobiology: The future utility of four concepts in four subdisciplines." *Social Biology* 39: 158–69.

Lieberman, V. (1999) "Transcending east-west dichotomies: State and culture formation in six ostensibly separate areas," in V. Lieberman, ed., *Beyond binary histories: Re-imagining Eurasia to 1830*. Ann Arbor, Mich.: 19–102.

Liebeschuetz, J. H. W. G. (2001) *The decline and fall of the Roman city*. Oxford.

Lilie, R.-J. (1993) *Byzantium and the Crusader states 1096–1204*, trans. J. C. Morris and J. C. Ridings. Oxford.

Liverani, M. (1979) "The ideology of the Assyrian empire," in Larsen, ed. (1979), 297–317.

Liverani, M. (1984) "Land tenure and inheritance in the ancient Near East: The interaction between 'palace' and 'family' sectors," in Khalidi, ed. (1984), 33–44.

Liverani, M. (1988a) *Antico Oriente: Storia, società, economia*. Rome.

Liverani, M. (1988b) "The growth of the Assyrian empire in the Habur/Middle Euphrates area: A new paradigm." *State Archives of Assyria Bulletin* 2: 81–98.

Liverani, M. (1990) *Prestige and interest: International relations in the Near East, ca. 1600–1100*. Padova.

Liverani, M. (1992) *Studies on the annals of Ashurnasirpal II. 2: Topographical analysis*. Rome.

Liverani, M. (2004) "Assyria in the ninth century: Continuity or change?" in G. Frame with L. Wilding, eds., *From the Upper Sea to the Lower Sea: Studies on the history of Assyria and Babylonia in honour of A. K. Grayson*. Leiden: 213–26.

Liverani, M. (2003) "The rise and fall of Media," in Lanfranchi et al., eds. (2004): 1–12.

Liverani, M., ed. (1993) *Akkad: The first world empire: structure, ideology, traditions*. Padova.

Liverani, M., ed. (1995) *Neo-Assyrian geography*. Rome.

Livi-Bacci, M. (1997) *A concise history of world population*. 2nd ed. Oxford.

Livingstone, A. (1989) *Court poetry and literary miscellanea*. Helsinki.

Llewellyn-Jones, L. (2002) "Eunuchs and the royal harem in Achaemenid Persia," in S. Tougher, ed., *Eunuchs in antiquity and beyond*. London: 19–49.

Lo, J-P. (1969)"Maritime commerce and its relation to the Sung navy." *Journal of the Economic and Social History of the Orient* 12: 57–101.

Lockyear, K. (1999) "Hoard structure and coin production in antiquity—an empirical investigation." *Numismatic Chronicle* 159: 215–43.

Loomis, W. (1992) *The Spartan war fund*. Stuttgart (Historia Einzelschrift 74).

Loomis, W. (1998) *Wages, welfare costs and inflation in classical Athens*. Ann Arbor, Mich.

Loud, G. (1936) *Khorsabad*. Pt. 1. Chicago.

Loud, G., and C. B. Altman. (1938) *Khorsabad*. Pt. 2. Chicago.

Lovejoy, P. E. (1983) *Transformations in slavery: A history of slavery in Africa*. Cambridge.

Lovejoy, P. E. (1990) "Concubinage in the Sokoto Caliphate (1804–1903)." *Slavery and Abolition* 11: 159–89.

Low, B. S. (1988) "Measures of polygyny in humans." *Current Anthropology* 29: 189–94.

Low, B. S. (1993) "Ecological demography: A synthetic focus in evolutionary anthropology." *Evolutionary Anthropology* 1: 177–87.

Low, B. S. (1994) "Men in the demographic transition." *Human Nature* 5: 223–53.

Low, B. S. (2000a) *Why sex matters: A Darwinian look at human behavior*. Princeton.

Low, B. S. (2000b) "Sex, wealth, and fertility: Old rules, new environments," in Cronk et al., eds. (2000): 323–44.

Luckenbill, D. D. (1926–27) *Ancient records of Assyria and Babylonia*. Chicago.

Lumsden, C. J., and E. O. Wilson (1981) *Genes, mind and culture*. Cambridge, Mass., and London.

Luraghi, N. (1994) *Tirannidi arcaiche in Sicilia e Magna Grecia*. Florence.

Luraghi, N., and S. Alcock, eds. (2003) *Helots and their masters in Laconia and Messenia: Histories, ideologies, structures*. Cambridge, Mass.

Luttwak, E. N. (1976) *The grand strategy of the Roman empire: From the first century A.D. to the third*. Baltimore.

Luukko, M., and G. Van Buylaere (2002) *The political correspondence of Esarhaddon*. Helsinki.

Lybyer, A. H. (1913) *The government of the Ottoman Empire in the time of Suleiman the Magnificent*. Cambridge, Mass.

MacDonald, B. R. (1982) "The import of Attic pottery to Corinth and the question of trade during the Peloponnesian War." *Journal of Hellenic Studies* 102: 113–23.

MacDonald, K. B. (1988) "Socialization in the context of the family: A sociobiological perspective," in K. B. MacDonald, ed., *Sociobiological perspectives on human development*. New York: 320–39.

MacDonald, K. B. (1990) "Mechanisms of sexual egalitarianism in western Europe." *Ethology and Sociobiology* 11: 195–238.

MacDonald, K. B. (1991) "On the concept of limited polygyny: A reply to Frost." *Ethology and Sociobiology* 12: 169–76.

MacDonald, K. B. (1995) "The establishment and maintenance of socially imposed monogamy in Western Europe," *Politics and the Life Sciences* 14: 3–23 (with discussion 24–46).

MacDowell, D. M. (1978) *The law in classical Athens*. Ithaca, N.Y.

Mace, R. (1998) "The coevolution of human fertility and wealth inheritance strategies." *Philosophical Transactions of the Royal Society of London*, ser. B., 353: 389–97.

Mace, R. (2000) "Evolutionary ecology of human life history." *Animal Behaviour* 59: 1–10.

MacGinnis, J. (2003) "A corvée gang from the time of Cyrus." *Zeitschrift für Assyriologie* 93: 88–115.

Machinist, P. (1983) "Assyria and its image in the First Isaiah." *Journal of the American Oriental Society* 103: 719–37.

Machinist, P. (1993) "Assyrians on Assyria in the first millennium B.C.," in K. Raaflaub, ed., *Anfänge politischen Denkens in der Antike*. Munich: 135–44.

Machinist, P. (1995) "The fall of Assyria in comparative ancient perspective," in Parpola and Whiting, eds. (1997): 179–95.

MacMullen, R. (2000) *Romanization in the time of Augustus*. New Haven, Conn.

Maffoda, G. (1999) *Il koinon Beotico in eta arcaica e classica*. Rome.

Magdalino, P. (1993) *The empire of Manuel I Komnenos, 1143–1180*. Cambridge.

Mahoney, J. (2000) "Path dependence and historical sociology." *Theory and Society* 29: 507–48.

Makra, L., and P. Brimblecombe (2004) "Selections from the history of environmental pollution, with special attention to air pollution. Part 1." *International Journal of Environment and Pollution* 22: 641–56.

Malik, K. (2000) *Man, beast and zombie: What science can and cannot tell us about human nature*. London.

Mango, C. (1994) *Byzantium: the empire of New Rome*. 2nd ed. London.

Mango, C. and G. Dagron, eds. (1995) *Constantinople and its hinterland*. Aldershot.

Mann, J. C. (1983) *Legionary recruitment and veteran settlement during the Principate*. London.

Mann, M. (1977) "States, ancient and modern." *European Journal of Sociology* 18: 262–98.

Mann, M. (1986a) *The sources of social power* I: *A history of power from the beginning to A.D. 1760*. Cambridge.

Mann, M. (1986b) "The autonomous power of the state: Its origins, mechanisms and results," in J. Hall, ed., *States in history*. Oxford: 109–36.

Manniche, L. (1987) *Sexual life in ancient Egypt*. London and New York.

Manning, J. G., and I. Morris, eds. (2005) *The ancient economy: Evidence and models*. Stanford.

Manson, J. H., and R. W. Wrangham (1991) "Intergroup aggression in chimpanzees and humans." *Current Anthropology* 32: 369–77.

Marcus, J. (1976) *Emblem and state in the classic Maya lowlands*. Washington, D.C.

Marcus, J. (1984) "Lowland Maya archaeology at the crossroads." *American Antiquity* 48: 454–88.

Markale, J. (1975) *Women of the Celts*. London.

Martin, B. K. (2004) *Under the loving care of the fatherly leader: North Korea and the Kim dynasty*. New York.

Martin, M. (1988) "The Venetians in the Byzantine Empire before 1204." *Byzantinische Forschungen* 13: 201–14.

Martin, T. R. (1985) *Sovereignty and coinage in classical Greece*. Princeton.

Matthaiou, A. (2004) "Peri tis IG i³ 11," in A. Matthaiou, ed., *Attikai epigraphai: Praktika symbosiou eis mnimin Adolf Wilhelm (1864–1950)*. Athens: 99–122.

Matthiae, P. (1999) *Geschichte der Kunst im Alten Orient (1000–330 v.Chr.): Die Großreiche der Assyrer, Neubabylonier und Achämeniden*. Darmstadt.

Mattila, R. (2000) *The King's magnates: A study of the highest officials of the Neo-Assyrian Empire*. Helsinki.

Mattila, R. (2002) *Legal transactions of the royal court of Nineveh, Part II: Assurbanipal though Sin-sarru-iskun*. Helsinki.

Mattingly, H. (1996) *The Athenian Empire restored*. Ann Arbor, Mich.

Maul, S. (1999) "Der assyrische König—Hüter der Weltordnung," in Watanbe, ed. (1999): 201–*14*.

Mauritsch, P. (1992) *Sexualität im frühen Griechenland: Untersuchungen zu Norm und Abweichung in den homerischen Epen*. Vienna, Cologne, and Weimar.

Maxwell, M., ed. (1991) *The sociobiological imagination*. Albany, N.Y.

Mayer, W. (1978) *Nuzi-Studien I: Die Archive des Palastes und die Prosopographie der Berufe*. Kevelaer.

Mazahéri, A.-A. (1938) *La famille iranienne aux temps anté-islamiques*. Paris.

McCormick, M. (1998) "Bateaux de vie, bateaux de mort: maladie, commerce, transports annonaires et le passage économique du Bas-Empire au moyen âge," in *Morfologie sociali e culturali in Europa fra tarda Antichità e alto Medioevo*. Spoleto: 35–118.

McCormick, M. (2001) *Origins of the European economy: communications and commerce, A.D. 300–900*. Cambridge.

McElvaine, R. S. (2001) *Eve's seed: Biology, the sexes, and the course of history*. New York.

McEvedy, C., and R. Jones (1978) *Atlas of world population history*. Harmondsworth.

McGinn, T. A. J. (1998a) *Prostitution, sexuality, and the law in ancient Rome*. New York and Oxford.

McGinn, T. A. J. (1998b) "Caligula's brothel on the Palatine." *Echos du Monde Classique/ Classical Views* 17: 95–107.

McGinn, T. A. J. (2002) "Pompeian brothels and social history," in T. A. J. McGinn et al., *Pompeian brothels, Pompeii's ancient history, mirrors and mysteries, art and nature at Oplontis, and the Herculaneum "Basilica."* Portsmouth, R.I.: 7–46.

McKay, J. W. (1973) *Religion in Judah under the Assyrians 732–609 B.C.* London.

McLennan, G. (1989) *Marxism, pluralism and beyond*. Cambridge.

McNeill, W. H. (1989) *The age of gunpowder empires 1450–1800*. Washington, D.C.

Mealey, L. (1985) "The relationship between social status and biological success: A case study of the Mormon religious hierarchy." *Ethology and Sociobiology* 6: 247–56.

Meiggs, R. (1966) "The dating of fifth-century Athenian inscriptions." *Journal of Hellenic Studies* 86: 86–98.

Meiggs, R. (1972) *The Athenian Empire*. Oxford.

Meiggs, R., and D. M. Lewis (1969) *A selection of Greek historical inscriptions*. Oxford.

Meijer, F., and O. van Nijf, eds. (1992) *Trade, transport and society in the ancient world*. London.

Menzel, B. (1981) *Assyrische Tempel*. 2 vols. Rome.

Merkelbach, R., and M. L. West, eds. (1967) *Fragmenta Hesiodea*. Oxford.

Meyer, P. (1990) "Human nature and the function of war in social evolution," in van der Dennen and Falger, eds. (1990): 227–40.

Millar, F. (1998) *The crowd in Rome in the late Republic*. Ann Arbor, Mich.

Millard, A. R. (1994) *The eponyms of the Assyrian empire 910–612 B.C.* Helsinki.

Millender, E. (1999) "Athenian ideology and the empowered Spartan woman," in S. Hodkinson and A. Powell, eds., *Sparta: New perspectives*. London: 355–91.

Miller, M. C. (1997) *Athens and Persia in the fifth century B.C.: A study in cultural receptivity*. Cambridge.

Miller, M. C. (2003) "Greece II: Greco-Persian cultural relations," in *Encyclopaedia Iranica* 11: 301–19.

Millett, P. (2001) "Productive to some purpose? The problem of ancient economic growth," in D. J. Mattingly and J. Salmon, eds., *Economies beyond agriculture in the classical world*. London and New York: 17–48.

Mitchell, T. (2001) "The limits of the state: Beyond statist approaches and their critics." *American Political Science Review* 85: 77–96.

Mokyr, J. (1990) *The Lever of riches*. New York.

Mokyr, J. (2002) *The gifts of Athena*. Princeton.

Montefiore, S. S. (2003) *Stalin: The court of the red tsar*. New York.

Moorey, P. R. S. (1999) *Ancient Mesopotamian materials and industries: The archaeological evidence*. Winona Lake.

Morabito, M. (1986) "Droit romain et réalités sociales de la sexualité servile." *Dialogues d'histoire ancienne* 12: 371–87.

Morley, N. (1996) Metropolis and hinterland: The city of Rome and the Italian economy 200 B.C.–A.D. 200. Cambridge.

Morris, I. (1991) "The early polis as city and state," in J. Rich and A. Wallace-Hadrill, eds., *City and country in the ancient world*. London: 24–57.

Morris, I. (1992) *Death-ritual and social structure in classical antiquity*. Cambridge.

Morris, I. (1997) "An archaeology of equalities? The Greek city-states," in D. Nichols and T. Charlton, eds., *The archaeology of city-states*. Washington, D.C.: 91–105.

Morris, I. (1998a) "Beyond democracy and empire: Athenian art in context," in Boedeker and Raaflaub, eds. (1998): 59–86.

Morris, I. (1998b) "Archaeology and archaic Greek history," in N. Fisher and H. van Wees, eds., *Archaic Greece*. London: 1–91.

Morris, I. (2000) *Archaeology as cultural history: Words and things in Iron Age Greece*. Oxford and Malden, Mass.

Morris, I. (2003) "Iron Age state formation in Greece," in D. Clark and Matthews, V., eds., *100 years of American archaeology in the Middle East*. Boston: 263–82.

Morris, I. (2004) "Economic growth in ancient Greece." *Journal of Institutional and Theoretical Economics* 160: 709–42.

Morris, I. (2005a) "Archaeology, standards of living, and Greek economic history," in Manning and Morris, eds. (2005): 91–126.

Morris, I. (2005b) "Military and political participation in archaic-classical Greece." Princeton-Stanford working papers in Classics, available at http://www.princeton.edu/~pswpc/papers/author/morris/morris.html.

Morris, I. (2006) "The growth of Greek cities in the first millennium B.C.," in G. Storey, ed., *Urbanism in the preindustrial world*. Tuscaloosa, Ala.: 27–51.

Morris, I. (2007) "Early Iron Age Greece," in Scheidel et al., eds. (2007) 211–41.

Morris, I. (forthcoming) "The eighth-century revolution," in K. Raaflaub and H. van Wees, eds., *The Blackwell companion to archaic Greece*.

Morris, I., and B. Powell (2005) *The Greeks: History, culture, and society*. Upper Saddle River, N.J.

Morris, I., and S. Tusa (2004) "Scavi sull' acropoli di Monte Polizzo, 2000–2003." *Sicilia Archeologica* 38: 35–90.

Morris, I., R. Saller, and W. Scheidel (2007) "*Introduction*," in Scheidel et al., eds. (2007) 1–12.

Morrison, J., J. Coates, and B. Rankov (2000) *The Athenian trireme: The history and reconstruction of an ancient Greek warship*. 2nd ed. Cambridge.

Morrison, K. D. (2001a) "Sources, approaches, definitions," in Alcock et al., eds. (2001): 1–9.

Morrison, K. D. (2001b) "Coercion, resistance and hierarchy:L local processes and imperial strategies in the Vijayanagara empire," in Alcock et al., eds. (2001): 252–78.

Morrisson, C. (1991) "Monnaie et finances dans l'empire byzantin Xe–XIVe siècle," in V. Kravari, J. Lefort, and C. Morrisson, eds., *Hommes et richesses dans l'Empire byzantin* II: *VIIIe—XVe siècle*. Paris: 291–315.

Morrisson, C., and J.-P. Sodini (2002) "The sixth-century economy," in A. Laiou et al., eds., *The economic history of Byzantium from the seventh through the fifteenth century*. Washington, D.C.: 171–220.

Morstein-Marx, R. (2004) *Mass oratory and political power in the late Roman Republic*. Cambridge.

Motolinía, T. P. (1951) *History of the Indians of New Spain*. Washington, D.C.

Mouritsen, H. (1998) *Italian unification: A study in ancient and modern historiography*. London.

Mouritsen, H. (2001) *Plebs and politics in the late Roman Republic*. Cambridge.

Mratschek-Halfmann, S. (1993) *Divites et praepotentes : Reichtum und soziale Stellung in der Literatur der Prinzipatszeit*. Stuttgart.

Mueller, U., and A. Mazur (1998) "Reproductive constraints on dominance competition in male *Homo sapiens*." *Evolution and Human Behavior* 19: 387–96.

Mullett, M. (1997) *Theophylact of Ochrid: Reading the letters of a Byzantine archbishop*. Aldershot.

Mullett, M., and R. Scott, eds. (1981) *Byzantium and the classical tradition*. Birmingham.

Murdock, G. P. (1967) *Ethnographic atlas*. Pittsburgh.

Murdock, G. P. (1981) *Atlas of world cultures*. Pittsburgh.

Murray, O. (1990) "Cities of reason," in O. Murray and S. Price, eds., *The Greek city*. Oxford: 1–25.

Na'aman, N. (1995) "Province system and settlement pattern in Southern Syria and Palestine in the Neo-Assyrian period," in Liverani, ed. (1995): 103–15.

Neumann, H. (1987) "Bemerkungen zu Ehe, Konkubinat und Bigamie in neusumerischer Zeit," in Durand, ed. (1987): 131–37.

Neumann, J., and S. Parpola (1987) "Climatic change in the eleventh-tenth-century eclipse of Assyria and Babylonia." *Journal of Near Eastern Studies* 46: 161–82.

Nevett, L. (1999) *House and society in the ancient Greek world*. Cambridge.

Nicol, D. M. (1972) *The last centuries of Byzantium, 1261–1453*. London.

Nicol, D. M. (1979) *The end of the Byzantine Empire*. London.

Nicol, D. M. (1988) *Byzantium and Venice*. Cambridge.

Nightingale, A. (1995) *Genres in dialogue: Plato and the construction of philosophy*. Cambridge.

Nishida, T. (1991) "Comment." *Current Anthropology* 32: 381–82.

Nissinen, M (1998) *References to prophecy in Neo-Assyrian sources*. Helsinki.

Nollé, J., and A. Wenninger (1998/99) "Themistokles und Archepolis: Eine griechische Dynastie im Perserreich und ihre Münzprägung." *Jahrbuch für Numismatik und Geldgeschichte* 48/49: 1–42.

North, D., and R. Thomas (1973) *The rise of the western world*. Cambridge.

Noth, A., with A. L. Conrad (1994) *The early Arabic historical tradition. A source-critical study*. Trans. M. Bonner. Princeton.

Nowag, W. (1983) *Raub und Beute in der archaischen Zeit der Griechen*. Frankfurt a. M.

Nriagu, J. O. (1998) "Paleoenvironmental research—tales told in lead." *Science* 281: 1622–23.

Oates, J. (1991) "The fall of Assyria," in J. Boardman et al., eds. *The Cambridge Ancient History* III.2. 2nd ed. Cambridge: 162–93.

Oates, J., and D. Oates. (2001) *Nimrud: An Assyrian imperial city revealed*. London.

Ober, J. (1989) *Mass and elite in democratic Athens*. Princeton.

Ober, J. (1998) *Political dissent in democratic Athens*. Princeton.

Obolensky, D. (1971) *The Byzantine commonwealth: Eastern Europe 500–1453*. London.

Oded, B. (1979) *Mass deportations and deportees in the Neo-Assyrian empire*. Wiesbaden.

Oded, B. (1992) *War, peace and empire: Justification for war in Assyrian royal inscriptions*. Wiesbaden.

Ogden, D. (1996) *Greek bastardy in the classical and Hellenistic periods*. Oxford.

Ogden, D. (1999) *Polygamy, prostitutes and death: The Hellenistic dynasties*. London.

Oikonomides, N. (1969) "Le haradj dans l'empire byzantin du XVe siècle," in *Actes du Ier Congrès international des Etudes Balkaniques et Sud-Est Européennes*, III. Sofia: 681–88.

Oikonomides, N. (1996) *Fiscalité et exemption fiscale à Byzance (IXe–XIe s.)*. Athens.

Olmsted, F. L. (1861) *The cotton kingdom: A traveller's observations on cotton and slavery in the American slave states*. New York.

Oppenheim, A. L. (1967) "Essay on overland trade in the first millenium B.C." *Journal of Cuneiform Studies* 21: 236–54.

Oppenheim, A. L. (1977) *Ancient Mesopotamia: Portrait of a dead civilization*. Rev. ed. Chicago and London.

Osborne, R. (1998) "Early Greek colonization? The nature of Greek settlement in the west," in N. Fisher and H. van Wees, eds., *Archaic Greece*. London: 251–69.

Osborne, R. (1999) "Archaeology and the Athenian Empire." *Transactions of the American Philological Association* 129: 319–32.

Osborne, R. (2004) "Keith Hopkins." *Past and Present* 185: 3–7.

Ostwald, M. (1992) "Athens as a cultural centre," in D. M. Lewis et al., eds., *Cambridge ancient history* V: *The fifth century B.C.* Cambridge: 306–69.

Otto, E. (2002) *Gottes Recht als Menschenrecht: Rechts- und literaturhistorische Studien zum Deuteronomium*. Wiesbaden.

Packer, C., D. A. Collins, A. Sindimwo, and J. Goodall (1995) "Reproductive constraints on aggressive competition in female baboons." *Nature* 373: 60–63.

Padden, R. C. (1967) *The hummingbird and the hawk: Conquest and sovereignty in the Valley of Mexico, 1503–1541*. Columbus, Ohio.

Papagrigorakis, M. J., C. Yapijakis, P. Synodinos, and E. Baziotopoulou-Valavani (2006) "DNA examination of ancient dental pulp incriminates typhoid fever as a probable cause of the plague of Athens." *International Journal of Infectious Diseases* XX.

Parker, B. J. (1997) "Garrisoning the empire: Aspects of the construction and maintenance of Forts on the Assyrian frontier." *Iraq* 59 (1997): 77–87.

Parker, B. J. (2001) *The mechanics of empire: The northern frontier of Assyria as a case study in imperial dynamics*. Helsinki.

Parker, H. N. (2001) "The myth of the heterosexual: Anthropology and sexuality for Classicists." *Arethusa* 34: 313–62.

Parpola, S. (1970–83) *Letters from Assyrian scholars to the kings Esarhaddon and Assurbanipal*. 2 vols. Kevelaer and Neukirchen-Vluyn.

Parpola, S. (1980) "The murder of Sennacherib," in B. Alster, ed., *Death in Mesopotamia*. Copenhagen: 171–82.

Parpola, S. (1981) "Assyrian royal inscriptions and Neo-Assyrian letters," in Fales, ed. (1981): 117–42.

Parpola, S. (1987) *The correspondence of Sargon II, Part 1: Letters from Assyria and the West*. Helsinki.

Parpola, S. (1993) *Letters from Assyrian and Babylonian scholars*. Helsinki.

Parpola, S. (1995) "The construction of Dur-Sarrukin in the Assyrian royal correspondence," in A. Caubert, ed., *Khorsabad le palais de Sargon II, roi d'Assyrie*. Paris: 47–77.

Parpola, S. (1997) *Assyrian prophecies*. Helsinki.

Parpola, S. (2003) "Assyria's expansion in the 8th and 7th centuries and its long-term repercussions in the West," in W. G. Dever and S. Gitin, eds., *Symbiosis, symbolism and the power of the past*. Winona Lake: 99–111.

Parpola, S., and Lanfranchi, G. B. (1987–1990) *The correspondence of Sargon II*. Helsinki.

Parpola, S., and K. Watanabe (1988) *Neo-Assyrian treaties and loyalty oaths*. Helsinki.

Parpola, S., and R. M. Whiting, eds. (1997) *Assyria 1995: Proceedings of the 10th anniversary symposium of the Neo-Assyrian text corpus project*. Helsinki.

Parpola, S., gen. ed. (1987–) *State archives of Assyria*. 18 vols. Helsinki.

Patterson, C. C. (1972) "Silver stocks and losses in ancient and medieval times." *Economic History Review* 25: 205–35.

Patterson, O. (1991) *Freedom I: Freedom in the making of western culture*. New York.

Paul, S. M. (1991) *Amos: A commentary on the Book of Amos*. Minneapolis.

Pecírková, J. (1977) "The administrative organization of the Neo-Assyrian empire." *Archív orientální* 45: 211–28.

Pecírková, J. (1987) "The administrative methods of Assyrian imperialism." *Archív orientální* 55: 162–75.

Peirce, L. P. (1993) *The imperial harem: Women and sovereignty in the Ottoman Empire*. Oxford.

Pelletier, A. (1984) *La femme dans la société gallo-romaine*. Paris.

Perikhanian, A. (1983) "Iranian society and law," in E. Yarshater, ed., *The Cambridge History of Iran III: The Seleucid, Parthian and Sasanian periods*. Cambridge: 627–80.

Perlin, F. (1993) *"The invisible city:" Monetary, administrative and popular infrastructures in Asia and Europe, 1500–1900*. London.

Pérusse, D. (1993) "Cultural and reproductive success in industrial societies: Testing the relationship at the proximate and ultimate levels." *Behavioral and Brain Sciences* 16: 267–322.

Pettegrew, D. (2001) "Chasing the classical farmstead: Assessing the formation and signature of rural settlement in the Greek landscape." *Journal of Mediterranean Archaeology* 14: 189–209.

Phang, S. E. (2001) *The marriage of Roman soldiers, 13 b.c.–a.d. 235: Law and family in the imperial army*. Leiden, Boston, and Cologne.

Phang, S. E. (2004) "Intimate conquests: Roman soldiers' women and freedwomen." *Ancient World* 15: 207–37.

Piérart, M. (1983–85) "Athènes et Milet." *Museum Helveticum* 40: 1–18; 42: 276–99.

Poggi, G. (1990) *The state: Its nature, development, and prospects*. Stanford.

Pollard, N. (2000) *Soldiers, cities, and civilians in Roman Syria*. Ann Arbor, Mich.

Pongratz-Leisten, B. (1994) *Ina šulmi rub: die kulttopographische und ideologische Programmatik der ak tu-Prozession in Babylonien und Assyrien im 1. Jahrtausend v.Chr.* Mainz.

Pongratz-Leisten, B. (1997) "The interplay of military strategy and cultic practice in Assyrian politics," in Parpola, ed. (1997): 245–52.

Pongratz-Leisten, B. (1999) *Herrschaftswissen in Mesopotamien*. Helsinki.

Porter, B. N. (1993) *Images, power, and politics: Figurative aspects of Esarhaddon's Babylonian policy*. Philadelphia, Penn.

Porter, B. N. (2000) "The anxiety of multiplicity: Concepts of divinity as One and Many in ancient Assyria," in B. N. Porter, ed., *One god or many? Concepts of divinity in the ancient world*. Casco Bay, Maine: 211–71.

Postgate, J. N. (1969) *Royal grants and decrees*. Rome.

Postgate, J. N. (1974) *Taxation and conscription in the Assyrian empire*. Rome.

Postgate, J. N. (1976) *Fifty Neo-Assyrian legal documents*. Warminster.

Postgate, J. N. (1979) "The economic structure of the Assyrian empire," in Larsen, ed. (1979): 193–221.

Postgate, J. N. (1980) "The place of the *āaknu* in Assyrian government." *Anatolian Studies* 30: 67–76.

Postgate, J. N. (1989) "The ownership and exploitation of land in Assyria in the 1st millennium B.C.," in M. Lebeau and Ph. Talon, eds., *Reflets des deux fleuves: Volume de mélanges offerts à André Finet*. Leuven:141–52.

Postgate, J. N. (1992) "The land of Assur and the yoke of Assur." *World Archaeology* 23: 247–63.

Postgate, J. N. (1995) "Assyria: The home provinces," in Liverani, ed. (1995): 1–17.

Potts, D. T. (1999) *The archaeology of Elam: Formation and transformation of an ancient Iranian state*. Cambridge.

Power, M. (1991) *The egalitarians—human and chimpanzee: An anthropological view of social organization*. Cambridge.

Prásek, J. v. (1910) *Geschichte der Meder und Perser bis zur makedonischen Eroberung*. Vol. 2. Gotha, repr. Darmstadt, 1968.

Preston, J. J. (1980) "Sacred centers and symbolic networks in South Asia." *The Mankind Quarterly* 20: 259–93.

Puin, G.-R. (1970) *Der Dîwân von ʿUmar ibn al-Hattâb*. Bonn.

Quinn, T. J. (1981) *Athens and Samos, Lesbos and Chios 478–404 B.C.* Manchester.

Raaflaub, K. (1979) "Beute, Vergeltung, Freiheit? Zur Zielsetzung des delisch-attischen Seebundes." *Chiron* 19: 1–22.

Raaflaub, K. A., and M. Toher, eds. (1990) *Between republic and empire: Interpretations of Augustus and his Principate*. Berkeley.

Radner, K. (1999) "Traders in the Neo-Assyrian period," in J. G. Dercksen, ed., *Trade and finance in Ancient Mesopotamia*. Leiden: 101–58.

Radner, K. (2003) "Neo-Assyrian period," in R. Westbrook, ed., *A history of ancient Near Eastern law*. Vol. 2. Leiden: 883–910.

Raeck, W. (1981) *Zum Barbarenbild in der Kunst Athens im 6. und 5. Jahrhundert v. Chr.* Bonn.

Ramsay, A. M. (1925) "The speed of the Roman imperial post." *Journal of Roman Studies* 15: 60–74.

Rathbone, D. (1991) *Economic rationalism and rural society in third-century A.D. Egypt: The Heroninos archive and the Appianus estate*. Cambridge.

Rawlings, H. (1977) "Thucydides on the purpose of the Delian League." *Phoenix* 31: 1–8.

Rawson, B. (1974) "Roman concubinage and other de facto marriages." *Transactions of the American Philological Association* 104: 279–305.

Rawson, B. (1989) "*Spurii* and Roman views of illegitimacy." *Antichthon* 23: 10–41.

Reade, J. E. (1979) "Ideology and propaganda in Assyrian art," in Larsen, ed. (1979): 329–43.

Redford, D. (1984) *Akhenaten: The heretic king*. Princeton.

Reed, C. (2003) *Maritime traders in the ancient Greek world*. Cambridge.

Reiser, E. (1972) *Der königliche Harim im alten Ägypten und seine Verwaltung*. Vienna.

Reiter, H. A. (1991) *Athen und die Poleis des delisch-attischen Seebundes*. Regensburg.

Renberg, I., et al. (2000) "Atmospheric lead pollution during four millennia (2000 B.C. to 2000 A.D.) in Sweden." *Ambio* 29: 150–56.

Renberg, I., M. W. Persson, and O. Emteryd (1994) "Preindustrial atmospheric lead contamination detected in Swedish lake-sediments." *Nature* 368: 323–26.

Reynolds, F. (2003) *The Babylonian correspondence of Esarhaddon, and letters to Assurbanipal Sin-šarru-iškun from northern and central Babylonia*. Helsinki.

Reynolds, S. (1994) *Fiefs and vassals*. Oxford.

Reynolds, V., and R. E. S. Tanner (1995) *The social ecology of religion*. New York and Oxford.

Rhodes, P. J. (1972) *The Athenian* boule. Oxford.

Rhodes, P. J. (2006) *A history of classical Greece (480–323 B.C.)*. Oxford and Malden, Mass.

Rickman, G. (1980) *The corn supply of ancient Rome*. Oxford.

Rilinger, R. (1988) *Honestiores—humiliores: Zu einer sozialen Dichotomie im Strafrecht der römischen Kaiserzeit*. Munich.

Roaf, M. (2003) "The Median Dark Age," in Lanfranchi et al., eds. (2004): 13–22.

Robertson, N. (1980) "The true nature of the 'Delian League,' 478–461 B.C." *American Journal of Ancient History* 5: 64–96, 110–33.

Robertson, N. (1987) "Government and society at Miletus, 525–442 B.C.," *Phoenix* 41: 356–98.

Robins, G. (1993) *Women in ancient Egypt*. Cambridge, Mass.

Robinson, E., ed. (2004) *Ancient Greek democracy*. Oxford and Malden, Mass.

Rogers, A. R. (1990) "Evolutionary economics of human reproduction." *Ethology and Sociobiology* 11: 479–95.

Rogers, A. R. (1995) "For love or money: The evolution of reproductive and material motivations," in R. I. M. Dunbar, ed., *Human reproductive decisions: Biological and social perspectives*. New York: 76–95.

Rollinger, R. (1998) "Der Stammbaum des achaimenidischen Königshauses oder die Frage der Legitimität der Herrschaft des Dareios." *Archäologische Mitteilungen aus Iran und Turan* 30: 155–209.

Rollinger, R. (1999) "Zur Lokalisation von Parsu(m)a(š) in der F rs und einigen Fragen der frühen persischen Geschichte." *Zeitschrift für Assyriologie* 89: 115–39.

Rollinger, R. (2003) "The western expansion of the Median 'empire': A re-examination," in Lanfranchi et al., eds. (2004): 289–320.

Rollinger, R. (2004) "Herodotus," in *Encyclopaedia Iranica 12*: 254–88.

Root, M. C. (1979) *The King and kingship in Achaemenid art: Essays on the creation of an iconography of empire*. Leiden.

Rose, H., and S. Rose, eds. (2000) *Alas, poor Darwin: Arguments against evolutionary psychology*. New York.

Rose, S., R. C. Lewontin, and L. Kamin (1984) *Not in our genes: Biology, ideology and human nature*. Harmondsworth.

Roskraft, E., A. Wara, and A. Viken (1992) "Reproductive success in relation to resource-access and parental age in a small Norwegian farming parish during the period 1700–1900." *Ethology and Sociobiology* 13: 443–61.

Rosman, K. J. R., et al. (1997) "Lead from Carthaginian and Roman Spanish mines isotopically identified in Greenland ice dated from 600 B.C. to 300 A.D." *Environmental Science and Technology* 31: 3413–16.

Ross, M. C. (1985) "Concubinage in Anglo-Saxon England." *Past and Present* 29: 3–34.

Rostworowski de Diez Canseco, M. (1999) *History of the Inca realm.* Cambridge.

Roth, M. T. (1989) *Babylonian marriage agreements, 7th–3rd centuries B.C.* Kevelaer.

Rougé, J. (1970) "La colonisation grecque et les femmes." *Cahiers d'histoire* 15: 307–17.

Rousselle, A. (1984) "Concubinat et adultère." *Opus* 3: 75–84.

Rowlands, M. (1987) "Centre and periphery: A review of a concept," in M. Rowlands, M. Larsen, and K. Kristiansen, eds., *Centre and periphery in the ancient world.* Cambridge: 1–11.

Rubel, A. (2001) "*Hellespontophylakes*—Zöllner am Bosporus? Überlegungen zur Fiskalpolitik des attischen Seebundes." *Klio* 83: 39–51.

Rubin, Z. (1994) "The Reforms of Khusro Anushirwan," in A. Cameron and L. A Conrad, eds., *States, Resources and Armies: Papers of the Third Workshop on Late Antiquity and Early Islam.* Princeton: 227–97.

Rubin, Z. (2004) "Nobility, monarchy and legitimation under the later Sasanians," in Haldon and Conrad, eds. (2004): 235–73.

Rueschemeyer, D. P., P. Evans, and T. P. Skocpol, eds. (1985) *Bringing the state back in.* Cambridge.

Runciman, S. (1970) *The last Byzantine renaissance.* Cambridge.

Runciman, W. G. (1983) *A treatise on social theory* I: *The methodology of social theory.* Cambridge.

Runciman, W. G. (1989) *A treatise on social theory* II: *Substantive social theory.* Cambridge.

Russell, J. M. (1991) *Sennacherib's palace without rival at Nineveh.* Chicago.

Rutter, N. K. (2000) "Syracusan democracy: 'Most like the Athenian'?" in R. Brock and S. Hodkinson, eds., *Alternatives to Athens.* Oxford: 137–51.

Saggs, H. W. F. (1995) *Babylonians.* London.

Sahlins, M. (1976) *The use and abuse of biology: An anthropological critique of sociobiology.* Ann Arbor, Mich.

Sahlins, M., and E. R. Service (1960) *Evolution and culture.* Ann Arbor, Mich.

Said, E. (1993) *Culture and imperialism.* New York.

Sailor, S. (2003) "Genes of history's greatest lover found?" *United Press International* (February 5, 2003); available at www.upi.com.

Saletore, R. (1974) *Sex life under Indian rulers.* Delhi.

Sallares, R. (1991) *The ecology of the ancient Greek world.* London.

Saller, R. (1987) "Slavery and the Roman family," in M. I. Finley, ed., *Classical slavery.* London: 65–87.

Saller, R. (1996) "The hierarchical household in Roman society: A study of domestic slavery," in M. L. Bush, ed., *Serfdom and slavery: Studies in legal bondage.* London and New York: 112–29.

Saller, R. (2002) = (2005) "Framing the debate over growth in the ancient economy," in Scheidel and von Reden, eds. (2002): 251–69 and Manning and Morris, eds. (2005): 223–38.

Salmon, P. (1978) *Étude sur la confédération béotienne (447/6–386).* Brussels.

Salmon, P. (1994) "La *koinon ton Boioton*," in *Federazioni e federalismo nell'Europa antica.* Milan: 217–30.

Samons, L. (2000) *Empire of the owl: Athenian imperial finance.* Stuttgart (*Historia Einzelschrift* 142).

Sancisi-Weerdenburg, H. (1987) "Decadence in the empire or decadence in the sources? From source to synthesis: Ctesias," in H. Sancisi-Weerdenburg, ed., *Achaemenid history* I: *Sources, structures and synthesis.* Leiden: 33–45.

Sancisi-Weerdenburg, H. (1989) "The personality of Xerxes, king of kings," in *Archaeologia Iranica et Orientalis: Miscellanea in honorem L. Vanden Berghe.* Vol. 1. Ghent: 549–61.

Sancisi-Weerdenburg, H. (2001) "*Yaunâ* by the sea and across the sea," in I. Malkin, ed., *Ancient perceptions of Greek ethnicity.* Cambridge, Mass.: 323–46.

Sanderson, S. (1999) *Social transformations: A general theory of historical development.* Oxford.

Saraswati, B. (1977) *Brahmanic ritual tradition in the crucible of time.* Simla.

Saunders, A. C. de C. M. (1982) *A social history of black slaves and freedmen in Portugal 1441–1555.* Cambridge.

Schäfer, H. (1939) "Beiträge zur Geschichte der attischen Symmachie," *Hermes* 74: 225–64.

Schafer, J. K. (1987) "'Open and notorious concubinage': The emancipation of slave mistresses by will and the Supreme Court in Antebellum Louisiana." *Louisiana History* 28: 165–82.

Schaps, D. (1982) "The women of Greece in wartime." *Classical Philology* 77: 193–213.

Schaudig, H. (2001) *Die Inschriften Nabonids von Babylon und Kyros des Großen.* Münster.

Scheidel, W. (1996a) *Measuring sex, age and death in the Roman Empire: Explorations in ancient demography.* Ann Arbor, Mich.

Scheidel, W. (1996b) "Brother-sister and parent-child marriage outside royal families in ancient Egypt and Iran: A challenge to the sociobiological view of incest avoidance?" *Ethology and Sociobiology* 17: 319–40.

Scheidel, W. (1996c) "Die biologische Dimension der Alten Geschichte: Bemerkungen zu Robert Sallares, *The ecology of the ancient Greek world.*" *Tyche* 11: 207–22.

Scheidel, W. (1999) "Emperors, aristocrats and the Grim Reaper: Towards a demographic profile of the Roman élite." *Classical Quarterly* 49: 254–81.

Scheidel, W. (2003a) "Helot numbers: a simplified model," in Luraghi and Alcock, eds. (2003): 240–48.

Scheidel, W. (2003b) "Germs for Rome," in Edwards and Woolf, eds. (2003): 158–76.

Scheidel, W. (2004a) "Demographic and economic development in the ancient Mediterranean world." *Journal of Institutional and Theoretical Economics* 160: 743–57.

Scheidel, W. (2004b) "Ancient Egyptian sibling marriage and the Westermarck effect," in A. P. Wolf and W. H. Durham, eds., *Inbreeding, incest, and the incest taboo: The state of knowledge at the turn of the century.* Stanford: 93–108.

Scheidel, W. (2005) "Human mobility in Roman Italy. II: The slave population." *Journal of Roman Studies* 95: 64–79.

Scheidel, W. (2007a) "Marriage, families, and survival: demographic aspects," in P. Erdkamp, ed., *The Blackwell companion to the Roman army.* Oxford and Malden: 417–34.

Scheidel, W. (2007b) "A model of real income growth in Roman Italy." *Historia* 56: 322–46

Scheidel, W. (in preparation) *Explaining empire: Models for ancient history.* New York.

Scheidel, W., ed. (forthcoming) *Rome and China: Comparative perspectives on ancient world empires.* New York.

Scheidel, W., I. Morris, and R. Saller, eds. (2007) *The Cambridge economic history of the Greco-Roman world.* Cambridge.

Scheidel, W. and S. von Reden, eds. (2002) *The ancient economy.* Edinburgh.

Schettler, G., and R. L. Romer (2006) "Atmospheric Pb-pollution by pre-medieval mining detected in the sediments of the brackish karst lake An Loch Mor, western Ireland." *Applied Geochemistry* 21: 58–82.

Schiappa, E. (1999) *The beginnings of rhetorical theory in classical Greece.* New Haven.

Schmal, S. (1995) *Feindbilder bei den frühen Griechen.* Frankfurt a. M.

Schneider, R. M. (1998) "Die Faszination des Feindes: Bilder der Parther und des Orients in Rom," in J. Wiesehöfer, ed., *Das Partherreich und seine Zeugnisse.* Stuttgart: 95–146.

Schuller, W. (1974) *Die Herrschaft der Athener im Ersten Attischen Seebund.* Berlin.

Schwartz, B., ed. (1975) *Wisdom, revelation and doubt: Perspectives on the first millennium* B.C. Washington, D.C.

Schwartz, M. (1985) "The Old Eastern Iranian world view according to the Avesta," in I. Gershevitch, ed., *The Cambridge History of Iran* II: *The Median and Achaemenian periods.* Cambridge: 640–63.

Scully, P. F. (1993) "Liberating the family? Gender, labor, and sexuality in the rural Western Cape, South Africa, 1823–1853." Ph.D. dissertation, University of Michigan.

Seaford, R. (2004) *Money and the early Greek mind.* Cambridge.

Sealey, R. (1984) "On lawful concubinage in Athens." *Classical Antiquity* 3: 111–33.

Segerstrale, U. (2000) *Defenders of the truth: The sociobiology debate.* Oxford.

Seibert, I. (1974) *Women in the ancient Near East.* New York.

Seipel, W. (1977) "Harim," in W. Helck and W. Westendorf, eds., *Lexikon der Ägyptologie.* Vol. 2. Wiesbaden: 982–86.

Service, E. R. (1962) *Primitive social organization.* New York.

Shaban, M. A. (1971) *Islamic history* A.D. *600–750 (*A.H. *132): A new interpretation.* Cambridge.

Shaban, M. A. (1976) *Islamic history: A new interpretation* II: A.D. *750–1055 (*A.H. *132–448).* Cambridge.

Shatzman, I. (1975) *Senatorial wealth and Roman politics.* Brussels.

Shaw, B. D. (1983) "Soldiers and society: The army in Numidia." *Opus* 2: 133–60.

Sherratt, S., and A. Sherratt (1993) "The growth of the Mediterranean economy in the early first millennium B.C." *World Archaeology* 24: 361–78.

Shotyk, W., et al. (1998) "History of atmospheric lead deposition since 12,370 C-14 yr B.P. from a peat bog, Jura Mountains, Switzerland." *Science* 281: 1635–40.

Siegel, B. J. (1947) *Slavery during the Third Dynasty of Ur.* Washington, D.C. (repr. Millwood, N.Y. [1976]).

Simonsen, J. B. (1988) *The genesis and development of the Caliphal taxation system.* Copenhagen.

Simpson, W. K. (1974) "Polygamy in Egypt in the Middle Kingdom?" *Journal of Egyptian Archaeology* 60: 100–5.

Singh, D., and S. Luis (1995) "Ethnic and gender consensus for the effect of waist-to-hip ratio on judgment of women's attractiveness." *Human Nature* 6: 51–65.

Skocpol, T. (1979) *States and social revolutions: A comparative analysis of France, Russia and China.* Cambridge.

Smarczyk, B. (1990) *Untersuchungen zur Religionspolitik und politischen Propaganda Athens im Delisch-Attischen Seebund.* Munich.

Smith, A. D. (1986) *The ethnic origins of nations.* Oxford.

Smith, A. D. (1993) "The problem of national identity: Ancient, medieval and modern?" *Ethnic and Racial Studies* 17: 377–99.

Smithies, M. (2001) *The customs of Cambodia by Zhou Daguan (Chou Ta-kuan).* Bangkok.

Snodgrass, A. M. (1977) *Archaeology and the rise of the Greek state.* Cambridge (repr. in Snodgrass [2006]: 198–220).

Snodgrass, A. M. (1994) "Response: The archaeological aspect," in I. Morris, ed., *Classical Greece: Ancient histories and modern archaeologies.* Cambridge: 197–200.

Snodgrass, A. M. (2006) *Archaeology and the emergence of Greece*. Edinburgh.

Southall, A. (1956) *Alur society*. Cambridge.

Southall, A. (1965) "A critique of the typology of states and political systems," in M. Barton, ed., *Political systems and the distribution of power*. New York: 113–40.

Spalinger, A. (1974a) "Assurbanipal and Egypt: a source study." *Journal of the American Oriental Society* 94: 316–28.

Spalinger, A. (1974b) "Esarhaddon and Egypt: An analysis of the first invasion of Egypt." *Orientalia* 43: 295–326.

Speidel, M. P. (1989) "The soldiers' servants." *Ancient Society* 20: 239–48.

Spencer, G. (1969) "Religious networks and royal influence in eleventh century South India." *Journal of the Economic and Social History of the Orient* 12: 42–56.

Spieckermann, H. (1982) *Juda unter Assur in der Sargonidenzeit*. Göttingen.

Spieser, J.-M. (1989) "L'évolution de la ville byzantine de l'époque paléochrétienne à l'iconoclasme," in C. Morrisson et al., eds., *Hommes et richesses dans l'Empire byzantin* I: *IVe–VIIe siècles*. Paris: 97–106.

Stampp, K. M. (1956) *The peculiar institution: Slavery in the ante-bellum South*. New York.

Starr, I. (1990) *Queries to the sungod: Divination and politics in Sargonid Assyria*. Helsinki.

Ste. Croix, G. E. M. de (1966) "The estate of Phainippos (Ps.-Dem., xlii)," in Badian, ed. (1966): 109–14.

Ste. Croix, G. E. M. de (1972) *The origins of the Peloponnesian War*. Oxford.

Steckel, R. H. (1980) "Miscegenation and the American slave schedules." *Journal of Interdisciplinary History* 11: 251–63.

Steckel, R. H., and J. C. Rose, eds. (2002) *The backbone of history: Stature and nutrition in the western hemisphere*. Cambridge.

Stein, B. (1977) "The segmentary state in South Indian history," in R. G. Fox, ed., *Realm and religion in traditional India*. Durham, N.C.: 3–51.

Stein, B. (1980) *Peasant state and society in medieval South India*. Delhi.

Stein, B. (1985) "Politics, peasants and the deconstruction of feudalism in medieval India." *Journal of Peasant Studies* 12: 54–86.

Stein, B. (1989) *Vijayanagara*. Cambridge.

Steinmetz, G. (1999) "Introduction: culture and the state," in Steinmetz, ed. (1999): 1–49.

Steinmetz, G., ed. (1999) *State/culture: State formation after the cultural turn*. Ithaca, N.Y., and New York.

Steymanns, H. U. (1995) *Deuteronomium 28 und die adê zur Thronfolgeregelung Asarhaddons: Segen und Fluch im Alten Orient und in Israel*. Freiburg and Göttingen.

Stol, M. (1995) "Women in Mesopotamia." *Journal of the Economic and Social History of the Orient* 38: 123–44.

Stolper, M. W. (1985) *Entrepreneurs and empire*. Leiden.

Stolper, M. W. (1999) "Une 'vision dure' de l'histoire achéménide (note critique)." *Annales HSS*: 1109–26.

Strauss, B. (1986) *Athens after the Peloponnesian War*. Ithaca, N.Y.

Strauss, B. (2000) "Democracy, Kimon, and the evolution of Athenian naval tactics in the fifth century b.c.," in P. Flensted-Jense, T. H. Neilsen, and L. Rubinstein, eds., *Polis & Politics*. Copenhagen: 315–26.

Strauss, B., and J. Ober (1990) *The anatomy of defeat*. New York.

Streck, M. (1916) *Assurbanipal und die letzten assyrischen Könige bis zum Untergang Ninevehs*. 3 vols. Leipzig.

Stronach, D., and S. Lumsden (1992) "UC Berkeley's excavations at Nineveh." *Biblical Archaeologist* 55: 227–33.

Stumpp, B. E. (1998) *Prostitution in der römischen Antike*. 2nd ed. Berlin.

Summers, K. (2005) "The evolutionary ecology of despotism." *Evolution and Human Behavior* 26: 106–35.

Syme, R. (1960/84) "Bastards in the Roman aristocracy." *Proceedings of the American Philosophical Society* 104 (1960): 323–27 (repr. in *Roman papers* II. Ed. E. Badian. Oxford: 510–17).

Tadmor, H. (1975) "Assyria and the west: The ninth century and its aftermath," in H. Goedicke and J. J. M. Roberts, eds. *Unity and diversity: Essays in the history, literature, and religion of the ancient Near East*. Baltimore: 36–44.

Tadmor, H. (1994) *The inscriptions of Tiglath-Pileser III*. Jerusalem.

Tadmor, H. (1999) "World dominion: The expanding horizon of the Assyrian empire," in L. Milano et al., eds., *Landscapes: Territories, frontiers and horizons in the ancient Near East*. Vol. 1. Padova: 55–62.

Tainter, J. A. (1988) *The collapse of complex societies*. Cambridge.

Tambiah, S. J. (1976) *World conqueror and world renouncer*. Cambridge.

Thalmann, W. G. (1998) "Female slaves in the *Odyssey*," in S. R. Joshel and S. Murnaghan, eds., *Women and slaves in Greco-Roman culture: Differential equations*. London and New York: 22–34.

Thompson, H., and R. E. Wycherley (1972) *The Athenian Agora* XIV: *The Agora of Athens*. Princeton.

Thornhill, R., and K. Grammer (1999) "The body and face of woman: One ornament that signals quality?" *Evolution and Human Behavior* 20: 105–20.

Thornhill, R., and C. T. Palmer (2000) *A natural history of rape: Biological bases of sexual coercion*. Cambridge, Mass., and London.

Tilly, C. (1975) "Reflections on the history of European state-making," in C. Tilly, ed., *The formation of national states in western Europe*. Princeton: 3–83.

Tilly, C. (1992) *Coercion, capital, and European states, A.D. 990–1992*. Cambridge, Mass., and Oxford.

Tod, M. N. (1948) *A selection of Greek historical inscriptions* II: *403–323 B.C.*. Oxford.

Tooby, J., and L. Cosmides (1992) "The psychological foundations of culture," in J. H. Barkow, L. Cosmides, and J. Tooby, eds., *The adapted mind: Evolutionary psychology and the generation of culture*. New York and Oxford: 19–136.

Treggiari, S. (1979) "Questions on women domestics in the Roman world," in *Schiavitù, manomissione e classi dipendenti nel mondo antico*. Rome: 185–201.

Treggiari, S. (1981) "Concubinae." *Papers of the British School at Rome* 49: 59–81.

Treggiari, S. (1982) "Women as property in the early Roman empire," in D. K. Weisberg, ed., *Women and the law: A social historical perspective* II: *Property, family and the legal profession*. Cambridge, Mass.: 7–33.

Treu, M. (1979) *Archilochos*. 2nd ed. Munich.

Trigger, B. (2003) *Understanding early civilizations: a comparative study*. Cambridge.

Tritton, A. S. (1954) "Notes on the Muslim system of pensions." *Bulletin of the School of Oriental and African Studies* 16: 170–72.

Trivers, R. L. (1972) "Parental investment and sexual selection," in B. Campbell, ed., *Sexual selection and the descent of man, 1871–1971*. Chicago: 136–79.

Tuplin, C. (1987) "The administration of the Achaemenid empire," in I. Carradice, ed., *Coinage and administration in the Athenian and Persian empires*. London: 109–166.

Tuplin, C. (1996) *Achaemenid studies*. Stuttgart.

Tuplin, C. (1998) "The seasonal migration of Achaemenid kings: A report on old and new evidence," in M. Brosius and A. Kuhrt, eds., *Studies in Persian history: Essays in memory of David M. Lewis*. Leiden: 63–114.

Turke, P. W., and L. L. Betzig (1985) "Those who can do: Wealth, status, and reproductive success on Ifaluk." *Ethology and Sociobiology* 6: 79–87.

Tyldesley, J. (1995) *Daughters of Isis: Women in ancient Egypt*. Harmondsworth.

Vallat, F. (1996) "Nouvelle analyse des inscriptions néo-élamites," in H. Gasche and B. Hrouda, eds., *Collectanea Orientalia: Histoire, arts de l'espace et industrie de la terre. Études offertes en homage à A. Spycket*. Neuchâtel and Paris: 385–95.

van Compernolle, R. (1982) "Femmes indigènes et colonisateurs," in *Modes de contacts et processus de transformation dans les sociétés anciennes*. Pisa and Rome: 1033–49.

van de Mieroop, M. (2003) "Revenge, Assyrian style." *Past and Present* 179: 3–23.

van der Dennen, J. M. G. (1990) "Origin and evolution of 'primitive' warfare," in van der Dennen and Falger, eds. (1990): 149–88.

van der Dennen, J. M. G., and V. Falger, eds. (1990) *Sociobiology and conflict: Evolutionary perspectives on competition, cooperation, violence and warfare*. London.

van der Spek, R. (1983) "Cyrus de Pers in Assyrisch perspectief." *Tijdschrift voor Geschiedenis* 96: 1–27.

van der Spek, R. (1993) "The astronomical diaries as a source for Achaemenid and Seleucid history." *Bibliotheca Orientalis* 50: 91–102.

van der Spek, R. (1998) "The chronology of the wars of Artaxerxes II in the Babylonian astronomical diaries," in M. Brosius and A. Kuhrt, eds., *Studies in Persian history: Essays in memory of David M. Lewis*. Leiden: 239–56.

van Gulick, R. H. (1974) *Sexual life in ancient China: A preliminary survey of Chinese sex and society from ca. 1550B.C. till 1644 A.D.* Leiden.

Vanderpool, E. (1964) "Themistocles' sanctuary of Artemis Aristoboule." *Archaiologikon Deltion* 19: 26–36.

Vehrencamp, S. L. (1983) "A model for the evolution of despotic versus egalitarian societies." *Animal Behaviour* 31: 667–82.

Vera Chamaza, G. W. (2002) *Die Omnipotenz Assurs. Entwicklungen in der Assur-Theologie under den Sargoniden Sargon II., Sanherib und Assurhaddon*. Münster.

Verdelis, N. M. (1956) "Der Diolkos am Isthmus von Korinth." *Mitteilungen des Deutschen Archäologischen Instituts, Athenische Abteilung* 71: 51–59.

Vining, D. R. (1986) "Social versus reproductive success: The central theoretical problem of human sociobiology." *Behavioral and Brain Sciences* 9: 167–87.

Voland, E. (1990) "Differential reproductive success within the Krummhörn population (Germany, 18th and 19th centuries)." *Behavioural Ecology and Sociobiology* 26: 65–72.

Voland, E., ed. (1992) *Fortpflanzung: Natur und Kultur im Wechselspiel. Versuch eines Dialogs zwischen Biologen und Sozialwissenschaftlern*. Frankfurt a. M.

von Reden, S. (1997) "Money, law and exchange: coinage in the Greek polis." *Journal of Hellenic Studies* 117: 154–76.

Waerzeggers, C. (2003/4) "The Babylonian revolts against Xerxes and the 'end of archives.'" *Archiv für Orientforschung* 50: 150–73.

Waldbaum, J. C. (1978) *From bronze to iron: The transition from the Bronze Age to the Iron Age in the Eastern Mediterranean*. Göteborg.

Wallace, S. L. (1938) *Taxation in Egypt from Augustus to Diocletian*. Princeton.

Wallinga, H. T. (1993) *Ships and sea-power before the Great Persian War.* Leiden.

Walter, H., and K. Vierneisel (1959) "Heraion von Samos: Die Funde der Kampagnen 1958 und 1959." *Athenische Mitteilungen* 74: 10–34.

Walters, K. (1983) "Perikles' citizenship law." *Classical Antiquity* 2: 314–36.

Waltz, K. (1979) *Theory of international politics.* Reading, Mass.

Watanabe, K. (1987) *Die adê-Vereidigung anlässlich der Thronfolgeregelung Asarhaddons.* Berlin.

Watanabe, K., ed. (1999) *Priests and officials in the ancient Near East.* Heidelberg.

Watanabe, K., and S. Parpola (1988) *Neo-Assyrian treaties and loyalty oaths.* Helsinki.

Watson, A. (1987) *Roman slave law.* Baltimore and London.

Watson, J. L. (1980) "Transactions in people: The Chinese market in slaves, servants, and heirs," in J. L. Watson, ed., *Asian and African systems of slavery.* Oxford: 223–50.

Weber, M. (1921) "Politik als Beruf," in *Gesammelte politische Schriften.* Munich: 396–450.

Weber, M. (1972) *Wirtschaft und Gesellschaft: Grundrisse der verstehenden Soziologie.* Tübingen.

Weber, M. (1988) *Gesammelte Aufsätze zur Sozial- und Wirtschaftsgeschichte.* Tübingen.

Weiler, I. (1993) "Ethnozentrismus und Fremdenangst aus althistorischer Sicht." *Ethica* 1: 377–98.

Weinfeld, M. (1972) *Deuteronomy and the Deuteronomic school.* Oxford.

Weisfeld, G. E. (1990) "Sociobiological patterns of Arab culture." *Ethology and Sociobiology* 11: 23–49.

Weiss, D., et al. (1997) "Atmospheric lead deposition from 12,400 to ca. 2,000 yrs B.P. in a peat bog profile, Jura Mountains, Switzerland." *Water, Air and Soil Pollution* 100: 311–24.

Weiss, D., W. Shotyk, and O. Kempf (1999) "Archives of atmospheric lead pollution." *Naturwissenschaften* 86: 262–75.

Welch, C. E., and P. C. Glick (1981) "The incidence of polygamy in contemporary Africa: a research note." *Journal of Marriage and the Family* 43: 191–93.

Wells, B., ed. (1992) *Agriculture in ancient Greece.* Stockholm.

Wertime, T. A., and J. D. Muhly, eds. (1980) *The coming of the age of iron.* New Haven.

West, M. L. (1966) *Hesiod, Theogony.* Oxford.

West, M. L., ed. (1991/92) *Iambi et elegi Graeci.* 2nd ed. 2 vols. Oxford.

Westbrook, R. (1988) *Old Babylonian marriage law.* Horn.

Westenholz, J. G. (1990) "Towards a new conceptualization of the female role in Mesopotamian society." *Journal of the American Oriental Society* 110: 510–21.

Westermarck, E. (1921) *The history of human marriage* III. 5th ed. London.

Wettlaufer, J. (2000) "The jus primae noctis as a male power display—a review of the historic sources with evolutionary interpretation." *Evolution and Human Behavior* 21: 111–23.

Wettlaufer, J. (2002) "Von der Gruppe zum Individuum: Probleme und Perspektiven einer 'evolutionären Geschichtswissenschaft,'" in S. Selzer and U.-C. Ewert, eds., *Menschenbilder—Menschenbildner: Individuum und Gruppe im Blick des Historikers. Werner Paravicini zum 60. Geburtstag.* Berlin: 25–52.

Whitby, M. (1998) "An international symposium? Ion of Chios fr. 27 and the margins of the Delian League," in E. Dabrowa, ed., *Ancient Iran and the Mediterranean world.* Kraków: 207–24.

White, D. R. (1988) "Rethinking polygyny: Co-wives, codes, and cultural systems." *Current Anthropology* 29: 529–58.

White, D. R., and M. L. Burton (1988) "Causes of polygyny: Ecology, economy, kinship, and warfare." *American Anthropologist* 90: 871–87.

White, L. (1949) *The evolution of culture*. New York.

Whittaker, C. R. (1994) *Frontiers of the Roman Empire: A social and economic study*. Baltimore and London.

Whittow, M. (1996) *The making of Byzantium, 600–1025*. London.

Wickersham, J. (1994) *Hegemony and the Greek historians*. Lanham, Md.

Wickert-Micknat, G. (1982) *Die Frau*. Göttingen.

Wickert-Micknat, G. (1983) *Unfreiheit im Zeitalter der homerischen Epen*. Wiesbaden.

Wickham, C. (1988) "Historical materialism, historical sociology." *New Left Review* 171: 63–78.

Wickham, C. (1991) "Systactic structures: Social theory for historians." *Past and Present* 132: 188–203.

Wickham, C. (2005) *Framing the Middle Ages: Europe and the Mediterranean, 400–800*. Oxford.

Wickler, W., and U. Seibt (1983) "Monogamy: an ambiguous concept," in P. Bateson, ed., *Mate choice*. Cambridge: 33–50.

Wierschowski, L. (1984) *Heer und Wirtschaft: Das römische Heer der Prinzipatszeit als Wirtschaftsfaktor*. Bonn.

Wiesehöfer, J. (1995) "'Reichsgesetz' oder 'Einzellfallgerechtigkeit': Bemerkungen zu P. Freis These von der achaimenidischen 'Reichsautorisation.'" *Zeitschrift für Altorientalische und Biblische Rechtsgeschichte* 1: 36–46.

Wiesehöfer, J. (1997) "Dekadenz, Krise oder überraschendes Ende? Überlegungen zum Zusammenbruch der Perserherrschaft," in A. Demandt, ed., *Das Ende der Weltreiche*. Munich 9–27.

Wiesehöfer, J. (1999) "Kyros, der Schah und 2500 Jahre Menschenrechte: Historische Mythenbildung zur Zeit der Pahlavi-Dynastie," in S. Conermann, ed., *Mythen, Geschichte(n), Identitäten: Der Kampf um die Vergangenheit*. Hamburg: 55–68.

Wiesehöfer, J. (2001a) *Ancient Persia*. 2nd ed. London and New York.

Wiesehöfer, J. (2001b) "Gift-giving II: In Pre-Islamic Persia," in *Encyclopaedia Iranica* 10: 607–9.

Wiesehöfer, J. (2002) "Kontinuität oder Zäsur? Babylonien unter den Achämeniden," in R. G. Kratz, ed., *Religion und Religionskontakte im Zeitalter der Achämeniden*. Gütersloh: 29–48.

Wiesehöfer, J. (2003) "The Medes and the idea of the succession of empires in antiquity," in Lanfranchi et al., eds. (2004): 391–96.

Wiesehöfer, J. (2004a) "'O master, remember the Athenians': Herodotus and Persian foreign policy," in V. Karageorghis and I. Taifacos, eds., *The world of Herodotus*. Nicosia: 209–221.

Wiesehöfer, J. (2004b) "'Persien, der faszinierende Feind der Griechen': Güteraustausch und Kulturtransfer in achaimenidischer Zeit," in R. Rollinger and C. Ulf, eds., *Commerce and monetary systems in the ancient world: Means of transmission and cultural interaction*. Stuttgart: 295–310.

Wiesehöfer, J. (2004c) "Das Wasser des Königs: Wohltat, paradiesischer Lebensspender und herrscherlicher Genuß," in A. Richter and U. Hübner, eds., *Wasser: Historische und zeitgenössische Probleme und Perspektiven in asiatischen und afrikanischen Gesellschaften*. Hamburg: 149–64.

Wiesehöfer, J., and R. Rollinger (forthcoming) "Königlicher Haushalt, Residenz Und Hof," in T. Krüger, ed., *Festschrift R. Bartelmus*.

Wilcke, C. (1984) "*CT* 45, 119: Ein Fall legaler Bigamie mit *naditum* und *sugitum*." *Ziva Antiqua* 74: 70–80.

Wilkinson, T. (1995) "Late-Assyrian settlement geography in Upper Mesopotamia," in Liverani, ed. (1995): 139–60.

Wilkinson, T. J. (2000) "Regional approaches to Mesopotamian archaeology: The contribution of archaeological surveys." *Journal of Archaeological Research* 8: 219–67.

Wilkinson, T. J., and D. J. Tucker (1995) *Settlement development in the North Jazira, Iraq: A study of the archaeological landscape.* Warminster.

Wilkinson, T. J., E. B. Wilkinson, J. Ur, and M. Altaweel (2005) "Landscape and settlement in the Neo-Assyrian empire." *Bulletin of the American Schools of Oriental Research* 340: 23–56.

Wilson, A. (2002) "Machines, power and the ancient economy." *Journal of Roman Studies* 92: 1–32.

Wilson, D. S. (2003) *Darwin's cathedral: Evolution, religion, and the nature of society.* Chicago.

Wilson, E. O. (1975) *Sociobiology: The new synthesis.* Cambridge, Mass., and London.

Wilson, E. O. (1978) *On human nature.* Cambridge, Mass., and London.

Winter, I. J. (1997) "Art *in* empire: The royal image and the visual dimensions of Assyrian ideology," in Parpola, ed. (1997): 359–81.

Winterling, A. (1999) *Aula Caesaris: Studien zur Institutionalisierung des römischen Kaiserhofes in der Zeit von Augustus bis Commodus (31 v.Chr.—192 n.Chr.).* Munich.

Wiseman, D. J. (1958) *The vassal-treaties of Esarhaddon.* London.

Wittenberger, J. F., and R. L. Tilson (1980) "The evolution of monogamy: hypotheses and evidence." *Annual Review of Ecology and Systematics* 11: 197–232.

Wood, E. M. (1988) *Peasant-citizen and slave.* London.

Wood, I. (1977/79) "Kings, kingdoms and consent," in P. H. Sawyer and I. N. Wood, eds., *Early medieval kingship.* Leeds: 6–29.

Woodhouse, C. M. (1986) *George Gemistos Plethon: The last of the Hellenes.* Oxford.

Woolf, G. (1998) *Becoming Roman: The origins of provincial civilization in Gaul.* Cambridge.

Woolf, G. (2001) "Inventing empire in ancient Rome," in Alcock et al., eds. (2001): 311–22.

Woolfson, A. (2000) *Life without genes: The history and future of genomes.* London.

Wrangham, R., and D. Peterson (1996) *Demonic males: Apes and the origins of human violence.* Boston and New York.

Wright, R. (1994) *The moral animal: The new science of evolutionary psychology.* New York.

Wright, R. (2001) *Nonzero: The logic of human destiny.* New York.

Wrigley, E. A. (1967) "A simple model of London's importance in changing English society and economy, 1650–1750." *Past and Present* 37: 44–70.

Wrigley, E. A. (1987) *People, cities and wealth: The transformation of traditional society.* Oxford and New York.

Wunsch, C. (1999) "Neubabylonische Urkunden: Die Geschäftsurkunden der Familie Egibi," in J. Renger, ed., *Babylon: Focus mesopotamischer Geschichte, Wiege früher Gelehrsamkeit, Mythos in der Moderne.* Saarbrücken: 323–42.

Wunsch, C. (2000a) *Das Egibi-Archiv I: Die Felder und Gärten.* Groningen.

Wunsch, C. (2000b) "Neubabylonische Geschäftsleute und ihre Beziehungen zu Palast- und Tempelverwaltungen: Das Beispiel der Familie Egibi," in A. C. Bongenaar, ed., *Interdependency of institutions and private entrepreneurs.* Leiden: 95–118.

Xue, Y., et al. (2005) "Recent spread of a Y-chromosomal lineage in northern China and Mongolia." *American Journal of Human Genetics* 77: 1112–16.

Yamada, S. (2000) *The construction of the Assyrian empire: A historical study of the inscriptions of Shalmaneser III (859–824 BC) relating to his campaigns to the west.* Leiden.

Yoffee, N. (2005) *Myths of the archaic state*. Cambridge.

Zahrnt, M. (1971) *Olynth und die Chalkidier*. Munich.

Zahrnt, M. (1992) "Der Mardonioszug des Jahres 492 v.Chr. und seine historische Einordnung." *Chiron* 22: 237–79.

Zaidman, L. B., and B. Schmitt-Pantel (1992) *Religion in the ancient Greek city*. Tr. P. Cartledge. Cambridge.

Zangger, E., et al. (1997) "The Pylos Regional Archaeological Project. Part II: Landscape evolution and site preservation." *Hesperia* 66: 548–641.

Zanker, P. (1988) *The power of images in the age of Augustus*. Ann Arbor, Mich.

Zawadski, S. (1988) *The fall of Assyria and Median-Babylonian relations in the light of the Nabopolassar Chronicle*. Poznan.

Zerja, T., et al. (2003) "The genetic legacy of the Mongols." *American Journal of Human Genetics* 72: 717–21.

Zimansky, P. E. (1985) *Ecology and empire: The structure of the Urartian state*. Chicago.

Index